This is the first typewriter co~_____ __ ___
showing the courseness and ragged edges of the individual characters.

Chapter the First - Antebellum days

Who does not remember the thrill of excitement that sent the
blood tingling through his veins, when, standing by the roadside,
he heard, for the first time in his life, the roll of the drum and
the blare of the bugle, and saw the militia, clothed in the gorgeous uniforms peculiar to his particular locality, and bearing
banners and guns, march past with measured tread? At that supreme
moment the prospective man turns to his meek-eyed sister with a
countenance expressive of lofty disdain, and exclaims —
"You can never be a soldier!"
I had mastered a few of the simpler elements of reading, and
was just beginning to dimly perceive the ideas embodied in printed
sentences, when a small pamphlet, containing a picture of the death
of Dr. Warren(1) at Bunker Hill, fell into my hands. I can vividly
recall the intense satisfaction with which I viewed the details of
that scene. The dying man reclines in the arms of a kneeling soldier, who turned aside a bayonet thrust aimed at his chief. About
them were others, Americans and Britons, engaged in a hand-to-hand
struggle. Upon the faces of each there rested a vengeful expression. Beyond this group, a dense smoke obscured partially the
field of battle.
This illustration awakened within me a strong desire to know
more about war; and, to gratify this desire, as soon as I was able
to read with ordinary fluency, I procured an old copy of the history of the American Revolution. The book was full of quaint
battle pictures, and in it was recounted in thrilling phrase innumerable incidents illustrating the prowess of our soldiery. Even
now I can feel my blood flowing as I recall those glorious deeds,
and the effect their recital had upon me. My slumbers were disturbed by warlike dreams, in which General George Washington, surmounted by a cocked hat, and on horseback, was the principal figure. The personal courage of Jasper(2) and Champlain(3) and Mad
Anthony Wayne(4) stood out in bold relief on those glowing pages.
I well remember that, when I closed the volume, there was another
earnest believer in the invincibility of the American Army. Later,
the patriotic feelings thus aroused found expression on fourths of
July, when I would arrange firecrackers in two lines, one to represent the British and the other the American forces; and, some how
or other, it was always so arranged that the latter came out of the
supposed conflict victorious.
At another time I secured the life of Napoleon Bonaparte. It
was written by a Frenchman, who, as a matter of course, was an enthusiastic admirer of the great general. That portion of the work
which described the incidents of his boyhood possessed for me an
especial interest. The little Corsican was duly imitated when the
winter came upon us; and the numerous snow forts that were successfully erected and stormed attested how faithfully the boys at the
old schoolhouse attempted to copy from the grand original. Like
other ambitious youths, I always wanted to assume the leading character, and will remember the difficulties I encountered when one
Willie Ferree(5) acted as the opposing army. Usually he declined

common soldier
Uncommon War

Sidney Morris Davis, an enlisted Cavalry Common soldier kept a diary of his days in the Civil War and from his notes and diary he reconstructed his day-to-day memoirs of life in the Civil War. The hand-written Manuscript of his Memoirs, written by him in 1871, was found among his literary papers by his great-grandchildren.

Sidney wrote many short stories, poetry and the great manuscript of the Civil War days. As a teenager he worked as a newspaper compositor on his hometown paper. After finishing the only schooling available to him in a one room schoolhouse in a small mining town, he traveled down the Monogahela River 16 miles to Pittsburgh to work on that city's large newspaper.

A newspaper hand compositor has the opportunity to gain and retain extra knowledge and increase his education if he has an inquiring mind. This Sidney had and as he continued to turn his editor's stories and reports into print, he gained great knowledge and the ability to express himself well. His later writing efforts proved this to be true.

In and out of the saddle
from 1861.

Army Life During the War;

the

~~Recollection of a very common soldier~~
~~Fortunes and misfortunes~~ of a Common Soldier.
Recollections of a very Common Soldier.

An Autobiographical Sketch.

By No. 28.

1861 — 1864

Washington City, D.C., July 16, 1871.

First page of Sidney's Memoirs, indicating his pondering over a Title. We trust that he would have approved of our Title change, though his final decision was *Army Life During the War: The Recollections of a very Common Soldier*. He tied it in sections with butcher's twine, and paper and twine are in excellent condition today.

COMMON SOLDIER

Sidney Morris Davis

Uncommon War

Life as a cavalryman in the civil war

Research and manuscript editing
by civil war historian Charles F. Cooney

Illustrations by Charles Dyker
Labyrinth studio

Published by John H. Davis, Jr.

Designed, edited and published by
John H. Davis, Jr.
5125 Edgemoor Lane, Bethesda, Maryland 20814

Calligraphy by William A. Bostick

Typeset by John H. Davis, III

Library of Congress Catalog Card № 94-094208
ISBN № 0-9638496-0-3

Printed in the United States of America
Port City Press, Baltimore, Maryland

Sidney's Original Dedication

To the memory of that dead brotherhood, whether of the Blue or the Gray, who, when the assembly sounded, mustered to defend the principles they proposed to uphold, without thought of rank or emoulument, these reminiscences are affectionately inscribed.

Added Dedication

To Sidney, a man we wish we could have known, for his intellect, compassion and good humor.

His Great-Grandchildren

REFERENCE NOTES AND ILLUSTRATIONS

The great National interest in our Civil War has resulted in most Civil War book readers knowing the circumstances of the Generals and other Senior officers.

Since this Book contains Sidney Morris Davises' recollections of his daily life in the Civil War and of his contacts with the men in his own Company as well as many others in his Regiment, we are restricting references to the people he knew best and with whom he rubbed shoulders throughout his presence in the Army. We are including, however, references to points of interest which may not have been found in the many Civil War books previously published.

Again, in the multitude of Civil War books we have seen, the authors have often picked up the same illustrations of various battles. We are not inclined to repeat this. The illustrations drawn by Mr. Charles Dyker are designed to depict the War from Sidney's unique perspective.

The Editor

Situations

By Way of Introduction

The Common Soldier presents his compliments, and expresses the hope that the humble volume he lays before you will be acceptable, if only on account of the old times to which it relates. The events therein recounted and the scenes depicted have at least the merit of being actual events and scenes. He has kept within the bounds of truth, even when its suppression would, in the opinion of some, perhaps have been of manifest personal advantage.

No effort has been made to display a knowledge of the movements of armies, save as these movements occurred under his own eyes. He was, simply, a "buck" soldier, proud of his company, regiment, brigade, division, corps, army, and flag.

He tried to do his duty under all circumstances, and is satisfied with the record. If every day of his term of enlistment was not devoted to active service, it was not his fault, surely; it lies with those in authority to whom he had surrendered himself for a specific period, in perfect faith, for the salvation of his country. His oath has been conscientiously consulted in all the steps taken, and he has not shrunk from any of its requirements.

If he has availed himself of the universally acknowledged and understood liberties of the common soldier, under conditions which did not and could not be productive of mischief to the flag, or to any person under it, no violation of that oath can be maintained.

For the one he asks no commendation, it was his duty; for the other he offers no apology, it was his privilege.

If he shall succeed in attracting your attention to the actual feelings and conditions of the private soldiers of your army, he will feel that his efforts have not been in vain.

He does not presume that his views as herein expressed upon matters of discipline will be fully concurred in; he is conscious that at best they are but crude suggestions; but perhaps they represent the average opinion of the men in the ranks, and exhibit their views of the questions involved.

The Author

Antebellum Days

Who does not remember the thrill of excitement that sent the blood tingling through the veins, when, standing by the roadside, he heard, for the first time in his life, the roll of the drum and the blare of the bugle, and saw the militia, clothed in the gorgeous uniforms peculiar to his particular locality, and bearing banners and guns, march past with measured tread? At that supreme moment the prospective man turns to his meek-eyed sister with a countenance of lofty disdain, and exclaims—

"You can never be a soldier!"

I had mastered a few of the simpler elements of reading, and was just beginning to dimly perceive the ideas embodied in printed sentences, when a small pamphlet, containing a picture of the death of Dr. Warren at Bunker Hill, fell into my hands. I can vividly recall the intense satisfaction with which I viewed the details of that scene. The dying man reclines in the arms of a kneeling soldier, who turned aside a bayonet thrust aimed at his chief. About them were others, Americans and Britons, engaged in hand-to-hand struggle. Upon the faces of each there rested a vengeful expression. Beyond this group, a dense smoke partially obscured the field of battle.

This illustration awakened within me a strong desire to know more about war; and, to gratify this desire, as soon as I was able to read with ordinary fluency, I procured an old copy of the history of the American Revolution. The book was full of quaint battle pictures, and in it was recounted in thrilling phrase innumerable incidents illustrating the prowess of our soldiery. Even now I can feel my blood flowing as I recall those glorious deeds, and the effect their recital had upon me. My slumbers were disturbed by warlike dreams, in which General George Washington, surmounted by a cocked hat, and on horseback, was the

1

principal figure. The personal courage of Jasper and Champlain and Mad Anthony Wayne stood out in bold relief on those glowing pages. I well remember that, when I closed the volume, there was another earnest believer in the invincibility of the American Army. Later the patriotic feelings thus aroused found expression on fourths of July, when I would arrange firecrackers in two lines, one to represent the British and the other the American forces; and, some how or other, it was always so arranged that the latter came out of the supposed conflict victorious.

At another time I secured the life of Napoleon Bonaparte. It was written by a Frenchman, who, as a matter of course, was an enthusiastic admirer of the great general. That portion of the work which described the incidents of his boyhood possessed for me an especial interest. The little Corsican was duly imitated when the winter came upon us; and the numerous snow forts that were successfully erected and stormed attested how faithfully the boys at the old schoolhouse attempted to copy from the grand original. Like other ambitious youths, I always wanted to assume the leading character, and will remember the difficulties I encountered when one Willie Ferree acted as the opposing army. Usually he declined to either surrender or retreat; nor could he be convinced that this was trifling with the serious truth of history. Poor boy! Little did we suppose, during these mimic contests, that his life blood would in after days stain the sod of a real battlefield, and that the pluck of the boy would so signally reappear in the man when the bitter end came![1]

Father and I seemed to be possessed with similar dispositions in respect to martial deeds and heroes. He could not read English, and there was at that time in our region a dearth of Welsh literature of the class desired; so I endeavored to fill the void from the books mentioned. As I recall them today, these were among the pleasantest hours of my life. In the old distillery, before a huge fire of free-burning bituminous coal, alone to ourselves, I reading aloud and he commenting at times in his odd way, the long winter evenings were a fitting close to busy days of toil. Sometimes we discussed the events narrated with some spirit, for I was a born American and he was still loyal to the English Crown, although he left the kingdom some thirty years before; but he usually employed summary means of closing the debate lest party feelings should too fully develop itself.

My cup of delight was full to overflowing when I happened to be in

[1]   Willie Ferree died at the Battle of the Wilderness in May, 1864

2

the company of persons who had at any time participated in the rough scenes of actual war; and perhaps my persistent efforts to draw out their reminiscences often led my many garrulous military acquaintances to impose on their credulous young listeners. Among those to whose utterances I was accustomed to give an undivided attention I recall one Joseph Gilmore, an old gentleman of patriarchal instincts and appearance; and his experiences in the Black Hawk War, as related by him—how he used to see the dead and wounded cover the ground, trampled underfoot by men and horses— invested the narrator in my mind with the prestige of a hero.

One experience in connection with my historical researches puzzled me for a long time. In the battle pictures before mentioned, I observed the soldiers usually represented with muskets poised at an angle, the breech apparently pressed against the right hip—in the position I have since learned as the "ready". Why were not the guns levelled at the enemy from the shoulder? To Mr. Gilmore I referred my query.

"Why," responded that grave personage, looking down on me patronizingly, "that's all right—that's the way they hold their guns when they open fire."

That was just the point needing elucidation; so I ventured to remark:

"Then they would shoot up into the air, and none would be hit."

"Ah!" he retorted, with a severe expression about the eyes, "boy, what do *you* know about war?"

Then, as if relenting a little, he continued:

"It's against the law of nations for men to aim at each other; that's considered murder. The gun is held that way, and fired at random, as it were, so that the killed and wounded are hit by chance, and no one can then tell that he has hit or killed a man, and the soldier's conscience can't trouble him afterward."

"But," I argued, "why do people go to war at all, if the killing of men in battle be murder?"

Probably because this question led away into another field of inquiry, the whys and wherefores of which were too interminable for present discussion, my old friend gave no reply. After reflecting for a few moments, I returned to the subject.

"Of what use are the sights on a gun, unless they are to be used? I once saw an old flintlock musket, and there were sights on it."

(This, to my mind, was the typical weapon of warriors, as I had yet to learn that a modern gun had long ago replaced the veteran piece that

3

carried our ancestors over bloody but victorious fields.)

The old man laid down his flail—we were threshing corn that day on the farm—looked at me steadily for a minute, and then slowly said:

"Boy, I see that you doubt my word, *(a pause)* however, I will explain the use of the sights *(another and longer pause)*. In olden times, when the country was full of wild game, the soldiers had to depend on the fruits of the chase for a living; and it was to enable them to shoot deers that these sights were put on their muskets. I hope, young man, that you are now satisfied."

Then by way of emphasis, for the next few moments his flail came down heavily on the grain. But I was not satisfied, though not daring to ask any more questions that day.

I regret to say that, at a later period of my life, the pretensions of Mr. Gilmore as a soldier were readily dispelled. Indeed it was boldly proclaimed by others of my acquaintance among the farm hands that he had never been within five hundred miles of a battle field. My boyish fancy, which had come to regard the old man as a veteran, was thrown into chaos by this unkind revelation.

My home was in southwestern Pennsylvania. It was a cozy spot, with peculiar and picturesque surroundings. A strip of land, varying in width from two hundred to four hundred yards, bounded on the south by the river Monongahela and on the north by hills that rose precipitately to a height of seven hundred to one thousand feet, comprised about all that could be cultivated. At the foot of the declivity, with a background of locust and peach trees, was the large stone house in which I was reared from the age of four, and around whose portals the feet of two or three generations played in years gone. Within a stone's throw there was a distillery, barn, stable, orchard, and family graveyard. The hills, rugged, uncouth, and seemingly valueless, were vast deposits I have noted, of bituminous coal. A heavy growth of oak, beech, maple, dogwood, and other varieties of timber clothed their sides up to the summit, where generally were clearings and cottages. Up the river, within a mile or two, one could count a dozen mines, perhaps, with their paraphernalia of cars and tracks and tipples, which were operated by individuals and corporations. Around each were clusters of cheaply built houses, with walls blackened by dust and smoke. The population as was usual in the coal regions at that day were mainly of foreign birth—Irish, English, Scotch and Welsh predominating in numbers. The village, as these groups of houses might be called, contained one church—a

4

structure devoted to the propagation of a somewhat primitive methodism —which, perched about midway up the hillside, reminded me of a huge carbuncle. Behind it was the graveyard of the community, surrounded by a broken fence, with the white headstones shining here and there among the tall weeds.

Many years before my advent here, and ere the coal business developed to the immense proportions to which it attained in later years, a Quaker farmer, Jesse Loeb by name, bestowed upon this section the vulgar cognomen of Limetown because of the numerous kilns that were located along the side of the river; and, although strenuous efforts were made, two or three decades afterward, to change the name to the more euphonious one of Pleasantville, the scheme had not yet been successful. Just how long the struggle would have lasted is hard to determine. A post office was established, called Coal Bluff, and this is slowly displacing the once appropriate impromptu appellation.

The religious elements of the community at that day were quite evenly divided between the Catholics and the Methodists. The latter were the more aggressive party and early located their tabernacle here. The skepticism of modern times had not yet invaded this region and, when the revival season began, the questions in the minds of the people were narrowed down to a choice of Heaven or Hell—to a conflict between dogged obstinacy and the conviction of sin. The victim could find no shelter in unbelief since the traditions of the fathers had never been questioned to his knowledge; so it was merely a matter of time so far as his following in their footsteps was concerned.

My little legs were scarcely sturdy enough to bear me to its portals when Mrs. Balsley, a good, motherly woman, called on my bachelor master, and appealed to him to send me to the Sunday school. This proceeding, probably, settled my religious status as a protestant. Here I was taught, among other things, to hate Satan and Catholicism. The objections to the former were quite clearly and conclusively stated; to the latter, somewhat vaguely, with appeals to profane history in proof of such allegations as were made. From what I could gather from the books, one was as bad as the other in their respective spheres. I soon manifested the result of this training by quarrelling with other little boys, with, whom, under different circumstances, I might have lived in peace; and I noticed my hostility was reciprocated in a way that suggested much as to their training. The picture of a revival scene presented below will be recognized my many. To prevent misunderstanding, let it be known that these lines are written with no disposition to sneer at religion, as some may conclude. I am convinced of its use as a factor of civilization; and, besides, the problems of existence are so profound that I cannot find in the perplexities and anxieties of my fellow man as he contemplates them anything for ridicule or amusement.

I have noted, I may say in passing, that in piety, as in other matters, human nature is the same. The peculiarities of thought and action find similar expression in different communities. The types are perfect, whether in the class or individual.

One hot summer night in July, when about ten years old, I attended a "protracted meeting," as it was called, at the church on the hillside. A terrible thunder storm, that for a time threatened to resolve all things into chaos, arose. The building, exposed to the winds from its porch, trembled under the mighty blasts that roared through the woods. A thick darkness, that was illuminated at intervals by flashes of lightning, hung over the valley. A few tallow candles threw a yellow glare over the hall, and tinted the faces of the frightened congregation with a ghastly hue. The preacher, a powerful young fellow, whose voice soon broke under the tremendous pressure to which it was subjected, chose as an appropriate text for the evening's discourse the scene of the judgement as described by Saint Matthew in his twenty-fifth chapter. As the storm increased in fury, the revivalist raised his cries and exhortations in a corresponding height. The "mourner's bench" was soon crowded with penitents, whose sobs presently developed into long-continued wailings. In the babel of voices I could only distinguish detached expressions now and then, as, "then shall the graves open"—I glanced out over the cemetery grounds, which just then were rendered visible by an unusually vivid flash of lightning, and would not have been in the least surprised if the sheeted dead had then and there appeared—"forgive me"—thunder—"pray on, brother"—more thunder—"the judge will open his mouth"—"O, my! O, my!" from a female's throat—"glory, glory!-"—"depart me, ye cursed"—"Amen! Amen!"—"lasting fire"—"hallelujah"—"for the devil"—"help me!"— "his angels"—and so on, for an hour or more. Then uprose the mighty men and women of the church. They deployed among the weeping ones, and offered to them the consolations of the scriptures. Soon the results were apparent. A man, noted for an inexhaustible vocabulary of obscene and profane epithets, roared out that he was saved; a woman, who rubbed snuff, and who was notorious for her gossipping proclivities, sprang high into the air, stiffened out, and fell prone and rigid across the legs of some young man, then rolled off onto the floor, and lay like one dead; the bully of the village, who had been on his brutal knees every night for a week past, suddenly arose, lifting with him two fat women, whose arms were encircling his neck, and shouted "Glory—hallelujah!" with the voice of a Stentor. A gaily dressed, handsome young man, whose means of livlihood were invisable to the people of the community, who had been writhing on the floor in pools of tobacco spittle, was taken in hand by a committee of the sisters, and presently announced, with a short demure smile, that his sins, which had been as scarlet were now as white as snow, and that he thanked God he had seen the errors of his ways. Then high above the roar of the elements rose the notes of the doxology, and the congregation, many of whom carried lanterns, picked their steps down the narrow pathway to their homes, little heeding the pelting rain that dashed on their unprotected heads

Rarely were the results of these phenomenal "conversations" visible after the lapse of three or four months. A percentage, it is true, maintained their pledges, and to this extent, it must be acknowledged, the world was the gainer; but with the greatest majority there was "backsliding" which last condition was much worse than the first, because of the recklessness and abandon that accompanied it.

The staid regulars of the church, anxious to encourage them in their new and holy calling, would appoint the most promising of the converts to sundry little offices of honor and trust, and give them prominence in many ways; and the wickeder the subject the greater the sympathy and attention shown. The man that was noted for his inexhaustible vocabulary of profane and obscene epithets became a leader in prayer, and turned his mental resources to account by regularly calling on God to "smite his enemies hip and thigh" the woman of gossipping proclivities grew conspicuous at experience meetings, and was a "power" in the church because of the fear that she excited from the free use of her tongue; the bully of the village seemed to gravitate to his natural place and took up the collections (I remembered his old vocation, and quailed under his eye when the necessary coin was not in my pocket); the gaily dressed, handsome young fellow, whose means of support were invisible to the eye of the community, was appointed a teacher in the Sunday school, and soon afterward, chiefly through the influence of the women, became its superintendant.

7

Entering zealously on the work laid out for them, these recruits to the cause rapidly rose in favor. They were pointed out with many approving nods as they wended their respective ways to the front rows of seats; at class meetings and love feasts they related the story of their lives with great particularity of detail, apparently to the infinite edification of their hearers; and they seemed to grow in popularity in proportion to their former depravity and present brazen-facedness of recital.

Does this seem over drawn? I have known gray-haired men who appeared to gloat over their previous sinfulness, and confessed to the commission of crimes that ought to have consigned them to dungeons, or outlawed them from respectable society, (and I can account for a different result only by supposing no one believed them) and young men who vied with the elder reprobates in unveiling in all its naked hideousness the wickedness of their lives. Standing apart from the congregation, and for the time being, shutting out the sympathies and customs of the hour, one could not help wondering how an individual managed to look at his fellows in the face while he narrated the story of his evil pranks, or how his audience could resist an impulse to lynch the self-confessed scoundrel.

The social lines were closely drawn in Limetown and its vicinity. The native born element looked on the alien portion of the community with an expression of lofty disdain. There was neither marrying nor giving in marriage outside of their respective groups, save in the few instances where the lovers were bold enough to bid defiance to public opinion. As a result of this policy, in the course of time one could trace, from family to family, the thread of consanguinity in an ever widening circle. Out of this state of affairs there developed a species of provincialism that was marked in many ways—particularly by a peculiarly swaggering carriage and attitude that I often recognized in other days at other places. Nor was this social exclusiveness, which had its origin in the heads of families, common only to the older people. It appeared in the public schools among the children, and led to quarrels that at times threatened serious results. I remember that once or twice the hostile feeling culminated in extensive stone battles between the river and hill boys, in which some youthful blood flowed from cut heads. This phase of the matter, however, led to a division of the school district, and the erection of another building for the accomodation of the people of the village proper.

How vividly do I recall the feeling of dismay that seized upon me when this latter scheme was announced. From the location of my home I was fated to attend the new establishment, with the class that I affected to dislike; but this was not the real reason of my discomfiture. To me the daughters of the farmers were fair to look upon —one of them, in particular. The transfer placed me in the forbidden caste, and she would no longer recognize my efforts to appear attractive. The current of my life flowed smoothly, until my nineteenth year. Of course, I had the usual boyish grievances, real or unreal—though, for that matter, they were all real enough at the time to me. My worldly experience, beyond driving home the cows morning and evening, and attending to the other ordinary duties pertaining to farm life, was rather limited. An interval of three years had been spent in a printing office, in learning the mysteries of the "art preservative," and a vacation of three or four months at the old homestead followed. In the fall I set out on a tour as a journeyman printer, drifting into the city of Cleveland, Ohio. Here I was indeed a "stranger in a strange land;" to me the busy, crowded streets were inexpressibly lonely; I felt cowed and disheartened, and dared not apply for work; and it was only by accident that I was thrown into the company of some compositors, who, as is usual among morning newspaper hands, were clamorous for "subs." From this time forward I found plenty of employment, and remained in Cleveland until the following spring.

For several years prior to this time I noticed the bitter language used in political discussions in debates and in the columns of newspapers, but attached no special significance to it. Crimination and recrimination seemed to be regarded as a necessity, beneficial in enabling the People (with a capital P) to secure proper men for office by exposing the defects in the characters of aspirants. No one appeared to dream of a sectional physical conflict. The John Brown affair at Harper's Ferry, Virginia; the acrimonious spirit manifested in Congress; and the hostile attitude of the Southern population during the presidential contest of 1860, however, were events that attracted universal attention; and now, for the first time, I began to realize something of the deadly hatred that was rapidly estranging the people of the free and the slaveholding States from each other.

I do not propose to write a history of those sad days, nor of the causes which led to this deplorable result. A world sits in judgement on the system to which our national woes are to be attributed. Probably the sentimentalism that led to the abolition of slavery did not understand the

9

philosophy of the movement, the result it sought to accomplish, nor the real gain that was to accrue to the beneficiaries; nor indeed, who in the end, were to be specially affected. These will be fully apprehended by a future generation, far removed from the passions and prejudices of today, and to it the true compensation to the country for its loss in blood and treasure will clearly appear.

I came home to the farm from Cleveland in the early part of April, 1861. In the quiet of country life I hoped to build up my health, which was rapidly failing under the close confinement and excessive labor incident to my peculiar employment. In my isolated condition here, however, I soon began feeling uneasy. Communication with other regions was, to some extent, interrupted; and the deep concern I felt in national affairs, and my feverish anxiety to hear of the progress of events, interfered greatly with the enjoyments I had promised myself. I would see a newspaper once a week, and during the interval between mail days felt entirely lost to the world.

Presently there came news of the bombardment of Fort Sumter; of the riot at Baltimore; of the capture of Alexandria and the killing of Ellsworth; of the concentration of troops—federal and confederates in Northern Virginia; of the engagement at Big Bethel. With each successive event of the war thus far I felt a fever grow upon me. I wandered around at night when I should have been in bed asleep; my hands went about their work mechanically, so that what I did often had to be undone; my appetite failed; and for days at a time I had little to say to my companions.

Limetown, like other villages in the United States during this eventful period, began to feel the delirium of popular excitement over political affairs. Party lines suddenly vanished. A meeting was called at the "upper schoolhouse"—the community was growing in numbers, and now needed two buildings to accomodate the children—and, when the people were assembled, speeches of an appropriate character explained the nature of the crisis that was upon the country. The event was Limetown's declaration of war against the Southern Confederacy, in advance of the formal action of the general government[2]. The leaders on this occasion, however, widely apart in the social scale, were one in purpose. Mr. French, an exhorter in the Methodist Church here, though badly affected with a stammering of speech, through very earnestness was the

[2] There is a slight error here. The Federal Government never declared war against the Confederacy.

10

personification of eloquence.   After explaining the irreconcilable differences that existed between the two sections of the country, and showing that the continent must be either all free or all under the domination of slavery, he boldly announced himself on the side of liberty, and expressed his intention of taking up his musket and fighting for the cause.   The audience, which was composed of all creeds and nationalities —for differences were now apparently blotted out —heartily responded to the sentiments of the speaker.

True to his promise, I may state here, Mr. French enlisted, and met a soldier's fate on the battlefield of Fredericksburg.

It was, however, on Mr. Thompson that most of the interest centered. For this there were several reasons. He was the rich man of the neighborhood, and by the people generally regarded as proud, cold, closefisted, and exclusive. To have him condescend to grace the meeting by his presence, and address these horny-handed, grimy sons of toil, was an event that demonstrated how grave indeed must be the political situation. So, when he arose from the bench where he had been sitting all this while alone, "grand, gloomy, and peculiar," and took his station by the schoolmaster's little desk, a breathless silence fell on the assembly. A few moments later the quiet was broken by tumultuous cheering. Mr. Thompson had announced, in a few words spoken in a matter-of-fact manner, that he would give nine hundred dollars toward the support of the families of those men who would volunteer to fight the battles of their country.   When the applause subsided, apparently stimulated by the reception of his offer, he further declared that, if this was not money enough, he would give nine hundred dollars more (renewed cheering.) No one's family should be allowed to suffer. (More applause). And he would, also, equip a man for the service with a horse, saddle, and bridle and everything else that was necessary. ("Hear! Hear!" from a stalwart young Irishman on my left whose brother had served the British Queen in the Crimea.)

It was quite late when the assemblage dispersed. As a result of the movement then inaugurated, the able-bodied men of Limetown volunteered en masse for the federal service, and vindicated their patriotism and manhood on many a hard fought field. I regret to be obliged to record, if popular rumor be true, that Mr. Thompson's promises, solemnly and publicly given, were not kept. It is said that he aided the government by investing in its securities, which was commendable; but the gifts he tendered to abandoned families never appeared; that, when some miner's wife appealed to him for food, at a later period of the conflict, he sent them to the field for "cow" pumpkins!

Without intending to make an odious comparison, or to exalt one class of citizens above another, I have selected Mr. French and Mr. Thompson as the representatives of those elements of our social life so vaguely defined as labor and capital. The one laid his all on the altar of his country without murmuring or questioning and passed into oblivion amid the wild throes of battle; the other was willing, provided a fair rate of interest was paid, and the principal secured to him, to speculate on the calamities of the Republic, and to remain at home out of harm's way sheltered under the wings of its armies. But of what use is complaint against that which seems to be the order of nature in all the departments of life?

My master, Levi Bentley, usually was too deeply engrossed in business affairs to take part in political discussions; but the condition of the public mind now began to arouse an uneasiness even in him, that manifested itself frequently. The States of the south were going out of the Union one by one, and the borders of the new confederacy were creeping nearer and nearer our home. But Virginia, whose frontier was forty or fifty miles away still adhered to her ancient vows, and on her loyalty we rested our hopes. "If Virginia can be held, all will yet be well," he would say. "Yet if the worst must come, the war should be fought out until the last waving of the banner."

These energetic expressions were a surprise to his neighbors, by whom he was regarded as a man of peace. Doubtless the sentiment as a result of mature reflection on the possibilities and effect of disunion, was by this time firmly fixed in every thoughtful mind in the north.

With me the fever was growing more and more pronounced in its manifestation. All my schoolmates were enlisting in various organizations, and this circumstance of itself added much to my feeling of unrest. An indescribable loneliness seemed to be settling over the neighborhood, despite the turbulent excitement of the times. It appeared as if the home of my boyhood was rapidly vanishing from existence through the power of some mysterious evil influence.

The grand hills were there, it is true, and the beautiful river; the smoky hamlet survived; but the dear faces wore different expressions; gossip over community affairs had been displaced by the weightier considerations of the state; the young men were rapidly disappearing in a maelstrom whose distant thunderings we seemed to hear; the usual sports and pursuits of life in a measure ceased; in everything and over everything was wrought a curious change; like the experience of one infected by malarial fever. To me the world was tinged by the dreadful hues of some impending calamity. With each day and hour the oppressiveness increased, until I realized it would soon be insupportable. Finally, one morning, while we were building a fence on the lower farm, I stopped for some minutes, forgetting I had a heavy rail on my shoulder, and gazed abstractedly on the ground.

"Well, Davis," said Hiram Taylor, one of the farm hands, who had been observing me, and understood the matter quite well, "I guess you had better go to the war."

"I guess I had," I responded, throwing down the rail, and striding towards the dwelling house. Within an hour I was dressed in my best clothing, and posted at the boat landing on the river, awaiting the arrival of the steamboat that was to carry me from Limetown to Pittsburg.

Enlistment and First Camp

This was on the 6th of July, 1861. It should not be supposed that I came to the conclusion to enlist in the army free from forebodings as to the result, personally; on the contrary, having always had a mortal fear of death, it required great effort on my part to bring my courage up to the mark. I had a presentiment—and the world knows that presentiments always fulfill themselves—that I should be killed; wounds or imprisonment did not occur to my mind—simply death. I well recollect the shudder that passed through my frame as I settled upon that dreadful conclusion—to go to war. It seemed as if my death warrant had already been signed. This was a grim test to my patriotism, but I felt that my steps could not be retraced.

I had seen an advertisement for recruits in a Pittsburg paper. The regiment[1]* belonged to the regular army; the term of service was five years. This force I proposed to join, although strong attempts were made by our volunteer officers, who were raising companies in the neighborhood, to dissuade me from it, and to induce me to go with them; but somehow or other I did not like to accede to their request. I was suspicious of these quasi-military men. It appeared to me that they had selfish ends in view. They were not men of high standing in the community, and the misgivings as to their individual capacity was not confined to me. The result proved as apprehended; in less than a year afterwards they were all back home, or in the ranks, and other and better men were pushed forward to take the place these men were not fitted mentally or morally to occupy. It was a long time to serve, these five years—a vast period out of a young life—with innumerable opportunities

* *Because of the number of notes in this chapter, they will appear at the end of the chapter.*

to get killed. The volunteers were called out for three years[2] of the war—to be discharged, it was understood, at the close of the war, or in no event to be held longer than three years. The regulars must serve out their terms of enlistment under all circumstances. The alternative was a fearful one to contemplate, but viewing the matter from all points I concluded that my resolution was the best, and I should join the regulars.

Of course, I thought I was in love—where is the youth of twenty years old that does not? Of an unusually backward disposition, I had not ventured to pay addresses to the young lady[3] in person, but, while in Cleveland, had written to her on matrimonial subjects.

There was some method in this, in my judgement. If she rejected me, I would not be present to have the blow fall upon me; I would be able to conceal my chagrin. But she did not reject me, and when I came home I mustered up courage enough to call and see her, and was graciously received by her and her friends. No obstacle appeared in the way.

To leave one's sweetheart and go to war has always been considered the highest test of courage and patriotism. The poets have ransacked their mighty brains to praise the heroic swain. They describe the parting in language that makes one's hair stand on end to think of it. But the return—that throws everything else into the shadows. I leave the reader to select passages to suit his own taste as to the parting of Sarah Jane and me, warning—him confidentially that nothing he can find will do the subject justice; as to the return, well, I think he need not trouble himself about that. In fact, in that sense I never—but I will not anticipate.

On the evening of the day before mentioned—July 6—I embarked on the steamer for Pittsburg. On board a company of young men, bound for the war, from Uniontown, near the Pennsylvania Stateline, had possession. It was evidently the first boat they had captured, and they did not seem to know exactly what to do with it. Here was a union of spirits, ethereal and material, and the effect was obvious. The cabin rang with yells; the tables and chairs were reversed in all directions; the floor was strewn with bodies—not dead, though I was tempted more than once to wish they were—and wearing apparel of all sorts filled all the corners. There was no quarrelling—it was all fun to them, but death to the comfort of everybody else. The ladies on board had retired affrighted into their cabins, and closed the door. To escape from the confusion I engaged a stateroom near the clerk's office, and locked myself within it.

There were two berths in this stateroom, one above the other, and they encroached upon each other so closely that the occupant was obliged to remain in a horizontal position. There was a chair, however, and upon this I seated myself, and tried to collect my confused thoughts. My head and eyes ached, and my heart—well, the less said about that the better. I did all I could to keep up my courage. Finally, about midnight, sleep visited my nervous lids—a troubled, feverish sleep—and I laid down.

I have a dim recollection of seeing long lines of battle, clouds of dust and smoke, of hearing the thunder of cannon and the tramping of squadrons of cavalry. It was the struggle for Manassas, the great stronghold of the Confederates in Northern Virginia. I awoke with a start, throwing my head against the ceiling above with such force that it seemed to rebound back upon the pillow, and making sparks of fire fly from my eyes, only to hear the rumble of the boat's machinery and the yells of the Uniontown men in the cabin. A sense of relief came over me as I thought it was only a dream after all; but I dared not close my eyes again for fear the terrible vision would return to haunt the portals of my brain.

The recruiting office of the Third United States Cavalry—the regiment I proposed to join—was located at the old National Hotel, Water Street, near Smithfield, Pittsburg. It was too early to visit the office when the boat landed at the Monongahela wharf, and as soon as day dawned I repaired to my old boarding house, 151 Third Street, where I procured breakfast, and then went to the National, which I reached about ten o'clock. At the door of the recruiting office I found an exquisitely dressed young German, whose name I afterwards knew was Frobin.[4] This romantic young man inquired, in very broken English:

"You want to go 'long—yes?"

"I want to enlist in the United States Army, Sir," I replied, somewhat impressed by the appearance of the young German.

"Lieutenant McGlain is not in shust now. You redurn at tree o'clock, and you be enlisted."

I wandered downtown again, looking listlessly into the windows, and running against somebody every few steps, and getting stared at in consequence, which made me more nervous, and I ran against people oftener in my efforts to get out of other people's way. Towards noon I went back to 151 Third Street for dinner, and then fell asleep on the sofa, awakening at two o'clock wonderfully refreshed in body and mind.

Punctually at three o'clock I was at the recruiting office, at the door of which I was met by the romantic young German, who led the way into an inner room, and, with great formality, introduced me to Lieutenant McClain[5] of the United States Army. This gentleman received me pleasantly. He was a good-looking officer, probably twenty-four years of age, with very black eyes and short black curly hair. His uniform added much to his appearance, and was scrupulously neat and clean.

"Well, sir, do you wish to join the army?" he asked, in a slow, well modulated tone of voice.

"Yes, sir," I replied.

"I suppose you know the nature of the duties upon which you wish to enter?"

"Well, sir, I suppose we are expected to fight for the United States." He laughed at this.

"How old are you?"

"I was twenty last March—the 6th of that month," I added, wishing to be precise as to the date, lest I should commit some breach of law by being vague in my answers.

"You are too young to enlist unless you can get the consent of your parents or guardian—you are not of age," he said. "Have you parents?"

"I have a father, that is all," I replied.

"Well, if you want to go, you can take these papers"—taking down some blanks from the top of a secretary—"and have him sign them, giving his consent to your enlistment."

With that he wrote rapidly, filling up all the blank but the place of signature, and handed the duplicate to me, saying:

"Take these, and if your father signs them, return within three days, and then perhaps I will take you."

I took the blanks and passed out of the room, glancing hurriedly at several sabres that stood in a corner, and a pistol holster that hung on the wall near the door, wondering if those would be the kind of arms we should have in service.

I confess to feeling a thrill of relief at the necessity of having father sign those papers, permitting me to enlist, for I was beginning to repent of the step I had taken. Here appeared an unexpected avenue of escape. Father would no doubt refuse his sanction, for he had already expressed himself as adverse to my joining the army, at least at this early stage of the war; then I could shelter myself from reproach under the parental wing—could retire gracefully from the position in which I had placed myself before the world.

I arrived home, and had an interview with father early next morning on the fatal subject. My astonishment and grief may be imagined, but cannot be described, when, upon my making strenuous exertions to induce father to permit me to enlist he promptly acceded to my request, and affixed his signature to the blanks. I would have gladly withdrawn my consent then, but it was too late; the die had been cast, and I had to set my teeth together like a vice to keep down the swelling in my throat.

I paid a farewell visit to my sweetheart that evening. We renewed our pledges of devotion to each other. It is hardly necessary that I should recapitulate those pledges here; it is to be presumed that every young man who abandoned his home under similar circumstances had a similar experience, and will understand it all without further reference. But my girl did make one remark that possessed a special significance, in view of my impecunious circumstances, and for other reasons that I shall not enumerate:

"I would rather be a poor man's darling than a rich man's slave!"

I left home, however, with a mock cheerfulness that surprised myself, and reaching Pittsburg on the 8th of July, reported promptly to Lieutenant McClain, and was ushered into the presence of the surgeon for examination.

My great modesty prevents me from giving a minute account of this surgical inspection. I suppose that to me it was almost as severe as any other surgical inspection. Suffice it to say that, after a series of remarkable jumps, kicks, coughs, and after I had thrown and twisted my nude body into all sorts of shapes and convulsions, till the fire leaped from my eyes, I was pronounced an able-bodied man, and the surgeon signed a certificate to that effect.

After this formal ceremony was over I was taken to another room, and there raised my right hand and swore to serve for a period of five years; to uphold the laws and Constitution of the United States; to obey the President and all officers appointed over me; and to defend the United States against all their enemies. So help me, God.

Such was the substance of that oath, as near as I can remember. I took it without any mental reservation, and I feel today that I have obeyed it conscientiously from first to last. As God helped me. This was July 8, 1861.

In another hour I was clad in blue, and my citizen's suit was carefully wrapped up and packed in my carpet sack, preparatory to sending it home. I felt wonderfully relieved now; I felt that the terrible suspense of which I was possessed before being sworn in had been removed; that I was indeed doing my duty. The future belonged to God alone. If it was my lot to die on the field, there would be some consolation in the fact that the cause for which I suffered was a good one, and the death honorable.

I was a good deal surprised to see, already enlisted, a number of my old acquaintances from up the river. I had thought myself to be the only one from my neighborhood who had joined the Third Cavalry, and was, of course, glad to find I was to have the company of some I had formerly known. The service would not seem so lonely to me, and there would be a mutual understanding and sympathy between us that might in after times prove eminently useful. These friends laughed at me heartily when I came among them with my uniform folded about me. This might seem to be a queer expression, but it is the only one that can do the matter justice. The pants, blouse, and cap must have been made for a giant of the pre-Adamite age, for the two former articles hung on my frame like a mourning gown, and the latter encased my ears.

We were quartered at the National Hotel. Up to the time I enlisted there had been sworn into the service for the Third Cavalry some fifty or sixty recruits. These formed a motley and diverse company, they being of several different nationalities, the Irish and German element predominating among the foreigners, with a sprinkle of Welsh and English. The larger number were of American birth. The party was under charge of a little Frenchman, named Strick, whom the lieutenant called "Sergeant," and who, evidently, had been in service before, judging from the manner in which he could handle a sabre. In short, in a few days we all looked upon Sergeant Strick as a sort of Mars; the fact that he was of French blood was sufficient to make him a hero in my eyes, such prestige had I attached to that People from reading the histories of their great wars. He was certainly quick and keen of eye, and soon showed himself prompt in dealing with offenders, compelling the respect of the whole company by his decisive measures and uniform politeness. It is but proper to say here that, although he did not remain with us to take the field in after days, he was commissioned an officer in the First Pennsylvania Cavalry regiment, and served gallantly, I believe, in that corps, receiving a severe wound in one of the many actions in Northern Virginia in which that regiment was engaged.

The recruits were soon put under the rod of discipline. Guards were posted at several places, in charge of one thing or another, with elaborate instructions to resist imaginary enemies. At night, patrols were organized, under charge of Sergeant Strick, by whom the squad was marched over town, picking up those of our number who proved to be unable to navigate the labyrinth of streets and alleys back to their respective quarters at the hotel on account of frequent potations. Such occasions were very amusing to all concerned, and the sergeant, when he wanted a squad to make these raids, had no difficulty in finding volunteers for the duty. The punishment of offenders was very slight, although they were often notified that they would be put into the Black Hole—a hideous prison supposed to be located under the floor of the bar-room; but so often had this threat been made, and the delinquents were so often pardoned, that we began to suspect the Black Hole existed after all in our affrighted imaginations only.

The quartermaster's office was located in one of the lower rooms of the Monongahela House, at which the officer in charge was domiciled. Here I was initiated into the mysteries of guard duty. How proud I felt, strutting with pompous step over the pavement in front of the door of the room, and halting, at night, everything that approached my beat, and uttering the challenge "Who goes there?" in stentorian tones, with my sabre pointed ready to deal the fatal thrust in case the object proved to be an enemy of these United States! It is needless for me to speak in detail of all that we said or all that we did during our pleasant sojourn at the National. How Flascher[6] quarrelled with the servant girl that wore a net on her head and had thrown another around Flascher's heart, and how he made such fearful grimaces as to bring down upon him the displeasure of the fat landlady; how we used to drill on the sidewalk, much to the discomfiture of non combatants, or learned to mark time, change step, go through the facings, and other movements in the military alphabet. How Conway[7] kept the neighbors awake in the vicinity by the rattle of his garrulous tongue; how Schumaker,[8] over his mug of lager beer. exhibited the most remarkable expression with his little snake-like eyes and huge mouth; how Old Blue[9] and Wilson[10] made their advent one day, and declared their respective determinations to "'list for sojers," and how the latter disappeared on the day following; how Christian Draker[11] rattled his tongue all day long about his "brother and nickel maul"; how Frobin stepped around with his tall hat and perfectly blackened boots—the clerk of our squad; how Evans,[12] and Charlton[13] and Brooks,[14] and Brown,[15] and Croy,[16] and Wallace,[17] and McMasters,[18]

21

and Ferguson,[19] and Iverson[20] kept the jokes swinging around their little circle; how Bopenhagen,[21] and Plate,[22] and Kettleburger,[23] and Scheide,[24] and the two Schillings[25] used to promenade with the German fair; how the two Gargans[26] kept drunk most of the time, and growled between themselves at everything we had to eat; of Todd[27]—quiet, shadowy Todd; of Parsell, once a member of the forces that stormed the Malakoff; of Kirk,[28] once of the Light Brigade—the immortal six hundred—who was taken prisoner in that charge; how Simmers[29] grew funny every evening, attacked by some comical disease; how the regularity of these symptoms was the subject of comment among the other members, who, upon consultation, decided to test his complaint by stealing his whiskey—an enterprise that was successfully carried out, to the infinite disgust of the smiling man. These days passed pleasantly enough, though at times we grew restless, and longed for a change from the monotonous life in the pent-up city. The concentration of the contending armies at Washington and Manassas Junction, the newspapers informed us, was vigorously carried on, and we felt a growing anxiety to be present at the battle which was certainly coming, and which most of us thought would be a decisive one. But few of us had ever seen more than one or two thousand men together on parade, and as the forces around Washington were reported to be composed of fifty or sixty thousand soldiers, we felt desirous of seeing this vast array. Curiosity is a powerful stimulus in some people—especially women, we are told—and I felt mine impel me to wish to be present at the seat of hostilities and look upon the pomp and circumstance of real war.

By and by there came rumors of the advance of the federal forces at the capital upon the enemy. The city was wild with excitement at the prospect of the collision. The newspapers contained full accounts of the magnificent pageant as it wound its way through the streets of Washington and across the Long Bridge and up the heights of Arlington. The soldiers sang patriotic hymns and songs—this I remember impressed me deeply; I thought soldiers that could go into battle singing must certainly be invincible. The hopes of the people seemed to have been aroused to the highest pitch; and when at last the movement culminated, when our proud army dissolved disgracefully before the Confederate hosts, the reaction was terrible. Never shall I forget the shudder that passed over me when I read the details of that engagement, and fully realized the shame, the degradation of that fatal 21st of July. Our visions of a speedy close of the war were dissipated; nothing now remained but to prepare for the struggle. We felt that a long vista of death and desolation had suddenly been opened before us, and there was no alternative but to walk therein.

Now came a hurrying of all available troops to the capital. Day after day the tramp of soldiers, the beating of drums and the rattle of crowded trains converglng upon one common center —Washington—resounded all through the loyal States. The record of the defeat at Bull Run was but momentary; the discouragement of the people soon passed away, although the sense of shame remained. But one common sentiment prevailed—to suppress the rebellion we pledge the last man and the last dollar. The reverse was of incalculable value in one respect at least—it taught the nation the nature of the task upon which it had entered. Besides it localized the war; it showed the limits of the virus of secession along the borders of the free States; it uncovered to its fullest extent the ramifications of our national disease—slavery; it confirmed the doubting rebel and developed the true Union man.

The real subject of disaster was the South. From that hour the downfall of its peculiar institution was a mere question of time. Here the term "disaster" has a limited sense, however. Events have shown that it was really a blessing in disguise to the whole country. The rebellion has been subdued; the land is under the shadow of one flag; slavery no longer exists; we have taken a departure on the road to national prosperity.

For this consummation—the salvation of the Union, the summing up of all the above benefits—we have every reason to be grateful. Upon our calendars the 21st of July should be set down as a day of Union victory and rebel defeat.

On the 29th of July we received orders to go into camp at Linden, a picnic resort formerly, located in the neighborhood of Oakland, and on the 30th marched out along the Fourth Street road to that beautiful spot. The day was oppressively warm, but the men bore up well, notwithstanding that, in addition to other difficulties, they were without food, and many of them unused to walking. Some of the boys procured, in a way known only to themselves—for every effort was made to prevent them from leaving the ranks—canteens of liquor, and, much to the horror of the denizens along the Fourth Street road, the air rang with a succession of sounds not mapped out in the symphonies of Beethoven. Finally, however, through the exertions of Sergeant Strick and the lieutenant, together with the entreaties of comrades, our exuberant brethren were safely deposited under the shade of the grove at Linden.

We were dusty, tired, and very hungry. A sort of cookhouse was located on the premises, in which a fat, sleek-looking darkey was duly installed to prepare our food. Though so much fatigued, and so hungry, we had to go to work to pitch our tents. First, the officers quarters—of these dignitaries we had by this time two—were to be established. Then lines were drawn, stakes driven, and "A" tents put up for the men; as we were new hands at the business, it was slow work; several times the canvas houses had to be taken down and realigned.

The officers were almost too particular in this matter, in our opinion then; we could not see the necessity of such great precision in the small matter of pitching tents. What had that to do with war, which in our minds, only meant blood and slaughter, and did not have reference to foolish exactitudes of less than an inch one way, or other, or slightly oblique positions. It was simply absurd; the officers were "putting on style," etc. But our growling availed us nothing; the work had to be done, to suit the official taste. I will confess, however, that, for my own part, I really felt proud at the comely army of white tents after we were done putting them up, and regretted that I had grumbled and found fault with the lieutenant for his exactions.

After we were through with this duty the men were assembled and told off into fours, and each quartette assigned to a tent. A thoughtful government had sent us lumber with which to make floors, and each party busily engaged itself in putting these down—an operation which was soon performed, and then our clothes and blankets transferred inside, mates selected, and everything made as comfortable as circumstances permitted.

By this time we were perfectly ravenous with hunger. Detachments of one from each tent were sent over towards the neighborhood of the cookhouse on reconnaissances, with orders to discover if possible whether any supper was being provided, but these returned with similar reports—nothing of that kind was in sight.

If the commissary department was engaged in its duty of procuring supplies, then the commissary department was eminently successful in keeping its operations invisible. The fat cook sat upon the top of an empty flour barrel, inside the bar, looking complacently upon the scene, and evidently contemplating the beauties of nature. So rapt in this admiration had the sleek looking African become that all our questions as to food fell apparently upon deaf ears; sometimes, however, the slight shrug of his ponderous shoulders assured us that life was not yet extinct.

Finally, some of the boys, in whom hunger aroused a hostile spirit, and who had come to the conclusion that our beloved cook was entirely too indifferent to our suffering, made a demonstration upon the commissary department with partial success. The result of the affair was the issuing of a piece of dry bread to each man, upon which he had to content himself until the next morning.

It transpired subsequently that the proprietor of the National Hotel had the contract of supplying us with food—an arrangement that fully accounted for the indifferent attitude on the part of the fat cook. In obedience to the general demand of the men, Lieutenant McClain cancelled this agreement.

Our experience this night demonstrated the great departure we had made from the comforts of the civil world. From the full table of the hotel to a piece of dry bread; from perfect liberty to strict discipine—these were fundamental changes of conditions. There was much grumbling among the men, and hints of leaving the service immediately were thrown out by a few; but the latter met with a prompt rebuke from their companions.

My own reflections at this period were not of a pleasant nature. Hungry and tired, my bed so cruelly hard, these conditions did not add rosy hues to the perception of the five years lying before me. I felt that now I was really an outcast; society was entirely closed to me; then all the ugly vicissitudes of war stood prominently exposed—death, mutilation, or imprisonment—I thought of all these misfortunes now. My excessive fatigue proved a boon, however, insomuch as it brought a deep slumber upon me, and I forgot my woes within its blessed oblivion.

At early dawn the bugle sounded the reveille. We were a little slow getting out, for the habits we had accquired during our three weeks stay at the National were rather of the indolent sort, and besides the previous day's work had worn us out with fatigue. The breakfast was somewhat better than our supper had been; additional to bread there was a very small piece of meat and about a pint of coffee—the latter, however, weak enough as a decoction.

At nine o'clock the men were assembled, and a series of orders were read, one of which designated our cantonment as Camp Scott, in honor of the Lieutenant General of the army. Our captain—Joseph H. Taylor[30]—had joined us by this time, and took command of the company. He was a small-waisted, slightly-built, cross-looking man, with a voice that astonished us—so fierce, and sounding so like the yelp of a bull-dog when he gave orders on drill.

Although our first impression of Captain Taylor was not assuring, yet time showed that he was one of the kindest of officers in the service. He busied himself about our welfare, giving us wholesome advice as to discipline, which afterwards proved of great benefit.

I here transcribe extracts from a letter written to a friend, under date Camp Scott, July 31, 1861, which exhibit the feelings of the Common Soldier at that time:

Dear Mrs. Samuels:

I seat myself beside a pile of luggage, which I have improvised into a writing desk, within our nice canvas tent—and, by the way, we have fixed it up to be as comfortable as a good house—to write you a letter.

While I am thus engaged most of the boys are exercising themselves on the green sward outside by feats of muscle. A shout of laughter has just greeted my ears, in consequence of a false leap by one individual, tumbling him head over heels on the ground.

We are all in splendid spirits, as though this war business was only, fun, and as though Manassas had been taken without a blow. Water-proof India-rubber coats have just been issued to us, and we can now stand out in the rain all day without getting wet.

Last night slept for the first time under canvas, on hard boards, with two blankets under me, and, considering circumstances, slept sound as a roach. (I use the term, "slept sound as a roach," because I have so often seen it quoted to show what a good night's rest one has had; my personal knowledge as to how a roach sleeps, however, is very limited; indeed, I do not think I ever saw one asleep.)

We had very, little to eat yesterday—the day of our arrival here—but are now better provisioned. Our captain made a speech to us this morning, and told us to be gentlemen, and he would treat us right.

I am very much obliged to you for your kindness in sending the towels and bandages, and for what you have always done for me.

Tell Taylor we have a jolly time here. We expect to get our arms soon.

The old lady to whom the above letter was written was the house-keeper at Bentley's. She had been a mother to me for over sixteen years—a good, kind mother, too. The item "bandages" mentioned in my letter she had sent me in the belief that I might need them in the field. Of course, I could not carry, a huge roll of muslin with me, but for her sake I held on to the articles as long as possible.

We now settled into the regular duties of camp life. Orders were issued establishing regular hours for drill, fatigue, and police duty; guard mounting took place daily, at nine o'clock in the morning; the Rules and Articles of War were read every second Sunday by the adjutant. Lieutenant Balk,[31] whose diction was not elegant, but whose emphasis upon the words "court-martial" and "shot" was faultless, tapering off so delicately upon the succeeding phrase—"or such other punishment as the court shall direct"—that few of us understood it, and were thus left with the shock of the extreme punishment upon our susceptible nerves.

Strange officers began to show themselves, some mounted upon gaily caparisoned steeds; new companies marched into camp and pitched their tents; and one day not long after our arrival here the whole command was marched out upon the parade ground to listen to orders read by Lieutenant Whitesides, the new adjutant.

The substance of these orders was an agreeable surprise to our party from Pittsburg. We were formally announced to be the Sixth Regiment of Cavalry, United States Army—a new regular regiment formed in accordance with an act of Congress approved July 22, 1861,[32] I think; our term of service was to be three years instead of five; our pay was to be thirteen dollars per month, instead of twelve; and we were to receive in addition to all this, one hundred dollars bounty. Our party from the National was designated as Company F, under command of Captain Taylor.

My experience teaches me that the most difficult part of the Raw Recruit to bring into a state of complete discipline is his stomach. He can easily master all the rudiments of military life, if he only goes about it in earnest; he can learn to yield a graceful obedience to those placed in command over him; if the occasion offers, he may even conduct himself heroically in the presence of the enemy; he can cheerfully endure fatigue; but I would not venture to say that he is ever fully satisfied with his stomach. That unruly portion of his anatomy refused to be comforted; it is forever suggesting stronger luxuries, forever wandering away from what should be its first, last and only love—army rations. It changes him into a midnight marauder; it tempts him to commit that most petty, most contemptible crimes of all—the theft of his brother soldier's rations.

During the first month of military life the struggle is a terrible one. Owing to the fact that the regulation allowance is much less in amount to the quantity he has been in the habit of gourmandizing when a civilian, the unruly stomach must be shrunken in its dimensions—a process of fearful torture; often yielding to its demands, he prolongs his sufficiency, or is driven wild by the persisting officiousness of civilians, who bring to camp baskets full of dainties for acquaintances. Words cannot describe the forlorn facial expression of a friendless recruit under the latter circumstances.

Such were precisely the difficulties that beset us at Camp Scott. When the contract with the proprietor of the National hotel was cancelled, and the sleek-looking African ousted from his stronghold, cooks were detailed from the company and the regular allowances dealt out to the men. This was a decided improvement every way—the allowances were somewhat larger, and much better prepared—in fact, the culinary department did its duty too well in this respect, as the men were able and anxious to eat so much the more—more than the proportionate increase of food permitted.

For a while it was customary with some to eat their daily allowance for breakfast, and fast the remainder of the day; others divided it into equal parts, and consumed a third part for each traditional meal, thus bringing their stomachs within a state of partial discipline; an example I recommend in preference to the first mentioned class.

My sister and my hostess at 151 Third Street, and one of my old schoolmates from Washington County, kept me well supplied with substantials and luxuries—in fact, the services of our entire quartette in the tent were necessary to devour the abundance proferred, and I need not say their assistance was promptly and cheerfully rendered. Owing to this additional source of supply I did not suffer so much as many others at Camp Scott; my misfortune in this respect overtook me after our departure from its precincts.

In time I grew used to my hard bed, and learned to sleep soundly from tattoo to reveille, our enforced habits in this respect proving of great benefit to me; and the open air life began to inspire me with, a good appetite and fresh vigor, such as I had not enjoyed for a long time.

Our camp was a model one in all respects. The tents were new and bright-looking, and pitched on lines drawn with mathematical precision; each company swept its streets twice daily with brooms improvised from the boughs of trees. At headquarters a large American flag floated from a staff, giving a completeness to the picture; and the masses of visitors that swarmed out daily to see us from the staid city grew larger. Under the training of our officers the regiment gradually assumed a soldierly appearance on parade, and the recruits began to exhibit a real pride in their new career.

I will not here recount the story of the haunted cookhouse, where almost nightly the sentry was visited by a "headless woman in white;" or how Cravar[33] was driven from this post by this apparition, and could not be induced to return to it; or how it threw Conway into a hysterical state until his yells brought the guard to his relief. Nor will I tell how McAlligot[34] and Charlton fought about a fair damsel whom both loved, and who lived in a house on the hill; nor how Weisenberger[35] and Frobin—two mighty men of war—exhibited their prowess in an encounter from which Frobin retired defeated with a gash on his marble forehead, whose grim proportions he unavailingly sought to conceal under his curly locks. An abler pen than mine is necessary to do justice to these themes.

During these days I often, when off duty, wandered away from camp alone among the woods, and in their deep solitudes pondered over the future, trying to lift the veil that shut out from sight the prospective grave vicissitudes of the three coming years of my army life. I was not ambitious; my sole desire was to be faithful as a common soldier. The question I earnestly propounded to myself was, "Will I be able to keep faith with my country? Will I, when brought into the presence of the enemy, be able to control my fears, and to do my duty or will I act the coward, and disgrace myself and my friends, and poor old father?" Then my reflections would invariable pass from, the future to the past—to my childhood, to my schooldays, to my old home by the river—and finally the tears would come to my eyes in spite of myself, and I would hasten back to the boisterous camp to forget it all in the hilarious confusion.

Another of my favorite places of resort was in the shadow of a huge oak tree. Here a little blue-eyed six-year old girl invariably came out to see me. The dear little creature, in the simplicity of her nature, made me presents of acorns and for fear of wounding her feelings I took them all to her apparent delight cheerfully loading my pockets. After this she brought her little baby brother out to see me. Then we had such a splendid time, romping, building Lilliputian bark houses and thatching them with leaves, and upon one, to distinguish it as a church, we affixed a spire.

The evenings at Camp Scott were really enjoyable. The white tents, illuminated by hundreds of lights presented an unsteady, ghostly appearance; the little groups of soldiers scattered here and there over the lawn laughing and singing old songs; the surroundings of gloomy woodlands; the glimmer of the river far below the hill; the red glare in the sky above the vast ironworks towards the city—these formed a scene uniquely picturesque.

And mornings—how shall I describe them? My eyes are open with the dawn, and I wander away off to the bluff above the river. Below me are myriads of boats, with huge black volumes of smoke issuing from the chimneys; there are villages stretching beyond the utmost range of vision; there are fields of grain; there are hills in the distance, whose summits found the horizon. The woods are full of singing birds; great flocks of sheep and herds of cattle swarm the hillsides. And over all the sun begins to pour his golden rays.

Hark! The blare of a bugle, at first dim and uncertain but presently swelling into the shrill notes of the reveille breaks upon my ear and rebounding along the hilltops. I immediately return to camp. There is a swift mustering of companies in front of their respective tents, a rapid alignment, and then "parade rest." The notes of many trumpets break forth, making melody; then comes the gruff command "Attention!" The roll is called; the sergeant wheels and reports "all present or accounted for," to the commissioned officer who is waiting to receive it, the line dissolves, and the men prepare themselves for breakfast, and the routine duties of the day.

NOTES

1. According to the regimental history, the regiment was recruited largely in western Pennsylvania, Ohio and upstate New York.

2. At the time that Sidney M. Davis enlisted, the term of three years for volunteers had only recently been established. When Lincoln called for 75,000 troops in response to the attack on Fort Sumter, their term was a mere 90 days.

3. See Chapter 4 for a fuller description of the young lady and the denouement of their romance.

4. Louis Frobin enlisted on July 3, 1861, in Pittsburg at the age of 21. He was born in Germany. He was discharged at the expiration of his term of service on July 3, 1864, at Lighthouse Point, Virginia. Virtually all of the members of Company F enlisted in Pittsburg.

5.   Hancock Taylor McClain was appointed 1st Lieutenant of the 3rd Cavalry on May 14, 1861, when the army expanded to add one regiment of cavalry. In August, 1861, there was a reorganization, and the 3rd Cavalry was redesignated the 6th Cavalry.

6.   Mathias Flascher enlisted on July 3, 1861, in Pittsburg at the age of 32. He was born in Konigsburg, Germany, and was discharged at the expiration of his term of service on July 3, 1864, at Lighthouse Point, Virginia.

7.   Michael Conway enlisted on July 3, 1861, in Pittsburg at the age of 32. He was born in Kerry County, Ireland. Conway died on January 1, 1862, of disease, at the camp east of the Capitol.

8.   John M. Schumaker enlisted on July 9, 1861, in Pittsburg at the age of 29. He was born in Germany, and was discharged for disability in Baltimore, Maryland, On April 15, 1863.

9.   "Ole Blue" has been identified elsewhere in the memoirs as James Stewart. He enlisted on July 26, 1861, in Pittsburg at the age of 20. He was born in Pennsylvania, and reenlisted in the field.

10.   James L. Wilson enlisted on July 17, 1861, in Pittsburg at the age of 23. He was born in Pennsylvania.

11.   Christian Draker enlisted on July 16, 1861, in Pittsburg at the age of 31. He was born in Hanover, Germany, and was discharged at the expiration of his term of service on July 16, 1864, at Lighthouse Point, Virginia.

12.   James Evans enlisted on July 22, 1861, in Pittsburg at the age of 19. He was born in Allegheny County, Pennsylvania, and was killed on July 7, 1863, at Funkstown, Maryland.

13.   Joseph Charlton enlisted on July 11, 1861, in Pittsburg at the age of 20. He was born in New Castle, England, and was discharged for disability on July 29, 1864, in West Philadelphia.

14.   Robert E. Brooks enlisted on July 6, 1861, in Pittsburg at the age of 21. He was born in Crownsville, Pennsylvania. He was discharged on February 8, 1864 so he could reenlist in a different regiment.

15.   John M. Brown enlisted on July 1, 1861, in Pittsburg at the age of 23. He was born in Pennsylvania, and was discharged at the expiration of his term of service on July 1, 1864, at Lighthouse Point, Virginia.

16.   Levi B. Croy enlisted on July 3, 1861, in Pittsburg at the age of 34. He was born in Butler, Pennsylvania, and was discharged in the field at the expiration of his term of service on July 3, 1864.

17.   Robert Wallace enlisted on July 6, 1861, in Pittsburg at the age of 28. He was born in Scotland, and was discharged at the expiration of his term of service on July 6, 1864, at Lighthouse Point, Virginia.

18. Robert H. McMasters enlisted on July 6, 1861, in Pittsburg at the age of 25. He was born in Canada, and was discharged at the expiration of his term of service on July 6, 1864, at Lighthouse Point, Virginia.

19. William Ferguson enlisted on July 3, 1861, in Pittsburg at the age of 32. He was born in Pennsylvania, and was discharged at the expiration of his term of service on July 3, 1864, at Lighthouse Point, Virginia.

20. Richard Iverson (the last name appears as Everson in other sources) enlisted on July 3, 1861, in Pittsburg at the age of 40. He was born in Newport, England, and was discharged at the expiration of his term of service on July 3, 1864, at Lighthouse Point, Virginia.

21. August Bopenhagen enlisted on July 3, 1861, in Pittsburg at the age of 21. He was born in Germany, and was discharged at the expiration of his term of service on July 3, 1864, at Lighthouse Point, Virginia.

22. Henry Plate enlisted on July 3, 1861, in Pittsburg at the age of 22. He was born in Hanover, Germany, and deserted to the Confederates in 1862.

23. Jacob Kettleburger enlisted on July 26, 1861, in Pittsburg at the age of 21. He was born in Altdorf, Germany. He died on Nevember 18, 1863, of pneumonia, while in Richmond as a prisoner of war.

24. George Scheide enlisted on July 6, 1861, in Pittsburg at the age of 23. He was born in Pennsylvania, and died on November 11, 1861, of disease, in Washington, D.C.

25. Jacob Schilling enlisted on July 11, 1861, in Pittsburg at the age of 25. He was born in Germany, and was discharged at the expiration of his term of service on July 11, 1864, at Lighthouse Point, Virginia. William Schilling enlisted on July 12, 1861, in Pittsburg at the age of 21. He was also born in Germany, and was discharged at the expiration of his term of service on July 12, 1864, at Lighthouse Point, Virginia.

26. James Gargan enlisted on July 6, 1861, in Pittsburg at the age of 29. He was born in Pennsylvania. He died on December 17, 1861, in Washington, D.C., of disease. Peter Gargan enlisted on the same day, in the same place, and was 34 years old. He deserted on January 27, 1862.

27. James Todd enlisted on July 9, 1861, in Pittsburg at the age of 21. He was born in Charlston, Indiana, and was discharged at the expiration of his term of service on July 9, 1864, at Lighthouse Point, Virginia.

28. Hugh Kirk enlisted on July 23, 1861, in Pittsburg at the age of 25. He was born in Belfast, Ireland. He deserted on January 17, 1863.

29. John P. Simmers enlisted on July 6, 1861, in Pittsburg at the age of 31. He was born in Germany, and was discharged at the expiration of his term of service on July 6, 1864, at Lighthouse Point, Virginia.

30. Joseph Hancock Taylor, a West Point graduate, was promoted on May 14, 1861, to Captain of the 3rd Cavalry (which was redesignated the 6th Cavalry in August, 1861. He received a brevet Lieutenant Colonelcy on September 5, 1862, for meritorious service in the Antietam campaign. He died on March 13, 1865.

31. Setphen S. Balk, an Englishman, was appointed a 2nd Lieutenant with the 6th Cavalry on August 20, 1861. He was promoted to 1st Leiutenant on July 17, 1862. Balk retired from the service on May 14, 1864. Virtually all of the lieutenants in the 6th Cavalry were previously enlisted men.

32. The regiment was organized in May, 1861, but the memoirs are correct in stating that the enabling legislation was not passed until July (although the date was July 29, not July 22).

33. John Cravar or Craven, enlisted on July 3, 1861, in Pittsburg at the age of 20. He was born in Galway, Ireland, and was discharged for disability on July 30, 1863, in the District of Columbia.

34. Charles McAlligot enlisted on July 9, 1861, in Pittsburg at the age of 20. He was born in Keery County, Ireland, and was discharged at the expiration of his term of service on July 9, 1864, at Lighthouse Point, Virginia.

35. John Weisenberger enlisted on July 15, 1861, in Pittsburg at the age of 24. He was born in France, and was discharged for disability on December 2, 1862, in Falmouth, Virginia.

A New Base and Learning Process

About the 22nd of August the command, now mustering some four hundred men, received orders to leave Camp Scott for the South. Nearly everybody appeared to be delighted with the prospective change, although it was, of course, an additional step in the round of progression toward dangerous scenes.

Then followed a day of confusion. Friends came to bid us goodbye, and make us their last presents of cakes, pies, and sandwiches; letters had to be written announcing our intended departure; clothing had to be drawn from the quartermasters department; rations for three days were distributed; articles brought to camp for comfort and amusement, which could not be taken along, must be left behind or sent home per express; and thousand things of a desultory character, never thought of on any other occasion, now forced themselves upon our attention, and we were compelled to attempt the impossible feat of attending to all of them at once.

Early on Monday morning we took up our line of march for the city, bidding farewell to Camp Scott, now to fade from our sight forever, to be remembered in the coming time as the spot where we took our first lessons in the art of war. As we emerged from its limits upon the Fourth Street road I found my little companions waiting to bid me good-bye, kissing me with the utmost simplicity. Dear little creatures! They could not realize the terrible meaning of that day's spectacle.

At Pittsburg, near the depot, we found the streets crowded with people, who had assembled to witness our departure. A large majority of these were ladies. As we filed along the train, loud cheers greeted us from the men and a cloud of waving handkerchiefs from their fair companions. This was glory, I thought, as I felt my nerves thrill with excitement like a shock from an electric battery. By common consent our lungs were simultaneously distended by one long, terrific huzzah. I hardly dare to trust myself longer with the memory of that scene.

Some of the boys, as usual, had managed to fill their canteens with a forbidden liquid. They were very boisterous, but otherwise conducted themselves with great decorum. After considerable effort on the part of Sergeant Strick, Company F was safely installed in a car, and awaited developments.

At this stage of affairs I have to note the first misfortune that befell me in my new career. A large carpetsack, filled with the choicest provisions, and which, from their delicate texture, required the utmost watchfulness on my part to preserve intact, was carefully placed on my side. While glancing hurriedly out of the window upon the crowded street, forgetting for the instant my treasure, Donaldson[1] came in with a face upon which rested a benign smile, and complacently sat down upon the mass of pastry, crushing it into a shapeless jumble.

My usual good nature received a great shock by this untoward incident, but Donaldson made such a graceful apology that I could not for the life of me refuse to forgive him.

At this moment the confusion was indescribable; nearly everybody was trying to get his head out of the car windows and shake hands with everybody else; Old Blue was interviewing his sister, who was giving him the excellent and patriotic advice never to desert his flag, while the tears were coursing down each of their comical-looking faces; Charlton was proclaiming to the assembled multitude that he was a Pittsburg boy. Ferguson, by some remarkable accident, fell into the gutter while trying to get to the car, but was promptly helped to his feet by the genial Evans; Croy was the personification of benevolence. Wallace's broad Scotch face grew broader and more Scotch in appearance as he looked upon the scene, while his sand-colored hair and red whiskers almost glowed; Flascher was discoursing upon the diseases of horses, and the Prussian cavalry; Draker still rattled about his "brother and nickel maul," with a persistency that was wonderful; Simmers had a severe attack of his periodic giggling, while by his side hung the Plethoric canteen; Todd's shadowy form rested half-reclining in a corner, while his resolute gray eyes were fixed upon the crowd, and a peculiar smile of satisfaction played upon his lips; the three Schillings and Scheide and Plate were bidding their German female acquaintances good-bye in

---

[1] This soldier has not been positively identified. There were three Donaldsons in the company.

stentorian tones; and Everson's[2] short body was stretched to its utmost extent out of the window, in a frantic effort to shake hands with some other short body.

But the whistle sounds at last; there is a rapid scattering of the crowd in the street from around the train; a few desperate women cling to the hands of their loved ones as though they would hold on to them forever, then there is a sudden jerk, that almost throws one headlong upon the back of the seat in front, and we are in motion towards the Federal capital. A shudder passed through me when I fully realized the import of the shrill whistle of that locomotive, and the steady rattle of the train that was carrying me away from my home and friends to fields of peril and suffering. As if sharing these feelings, most of the men grew silent and thoughtful as they watched the city recede from sight—to many of them, as it afterwards proved, forever!

Our old joyousness soon returns, however. The genial Evans hurls a joke full at the head of Charlton, "the Pittsburg boy;" Old Blue's comical face frightfully distends in a vain effort to sing; Ferguson has been safely coiled up in a corner; Flascher, "the horse's doctor," as he calls himself, is pouring forth a stream of lingo that sounds for all the world like the rattling and spitting of an ignited bunch of firecrackers into the ears of his German friends; shadowy Todd settles himself into his seat with his hands thrust deep into his pockets and half shuts his gray eyes; Wallace and Croy sit together, the former's broad Scotch accents mingling with the soft Yankee purl of the latter; the three Schillings, and Scheide, and Plate, to judge from the great display of photographs and delicate-looking notes, and the occasional "charming maid" I hear, are discussing the German fair; and poor Simmer's face is still wreathed in that periodical comical smile.

At every village along the road we were met by crowds of people, who welcomed us with hearty cheers, and displayed the American flag. The whole country through which we passed seemed to be fairly ablaze with enthusiasm.

There is nothing, I think, which so repays the common soldier for his services as the expressed gratitude of the people for whom he takes the field. When they sullenly pass him by without recognition, he loses spirit in the contest, and begins to flag in his patriotism. Dollars to him are nothing; there are times in his life, during the cruel scenes of a

---

[2] This is probably the individual identified in the notes to chapter 2 as Iverson. Varient spellings of names is very commonplace in the records.

37

campaign, when he would give millions of them to be from the field an hour. Extend to your soldiers your hearty sympathy, and you make your army invincible.

I greatly enjoyed the ride over the Pennsylvania Central Railroad. The ever-changing scenery of hill and dale and river, of woodland and field, was a source of exquisite pleasure. I hoped we would reach the Allegheny mountains before nightfall, for I had heard much about their wonderful grandeur and I longed to see them for myself, but in this I was destined to be disappointed. Darkness came on before we reached their base.

The train stopped at Johnstown for a few moments. Here the great gleaming sea of fire was an object of interest to most of us, for few had seen such a vast establishment as the Cambria Ironworks, with its myriads of workmen, who flitted about among the flames like so many demons. It took but little effort of the imagination on one's part to work up a perfect picture of the bottomless pit.

While standing on the platform of our car about ten o'clock that night, watching the lights that seemed to dash past us in a headlong career, a spark from the locomotive fell into my right eye. For a time this gave me great pain, and obliged me to return within the car. The agony continued until towards morning; but finally I fell asleep with my head resting upon the back of the seat.

Shortly after daylight I awakened, and found that we were running along the banks of a beautiful river. Its margins were fringed with dark green forests and its bosom studded with small islands. Upon margin and Island dense forests crowded to the water's edge. This was the famous Susquehanna.

At Harrisburg the command changed cars. A short delay occurred here, the monotony of which was somewhat broken by threatened hostilities between Thomas[3] and Powell[4]—the latter, a large, quarrelsome Irishman had accidentally received a blow with a small pebble stone which brought the blood spouting from his scalp—we were packed away in filthy cattle-cars.

[3] John Thomas enlisted on July 6, 1861. He was 24 at the time, and was born in Rockland County, New York. He was discharged at Lighthouse Point, Virginia, at the expiration of his term on July 6, 1864.

[4] Patrick Powell enlisted on July 4, 1861, at the age of 23. He was born in Clare County, Ireland, and was discharged at the expiration of his term of service on July 4, 1864, at Lighthouse Point, Virginia.

At the first station outside of Harrisburg a rumor that an attack was meditated upon our party by the secessionists of the Monumental City[5] found frequency. As this sort of amusement had already been practiced upon the Sixth Massachusetts volunteers under somewhat similar circumstances, the rumor assumed a phase of disagreeable plausibility. A good deal of nervousness was manifested by most of the men, and some criticism upon the action of the government thus in sending soldiers through such a dangerous section of country without arms found expression.

Near Baltimore we came upon the first signs of our approach to a hostile community. These were sentries on duty along the rail-road to protect the track and keep open communication with the capital. As we dashed by the guards halted on their beats, faced the train and presented arms. There were numerous little encampments, and at these the soldiers would fall in under arms and salute us, while our men thrilled the old Maryland hills with cheers. It was a curious sight to me—these camps, these sentries, and these armed lines, on actual duty guarding the railroad. Even now I could hardly realize that there was really a war.

The train reached Baltimore some time after dark, and the men disembarked from their disagreeable quarters. We were somewhat reassured by the silence of the surroundings. But few people were seen, and these were apparently indifferent to our presence. Orders were given to the men to preserve perfect order and quiet on our march to the Washington depot, which was fully observed, although, on account of the pleasant greeting extended to us by citizens of all ages, sizes, and colors along the route, it was as much as we could do to refrain from breaking forth into cheers. These demonstrations were a wonderful, and, I need not say, an agreeable surprise to us all. Instead of a hearty "welcome to hospitable graves," as we had been led to anticipate by the numerous newspaper articles published at that period, the warm commendations and display of loyal bunting were equal to that of any place along our route, and much greater than at Harrisburg.

At the Washington depot we found four or five hundred recruits—a ragged, motley crowd of men, in citizen's clothes. They were apparently in very high spirits. A number of women and little girls maintained a thriving business in provisions. At first these were regarded with some suspicion by our hungry squad, owing to the many rumors of cases of

[5]   This refers to Baltimore and the Washington Monument on, appropriately enough, Monument Street. The Washington Monument in the District of Columbia was only partially erected, and funds for further construction were not available.

39

poisoning afloat; but their famished stomachs at last overcame all opposition, and they soon joined with the recruits in purchasing largely of the palatable luxuries. Some little excitement was occasioned by a quarrel between a white citizen and a colored boy, and quite a crowd gathered, but the affair was soon checked by the arrival of some policemen and the prompt arrest of the aggressor.

Two or three hours after our arrival at the depot another train of cattle cars were assigned to us, but this did not start for Washington until after daylight next morning. In the meantime the men in their agony of fatigue stretched themselves out at all available points, the writer occupying a broken bench that he was fortunate enough to find bolstered up behind an old building near the depot.

When the cars started I located myself in a convenient spot near the car door, that I might observe the scenery as we passed through the country. A partial view of Baltimore, with its harbor and shipping rewarded my efforts; but the level land, covered with low pines, and disfigured here and there with squalid cabins and dilapidated farm houses, formed an unpleasant picture, and I was glad when, two hours later, the train halted at Hyattsville, some six miles from Washington. It was a forlorn looking village, but the surrounding country was quite attractive.

Here we found Company H, which had arrived several days before, snugly ensconced in tents along the bank of a fine brook, which forms, I think, the headwaters of the Eastern Branch of the Potomac. The site selected was a very pleasant one, about half a mile from Bladensburg—a meadow skirted on the south by the brook and woodlands, which formed the limits of the camp on that side. The clear pools of water were very inviting to men whose opportunities for washing had been curtailed for some days past, and whose bodies were begrimed with dust and smoke from the locomotive, and in a short time everybody was vigorously applying soap and water to his person in a manner that showed his appreciation of the boon.

By nightfall our tents were pitched, a good hearty supper eaten, and all the men were hilarious but sleepy. When tattoo sounded that evening it found a willing and prompt obedience on the part of the command.

I transcribe here extracts from a letter dated Bladensburg, Maryland, August 29, 1861—a few days after our arrival—as exhibiting the feelings and sensations of the common soldier at this stage of his military life:

Our company left Pittsburg on Monday afternoon for the south, and arrived here about ten o'clock on Wednesday morning, after the jolliest kind of a trip, having been received by the people at all points along the route with demonstrations of joy and satisfaction. Even in Maryland the people seemed glad to see us, for at almost every house a flag or handkerchief was waving, while at Baltimore, where we looked for treatment of a different character, old and young, men and women, black and white, all welcomed us with apparent sincerity. I did not hear an insulting remark or see a solitary rebel flag in Baltimore, although from newspaper accounts I had been led to expect both.

We are now encamped about six miles from Washington, near Bladensburg, surrounded by our secession friends, who, rumor says, are altogether too familiar with the infantry pickets in the neighborhood, one of whom was shot dead the other night by some unknown person, a couple of miles from here. Such rumors are not reassuring to our party, as we have no arms except sabres, and these are not available as against rifles.

I understand that by air line the distance from this point to Bull Run is about thirty miles. Occasionally we hear some cannonading, which often gives rise to rumors of battle; but these so far have proved untrue, being merely the artillery practice of some of our batteries.

We now realize that all this parade of troops is not a meaningless display; that there is really a state of war existing, and that we are not far from that line that divides the hostile forces. The men seem cheerful, though somewhat sobered down from their former hilarious enthusiasm—a change, I take it, for the better, as it brings them to a serious consideration of the work in hand.

We have settled down to the regular conditions of camp life; we have tents, and sleep upon the ground, and have hard bread, coffee, and pork and beans for our rations. The change of life so far seems to prove beneficial to my health, and, with exception of the circumstances which called me to the field, I have no reason for regrets.

Shortly after our arrival a startling story reached us that a force of the enemy was encamped in the woods some ten miles south of us; and the particular instructions given to the guards after nightfall to keep a sharp lookout gave it an ugly plausibility. As a result, the men felt somewhat uncomfortable for a time. This, however, turned out to be one of the thousand fabrications of the nervous element in camp, which was perpetually suggesting some horrible contingency or inventing some disquieting story.

One night, while some such rumor was afloat, I was a member of the detail for guard. It was my lot to occupy, during the "wee small hours" a lonely beat along the edge of a campfield that was located on the east

41

side of the camp. I had been on post perhaps an hour, cogitating on various old ghost stories I had heard long years before, and at intervals peering sharply along the green rows of corn, when a bugle in camp struck up a shrill, nervous call, quite different from anything I had yet heard. Following this almost instantaneously came the voices of officers, giving orders to "turn out, fall in," and in another moment the company streets were alive with men mustering in hot haste. I hurriedly surveyed all the surrounding country as far as my limited vision would reach, but could see nothing unusual. Then came great shouts of laughter from camp, and a sudden disappearance of half clad forms into their tents, and in a moment more all was as quiet as before.

It transpired that the captain of Company H, having reason to suppose that some of his men were absent without leave, had ordered his bugler to sound "assembly," in order to discover if such were the case; but the inexperienced trumpeter, whose dreams perhaps had been of a troubled character, sprang to his feet and sounded "to arms."

There was a good deal of merriment in camp the next morning over our first alarm. When I went down to Company F's tents for breakfast, a perfect babel of voices was discussing the event. One of the Gargans, the growlers, was telling how he had jumped up when the bugle sounded, and had buckled on his sword, and that he was the first man on the company parade ground; Iverson was explaining to Wallace how he had turned out at the first note of alarm, and buckled on his sword, and that he was the first man on the company parade ground; Flascher was informing Simmers, the smiler, how he had buckled on his sword, when the bugle sounded, and that he was the first man on the parade ground; the mercurial little Irishman, Leonard,[6] instantly met Flascher with a counter-claim as to who was the first man under arms on the parade ground. All efforts to learn, from these discussions, who was the honest man in the company were in vain.

There was a general interchange of articles of clothing that morning among the men, who, during the excitement the night before, had snatched whatever came first—and from all accounts the efforts of some large people to crawl into the boots and pants of smaller people must have been ludicrous. To imagine the burly Powell endeavoring to get into the neat boots of the diminutive Cravar, and the diminutive Cravar putting on the larger boots of the burly Powell; or the giant Wallace

[6] John Leonard enlisted on July 10, 1861, at the age of 22. He was born in Staffordshire, England. He was discharged on July 10, 1864, upon the expiration of his term of service, at Lighthouse Point, Virginia.

trying to buckle on the sabre of the shadowy Todd, and the shadowy Todd trying to buckle on the sabre of the giant Wallace!

This false alarm was very beneficial in one respect, at least. It learned the men to put their arms and clothing in accessible spots, and demonstrated the wisdom of the regulars to fall in for roll-call under arms upon all occasions and under all circumstances. Perhaps the history of many a surprise by the enemy among the volunteer troops during the war would not have been written if this requirement of discipline had been rigidly enforced.

Some few nights after this event I was aroused from my slumbers by the loud pattering of rain upon our tent. For a short time I laid still listening to the fierce storm; but accidentally putting out my hand, I made a frightful discovery—the tent was flooded with water! My blanket had been wrapped so tightly about me that the fluid had not yet soaked through it. I sprang to my feet, and caught up my clothing. Fortunately, the water had not yet reached these indispensable articles. Our sabres were safe enough, as they were hung up by the cross-bar of the tent.

In a few moments the entire camp was swamped, and several hundred disconsolate-looking men might have been seen wandering about for the balance of the night.

I confess that this experience was a severe test to my patriotism and patience. I would have given a portion of my bounty to have been home, with the poor privilege of sleeping in the pig-sty, for I remembered that was dry and warm. It was astonishing, however, how soon we forgot our discomforts the next morning, when the sun arose in a clear blue sky. By nightfall our blankets were all dry, and a few pine boughs protected us from the ground.

We, too, had a field of honor in Bladensburg,[7] in imitation of the fiery statesmen of the early days of the Republic, but the affairs were not so sanguinary as their prototypes. The weapons used were those with which nature had provided the combatants, and used according to the rules of the ring. It was the custom whenever a dispute had passed beyond the control of diplomacy for the parties thereto to go outside the limits of the camp to this sequestered spot and appeal to arms.

A sad joke in this connection was perpetrated upon the men by Dietz and another bugler. A sudden quarrel rose between them, and coats and caps were flung recklessly to one side, sleeves were rolled up and the

[7] The reference is to the dueling ground at Bladensburg. While noted for the duel between Stephen Decatur and Commodore Barron, it was also the scene of several duels between Congressmen, and by newspaper editors and people impugned in print.

combatants strode with scowling faces towards the cornfield.

"A fight! A fight!" shouted several voices at once when this proceeding had been observed.

This was the rallying cry, and as usual eager crowds of men swarmed out of their tents to see the impending conflict.

On marched Dietz and his foe, cursing each other in the most vicious manner, and shaking their fists under each other's noses. On followed the immense audience in a state of great excitement over the expected fight. When at last the scene of combat was reached, and the multitude had surged up into a sort of clumsy ring around them, they—well, I may not say what they did, these hateful principals, but there was no fight.

The disgusted crowd, feeling itself very badly sold, retired precipitately from the spot. From that time to this no one has been found who went out to see the battle between the two buglers.

During these days we were initiated into the several modes of punishment employed in the army for the preservation and enforcement of discipline. The inebriate were, as a general thing, taken down to the creek by two stalwart guards, and submerged at intervals until they became completely sober. Minor offenses were punished by extra duty details, or incarceration in the guard-house. Those of a more serious nature were expiated by the perpetrator in another novel way—he was attached to the "cord-wood brigade," and doomed to walk at stated periods around a ring with a log of wood on his shoulder. A still severer mode was to tie the culprit up by the thumbs to a post; in this case the weight of the body rested almost entirely upon those members, the toes barely touching the ground, and the suffering was intense. Still another mode, generally enforced when men became violent and threatening, was to "buck and gag" them. "Bucking and gagging" consisted in tying the hands together by the wrists in front, and then forcing the knees up between the arms, running a stout stick through under those joints and over the elbows, so that all struggling was impossible, the victim being thus placed in a very painful position; then inserting a wooden stick like a bridle-bit between the teeth, and fastening it securely by a rope or strap behind the head.

By common consent the prisoners in the guard-house were called Company "Q".

One surprising circumstance, or coincidence, if one chooses to so regard it, was the invariable reply given to a certain question; "For what offense are you imprisoned?" when addressed to the inmates of a guardhouse. I found this peculiar similarity not confined alone to our regiment, but all others with which I have come in contact throughout the army. The answer was, almost invariably, "Nothing!" I have not the least doubt that my many comrades will recognize the truth of this assertion. It is possible that this uniformity can be accounted for on psychological principles, and to the able professors of that science I leave it for solution.

Our duties during this period were light but incessant. First, reveille aroused the slumbering Raw Recruit, and the roll was called; then followed lessons in sabre-exercise, which gave us an appetite for breakfast; after this meal came a drill in field maneuvers, which materially assisted digestion; then dinner, and after dinner another field drill; and at five o'clock the labors of the day were closed by dress parade. After that, at sunset and nine o'clock, we had, respectively, retreat and tattoo, at which we simply fell in under arms and answered to our names at the roll call.

In addition to this daily routine, there was guard mounting, details for camp, and cook's police, and fatigue parties. The man who came off guard one morning went on camp police the next, and was expected and required to keep the company streets and the grounds around the officer's quarters swept clean. On the succeeding morning he was detailed as cook's police, and was obliged to carry water, split wood, and otherwise assist that august chief of the pots and kettles, and to carry water and wood for the laundresses of the company. These latter appendages of the camp, however, were dispensed with when the regiment took the field.

Four women, the wives of enlisted men, were allowed to each company as laundresses. They were quartered in wall tents, which, to secure a degree of privacy, were located at some distance from the company. They were expected to wash the clothes of the soldiers of the company to which their husbands belonged, and were by the government allowed one ration per day in all respects similar to that issued to the men. The price fixed per piece by the council of administration for the regiment as compensation for their labor was five cents for shirts and under clothing and ten cents for pants. A guard was posted in front of their quarters to protect them from insult or violence.

I have stated above that our laundresses did not follow us to the field. There was one exception. A woman attached to Company D donned a uniform and followed her husband all through the Peninsular campaign, remaining with the wagon train while the soldiers were marching and fighting, and rejoining them when they encamped.[8] The men seemed to be somewhat proud of her, although she was not at all good looking. When the Army left the James river and came back to the Port of Washington, both she and her husband, I understood, disappeared from the service.

Upon the breaking up of our camps at Washington the other laundresses were detailed as matrons in hospitals, and for this service were paid a salary of twelve dollars per month and allowed one ration per day.

We were obliged to keep our arms in the best condition and our clothing clean, and on inspection and guard mount shoes had to be polished and white gloves worn. The man who presented the best appearance in the guard was detailed as orderly for the commanding officer of the camp, and the next best as orderly for the officer of the day.

This position as orderly was desirable in one sense, and very undesirable in another. His duties for the day were generally supposed to close at taps, and he was permitted to retire to rest at his quarters, "getting that night in bed," as the saying was with us. But the unpleasant feature of the matter was the fearful feeling of constraint and the excessive military etiquette the soldier was obliged to suffer and practice. I suppose, as a general thing, native American soldiers thoroughly detested this stiff presence, this standing to attention, the humble subservience to every beck and call and whim of official position. As a result, the competition for these positions was almost exclusively confined to the foreign-born members of the army, who seemed to be of much better material for such duty.

I do not mention this to deprecate the services of our foreign fellow-citizens, but as a statement of fact, as I observed on numerous occasions, and perhaps almost universally noticed throughout our army.

Although the discipline of the camp was strictly maintained, and the entire force, during a certain number of hours during the day, industriously employed in some duty, the men were not entirely deprived of the means of enjoyment. In the evening, after retreat, many of the men indulged in a bath in a creek, giving themselves a thorough cleaning; then the balance of the time until tattoo was occupied in singing songs, telling stories and playing cards. Half an hour after tattoo the

[8] There were several instances of women wearing a uniform and serving in battle during the Civil War that have been verified; countless others exist, but have not been proven.

46

bugle sounded "Extinguish lights," when every candle was blown out unless excepted by order of the officer of the day. Unless this call was observed the guard were sent around to enforce it.

On Sundays we were allowed to attend religious services in military style, under charge of a corporal or sergeant. Although, this seemed to us an unnecessary humiliation, a number of the men participated quite regularly with the different congregations in the neighborhood in the meetings held by them.

At the church in Hyattsville I could not help noticing the peculiar physiognomy and dialect of the natives. Their long hair, narrow faces, and slovenly dress, added to the apparent lack of enthusiasm in their devotional exercises, were all different characteristics from those I had been familiar with in the Methodist churches at the north. The dialect surprised me most, as it was similar to that I had heard spoken by the colored people in the streets of Baltimore and on the farms near Bladensburg; and to test it I would shut my eyes so that I could not see, and then sometimes found my judgment completely at fault as to the color of the speaker.

Our reception at church, too, was very different from that usually extended to visitors at such places in the north—cold, formal, unwelcome; there could be no mistake about the latter. The spiritual welfare of Yankees, as the federal soldiers had by this time become universally known in the south, seemed to be of no importance to them.

We showed them how well we could behave ourselves, however, and by our cordial greetings and conversation made the better educated portion of the congregation feel ashamed of themselves, I think, as there was a slight softening of manner towards us in time, and even invitations to return were finally extended.

During our stay at Bladensburg orders were issued from the War Department detailing field officers for the regiment. David Hunter[9] was assigned as Colonel, W H. Emory as Lieutenant Colonel, James H. Carlton and Lawrence Williams as Majors. Lieutenant Colonel Emory took command of the camp; the others mentioned, with the exception of

---

[9]   David Hunter was born on July 21, 1802, in Washington, D.C., and graduated from West Point in 1822. Although he was appointed Colonel of the 3rd (later redesignated the 6th) Cavalry, he chose instead to accept appointment as Brigadier General of Volunteers, rising to the rank of Major General. His most notable service came at the end of the war, as a member of the military commission that tried the Lincoln assassination conspriators. He died in Washington, D.C. on February 2, 1866.

Major Williams,[10] did not join us during the war.

Of Lieutenant Colonel Emory I suppose there was but one opinion among the common soldiers in the Sixth Cavalry—that he was a good-hearted man and a lion-hearted soldier. Although a strict disciplinarian, he was free from the mean caprices which curse the character of so many of our commissioned officers, and which seem to be born of the almost absolute powers they possess over the victims under their charge. The necessities of the dry details and severe requirements of military life he sought to make intelligible to the men, and was highly successful, and thus secured a willing obedience, in many instances, where before men had been inclined to shirk their duties under an impression that those duties were imposed upon them simply for the purpose of keeping them employed.

While I do not pretend to hold that a commissioned officer is morally obliged to be profuse in his explanations of this, that, or the other specialty in military service, or to lower the standard of his dignity before enlisted men, yet it seems to me that a patient rehearsal of the various duties required, with their accepted results and necessities and general effect, would have a wonderful influence on them in securing a cheerful acceptance of the situation, however onerous it might be. Fully four-fifths of the cases of disobedience of orders can, I believe, be traced to the existence of an idea in the minds of the perpetrators that the order disobeyed was the creation of official whim, of no moment or importance, and that they were the victims of a stupendous hoax.

I know it will be said by some that this would not be discipline—that the soldier has no right to think anything about it; that he is for the time being a machine, subject to the absolute will of the officers placed over him, and must obey without questioning. No matter what the order, he must obey it, however much of an outrage it should perpetrate upon himself or others—he must obey, and complain afterwards. This is his poor privilege—he can complain to a superior power after obeying the order, and the outrage, with all its deleterious effects and results, shall have been committed.

A few words will demonstrate that this supposed foundation of

[10]   Lawrence A. Williams was appointed to the 6th Cavalry after having served as a Captain in the 10th Infantry. He was also a relative of the Lee family. During the Peninsula Campaign, he was arrested for communicating with the enemy, apparently in the aftermath of sending a note to Mrs. Robert E. Lee. He demanded an investigation, but the investigation never came about. He was later returned to duty in New York City and remained there until he was dismissed from the service on March 11, 1863.

military government is no foundation at all—that the soldier must, occasionally, at least, have some latitude for discrimination. Suppose he should, under orders, shoot down a citizen of Pennsylvania whom he met on the public highway without any other justification; would he or the officer who gave the order be subject to conviction for murder? Here an illegal order is issued, and consequently, if illegal, is void—no order at all, in the eye of the law, and the man who fired the shot would do so upon his individual responsibility. Yet the above class of military reasoners would compel him to obey that order, and complain afterwards, according to their principles.

To show that the rule—obey first and complain afterwards, but obey at all hazards—is no idle fiction of the brain, but is taken to be a necessity absolute and without the capacity of modification, I quote from a decision rendered by the commanding general of the department of the East published June 29, 1871, in the cases of Privates Robert Thier, Sanford Butler, Thomas Smith and Henry Miller, of Battery C, First Artillery, who were arraigned and tried before a general-court-martial, which convened at Fort Hamilton, New York. In his review he says:

In ruling that the order disobeyed was not a proper one, it is also to be well understood that the order did not require of these soldiers anything in violation of the moral or civil law—nothing devolving personal degradation. That in complying with it, it, at most, only established ground for application for redress of a grievance, and that in taking on themselves to judge the case they but brought on the trouble, cost, and confinement to a trial, whereas, had they obeyed the order first, WHICH IS THE SOLDIER'S RULE, and complained afterwards, their complaint would have been heeded, and they would have been spared the punishment they have already undergone, part of which was also due for the terms in which the order was replied to.

These men had been convicted of disobedience of orders, and sentenced to be confined at hard labor various periods, and to forfeit a portion of their monthly pay during the term of their imprisonment. It will be seen that the commanding general ruled that the order disobeyed WAS AN IMPROPER ONE, and upon this ground ordered the remission of the sentences. But it will also be observed that he lays down what he calls "the soldiers rule"—obey first, and complain afterwards. It does not matter whether the order given these men was a violation of moral or civil law—it is enough that it was an improper one, as admitted. The principle is the same.

49

It does not appear that proceedings were taken against the officer who issued the improper order, nor even that he was reprimanded; the implied censure rests entirely upon the victims of the court-martial, whereas they were really entitled to commendation.

As if to emphasize the statements I have made in this regard, there comes to me, through the associated press dispatches, the story of the deliberate killing, without a shadow of justification, of a bugler, on the order of Lieutenant Collins, by one of the enlisted men under his command. It appears that the company were at target practice, and the lieutenant ordered one of the soldiers to shoot the bugler, and it was done. Lieutenant Collins, it may be said with grim satisfaction, was dismissed from the service of the United States! That was all.

I have drifted into the discussion of this question almost unconsciously.

The affection of the men for Lieutenant Colonel Emory, Captain Sanders, Captain Taylor, and Lieutenant Ward,[11] and their willingness to follow them through any peril, and their cheerfulness to discharge all their duties fearlessly, as the records of actions will show, were in striking contrast with the dislike, the restlessness, and the indisposition to service manifested on subsequent occasions under other officers—occasions which can readily be recalled by any man who was then a member of the regiment.

In due time horses arrived in camp, and were corralled ready for assignment. Cavalry equipment also appeared at the quartermaster's office—a great pile of saddles, curb-bit bridles, nosebags, and watering bridles. Then commenced a season of excitement among the men, everybody wanting to pick out his stud for himself.

It was surprising to see what a large number of men fully posted in equestrianism we possessed—to hear the learned remarks about "clean limbs, high withers, bald faces, white fat, good eyes, easy kept, high-spirited" animals. Nobody could learn anybody else anything about horses—he knew all about it himself—it was a positive insult to suggest anything. Flascher had been in the Russian cavalries—it was the height of impudence to mention "horse" to him; Christian Draker's "brother" was a farmer—that was clear evidence of Christian's capacity as a judge

---

[11] Isaac M. Ward was appointed 2nd Lieutenant of Campany F of the 6th Cavalry on October 26, 1861. He was promoted to 1st Lieutenant on October 10, 1862. Ward was killed at the Battle of Brandy Station on June 9, 1863.

of horseflesh; Cravar, though a puddler[12] by trade, and never having been on one's back, had seen them at race courses, and was acquainted with one or two of the riders, and they "ought to know, you know;" and so all around.

The horses were rather above the average as to quality, owing no doubt to the great care of our regimental quartermaster, Lieutenant Spangler,[13] who was certainly a capable and efficient officer for the duty to which he was assigned. A few very vicious animals were among the number, but these were soon brought into subjection by some of our best riders, who at once took them in hand.

I recollect one horse in particular—a tall handsome animal which had an ugly habit of walking around on his hind legs when one was on his back, and varying his maneuvers by taking wicked leaps and distending his jaw to fearful dimensions. It required some time to conquer him, but at last it was done.

When the time had arrived to make the assignments of the horses, to prevent confusion and jealousy among the men, a sort of lottery was arranged; the non-commissioned officers, however, were first allowed their choice in order of rank. Paper tickets were cut and numbered, and corresponding numbers marked upon the halterstraps of the horses as they stood hitched to the picket-line. The tickets were thrown into a hat and well shaken up, and then a soldier put his hand in and picked out a ticket without seeing what the number was, and his lot fell to the horse upon the halter of which was marked its counterpart.

There was much amusing excitement during the progress of the drawing. When a soldier pulled a number out of the hat he would hurry along the picket-line looking for his prize. If the animal pleased him his face would show it, and he would return amid the congratulations of his comrades; if it was an ill-favored one, his disappointment would be clearly manifested by scowls and curses, if a profane man, or less emphatic language, if a Christian, and he would perhaps hide himself to escape from the jeers and shouts of laughter that were sure to greet him upon the discovery of his misfortune.

With my usual luck I secured the worthless horse of the company—small, slow-walking, scrubby, chubby fellow, whose only practical use was to aid in making a demand for oats and hay; for this

---

[12] A puddler is a workman or artisan involved with iron fashioning.

[13] John W. Spangler had risen to the rank of Sergeant with the 2nd Cavalry. He was appointed 2nd Lieutenant in the 6th Cavalry in June, 1861.

duty he was eminently qualified.

Now came a season of diversion. Our horsemen, desiring to test the qualities of their respective steeds, and also to establish their reputation as riders among their fellow-soldiers, took every opportunity that offered to have races. The most favorable time for this was when the company rode out to water morning, noon, and night, under charge of some non-commissioned officer, to a deep place in the creek some distance below the cook's quarters and out of sight of the camp. Upon these occasions watering bridles were used, as the curb-bit bridles interfered with the comfort of the animals in drinking; no saddles were allowed, the men using the saddle-blanket only, which was secured on with a surcingle. Spurs were not permitted to be worn upon these occasions but the men constantly violated this order in spite of the watchfulness of the non-commissioned officers, whose duty it was to enforce it.

Everything would, perhaps, be properly conducted until the men had allowed their horses to drink. When your horse was done drinking you were supposed to ride out of the stream and permit your comrade to go in, while you fell into column ready to march back to camp. Somehow or other, however, by some singular accident, there was almost invariably a stampede—the horses, becoming unmanageable, would dash off at a fearful rate across fields and ditches, the riders apparently holding back powerfully on the reins; but a close observer could easily discern a pair of spurred heels tightly clamped in upon the quivering sides of each runaway animal, and when at last they succeeded in reining up, under the imperative orders and physical demonstrations of the non-commissioned officers, you could hear sly remarks made about the running qualities of their respective steeds by these men, and something was almost always said about imaginary bets of vast sums of money, and that they would see about it tomorrow, if they were not detailed for guard, or on some other duty, etc.

On most of these occasions some robust son of Mars found himself tumbled off into the sand, while his steed careened proudly over the plain, to his great disgust and the infinite amusement of his comrades. Once in a while this feat was accomplished by the animals in the creek, where, by a sudden movement, the rider was quietly deposited in the water, giving him an involuntary bath, out of which he would come savage looking and growling at his horse.

One of the most comical-looking men in the command was Conway,[14] who had drawn a tall, bony mare, which proved to be a complete termagant. Almost every day she would run off with him while coming from water, and dash across the commons at a rate of speed fearful to contemplate. At these times Conway's cap would fly off, his hair would float out behind, and he would lie back upon the halterstrap with a death-grip, while his spurred heels would be bored into her sides in a way that must have been unpleasant for the mare. She generally stopped when she came in contact with a fence, or ran in among a crowd of horses.

One day, however, unfortunately, she carried Conway against the projecting stump of a limb, which struck him in the side, throwing him heavily to the ground, and injuring him internally, from which he did not recover, dying in two or three months afterward.

Schumaker was a wonderful rider — in his own estimation. To see him mounted on his long lank horse, dashing along at a full gallop, with his ungainly form, wide mouth distended by a broad grin of excitement, his remarkably small, black glistening eyes starting from their sockets, his short curly hair, his legs bent into two sides of a sharp-angled triangle, his uncertain poise, and his desperate grip upon the animal's mane, was to behold a picture which, to be appreciated, had to be seen.

And Simmers—how shall I describe him as he appeared during these days? The periodical grin was visible on his countenance on fewer occasions now than formerly; he was evidently improving from these comical attacks. He, too, was a horseman of some accomplishments; but Simmers was sharp enough to attempt no displays in the presence of the company. It was only when he had succeeded in getting alone that he stood out in full relief as a cavalryman. Then you could see him—if he did not see you—perform some of the most remarkable of maneuvers. He would lean forward, with his face almost between the horse's ears, twist both his hands carefully into the mane, clap his spurs into the animal's flanks, and away they would fly like an arrow from the bow. His favorite mode of getting his steed halted was to roll off on the ground, in which case the animal made his way to the company stables, leaving Simmers to walk in alone.

Flascher was now duly installed as the "horse's doctor" and blacksmith for the company. As a veterinary surgeon I do not think he was successful in many instances, though he would stand for hours

[14] Conway died on January 1, 1862.

54

grandly contemplating his patients. I have often fancied he would rather attend to the professional duty than the mechanical, would rather doctor a sick horse than wield his hammer in the blacksmith shop, but in this I may have been mistaken. He was wise in his generation, however, giving preference to those men who wanted their horses shod—and who paid for the work.

Whatever might be said of Christian Draker as a cavalryman, there could be but one opinion as to his ability to take care of his horse. That querulous little Dutchman would buy or fight for feed for the little animal he rode—though it should be remarked that he would rather fight than buy. Stable-call was of little moment to Draker; he was sure to be found in the stable at all times, cleaning his horse, if he was not on guard or other duty. The querulous little animal thrived and grew fat in consequence of this liberal treatment, and seemed to fully understand the language of his master.

"Me no use mine spores," he would say, when you asked him how he kept his horse in such good condition, "like some of these tam doom a raisels, nockel maul. He be's mine freund, and I treats him right."

Cutting Ties—On to Washington

Iverson had been made commissary sergeant, and now had charge of the cook house. The bustling little man seemed to be in his element here, for he managed the culinary department in a way that suited himself, if not the men. Of course, promoting a man to be commissary sergeant was to place him in a position of constant hostility to the men, or rather the men to him. Those who possessed small stomachs were not satisfied because they could not eat all their rations, while those with large stomachs were not satisfied because they could eat more than their rations.

At almost every meal Iverson and Draker opened on each other a sharp fusillade, Draker bestowing upon Iverson the title of "cook's police," in a mock squeaking tone of voice intended to resemble that of our worthy commissary sergeant when he called these functionaries for duty, at the cook house, while Iverson would respond with some savage remark intended to annihilate Draker but which the cunning Dutchman did not care to understand.

A pleasant fiction connected with the commissary department of the company was the reported accumulation of what was called the "company fund." This fund was made up by the commutation of rations over and above what the company did not draw from the regimental commissary, and was to be credited to the company account as cash. With this money, we were supposed to be furnished little comforts not provided for in Army regulations, such as scarfs, mittens, gloves, etc. Of course, this fund ought to accumulate very rapidly during active duty in the field, when the men foraged a great deal, and often were without government rations several days at a time; but beyond half a dozen pairs of white cotton gloves, worth perhaps in the aggregate seventy-five cents, I never saw anything that indicated the existence of such credit. If we needed mittens or scarfs in the winter we went down to the sutler's quarters and bought them out of our monthly pay, and paid rather good prices for the articles, to say the least.[1]

Just here I want to say a few words about sutlers. This individual — our sutler — joined us about the third month of our service, if I remember aright. His stock in trade consisted of writing paper, envelopes, tobacco, cigars, and some other notions, among which was very poor whiskey put up in pint bottles and labelled as some sort of patent medicine. The army regulations provide that only a limited amount of the soldier's monthly pay—two dollars, perhaps—shall be issued in tickets by the sutler as an advance upon such pay, the sutler accepting these tickets in lieu of cash, a settlement, however, to be made on each pay-day. Outside of these tickets the soldier could spend all the money he chose.

For these tickets we could receive articles, but the prices were fearful—possibly double what they should have been, judging from the rates charged in stores in the neighborhood. It is true the regulations provide that the prices of sutler's goods shall be fixed by the council of administration, but I never could discover that there was any protection extended in our case. It was rumored—I will not say upon what foundation—that there was a collusion between the sutler and the officers; that by the judicious distribution of brandy and luxuries of the mess these exorbitant charges upon articles sold to the men were winked at and ignored.

It is far from being my purpose to reiterate these charges of corruption. Of one thing there is no doubt in my mind—that the sutler's dealings with the men were simply a repetition of downright swindles from first to last. It would have been much better for the morale of the regiment to have driven off this individual, and compelled the quartermaster or commissary to furnish the articles required at cost prices. This could easily have been done under all the circumstances in which the sutler was with us. Then no suspicion of corruption could have been entertained.

It seems to me that this plan is especially feasible in time of peace at all places where there are now post sutlers. Let the commissary department furnish or keep on hand, outside of what it is now required to provide, an assortment of goods or imperishable articles in common

---

[1]   Sutlers were officially appointed purveyors of a prescribed list of goods. In the field, the sutlers had a monopoly on the soldiers' business, and inflated prices and scandalous credit arrangements were extremely common.

use among the men; let that department be accountable to the same authority for its conduct in the purchase and sale of these articles or goods as it is in the discharge of its duties proper; assess the charges for freight and all incidental expenses and add to the first cost, and issue to the soldiers at the actual rates paid as assessed. The enlisted men will then be satisfied that the whole matter is an honest transaction, and the demoralizing influences invoked by insinuations as to collusions between officers and sutlers will be avoided, for there will then be no ground upon which to field such a charge.

It is well known that immense fortunes were made during the war by the vultures that swarmed after the army under the protection of commissions as sutlers, and that the evils they introduced and aggravated far outweigh the good they accomplished under the most liberal estimate.

After the men had been furnished with all their equipment they were numbered off as their names appeared alphabetically on the roster, and each article of public property in each soldier's charge was stamped or marked with his number, the letter of his company, and the number of his regiment. For instance, mine stood thus: 28F6Cav. Anything so marked I could claim, for this was my assigned company number, letter of my company, number of regiment, and arm of service, and was the evidence of my ownership.

The superiority of this mode of designating men and property over that of using names is obvious. There may be duplicate names, but there are no duplicate numbers; besides, neatness and uniformity, unattainable under any other mode, are thus secured. The system is, I believe, in vogue in the British army, but there the whole number of men who have served in a company from its organization can be known at a glance, the last man enlisted receiving the last number. An acquaintance of mine, who had served in one of the English Grenadier regiments, told me that his company number was between 3,000 and 4,000—I do not remember the exact figure—showing that, up to the time he had been enlisted, a certain number of men had served in that company before him. Of course, the regiment was an old one; perhaps several hundred years had passed since its organization.[2]

I think this mode preferable to ours, for in the American Army when the soldier dies, or deserts, or is discharged, his number reverts to some one else, and the soldier originally known by it thus loses his identity. In the other case, however, the company number becomes his military

[2]   This description is an accurate account of some European army arrangements.

name on the rolls of the army forever; he has a perpetual interest in it; it is his coat-of-arms, and it is in his power to make it a glory or a shame. There may be two John Smiths in a company; the number of one may be 44 and that of the other 45; one may be a brave soldier, and the other may be a deserter; under their civil names there may arise confusion in after times, but under their military names the identity would be secure .

Sometime in September, 1861, while I was thus faithfully serving my country at the camp near Bladensburg, occurred one of the little episodes of my life—a fitting sequel to my romantic step of a few months before. I had kept up a regular correspondence with the lady referred to in a former chapter ever since I had left home for the war. My treatment by her before my departure, I am fain to believe, would have convinced one far less credulous than I that she actually loved me; there was scarcely any limit to the affection she had exhibited. She had hugged and kissed me; she had called me pet names until I was actually ashamed of myself; she had declared my rival, a young man who was then employed as a laborer on one of the tow boats running on the Monongahela river, "a goose," and had given such instances of foolish conduct on his part that I thought he ought to be ashamed of himself; in short, from what she said, there was nobody on the earth, nor under the earth, nor above the earth, that stood as high in her affection and esteem, as the humble individual who pens these lines; and I believed it all!

After I had been away for a few weeks, however, and had time to reflect carefully upon the situation, without the danger of being influenced by her beautiful face and form—for she was certainly very handsome—it occurred to me that I had been guilty of a very foolish, not to say criminal, act. I had not yet attained my majority; my earthly possessions did not exceed twenty dollars and my suit of blue; my father was actually dependent upon the care of friends; and there was a very bad prospect of my returning without some of the bodily appendages that go to make up a complete man, if I was permitted to return at all. Through my efforts she had been led to pledge herself that she would wait for me until my term of service had expired, if not sooner shot; she wanted me to serve my country, like a true daughter of the mothers of 1776; she related a story she had somewhere heard, about a reply made by some patriotic young lady whose poverty-stricken young man was in the Army, and who had been wooed in vain by some other young man who wasn't in the Army, but who was very rich. Said the patriotic young lady, whose poverty-stricken young man was in the Army, to the very rich young man who wasn't in the Army, with commendable emphasis on the proper words, "I would rather be a soldier's widow than a rich man's slave!" Of course, I was delighted to hear my Sarah Jane tell this anecdote; it showed she appreciated my efforts for my country properly; but the question that was in my mind now was whether I had not done wrong in thus binding the dear creature to me under the ugly circumstances in which I was placed. Still, as there had appeared no mark of regret in her letters to me, and she seemed only gladly anxious, if this be a proper phrase, about my welfare, I felt it to be my duty to fulfill my part of the contract, and keep faith with her.

This brings me down to the time of which I speak—to the episode. The mail had just been distributed to the company, but no letter had come for me, though I had been anxiously expecting one from her. Wandering disconsolately along the line of tents, I happened to pass behind Corporal McMasters, who was sitting down reading a letter he had received. The corporal came from my neighborhood, by the way. I cannot say how it occurred, but I noticed the empty envelope in his right hand—so upturned that the handwriting was plainly visible—and curiously scrutinized it. The hand that wrote the address on that letter was the hand that wrote the letters purporting to come from my Sarah Jane—of that there was no doubt in my mind. I started on making this discovery, but said nothing, and passing along entered my tent in a peculiar frame of mind. My impression was that there was something in that letter affecting me; and sure enough, in a few moments along came Corporal McMasters, with a grin intended to be sympathetic or sardonic—for the life of me I could not tell which—holding the open letter in his hand; and he read therefrom the announcement of the marriage of Mr. James Rose and Miss Sarah Jane Anders, upon a certain date, which date I found, upon comparison, to be the one under which my Sarah Jane, or rather his Sarah Jane, had written her last letter to me. It is proper to remark here that Mr. James Rose was the name of the rival, who was a laborer on the tow boat, and whom she had called a goose, and who had been guilty of the foolish conduct, and whom I thought ought to have been ashamed of himself. The letter went on to remark that the young lady's parents had given her a good scolding for her duplicity, and used language calculated to convince her that I was the better fellow; and that her husband had enlisted the next day and left her to go to the war. These two pieces of information were a source of pleasure to me in spite of myself, though I tried hard to call up my sense of manhood to repel the base instincts; the first flattered me, while the second inspired me with a savage satisfaction which showed how much I was chagrined at her conduct though I affirmed the utmost indifference, and even declared I was glad the burden was off my hands that nothing she could have done would have given me more satisfaction.

Did I take my revolver and retire to some shady nook by the riverside, and then and there blow out my brains? I do not think I did. Did I immediately get a leave of absence, and go down to the saloon at Bladensburg—if there was one there—and drown my sorrows in the flowing bowl? I do not think I did. On the contrary, cautious man that I am, I took time to reflect upon the matter, and after mature deliberation, as the court-martial record says, decided upon my course. Gathering up all the letters from her, and her likeness, and putting on my revolver belt, I jogged out of camp away across the woods, so far off that the reports of my weapon would not be noticed at headquarters, and then selecting a pretty little cedar tree, reverentially buried beneath it these mementoes of a lost love, covered the spot with green boughs, and fired the traditional three rounds over the grave. I felt better for this deed; all my transactions with Sarah Jane had now been respectfully blotted out forever. She was to me now as if I had never known her, and I could freely wish her and him long life and happiness without a single mental reservation.

I may here add that I have heard from this couple since the close of the war; and I may further add that, upon information furnished by one who ought to know, Mr. James Rose served with honor through his entire term, and came home without a wound; that his wife, who was once my Sarah Jane, went out to work for herself, and earned her own living, and saved the money sent her by her husband; and that they are now living together happily and comfortably, with a family, in Monongahela City. And as I said that bright September day so say I now—May they live long and prosper!

Our duties since the assignment of our horses were materially changed. Immediately after roll-call at reveille the bugle sounded stable-call, and the men mustered in the stables and fed and groomed their horses. This lasted one hour, at the conclusion of which a commissioned officer passed around, inspecting each horse, and seeing that the work was properly done, and that the animals of those soldiers on guard or other duty were not neglected. Instead of having troughs in which to feed the horses, the government issued what were known as nosebags; these were fastened up to the mouth by means of a strap passing up over the head behind the ears. It took the animals a short time to learn to eat out of the bags, but they soon became used to them. Very particular care had to be taken to groom the horses properly, as this is one of the most important duties connected with the life of a cavalryman, and the manner in which it is done is deemed a fair test of the character of the soldier. A proper disposition to make of an enlisted man showing a deficiency in this respect would be to transfer him to the infantry, or discharge him from the service altogether; the government will lose much by retaining him in the cavalry.

There was a good deal of adventure connected with these grooming duties occasionally. What was known as the stable was simply four heavy posts set deep in the ground on a line along the company street, in front of the tents, at intervals of perhaps twenty feet; and to these, beginning on the right, where it was fastened to a short stout post inserted at an angle in the ground at greater depth than the others, was attached a very strong rope, known as a picket line, passing from one to the other through a hole bored in the top and drawn as tightly as possible to prevent it from becoming slack, and fastened on the left in the same way it was on the right. To this the horses were tied, each noncommissioned officer's squad keeping together, and occupying opposite sides of the picket line.

Many of the horses had vicious dispositions, and often used their heels in such a lively way that one had to beat a hasty retreat; on such demonstrations being made his rider would be compelled to take him away from the line and groom him alone. Other vicious animals, getting impatient, would throw up their heads and toss off their nosebags, and then, made angry by this mishap, would reach around and nip with their strong fore teeth, some individual close at hand, who was stooping over in a state of blissful ignorance as to the fate that lay in store for him. Then there would be a sudden yell, intermingled with emphatic protests and often times vigorous kicks and blows, which would cause the culprit to surge over against his mates with such force as to throw the whole line on that side of the picket line into confusion, driving the men from among the animals to avoid being trampled upon by the myriad of hoofs.

The drills now, instead of being conducted on foot, were mounted. To this stage of our military life we had looked forward with some anxiety, for it was in the capacity of mounted troops that we were to take the field, and but few men in the regiment had ever had any experience in cavalry service before, and the reminiscences of these were not altogether reassuring. Kirk, of the British fusiliers, who had gone through the ordeal at Balaklava,[3] and Sergeant Stoll, of one of our old mounted regiments, were the only enlisted men in our company who had served in cavalry in actual battle; and the story of the fierce charge in the Crimean war, "with cannon to the front of them," etc, as related by the former, and the ugly fights with the Indians on the frontier, as told by the latter, gave rise to many forebodings and reflections in my mind as to our probable future adventures.

This drilling on horseback is not so pleasant a thing as many would suppose, especially when both men and animals are recruits. That this is the case I respectfully refer you to any cavalryman who has had experience as proof. It can be accounted for upon the following grounds, among others: The men are utterly ignorant as a general thing of equestrianism, many of them, perhaps, never having been astride a horse previous to their enlistment. Their heels are shod with keen spurs, which they are sure to keep at work with a fiendish activity. The bridles are made with curbs that are intended to control the animal during its highest state of excitement, and needs to be carefully operated by the rein, as these curbs are very severe, often cutting the tongue and mouth in an ugly manner; the inexperienced rider is sure to jerk on the rein, causing intense agony to his horse, which will then throw up its head wildly, sometimes, I feel gratified to say, giving the idiot on its back a good sharp blow on the nose. Besides this, the new horses get peculiar notions in their heads; for the first two days they do not want to form in ranks at all; will bite and kick each other in a furious manner. Then, in a few days more they gravitate to the other extreme, and you cannot get them out of ranks; they will actually lean against each other heavily. I have many painful recollections in this connection; my poor legs have been gored terribly by the tongues of numerous buckles, which were sure to fly open on such occasions, for the express purpose, it seemed to me, of pronging my diminutive calves. To remedy this I purchased a pair of long legged boots, which reached up to my knees, and certainly proved of vast benefit.

In addition to all this, our four footed outlaws had such an ugly way of "kicking up behind," when the man in the rear rank rode too close to

---

[3]   The charge in the Crimean War that inspired the poem "The Charge of the Light Brigade."

64

those in the front rank; but I cannot blame them for this, as it was their only means of protection in cases when the careless rear rank man rode his horse upon the heels of the file leader, and bruised them.

But the most terrible of all movements was the company or squadron wheel. Unless remarkably great care was taken, the men on the marching flank would move too fast or the men in the center would move too slow—both productive of the same results—and the inevitable consequence was the curving of the line instead of being kept "well-dressed up," as the common expression has it, or aligned; and when the wheel was completed the company or squadron would be crescent shaped, the two wings projecting far beyond the center. Then what crushing of legs there was as the center forced itself into alignment by sheer strength! It makes my pedal extremities ache to think of those days!

But officers began moderately with us, first instructing us as to the proper mode of saddling and bridling up, rolling up and strapping on the pommel and cantle of our saddles our overcoats and blankets, and carrying forage and rations on horseback; but in consequence of orders having been issued shortly after we received our horses for a grand cavalry review at Washington, we were hurried along into company and division drills with an energy of purpose commendable, perhaps, in the officers, but severe on the men and horses.

This review took place on the plain east of the Capitol, and perhaps three-quarters of a mile distant from that structure. To our inexperienced eyes it was certainly a grand affair. Six thousand mounted men, so the newspapers afterwards said, in their notice of the affair, took part, and marched in review by column of companies before the President of the United States, members of his cabinet, Lieutenant General Winfield Scott, diplomatic representatives of foreign countries, and numerous smaller dignitaries. An immense crowd of people were present.

I did not see anybody but Abraham Lincoln particularly who was prominent for his long, lank, ungainly figure; I was anxious to have a view of the lieutenant general, but just at the critical moment, as the company marched in column past the cluster of dignitaries, with sabres presented in salute, we were so busily engaged in keeping our lines dressed that few of us dared look up. I glanced hurriedly back as soon as we came to a "carry sabre," but failed to see him, looking for him among the crowd of mounted staff officers. I afterwards learned that he was seated in a carriage was unable to ride on account of a severe attack

of the gout. This was certainly a memorable day in the experiences of the raw recruit.

The regiment returned to the camp at Bladensburg in the afternoon, a very tired, hungry, muddy body of men, having been in the saddle during the whole day. As this was, practically, our first appearance in public, and as the newspapers spoke highly of our apparent state of discipline, it furnished a theme of conversation for some time among the men.

One Sunday, shortly after this review, I rambled off from camp as far as Fort Lincoln[4] to see the mode of building earthworks. I was particularly interested in the peculiar shape of the angles at the corners, so constructed as to give its defenders an opportunity to beat off assailants who reached the ditch and tried to scale the parapets, and the admirable support furnished by the rifle pit lower down the hillside. While thus inspecting the work my nose began bleeding profusely from some cause, and running to the parapet, I allowed it to trickle down the side of the earthworks, to have it to say in after days that the first blood by me shed in the war was at Fort Lincoln.

One day, about the middle of October, orders came to break up the camp at Bladensburg and move to Washington; and so, early on the following morning, our tents were taken down and packed in the company wagons, our blankets and overcoats rolled up and strapped to their respective places on our saddles, the horses saddled and bridled, and the Sixth United States Cavalry marched majestically from the scenes of its first lessons in the school of the trooper mounted.

This was another step towards the stage upon which we were to play our part in the coming tragedy, but I doubt if there was any regret felt by the majority of the men. There was steadily developing in them an *esprit de corps*—the result of careful efforts on the part of our officers—and a certain robustness of body, especially among those used to sedentary employment, that foreshadowed a future full of glory to our regiment. They were restless, too, for a change, and the prospect of one filled them with a sense of pleasurable excitement, owing to which they did not stop to think of the actual significance of these successive movements toward the front.

Our new camp was located upon the ground over which we had been marched in the late grand review, close to the city workhouse and the

---

[4]   Fort Lincoln is just south of the Bladensburg dueling ground and is now a private cemetery.

Congressional Cemetery, and not far from the Eastern Branch of the Potomac. It was named in regimental orders "Camp East of the Capitol." In most respects it was a desirable spot for our purposes, being surrounded by a large plain upon which to drill, and the river furnishing water for our horses, but the great marsh to the east of us was sadly suggestive of chills and fevers. The hills all around were occupied by numerous bodies of infantry and artillery, giving the country the appearance of one vast camp, while at night, before tattoo, the illuminated tents stretching over miles of territory formed a rare picture. One fort was visible on the heights beyond the branch, guarding the approaches to the city from the east, though, to our inexperienced eyes, it looked very much like cowardice on the part of our authorities to erect defenses on the north bank of the Potomac. With the mighty hosts then assembling around Washington at the rate of thousands of men per day, it certainly seemed like an absurd expectation to look for an attack on the Virginia side, and a much more absurd one to suppose the enemy would cut loose from his base of supplies, and commit the irredeemable mistake, in our crude military opinion, of coming around to the opposite side of the capital. But as subsequent events proved, the precaution was a wise one.

On the night of the day of our arrival at Camp East of Capitol I was detailed as stable-guard, and went on post at eleven o'clock. About an hour later, I saw a horseman ride down from the direction of the city to the tent of the commanding officer, Lieutenant Colonel Emory, and in a few moments, the latter's orderly passed from one to the other of the tents of the company officers. It was evident something was up, and I anxiously awaited developments, hoping, however, from the bottom of my heart, that we would not be compelled to march this night, for I was very tired, and would gladly have laid down to rest. A short time after the orderly returned to the commanding officer's tent, the company officers issued forth, and went straight to the quarters of the first sergeants. Listening attentively I caught the words "three days' rations," "saddle up," "Chain Bridge," and then there was a "hurrying to and fro" among those noncommissioned functionaries.

The men were armed, ordered to pack their clothing, and saddle up; and then came, for the first time in our military career, that ominous command, "load your arms." What could be the matter? The confederates certainly could not have concluded to attack us? We were beginning to realize fully the meaning of the word "soldier". Here we are, thought I, ordered to load our arms, not to kill animals, but to take the life of a fellow man, and—which was not the least of the subjects of my reflections—to run a decided risk in getting killed ourselves.

For a time confusion reigned supreme. The men, aroused from a sound sleep, and fully impressed with the belief, from the nature of the orders issued, that they were on the eve of bloody work, were very nervous, and appropriated each other's clothing promiscuously. Jim Gargan threw on his saddle in a state of great trepidation, buckled the girth so tightly that the animal could scarcely breathe, and then made frantic efforts to get the crupper-strap under the tail; he also endeavored to load his revolver by inserting the cartridges in the muzzle of the barrel, instead of in the cylinder where it belonged. Draker is reported to have loaded his pistol by reversing the charge, putting the ball in first. Gardner gave his bridle such a savage jerk that his horse rose upon his hind feet and fell to the ground.

I confess to feeling very nervous in regard to the proposed expedition, though for the life of me I could not understand what all this mustering was for, and consequently could not believe that we were likely to meet with any danger. I felt satisfied that the enemy had no intention of attacking our vast force in the defenses of Washington; and that our Army was going to advance just then was very improbable, for the newspapers had given out no such intimation; and at that stage of the war, this was very good evidence.

All this speculation on my part, however, did not delay the preparations for marching. In half an hour from the time the cavalryman made his appearance at the door of the tent of the commanding officer, the regiment silently mounted their horses and rode out of camp. Anxious to divine as quickly as possible the object of this hurried movement I watched the course of the head of the column as it marched off, and found that we were approaching the Capitol. This, in connection with what I had heard about the Chain Bridge,[5] confirmed me in the belief that there was to be our destination.

We passed the Capitol, and kept on up Pennsylvania Avenue to Georgetown, and through the latter place to the river road above the aqueduct. I remember how wistfully I looked into the silent houses as we rode along, thinking how happy the occupants must be, without our trials of mind and body. The blessings of peace never before had

---

[5] Chain Bridge still exists. It crosses the Potomac between upper northwest Washington and Virginia.

appeared too attractive to me. Then, in my half dreamy mind, I wondered how fared my friends at the old home by the riverside. Doubtless at that hour they were asleep, little thinking of their poor boy plodding his weary way to the front, with the perils of war gathering rapidly and thickly about him.

A death-like silence reigned throughout the length of the column; we were truly a solemn-visaged regiment. The sad river flowed past us with a mournful tone in its rippling voice; the wind, coming down the river freighted with a chill, sighed among the bleak hills which stood out in black relief against the cold gray sky. In the dead silence the river, the wind, the hills, and the sky were as so many personified enemies of ours; we were being marched out to execution, and they were all looking on with unpitying eyes; we were cut off by an impassable barrier from the world of sympathy we had left three months before.

The column at length halted, and orders were given to dismount and "stand to horse." After waiting for some time the men began to lie down by the roadside and fall asleep; but the weather was too cold for me to remain still, and I was compelled to walk about and beat my arms around me to keep myself comfortable.

Just at dawn a balloon, which had been anchored on the opposite hill, broke loose and went careering off toward the southeast.[6] As it grew lighter the outlines of a battery became visible against the sky on the top of a high hill toward the southwest. I afterwards learned that this fort commanded the approaches to the Chain Bridge.[7]

As soon as daylight was fairly upon us, the men straggled wearily down to the canal and bathed their heads and faces, and dived into the recesses of their haversacks for eatables. At nine o'clock the bugles sounded "to horse," the regiment mounted, and a few moments later the head of the column countermarched slowly toward the city. The alarm, if one, was apparently now over.

I suppose a more joyous body of men could not have been found than we were upon this discovery. The glad sunshine now bathed the hills, and they no longer looked bleak, but grand; the river sang carols of gladness; the wind was balmy. A great many jokes were passed as to who was the worst scared man in the company, but I doubt if that was within the possibility of decision. Late in the afternoon we reached our

[6]   At this time numerous balloonists were vying to interest the government in using balloons for observation, and, in one case, aerial bombardment.

[7]   This is probably Fort Marcy

70

camp, cleaned up our horses and took a good rest for that night, for we were sadly in need of sleep.

In all our subsequent campaigns, where the danger was actually great; when days and nights were consumed in long marches in hostile country; where no food for man or beast could be procured perhaps for forty-eight hours at a time, I was never so deeply impressed with the horror of my situation as I was upon the cold, gloomy march up the Potomac.

Activities—Camp East of Capitol

After we had become well settled in our new camp I improved every opportunity which presented itself of visiting the different points of interest around and in Washington, and spent hours in meditation upon the patriotic associations connected with them. In the simplicity of my heart I admired all the works of art adorning the public buildings and squares, even to the statue of the Father of his Country in the eastern portion of the Capitol grounds, and rested in the conviction that there was nothing on the globe to be compared with them; and, no doubt, would have continued of the same opinion until the present Year of our Lord 1871, had not this conscious national pride in American specimens been woefully shaken by the well-sustained war between the artists contending for huge contracts for works of art, or rather, perhaps, contracts for huge works of art—they each seem to have the same object in view, a share of our venerable Uncle's money—and the terrific showers of criticisms poured upon each other's efforts, which is, perhaps, fair, and the bitter personalities indulged in toward each other, which is, perhaps, unfair.

Now I have given the whole matter up as an unanswerable conundrum, and when I look at a work of art I am afraid to form an opinion upon its merits until I see which faction has the last word; if its detractors, I denounce the thing as simple trash; if its supporters, I clap my hands in enthusiasm, and declare that it is one of the finest, if not *the* finest, piece of workmanship extant.

I was badly deceived in one instance, however. When Miss Vinnie Ream[1] brought her statue of Abraham Lincoln, and unveiled it in the rotunda, I went to see it, and, being fairly stunned by the acclamation

[1] Vinnie Ream Hoxie was the sculptor for a statue of Lincoln that was placed in the Capitol building shortly after the Civil War. She is buried in Arlington Cemetery.

with which it was greeted by the large audience there assembled, and the fine address of Senator Carpenter[2] on the occasion, I grew extravagant in my expressions of commendation. I was further influenced in the matter by being a woman's rights man, and consequently proud of the achievement of Miss Ream. Judge my horror, when, a few days later, I read the columns of criticism that filled the New York and other eastern papers, by which it was proved beyond doubt to the unprejudiced mind that as a work of art it was a complete failure, and the insinuations thrown out that my champion's personal beauty and accomplishments had more to do with the extraction of the ten or fifteen thousand dollars from the pockets of an unwilling people through their susceptible representatives in Congress assembled, than the intrinsic merits of the Statue!

In this case, however, I cannot help thinking that, under all the circumstances, Miss Ream's effort is a remarkable success, and should be very encouraging, and my hope is that she may yet achieve something which will put to grief the foul-mouthed art bigots of the east.

A trip to the dome of the Capitol repaid me for the numerous difficulties I encountered in making the ascent.[3] The day was a beautiful one, and the scenery that stretched for miles around was indescribably grand. It is not very likely that the picture I gazed upon that day will be exhibited again.

Soon after Camp East of Capitol was established the regiment was attached to a brigade under the command of General Philip St. George Cook,[4] an old army officer, and, in addition to our usual course of military exercises we were treated to a brigade drill every few days. These were occasions of much interest, though very fatiguing to both men and horses. The brigade was made up of three regiments, I think, numbering in the aggregate, perhaps, twenty-five hundred men.

After a few days of practice, when the officers seemed to have the men pretty well in hand, we began to charge by company over the plain,

---

[2] Senator Carpenter's address was extremely laudatory. Some newspapers, however, criticized the statue as mentioned herein.

[3] The dome of the Capitol was under construction at this time which explains his difficulties in climbing up.

[4] Philip St. George Cook was born in Leesburg, Virginia, on June 13, 1809, and graduated from West Point in 1827. He was commissioned a Brigadier General on November 12, 1861, and given command of cavalry forces in the Washington, D.C. area. His failure to retain command of the cavalry in the field may be due to his being the father-in-law of J.E.B. Stuart.

and after that by regiment, and finally by brigade. All this was amusing, except, perhaps, to the few unfortunate heroes who were tumbled into the mud, or whose horses fell floundering on top of them, while a dozen companies dashed over them. Although such accidents were of common occurrence, but few injuries were sustained. The most serious case was a broken leg. I had my ear gouged by a dull sabre-point owing to the carelessness of the drunken soldier who carried it; but beyond bleeding profusely, this was of no consequence.

Once my horse fell so suddenly that I found myself standing fairly upon my feet half a dozen paces beyond him with my sabre sticking in the mud the same distance beyond me before I realized what had happened. When I looked around, I discovered him lying flat on his right side, with all four legs sticking straight out, and my saddle ploughed into the mud several inches deep. I had made a narrow escape, evidently. The animal was not hurt, but laid still until I went and gently urged him to rise.

Captain Abert furnished us with an example of coolness on the occasion of a charge by his company which I was obliged to admire. They moved off at a walk, then took up a trot, then a gallop, and then the charge, and went over the plain at a fearful rate, with Captain Abert in advance, when his horse fell and the company dashed headlong over them both. Just as they had cleared that odd-looking heap of upturned legs the captain raised his head, looking like a huge frog coming out of a pond and shouted:

"Attention, company! Gallop; trot; walk; halt!"

As these successive orders were given they were promptly obeyed, and Captain Abert raised up his horse, remounted and rode up to his company with dignity undisturbed.

In addition to our drills in field maneuvering, a course in sabre-exercise, mounted and dismounted, was instituted, by which we progressed favorably in this important branch of a cavalryman's education. After this came target-practice with our revolvers, dismounted.

I recollect our first experience in this line. There was a good deal of trepidation among the men in regard to the manipulations of this weapon, many of them never having seen one prior to their coming into service, and but one or two only had actually fired a shot out of them. We got along very well, however, for beginners, until it came Jim Gargan's time to shoot. Gargan was very nervous fellow anyhow, and this tendency had been greatly increased by the many potations in which he indulged upon every opportunity; so when he marched up and took position in front of the target a very perceptible tremor ran through his frame. Cautiously drawing the weapon from its holster at the command, "Draw pistol!" Gargan proceeded to obey the subsequent commands in a way that would lead one to think he was expecting an order to shoot himself instead of the board containing the bull's eye, and when the words, "Aim, fire!" were uttered, there was no response. He stood there still pointing the pistol at the target.

Captain Taylor asked him sharply why he did not obey, and Gargan lowered his pistol carefully and looked at it, and then went through the motions with similar success; but there followed no report.

"What do you mean, sir?" asked Captain Taylor. "Why do you not fire?"

"I can't get it off," tremblingly replied Gargan.

The captain took the revolver and, examining it, pronounced it all right, and handed the pistol back to the soldier.

Gargan tried again, with no better success; the hammer would not fall, he explained.

Captain Taylor again examined the weapon, but nothing appeared to be the matter with it; the cylinder revolved and the hammer operated as well as in any other well-behaved pistol.

Once more Gargan attempted to shoot, and the countenance of the captain, who was watching him closely, was observed to suddenly break into a smile and as suddenly regain its severe dignified expression.

"Why, you damned fool," he said, in tones that made Gargan shake harder than ever, "no wonder the hammer won't fall. You are holding it back!"

And, sure enough, Jim had securely held the hammer back with his thumb, while with his forefinger he pressed with great vigor upon the trigger! A loud laugh went up at Jim's expense.

Another amusing incident occurred when Christian Draker came to take his turn at firing. That querulous little Dutchman, who, in his own estimation, had no equal with the "sable," as he called his sword, was somewhat afraid of his revolver, but took up his position and opened on the target with a great show of confidence, the revolver, however, merely responding by a series of snaps. Captain Taylor ordered Draker to put on fresh caps, but the result was the same.

"What the devil is the matter with your pistol?" angrily exclaimed the captain, jerking the weapon out of Draker's hand.

The little Dutchman meekly replied:

"I cannit tell what ish de matter mit de pistol."

The captain looked a moment at the revolver, and almost threw it at Draker, exclaiming:

"Get out of this, and load your pistol; and if you come here again with it empty I will send you to the guard house!"

The Dutchman had simply put caps on the nipples of the cylinder, without completing the preparations for target practice by inserting charges of powder and ball.

The slightest reference to this joke in after times was sufficient to arouse Draker's fiercest indignation.

When it came Schwab's turn to fire, he marched up to the designated spot deliberately—Schwab always was deliberate—and took aim at the utterance of the proper command. It so happened that a dog, which had for some time been with the company, had assumed the role of a spectator, and was seated with dignified mien off some distance to the right of the target. The thoughts of Schwab on this occasion have never transpired—whether or not that deliberate individual, as he stood there taking deliberate aim, had made up his mind that there was not much difference between a bull's eye and dog's eye anyhow; suffice it to say that, "after due deliberation," the trigger was pulled, and, contrary to our expectation, and much to our surprise, the bull's eye was not hit, but the dog was, and the latter retired at a limping gait, and with loud yells to the company quarters. If Schwab had made up his mind that there was not much difference between bull's eye and dog's eye anyhow, and had acted accordingly, that deliberate individual must have possessed a wonderful faculty for feigning astonishment, to judge from the way his eyes followed the dog's retreating form.

After the men had become partially accustomed to the use of their arms we were required to attend target practice mounted, in order that our horses might be broken in and exhibit no alarm upon hearing the report of guns. While this furnished a source of amusement it was by no means unattended by danger, as from the prancing about of the animals, and the great awkwardness of many of the riders, there was a probability of revolvers being discharged involuntarily. Fortunately no accident of any kind occurred. In course of time the company exhibited commendable steadiness on such occasions.

One day, while on post as stable-guard, my attention was attracted to an apparent quarrel going on between Powell and McKeefery. Powell was a very large, athletic man, while McKeefery was small. Both were Irishmen.

Powell held in his right hand a heavy-bitted curb-bridle, which he grasped by the head-stall. After some time spent in disputing—a moment or so—Powell swung the bridle overhand, and brought it down with savage force upon the head of his diminutive opponent, the iron curb striking the skull with a sickening thud, and the victim fell prone to the earth with a deep groan, quivering in every limb. I felt sure he was killed, but he recovered partially in the course of a few months, though I believe was never fully restored to health.

About the 1st of November Mrs. Hargraves, one of our laundresses, received a furlough to go home for a few days. As she came from the neighborhood of my old home I embraced the opportunity to send away some articles I had up to this time carried with me, but which I had found were obstructions rather than of benefit. I suppose next to getting a leave of absence himself the soldier enjoys one procured by some one else whose residence is located at or near his own; at least, this was the case with me. Letters from home are good—it is, perhaps, impossible to overestimate their benefits—but when one can communicate with his friends through some tangible medium—one whose eyes you are sure saw the old place and looked upon the forms of the loved ones, and whose tongue can describe, in a manner infinitely more graphic than pen, their actual condition—it is almost as gratifying as if you had been present yourself. With such an interest was this visit of Mrs. Hargraves imbued, and when she returned I kept the poor woman talking for hours upon that subject of engrossing interest—home, from which I felt I had been absent for an age. She willingly gratified me, however.

I was very much annoyed by the conduct of my tentmates, who, up to this time, had behaved themselves very well, but now began indulging in poisonous whiskey, with its usual disagreeable effects. While in this state they would stalk into the tent without attempting to cleanse their feet, and trample upon my blankets and clothing, or, what was infinitely worse, made no effort to get out when they grew sick. I bore this quietly for a while, but finally remonstrated with Corporal Purcell, who, though a good fellow when sober, was quite different when drunk. He became very angry at my impertinence, and remained away altogether for several nights; was reduced to the ranks and thrown into the guard house, and finally deserted. Although sorry at the course he pursued, I was much gratified at being relieved of his presence. The others were more easily managed, and it was soon pleasant again.

About the 1st of December the men were ordered to have their sabres ground, and for this purpose a detail was made from each company. This was rather unexpected, as up to this time we had been under the impression that it was against the laws of war to have sharpened sabres. I have no doubt if I had asked Joe Gilmore about the matter he would have told me that it was not permitted in his military time. They were ground from the point down about fourteen inches along the edge proper, and then in the same manner about four inches from the point down on the back, thus making them very sharp on both sides, and rendering the sabre a dangerous weapon either for a stroke, or more especially for a thrust. This evident preparation for butchering sent a shudder through me. It was another step toward the front.

In November a large force of men were set to work building stables for our horses and barracks for the men, and these, during the first week in December, were finished and occupied. We were furnished with an extra blanket apiece, and a bed tick, which we filled with straw. Large stoves were put up in the barrack room. The kitchen outfit was complete. A bake house was built to furnish us with soft bread. Altogether we were getting along remarkably comfortable for soldiers in time of war—too much so, I thought, as reference to a letter written December 31, 1861 shows. An extract from it on this subject says:

I have been almost six months in the army, and have not yet seen an enemy, to my knowledge. There is no glory in soldiering among friends. There is too much partiality shown to the regulars. We have good winter-quarters, while the volunteers have to rough it in the woods with no shelter except tents. If they do not let us fight, I shall ask for my discharge. I did not come to soldier for fun; I thought to be of some service to my government, but have not earned my salt yet.

I have not a single word to say in defense of the above. It was written before we had received our baptism of fire, and betrays the crudeness of the writer in war matters. I am free to say that after the experiences of the succeeding six months, it is exceedingly doubtful whether my brain would have been invaded by such thoughts. I should have been glad to have received such comforts, and would not have dreamed of complaining of them.

About the middle of December a letter from home brought me the

79

painful intelligence that father had met with an accident by which his collar bone had been broken. This caused me great uneasiness, as he was in his sixty-first year, and the prospect of recovery was not good. My forebodings, however, were relieved in a week or two with news by mail that he was making fair progress. I am glad to say that he entirely recovered.

A day or two after the battle of Dranesville[5], James M. Davis, a fellow-apprentice with me in the office of the Monongahelan Republican in ante-bellum days, and who was now a member of the Twelfth Pennsylvania reserves, walked over from his camp to see me. His regiment had participated in that action, and Jim came to tell me how it went. He had an admiring listener, for I looked upon him with pride as one who had done service for his country. His description had a reassuring effect on me as to the future, for the enemy seemed to have shown but little resistance, retreating in great disorder before the reserves.

About the middle of December, upon the conclusion of dress parade one day, the lieutenant colonel announced to us that, on account of our uniform good conduct and efficient discipline, we had been detailed by the Secretary of War[6] as a guard for the city.

The next day a squadron was sent out with two days rations and forage for this duty. They presented rather a comical appearance, mounted on their horses with haversacks full of bread and meat hanging by their side, and a bag of oats and bundle of hay stowed upon the cantles of their saddles. This was a feature the men did not like; it detracted from their soldierly appearance, and besides, the horses were constantly making raids on each other's forage.

Great curiosity was felt to know what the nature of our duty was, and when the squadron was relieved by another, and returned to camp, the men were besieged for information. To our great disgust it proved to be a sort of police service—to arrest drunken soldiers, strip all negroes of government clothing, and stop all ambulances from carrying more able-bodied men than the driver, and to prevent all fast driving.

The rainy season commenced about the middle of November. Before the men had occupied their barracks. The exposure to the cold and wet weather and the sleeping on the damp ground—for the tents were without

[5]   The Battle of Dranesville, between the forces of George B. McClellan and Joseph E. Johnston, was fought on December 20, 1861.

[6]   The Secretary of War at this time was Simon Cameron, a Pennsylvania politician.

flooring—began to have their effect, as was visible from the rapidly-filling hospital. Four of Company F died—Scheide, Conway, Jim Gargan, and Schaffer—and were buried with the honors of war. The funeral service of the cavalry was to me very impressive. An escort was detailed from every company in the regiment to accompany the cortege to the grave. The six pall-bearers were men chosen from the company of which the deceased was a member; the escort proper was composed of eight men, also of the same company; the coffin was enveloped in the American flag, and carried upon a hand-barrow. The regimental band preceded the remains, playing a mournful dirge; then the pall-bearers carrying the body; then the horse of the deceased, saddled and bridled, with crepe attached to each side of the bridle-bit, while from the saddle hung the boots and sword; after the horse the escort, carrying their sabres reversed; after these followed members of the company and regiment, wearing side arms only. At the grave an officer read the Episcopal funeral service, and some appropriate chapters from the Old and New Testaments; then the coffin was carefully lowered into the grave while the escort presented sabres; a few shovelfuls of earth were thrown in on the coffin, while the escort returned sabre and drew their revolvers; then three rounds were fired over the grave, and the men were silently marched away for some distance, when the band recommenced playing a dirge. In some instances there was no band, in which case buglers took their place. At these times the bugles sounded, as the earth was thrown in, the appropriate call of "Extinguish lights."

One of those events, which sometimes occur to give a shock to the sensibilities on such occasions, took place at Jim Gargan's funeral. I was one of the pallbearers. When the hour for the funeral had arrived, the F Company escort marched over and took position in front of the dead house[7] where they were joined shortly after by the soldiers from the other companies. Several of the pall-bearers went in and found the coffin, already closed up, deposited on the hand barrow, and proceeded to wrap it up in the colors. After this was done, we took hold of the handles of the barrow and carried it outside, where the escort came to an attention, faced us, and presented sabres. We then took our proper positions in the line.

The wife of the deceased, who was one of our laundresses, soon after arrived, dressed in deep mourning. When all was in readiness, the

[7] The "dead house" was the name given to the shed or barn used to store dead bodies. It was usually located near the hospital.

81

column moved off towards the Congressional Cemetery[8], where our men dying at Camp East of Capitol were buried. We had marched a short distance when the hospital steward came running after us, calling out to halt—that the body was not in the coffin, but in the dead house. An awkward confusion followed, of course, but we marched back after the corpse, put it in the coffin and started again for the cemetery.

> *Sleep, soldier, though many regret thee*
> *Who stand by thy cold bier today,*
> *Soon—soon shall the kindest forget thee,*
> *And thy name from the earth pass away.*
> *The man thou didst love as a brother*
> *A friend in thy place will have gained;*
> *Thy dog shall keep watch for another,*
> *And thy steed by a stranger be reined!*

Up till the 31st of December, 1861, we had lost out of F Company eight men by desertion—a large percentage—but I think the Government was a gainer rather than a loser by their absence.

One night—I think it was the 8th of January, 1862—I met with an adventure which, though unimportant in itself, was a lesson I took care ever afterward should not be forgotten. Our company was on duty that day in the City and were quartered in a large brick house on Maryland Avenue just west of the Capitol grounds, near the canal. Early in the evening Sergeant Brown came to me and asked to exchange revolvers for the night, saying that he wanted to go out, and his pistol was unserviceable—the cylinder would not revolve. As I did not expect to go on duty that night I agreed to the exchange, and took his pistol and placed it in my holster. Lieutenant Paulding came around to our quarters and ordered me to go, in company with another private soldier, to arrest a citizen who was selling liquor to soldiers. Off we started, the lieutenant coming along to show us the culprit, and after a tiresome tramp of several squares the house—a small frame shanty—was found. The proprietor and his wife—both natives of the Emerald Isle—stood behind a rickety bar, unsuspecting the fate that was impending over their devoted heads.

Our little party entered and the lieutenant pointed to the man, and ordered us to arrest him. This was done, and we received further orders to take him to the central guard house. Being unacquainted with the

---

[8] Historical Congressional Cemetary where Sidney was buried on 1/12/1899.

location of that establishment, and feeling unable to comprehend the description given by the lieutenant, I was in a quandary about the matter. A carriage had in the meantime driven up to the door, in which our prisoner proposed to drive us to the guardhouse, but Lieutenant Paulding objected, and ordered us to walk, and then left the premises.

To add to the dilemma in which I was placed, a crowd of very rough-looking men began to throng about the house and the thought occurred to me that it might become necessary to use my revolver when, to my horror, I recollected that I had made an exchange with Sergeant Brown. A few whispered words to my companion revealed the fact that his pistol was not loaded; so here we were alone with a mob, in a part of the city utterly unknown to us, without a serviceable weapon except our sabres.

An ugly sort of muttering could be heard through the crowd, which showed us clearly that they were not at all satisfied with our proceedings. The saloon-keeper was a friend of theirs, apparently. However, off we started, followed by the crowd, whom we ordered to stand off, laying our hands upon our useless revolvers; this had the desired effect, and we proceeded unmolested, allowing our prisoner unconsciously to act as a guide, and in due time delivered him to the guard in charge at the Central. Some of his friends appeared, and offered to go his bail, but these were informed that bail was accepted only for prisoners confined by order of the military. A small party followed my companion and I several squares as we came away, but finally disappeared, and we reported at the company quarters, rather glad of our escape.

To show the reader how the Common Soldier felt, what he thought, and how he looked at this period of his military career, I make some extracts from a letter written under date of January 22, 1862, from Camp East of Capitol. It is a curiosity in its way, and makes me smile every time I see it and compare it with the history of subsequent events.

Dear Friend;

I got your kind letter yesterday evening, after coming off guard, and felt so happy to hear of father's progress towards convalescence.

The weather here is very disagreeable, and our camp, owing to the frequent rains and the trampling of horses, is one vast mire of mud.

I continue to have good health, though just recovering from a severe cold and sore throat, having been off duty, however, only one day.

We had a brigade drill last week. About two thousand mounted men were on the ground. Our regiment made a charge, our squadron leading off, followed by company after company in succession, each of whom as they came up to the line we had halted formed on our right. The mud flew in a perfect shower, and covered both man and horse. I had to laugh as I looked back and saw, as each company dashed across the plain, the unfortunate boys whose horses had fallen rolling into the mud. I had managed to hold mine up, or perhaps would not have felt so much amused.

A whole regiment on a charge looks terrific, with their sabres—in the front rank at a pierce point, and in the rear rank at a front cut—gleaming, and the men cheering. I wish we could get a chance at the rebels.

There are rumors that we shall move soon; also others that our regiment will be discharged when the war is over—the latter is reported to be the statement of an officer, and we privates think an officer ought to know everything. I suppose in that case shall have to reenlist, as this is the best life I have found; there is just enough of work to make one feel right all the time.

I am convinced that the war will be over by the 1st of July and I think it may end sooner. The defeat of Zollicoffer in Kentucky has proved a severe blow to the enemy. I have full confidence in General McClellan, and think the papers ought to give him a chance and not be too impatient. There will be hard fighting during the next four months.

If Johnston is conquered at Bowling Green the war may be considered at an end, for the enemy can hold out no longer. We cannot risk a defeat here, for if the Southerners took our capital their confederacy would be recognized by the European governments.[9]

The widow Gargan is still here, and report says she is to be married soon. She has a tent to herself, near Sergeant and Mrs. Hargrave's quarters and she is allowed a guard. She is to get one hundred dollars bounty.

The authorities are getting to punish the men harder than formerly, as the regiment grows older; they think we ought to be well disciplined by this time.

You ought to see me now, with my whiskers, and cap, and dress-jacket, and sabre and revolver, and blue pants, and long-legged boots, and spurs, mounted on my steed, "Pips," a sorrel horse for which I have traded the little nuisance I first rode. You would hardly know me.

We expect to be supplied with carbines soon.

We were paid today; I have twenty dollars in my pocket, and feel quite rich.

I went through the Patent Office yesterday, and among other curiosities saw the coat that Jackson wore at New Orleans, and the old printing-press of Benjamin Franklin.[10]

[9] The Confederacy sought recognition by European governments eagerly. While England gave surreptitious assistance through building sea raiders and blockade runners, no government formally recognized the Confederacy.

[10] At this time, the old Patent Office was probably as close as Washington came to having a museum. In addition to the items mentioned, the Declaration of Independence was on display there.

Such was my admiration of Jackson at this time that I almost felt like worshipping that old coat.

Our guard duty during the winter of 1861-62 was very severe. The quarters for the prisoners and reliefs consisted of a small barrack room built off some distance from the regimental quarters, and was not large enough to accommodate the force, and sometimes we would scarcely find food for the prisoners.

One diminutive fire was all that was allowed to keep us warm, or with which to dry our clothing. Sometimes we went on guard mounted, and rode instead of walked post; I suppose this is occasionally the custom, although we never repeated it after leaving Camp East of Capitol, unless going on picket. The practice, however, was soon abandoned, and camp guard duty was subsequently performed dismounted.

The posts or beats extended around the entire camp and through the camp. The orders usually were, to those on the outside to prevent any soldier or horses from passing out of camp and to those stationed between the barracks to watch for fights or fires. All the guards when on post were expected to salute all officers according to rank. This was an order the particular use of which could not be understood by the men, and was the theme of many an angry discussion among them, and the cause of numerous arrests for disobedience. They generally thought it was required to humiliate them, and were always rebelling and refusing to obey it, or seeing some pretext for shirking it.

One of the posts was located in an old cemetery used by the colored people just outside of camp. The guard here had no particular orders except that universal one, "salute officers according to rank."

Shortly after this line was established Evans was placed on post, and went on duty about midnight. As he was walking his beat a cart drove up with a coffin in it, and in the coffin a corpse evidently, from the weight with which it slid out of the cart when the bow of the latter was tipped up by the only person with it—the driver. The latter remounted the cart and drove rapidly away. leaving the coffin where it had fallen. Evans was somewhat puzzled by this performance, but said nothing, as he had no orders to meet such a contingency, and proceeded to walk his post as usual. As it lay directly across his path, he was obliged to step over the coffin each way. At length he became fatigued with his duty, and finding the coffin quite convenient, sat down upon it.

It is needless to say that Evans was made just a little uncomfortable next morning, while standing his last turn of guard, when an old colored man, who arrived and proceeded to bury the corpse, remarked, in reply to his inquiry as to the case, that "that dar nigger died of de small-pox!" However, he did not take the disease.

It was customary in the morning, after the guardmount, for the detail relieved to retire above the guardhouse and discharge their weapons. This was done at will, and the men often did a little target shooting on their own responsibility. Sometimes this was rather dangerous to the residents of that neighborhood, especially when Sergeant Hargraves began to fire—his revolver being generally elevated at an angle of forty-five degrees or less, when the shots would go singing among the houses beyond.

I recollect on one occasion an old man came running out, and threw up his hands in the wildest manner. After the fusillade was stopped it was ascertained that several bullets had passed into his house, endangering the lives of the members of his family, but fortunately injuring no one. Owing to the vigorous protests and representations of the citizen the officers checked future amusements of this character in that neighborhood.

Stable guard was not so exacting in its demands as camp guard. No arms were worn; the duty was simply to see that no grain was stolen, to tie up horses that should happen to get loose, or release them when they became entangled, and to keep them from fighting among themselves. The officer of the day seldom disturbed us on this duty.

The scene in the barrack-rooms during the winter evenings was a curious one, if not picturesque. A few rude chandeliers, made of pine boughs, hung from the ceiling at intervals of perhaps twenty feet, and from these a number of tallow candles shed their dim light. At almost every bunk or berth—each of which was occupied by two men—a half candle generally was burning. In little clusters along the upper tier of bunks—these presented better facilities for such purposes than the lower ones, as there was room for one to sit upright upon them—a number of men could be seen, some playing cards, some writing letters, and others smoking and conversing. In F Company's quarters, the German element usually gathered together, and sang songs of the fatherland, or played poker for "gelt," as they called money. Around the stoves, other squads collected and sang, or talked of scenes in their homes, or of their boyhood. Sometimes a space in the room was cleared, a couple of pairs of boxing gloves brought in, and a friendly set-to maintained by the experts at such things. Occasionally two of our stalwart German members could be induced to put them on, and awkwardly knock one another all about the room, to the edification of the lookers-on. Then we had "stag-dances," presided over by the traditional long-legged fiddler—who ever saw a fiddler who was not long-legged—and amid the dust they shook up the boys would "hoe it down" in a manner that was astonishing.

Some time in January, F Company enjoyed a sensation in the shape of a marriage between two of its members, upon due application for, and the granting of, permission on the part of Lieutenant Colonel Emory, as I understood, as a recognition of his authority in the premises. The happy couple were Private McKibben and laundress Gargan, Jim's widow. A great jollification on account thereof was indulged in by a number of the men, some of whom became temporarily attached to "Company Q" in consequence of their too boisterous demonstrations.

As if to complete our domestic circle, Mrs. Pete Gargan, also a laundress, gave birth to a fine boy. I suppose he was one of the youngest soldiers on record, drawing his first breath of life within the military enclosure of a wall tent. The incipient regular was named after Lieutenant Colonel Emory, who recognized the honor by an appropriate gift. I am sorry to say that they all subsequently deserted—private, laundress, and incipient regular.

Schumacher paid his first visit to the guard house during these halcyon days. It seems that this handsome man, making a visit to some of his female friends in the city, was so overcome by their blandishments that he shared with them an indefinite amount of lager beer. As a consequence, when he returned to camp, he unwittingly came under the notice of Lieutenant McClain. The latter, seeing his unsteady gait, and drawing the circle every few steps, ordered him, to be tied up by the thumbs to a post. This did not at all suit the festive Schumacher; so he raised a great howl, of such mournful numbers, as Longfellow[11] has it, and for such a long period, that our regimental surgeon decided his life to be in danger, and ordered him, to be let down. It was then decided to vary Schumacher's occupation, and accordingly a piece of timber—it was too large to be called a stick, and too small to be called a log was placed upon his right shoulder, and he was ordered to walk around a ring for a specified time. No sooner had he felt its weight, however, than he doubled up under it in the most helpless way imaginable, literally

[11]   The reference is to Henry Wadsworth Longfellow.

crushed to earth. His face assumed a sickly smile; his small eyes closed languidly; his close-curling hair had absorbed a great quantity of mud; and taken altogether, he was a most comical object. It was finally decided that the man was in such a bad way as to render it advisable to release him and send him to his quarters, and two men were detailed to support him on the way. After considerable effort on their part, he was at length safely deposited in his bed, and the men returned to their duty at the guard house; but Schumacher, as the door closed behind them, scrambled out of his berth, changed his clothes, washed and combed his head, and appeared his own cheerful self again, as though nothing had happened.

Our duty in the city was demoralizing to many of the men; liquor was too easily procured. As a specimen of its effects, it may be mentioned that Draker was found near the place where he was supposed to have been posted as a guard, lying helplessly on the sidewalk, with his horse standing over him, looking piteously at his master's prostrate form. In consequence of this fearful breach of discipline, Christian was ignominiously thrown into the guard house, but escaped further punishment after a few days of confinement. Court martials were painfully frequent, and inflicted severe punishments on each successive case, to restore the diminishing discipline. For this reason, as well as for the additional one that the duty at most was rather dishonoring than otherwise, I was glad we were relieved from such service, and returned to the more legitimate occupation of the camp—constant preparation for the field.

During the first week in January, the regiment marched to the White House and paid its respects to President Lincoln, passing in review, with the usual salute. I had not seen him since the fall of 1860, during the presidential campaign. A great change seemed to have taken place; for the life of me I could not help pitying the sad-looking face of him who stood upon the portico that day and bowed as we presented sabres.[12]

After the ceremonies at the Executive Mansion were concluded we called on the Secretary of War, and saluted him. The robust man that returned our salute looked a wonderful contrast to his chief, both in body and mien. The depressing sense of the responsibility that weighed down Lincoln, and which communicated an uneasy sensation to the men while in his presence, was not so visible in Stanton, whose figure was a type

[12] The greatest change that had taken place regarding Lincoln's face after the fall of 1861 was the growth of a beard.

of the energy with which the latter subsequently carried on the great war.

Some time in February, if I remember aright, my attention was attracted to an article in one of the Washington newspapers—a communication from a soldier, in which an account was given of an occurrence during the Mexican War. It went on to state that, on the occasion of General Scott's advance against Mexico City and when his army had halted before its gates prior to making the attack, and while the hero of Lundy's Lane was in a quandary as to the best mode of procedure in the proposed assault, his notice was called to a young lieutenant of engineers as being a man likely to give him the proper advice in the matter. An interview was ordered, upon which occasion the young lieutenant of engineers unfolded his plans, to the great satisfaction of his chief, who adopted them, and the City of Mexico succumbed.

According to this communication to him belonged the honor of the capture. Now who was this young lieutenant of Engineers? Why, General George B. McClellan, of course.

I was much impressed with the story, but thought its peculiar style was familiar. Sure enough, a few days thereafter I received a letter from Lieutenant Chill Hazzard of the Twelfth Pennsylvania volunteers, detailing to me that he had been on picket recently, and how he had, to while away the time, written this article, closing his communication substantially with these words, "And now, Sid, I pledge *you* my word I scissored none of it. It was manufactured out of whole cloth." So it transpired that the story was a fabrication of Chill's fertile brain, and no other foundation upon which to rest than the delicate texture of his brilliant imagination.

The story in question went the rounds of the different newspapers throughout the country, and has not yet been denied, so far as I have heard. There are those who claim that subsequent events have proved the military reputation of General McClellan to rest upon a foundation as fragile as that of Chill's romantic statement.

Another anecdote of Lieutenant Chill was related to me, which I think is too good to be lost. Some years later in the war he became adjutant of the regiment, and in this capacity was often importuned for guards by the inhabitants of the different neighborhoods in which his regiment was encamped. One day, while the reserves were located in the neighborhood of Warrenton, Virginia, a woman importuned him for a guard to protect her property, alleging that the soldiers were stealing her vegetables. After much discussion Chill finally promised her that if she would do one of two things he would furnish the guard—"pray to the Lord for the success of the Union armies, or bring him a mess of cabbage." She brought him the cabbage.

One day, Simmers, who had been down to the Eastern Branch watering a couple of horses, came riding back in proud state to the stables. In the company street he met our teamster driving down towards the stable; both approached rapidly, Simmers on the gallop. They met—the led horse pulled off towards the right, and the one he rode swung suddenly to the left. The teamster's animals halted and threw up their heads. The latter appendage of the off horse, not being able to get out of the way, came in fierce contact with the stomach of our smiling cavalryman, and landed him in a comical way into the mud. Simmers was not injured in body, but this ignominious fall before the faces of his comrades wounded his feelings severely, and he hurried away to hide his diminished head. Late that evening, however, Simmers appeared, suffering from an attack of his periodical disease, and actually singing a song about some "chaney madel" of his fatherland.

Sergeant Hargraves—who, by the way, had seen service in Her British Majesty's infantry forces in the East Indies, and was, therefore, an old soldier—was the possessor of a fine, large, though somewhat clumsy mare. I do not know whether or not the sergeant, looking ahead to the troublous days in store for us, when a clumsy animal would be at a discount, imagined that it might be worth his life or liberty to keep her; at all events he endeavored to induce Private Snell[13] to make a trade, offering something as a bonus to the susceptible Snell. Snell also possessed a mare, but she was remarkably fleet of foot, and otherwise attractive to a cavalryman, and every way worthy of the animal the sergeant proposed to reduce to the ranks, and to whose position he desired to promote her. At length the susceptible Snell agreed to an exchange, and Hargraves, before finally closing the bargain, proposed to ride her down to the Branch at water call. Promptly upon the sounding of the first bugle notes Hargraves was at the stable. He did not think a bridle would be necessary, although Snell urged him to put one on; the halter strap was all he would need. Sergeant Hargraves was a magnificent rider—in his own opinion—and for any person to hint otherwise was to invoke upon that person's head the vials of the

[13]   James Snell enlisted on July 5, 1861, at the age of 22. He was born in Pennsylvania. Snell was discharged at Lighthouse Point, Virginia, at the expiration of his term of service on July 5, 1864.

sergeants wrath. Snell understood this, and did not long urge him to put on a bridle, lest the sergeant should deem it to be a reflection upon his ability as a horseman. The mare walked prettily all the way down to the Branch, actually looked solemn under her official load; went into the water and drank properly; came out and moved back towards the stables with a dainty step; in short, was all any one could desire.

Sergeant Hargraves was delighted with her; if Private Snell had been present then, and of a practical, business turn of mind, a much larger bonus might have been secured while the sergeant was in that satisfied mood. I wish I could continue to describe how well he was pleased with her; how the trade was finally consummated to the excessive satisfaction of both; how the sergeant rode that dainty-stepping mare at the head of the column at all future stable calls, but I have not been permitted to do so. Unfortunately, at the very moment he had halted, after leaving the water, to await the formation of the column preparatory to marching back, Christian Draker, on his little sorrel, and the smiling Simmers, on his horse, dashed up past Sergeant Hargraves and Private Snell's mare and across the field, in a headlong race. The mare threw her ears forward, gave one earnest look, and struck out after them. The sergeant was taken by surprise, but made a frantic clutch for the mane, clamped his short legs against the mare's side, and managed to keep mounted. His cap fell off, and his ambrosial locks streamed on the breeze; he bowed his head low. On went the mare.

I doubt if, at this instant, Private Snell could have induced Sergeant Hargraves to give a bonus, unless, indeed, it had been a bonus for the privilege of dismounting. Still on went the mare.

A loud cheer greeted the twain as, like a flash, they swept past the companies marching along the hill. Now she moved straight toward a fence. Some curiosity is excited as to the final result. This is soon satisfied, for with a sudden swing she wheels square to the right, while the burly form of Sergeant Hargraves, late of Her British Majesty's Royal Infantry in the East Indies, rises into the air like the thrust of a porpoise in the sea, and passing clear over the fence, landing in a heap on terra firma while great shouts of laughter go up from the unsympathetic mob above. The damage sustained by the Sergeant was two broken ribs.

On the afternoon of the 24th of February, 1862, a terrific gale of wind arose, and soon grew so strong that the boards on the roof of the stables of Companies C and L began to be torn from their fastenings.

The orderly bugler sounded some sort of a call, and a soldier shouted "to arms," creating great excitement. It proved to be "assembly," to turn out the men to rescue the horses from the falling stable. This was successfully accomplished.

As spring approached there were many rumors of the early advance of the army. As usual, the newspapers teemed with accounts as to what was to be done, by whom it was to be done, and how it was to be done. On the 9th of March word came that the forces south of the Potomac were under marching orders. On the morning of the 10th I wrote a letter home, and had scarcely finished it when the first sergeant came in and announced that Camp East of Capitol was to be broken up. I had barely time to pen the following postscript:

We have just received marching orders, with three days rations and ammunition. Destination unknown. Goodbye.

It was hard for us to turn out of our comfortable quarters that dark, cold, drizzly morning, but there was no alternative. Extra blankets and clothing had to be abandoned. An impression prevailed that we were to return soon, and this reconciled us somewhat, as we thought we could secure what we had left behind in that contingency.

The regiment, with the exception of C and L Companies, formed in line on the parade ground, fully eight hundred strong. After the first sergeants had made their reports to the adjutant and the company officers gave their customary salute, Lieutenant Colonel Emory called for our standard bearer, took the banner in his hand, and said, holding it aloft;

"Soldiers we are to take the field. I want no man to abandon this flag."

A death-like silence followed, broken only by the clinking of sabres as the officers took their positions on the right of their respective companies. Then came a bugle call; the command broke by fours to the front, and in a few moments the soldiers of the Sixth Cavalry bade farewell to their camp, and moved up the street towards the Capitol.

How well they performed their duty in succeeding years let the graves in Virginia, Maryland, and Pennsylvania answer!

Washington to Yorktown to Chickahominy

As the regiment marched past the camps of artillery that stretched along the streets east of the Capitol it was greeted with cheer after cheer by the soldiers that mustered within them to see us depart for the front.

"Go ahead boys—God bless you! We will all be along soon!"

Our hats were off in an instant, and one long, loud, deafening shout went up from our ranks in response.

Can I trust myself to describe the scene at the Capitol—of the throng of fair ones on the northern balcony who cheered us in the feminine way by waving their snowy handkerchiefs? I fear not. I can only say, for myself, that I felt my flesh tingle with excitement; I wanted to yell with an exceedingly great noise. That hour was worth years of suffering!

The rain was still falling as the regiment marched across the Long Bridge, but ceased within an hour later. By one o'clock we were well on our way to Fairfax Courthouse. The vast encampments were all abandoned by their occupants, no soldiers remaining, save a few stragglers, who were plodding about picking up articles from among the piles of debris which were scattered around. A few citizens, who stood by the roadside at intervals, looking upon the scene in a sort of daze, and replying to our questions as to the surrounding country in a hesitating, bewildered way, were all of that class visible. The pictures everywhere presented were the same—trodden, fenceless fields, ruins of houses, silent woods. We began to realize the full meaning of the phrase, "war's desolation;" here it was stretched before us, protesting in its sickening silence against the cruel absurdities which place man in bloody antagonism to man.

Darkness came on before we reached Fairfax Courthouse. The scene just beyond the village was grand and inspiriting. Thousands of bivouac fires stretched along the road and far off to the east, lighting the horizon with a liquid glare. Fully sixteen thousand infantry, several batteries of artillery and two or three regiments of cavalry were crowded upon the surrounding fields. As I stood looking upon this mass of men and horses I could not help asking myself, "Who can resist this mighty force?"

The regiment halted here, and after a short delay was marched into an orchard on the right hand side of the road, formed in columns of companies, dismounted, and ordered to "stand to horse." After another delay, we were permitted to feed and rub down the legs of our tired animals, and loosen the saddle-girth. About midnight the men, worn out by their long march, fastened their horses to various stakes and limbs by sundry means and devices, and stowed themselves away in different corners to enjoy a little rest. The air became very chilly, and I was obliged to move around to keep myself warm. The sky had become entirely clear, and the stars glittered coldly upon us.

I had abundant opportunity for reflection now; the excitement of the day had completely passed off, and the cruel realities of our condition were fairly presented in all their fearful colors. This was one more step upon the stage—the curtain would soon rise, and the tragedy begin. We had as yet heard no news from the front. Centerville, the fortified outpost of the confederate army was but a few miles distant. Doubtless the coming day would usher in a bloody engagement. Where shall I be at this hour tomorrow? In this world, or in another? Perhaps, by that time, the great mystery of this life shall have been solved. Sitting down behind an outbuilding where I was partially sheltered from the northwest wind, full of these thoughts, I fell into a troubled sleep. About midnight an order came to unsaddle and rub off our poor horses' backs as soon as they should dry a little. This was done, and in a short time we were wrapped up in our blankets, with our heads upon our saddles, and our arms carefully arranged beside us so that they could be seized without confusion.

The shrill notes of a bugle aroused us while yet the stars glittered in the clear cold sky. A few moments later the air trembled with the roll of drums and the blare of trumpets. The bivouac fires, which had burned low, started up with fresh vigor; the hum of preparation could be heard all around. Horses were fed and groomed; our breakfast, consisting of pork and crackers and coffee, was soon eaten.

Seven o'clock came, but there was no sound of war. At that hour "boots and saddles" rang out, and half an hour later we were upon the road again. To our surprise, no one marched or showed signs of moving except our regiment. Our route stretched towards the front; there could be no mistake as to that; perhaps we had been selected to open the attack. If this was the case, surely some support would be visible; here there was none. As the columns moved past the different regiments bivouacked by the roadside the men looked at us with a curious indifference. At last we had left all these behind, and rode into a dense forest of scrub pines, over innumerable ravines, and past occasional clearings with a farm house and barn visible here and there. Finally, after a ride of two hours, we halted, dismounted, and "stood to horse." Presently couriers galloped from front to rear. By and by we hear that we have marched on the wrong road for several miles; then the men are ordered to remount; the head of the column, preceded by Brigadier General Phillip St. George Cooke, appears coming down the road, and we crowd our horses off up against the fence to give them room to pass.

As soon as the countermarching movement had been completed the regiment broke into a trot, filing by twos over paths through solitary woods, the men dodging the limbs as best they might, jumping ditches and logs at short intervals. Then we emerge upon an open sandy field, and forming fours at a gallop—numerous bare heads and scratched faces are visible as I glance around—dashing past a small guard of infantry scattered in an unconcerned way along a fence. Finally we reach a road, and come down to a walk. This change from the hard jolting gait of the previous hour was a wonderful relief to me, at least, for a keen pain had just begun to develop itself in my right side.

We had slowly marched a mile, perhaps, when, emerging from, a heavy growth of timber, a long regular rising slope broke upon our view, on which, just where it ran up to the horizon, stood strong looking entrenchments, and out of the embrasures peered what seemed to be the black muzzles of many cannon. Not a human being was in sight. I anxiously looked for some sign of hostile troops, but all was still. Presently a small flag was detected floating from the crest of the parapet close to the road, and this was soon announced, to our great satisfaction, as the stars and stripes. The enemy had abandoned all his strong positions without a struggle. The threatening guns in the works proved to be harmless logs, to our disgust, for our first impression was that we had made great captures. These were the heights of Centerville.

The column halted here a few moments, and then moved up the hill past huge boulders of rock that threatened the legs of horses and of riders. On the crest we halted again for a few moments, looking at a dull mass of smoke rising from distant plains toward the south. The cloud proved to be hovering over the famous fields of Manassas.

The bugle sounded again, and away we went on that hateful trot—the sharp pain stinging my side—our poor horses panting and covered with perspiration. Our route stretched along the corduroy road down the hill towards Bull Run, past numerous clusters of log huts. We caught a glimpse—as we learned afterwards—of General Beauregard's headquarters, and then dashed into the woods again, with dead horses and broken-down wagons impeding the way at intervals; now across the celebrated stream, and up the hill and through woods, past rifle-pits stretching to the right and left of the road, and halting at last at the once dreaded Junction.

At Manassas we found about eighty wagons parked in a sort of yard. They were generally useless, apparently the refuse of southern plantations. The confederate commissary buildings were still burning, and flour, rice, sugar, broken muskets, bayonets, shot shell, bullets—all the paraphernalia of war without its pomp—were scattered along the railroad and among the fortifications.

We had but little time to examine the curiosities; a halt of perhaps ten minutes in duration was made, and then the bugle sounded and we were off again. The column followed the railroad for some distance, capturing a solitary confederate, who, somewhat inebriated, and mounted upon an old gray horse, shouted as we came up that he "was the last of the Mohicans," and burst out into a loud, drunken laugh. Then the column dashed down one hill and up another, through forests of low scrub pines and past trees in which bowie knives—a few of them that one of our sergeants examined bore the name of some Mississippi organization—were sticking. Then over graves, partially broken down fences, into roads and off roads, then into a field, and finally forming in column of squadron under a ridge, with the order, as soon as the abridgement was completed, "Draw sabre!"

A rumor was immediately started that we were in the presence of the enemy, and much curiosity was manifested to see them—a great stretching of necks to peer over the heads of the men in front, but all in vain.

I afterwards understood that a few pickets were visible on some distant hill, who had, by the time the regiment was formed, quite disappeared.

In a few moments we were ordered to "return sabre," and pushed forward again, passing down a hill to a stream, where we gave our famished beasts water; thence around the base of the hill to the right, filing through the woods into an unknown road; then striking into a trot again, stumbling over huge stones in the darkness that by this time had fallen upon us, dashing through what were either many creeks, or the same creek many times—I do not know which— and finally, about nine o'clock, reaching Centerville once more, very sore, hungry, and tired, and thoroughly disgusted with the cavalry service. The great majority of our poor horses were now staggering on their weary limbs.

I wondered what all this hard riding was for? It looked very much like the movements of that celebrated potentate who marched up a hill with forty-thousand men, and then marched down again, though I question if his forces were so badly used up as ours on this occasion. General McClellan had joined us shortly before nightfall, and rode at the head of the column until we returned to Centreville. He must have been cognizant of our condition. If the movement was designed as a pursuit of the enemy to bring him to bay, it was commenced at too late an hour. At the time we halted at Centreville the enemy were beyond the Rappahannock.

We had passed over a field during the day on which the famous Black Horse Cavalry met the no less famous Fire Zouaves at the battle of July 21, 1861. Of course, one would have supposed, from reading the graphic newspaper descriptions of this charge of the knights of Virginia upon the invincible zouaves—you recollect how it was said that the latter, indignantly discarding the usual modern methods of war, met their antagonists with knife in hand, snatching them off their horses, and hewing them to pieces—that the ground would have shown some of the marks of that sanguinary conflict; but it did not. The remains of two horses only were visible, but not a human grave.

I had a conversation some two years afterwards on this subject with a member of the First Virginia Cavalry—a portion of which was once known as the Black Horse—whom we captured on the Rappahannock, and he assured me their loss on the occasion referred to was men wounded and two horses killed. His description of the affair reflected little credit upon the fighting qualities as there displayed by our pet zouaves.

Our fires were soon kindled, and the coffee simmering on the coals in our tin cups, and the pork crackling melodiously on the ends of sticks over the blaze, and our tongues busy recounting the scenes and

97

sensations of the day. For one I enjoyed the rough fare that night with wonderful relish; that long fearfully rough ride proved a remarkable appetizer.

It must not be thought that in our anxiety to make ourselves comfortable our poor horses were forgotten. As soon as they had recovered their breath they were fed and groomed in the most thorough manner, and had saddle blankets wrapped around each one of them to keep from cooling too quickly, and everything within our means was procured to counteract the effects of the sad usage they had received. When everything was ready we laid down with our heads on our saddles and arms, wrapped our blankets around us, and fell into a deep sleep, to dream over the excitement of our first day of actual service in the field.

Reveille did not sound until long after sunrise the next morning, giving us ample time to rest—a boon fully appreciated by all. We found many of our horses stretched upon the ground unable to rise—that day's ride had killed them. Those that were on their feet were stiff, and scarcely able to move. Poor creatures! They had been faithful unto death.

It was evident that we would not move camp this day, at least, so after our duties at the stables were completed, I took a stroll around among the fortifications and log huts that the enemy had occupied as winter quarters. The latter teemed with what, to me, were great curiosities. A vast number of books, magazines, Southern papers and letters—some of the latter received from the south had not yet been opened, some had been read, and others were written in camp and sealed, but not sent away—were scattered around. Here was a fine opportunity of discovering the private feelings of the confederates upon the question of the war, and I availed myself of it. The letters from the people to their soldiers in camp were generally full of sanguine expressions, those from fathers and mothers being moderate, telling their sons to "trust in God," while those of younger persons, and especially the fair sex, were immoderately abounding in exhortations to their friends and lovers to "do their duty," and "kill the Yankees." One young lady, in particular, modestly requested her affianced to bring home a scalp. Those written in camp to friends and relatives at home were less hopeful as a general thing. One man wanted his father to get him elected constable, so that he could come home with honor and get out of the army without being suspected of cowardice. Another, written by a South Carolinian, a member of General Evans's brigade, dated at

Leesburg and addressed to his brother at Centreville, gave an interesting description of the part they took in the battle of Ball's Bluff. He stated that their force, all South Carolina soldiers, had been attacked by a large federal force, which had crossed the river for that purpose; that the confederates, all told, mustered about fifteen hundred men, but that the regiment to which he was attached was the only body engaged on their side, that the federals were soon repulsed and driven back to the water's edge, where they crowded at the foot of a bluff, completely at the mercy of the confederates, with no chance of succor, and apparently abandoned by their more fortunate comrades on the Maryland side of the river. He supposed the federal loss to be fully nine hundred men.

I also picked up a diary, in which the first entry was dated January 1, 1862, and the last March 6—four days before the evacuation. The last memorandum stated that it was rumored the "Yankees are about to advance, and it is most likely our army will fall back." From other entries it appeared that the writer was a member of the Nineteenth Virginia Infantry, and had graduated at the University of Virginia.

In the hut where the diary was found were numerous copies of Little's Living Age, and other literary papers, and from memorandums made on various books I was satisfied that the members of one company, at least, of the Nineteenth were graduates or members of that institution of learning. Some classical works, Latin dictionaries, and a few copies of DeBow's Review still adorned the rude shelves. Coffee, sugar, rice, flour, and salt pork must have been plenty among the confederates, as there was still an abundance of these articles of food scattered around the fireplaces. The cooking utensils consisted of cast-iron pots, heavy skillets, and "Dutch ovens." A few muskets and plenty of ammunition remained strewn about the floor. Gray jackets trimmed with scarlet, gray pantaloons with red stripes down the legs, and gray caps with red bands around the base of the crown, which I found thrown here and there, belonged, I supposed, to their artillerymen. Numerous trees perforated with musket balls, all over the camp, clearly demonstrated that in their army close attention had been given to target-shooting—a feature essential in military training, but which had been, so far as I could judge, woefully neglected in our own.

Regiments of our troops, though in service six or eight months before, were led into battle without once having the opportunity of discharging their pieces until in the presence of the enemy. In this respect I think our government acted on the penny-wise, pound-foolish principle. Nothing gives the soldier so much confidence in his weapon, and adapts it so well to his manipulations, as target practice.

The discovery of an old guidon, adorned with stars and bars, showed me the banner of the confederacy. It had an ugly look to me—a brazen, impudent look.

On my return to camp I saw a regiment of zouaves, which proved to be the Fourteenth Brooklyn, deploying along the fortifications on the hill. Beyond them appeared other regiments of infantry, coming up, I suppose, to support the mounted men in case the enemy showed a disposition to return.

On the 14th a portion of our regiment, supported by a brigade of infantry, left on a reconnaissance towards the Rappahannock, while the remainder of us started for Alexandria, camping that night at Fairfax Station, on the Orange and Alexandria. Towards morning a cold, drizzly rain began to fall, and by daylight we were completely drenched to the skin. We marched at nine o'clock for the Potomac. The storm continued all day of the 15th and upon our arrival at Alexandria we were covered from head to foot with mud—a disgusted, querulous body of men.

The command was marched into a low meadow on the right of the road just north of the town, dismounted, and ordered to "stand to horse." In ten or fifteen minutes the meadow was covered with water some inches deep, and we were compelled to move. Then we were marched to the left of the road up the side of the hill upon which stood Fort Ellsworth and ordered to unsaddle and feed. The prospect of passing the night here was anything but pleasant; the field had been in grain the summer before, and consequently was not covered with sod, and a few moments after our arrival became a vast mire. Into this mass of mud our saddles and arms were deposited, but few poor fires were started, for wood was very scarce. Our rations were exhausted. The horses broke loose every few moments, and went tramping around among the men, who had thrown themselves upon the ground in a vain effort to sleep, and had to be caught and tied, or held if one could find no place to tie them.

I managed, however, to slip off to Fort Ellsworth, into which I was passed by the humane sentry, though against orders, under the convoy of another humane private—we common soldiers sympathize with each other in defiance of regulations sometimes—and soon found myself in a great Sibley tent, beside a warm stove, stripped to the skin, and my clothes hanging up to dry, and a great bowl of mill in one hand, and a huge piece of nice cake in the other. For once in my life my heart was too full of gratitude for utterance; I had often read of other people's hearts being in that condition, but never fully realized it until now. And the kindness of this generous squad—I know they were brave, for men with such hearts are always brave—did not stop here; I was tumbled into a nice soft straw bed, which soon soothed me into a deep slumber. I have a dim recollection of saying something in apology for occupying one of their beds, and of inquiring where its owner was to sleep, but they said he was on guard and would not be in tonight. Happening, however, to wake up some hours later, and beholding a man actually sitting up and drying my clothes, in a sleepy way asked him why he was not in bed. He replied that he was on guard, and came in for a lunch, and that while here he thought he would turn the outside of my clothing to the fire. I subsequently learned that this was a pious fib. He was not on duty; it was his bed I occupied; and the men in the tent took turns in sitting up and drying my wet clothes.

The next morning I was wakened by the bugles of the regiment, hurried on my now dry clothing, ran down the hill, and was fortunate enough to find my horse all right, except that he had been rolling, and was covered with a mass of mud. The poor boys who had remained in the field showed traces of weary, wretched night on their wan faces. If this meets the eye of any of my hospitable friends of Fort Ellsworth, they may rest assured that their kindness is still unforgotten.

The sky had cleared off, and the sun rose bright and warm that morning. Rations of crackers, salt pork, and coffee were issued to the men, and feed for the horses. Most of the day was occupied in cleaning our animals and weapons, and towards evening the regiment was marched to a pleasanter site a short distance away, where Sibley tents were pitched, the men made comfortable, and the unnumbered woes of the previous night forgotten.

It was several days before the balance of the command rejoined us at Alexandria. They had been on a long reconnaissance towards the Rappahannock and had found the enemy in small force on the south bank. They seemed to have enjoyed themselves very well, and had wonderful stories to tell us—how they fared and what they had seen in that unknown land. For a time they were the lions of the regiment.

By the 18th of March the larger portion of the Army of the Potomac was encamped around Alexandria. About this time it was rumored that most of us were to be sent to Fortress Monroe, but as to future destination all was in doubt. The general opinion seemed to be that an expedition against Norfolk was in progress, and that an attempt would be made, with that city as a base of supply, to penetrate the confederacy and thus compel the abandonment of Richmond, which was now the capital of the insurgents. The appearance of an innumerable fleet of all sorts of boats in the river off Alexandria gave color to these speculations—at least showed conclusively that some movement was intended.

By the 21st thousands of men had been embarked on boats, and soon disappeared down the river. On the morning of the 28th the Sixth Cavalry was marched on board two-masted schooners—our squadron, G and F Companies, embarking on the same boat. The horses were picketed on deck, and men were crowded away into dark holds upon the ballast of coal. Toward the afternoon a transport, loaded with troops, appeared, and took us in tow. That night we anchored off Fort Washington, some eight or ten miles from Alexandria. At early dawn the next morning the anchors were drawn up, and our tug started with us again. I was anxious to enjoy the scenery of the river, but a heavy rain set in, and did not cease until afternoon.

Our fare was still more frugal now—raw pork, crackers, and water—coffee was out of the question, as there were no facilities for cooking on board. Towards evening one of the employees on the boat dipped up a bucket of water, and let us taste it. It was brackish, and now we could say we had floated on real brine. I have said that there were no cooking facilities on board. This is to be taken in a partial sense. The boat's crew had means of cooking for themselves, but of course the arrangements were far too limited to accommodate the soldiers. The worthy Fenton who did the cooking for G Company while on land, and who on water assisted the commissary sergeant to deal out rations, and made himself generally useful, planned a surprise for the squadron. That he was eminently successful the sequel will show—so far, at least, as the surprise was concerned.

One morning, about the hour we were wont to have breakfast, he suddenly appeared on the scene and announced that he had prepared hot coffee for all of us. Everybody was delighted. For a time there was imminent danger of a meeting being called, and a vote of thanks tendered to that functionary. The old Dutchman had importuned the boatmen for the use of their stove for once on our trip, and this they had reluctantly granted, and here was the evidence of his triumph. If I remember aright, tin-cups were in demand during that memorable morning. Those who were fortunate enough to possess them looked with pity on those who were unfortunate enough not to possess them. A great throng crowded around the camp kettles, sniffing the odorous perfumes that arose from the seething nectar. The enterprising creature that had his first cooled enough to taste cast a triumphant glance around upon his fellows as much as to say, "Just look at me"—which they did. He imbibed cautiously—it was still too hot for comfort and we all gazed upon him to see how his lips would smack with pleasure—which they did not. A wry sort of smile passed over his face, but he said nothing; it was noticeable, however, that the application of the cup became more and more infrequent. Soon somebody else, who had allowed his coffee to become moderately cool, took a long drink, but he hurriedly spit it out again and showed signs of a swelling in the throat.

It soon transpired that the trouble with the coffee was of a fatal character—that the water of which it was made was too brackish to be palatable.

Nor were our opportunities and conveniences for sleeping at all satisfactory. The ballast of coal on which we were obliged to lie was a bed full of ugly points that were sure, when one laid down upon it, to find the most sensitive parts of one's body, and keep one constantly turning from side to side to ease one's misery. Then the horses on deck were continually tramping heavily, setting one's sensitive nerves on edge, and making one feel as though they would probably come through the flooring upon him; this was another condition not conducive to peaceful slumber.

It will thus be seen that, from lack of the vital pleasures of man—eating and sleeping—our experience as tourists was not inviting. It might be thought, perhaps, that in consequence of this, we did not enjoy ourselves, but we did, after a fashion. The constant changing of scenery was a source of well-defined pleasure. The rigors of discipline were relaxed, and all duties dispensed with save those actually necessary. At night the vessels were always anchored—for fear of accident, I suppose. Some of the soldiers became seasick after we reached the Chesapeake Bay, exciting the merriment of their more fortunate comrades by their frantic efforts to turn themselves inside out.

On the 1st of April our schooners were safely anchored in the magnificent harbor of Hampton Roads, off Fortress Monroe. The scene here was very inspiriting. The water was covered with innumerable boats of all descriptions, loaded with troops and military stores. One or two English and French war vessels were also at anchor in the roads. The fortress, a grand and imposing structure, frowned upon us with its myriad guns. Along its base the clear sward, just brightening under the influence of the early spring sun, stretched like an emerald carpet. A short distance from the water's edge stood an earthwork, and in this was mounted the huge gun from Pittsburg—a veritable monster of its kind. Then there stood the Rip-raps, of which we had heard so much, but of which we had not been able to form a conception—a huge pile of unfinished masonry work rising out of the bosom of the waters directly across from Monroe, whose younger brother it was, built to aid in the defense of the approaches to the harbor. Directly across from Rip-raps extended a strip of lowlands which, it was understood, was yet in the possession of the enemy. On the right we could see the mouth of the Elizabeth river, and beyond this the Point of land lying between the Elizabeth and the James rivers, upon which the confederates had established batteries. Then came the wide-mouthed James, and Newport News, occupied by some of our infantry, completing the circle of vision.

Early on the morning of our arrival huge puffs of white smoke could be seen shooting up from the strip of land between the Elizabeth and James rivers, followed by loud reports that sounded like distant thunder. The enemy, we were informed, was practicing with his artillery.

A few days before our arrival in Hampton Roads the famous contest between the Monitor and Merrimac, preceded between the latter and three of our wooden men of war, the Congress and Cumberland and Minnesota, all of which had been disabled or driven off, had occurred within its waters. Although the Merrimac seemed to have been defeated and retired from the fight upon that occasion, it was rumored that she intended to return soon and attempt to destroy the shipping in the harbor which certainly presented a very tempting object, and we found everybody waiting in anxious expectation for the raid.

It was not pleasant to contemplate, especially for one who had no nautical experience—the prospective advent while shut up on board an old schooner, and anchored some distance from dry land, of a marine monster which was to blow one to atoms or sink one to the bottom of the sea—the result in each case being the same. This was taking one who had no nautical experience at a very awkward disadvantage, and it may be inferred that the Sixth Cavalryman in the above mentioned predicament was filled with anxieties, and realized the gravity of the occasion with a painfully clear conception.

One consolation was ours, however; the schooner was anchored but a few yards from the gallant little Monitor. This nondescript kept a full head of steam on, ready for the fray. The marks of conflict were visible her turret, the indentations of the huge shot from the guns of the Merrimac being distinctly perceptible.

On the second day after our arrival, a dapper little vessel carrying a small white flag and a very large confederate flag of the stars-and-bars pattern, made her appearance out of the mouth of the Elizabeth river, and steamed down in the direction of the fort. One of our small boats met her, carrying a white flag and the stars and stripes. These were understood to be flags-of-truce, and that the United States and confederate authorities were now in communication.

This scene made a strange impression on my mind. During my experience so far I had seen nothing of the enemy except the drunken dragoon at Manassas, and there was little in his appearance that indicated an enemy; he wore no arms, and might have been a citizen instead of a soldier. The camps at Manassas and Bull Run and Centreville, with their military debris, were unoccupied, rather resembling a peaceful mustering ground, and, to the mind of one who was unacquainted with the situation, might have been presented as the quarters of our own troops. The change from the old-time peace was so made, and so irreconcilable with my feelings, that I could not bring myself to properly realize it. I felt no ill-will against the common enemy, for I had not seen him or felt him, though I had seen his effects; but these effects were continually confounded with those of our own soldiers—that is, from their similarity—that the impressions were confused and inseparable. It was only in after days, when I had witnessed the rude shock of conflict between the gray and the blue, and when the gray awakened in my heart a strange anger, that this old uncertainty and hesitation were driven away.

The arrival of troops at Fortress Monroe steadily continued. The debarkation of the infantry received attention in preference to the cavalry and artillery, and, as a consequence, we did not reach terra firma until the 3d of April.

The mode of disembarking horses was comical. The wharves were monopolized for other purposes, and unapproachable so the horses had to be pushed overboard into the water and swim ashore. The poor

frightened beasts as they were plunged into the bay, evidently thought, if an animal does think, that their last day had arrived. They would go down out of sight under the water, but rise in a moment, and strike out for the shore with the promptitude and skill of old swimmers.

By waiting until the proper moment our horses were spared this unpleasant process of debarkation, as we finally secured a chance at a wharf, but here great urging was required before they would trust themselves to the mercy of the gangway. We had been on board the schooner six nights and five days.

After the regiment had been safely mustered on shore it was marched beyond Hampton to camp, while Barlow and I were left to guard the forage belonging to the command on the wharf. The next day Barlow was called away to join the company, and I was left alone to perform the duty. Here I passed the following night alone. On the 5th Barlow returned, bringing orders for me to hurry on with him to camp and leave the forage. We pushed rapidly to the neighborhood where Barlow had left the regiment, but by the time we arrived it had left, and gone no one knew whither, or rather, what amounted to the same thing, had gone everybody knew whither, the trouble being that of the everybody of whom we inquired no two would name the same destination. Here my knowledge of the topography or rather geography of the country, gathered from the war maps at that time published, came into service. We were on a peninsula bounded on three sides by water and on one side by the enemy. It was evident that the regiment could not travel through the water, but had business, in common with the balance of the army, with the enemy; so after debate Barlow and I unanimously arrived at the conclusion that the road leading to Yorktown was the one we wanted to find. This was easily done, and away we went, catching up to the rear guard of the command—here was a new feature of our military experience, the rearguard just at dark. The regiment bivouacked for the night in a peach orchard on the left of the road.

I had drawn, in common with the rest of the company, one day's rations on the 3d; that was to last until the 4th. I rejoined the company on the night of the 5th; on the 4th they had drawn two day's rations, to last them until the 6th. Of course my rations had given out—this hard outdoor life accelerates the consumption of food—at the appointed time, but there was no more to be procured. Though ravenously hungry on the night of the 5th I was too tired to notice it and fell asleep as soon as I had cleaned and fed my horse and thrown myself on the ground.

The 6th of April is prominent on my list of memorable days as being the one on which I first heard the sound of hostile cannon, as it was understood to be, firing upon United States troops, and resisting their advance. From the sound it must have been several miles away. The regiment marched early, but had not proceeded more than a few hundred yards, perhaps, when a sound like the reverberation of distant thunder, broke upon our ears, from the country towards which we were advancing. A few moments later we halted, and after a short interval the sound was repeated; then we marched a short distance further, then came to another halt; then another dull report. For ten long hours our progress was simply a repetition of these—I had almost said measured—incidents, the intervals of march and halt and peal were so regular in their succession. We must have been a sort of rear guard that day for the army, for we were no nearer the sound, apparently, in the evening than in the morning. From what we afterwards learned through the newspapers, the enemy made but a slight resistance to our forces, falling back in good order upon his works at Yorktown, and merely showing his teeth at intervals to demonstrate that he meant to fight us by and by.

Our movements this day were continued long after dark. A great gale of wind, keen with cold, arose about dusk, making us shiver until our teeth chattered together. Finally about midnight, perhaps, the regiment halted in a dark, desolate looking valley out of which arose a stench so dense that we could hardly breathe. Here we remained until daylight.

It subsequently appeared that we had lost our way, and morning revealed the fact that we were bivouacked near a pound where the enemy had corralled and slaughtered cattle for his forces. We hurried from here, and went into camp two or three miles distant, but the tents had barely been pitched before orders came for us to move, and they had to be taken down and packed up, and we were soon in the saddle again. Our route laid through forests of small scrub pines and over barren fields, where at places whole companies of men and horses would sometimes drop down suddenly as though they had fallen through a floor, and could be extricated only after serious efforts on their part. These accidents were occasioned, I understood, by the veins of quicksand that run all through this region. The houses along the route were deserted, with very few exceptions.

At noon we came in sight of what appeared to be a bayou which extended for some distance on both sides of the land here, and on the cape thus formed we found a breastwork for infantry and artillery, built so as to face the water, on the inner side of which were erected huts similar to those I had seen at Manassas and Bull Run. Inquiry at a house close by revealed the fact that this place was called Shipping Point, and this earthwork and these huts had been prepared and occupied by a small force of confederates up till within a day or two, when, becoming untenable upon the advance of our forces along the Yorktown road, the soldiers had been withdrawn from it.

The command halted at Shipping Point, and details of foragers were sent to a barn for corn for our horses—a duty which was promptly performed. After feeding our animals, and while they were eating, I wandered along the shore of the bayou, where I discovered some oyster shells lying out in the clear water. I will here say that the rations we were to draw on the 6th had not been issued, nor had we yet received them although this was now the afternoon of the 7th. I had had nothing to eat since the morning of the 4th, and the balance of the men had been without food since the morning of the 6th. From this statement it will be inferred that my appetite by this time could with propriety be described as ravenous. I had never been able to eat oysters, regarding them with feelings of disgust upon other occasions; but these shells, as they lay there in the water, suggested a meal with such vividness that I could not resist the temptation of tasting them. I pulled off my boots and waded in, securing the few in sight. They were very small; what had appeared as the large shell of one oyster proved to be a conglomerated mass of little shells inhabited by very minute bivalves; but as these were better than nothing, I pounded them out of their fortifications with stones, and ate them with great relish.

Altogether, however, they would not have filled the half of a tea-cup, and served only to sharpen my appetite. When I returned to the command I parched a little corn and devoured that, but was afraid to eat much lest it should be followed by results of a serious character.

Towards evening the regiment remounted, and we retraced our steps of the forenoon for a part of the time at least; but darkness came on, and I was too bewildered to understand toward what point of the compass we were moving. After a long ride, sometimes on roads, sometimes across fields, and sometimes through woods when no road was visible, the men dodging the limbs and scuttling like foragers to get past the trees, and sometimes dropping into veins of quicksand, where they would flounder about like porpoises—I particularly recollect Ferguson's adventure of this sort—we came in sight of numerous fires. To our great joy it proved to be our new camp, where we found that the cooks and stragglers had pitched our tents, put up picket lines, and prepared an immense supper with double rations of strong coffee. As this was the first coffee I had tasted since leaving Alexandria on the 8th of March, it was deeply appreciated. I suppose I never enjoyed Uncle Sam's allowance so well before or since as I did on that eventful night. The horses, too, rejoiced over a good feed of oats, and were well groomed before we retired to rest. I think it ought, in justice, to be put on record here that the comforts and necessities provided and work performed for Company F were done under the supervision of our worthy commissary sergeant, Everson, and his assistants, Sam Hamilton and Evan Davis. I doubt if any other company could boast of equal preparations for their reception.

Our camp here was a very good one in most respects, excepting that one of great importance to cavalry—the plenitude of water. However, we were not allowed to remain here long, but returned to Shipping Point for the reason, it was stated, that the facilities for procuring forage and other supplies were much better, as schooners now came up to the point and there discharged their freight.

I suppose that the recollections of our experiences at Shipping Point are remarkable only for the vividness with which they recall the hardships there endured, and the hopes and disappointments that followed each other in rapid succession, and in the order here written. Our old commanding officer, Lieutenant Colonel Emory, had left us, having been assigned to the command of an infantry brigade, and made brigadier general, and the regiment was now under the control of Major Lawrence Williams—an officer distinguished for his rigorous discipline and haughty bearing. Though intensely hated by the men, he seemed to have the welfare of the regiment, so far as its military reputation was concerned, at heart. If earnestness in matters of discipline and drill is evidence of a good officer, he was certainly entitled to be called such; but he lacked the peculiar trait of character, which, while at all times controls a soldier, still excites affection for the possessor.

We reached Shipping Point early in the morning. and immediately set to work building stables and corduroying the floors thereof, and the roads leading to and from camp on each side. To corduroy a road was to cut pine trees of small growth into length of twelve or fifteen feet, and to lay these closely together side by side, thus forming a causeway of wood. The work had been nearly completed by late in the afternoon, and the men were congratulating themselves on that fact, when, to our intense disgust, an order came to abandon this location and to go into camp about two hundred yards nearer the landing. It is no exaggeration to say that curses, not loud, but deep, followed this announcement. In addition to the many other difficulties encountered, our wagons became mired in quicksand, and heavy details of soldiers had to be made to extricate them; this was done only after peculiar efforts, by lifting them bodily to the surface.

After two or three days of hard work here, followed by several more of severe drilling, during which time, in addition to these duties, larger details were made out daily to unload schooners of forage at the point. This forage consisted of baled hay, threebushel sacks of corn, and oats, and had to be hoisted out of the hold of the vessel and carried upon our backs, with the exception of the hay, which was rolled away up on the bank. We had not yet, under the McClellan pro-slavery policy, been able to utilize the colored force in that section for the purpose. The command was ordered into camp at another place, perhaps four miles distant, and in rear of the troops operating in front of Yorktown. The spot selected was much better every way for us than the one we had left, and the change was peculiarly gratifying to the men. It was an open space just large enough for the regiment, completely surrounded by a dense forest of pines.

One of the great reliefs brought by this movement was our delivery from the heavy work of unloading schooners. Our attention was now devoted to the legitimate duties of a soldier—series of drills, mounted and dismounted, by company and by regiment being instituted, and of such frequency as to take up our entire time. Each company hunted up an available field, made ditches, erected poles, put up posts to represent men, with bags stuffed with hay for their heads, at each ditch and pole, and at intervals between, and went through such a course of exercises as we had never before experienced. These riding schools were very popular among most of the soldiers, and were of much value in making them feel at home in the saddle. First, we had to ride around at a walk, avoiding the poles and ditches, and strike off the heads on the posts; then this was repeated at a trot and then at a gallop. After this we galloped around the ring, learning to jump the poles and ditches, and then to strike off the heads while our horses were in the act of leaping, and in the succeeding intervals, being obliged by the latter requirement to recover ourselves instantaneously from the shock. These performances were repeated with revolver in hand; and then, instead of striking, we had to shoot the heads.

I must say that this was such an innovation upon the usual order of things in service—that is, such a really useful drill that its execution occasioned much surprise and pleasure among the men. Its effect was soon visible in the soldiers, when mounted, to one of perfect freedom and ease, and an apparent "at-homeativeness"—for want of a better expression—in the saddle. No one would have thought, to have seen us after a few weeks of instruction in our riding school, that this was the squad of green men, most have whom had never been astride of a horse, who had left Pittsburg the summer before.

The news of the battle of Shiloh was received on the 8th or 9th of April and occasioned much excitement. Although it seems that our troops reoccupied their camps and regained all their lost ground, thus winning a sort of questionable victory, this engagement demonstrated that the army of the enemy was made up of good material, and served to dispel the prevalent opinion, created in part by the newspapers, that the confederate soldiers would not fight bravely. The action at Shiloh taught our men and those in authority at Washington that the war was to be no child's play.

We heard plenty of cannonading during the latter part of April. The guns of the enemy's batteries and those of our gunboats, as we learned, startled us by night and by day with their oft-repeated thunder at irregular intervals. Reports from the front indicated that a siege was in progress. It was said that twenty-five thousand of our troops were on each relief engaged in digging entrenchments and parallels towards the confederate works. The enemy's forces were represented as being ninety-thousand strong, though subsequent events showed this to be too high an estimate. Our strength was supposed to be one hundred and twenty thousand men of all arms, but this, too proved to be a great exaggeration.

The men at the rear received their information as to matters at the front through the agency of the newspapers published in Philadelphia and New York, and occasionally picked up a little from stragglers and visitors.

Everybody felt that the campaign had now opened in earnest, and all were sanguine as to the result. The Sixth Cavalry had no duty to perform as yet, however, that brought the men under the fire of the enemy's artillery, and the ordinary routine of camp regulations made our life a weary monotony.

About the 1st of May the newspapers announced that General McClellan was about ready to storm the confederate lines. It was also stated that our siege guns were in position, our parallels pushed to within striking distance of the opposing forts, and that, with the active co-operation of the navy, our success was assured.

On Saturday afternoon the roar of cannon came through the wood with increased vigor, but from what batteries we could not determine; there was an impression, however, that a general engagement was imminent. The firing continued until towards Sunday morning when it gradually ceased. The men, who had by this time become used to cannonading, paid little attention to it, but fell asleep at their usual hour.

I have some reason to remember this Saturday night. I was on guard, having been regularly detailed in the morning, and the post to which I was assigned was at the quartermaster's tent. As near as I can recollect, my turn to be on "beat" was from ten to twelve o'clock that night. Shortly after I was posted Lieutenant Spangler the quartermaster or some other officer, who had been to the front, arrived, and went into the quartermaster's tent. Several other officers were there, playing cards, and evidently drinking. The officer who arrived announced that the enemy had been making unusual demonstrations all afternoon, and that it was his guns that were thundering during the day. After some conversation the game of cards was resumed. Presently a dispute arose between Lieutenant Hutchins and Captain Savage. The former sprang up and shouted:

"It is false—as false as hell!"

Then a great uproar followed. The table appeared to be upset; the light went out in an instant; there was a rattling of glasses; a sound as of struggling, and some oaths. Then it quieted down, apparently through the intercession of Lieutenant Ward, and the belligerents came out of the tent to cool themselves after their exercises. However, everything was soon in a satisfactory condition; explanations followed, regrets were expressed, and the officers returned to their game and their cups.

I had no particular interest in the result of this affray, further than to know what my duty was in the premises. As I understood the regulations, I could not leave my beat until regularly or otherwise relieved by the proper officer or non-commissioned officer, and consequently could make no arrests. Then it occurred to me that it was my duty to call the corporal of the guard, and state the case to him; but to do this or anything else would be to incur the fierce persecution of my superiors under the law without any means of self protection, and as I did not care to incur their ill-will, I made up my mind to let matters take their course.

On Sunday morning, May 4, we received orders to prepare for the regular inspection, which was to take place at nine o'clock. The usual confusion incident to cleaning arms, polishing boots and saddles, brighting buttons, etc., followed, and at the appointed hour we were in the saddle, with haversacks on, blankets and coats neatly rolled up and strapped on the pommels and cantles of our saddles. We were marched out upon the parade ground, and formed for inspection, but to our surprise, after a few moments of delay the head of the column moved out upon the road, and started for the front. After travelling for some distance through the woods we emerged upon an open plain, where we found several infantry camps. At one of these we saw two men carrying a stretcher literally covered with blood, and the sight of this sent a sickening thrill through my frame. In a short time we had arrived in full view of the enemy's batteries at Yorktown, from one of which the stars and stripes proudly floated. The mystery was now solved—the confederates had abandoned their stronghold.

Off to the right lay the magnificent York river, upon whose quiet bosom rested several war vessels at anchor. To the right and left of the road long lines of parallels ran zig-zag towards the once hostile batteries, with the loose earth cast out upon the side next to the enemy. As this was a new feature of our military experience, I could not help regarding it with some curiosity. This was what was meant by "digging out your enemy." "Spades were trump this time," as the newspapers had duly announced; but the process had involved a month's delay of invaluable time, as events subsequently proved.

As the command moved up the broad road leading into the enemy's works, proceeded by a battalion of cavalry which had joined us somewhere as we had marched from camp, and while all the men were gazing awe-stricken at the strong walls built with bays of earth, and perhaps twelve or fifteen feet in thickness, and mounted with huge guns—no wooden ones this time—which looked out threateningly from the embrasures, an explosion was heard. Rising in my saddle I sought to see what had happened, but at the same moment everybody else rose in their saddles for the same purpose, and my efforts were thus neutralized. I caught a glimpse, however, of a commotion in the ranks of the battalion—the McClellan Dragoons, I think—as the regiment came to a halt. After a few moments word was passed along the line that a torpedo had exploded in the road as the dragoons were marching over it, killing a horse and severely wounding the rider. This torpedo had been placed there by the enemy for our discomfiture, and consisted simply of a shell set in the road with its apex projecting just above the earth, capped with fulminate in some way, so that when trodden upon it had been ignited. It subsequently appeared that there were many of these shells planted around in various places, and the spots were marked as soon as found by small red flags so that the troops could avoid them. From the newspapers we afterwards learned that several men had been killed by them, and that General McClellan employed prisoners captured from the enemy's forces to remove them.

As may be inferred, this little episode took the men by surprise. It was a species of warfare for which they had not been prepared. For some time after this every little projection in the road was regarded with a painful suspicion.

After a short delay the column moved forward again into the works. As we passed the spot where the tragedy had occurred I caught a glimpse of two or three men carrying a bloody object away towards a tent. In the road lay the horse, not yet dead, struggling in his agony, covered with dust and blood, with one of his forefeet—the one, doubtless, that had trampled upon the torpedo literally blown to atoms, and the bone as far up as the knee stripped of skin and flesh as completely as if one had scalped them off with a knife. How my heart ached at the sight!

Another halt took place after the command had reached the village of Yorktown, and this time word was passed along the column to "load at will." This evidently meant business. The dragoons here retired, leaving the Sixth Cavalry alone. In a few moments all preparations were completed, and the command pushed forward along the road, which wound down a hill, and on either side of which were smoldering embers of commissary and quartermaster's stores. The way was literally strewn with all the paraphernalia of a camp, from a tent down to a stool.

The head of the column plunged into a dense pine forest that soon completely shut us out from the sight of our people at Yorktown. Presently we came to the smoking ruins of a wagon, to which was still hitched the dead body of a horse. The regiment halted here, and I saw our carbinier squadron, company band H, separate from the balance of the command and ride forward at a gallop, with their pieces at an "advance," and disappear up the road. Then an order came to our company to detail twelve men as flankers, and Sergeant McMasters took charge of this squad, of which I happened to be one. We were armed with revolvers and sabres, and on this occasion rode off to the right and deployed across the fields and through the woods, carrying our pistols at a "ready."

It occurred to me at this juncture that matters were growing decidedly serious. Here I was riding through all sorts of places in a strange country, carrying in my hand a deadly weapon, with which I was expected to shoot at, if I saw one, and, if possible, kill, a man whom I had never seen, and against whom I could certainly have no personal feeling, and whom I was to distinguish from our own people simply by the color of his clothing. That was disagreeable fact number one. Then this same man with numerous other men dressed in similar clothing, were supposed to be somewhere near us, watching with vengeful eye for our appearance, when they would shoot at, if they saw us, and, if possible, kill, a man whom they had never seen, and against whom, they could certainly have no personal feeling, and whom they were to distinguish from, their own people simply by the color of his clothing—which was myself; I never thought of anyone else getting killed. That was disagreeable fact number two—the most annoying of them both. Still, I felt a sort of pride, after all, in this unrestrained rough-riding, and would dash up to house and demand if there were any rebels there. The answer invariably was, "There are none," from white lips, and scared looking faces would peer out from behind half-open doors.

"Well, have you seen any lately?"

The answers to this were varied; sometimes they had; sometimes they had not.

"How many did you see?" to those who reported that some had passed them.

The answers to this question, too, were varied, some said about a thousand; one old darkey said he "seed two hundred thousand men."

"How did you know there were that many? Did you count them?"

The old darkey scratched his head.

"Well, massa, dey fill dat road from behind dem trees dar clear up past de barn yonder."

This was satisfactory; there would be about four hundred if mounted. In answer to that question, he said they rode horses and wore swords.

116

These men had been there within an hour. From this it would undoubtedly not be long before our advance guard would come in contact with them, and a fight would probably ensue.

Shortly after this we were recalled to join the company, and rode back to the column and reoccupied our proper places in ranks. Presently we passed another wagon, which was burning briskly, the spokes of the wheels of which were hacked with a hatchet or ax, so as to render them unserviceable, and another swamped horse, still alive; the road all about the wagon was covered with forage and soldier's rations thrown around in a manner that gave evidence of a hasty flight. The chase was certainly getting exciting.

Now we came to a solitary confederate, dressed in a well-worn, greasy-looking suit of gray, with his head encased in a close-fitting red skull-cap, from the top of which hung pendant a yellow tassel—a thin, sallow-looking man, without weapons. The men regard him with some curiosity, a few curse him; but he simply looks at them and says not a word. This is our first prisoner, and we leave him with his guard, a Company K man.

Now a shot is heard in the distance towards the front—the men looking at each other with faces just a little changed—then three or four men in quick irregular succession. We break into a trot now, for the game is at bay, and the carbiniers must be supported. The hard jolting of my horse keeps me from thinking of much else beside the agony in my side—for I always suffered from this during the continuation of a trot. Perhaps it is as well, for I am too much occupied to get frightened, and I am thus carried forward in spite of myself. The chase becomes more exciting, as we press forward a sort of rattling is heard, quite faint in the distance; so we know that the enemy is replying to our skirmishers with a volley. We leap into the gallop, but have not gone far before we come to a sudden halt that throws the rear men upon those in front, and causes some confusion. Some of Company H come dashing in from the woods on the left, capless, and with faces scratched by limbs and bushes, carrying their carbines at full cock. Now we are ordered to give way to the right, and as we crowd over the side of the road two pieces of light artillery—to our surprise, for we were unaware of their presence—dash up past us, the drivers lashing the horses with short whips. As soon as they are out of sight we follow at a gallop, coming to the top of a low hillock where we find the guns already unlimbered in a field to the right of the road, and the cannoneers busy around them. Then the head of our regiment pushes into the same field, and we follow and form in close columns of squadron to the right and rear of the pieces. Next comes the order "Draw-sabre," and the air is glittering with steel. The artillery opens now, with an ear-splitting roar; we hear the shells shrieking a moment and then in another instant their explosions in the distance. I feel the concussion of the air; the smoke sweeps into our faces; the sweat springs out of my flesh like a deluge. The scene is a curious one to men. These are the first guns I have seen fired in anger. No enemy has been visible to me yet save the unarmed prisoner; but I realize they are not far away.

Only two rounds are fired; the gunners pause a moment, and then begin limbering up their pieces. The regiment breaks by fours to the front, and the head of the column wheels into the road again, and we move forward at a trot. I begin to wonder how this will all end. As I ponder, we dash down a hill and across a stream, coming to a mill-race and an old mill. There are slight earthworks to the left of the road and this was the spot at which the enemy had been posted to resist our advance a moment before. Now we hurry up another hill, into a dense wood; then past open fields, with a white frame house and a barn to the right of the road. Then there are more dense woods. As we enter these the regiment comes down to a walk. A dull sound, like distant thunder, breaks upon our ears; something comes crashing through the treetops, and bursts a little distance away with a sound as loud as that of a cannon; and the men make their first involuntary bow to a confederate shell. Then comes another roll, and another shell, and we bow again. Now we halt; there is a pause of a few moments and then the head of the column countermarches to the rear, while we give way to the right to allow it to pass. Presently we are all in motion, and, as we emerge from the woods, instead of keeping the one we had advanced upon beyond this point, we here file off along another road that follows the skirt of the woods northward. This road, after we have gone a short distance, turns abruptly to the left, and bears in the same general direction as the one from which we have just retired. By and by we emerge from the dense timber and find ourselves on the edge of a great open plain. Directly in front of us the road leads down into a narrow marsh; beyond this marsh there is a peach orchard; beyond this peach orchard an earthwork, from which great puffs of smoke arise at short intervals followed by successive reports of cannon. The shots seem to be directed upon a point away off to our left, just at the skirt of the woods, where we see their shells bursting, from which there are occasional puffs of smoke and reports of guns apparently in response to their fire. Which are friends or foes we cannot tell.

To the left of the fort where we see the battery at work, stretching as in a line across the plains are other earthworks but they seem to be unoccupied. We move across the marsh, and leaving the road proceed at a trot, with drawn sabres, in column of companies, across the peach orchard, and straight towards the smoking earthwork. There are no skirmishes in advance; we march as though we were going through a drill, the officers constantly looking to see if we keep our alignment, and retain our proper distances from the companies in front of us. This puzzles me more than ever, and I wonder if those men in the fort are our friends. The head of the column reaches the ditch outside of the parapet, and advances along its side until they encounter a fence at the rear, and then the regiment halts.

The movement has brought us within thirty or forty paces of the cannoneers. I look in upon them, and see that they are dressed in gray; still I think they may be our men, as I had often heard that some of our Western troops were clothed in such uniforms. They are busy with their guns, and seem to take no notice of us. The rear of the earthwork is filled with huts like those in the camps around Manassas. No other soldiers are visible.

A number of our troops dismount and begin to tear down the fence leading to the rear of the earthwork, and pitch the rails into the ditch. Lieutenant McClain turns in his saddle, and looking upon Company F, sternly cries out

"When we enter this fort, I want every man to cut right and left!"

The mystery is over now; these are our enemies.

At this juncture a man apparently dressed in civilian clothes is seen upon the plain towards the spot from which we have just emerged, and beckons with his hand. Some one calls Major Williams' attention to this, and he seems to understand it, for he orders the men to remount, and then, riding off a little to one side, he calls out,

"By fours, right about wheel-march!"

This brings the regiment left in front. When the wheel is completed, and the line is dressed, and the column is in motion, I look back over my right shoulder to see what is going on in the fort. It has occurred to me that we were not to be released so easily. I see the artillerymen wheel their pieces around, and train them upon us. The next instant there is a roar, and smoke leaps from the mouth of one of the guns, and a shell comes over our heads with a hissing sound that makes me think of white-hot iron in water. We bow to the necks of our horses, but in their excitement they have fired too high, and no one is hurt. Two or three more follow, with like result.

As each report dies away I timidly look around. Presently I see a regiment of cavalry, dressed in gray, with frock coats and low-crowned hats trot out from behind the fort we have just left, and to its right as it faces us, and come across the plain towards us. The head of our column has just reached the swamp, and we are obliged to halt and break by fours to pass down the narrow ravine leading to the crossing. The enemy have evidently divined our difficulties, for they leave the trot for the gallop. Some one by this time calls out in rear, "Cavalry coming!" and this warning is passed from company to company to the major, who, by this time, is across the marsh with the head of the command and is reforming the men into columns of companies as fast as they regain that side. The artillery of the enemy has ceased its firing, for their mounted men are between us and the fort, and in the range of their guns, closely pressing on our rear. The crackling of small arms, evidently revolvers, begins. Our men struggle hard to get across the swamp, crowding one another fearfully in their fierce efforts. The horses sink up to their breasts into the now boiling marsh, and plunge wildly forward. A great log forms an additional obstruction.

I hardly know how to get across, but I find myself riding up the slope on the safe side. Presently the men are all over, and fall into ranks, their tormentors dashing into the marsh and across it in the ardor of their pursuit. They swarm up the side of the slope like bees.

A loud, clear voice, which still rings in my ears, rises above the tumult:

"Sixth Cavalry—right about wheel!"

Everybody within the reach of its sound seems to comprehend instantly its import. Two or three hundred men execute the movement, which brings them face to face with the foe, and in another moment they sweep upon them, with glittering sabres, like an irresistible avalanche, and crush them back into the marsh. Hoarse shouts of vengeance go up as the sabres flash and the strokes fall rapidly in all directions. It lasts but a moment, for our enemies retire in disorder across the plain towards their fort. Major Williams had, in the meantime, gone on with the balance of the regiment.

When the rush was made towards the swamp, my previous experience in that pool of mud warned me not to risk another submersion; so I ride to one side and begin firing upon a squad of the enemy who are huddled upon the opposite side and are shooting into our ranks. I hear the bullets in the air, and I think of Virginia hornets. I am anxious to fire rapidly for fear I shall be disabled before I can repeat the shots. I feel a thud on the back of my head, and look around, and see Schumacher, who has raised the point of his pistol, fully cocked, against it in his efforts to get a shot at the enemy.

By this time the confederates have retreated, and I ride slowly up the hill to rejoin the forming squadrons. I find Merkle of E Company, on his knees, with his eyes raised toward the sky and with a ghostly look upon his face, I stoop down and ask him where he is hurt for I feel that he is grievously wounded. He raises his clenched hands in an uncertain way to his breast, and groans. I stoop over, and try to raise him by the shoulders to his feet, and think to help him out of the way of the surging horses into a fence corner, but am nearly thrown from my saddle by a squad that now dashes up and over him, and carries me away with it. When I am extricated from this I see a confederate soldier, with no arms, hatless, and dismounted, struggling with a half a dozen of our men, who in their mad excitement do not seem to comprehend that he has surrendered, and are trying to hew him down with their sabres, but are prevented by their horses' heads, which are so crowded in upon him as to form an effectual shield from their threatened strokes. He throws himself on the ground; I tell them he has surrendered, and they seem to know it now, and leave him to me. He rises to his feet and we start after the retiring squadrons. He is a man apparently about thirty-five years of age, and has a bald spot on the top of his head. His long beard is covered with froth; his clothing is drenched with sweat as though they had been submerged in a river. He pulls out of his pockets a pair of heavy woolen mittens, which are knit with the trigger finger detached, and reaches them to me. I tell him to keep them—I have no need of such articles this hot weather. The man is evidently partially delirious after his terrible struggle for life. He tells me he is a member of the First North Carolina Cavalry.

On our way to the rear I find Brooks in a dilemma. His saddle has slipped back upon the horse and has turned under the animal's stomach. Brooks is devising ways and means to right it, but the horse is excited and threatens to kick when he approaches the saddle. Time will admit

121

of no delay, so he manages to get the saddle ungirthed and lets it go, but with commendable presence of mind saves his haversack containing the rations, and mounts the animal bareback. We ride after the company. The enemy throws a few shells into the woods, but they do no harm. Here I turn the prisoner over to Brooks, who takes him and starts to report with him to Major Williams.

The regiment regains the open fields where stand the white frame house and the barn and there forms in column of companies; the lines are carefully dressed; the men count off by fours again; the roll is called amid profound silence, and when one does not answer to his name his comrades are asked if they know anything about him, and if any one can tell his fate he responds. We find that there are thirty-one men dead, wounded and missing.

As we sit on our horses, a man—a member of the First Cavalry which regiment had been sharply engaged on our left, and upon which the fire of the battery we had encountered was at that time directed—is carried past us on a stretcher. His pants are unbuttoned and thrown open, and his shirt pulled up, and a great wound in the pit of his stomach gapes open like a bloody mouth. I cannot say that he is dead or alive.

The regiment is dismounted after being marched still further to the rear, and into a field that has been newly cleared and is full of stumps, and we are ordered to "stand to horse." The shadows of evening are gathering around us. Fires are kindled, and we cook our coffee and feed our horses, amid the chattering of many tongues, all talking at once about the fight.

No further order comes during the night, so they now gradually struggle out of ranks and tie their horses to shrubs and stumps or to the handles of their sabres, which they thrust deep into the ground for stakes, and lie down to sleep, completely worn out with the fatigue and excitement of the day.

The Sixth Cavalry has received its baptism of fire, and I feel that, under the circumstances, the regiment has acted nobly. It is, perhaps, as well to say that the man who beckoned us back from the fort was Prince de Joinville of McClellan's staff, as we afterwards learned.

The dead body of poor Merkle was found, among others, two days after the Sunday fight by some of our men, and duly buried.

About two o'clock the next morning I was awakened from slumbers by hearing some musketry firing in the woods towards the front and left of the field in which we had bivouacked. The rain was falling in a steady shower, and the ground where I had made my bed had become a pond of small dimensions, though the water had not yet penetrated through my blanket and clothing. Cold and shivering, and somewhat bewildered, I arose from my uninviting bed, and searched for a fire. A few smoldering embers remained of one nearby which I endeavored to resuscitate, but with indifferent success. A few of the soldiers were wandering around like so many ghosts, but the rest still slumbered on the wet, cold ground, and with the rain drizzling over their faces and through their hair. Many of the horses were loose, wandering around among the sleeping men, trailing the stakes attached to their halter straps, and occasionally greeted with a sleepy growl from somebody over whom they had stepped and dragged their anchors, and thus partially awakened. The regiment was so scattered that it occupied fully seven acres of ground. The company lines were entirely indistinguishable.

The scattering shots on our left and front—of course, I refer to the position we had occupied at halting on the evening before; as we now lay huddled there was no left or front—continued at intervals, and demonstrated that other troops had arrived and were in contact with the enemy. Just at dawn the confederates opened with a few cannon shots, apparently, by the sound, from the fort to which we had advanced the day before. Bodies of infantry began to appear, and as fast as they marched up were deployed in long lines across the front of the woods, into which they then disappeared; and soon the shots began to fall thick and fast, showing that they had already become engaged. It was evident that the enemy had made up his mind to resist our advance at this point, and judging from the number of men appearing on our side, the fight was likely to be a serious one. Owing to the nature of the ground but few of our cannon could be brought into action—and this gave the enemy great advantage, as his guns were left free to deliver their shots upon our troops. As the day wore on the firing increased in vigor, and towards noon we were ordered to mount and were marched across to the road. A battery galloped up and took position in a wheat field to the right and rear of the frame house, unlimbering and training their guns upon the woods on our right side. To the right and rear of these guns our command was formed in line, evidently as a support, while on our right a regiment of cavalry—the Eighth Illinois—also formed, the two mounted bodies extending far across the fields towards the spot where we had bivouacked the night before. A regiment of infantry marched past and deployed along the woods to the left of the battery. Here we remained, the infantry standing in line as on dress parade; the artillerymen occupying their respective positions about the pieces ready to open fire, and the cavalry sitting on their horses, with sabres drawn—the attitude of the whole force being one of evident expectation. I kept my eyes fixed upon the woods in front, waiting to see every instant the long gray lines of our foes swarm out of them. The rain fell faster than ever; a few of the men unstrapped their overcoats from the pommels of their saddles, and threw them around their shoulders but were quickly ordered to replace them as before. The wheat was, perhaps, two or three feet high; the ground was soft, and our horses were continually sinking to their knees, and as constantly endeavoring to extricate themselves, an exercise that was fatiguing to the rider.

During this time the fighting on the left seemed to increase in severity. Our advanced line in that quarter appeared to be heavily pressed. Hancock's brigade early in the afternoon marched up, the men covered with mud, but carrying themselves proudly, deployed across the fields in our front, and pushed out of sight into the woods. The battery and our regiment were now moved from the wheat field and took up another position in front of the white frame house, and on the left of the road, apparently to support our infantry here which was showing signs of giving way. Just as we formed in columns of squadrons a great flock of birds, which evidently had been frightened by the tumult in the woods, arose from out of the tree tops and flew away through the falling rain. A constant stream of wounded men was flowing down the road to the barn, which had been turned into a hospital, and in and around which hundreds of unfortunates were collected.

About four o'clock General McClellan, accompanied by his staff, arrived from the direction of Yorktown. He turned off the road when he had reached the point at which we were stationed and rode up to Major Williams, and, through the latter, tendered his thanks and compliments to the regiment for what he termed as gallant conduct the day before in front of the enemy's works.

"Thank heaven!" ejaculated Lieutenant McClain, as he caught sight of the general, "we are all right now!"

The regiment gave three hearty cheers in acknowledgement of his presence, which was instantly taken up by other troops, and soon ran along the line to the left. Just at that moment heavy volleys on the right showed that Hancock's men had become fiercely engaged with the confederates in that section. Then dying away almost as soon as it

124

began, the firing slackened and ceased altogether, save a few stray shots, and the battle was over. The enemy seemed to have been repulsed at all points, and retired to the shelter of his works.

We were marched back to our old bivouacking ground of the night before, but under somewhat different circumstances. Every one seemed to feel that we had gained a substantial victory under discouraging circumstances, and were well satisfied with the result. Our poor horses were unsaddled now, and carefully groomed and fed; the picket line was put up, to which they were properly fastened, and our inner man—or men—indulged to the extent of several crackers, some pickled pork roasted, and an abundance of coffee.

As we sat around the fires that night squads of wounded men, haggard and bloody and hungry, all of whom belonged to the infantry, gathered among us and related the scenes of the day on their part of the line. Poor, noble fellows! How gallantly they bore up under their misfortunes! We shared our little stock of rations with them, glad that we were able to do something for their comfort. This had been their first battle, and it was amusing to hear them speak of their peculiar sensations while under fire, and when shot. From them we learned enough to show that the action had been a most stubborn one, and that, throughout the day and up till the time of the arrival of Hancock's brigade, our troops had all they could do to hold their own against the enemy.

The next morning the sun arose in a clear sky. A dead stillness rested upon the field where fifteen hours ago over twenty thousand men had struggled for victory. Our forces the night before had carried a redoubt at the point of the bayonet, killing about one hundred men in the assault. It was now understood that our advance had reached Williamsburg, and held that town, while the enemy had retired hastily along the road leading to Richmond.

About noon our bugler sounded "boots and saddles," and an hour later we were on our way to the front. Just as we entered the woods out of which we had retired on Sunday—where we had received our first shells—I met several friends from Washington County, who were now members of the One-Hundred-and-Second Pennsylvania infantry. From them I learned that their regiment had been engaged in the battle, having formed part of the line on the left. The Washington County men had all escaped injury, fortunately. They seemed to be in good spirits.

Our route led us directly across that part of the field where the conflict had been the heaviest and longest sustained. We had proceeded but a short distance when the marks of the day's fight began to be visible in the trees cut by the enemy's cannon shots. As we approached still nearer the line of separation of the two forces, bullet marks, few at first, but increasing in number until the trees and limbs and shrubs were literally clipped and riddled with them, showed that a real storm of lead had swept this portion of the line. I found myself wondering where the troops could have been during all this shower of missiles. Every six square inches of timber bore at least one scar, and frequently several. Not a single dead man of our side was to be seen, having all been gathered and taken away somewhere. When we reached the edge of the woods where it bordered on the great plain upon which the enemy's forts stood, the position of the confederates as occupied by them during the conflict was visible, and marked by numerous dead bodies. They had made an abatis by felling trees all along the edge of the dense forest with their tops towards Yorktown, so as to completely obstruct and break up any line of battle advancing from that direction, and to detain troops long enough to enable them to destroy them by the fire of their infantry lines, which had stretched across the plain at an average distance of perhaps one hundred and fifty yards from the edge of the woods, assisted by their artillery in the redoubts.

Although partially prepared for the sight, expecting to see dead men as a matter of course on a field of battle, I could not help shuddering when they became visible on the plain as we emerged from the woods. The right and left and front they lay scattered, almost as far as we could see—not thickly, as I had expected, but with irregular intervals of perhaps from twenty to fifty yards between them. Some lay as they had fallen; others had evidently dragged themselves short distances, marking the earth with their blood; some were drawn up as if by a great spasm; others looked as though they were asleep, so natural was the position of the body. Over many some friendly hand had cast blankets to shut out their dead faces from the curious stare of the living. At one spot lay a poor old man dressed in civilian clothing, the little hair on his head white with age, his hands clenched, and his knees drawn up to his chin as if by a mighty convulsion. By his side was a small dog, evidently once his property, which ever and anon licked with his tongue a great gaping wound in the neck of his old master. Another, who seemed to have crawled some distance from the spot upon which he had received his mortal wound, held in his dead hand what appeared to be an open letter.

We found Williamsburg with a hospital flag on nearly every house. The people peered out from behind half open doors and shutters as though frightened at the masses of federal soldiers who were marching through and encamping around the town. The streets were badly cut up by the passage of artillery and wagon trains and cavalry.

I was pleased with the quiet beauty of William and Mary College and grounds, and thought of its old historic connections and the memories that must cluster around it. A guard of honor was placed in charge, while at the entrance two brass pieces of artillery were posted with their muzzles bearing down the street.

Our regiment halted in a wheat field on the southeast side of the town, and here rested for the night, the men giving their horses a thorough grooming and feeding them well, and indulging in a hearty meal themselves .

At dawn the clear notes of the bugle aroused us from our slumbers, and, refreshed and vigorous, we prepared for the march. At eight o'clock the command was in saddle, and mustered in line ready for the road. Major Williams announced that, on account of our meritorious and praiseworthy conduct in action on Sunday, we had been assigned the post of honor, and should lead the advance on Richmond.

By half past eight we were out of town and on our way towards the Confederate Capital, marching along the Williamsburg stage road. The telegraph line along the route was broken down in many places, and the wires seemed to be trampled into the mud at intervals. Some of the men amused themselves by catching hold of the wire as they rode along it and by swinging it back and forth, knocking off the caps of those in front or rear. During one of these pleasantries, just before the head of the column entered the woods beyond Williamsburg, and where the wire descended into the mud some distance beyond us, a shell burst at that point throwing the earth around, but doing no further damage. The enemy had planted this shell in the road and affixed the wire to it for an evil purpose, which, owing to the fun-loving proclivities of our men, had been completely foiled by a premature explosion. It is, perhaps, needless to say that the telegraph wire, so far as the Sixth Cavalry was concerned, remained undisturbed during the remainder of that day.

Some distance in the woods we met about half a dozen mounted men, who were attached to the Signal Corps, and who told us that "they were waiting for us"—meaning the enemy's troops. This announcement was not a pleasant one, and had a marked effect upon the soldiers;

conversation was suspended, each individual seeming to be communicating with himself. Presently we reached several broken down wagons, two or three dead and dying horses, and four pieces of heavy field artillery. The latter had settled so deep in the mire and quicksand that the enemy were unable to extricate them, and had abandoned them, taking the precaution to chop the wheels of the gun carriages to render them unserviceable to us.

As we emerged from the woods into the open country a party of the enemy's dragoons were seen, sitting on their horses on the rising ground to the westward, distant perhaps three-quarters of a mile. The regiment halted as soon as it was clear of the timber, and the carbiniers were sent forward as an advance guard to attack them, but had not proceeded far before the enemy disclosed his artillery, and sent a shell into the road just ahead of them. They retired upon the main body, which by this time had formed in column of squadrons on the open field on the right of the road. The artillerymen now turned their attention to us. First we saw a puff of smoke, then presently heard the report of the gun, and simultaneously with that the whistling of the shell in the air as it came. It fell short, however, throwing up a column of dirt unpleasantly suggestive. The next one exploded in our front, perhaps fifty yards away, and the pieces went singing over our heads. The entire command bowed involuntarily. Another came still closer, not bursting, however, but striking the earth close to our right, throwing the sand all over us, and then rebounding into the woods in our rear, crashing through the trees as though they were so many imaginary pipe-stems.

This affair was getting to be one of painful interest to us. It was not pleasant to sit there and have these artillerymen take their time about getting one's range. So "attention" was called; our company was sent off to the right and another to the left at a gallop, while the portion of the command was moved and took position a short distance to the left so as to disturb the enemy's line of fire.

A number of men—the writer among them—were dismounted, and tore down the fence in rear to make room for the maneuvering that might become necessary. When this work was done, we were ordered to remount. While in the act of doing this the column started at a trot, my horse in the ranks with the others, while I, with one foot in the stirrup, and both hands grasping the pommel and cantle of the saddle, clung on, without being able to get up or daring to get down. By and by, after herculean efforts, somewhat frightened by my situation, I managed to climb upon my horse's back.

At this juncture two regiments of Infantry—The Ninety-Eighth Pennsylvania and Second Rhode Island—came up at the doublequick to our support, proceeded by four pieces of the Second Artillery. The enemy immediately limbered up and retired, and the command pushed forward and occupied the position thus abandoned. Here a halt was ordered, the artillery placed in battery, a line formed, pickets thrown out, and the necessary preparations made to hold the ground until the army at Williamsburg should march up within supporting distance.

We were now ten miles from the battlefield of the 5th of May. Cannonading could be heard at intervals and shells were seen to burst in the air far away toward our front. This was a mystery to us, which was afterwards solved by reading the accounts of that rather unfortunate battle at West Point on the York River. Fresh meat for ourselves and forage for the horses were procured here, and towards evening the Sixth Cavalry marched a few miles further toward the front, leaving the infantry and artillery in position, and halted for the night in a clover field. The command was not allowed to unsaddle, but the girths were unloosened, and the legs of the horses rubbed down. We "stood to horse" during the night. On the 8th the advance was continued, at a very slow pace, until we reached a place called Barhamsville, if I remember aright, meeting with no resistance on the way. It was about five o'clock in the afternoon when the halt was ordered. Pickets were thrown out, horses unsaddled and fed and groomed, and preparations to bivouac for the night were made. Scarcely had all this been done before the bugle sounded "boots and saddles." Our first impression was that the enemy were about to attack us, but the sergeants notified us to leave all our clothing; we were to go light. In a few moments the regiment was in motion, advancing up the road toward the front at a sharp trot. We had not proceeded far before I noticed several muskets scattered over the ground on the left of the road, and a few moments later several of the enemy's infantry pickets were passed, leaning on their muskets, and looking at us in a bewildered way, but making no hostile demonstrations. On we went, through forests, past houses and open fields, up hill and down hill, across streams and past gloomy ravines, at the gallop and trot alternatively—the latter starting that agony in my side, as usual. In the twilight we dashed past a house on the right of the road on the porch of which was a whole bevy of girls, who waved their handkerchiefs, to our inexpressible astonishment—a proceeding not to be expected in that

129

section of Virginia, where all the feeling and sympathy seemed to be for the other side. We would gladly have cheered, but had received express orders to suspend conversation and make no noise whatever; so we had to content ourselves by raising our caps.

It is, perhaps, proper to remark here that that was the only union demonstration I saw among the residents during my stay on the peninsula.

We were past in an instant, however, and plunged into a forest of pines, when a trio of shots came from as many confederate soldiers, and to these our advance guard promptly responded. A sudden halt was made, the regiment formed in close column of squadrons among some low scrubby pines on the left of the road, and sabres were drawn, ready for action.

It appeared, however, that the force in our front was the whole rearguard of the confederate army, and consisted of ten regiments of infantry, a brigade of cavalry, and a battery of artillery. Of course, an attack by our force, which consisted of not more than six or seven hundred men, was out of the question. I have always regarded it as a fortunate circumstance that we escaped capture, as we were fully ten miles from our supports. No assault was made on us, however, and we retired to Barhamsville, reaching our camp some time after dark. There was now great confusion. In the haste that followed to leave camp, the spots where we had deposited our individual commissary and quartermaster's stores had been but vaguely fixed in our minds, and as a consequence, everybody made a rush for property that belonged to everybody else. However, after a great deal of swearing and growling, the camp quieted down and the men settled into a profound sleep after their "ten mile ride." Many remarks were made among the troops subsequently about this affair, indicating certain suspicions in regard to Major Williams, but as they are not traceable to authentic sources I refrain from dwelling upon them at length.

The command remained at Barhamsville during the 9th of May. On the morning of that day Sergeant Wallace, with a detail of four or five men, including the writer, was sent to picket a road that approached from the southwest, as near as I can remember. We rode out a few miles, and halted near an old fashioned house standing on a hill, where we posted a picket. A visit to this house revealed that fact that it had been deserted by its late occupants, so hastily that the table still bore upon it the unfinished breakfast. An examination of the books in the library showed that it was the home and property of Joseph Mayo, ex-Mayor of Richmond. This was a surprise to us; and as he had the honor to preside over the capital of the Southern Confederacy, I thought it would be pleasant to take something away as a trophy. Two books were selected—one a copy of Cleveland's compendium of English Literature, and the other a copy of the poems of Robert Burns. The latter I intended for Sergeant Wallace, a Scotchman, and the other for myself. On the fly-leaf of the Compendium of English Literature was written, in a neat manner, "Susan L. Mayo, October 10, 1860." Scattered through the pages at intervals other memorandums were traced, indicating that it was the property of an intellectual young lady—and I am tempted to believe that she was handsome.

I carried my trophy several months, and finally, securing an opportunity, sent it to my home in Washington County. After the war was over I secured it again. I confess that its perusal during and after my term of service whiled away many a painful and weary hour. About the 1st of May, 1870, I conceived the idea of restoring it to its former owner, if she were to be found and accessible, and as a step towards this result addressed a letter to the postmaster at New Kent Court House, inquiring if he could furnish me with her address. In due time I received the following note:

Cedar Hill,
near New Kent Court House
May 6, 1870

Sir:
   I have before me at this time your letter bearing date of 2nd of May, which letter was forwarded to me by the postmaster at New Kent Court House.
   You are correct in your conjecture concerning the relationship I bear to Mr. Joseph Mayo. You will please inform me at your earliest convenience why you wish to know my place of residence, &c.

Most Respectfully,

Susan L. Mayo

I immediately sent the book to her address, accompanied by a letter of explanation. The trophy was restored, after an absence of eight years from its old home, and after having passed through many vicissitudes in the field. The following letter was received acknowledging its arrival:

Cedar Hill, near New Kent Court House
May 19, 1870

Sir:
You will please accept my thanks for the return of the volume forwarded by you some days since, the sight of which brought up the reminiscences of the days of "auld lang syne," as it had been my daily companion when I was pursuing my studies as a school-girl.

You brought up vividly before my mind's eye a true picture of the day "when wild war's dreadful blast was blown" in the allusion you made to our place of residence when you last saw it. If your memory does not fail you, you will remember that I was not at home on the memorable "May morning" alluded to in your last letter. I have had statements, however, from several sources of many things which transpired. Could you look upon this place the present month of May, it probably would not bring about a forcible reminder of the day's of yore. Nothing remains to mark the desolated place where our homestead once stood save two chimneys and the brick foundation. It was laid in ashes during the war by a party of raiders, who made their headquarters here. Not only did they apply the torch to the house, but destroyed the entire lot of household furniture, and we were compelled to commence life anew in the most desolate condition.

Hastily, but respectfully,

Susan L. Mayo

When I read this letter I wished from the bottom of my heart I had been able to restore the old homestead as it had stood in antebellum days.

On the 10th the command advanced to Burnt Ordinary, where it encamped for the night, the result of the days operations being the capture of one prisoner and an exchange of shots with the enemy's pickets near Slatersville. The next day the regiment engaged the rearguard of the confederates at Slatersville, and after a sharp encounter, during which our artillery, consisting of four pieces, was fully used, and two sabre charges were made, the enemy retired with a loss of sixteen men killed and a number wounded. Our loss was only three men killed—two of whom were shot after their capture by the confederates.

132

Major Williams showed great ability in conducting this action. The carbiniers were posted, with two other companies, along the edge of the woods directly in front of the enemy's line, deployed as skirmishers, to engage their attention, while four companies were sent around to make a descent on their rear. The plan succeeded admirably. While the enemy's cavalry was busily watching our skirmishers at the edge of the wood, our men quietly outflanked them and suddenly came down upon them in a sabre charge, cheering vociferously. The confederates immediately broke up and fled in great confusion.

The killing of the prisoners after capture was fully confirmed. I saw one of them at the spot where he had fallen. He had been placed with his back against a tree in a sitting position, and then shot several times in the head, which was literally riddled with bullets. The sight was indeed a ghastly one. The other man was found dead in the road perhaps a mile or so further on, having been shot through the body. Without a full knowledge of the circumstances attending the killing of these men, it would, perhaps, be unfair for me to presume that it was altogether unjustifiable. The excitement of men of the command was raised to the highest pitch by the circumstance, and threats of retaliation were freely made.

The killing of prisoners was not confined to the enemy on this occasion. One of the members of M Company, having in charge a confederate major who had been captured at an early stage of the engagement, started with him toward the rear. They had not proceeded far before a threatening demonstration was made by the enemy, which was noticed by the major, who slackened his pace in disobedience of the orders of his guard, and even grew defiant at the prospect of being recaptured. The federal, finding he could not escape with him from the advancing line, deliberately shot him through the head, and then galloped off to his company.

When the confederates retired from the field they were crowded together at the entrance of a lane, where the road leaves Slaterville for Richmond. Into this mass of men and horses our artillery hurled a shell, which exploded, killing thirteen soldiers. Several prisoners and a number of good horses fell into our hands during the action.

The scene at the opening of this engagement was amusing. The enemy's pickets were posted a short distance east of Slatersville on the road where it left the open country and entered the woods. As our advance guard came up, a number of colored men could be seen working

133

in a cornfield on the right of the road. When the first shots were fired, they looked up, with great astonishment depicted upon their faces, and the next moment hastily unhitched their mules, mounted them, and rode off rapidly in a direction decidedly opposite from the spot at which the skirmish was in progress, scarcely stopping for fence or ditch long enough to tear it down or find a bridge.

The occupants of an old-fashioned farmhouse here, near the junction of the roads leading respectively to Richmond, West Point and Yorktown, were an old man and woman. The enemy had taken up a position at and around this house, their line stretching out through the yard into the fields, so as cover both Yorktown and West Point roads. The firing so frightened the elderly twain that they sought shelter in the cellar. When the enemy gave way, and our troops had undisputed possession of the field, the old man ventured out of his hiding place, evidently feeling, in his alarm, much chagrined at the defeat of the confederates, but, being afraid to openly express his disgust, bemoaned alternately his hardship, and the sickness of his wife, who, he said, was so prostrated by nervousness that he feared she would not recover. We found an ample supply of corn for our horses in the cribs and barns about the place, which was really of much importance to us, though the farmer seemed to think that the appropriation of the cereals was adding injury to insult. After all, though deeply sympathizing with the affectionate old couple, I could not help laughing at the grim sarcasm of their remarks.

The night following this day of excitement is marked down on my calendar as one fraught with unusually unpleasant experiences. The enemy were reported as being in heavy force in our immediate front and would probably make a demonstration upon us to test our strength. To meet this emergency the men were ordered to "stand to horse" during the night. This requirement was soon modified, permitting us to lie down in front of our horses; but we were expected to hold the reins in our hands, and not to sleep. Every half hour an officer would pass along the lines and arouse the tired men out of the slumber into which they were sure to fall during the interval.

The artillery was posted in battery along the crest of the hill, with runners around each piece, ready to open fire upon the enemy should they advance. A long line of fires were built in front of the guns, and distant therefrom perhaps one hundred and fifty yards, to enable the artillerymen to get the range of an attacking column. Every preparation was made to give the confederates a warm reception. The many fires built must have given the place from a distance the appearance of a larger camp.

During one of the intervals between these periodical rounds of the officers, I had fallen into a partial sleep, when I was aroused by a terrible hissing noise. I sprang to my feet in a state of great consternation, under the impression that it was a shell from the other side, but much puzzled to hear no report of cannon. It proved, however, to be a rocket sent up from our lines, evidently as a signal.

The mules kept up a doleful braying around the wagon train, adding to the hideousness of the scene. About ten o'clock, however, after we had passed several hours in a fearful state of suspense, we heard a dull humming noise in the woods off to the eastward, and in a few moments more the undistinguishable buzzing had resolved itself into the sound of many voices, and the welcome intelligence was received that Franklin's force from West Point was marching up to our support, and, sure enough, in a few moments, the woods and fields on our left were alive with infantry. The regiment was now permitted to unsaddle and rest.

About three o'clock in the morning a detail from the different companies was made to picket the West Point road for the purpose of keeping open our line of communication with the navy, and to serve as a protection to our trains, which were sent down there to obtain supplies. As this happened to be my first night on picket guard, it marked another epoch in my military career, and I must confess that, sitting there on my horse, alone in those dark woods, fully a mile from any of my companions, in the midst of a hostile community, armed only with a revolver and sabre—though weapons are of little account when one is so exposed to assassination by an unseen enemy—I felt considerable uneasiness. This disquietude, however, wore off partially in a short time, though I watched with as much vigilance as if my very existence were involved. The only noise I heard was a rustling of dry leaves in the forest beyond me, which, after a great deal of cautious peering, I discovered to be caused by a huge dog.

On the 12th of May the command reached New Kent Court House, not very far distant from the Chickahominy river. At this point our squadron was detached from the regiment, and sent northward along one of the gloomiest of roads. The obstructions consisted of streams of water and fallen timber. About twelve o'clock p.m, our party arrived in the vicinity of Cumberland, on the Pamunky river, where, very tired and hungry, we bivouacked for the night.

When we halted we were not aware of our close proximity to the river, and at dawn next morning, was astonished at receiving a challenge from a gunboat lying at anchor here.

"What troops are those?" shouted a gruff voice from the vessel.

"United States troops," was the prompt reply.

"Well, boys," said the voice, "I almost had opened fire upon you. I thought you belonged to the rebel army."

Then, as if by magic, the rigging of the gunboat swarmed with nimble boys in blue, who greeted their brothers-in-arms on shore with vociferous cheers, to which our men responded with a will. Then followed those hearty courtesies which are only to be appreciated by those whose good fortune it has been to witness and receive them.

Our men took the opportunity here afforded to enjoy a most delicious bath in the limpid waters of the Pamunky. This they badly needed, owing to the accumulation of dirt during their continuous and arduous duties. Their clothing also received due attention. This accomplished, we felt like new creatures, and gratefully enjoyed the respite granted us.

I think I have never seen a place of more beauty than Cumberland was at that time. The great broad, rich bottom lands, with the alternate fields of grain and clover and grass, the background of low hills, and the pretty river fringed with dark green woodlands, certainly formed a magnificent picture. I cannot help envying the proprietors of those green acres, Old Dominion mansions, and dreamy forests.

We were informed that on the opposite side of the river a number of Indians, remnants of the once powerful tribes that in the early history of our country controlled all this region, were still living. As no opportunity presented itself I was unable to visit them, as I had desired.

On the 15th the regiment, which by this time had been collected together again, encamped at the celebrated White House, not far from Cumberland. Here we found a magnificent plantation. There were a large number of negroes on the farm, who informed us that they were the property of General Robert E. Lee.

The enemy occupied the hills overlooking White House, but retired upon our advance, which was supported by the Navy, to Tunstal's station, on the York River railroad, leaving a few cavalrymen to watch our movements. For a day or two they were undisturbed.

Our pickets were posted on a line stretching across the broad open fields from the river, which protected our right flank, to the woods on the left. Here the guards of the Sixth Cavalry connected with those of the First New York Dragoons, the latter extending off towards the mouth of the Chickahominy.

At this time, while Company F was guarding the right, Lieutenant Ward was in charge of the line. He rode around the entire front, going from point to point, giving instructions to the men, and inspecting the country. A confederate, who doubtless knew him, to be an officer, rode down the hill to within a reasonable distance of our line and, raising a rifle to his shoulder, deliberately fired at the Lieutenant, but without effect. The latter responded by a wave of the hand, and rode on as though nothing had happened. His coolness on this occasion raised him, high in the estimation of the company as a soldier, as his humane treatment had previously endeared him to them as a man.

In the course of a day or two the enemy's pickets were forced from their position on the crest of hills, and the ground thus abandoned was taken possession of by our regiment. A large force of our infantry arrived, and went into camp near the White House. This was now made a depot of supplies for the army.

One miserable rainy night Company F was detailed to picket a line to the left and rear of camp, to establish and keep open communication with our forces at New Kent. So long was this line that but one relief could be formed of the company, the few who were not on post being held at the reserve quarters as messengers and supernumeraries. About midnight word was sent in by Sergeant Brown, who had charge of the pickets, that the enemy was advancing in force upon the line. Of course, this announcement caused some sensation among the men on reserve, but as there were none to spare, instructions were sent to Sergeant Brown to hold the position as long as possible. After the courier had left to notify the sergeant of the decision in the matter, Lieutenant McClain ordered Corporal McMasters to take two men and proceed to the threatened point, and report on his return the actual condition of affairs. I happened to be one of the detail, and our party rode cautiously through a dense forest of pines over a terrible road, arriving finally at an open space, where we were peremptorily challenged by a sentry. Here we found ten or twelve men deployed along a fence, keeping a close watch upon a mass of woods on the opposite side of a cleared field that stretched for some distance along their front.

Sergeant Brown seemed to be in a state of great trepidation, and anxiously called our attention to a line of dark objects, apparently about one hundred yards distant, which bore some resemblance to a party of skirmishers. He also stated that he had observed signal lights, but these our matter-of-fact corporal decided to be fireflies, to the great indignation of Sergeant Brown. Our whole party continued to watch these objects for some time, but there was no movement; everything was still. The rain had long since ceased to fall, and the fireflies were quite numerous, but the supposed skirmishers never stirred. After some time thus spent, Sergeant Brown ordered me to ride cautiously through a piece of woods on our right, and reconnoiter. Although I had, previous to the reception of this order, laughed at the apprehensions of the sergeant, and suggested that the apparent line of skirmishers was really a line of bushes, I began to feel uneasy at the thought of having to venture off by myself outside our line of pickets, and especially on horseback, for the reason that the feet of the animal could be easily heard for some distance. There was no escape, however, without a display of cowardice on my part so I disguised my alarm and started. A thorough search satisfied me that no enemy was in that neighborhood, and in due time I started to return, riding along leisurely and carelessly. After travelling some distance I was startled by a gruff "Halt!" and saw the indistinct form of a man and horse loom up before me distant about ten paces. My horse seemed to stop involuntarily, no doubt, however, through the agency of a nervous jerk on the reins. I answered the challenger promptly, and was gratified to find that my supposed enemy was Billy Barlow, who had been placed upon this post after I had been sent out, but who, owing to the carelessness of the non-commissioned officer who had put him there, had not been notified of my absence at the front. As the enemy was supposed to be close, and as he had received no orders to challenge any one approaching from that direction, I consider my escape a rather fortunate one, due to Billy's thoughtfulness in halting me. I reached the party along the roadside in safety, and reported to Sergeant Brown the result of my observations.

At dawn four or five men were deployed across the field and advanced to the woods beyond on a reconnaissance, but failed to find an enemy. After some time spent in making examinations and questioning the occupants of a house found out there, we started on a return. As we came in sight of the road we observed a body of strange looking troops drawn up where we had left our company, who deliberately levelled their carbines upon our party. Just then Sergeant Brown, who had been somewhere in the vicinity dashed up to the carbiniers and notified them that we were his men, and thus saved us from a volley from the First New York dragoons.

Our duties during these days were arduous in the extreme. The cavalry force was so small, and the extent of country to be guarded so great, that the men were obliged to picket roads singly, and at distances from each other varying from one to four miles. Sometimes they were obliged to sit on their horses twelve hours at a time without relief or food. At some part of the line or other the confederates were in sight all the time, and needed close attention. In spite of all these hardships the men grew robust; the very dangers of their military life seemed to give zest to their existence. Shadowy Todd was no longer shadowy; the thin form was filling out to fair proportions; the resolute gray eyes no longer shone out from a pale emaciated face, but gleamed from a wellsounded though bronzed physiognomy. My own health had been vastly improved, though I scarcely ever found time to cook anything, and ate my crackers and pork raw.

Upon our return from picket duty one day, we were informed that Major Williams had been arrested, and was confined in his quarters under a strong guard; and, sure enough, a glance at the tent once used as headquarters disclosed four carbiniers—one on each side—walking past, and keeping a lookout upon it as though they were expecting a tiger to leap from the enclosure. The cause of this, it was understood, arose from the capture of a confederate mail carrier, in whose possession was found a letter addressed either to or from Major Williams to or from General J.E.B. Stuart, in command of the enemy's cavalry. Some relationship—I think by marriage—existed between them. Captain August Kautz was now in command of the regiment.

I suppose this will be a proper place to record the conclusion of this arrest, and the subsequent career of Major Williams, so far as I have been able to learn.

He was released from confinement after the lapse of several days by order of General McClellan, as the newspapers stated, upon the application of his sister—a lady residing in Philadelphia at that time—and returned to the command of the regiment. After the battle at Hanover Court House he was placed on the sick list, and sent to Washington. Some months after—in 1863, I think—he was ordered to rejoin his regiment for duty, but failed to do so, and was in consequence of disobedience to orders dismissed from the service of the United States. Shortly after this disgrace he went across the lines to the enemy, and was appointed chief of artillery in the army operating in Tennessee and Kentucky under General Bragg.

When Cincinnati was threatened, in 1864, he was arrested, with another man in that city, having in his possession drawings of the fortifications, and other data as to troops and their dispositions for the defense of the place. He was tried as a spy, convicted, and executed.

Such was the tragic close of the life of one whose military attainments promised an unusually brilliant career as a soldier, and who, but for his peculiar disposition, might have risen before the close of the war to the command of armies.

About the 20th of May the command reached Gainesville, where a force of the enemy made a short stand, but were driven with small loss across the Chickahominy at New Bridge. None of our men were engaged except the carbiniers.

After the skirmish, when we had halted for the night, while foraging for horse feed, I discovered a bloody trail, no doubt that of a soldier, and followed for a long distance, hoping to find the wounded man, but without success. It must have been that of a confederate, for none of our men had been injured. The trail was very distinct—the drops of blood smeared the crossings at fences and sprinkled the ground and grass.

Chickahominy to Yorktown—Cast Adrift

Alas for the pleasant peace we knew
    In the happy summers of long ago
When the rivers were bright and the skies were blue
    By the homes of Henrico.

We dreamed of wars that were far away,
    And read, as in fable, of blood that ran
Where the James and Chickahominy stray
    Through the groves of Powhattan.

'Tis a dream come true, for the afternoons
    Blow bugles of war by our fields of Grain,
And the sabres clink as the dark dragoons
    Come galloping up the lane.

The pigeons have flown from the eaves and tiles;
    The oatblades have grown to blades of steel,
And the huns swarm down the leafy aisles
    Of the grand old Commonweal.

They have torn the Indian fisher's nets
    Where the gray Pamunky goes toward the sea,
And blood runs red in the rivulets
    That babbled and brawled in glee.

The corpses are strewn in Fair Oaks' glades;
    The hoarse guns thunder from Drury Ridge;
The fishers that played in the cool deep shades
    Are frightened from Bottom Bridge.

I would that the year were blotted away,
  And the strawberries green in the hedge again;
That the scythe might swing in the tangled hay,
  And the squirrels romp in the glen;

The walnuts sprinkle the clover slopes,
  Where graze the sheep and the spotted steer,
And the winter restore the golden hopes
  That were trampled in a year!

George Alfred Townsend

We had now reached the dreaded Chickahominy where it was expected that, if anywhere, the enemy would make his last desperate stand. He had retired to the west bank, so that all the section of country lying east of a line drawn from New Bridge on the Chickahominy northward to the Pamunky, and southeastwardly to the James river was cleared of confederates.

The regiment was bivouacked that night after the skirmish at Gaines' Mill about a mile from New Bridge, awaiting the arrival of support before making another advance. The next morning a reconnaissance was made by six companies towards the Chickahominy for the evident purpose of feeling the enemy's lines here, and securing a lodgment on the west side if circumstances proved favorable. We marched to within half a mile of the bridge and halted, while Corporal McAleese, of Philadelphia, belonging to M Company and four men were sent forward as an advance guard. They found a soldier posted on the bridge.

As soon as the picket discovered the advance he made a motion with his hand, as if to wave our men to go back, though it might have been a signal for a different purpose. Corporal McAleese raised his revolver and shot at the guard, and at the same instant a dozen or fifteen confederates, who had been lying in ambuscade in the bushes as our men rode past, sprang to their feet and fired a volley at them from a distance not exceeding twenty paces. Corporal McAleese fell dead in the road; the blacksmith of M Company received a severe wound in the back and mouth, in spite of which, however, he managed to ride to the rear; and two horses were shot, their riders being compelled to retreat on foot. As this affair proved that the enemy's infantry occupied the line of the river, the regiment returned to its halting ground near Gaines' Mill, and established patrols and pickets on all the roads in the vicinity.

That evening, about six o'clock, it was my fortune to be placed on picket about one hundred and fifty yards from the bridge, and to remain there until one o'clock next morning. The enemy had now five infantrymen on the bridge who, however, made no hostile demonstrations upon us—there was a mutual understanding, it seemed, that pickets should remain undisturbed so long as no advance was attempted. Three stood post while I was there, and two sat on a fence close by, reading newspapers while it was yet light. Fifty yards behind me we had another picket, while a distance behind him was another—each man had his horse reined up under the dark shade of a tree. At nine o'clock I heard tattoo beat in four different camps which showed that the enemy was in heavy force in our immediate front. Towards midnight I became very sleepy. By midnight this desire to sleep became unsupportable, and I began to nod in my saddle. Just then a gun cracked in my immediate front, and a bullet went singing up the road past me. I was wide awake in an instant, and peered anxiously down the road, expecting to see an enemy slipping toward me, or to hear him in the bushes. Nothing was to be seen or heard. In spite of my anxiety I was soon nodding again when the shot was repeated. Once more I aroused myself and tried to pierce the thick gloom, but could not; all was still. I tried my best to keep awake, fully realizing the responsibility of the position I occupied, but it was of no use. It seemed to me as if my eyes would go shut, even if the whole confederate army were marching down that road. Fortunately, while I was on the point of toppling over again I heard the clicking of sabres behind me, and in a moment more the relief was by my side, accompanied by Lieutenant Ward, who inquired about the shots. I reported all I knew about it, and rode gaily up the hill to the reserves, full of delight at the prospect of securing some rest. I do not think it was many minutes after I had hitched my horse to a tree, and laid down with my head on a rail, that I had forgotten all my woes in a sound, sweet sleep.

That I was not the only one utterly exhausted from want of sleep, the following anecdote of Schwab—deliberate Schwab—will show. This individual stood on post at the same time, though he was located under a tree on the slope of the hill, perhaps half a mile north of the road, in a field. When Corporal Croy visited the stations to ascertain if the men were all right, about ten o'clock that night, he found Schwab in a state of great consternation. He pointed through the darkness to some trees below him, and declared that they were coming up the hill. Corporal

Croy looked at Schwab, astonished at these remarkable revelations, but there he stood with his eyes wide open, and looking ludicrously in earnest, and still insisting that the trees were walking up the hill. The deliberate Schwab was, without doubt, as much asleep at this time as he ever was in his life. I shall relate on another page the curious effect the loss of sleep had upon me on another occasion, which will demonstrate how unreliable the sense of sight becomes under such circumstances.

About the 21st of May General Fitz John Porter's corps reached New Bridge and relieved the regiment from duty at that point, and we were allowed two or three days of quiet rest. Colonel Lowe[1] with his balloons arrived soon after, and went into camp, and prepared to make bird's-eye observations of the enemy's lines. I had never witnessed a balloon ascension, except the involuntary one on the memorable morning of our advance on Chain Bridge the year before; so I made it my especial business to be present on this occasion. A large crowd of colored people had gathered in from the surrounding plantations, and were on the hill above the spot from, which the ascension was to be made; and as this position afforded a fine view of the proceedings, I posted myself there, and awaited the event.

As the balloon swelled out with the gas, the colored folks gave vent to their surprise in numerous ejaculations, while their black faces twisted into all sorts of grimaces, and their white teeth glistened and their eyes rolled.

"I am clar done gone!" exclaimed an old fellow, with a great bushy head who, it appeared, was a sort of preacher.

"I am clar done gone!" sounded in a chorus all over the field.

Finally the balloon was ready to go up, and General McClellan and the aeronaut entered the bucket, and the huge pile began to arise.

"I am clar done gone!" shouted the preacher.

"I am clar done gone!" rose the chorus.

It was evident that somebody else imagined themselves "clar done gone" before that balloon descended. After it had attained a proper altitude, one of the enemy's batteries opened upon it in a manner that must have been unpleasant to the occupants of the basket. The shells burst all about the fragile bubble, and every moment I expected to see it come down collapsed but it did not. Somebody called down to the men who were operating the windlass to hurry and pull down the balloon, which they did in a few moments, the vengeful shells following it until

[1]   Thaddeus S.C. Lowe became the Army's first balloonist late in 1861.

it was quite low. Stepping out of the basket as soon as it had reached terra firma, General McClellan said that he had seen Richmond.

On the 23d of May the Sixth Cavalry 2nd and one or two regiments of infantry moved up along the crest of hills enclosing the Chickahominy on the east towards Mechanicsville—a small village said to be about five miles north of Richmond on the road leading to Fredericksburg. At this place the enemy was encountered in small force with artillery. The road upon which we had advanced was at some points under fire, and we were obliged to hurry past these exposed places at a trot. A short distance from Mechanicsville we reached a mill, and in order to get into position were compelled to ride along the bank of the water-race course by file—a movement that brought us close under the enemy's guns, from whence we could distinctly see their movements. From this race-course we dashed up and over a ridge, and under its friendly shelter formed in close column of squadrons, with sabres drawn, and with a line of skirmishers deployed across the field on our right flank and front. At nightfall the firing ceased and we were marched across to the left of the road into an orchard, where the command bivouacked until morning. At dawn there was more artillery firing, but this soon ceased, and our forces advanced and occupied the village. Some of the houses here had been seriously damaged by our shells.

The command remained at Mechanicsville during the day. The view from this point towards Richmond was magnificent, the ground descending gradually towards the Chickahominy, and as gradually rising beyond. It has been said that some of the spires of the churches in the city could be seen from this point, but my eyes failed to detect them. No troops, save a cavalry picket were visible; these were stationed at the point where the road crossed the swamp. Contrary to our expectations, not a single earthwork was in sight, though from rumors we had supposed Richmond was enclosed with an impenetrable wall. I was surprised to see after our arrival our infantry march up with spades in hand, and commence digging and shovelling, thinking all the while that we were to continue our advance until the enemy was found in such great force as to justify siege operations. On the same day that our soldiers commenced throwing up their redoubts the enemy marched into sight on the opposite hills, and began constructing their redoubts; the only difference was that the latter were finished first, and the confederates were enabled to annoy our men with the guns they had placed in position.

Some of our infantry, during the day after our occupation of

Mechanicsville, strolled off down the road towards the cavalry picket on the bridge with the avowed purpose of shooting him. As this was a violation of the mutual understanding between the hostile armies that pickets should not be disturbed unless demanded by the necessities of an advance, I was so shocked that I hurried away from the spot anxious to shut out from my view what I was convinced should be properly designated as the crime of murder.

Our camp was now established in a pine forest some two miles north of Mechanicsville. I do not know that, properly speaking, it was a camp, because we had not seen a tent since the evacuation of Yorktown. We tied our horses to trees. and made a sort of shelter out of our blankets, and slept on some pine boughs we had gathered. On the 27th of May the Sixth Cavalry marched toward Hanover Court House, for the purpose, as I at that time understood, of opening communication with General McDowell, who was then reported to be advancing from the north, with an army of sixty thousand, and was said to have reached Bowling Green—a village fifteen or twenty miles south of Fredericksburg. The latter place is, I believe, sixty miles north from Richmond, and Hanover Court House some fifteen miles, so that by the time our forces had penetrated five or six miles beyond the Court House, the two bodies of United States troops must have been within twenty or twenty-five miles of each other. We were supported in the movement by several batteries, a division of infantry, and two or three regiments of cavalry—in all some fifteen thousand men. Two and one-half miles south of the Burnt House, at the junction of the White House road with the road running from Fredericksburg to Richmond the enemy was found in strong force, covering the latter road, and evidently contemplating a strong resistance to our progress. As soon as we reached the enemy's pickets the regiment dashed forward, supported by four guns of the Second Artillery, and took up a position on the White House road—one portion of the command, with two guns, facing southwest, engaging a confederate battery posted near Ashland, and the other portion, with two guns facing northwest, engaging another battery posted on the opposite side of a wheat field in the direction of the Court House. Each of the enemy's batteries was supported by a strong force of infantry. Our troops on the left were soon successful in silencing the enemy's guns, but our battalion, though formed under the cover of a ridge in rear of our pieces, was much annoyed by the shells. The wheat field mentioned above served as admirable cover for the enemy, as the smoke from their guns clung to the masses of wheat and spread out over the field in such a way that it was next to impossible to locate the pieces excepting at long intervals. Their fire was so efficient that our gunners were obliged to change position every few moments.

One of the members of the Second Artillery, who was with the guns our battalion supported, had completed a term of enlistment for five years on the day before this action occurred, and had intended to leave for home in the morning. When it was understood the battery was to take part in this movement the brave fellow said that he would accompany it for the last time. During the engagement he took no active part, but stood at one side of the pieces, watching the explosions of the enemy's guns. As each fresh cloud of smoke rolled up, he cried "There she comes!" as a warning to his comrades. On one of these occasions he had turned his face toward the gunners with this exclamation, and then looked back towards the confederates. At that instant, the shot struck him square on the forehead, carrying away the upper half of his head, and the lifeless body fell backward upon the ground. He had indeed accompanied the battery for the last time.

In spite of the horrors of our situation there, occasionally expressions made by some of the men were full of a dry humor from their very grimness. For instance, Croy proposed, when the enemy's fire had become almost intolerable, that some one should ride up and read the riot act to the enemy. The genial Evans kept those next to him enlivened by his antics, and did not seem to notice the shrieks of shots as they flew over our heads.

The major, upon forming the men in close columns of squadrons, with drawn sabres in rear of the guns at the beginning of the action, after the lines were dressed, looked a moment upon the men, and said, "I believe I can trust you; I have seen you in action before." and then coolly dismounted and cast himself upon the ground awaiting developments.

One shot struck the ground on the ridge, and rebounded high into the air, falling through the timber with a crash, and being plainly visible in its descent. It made a curiously fluttering noise in its flight, that could have been heard fully half a mile.

Our infantry now appeared upon the field, marching proudly, filed between and to the right and left of the two sections of artillery, and deployed across our front. Our pieces now ceased firing, and in a few moments the sharp cracks of rifles showed that the "dough boys" were already engaged. Presently squads of prisoners began streaming to the rear, apparently without guards. The sound of musketry died away suddenly, and our sections limbered up, the regiment broke by fours to the front, and pushed forward in pursuit of the flying foe. The sight was a curious one when we reached the field in which the enemy had been posted. Quite a number of dead and wounded men were lying around, while the ground was literally covered with muskets standing up like stalks of corn, with the bayonet driven into the earth. A long line of knapsacks stretched across the open ground, where the confederate infantry had slung them before the attack commenced. One brass gun had been left behind as a trophy to our men. Lying near it, with his hand still clutching a rope fastened to the end of the limber, was a dead soldier. He was a young, beardless man, with fair, freckled skin and very light hair. One eye stood wide open, while the other was shut, and his lips were distorted by what might have passed for a sardonic smile. His death wound was in his neck, where a bullet, plowing its way through, tore open a great gash in its course, from which the life blood had sprinkled his gray uniform.

The regiment had marched perhaps a mile or two when the sound of a cannon in our rear awakened in our minds a strange disquietude. Can it be possible that this sudden retreat of the enemy was simply a ruse to enable them to cut off ours? The gun roared again. A few sharp cracks of muskets followed, demonstrating that the confederates were actually between us and our army. All the forces then advancing towards the north countermarched toward the exposed point, and in a short time the firing became quite brisk not by volleys, however, but by file. As we came in sight of the field where the first action had been fought the scene was certainly inspiriting. On the left stood, formed in a long line across the field, the Sixth Pennsylvania Cavalry,[2] then armed with lances, fully one thousand strong, and making a fine display, reminding me of the engravings I had once seen of the Mexican cavalry at the war of 1848. In front, supporting our guns, were the infantry, while on the right a brigade of the latter was deployed in line extending far along the slope of a hill, looking as bright and new as if going on dress parade, with an alignment that was faultless. In a few moments this line moved forward

[2]   This unit is also known as Rush's Lancers. Consisting of the Philadelphia upper crust, Rush's Lancers were equipped with nine foot long lances tipped with an eleven inch blade with three edges. In June, 1863, the lances were replaced by carbines. The regiment served throughout the war and was conspicuous during the Peninsula campaign and at the Battle of Brandy Station.

up the slope. The picture was magnificent at this juncture. The sun was just sinking in the west, and his golden rays tinted the whole landscape. The long line of lancers, with the little red ribbons fluttering in crimson ripples from below the spear heads of their peculiar weapons—the smoke rolling up from the billowing guns, rendering almost indistinguishable the springing figures around them—the blue lines of support—the brigade on the right moving as one man up the greensward of the hill, their colors several paces to the front, the folds of the flags catching just enough of wind to carry them in waves from the staff, illuminated by the yellow beams from the west—this is the scene upon which my vision rested on that eventful evening, and which I can now unfold at will to my mind's eye as it then existed—an invaluable treasure in my little collection of gems of those stirring days.

But all this changed with the rapidity of the colors of a kaleidoscope—the line reaches the crest of the hill and disappears beyond it, and a moment later a heavy volley rolls back, reverberating along the horizon—a few spluttering shots follow, and all is still. The battle of Hanover Court House is over.

It was dark by the time the troops had mustered, and dispositions were made to pass the night. At nine or ten o'clock—it is so hard to remember hours amid such exciting scenes—our regiment bivouacked upon the field of battle, and, barely taking time to secure my horse, I flung myself on the ground beside some one who had already lain down, and was asleep in a moment.

The sun was shining in my face next morning when I awakened. The first object on which my eyes rested, lying within three feet of me, still with one eye open and the other shut, with a sort of leer that seemed intensified by the sardonic smile on his bloodless lips, his short white hair sticking straight up and wet with dew, and with the great ghastly gash in his neck, from which a pool of clotted blood had been built up upon the ground, and with the freckles standing out in relief upon his livid skin, was the dead confederate, with his hands still clutched, though the rope was no longer between them. This body I had supposed to be a sleeping comrade the night before.

I heard something about this dead soldier afterwards from a prisoner. When the retreat began during the first engagement, and the gun was about to be abandoned, he begged his comrades to help him haul it off by hand, deeply feeling the humiliation of losing a portion of the battery to which he was attached. Failing to induce any one to assist him, he caught up the rope, and tugged at it alone, when a bullet from our side felled him.

The gun had made an about face, and was used upon our troops a second time by the enemy when they came up in our rear. It had been left by our soldiers in the position where captured without a guard, was lost and retaken during the day.

I strolled over the field, impelled by a sort of curiosity. Our men were asleep yet, with very few exceptions. The dead confederates were scattered here and there, some covered with blankets and others exposed as they had fallen. Corporal Welch was lingering around a body, and presently thrust his right hand deep into one of the pockets. He did not observe my presence. A sickly look came over his face; he drew out his hand, which was now covered with blood; a great wrinkle appeared across the bridge of his nose as he contemplated the gore; and then he made frantic efforts to wipe it off. Just then he saw me.

"I was hunting for tobacco," he said, apparently by way of explanation, as though he did not want me to think he would take valuables if any should be found, instead of the article mentioned.

"Ugh! This makes me sick!"

Wandering over the field we came to a spot where five men were covered with a blanket.

"Poor fellows!" said Welch, sympathy. "Here are five in a bunch."

Thus speaking, he gently and reverently uncovered their heads to have a look at them. The supposed dead men opened their eyes with a rather surprised expression of countenance. They proved to be some of our own soldiers who had been asleep during the night.

Our loss at the battle of Hanover Court House was fifty-three men killed and three hundred and fifty-seven wounded. The enemy's loss in killed and wounded must have been considerable, owing to their great inferiority in numbers; our captures footed up to nearly eight hundred prisoners, one gun, and a railroad train loaded with tobacco—the latter of great importance to some of our soldiers, some of whom laid in a goodly store for the future.

For two days after the action confederate stragglers came into our lines from their hiding places, from which they were driven by hunger. I believe that they were all North Carolinians. Most of them expressed themselves tired of the contest, and anxious to get home. This declaration seemed to us at that time to be of great importance, but since then we have learned that it did not make so much difference after all;

150

that these same men, when they were exchanged and returned to duty, would most likely fight as hard against us as the most outspoken, radical confederates.

In the afternoon the regiment marched five or six miles from the Court House up along the Pamunky river, and destroyed several bridges, and the telegraphic communication between Richmond and the confederates in Northern Virginia.

An amusing incident occurred during our advance to this point. A few miles from the Court House a crowd of people appeared on a low hill two or three miles away. The impression prevailed that these were confederates and that they had a battery posted up there to give us a warm reception. After a good deal of preliminary delay and examination, the supposed hostile party developed into a squad of contrabands,[3] who had gathered here to see us, some one having advised them of our arrival.

After the objects of the raid had been accomplished, the command returned to the Court House, where it remained until the evening of the 30th of May. Then followed one of those long, miserable night-marches, which are tenfold more demoralizing than the actual conflicts of a war. At this time occurred to me the curious phenomena of sight mentioned elsewhere. As I rode along, almost utterly overcome from want of sleep, the actual surrounding disappeared, and I seemed to be marching along a different road. It was in broad daylight. On each side of our column, going in the same direction, and keeping abreast of it, were trains of wagons and batteries of artillery. On the outer flank were brigades of infantry, carrying their muskets at a right shoulder shift. Then the scene changed. It was night again, and we were marching along a long road, through woods, beset on all sides by mysterious enemies, whom we were unable to resist, and who seemed to be impervious to our shots. All this time I was conscious of a rocking or swinging sensation. I could plainly see my right hand man—we were marching by twos—never made a mistake as to him, and occasionally carried on a conversation with him, and understood his replies. Beyond this, however, the optical illusions were perfect.

Towards morning we halted somewhere in the vicinity of Coal Harbor, dropping down asleep as soon as the horses were dismounted

---

[3] Contrabands was the name given to slaves leaving their masters' and going to Union camps. General Benjamin Butler declared that fleeing slaves were contraband of war because otherwise they could be used for the construction of fortifications and trenches for the enemy.

151

and unsaddled. After daylight a camp was organized, picket ropes put up, horses thoroughly groomed and fed, and our haversacks replenished, the men forgetting their fatigues of the night before in the prospective rest before them. About one o'clock, while we were still "standing to horse," awaiting final orders to march, a muttering of cannon and small arms could be heard away off towards the south. This increased in volume, until it became evident that somewhere a full-fledged battle was in progress. The crash of muskets was continuous, amid which the artillery fire could only be distinguished by a succession of heavy thumping sounds. Although the soldiers around our neighborhood were much concerned about the action, no excitement was visible about the different headquarters; so we were constrained to suppose that everything was going on well. The tumult of battle continued until sometime after dark dying away at last in a few nervous explosions of cannon.

At dawn the next morning the roar again came up from the south, showing that the fight was not yet over. We now began to think that final operations for the capture of Richmond were actually in progress, and grew quite enthusiastic over the prospect, but after two or three hours the firing seemed to cease, and instead of packing up our military fixtures and entering the Capital of the Confederacy, as we had hoped, the regiment merely went about the routine duties of a long established camp. The engagement proved to have been the battle of Fair Oaks, and instead of culminating in the capture of Richmond, it had almost ended in irretrievable disaster to our arms.

The quiet which settled upon the lines of the Army of the Potomac from the 1st until the 26th of June brought to us a succession of duties. Owing to the small force of cavalry and the heavy drafts made upon it for headquarters and other service, the execution of the legitimate purposes of a mounted force—to guard the flanks and rear, and patrol all roads surrounding an army—fell upon the few left to fulfill them with a cruel force. Details were daily made to scour the country lying between the right wing and the Pamunky river, and as far west as Marion Court House. These scouts were generally made with two days' rations, but we rarely managed to return to camp within three or four days, and consequently these extensions of time were very exacting upon our stomachs.

On one of these expeditions our squadron halted at the residence of Fitzhugh Lee—then a general in the confederate service—a beautiful mansion located in a delightful country, a short distance from the

Pamunky river. The house was locked up and deserted. Several of us entered through a window and took a survey of the interior. The furniture seemed to have been left in its accustomed places. The splendid library, and the cabinet of curiosities—two collections which must have been of wondrous value—were rooms of great interest to me, and, had I possessed means of moving them intact to some point where I could have had the benefit of them in after life, the temptation to do so would have been great. As it was, however, our party disturbed nothing.

Leaving Fitzhugh Lee's house, the squadron was marched to the Pamunky and halted at a comfortable old-fashioned mansion surrounded by a beautiful grassy lawn and delightful old trees. While here a carriage drove up, from which a lady, closely veiled, alighted, and went into the house. The colored people here informed us—the enlisted men—that this was Mrs. General Longstreet,[4] and it was also rumored that she had a permit from General McClellan to pass our lines. Afterwards I saw a statement in the newspaper, giving substantially the same facts, substituting, however, the name of Mrs. General Lee for that of Mrs. General Longstreet. This permit from McClellan seemed to be a subject of comment by the press, and an effort was made to connect the lady's advent and exit into and from the federal lines with the events that occurred shortly afterward—the raid made by General Stuart around our army with his cavalry.

I have been impressed, however, with the injustice of this criticism. Without relying upon her sense of honor, which must have been pledged to secure the permit, and which, in itself, it seems to me, to be satisfactory, it also is a fact that she crossed the river at a point remote from General Stuart's force, and the confederates at that moment were on their way.[5]

Our party bivouacked that night in a pleasant field of clover where, on corn and grass, our horses fared sumptuously. The night passed pleasantly to us, sleeping there under the blue sky, amid the sweet-smelling clover blossoms. Reveille sounded at dawn, and, refreshed and vigorous, the squadron marched toward Hanover Court House. The road was a delightful one, running through a long straight vista of trees, bordered with a profusion of leaves and flowers, and bounded on the right and left by a landscape of marvelous beauty. The

4 The reference is to the wife of Confederate General James Longstreet.

5 J.E.B. Stuart's ride around McClellan took place June 12—16, 1862.

153

broad well-cultivated fields of grain, elegant real Old Dominion homes, low dark green hills, with occasional glimpses of the pretty serpentine river, would have driven the soul of an artist wild with delight. The fresh balmy air, the clear cool sky, the elastic, cheerful tread of our horses, and our exhilarated spirits rendered the journey a remarkably pleasant one, though through a hostile country, where we momentarily expected to come in collision with our enemies.

No confederates were encountered until we reached the Court House. Here we found thirty cavalrymen drawn up across the road, apparently determined to dispute our progress. As our force was very small, and as we were then perhaps ten miles from any of our people, judgement and caution were necessary in conducting operations. When within a quarter of a mile of the enemy the command halted, and three men were sent forward to reconnoiter their line. These men were allowed to approach within forty or fifty paces, and were then challenged with:

"What do you all want?"

To this no reply was made, and our men retired towards their supports.

In all this no hostile demonstration was made by either party. The actions of the confederates indicated that they were well prepared for an encounter, and our officers, deeming an attack upon them under the circumstances imprudent, we were withdrawn from their front at a slow pace until out of their sight—they made no attempt to follow—when we took up the trot until we reached the scene of the battle of Hanover Court House. Some of the enemy's pickets were found here, but these retired precipitately towards Ashland.

I was much annoyed on our way from the Court House to the battle-field by the sarcastic remarks of Christian Draker, whom it was my misfortune to have as my right hand man in the ranks. Naturally expecting that the enemy would make a demonstration upon us while retiring from their front—a movement they would not fail to recognize as an evidence of our weakness—I cast many—and, perhaps, they were anxious ones—glances over my shoulder toward the rear. On one of these occasions I noticed a cloud of dust rising above the tree-tops in the distance, and mentioned it to some one, supposing that it was caused by the movement of a column of the enemy, and desirous of having the attention of the commanding officer attracted to it, so that we might not be surprised and attacked. The querulous little Dutchman seemed to regard this as an unmistakable evidence of cowardice, and growled out

154

in that cracked voice of his:

"Vat you 'fraid of? For vat you come to war, if not to fight mit de rebels?"

Knowing that he would regard it simply as further evidence of fear, I made no reply, but merely cast upon him what I intended should be a withering look of contempt. He received this with a disdainful laugh, and then began talking with someone else on the same subject.

Two hours after our withdrawal General J. E. B. Stuart, with a force of three thousand mounted men, started out of the woods beyond the Court House on his celebrated raid around our army. From this it may be inferred that our escape was by the sufferance of the enemy, who, no doubt, was not at that moment prepared to have their movements disclosed to our forces.

Corporal Sweeney, of Company K, was captured while on duty on one of the roads leading to Hanover. First there passed him three men dressed in blue uniforms, but they also, he noticed, wore gray caps. He supposed they were United States soldiers, though somewhat puzzled at that portion of their costume. Following these came a squad of perhaps a dozen in similar attire. One, who seemed to be an officer, halted the party, and said to Corporal Sweeney:

"Well, I guess you might as well give up those arms. You are our prisoner."

The astonishment of the corporal at this denouement may be imagined, but not described. There was no escape, however, and he submitted to his fate with as good grace as possible. These were the enemy's scouts.

He was taken to Stuart's headquarters. The general made inquiries as to his command, and its different officers, with most of whom he seemed to have been acquainted before the war, and especially in regard to Major Williams. He then ordered Sweeney to be paroled, and by him sent word to Major Williams that he would like to meet the Sixth Cavalry in a fair hand-to-hand fight, some day.

That night our party bivouacked off the road in an out-of-the-way place several miles from Hanover Court House. The officers exhibited some anxiety of mind, and maintained a vigilant superintendence over the picket guards. The next day we marched to a place known as Raines' Shops, and there halted, and communicated with General Fitz John Porter. When the courier returned, pickets were established well out on all the intersecting roads, and we remained here until the next day.

155

About midnight, one of our guards was startled at discovering what was first supposed to be a body of infantry advancing along the road towards his post. Corporal Frobin was in the vicinity at the time, and, being notified, reinforced the sentinel in person, and challenged the advancing host. To this no answer was given. A second challenge met with a like silent reception. The third was given, and the revolvers duly presented, when several voices with a peculiar dialect, called out:

"Its we alls, massa."

This explained the whole matter. They were slaves, of both sexes, and of all sizes, escaping from their masters, having traveled from the country north of the Pamunky. They were convoyed to the presence of the commanding officer. From them we learned that the enemy's cavalry, in large force, had passed along the road leading from Hanover Court House to White House. Dispatches containing this information were immediately sent to General Porter by a courier.

These refugees were a great source of amusement to our men, who kept them dancing "Juba" all morning. No one was exempted from this requirement, from the child just able to walk to the decrepit old man in charge of the party. The negroes would grin at the evidences of their success in pleasing the "Yankees," and seemed delighted with the new life and prospects that were before them.

An old fellow of pious mien, utterly refused to dance. He belonged to church, he said, and was not permitted to dance; he was willing to sing hymns and pray. So he sang all the hymns he knew, some of them several times in succession. When these were all exhausted, the boys told him he must dance "Juba"—to dance "Juba," and they would shoulder the sin. It was all of no use, however. Then Leonard, taking his lariat rope from the saddle, made a noose, and, slipping up behind the old man, dropped it over his neck. He threw the other end over a limb. All the while the soldiers maintained, though with some difficulty, serious countenances.

"Now, sir, you must dance 'Juba,' or you are a dead man."

This was sufficient; the old fellow surrendered, and gave us one of the most successful performances of the day. It had been a long time, he said, since he had danced, but he thought he had not forgotten how to swing the heel. In this opinion our party unanimously concurred.

After the conclusion of the fun, the soldiers shared with them what little rations they had left, and sent them on their way rejoicing to General Porter's headquarters.

Our party left Raines' Shops about nine o'clock, and reached camp at noon. We found it entirely deserted, with the exception of a few stragglers. These reported that the enemy were at White House Landing, and that the remnant of the regiment were in pursuit of them. Instructions had been left for us to follow the command to Old Church Tavern, and after a moment's delay we were on the road. At Old Church Tavern we found General Philip St. George Cooke with all the available mounted force in the army—some fifteen hundred men. The remains of the camp of a squadron of the Fifth United States Cavalry, which had been on picket duty here, and a number of freshly made graves showed that the enemy had been resisted at this point. The squadron had performed its duty faithfully. When the confederates made their appearance the little band resisted to the last, actually making a sabre charge on their foes, though outnumbered thirty to one. The shock of the charge threw many of them from their saddles. Of course, they were defeated; their camp was destroyed, and the men were obliged to escape as best they could.

The landlord of the Old Church Tavern was arrested and sent north on account of insulting language used toward our troops when the attack was made, and for displaying the confederate flag.

After "standing to horse" all night, and learning that General Stuart had crossed the Chickahominy at a point southeast of our army, the regiment was marched back to a camp near Coal Harbor, where we were allowed a brief interval of rest before the beginning of the celebrated Seven Days[6]—a boon which we had learned by this time to fully appreciate. Our duties during this short period were confined to those ordinarily pertaining to camp life.

To show how the Common Soldier felt and what he thought at this stage of his military career, and how his heart yearned for the sympathy of his friends at home, I subjoin the following letter, written under date of June 22, 1862, at Camp of Cavalry Reserve:

Dear Friend:

You cannot think how glad I was to receive your last letter. I had almost come to the conclusion, as four of mine had been sent from here without the

[6]   The Seven Days Campaign took place June 25—July 1, 1862. These were the pivitol battles in the Peninsula campaign. During these battles, the Confederates, now led by Robert E. Lee, and with incoming troops from Stonewall Jackson's force, repulsed the Union efforts to capture Richmond.

appearance of a reply, that you were either sick or had forgotten me. I used to wonder what could be the matter, and felt so restless that I knew not what to do. Home influences have been all-sustaining to me in the troublous days upon which I have entered. I thought of home on the field at Hanover Court House, as I sat on my horse there waiting to be killed, as the enemy's shot and shell whizzed and bursted over our heads and in our faces, and thought that I could die like a soldier if I only knew that my old friends remembered me kindly, and applauded my devotion to the cause.

For your dear sakes I will bear all and suffer all.

We are getting some rest now.

No doubt you have heard of the battle of Seven Pines. We took no part in that engagement. We had strong hopes that operations would be kept up until matters were brought to a crisis. Would to God that fight had been continued until Richmond had fallen, or our army had been annihilated. These drawn battles look as though our troops were inferior to those of the enemy, and are annoying. As it is, the great battle is still to be fought. Let our generals take us into action, and no recall until we ask them to do so, and the world will see of what manner of men the United States Army is composed.

Ask Levi if he recollects the last words he spoke to me, which were, "keep wide-awake, Sid"? I have had occasion to remember them, I can assure you. It requires much effort at times to obey this mandate, especially after several nights spent in marching and "standing to horse."

I have got another horse now. I call him Bob. He has carried me through one battle.

I am sorry to hear that Levi is sick.

On the morning of June 26 I happened to be on guard at headquarters. The regiment broke camp early and marched out toward the Pamunky river, leaving the guard behind. For two days past it had been rumored that the confederates, under Stonewall Jackson were advancing upon our right flank and rear from northern Virginia and meditated an attack in force on our army at Mechanicsville.

About two o'clock we received orders to pack up headquarters, and move the trains to Woodbury bridge on the Chickahominy. As yet only the usual cannonading—it may have been more constant—could be heard along the lines of the army. It was evident, however, that something was expected by our generals, judging from this significant movement from our late camp.

The trains, after some delay, moved out to Gaines' Mill, having been hurried off at the last moment by our regimental quartermaster, who was said to have declared that the enemy was then rapidly approaching. One or two shells burst in unpleasant proximity to us as we drove up the hill through the woods at Gaines', apparently from the enemy's siege guns located beyond the Chickahominy, which seemed to have a complete range of that portion of our line. When the road leading from Woodbury bridge to Mechanicsville was reached, our wagons turned to the left and moved towards the former.

This movement of trains must have been fully visible to the enemy, and showed him in advance that we had made up our mind to be defeated in the impending battle. It was, to say the least, a grave blunder thus to expose our intentions and invite and encourage attack. Other roads were available—why were they not taken?

The condition of our army at this moment was a perilous one. Although we had fully forty-eight hours in which to decide whether to fight or retreat, nothing was done until the last moment, and then in a half-hearted, undecided way. The cavalry was sent out to fell trees, tear up bridges and culverts, and otherwise impede the advance of the enemy, and yet the right wing of the army was allowed to remain stretched out, with unprotected flank and rear, during all the precious hours thus gained.

Three plans were open to McClellan, with time sufficient to adopt and execute any of them: One—which would have been deemed dishonorable, but which would have at least avoided the tremendous losses that ensued—was to retreat without a battle back to Yorktown, or some other point near a base of supply. Another, to concentrate his entire army, after the attack began, to the right bank of the Chickahominy, and then destroy the masses that were thrown by the enemy upon that portion of the line, after which, if so desired, our old lines could have been re-established, if nothing more. The third was to withdraw all his force to the south side of the Chickahominy, and move by the left flank upon the James river, and there establish his camps for future operations. In that case he would have been close to a base of supply, and at liberty to carry on the siege directly against Richmond as he had against Yorktown, or indirectly by operating on the south side of the James river, as was afterwards accomplished by Grant.

Instead, however, of adopting any measure to secure his army from defeat, much less to capture the Confederate capital—the object for which he had been sent—McClellan adopted the disastrous means, which if it did not end in the total loss of his army, placed it in a position where it existed only at the sufferance of the enemy.

This may seem strong language, but I believe it is justified by the actual circumstances. The country will never realize how nearly it had lost the Army of the Potomac, fully seventy-five thousand strong, on that dismal fourth of July, when, huddled like a great mob upon the right bank of the James river, along the lowlands bottom, the fire of the confederate battery was opened upon it from the range of hills on the north. There it was, a helpless disorganized mass—I had almost said swamped in the vast mire—with an impassible river on one side, and a powerful enemy on the other, whose out post had already been established in a position from which it could control our troops, but which, through one of those mysterious providences that so often befriended us during the war, they had neglected to strengthen. For twenty-four hours those hills had been left at the service of the confederates, and it was only when the battery mentioned had disclosed itself prematurely that our commanding general was apparently brought to realize the extreme peril in which his army was placed.

Perhaps it is not worth while at this late day to criticize McClellan's campaign on the peninsula; perhaps, too, the opinion of a common soldier is of little moment in an undertaking in which he is only an atom of the force to be used; but it is a melancholy satisfaction to me to testify in my humble way to the patriotic devotion of the poor boys who made up the Army of the Potomac during those memorable days of peril, when their heroic effort certainly deserved success, and under the direction of George H. Thomas or Phil. Sheridan would undoubtedly have achieved it.

In common with the rest of the soldiers I loved McClellan in those days. He was my idol. I accepted everything that he ordered as for the best, and God knows I was willing to do anything in my humble capacity to make his operations successful. I am prouder of that portion of my military career than of any other; my patriotism was fresh and all-sustaining; my heart had not yet been invaded by a single misgiving as to the ability of our commanding general; my spirit had suffered no humiliation, and my duties were performed with a hearty cheerfulness. This much I say to show that the reflections I have indulged in were not the outgrowth of prejudice. but were forced upon me by the influence of sober conviction after a review of the whole field of action.

There was one thing I noticed after leaving the woods and passing in rear of our works opposite Gaines' house, which, in the light of subsequent events, fully confirms the opinion entertained as to McClel-

160

lan's peculiar indecision. Although the confederates were known to be advancing upon our right flank and rear, and at that moment must have been close to our lines, our men were still working upon the entrenchments facing toward the south, instead of making preparations to resist the attack which was impending from, the almost opposite quarter, and which afterwards rendered the works utterly untenable. Everything was progressing in the usual manner, as though there was not the least danger. It is to be borne in mind that this was at least twenty hours before the confederates reached Hogan's farm, from which they attacked our position at Gaines' Mill, thanks to the determined resistance of our force at Mechanicsville—a period of time sufficient for our troops to have very good rifle-pits that might have proved of great benefit afterwards.

An incident, amusing to those who hear of it, but not to the parties affected, occurred during out temporary halt at Gaines' house. Our regimental band, desiring to make a display, as my sinister spirit suggests, rode out in a body, upon the ground on which stood one of our redoubts and surveyed the country on both sides of the Chickahominy. They had been warned by an artillery sergeant that they exposed themselves to the fire of the enemy's large guns which were located on the range of hills opposite. To this friendly admonition, however, no attention was paid. Presently a white cloud puffed into existence from the enemy's line, and a moment later a huge missile came shrieking over their heads, so low that everyone seemed to think he was hit, striking in a field far to the rear, throwing up a huge column of earth high into the air. It is unnecessary, to say that the band needed no further hint to withdraw.

When we had reached a point about one mile beyond Gaines', I noticed that quite a heavy cannonade had sprung up and was going on away off to the right, intermingled with some spluttering volleys of musketry. In a short time the well-sustained roll of guns showed that a hard-fought battle was in progress, which after some time I was able to locate in the neighborhood of Mechanicsville. It was evident that the expected attack had begun in earnest, and that the next few days to come were fraught with events important to the army and the nation. The roar of conflict continued all afternoon without intermission, and late into the night, and seemed to keep about the same position, neither receding nor advancing. This fact was of itself a great consolation to me.

Our train reached Woodbury bridge about sundown, and halted for the night. After eating a hearty supper and feeding and grooming my horse, I selected a wagon under which to make my bed, spread out my blanket on the ground, procured a piece of flat fence-rail for a pillow, laid down and was soon asleep. Sometime in the night I awakened, and heard two men who occupied a tent that had been pitched by them and whom, I supposed from their conversation, to be officers talking about the battle. From them I learned that the action had occurred near Mechanicsville; that on our side it had been fought by McCall's division of Pennsylvania Reserves, and that of the enemy by Stonewall Jackson and some troops from the vicinity of Richmond; and that our men still held their ground, having suffered a loss of some twelve hundred in killed and wounded. I was gratified that no disaster had yet befallen our troops—a misfortune I could not help dreading under the peculiar management thus far displayed by the commanding general.

At daylight firing was again heard on the right, apparently at the same point as on the day before; but this was of short duration, and was succeeded by a lull, broken only at intervals, for some hours.

The trains now moved across the bridge and up the rising ground to army headquarters, where the wagons were parked for the day. The guns across the river at Gaines' Mill began to roar, and heavy volleys of musketry at that point forced upon me the painful conviction that our troops had been compelled to abandon their position on the right, and were now being pressed around to the left. There was still hope, however; in fact there was some encouragement in the situation. The enemy attacking was constantly being withdrawn from his lines of support, while our troops were gathering strength by concentration. By energetic movements the twenty-five thousand men on the right could in two hours receive the support of forty thousand fresh soldiers from the left—a force amply sufficient to destroy the confederate army. Thus the Common Soldier soliloquized.

The two lines of battle—blue and gray—could be seen running from the swamp on the left up and across the hill to the eastward. As the fighting became severe a dense cloud hung over the field illumined at rapid intervals by flashes of lightning, while peal on peal rolled up from its depths. A terrible mystery—the culmination of the evil passions of this world—was veiled by that white bank of smoke. Fully sixty thousand soldiers, members of the same great family, once under the same flag, were here engaged in mortal strife. The old flag was indeed there, but a strange banner, which the world had seen for the first time but a few months before, had reared its bloody crest in front of the

162

stripes and stars, and was pressed forward with a cruel force.

About three o'clock the hitherto loud roar of guns grew suddenly almost deafening. It was evident that new forces had been precipitated into the conflict, and as none had passed the bridges from our left to the right, they must be confederates. And so it proved. These were Jackson's men swinging in upon the right and rear. Our lines had already been extended to their utmost capacity. Some of the batteries were left without support in the great effort to save the flanks, and this fresh overlapping force, mustered with their peculiar rapidity and thrown into the engagement with a rush, decided the action at this point. Loud yells told us of the defeat of our arms; most of the artillery had been captured, and the federal troops began retiring towards Woodbury bridge, maintaining, however, very good order in their ranks.

The excitement incident to a battle creates great confusion in one's mind as to time, unless one possesses a watch, which I did not, and frequently refers thereto upon the occurrence of each distinctive epoch or phase of the engagement. This much I write in explanation of any discrepancies that may appear as to the different hours fixed in my memory or expressed in my memorandums as those during which occurred the movements I relate.

About four o'clock I saw a brigade march across Woodbury bridge from the south bank to the north bank of the Chickahominy, apparently for the purpose of reinforcing our crushed ranks then retiring from the enemy's front at Gaines' Mill. These men wore straw hats, which distinguished them from the balance of our army. Meagher's Irishmen were also thrown across, reaching the field in time to relieve Porter's troops from the overwhelming pressure the enemy was bringing to bear upon them. After a short struggle the advance of the confederates was checked and our lines remained undisturbed during the remaining portion of the day.

During a part of the time our balloon had been up in the air, overlooking the movements of the different armies. I went over to the spot where it was stationed, hoping to glean some information from its occupant as to the gravity of the situation. He descended once, and reported that our left wing would be in Richmond within half an hour. That was certainly consoling and immediately I censured myself for having found fault with General McClellan. From, this declaration I inferred that operations had been commenced on our left, and that the enemy, by stripping his right of troops to take part in the action on the north bank of the Chickahominy, had overreached himself and was now likely to suffer for the indiscretion; he would return from his fruitless efforts on the north to find himself confronted in his capital on the south.

The balloon ascended again. Anxious to hear the result of the movement on our left, I awaited in a state of suspense for the lapse of that pregnant half hour. When at last the signal was given to lower the balloon there was a rush to hear the news.

If the aeronaut said anything about the occupation of Richmond I did not so understand him. All that I could hear was an order given to pack up, and this duty his assistants proceeded to perform with a vigor that was really astonishing. This movement had a double meaning, either branch of which commended itself to my mind. He might be preparing himself for retreat, or he might be intending to follow the army in its advance. Full of doubt as to the matter I quitted the spot.

That evening, in company with Sergeant Hargraves and Private Samuel Hamilton, I rode over to the camp of the One-hundred-and-Second Pennsylvania Infantry, to see how fared our Washington County friends. We found their quarters, around which they had thrown up entrenchments, deserted of all save a number of sick soldiers, among whom were a few of our acquaintances. From these we learned that the regiment was on picket duty at the front, and would not return until the next day. By invitation we concluded to pass the night here, and return to headquarters next morning; so I unsaddled Bobby, fed him, ate my own supper, and, after having indulged in a long talk with my friends, laid down in one of the vacant tents to sleep.

About two or three o'clock the next morning, my profound slumber was broken by a fearful crash of musketry, apparently but a few yards away. This was followed by the explosions of cannon. I sprang up, and rushed out of the tent. All the sick soldiers who were able to stand mustered along the entrenchment with their muskets. The scene just now was one of terrific grandeur. That darkness, at times, was impenetrable; but at moments the dense pine forest was blazing with flame. The air was full of missiles, large and small, and I could readily distinguish the shriek of the shell from the ragged zip of the rifled musket bullets.

The scene, while it lasted, was wonderfully suggestive of Pandemonium. I felt a strong desire to retreat from my self-imposed peril, but was not exactly able to tell whither to fly. Fortunately the affair was over in a few moments, dying out almost as suddenly as it had begun. However, there was no more sleep that night. The troops remained

164

under arms until daylight.

As soon as practicable I returned to army headquarters. Our horses were already hitched, but the trains had not yet moved. Here I found the remnants of Porter's corps and the Pennsylvania Reserves who had retired across Woodbery Bridge during the previous night, and who were now huddled on an open field along the banks of the Chickahominy. The bridge had been destroyed as soon as our troops were over on the south bank, but some three hundred stragglers who had thrown themselves upon the ground in the woods on the north side and utterly refused to stir, were left behind and fell into the hands of the enemy.

On my way from the camp of the One-Hundred-and-Second I had met a train of ambulances. These were loaded with wounded soldiers. I estimated it to be two or three miles in length. The blood from many of the occupants had trickled down through the boards and out upon the wheels. In others the poor wounded bodies had given up their spirit and lay stark upon the floor, no longer conscious of their old agonies. Scarcely a groan from all this mass of mutilated humanity reached my ears; they seemed to bear their sufferings with a heroic patience in keeping with the sublime courage they had displayed on the field. The ambulances were now on their way to Savage Station, a point not far from Bottom Bridge, on the York river railroad.

It was now evident that our army was cut off from its communications with the north. The enemy occupied the country between us and Washington and Fortress Monroe, and occasionally threw shells across the Chickahominy to show us they were there. Matters were reaching a crisis. Rumor, always busy in such times of deadly peril, said that we were going to march to the James river and renew the campaign on the south bank of that stream; that pontoons had already been thrown across in anticipation of this event of withdrawing from our base of supply at White House; and even went so far as to assert that all this fighting and apparently retreating was in conformity with some great plan of General McClellan.

Whether true or otherwise, one great benefit grew out of these speculations. They kept up the spirits of our humiliated soldiers. It actually mattered little or not whether we were fully aware of the gravity of our situation; we were in no position to make suggestions to our commanding general. All that remained to us was obedience to his orders and reliance upon him, under Providence, for the success of the campaign he had begun and thus far conducted.

While at headquarters, I concluded to go over to where the Pennsylvania Reserves were bivouacked to see my friends in the Twelfth regiment. After searching for some time, I found Lieutenant Chill Hazzard and Corporal Davis. They were unhurt and gave me an account of the action on the previous day. By their reports someone was to blame for non-performance of duty. The lieutenant said he did not see a general officer except during intervals of three hours or more. There seemed to be no unity of operation—no direction to affairs. The men had held the lines until the pressure became too great for human endurance.

One of the Reserve regiments was making a great display of a confederate banner it had captured. This was fastened to the staff of the stripes and stars, below its folds, and turned upside down.

While we were conversing, a great crash of musketry rolled up from the woods adjoining the field in which the Reserves had halted, and the men looked at one another with dismay pictured in their faces. Many rushed to arms. It proved, however, to have proceeded from our own troops, who were firing off their pieces to clean them. The confusion was of short duration.

After leaving my friends of the Reserves, I returned to army headquarters. Here I met with three young men—mere boys in appearance—each riding a horse. They applied to us for feed for their horses, and something for themselves, if we could spare it. From them I learned that they were members of Captain Eastman's battery,[7] if I remember the name aright, and had been attached to McCall's division. They had taken a prominent part in the late battles, but had lost all their guns. So far as they knew, they were the only survivors of their company. The captain had died by his pieces. During part of the time they had been supported by an infantry regiment, but this had been withdrawn to extend their line on the right, and then the enemy had charged upon them and secured the guns. They had kept up a heavy fire as long as possible, sometimes using double charges of grape shot; but it was all of no use; the confederates closed in and knocked the gunners right and left with the butts of their muskets. The young men had escaped by mounting their horses and galloping away.

This story opened our hearts at once; we shared with them our little stock of provisions, and gave them horse feed enough for two or three days.

[7]   A Pennsylvania artillery unit.

Our train now started for Savage Station, but I lingered about headquarters for a time, hoping to discover something definite as to the future intentions of the general-in-chief. I have now concluded that at this time the general-in-chief had no future intentions; that his line of movement was so dependent upon that of the enemy as to preclude the possibility of his having future intentions.

About noon I rode down to Savage Station. Here were large numbers of our wounded, occupying tents, and attended by surgeons and nurses. The train had already departed from this point, and nothing remained for me but to follow it. I found the wagons halted at Bottom Bridge Cross-roads, and as the day was near its close, I selected a tree under which to bivouac for the night. Columns of infantry and batteries of artillery were constantly passing along the road on their way to White Oak swamp. As I saw the men and heard their frequent cheers, I could not believe our troops had been defeated. The army was still proud and defiant. The disaster at James' Hill happened to a portion of it only; the main body was yet untouched. At nine or ten o'clock the noise ceased somewhat, and I fell asleep.

About midnight Hamilton awakened me, saying that the entire army was rapidly moving towards White Oak swamp, and that he thought we had better keep with it. After a survey of the situation, I made up my mind to stay where I was, and rest myself and horse. At daylight I rode down after the retreating columns. They were then crossing the swamp. Here I concluded to halt for the day, as large numbers of our troops were already bivouacked, and trains parked. At this time heavy firing could be heard in the rear, which afterwards I learned was from the battle at Savage Station, where the enemy had attacked our rearguard. Great clouds of smoke, arising in the direction of the battlefield, showed that McClellan was destroying his stores of provisions and ammunition to prevent them falling into the hands of the enemy. This was one of the discouraging features of the retreat. So long as we had been able to bring off our trains and artillery, and had been compelled to destroy nothing, it was an evidence of our strength; this burning of material, however, was an acknowledgement of our inability to defend it.

This was on Sunday, the 2th day of June, and the fourth day of the famous seven. Some of the troops had by this time marched perhaps forty or fifty miles, and passed through some heavy fighting; food was getting scarce; the constant pressure upon their physical and nervous organizations was beginning to show itself; the prospect was becoming gloomy. Still that pious fib about the pontoon bridge at James river was a support through it all.

That evening Hamilton, Hargraves, and I discovered a well filled barn not far from the field in which our train was parked, and occupied it for the night, giving our horses a good supply from its granaries. The next morning Hamilton and I rode about a mile down along the swamp, where we found a farmhouse. At this establishment we proposed to purchase something to eat. The occupant, a pleasant-looking old gentleman, met us with a smile, and invited us to dismount and partake of breakfast at his table; but that smile of his was something so unusual for us to find on the face of a citizen in this section of country that we were suspicious, and took the precaution to leave the gates open and the bars down. I declined to dismount, but held Hamilton's horse while he went in, all the while keeping a sharp lookout upon the woods and fields around me, having a presentiment that the enemy's cavalry might be in that vicinity. Hamilton made a very successful negotiation with the old gentleman for supplies, bringing out a great loaf of bread, meat, buttermilk, etc., which in the dilapidated conditions of our stomachs, were very acceptable.

As we rode away this astute forager informed me that his purchases had been made with his new currency—some bogus confederate notes which, about that time, an enterprising firm up north was printing and forwarding to the army for the low price of twenty-five cents for one hundred dollars.[8]

These notes were of a far better material and the engravings executed in a much better style than those of the genuine, and were often accepted in preference to the latter. Some how or other I always felt uncertain about the moral right of using this spurious money, although I plead guilty to eating the provisions supplied by Hamilton at this time.

In the course of half an hour we reached our train, where it was parked near White Oak swamp bridge, and then rode out upon the brow of the low hill which rises from the south side of the marsh, and took a survey of the situation. On the opposite side there was another low hill. This at one time had been held by Casey's division as the left of our line

---

[8]   There is an interesting story here.   After the Confederate government was established, but prior to the attack on Fort Sumter, printing Confederate currency was contracted to a New York city firm, the American Banknote Company. After the attack on Sumpter, the printing was done by the Archer & Daly company in Richmond, and by Keating & Ball in Columbia, South Carolina. In an effort to further undermine the economy of the Confederacy, counterfit *confederate* notes were issued in profusion by the *New York company*.

of investment of Richmond. A rifle-pit had been constructed by his troops as an additional defense to his position. A few Sibley tents stood back some distance from the rifle-pits, partially hidden by the timber.

To our great astonishment a force of the enemy marched down the road along which we had retreated, and, instead of attempting to come across, abandoned the road and filed to their left along the brow of the hill, and disappeared into the woods. Some of our regiments of infantry were sent along to the right on our side of the swamp, to watch and oppose any movement upon our lines they attempted to make. They evidently intended to outflank our forces, if possible. The bridge at this point had already been destroyed.

Additional bodies of confederates marched down the road, and followed in rear of the first. At this time a number of our batteries were in position here but the gunners and infantry supports were lying asleep under and around their fires. No effort was made to shell the gathering hosts. A few of our infantry—not a dozen in all—were down by the edge of the marsh on our side, practicing, on their own account, with their rifles upon the enemy's ranks, but their few shots were apparently unheeded.

While we were watching the different phases of this curious scene, a man approached the writer and asked for something to eat. I divided with him, and incidentally called his attention to the enemy's troops.

"My God!" he exclaimed; "I do wonder where Smith's division is?"

"I do not know," I responded; "I suppose it has gone on."

"Why, it hasn't crossed the swamp yet," he returned.

This was unpleasant news. Where could Smith's division be?

After the soldier had eaten his lunch, he held up his canteen, and invited me to take a drink. As I was a teetotaller in those days, the proffered potation was politely declined, but I referred him to Hamilton, who, I thought, would do him justice; which the astute forager did without delay.

The enemy's columns filed out of sight into the dense woods. While we were awaiting their reappearance, an artillery officer, apparently attached to one of the batteries at this point, called out to our little party:

"Move over to the left. When the enemy shows himself again I intend to open fire."

Of course, this hint was sufficient to us. We rode some distance to the left, and gave him a clear field for practice. The confederates, however, did not reappear as expected. A single individual, mounted on

169

a gray horse, rode out by the Sibley tents, and surveyed our lines. At last, tired of waiting, I rode off after our train which, by this time, had departed, and left Hamilton at the swamp with his new found friend of the canteen.

I lingered a short time among the hundreds of wagons standing in rear of the batteries. They were all hitched and ready for the road, as soon as those in advance were in motion. Then I rode very leisurely through the woods out of the way of the trains. I suppose by this time it must have been eleven or twelve o'clock.

I had not proceeded more than half a mile when suddenly the enemy opened with his artillery. The shells came tearing across the hill on which our wagons were parked. The whole mass was soon in an apparently inextricable confusion. Our batteries on the verge of the swamp, although unlimbered and ready for action, were unable to respond; the gunners had been caught napping in a literal sense.

The panic among the teamsters threatened to result disastrously, and no doubt would have done so, were it not for the almost superhuman exertions of the several quartermasters and wagonmasters in charge. By the fierce application of horsewhips over the heads and shoulders of many of the drivers, and the pressure of the muzzles of revolvers against the breasts of others, something like order was brought out of chaos, and the trains pushed along the road to a place of safety. The guns kept up a terrific fire for some time, sending their shells screaming across the field and smashing through the timber. The action extended along the lines to the right with great violence, and occasionally flashed up on the left, covering a mile or two of our front.

It is hardly necessary to say that I did not remain longer in this locality than necessary; I hurried along until I found the field in which our wagons had halted, and, proceeding a short distance further, stopped under the inviting shade of a tree and dismounted. Tying Bobby to this tree, I threw myself on the ground, and, in spite of the heavy firing, soon fell asleep and forgot the fearful scenes then enacting only a short distance away.

I suppose it is proper for me to give Hamilton's statement of the beginning of this battle of White Oak swamp. That astute forager was still conversing with his friend of the canteen when the man on the gray horse appeared at the edge of the woods beyond Casey's rifle pits. A number of our men began firing upon the confederate, and he retired from sight.

"Hold on," said the canteen friend, "let *me* try him once."

So saying, he picked up his gun, bade Hamilton good bye, and marched down to the edge of the swamp. He halted a moment here, looking across the stream intently, and then turned toward our man, saying:

"I shall slip across to that big log, yonder, and when he comes out I will bring him."

This was a bold proposition. The log was more than half way over, and, if the enemy should appear, the chances of the canteen friend's getting shot to death were numerous.

He went, however, and reached the log in safety. No one was yet in sight. Our men held their several breaths in suspense. As he stood here he took another cool survey of the surroundings. Then, throwing off his coat upon the log, he kept on across the swamp, and began creeping stealthily up the hill. Still no confederates appeared. Presently he leaped across the rifle-pit, and strode up to the edge of the timber, when, to the astonishment of all, the man on the gray horse rode out from the woods and shook hands with him.

It was all out now. Our canteen friend was nothing more or less than one of the enemy's scouts. There was some swearing, and a fierce cracking of muskets just then, but the two, after a momentary pause, walked slowly and deliberately back into the forest, and were soon lost to sight.

While Hamilton stood there reflecting upon this mysterious affair, and explaining the nature of his acquaintance with this man to the infantry, who now regarded the astute forager with some suspicion, a body of cavalry marched down the road and formed in line on the crest of the hill back of the rifle-pit. They remained in this position for a short time, and then, breaking to the right and left, uncovered two or three batteries of artillery, which, as soon as the mounted men had passed from their front, opened savagely upon our lines.

The astute forager immediately decamped .

I do not know how long I remained asleep under the tree; at all events, I was awakened by the trampling of horses' feet, and heard, as in a dream, the command:

"Forward into line—trot—by section right wheel—in battery!"

This was sufficient. Jumping to my feet, and looking around, I saw the artillery execute the movement, and unlimber for action. I mounted my horse, and awaited developments for a few moments, but no enemy appeared. I turned my horse's head towards the road, and left this spot.

It was now late in the day; I began to feel hungry, and concluded to ride off the main road and forage for the inner man. Judging from what I had seen, it occurred to me I had better keep shy of the Richmond side, and so turned to the left along a rarely-travelled path. About half a mile from the main road I met two colored girls, who were coming down to sell the soldiers some cornbread and buttermilk, and from these I purchased heavily. Though a different dish from that provided by our worthy Uncle, I think I did that meal justice. After this, I concluded to take a short scout off to the right, or Richmond side of the road, but kept within hearing distance of our trains. The forest was dense, but by and by I reached a clearing, and found that so far I had kept a parallel course with the road.

Just then a battery dashed up, followed by infantry at double quick. Great consternation was apparent among the teamsters, who began to whip their horses into a run. The artillery wheeled into position and unlimbered. As I was directly in front of the pieces, I put spurs to my pony and attempted to reach an interval between the guns. Bobby, when he felt this unusual attack upon his sides, made a brave effort, apparently knowing that the application of the keen rowels was a signal of serious import. We had barely passed the line of fire when the guns opened with a savage roar.

At Bay on The James River

The trains were hurrying along to Malvern Hill, and I followed them. As we emerged from the woods into the open country where the road ascends the plateau, the scene presented was a memorable one. Along the right some soldiers were busily felling trees, apparently for the purpose of forming a sort of abattis along the edge of the forest as an obstruction to the enemy's advance. The broad open plain which forms the top of the hill was crowded with wagons. Their numbers were constantly augmented until, in a short time, the whole expanse seemed a mass of moving trains. On the right of the road stood a white frame house, which was now filled with our wounded soldiers, and over which a hospital flag was displayed. A short distance past this house, and beyond a narrow strip of woodland, our eyes rested upon the goal of our army—the beautiful James river, with its broad bosom dotted with densely wooded islands.

My first impulse was to ride down to the river and see the pontoon bridge. A large number of wagons were passing down a tolerably steep road which wound around the hill on the right as we faced the river, and these I followed. Alas! for human expectations. No pontoon bridge was visible. No gunboats were lying in the stream opposite the hill. The trains were quietly going into camp upon the low bottom lands. From the absence of all preparations to cross the bridge, I was forced to the conclusion that the story of a campaign on the south side of the James was a harmless myth.

The sun went down behind the forests beyond the river. Feeling lonely amid the multitudes around me, I led my tired pony into a field, and turned him loose to browse upon its rich burden of clover. Several artillerymen were here, with their overworked horses. Two hours later I gathered together the few broken crackers that yet remained to me, tied

173

my pony to a shrub, spread my blanket upon the grass, and laid down for the night.

I did not rest well. The disappointment in not finding a bridge across the river, the tearing down of all the bright castles I had built of our glorious successes in the Richmond campaign; the realization that, instead of a victory, we had really sustained a disastrous defeat; the grim conviction that the struggle was not yet over, that the enemy was in great force in our rear, and an impassible river in our front—these were reflections not well calculated to induce repose. I was much disturbed, too, by the constant arrival of teams. These were crowding into the fields all around the spot I had selected, and likely at any moment to be driven over me. The doleful cries of the mules and the curses of the drivers mixed in a hideous concert. Some time after midnight, however, I fell asleep from sheer exhaustion.

The sun was shining in my face when I awakened next morning. My pony had pulled himself loose from the shrub, but was quietly grazing near my rustic couch. The artillerymen had disappeared.

The lowlands were crowded by teams. Our train was not among them, but a member of Company K, whom I accidentally met, stated that it was near a brick house which stood on the hill; this house was afterwards known to me as Crew's Mansion.

Thither I made my way along the road by which I had reached the river the day before. Here I found numerous guards, who were permitting wagons to pass, but stopping all infantry soldiers, and turning them back to the hill. I found our wagons at the spot designated. The horses were unhitched, and fastened one to each wheel. After procuring supplies for my pony and myself, I rode over to the brick house, selected a shady spot under a tree, tied my horse to a limb, sat down with my back against its trunk to contemplate the scene, but presently fell over asleep on the ground, exhausted by the nervous excitement and loss of rest the night before.

I do not know how long I thus slumbered. I was awakened by hearing a colored man exclaim that "there were a hundred thousand men out there." When I arose I saw several members of McClellan's staff at the Crew Mansion, from which I inferred that the commanding general had there established his headquarters. Thinking that, perhaps, this remark had reference to reinforcements by river from, the north to our army—a hope that more than once had presented itself to my mind—I rode out upon the great plain to see for myself.

The scene unfolded to my view was at once inspiriting and exciting. On a field not over a mile square in extent, fully seventy thousand men were massed, ready for battle, with their flags floating proudly upon the breeze, and their muskets gleaming like a forest of steel in the sunlight. Stretching along the brow of the hill facing the northwest, with their gunners standing around them, were about one hundred and fifty pieces of artillery, from the tenpounder up to the siege Parrott, silent as yet, but unlimbered for action. Off towards the north, near the white frame house, which I had noticed as a hospital the day before, were a few wagons moving hastily from the presence of some of the enemy's skirmishers, who were located in the dense woods on the Richmond side of the road. As far as I could see on the northwest, the lowlands were covered by a dense forest of pines. Off to the northeast an open country extended for perhaps two miles, seemingly unoccupied except by a small force of cavalry. These were so far away that I could not determine to whose force they belonged. They were apparently dismounted, and standing to horse. The attitude of the whole army was one of evident expectation.

The United States forces were now standing at bay. The enemy was on one side—a numerous, energetic force, as we had reason to believe from the operations of the last few days—and the great river on the other. To lose here was to lose all. The storm which had beaten against the Army of the Potomac for the past six days would now exhaust itself or annihilate that organization. It is a curious fact that the men in ranks felt hopeful here; no one seemed to realize that a disaster had occurred, and in the action now impending appeared to expect the enemy to be badly beaten. The grand old army seemed to have risen in its strength, like Sampson of old, to shake off its relentless pursuers and scatter them to the winds.

The gunboats on the James now began throwing ponderous shells into the dense woods on the lowlands northwest of the hill, their fire being directed apparently by a signal officer, who had mounted one of the buildings at headquarters. A few artillery shots from the enemy came down the road from the direction of White Oak swamp, striking the ground, throwing up clouds of dust, and then rebounding savagely into the air clear over the heads of our troops. The head of a column of confederate infantry appeared at the edge of the woods at the right and rear of the white frame house, but disappeared into the forest under the fire of one of our batteries.

I rode over to the brow of the hill on the west, to the left of our line of cannon, and took a survey of the country beyond, expecting to see some signs of the enemy for whom such vast preparations had been made by our army. Not a soldier was to be seen. The slope of the hill descended with an easy grade to the bottom, and here the woods bounded it from north to south like an impenetrable fringe. This forest stretched to the river bank, and, looking toward the west, seemed illimitable in extent. From this timber, judging from the ample provision that had been made, the chief confederate attack was expected, and into their depths the great shells from the gunboats dropped at regular intervals.

While I was sitting here looking sharply into the woods for the appearance of the enemy, and wondering where the confederates were hidden, a cloud of smoke suddenly rolled up from under the edge of the timber at the foot of the slope, just at the point where the road leading from the hill towards the west entered the woods, and a shell came whistling toward and past me, so close that I fancied the air was hot upon my face. I bowed low upon my pony's neck, but had barely done so before another and another came, so rapidly in succession that I did not dare to raise my head. A glance down the hill revealed a bluish white cloud, which had settled along the treetops. Presently, there was a momentary lull, and during it, I took the precaution to retire from the exposed point.

I had retraced but a few steps when the guns all along our line became engaged. Their reverberations shook the solid earth. The roar was absolutely terrific. In a few minutes a great cloud rested upon this portion of the line effectively veiling from sight the operations in front and beyond them.

The fire of one confederate battery was directed upon the solitary man who waved his flag from his station on the top of the house at headquarters. That the success of this individual in directing the fire from the gunboats was a wonderful annoyance to the enemy was clearly evident from the savage efforts made to dislodge him. Shells burst all around his person with such rapidity that at times he would be lost from sight in the smoke, and I was in doubt about his fate, but that flag was seen to appear again, moving with increased energy. I could not help admiring the gallant bearing of this unknown man. He did not act as if "weary of his life," but with a vigor which showed that he gloried in his perilous position.

Before the battle had fairly begun, my attention was attracted to a

176

scene unusual upon such occasions. A band of music, which was discoursing stirring strains, was located not far from the brick mansion, and close by it some cavalry patrols were gathering up infantry stragglers and placing them in ranks, preparatory to marching to the front. About twelve hundred men were thus collected, whose spirits were so aroused by the delicious music that they marched away with loud cheers.

I rode over towards the center of the field to a large tree. I dismounted, and from this comfortable position watched the progress of the fight. Owing to the points occupied by the enemy's batteries—they were so much lower than those held by our troops, and consequently their shots flew upward at an angle, and passed clear over our army—but little damage was done by their fire.

The position of our army on Malvern Hill was a strong one, as against an advance from the quarter from which that attack by the confederates begun, although, if it had been made from the northeast, the result might have been different. From the latter point their artillery could have swept our masses on the open plain, with an effect which I shudder to contemplate. A disorganized host of seventy thousand men dashing in a panic down the steep hill towards the river would have completed a calamity unparalleled in modern history.

While I was intently watching the changing phases of the battle, two infantrymen ran to the spot where I stood, deposited their guns beside me, and threw themselves on the ground. For a moment I could not divine the meaning of their curious movement, but, on looking in the direction from whence they came, saw through it all. The cavalry were still gathering stragglers and sending them to the front. These men proposed to assume that they were under my charge as prisoners, and thus check the pursuit of the relentless mounted men.

"We are completely worn out." said they; "We have had nothing to eat for three days, and can scarcely stand up."

Being a straggler myself on these memorable days, without any commanding officer except the regimental quartermaster, who had not been visible more than once or twice since the retreat began, and with whom it was an utter impossibility to keep in contact, I suggested that I possessed no power to protect them.

"Never mind that." they responded; "You need not say a word. We are your prisoners, and that is sufficient."

The dreaded guards came along, looked at us sharply, and then passed on without saying a word, to the great delight of my "captives." As at

177

that time the fight was progressing favorably, their individual presence at the rear was perhaps of no especial detriment to the cause, though, of course, wrong in principle.

The battle continued throughout the afternoon, but by sundown it was clearly evident that the confederates had exhausted themselves, and that the storm of the past six days had indeed culminated and spent its force. They were repulsed at all points with considerable loss, and the Army of the Potomac, as if to show the world how easily it could hold its own, was victorious without even half an effort. It stamped the assertion that it suffered defeats from a want of prowess on its part as a base lie, and today, had it been under the control of a brave, vigorous soldier, would have driven its enemies into their entrenchments at Richmond. The heaviest of the firing was over before dark, though a desultory contest between skirmishers was kept up until late at night.

I was now constrained to resort to my own resources for food for myself and pony. The rations at the train had been exhausted by the constant drain of the past week, and the presence of a large body of hungry men in a few hours rendered the country utterly destitute of provisions. Just before dark I left the hill, and rode down along the bottom to the vicinity of my stopping place of the night before. Another clover field stretched its inviting limits before us, and, tearing down the fence, I led Bobby among the great masses of grass. We were both happy now—the pony whinnying at the prospect of an abundance of pasturage, and the Common Soldier at seeing the horse show in his peculiar way his great satisfaction. To procure water it was necessary to ride yet another half mile where we found a nice running stream in which we severally quenched our individual thirsts. Though not so cold as I could have desired, still it was excellent.

It was very dark before we left the brook. In my perambulations to secure a high and dry spot beside some shrub to which I could fasten my pony, I became somewhat bewildered, and was unable to distinguish one thing from another in my surroundings. All at once, as if he had been brought in contact with a stone wall, so hard and so rigid did he brace his limbs, the pony stopped. Not a step further would he move. To all my entreaties and persuasions and gently applications of spurs he maintained a decided though taciturn opposition. Nothing remained but to dismount, and investigate the difficulty. An examination showed that he had planted his forefeet within half a yard of a deep ditch, into which another step would have hurled horse and rider to unknown depths. My gratitude to my pony for this fresh evidence of his wisdom and care was unbounded. I patted him on the head and neck, and said:

"You were wiser than I, my poor child. While I was half angry with you for stopping, you were trying to save my life. You must overlook my harsh treatment."

As was his wont at every opportunity, the little fellow rubbed his head against me with affectionate vigor, showing that, whatever might be his fault, a vindictive recollection of past wrong was not one of them. Leading him some distance from the spot, I threw off his saddle and turned him loose to use his own blanket, took my last cracker from my haversack and devoured it, rolled myself up to sleep hungry but happy. About midnight I awakened, and found Bobby lying beside me asleep, evidently satisfied with himself and the world.

The next morning my pony took another feast of grass, while I filled my empty stomach with blackberries, of which there was an abundance. After we had partially satisfied our hunger, I saddled up and started to find the train. I could hear cannon booming in the distance, apparently down the river, and bodies of troops were marching in that direction; so I concluded that must be the route I ought to pursue. Two miles from my bivouac of the night before I emerged from the woods upon a great plain, on one side of which there was a large drove of cattle and a vast number of wagons, and on the other, with their lines running across into woods, and with batteries in position, were some sixteen or twenty thousand men, seemingly waiting for an attack. The gunboats were throwing shells over the heads of our troops into the forest in their front, in which the enemy were supposed to be; but if any confederates were there, they remained invisible.

A short distance beyond this I met one of our musicians, who informed me where the train was to be found. That evening I reached Harrison's Landing, where our party had parked the wagons in an orchard, pitched their tents, and were rejoicing in plenty of rations and horse feed, which they had drawn from the stores that had already been landed from the numerous transports lying in the river at this point. Our horses received a good grooming, and the men indulged in a bath in the river. That night we felt like a new set of creatures.

Thus closed our wanderings, which had begun at a point near Coal Harbor, and ended at Harrison's Landing. The Army of the Potomac had been transformed from a besieging force into a besieged one; instead of encompassing the enemy within four miles of his capital city we were

179

cut off from our own, and crowded together on the bank of a great river twenty or thirty miles from our original objective point. The labor, expense, and sacrifice of the nation had apparently been in vain. We had been defeated in a series of actions in each of which we had really been victorious; and all this the result of a curious timidity which held dominant sway in the breast of one man.

Through all the times of suffering and death there seemed to be in the ranks of the army no lack of confidence in McClellan. I did not hear a single soldier express any misgiving as to the abilities of their commanding general. His amiable manners to all the common soldiers, his anxiety for their personal comfort, and his humane treatment of the wounded won for him a love that was blind to everything but the man. This was the great secret of his hold upon the affection of the army. I had seen him vacate his own tent to make accommodations for poor mutilated fellows; turn from the brilliant crowd of officers around him, to speak to them as they limped by, always with a kind word for every one.

Upon one occasion I was riding along past a train of wagons, picking my way very leisurely, when I became conscious that someone was riding behind me. I did not look around, however, but kept on, stopping at one moment to look at something; catching hold of limbs of trees at another—in short, taking my time in a literal sense. After awhile I swung off to one side into an open space, and then saw, to my great astonishment, the general ride past me. He had kept behind me all the while, stopping when I stopped—the path was too narrow to permit him to pass without crowding—and accommodating himself to my whimsical gait in a way that demonstrated a remarkable degree of patience. No one was with him. Had many second lieutenants occupied his saddle at that time, I could have expected a volley of oaths and curses, and peremptory commands to get out of the way.

What a power, resulting from this happy disposition towards his common soldiers, could General McClellan have wielded on the field of battle, had it not been for that unfortunate timidity! Their enthusiasm in and love for him was not of a light character to be dispelled by threatening danger, but deep-seated and enduring.

Rain began to fall during the night, and by morning the earth was sodden and miry. Shortly after daybreak a few cannon shots were heard in the distance, and the bursting of shells just outside of our camp disturbed our equanimity. It was evident that our relentless foe was following us up, and proposed to drive us into the river if possible. The army did not seem to me to be in a favorable position to resist attack. The masses of men huddled together over these fields seemed to possess no organization. The ground was low, and commanded by that on which were located the enemy's guns, while a range of heights on the north, if occupied by the confederates in force, would form a barrier on that side of formidable proportions. Fortunately, however, for the Army of the Potomac, the battery which had begun firing upon us was not supported, but seems to have been pushed to that point by an adventurous confederate spirit, and was captured by some fresh troops sent here from the valley of Virginia, with cannoneers, horses, drivers, and caissons, and the whole marched triumphantly into our lines within a short time after the firing of their first shot.

That afternoon we were ordered out—there were sixty men belonging to the Sixth Cavalry here—to go on an unknown mission. In the confusion my forage cap mysteriously disappeared, and in its place appeared a chip hat, around the crown of which was sewed a flaming red band. There was no time to lose, so I donned the hat and rode into the ranks, an object of amusement to the men.

After leaving camp, and reaching the road along which the army had retreated, the scene was one of a painful character. The ground had been worked up into a mass of mud by the wagons, hundreds of which were still straggling toward the landing. They swamped at every few steps, and the men were obliged to wade in and literally lift the wagons forward to harder soil. The poor horses were almost exhausted with their fearful labors. Through the woods and along the road numerous wounded men, pale, haggard, and bloody, toiled on their painful course, while empty ambulances, driven in most instances by colored men, dashed past heedless of the cries of distress that rose from all sides on their appearance from the poor maimed fellows that wanted to be taken up, and followed by curses as they receded from sight. Among these wounded were some with shattered legs who actually crawled upon the muddy ground and dragged their mutilated limbs after them.

There were generals, some with and others without escorts; a few cavalrymen; a few infantry stragglers, some without guns; many contrabands; occasionally a battery of artillery dragged slowly along—I had almost said by horses more dead than alive—all drifting towards the landing. At one place we came upon an old woman and her two sons, both of whom were soldiers. They had stopped by the roadside, and the faithful old mother was cooking their dinner for them. General McClellan rode up just then, and addressed a few questions to this model matron, who said that she had followed her boys ever since they had joined the army, and that she hoped she could remain with them.

At another point we found a wagon train mired, without help, and dismounted and sent it on its way rejoicing—the job was to us, however, a rather unpleasant one. A few miles further on a halt was ordered, and we marched into a field and dismounted to rest our horses. I tied Bobby to a limb and crossed over the field to some fallen timbers, where I found many members of the Pennsylvania Reserves cooking their rations. The troops were recounting the fearful scenes through which they had passed since the morning of the 26th of June. Tears came to the eyes of some as they spoke of their dead comrades. While there was sadness among them, there was no despondency; a sort of sullen determination to fight out the war was plainly manifested. I found this feeling everywhere among the soldiers—the same unconquerable disposition to struggle for the cause they had espoused. Cheer upon cheer arose whenever the commanding general made his appearance—a tumultuous display of enthusiasm that would make one unacquainted with the circumstances imagine they had been led to achieve great victories instead of suffering disastrous defeats.

Towards evening our party returned to camp at Harrison's Landing, having accomplished nothing except to fatiguing our horses, unless the assistance rendered that solitary train of wagons should be deemed as something. Our animals were taken to the river and relieved from the great masses of mud that had enveloped them from the tips of their ears to the ends of their tails, and then rubbed dry and fed. The soldiers also took a bath, and did justice to their frugal rations on this eventful Fourth-of-July eve.

The regiment did not rejoin us until about the middle of July. It had been cut off by the confederates in their rapid advance against the right wing of the army and, with some infantry and horse artillery, retreated upon Yorktown. These had done good service, however,—had succeeded in drawing a large force of the enemy away from Porter by showing a front which indicated a force of quadruple the strength they really possessed, and aided in their deception by building a great number of fires at night at points inside of their picket lines. At White House they helped remove the stores to the transports, and destroyed what could not be shipped. It was from the flames of these burning munitions of war that the White House is supposed to have caught fire and been reduced to ashes. The command enjoyed itself hugely among the abandoned sutler's stores, indulging in wine and brandies, and procuring almost every man a white felt hat. The white hats had, however, to be abandoned in time, as these memoirs will in due form relate.

A day or two before they arrived we had moved down to Westover, a few miles below Harrison's Landing. As the regiment rode into camp there were hearty greetings exchanged between the bronzed boys in blue. All were glad to meet their old comrades again. There was the querulous Dutchman, Draker, still talking about that everlasting "brother and nickel maul;" there was Old Blue, who had not deserted yet; there was the benign Croy; the big whiskered Scot, Wallace; Charlton, "The Pittsburg boy;" the genial Evans; the romantic Ferguson; the once shadowy but now rather burly Todd; the deliberate Schwab; the resolute McMasters; the redoubtable Schumacher; the dapper Frobin, who no longer wore his tall crowned hat as in those days at the recruiting office. Flascher, "the horse's doctor," had been lost on the retreat. I might as well state that this individual, like bread cast upon the waters, returned to us after many days, having retreated on his own account overland to the Potomac river at a point not far from Aquia creek, reaching our lines in safety.

Schumacher had an adventure since we separated in the camp beyond James' Mills, which I deem worthy of record here. On the memorable 26th of June a part of the company—perhaps a dozen men—were sent out on one of the roads beyond our lines at Mechanicsville, with orders to tear up the culverts and bridges and otherwise blockade and impede the enemy's advance. While hard at work upon a small bridge over a stream, the party were startled by the voice of an old colored woman, who ran out of a cabin and shouted, in stentorian tones:

"Lord! Massa, de rebels are comin'!"

Of course there was a "mounting in hot haste" just then, and a retreat more rapid than graceful. It happened, however, that our Teutonic friend, the redoubtable Schumacher, discovered after they had galloped a few rods that he had forgotten his jacket—which, owing to the extreme heat, he had thrown upon a log—and, true to his national instincts of economy, rode back alone after it. The balance of the party kept straight toward camp. Schumacher reached the bridge again, and drawing his sabre from its scabbard, made a lunge at the jacket to catch it on the point of his blade, and thus raise it to his left hand. During this act he

183

heard the sharp crack of a gun on the hill above him, followed by the "wish" of a bullet, and on looking up saw three mounted confederates coming down the slope at full speed. Schumacher was obliged to abandon his jacket. He took no time to return his sword to its scabbard, but wheeled his horse and dashed off at full gallop in the direction taken by his comrades.

Now began a race second, perhaps, only to that of Israel Putnam and his British pursuers. Up hill and down hill, through woods and through clearings, over logs and amid stumps, each party bringing their horses to their utmost speed, flew this blue bird and the three gray hawks. Schumacher happened to have a fleet animal, and soon distanced two of the confederates, but the other constantly gained upon him, and by and by his horse's outstretched nose was upon the right flank of our Teutonic friend.

Schumacher, who still clung to his sabre, turned partially in his saddle, and giving expression in his cracked voice to an epithet I will leave unrecorded here, administered a severe blow on that outstretched nose. This checked the animal to the great disgust of the confederate, who applied an epithet of similar import to Schumacher. Why Schumacher did not draw his revolver, or why his pursuer made no attempt to use one, can only be accounted for by supposing that both labored under great excitement, and did not think of these weapons. Possibly the confederate may have desired to capture his prisoner alive, thinking to thus gain information as to army movements on our side. It is also possible that Schumacher, remembering his experience in target practice at Camp East of Capitol, deemed it safest after all to keep hold of his sword, and not trust the—in his hands—unreliable pistol.

The check given to the horse of the confederate was but momentary. Again the distance between them began to diminish. They had left the main road now, and were dashing blindly across a field covered with low pines. The crisis was rapidly approaching—the confederate had closed up the gap between them—and Schumacher's horse strikes a great ditch that extends across their path, and with one tremendous spring clears it. Not so fortunate, however, the confederate. His stud falls short, and strikes the bottom of the ditch "all in a heap." That ended the chase.

Schumacher, in the excitement, had lost his way, and now made an effort to find his old camping ground, supposing that there he should discover the regiment. Here, however, he found Jackson's corps of Confederates, who were just deploying their lines of battle for an attack upon Porter's flank. The absence of his blue jacket saved him. His presence was not noticed, and, halting but a moment, until he could gather together his somewhat scattered senses, he galloped toward the left and front of the enemy's lines, and soon after found himself in the midst of one of the federal zouave regiments. An hour later he rejoined the command.

To see Schumacher's distended eyes as he related this adventure, and to hear the intonations of his cracked voice at the exciting parts, added tenfold to its interest and amusement.

The camp at Westover will long live in the memories of those who endured its misery during those eventful July days. I should have used the plural of the term, for our woes were manifold. There was the extreme heat; the fierce flies during the day and the savage mosquitos during the night, and the sultry air was loaded with poison from the carcasses and offal of dead animals all around us. Our horses died rapidly from some peculiar disease, a vast swarm of the vicious flies settling on the poor brutes like a cloud when attacked by it; and a majority of the men were suffering constantly from chronic diarrhea, and other complaints incident to our pestilential surroundings. During the day the hot sun baked down upon our quarters till they glowed like a furnace, and we were glad when night came to shelter us for awhile from its relentless rays.

For a short time we were obliged to depend upon the springs that spouted up out of the ground along the river for our water supply, which was limited on account of the large number of persons dependent upon them; but one day nine men of Company F, under the leadership of Hamilton, the astute forager, determined to make an effort to rectify this want by sinking a well close to their cookhouse. They went out to the forest, and cut wooden forks, and improvised a windlass, which they set up at the proper spot, and procured a rope, which they fastened by the middle to the windlass roller and to each end of this rope they attacked a camp kettle. The work began at nine o'clock that morning; the squad was "told off" into their reliefs, and by nightfall these nine men had dug and successfully completed a well twenty-seven feet deep out of which the company had the satisfaction of using water with which to cook their breakfasts the next morning. The success attending this experiment encouraged other companies to make like attempts, and though they all obtained water, none dug their wells in the same number of hours. I considered this little piece of sapping and mining quite an achievement.

An incident occurred during our encampment here which was the occasion of much comment among the men. There joined the command a private named Carpenter, whose peculiarities were the object of conversation on many occasions among his comrades, whose opinions of him, as a soldier were altogether unfavorable. For some reason or other, however, he seemed to be regarded as a sort of favorite among the commissioned officers, and was soon invested with the stripes of a corporal, over the heads of others whose claims to the position were thought to be superior by the men in the ranks. Following this, after a very short interval, came a commission from president Lincoln as second lieutenant in the Sixth Cavalry, and assigning him to one of the companies. This unmerited promotion of a man whose knowledge of military life must at best have been very limited, while the regiment possessed a large number of sergeants whose terms of service already numbered many years in succession, whose practical military capacity were superior to many who had won honors at West Point, was very demoralizing, and demonstrated that, after all, hard and honorable service in the ranks was likely to be disregarded at Washington as worthy of reward. This demoralization was increased when it was afterwards whispered among the enlisted men that Carpenter was a nephew of General Dix and it was felt that the influence of the latter had something to do with this commission. I presume the records at the War Office will show the truth of this feeling. He is at this writing a captain in the Tenth Cavalry, United States Army.[1]

I have no comment to make upon this appointment further than to say that I believe many of our disasters during the war are to be traced to just such cases. Apart from everything else, it had a bad effect upon the men in that it discouraged attempts to win commissions by distinguished gallantry on the field of battle. After all our boasted superiority over other countries in the democratic administration of our military affairs, the men actually raised in the service from the ranks for meritorious conduct alone were few in number. I do not include the announced promotions after the war was over. These were brevet ranks and

---

[1]   While Sidney Davis may not have thought much of the military knowledge of Louis Henry Carpenter, who joined the Sixth Cavalry on November 20, 1861, and who was promoted to Second Lieutenant less than a year later on September 20, 1862, but the army apparently did. By the end of the Civil War, Carpenter was the colonel of a volunteer regiment. He made the army his career and retired as a Brigadier General of volunteers.

attached to the names of those who had been commissioned officers.[2]

I make extracts from the following letter, dated at Camp of Cavalry Reserve, near Westover, Virginia, July 10,1862, which will show the feelings that animated the Common Soldier at this stage of his military career:

Dear Old Friends—

I was glad to receive your letter, though saddened by the news it brought me of Levi's death. I should have been glad to have seen him before he died, for I esteemed him highly and loved him. The confidence he evinced in me when I enlisted that I should faithfully perform the duties allotted to me to the best of my ability, and the kind words he spoke at our parting on the wharf at the Old Mill, will not soon be forgotten. I have thought of him and of home hundreds of time since I left it—times when I was placed in perilous and responsible positions—and, when I felt that I was the representative of the old homestead I grew proud, and determined to allow no reproach to fall upon it through me. While I have not volunteered to perform duties not assigned to me, I have not failed to obey any order given me, however perilous the service designated.

Since the 4th of May the troops attached to the army have participated in thirteen skirmishes and ten pitched battles resulting in a loss on both sides of fully sixty thousand men, dead and wounded.

From sickness and fighting I think Richmond has already cost us over thirty thousand men . . . . I have beheld such scenes of suffering as memory shall not soon forget.

I do not want you to think we are conquered here yet.

It appears that the enemy fought with the greatest desperation, and it is rumored that whiskey was freely used among them to stimulate their courage; but this I doubt. I have not much confidence in liquor under the circumstances; the intense excitement to which one is subject, unless he had imbibed an overwhelming quantity, would be likely to sober him up; in the contingency above mentioned it is not likely he would be fit for much as a fighter.

It is related that in one instance, when a battery was attacked by the confederates, the support of which had been withdrawn to another point, they came up in masses in its front, carrying a flag, which was shot down four times in succession by the discharges of the guns. On each occasion, however, it was

---

[2]   Brevet rank was, essentially, a reward for meritorious service. Until the Civil War, there were no military decorations and brevet rank served to notice gallantry, bravery, etc. In 1862, the Congressional Medal of Honor became the only decoration in the army (though there were several unofficial decorations handed out by individual army, corps and division commanders). After the Civil War, new decorations were established and eliminated the utility of brevet rank. The last brevet rank was given out during World War I.

pushed still further along until the pieces were wrested from our men by sheer force.

It is hard to tell when I shall see you again—perhaps never. I feel disposed to fight it out to the bitter end. If I am killed, all I ask is to be kindly remembered at the old homestead, and talked about in the sweet June evenings, when the moon is full and the crickets and katydids and black birds sing in the hearth and rose bushes and the cedar tree in the garden.

Good bye. God bless you all. Pat Caesar on the head for me, and if old gray Tom is still alive, give him some salt in my name.

Caesar was my old favorite dog—the companion of my boyhood—and gray Tom was the blind horse I used to drive upon the farm.

One day, while we were at the river watering our horses, I saw a member of Company I stealthily approaching one of his sergeants, who was sitting on his horse a short distance out in the stream, apparently unsuspecting the evil in store for him. Presently he threw a large round boulder, which struck the upper part of the latter's head, and ricochetted off into the water. A stream of blood spouted up ten or fifteen inches high from the wound. The sergeant, who was a large, powerful man, reeled a moment in his saddle, as if stunned, and then wheeled his horse toward shore. The soldier who threw the stone stood a moment, as if hesitating, and then attempted to run away, but the sergeant rushed his horse against him, knocked him headlong upon the ground, and then dismounted and thrashed him soundly. The sympathy of the men in this case was entirely with the sergeant.

The long, hot, weary month of July drew to an end at last. I have some reason to recollect the night of the 1st of August. The weather was very sultry, and the mosquitos more than usually abundant. We had talked in our tent until a late hour, and finally became quiet, and I had settled down into a sort of feverish sleep, when the sound of a cannon, which fell upon the air like a clap of thunder, startled me from all sense of propriety. I sprang to my feet, and thrust my head through the opening of the tent just in time to see a great flash of fire blaze up from the opposite side of the river and a curious looking jet of flame going through the air till it reached some distance inland on our side, and then, bursting into a broad bright sheet, disappearing into total darkness; this was followed by two other stunning roars in succession. The one report was from the gun; the other from the shell it had thrown. These explosions were multiplied an indefinite number of times before I awakened from my state of bewilderment. The line of fire seemed to me to be two or three miles in length, and to be kept up by from twenty to thirty pieces of artillery. The air seemed to be full of screeching missiles of death.

It is possible that I was not scared; I did not take time to put on any more clothing—a confession which may throw some light on the vexed question. It occurred to me intuitively that the lowest ground I could find was the spot for me to select; the broad bottom upon which our camp was located was so very level that not the least sort of ravine could be found in which to take shelter. Besides this drawback we appeared to be coming in for our full share of these terrible shells, and whatever was to be done must be done quickly.

I started for the river shore at a gait which was, if not a run, then a rather rapid walk. At the lower end of the company quarters another object, dressed in the habiliments of the grave, it appeared to me, with a face as colorless as the apparel, came into a sharp collision with me. That form dressed in the habiliments of the grave was a solid substance—some other individual, who seemed to be moved by the same inspiration which controlled me, only he was taking a route at right angles with mine, and was making for Herring Creek swamp, on the east of our camp.

"Where are you going, sir?" I asked, in a tone of command, that he might think I was an officer, and not the least frightened.

"I—I—am—am—"

It was getting too hot—decidedly too hot—for me to wait longer for the termination of this singular speech or I should have stayed to hear the end of it that I might have recorded it for the benefit of posterity. My decision of character—this is my stronghold, my forte, this decision of character—prompted me to complete the journey upon which I had set out, and I rushed immediately to the river shore. By this time I discovered that there were many of my opinion—a great crowd of half-dressed soldiers were swarming down the banks, and there intermingled with them a large party of contrabands, of all sizes, ages, and conditions. The latter element of this disorderly mass very properly thought, and not a few of them remarked, "Lets follow de soldiers—dey knows where to go." If anybody should know where to go in time of danger, soldiers ought—though from their actions on this eventful occasion they were the least bit puzzled. After the crowd reached the shore it streamed along the water's edge and swept down the river as far as it could, being finally intercepted at the cape where Herring Creek joins its stream to that of the James. When it could go no further it floated up to the end of the cape like a great mass of animated drift wood, lying in heaps upon the wet sand. It was amusing after all to see this terrified lot of wretched human beings, in their blind rush for safety, tumble head over heels upon the piles of offal that had lodged along the shore, and into which their toes would become entangled. If it had been a proper period in which to indulge in fisticuffs we would have enjoyed a plentiful number; but the warriors could take only a sufficient length of time to let out a vigorous oath, and then kept straight on. Our band was augmented in numbers by a crowd of white civilians, who swarmed off the transports in the river in all sorts of ways and by all sorts of methods. Our little colony at the cape grew to respectable proportions in the course of fifteen or twenty minutes—if the word respectable could be applied in any manner to that miscellaneous populace. It was a sort of republic, in which there was no privilege denied on account of race, color, age, sex, or previous condition of servitude—all shared alike in the terror and discomforts of the situation.

We had been here thirty minutes, perhaps, when suddenly there burst forth a great flash of lightning from the bosom of the waters just beyond us, as it seemed, followed by a deafening roar, and our party dropped upon the ground in a state of great consternation. To our affrighted imaginations it appeared that the enemy had opened a fresh battery, and that the sense of security we were just beginning to feel was about to be knocked to pieces by the cruel iron; but the fortunate discovery was soon made that this gun was on board one of our war vessels, which displayed no lights, and had up till now been lost to our sight in the dull background of forest and shaded river. The huge shell hurtled through the air up the stream and burst in close proximity to one of the enemy's batteries, no doubt developing in the minds of the confederates operating the piece a new sensation. As soon as the missile exploded the silence that had hitherto been observed on board the boat was broken, and I could hear the voice of one, whom I suppose was the commander of the vessel, speak in terms of commendation of the gunner who sent it on its errand. Other guns followed in quick succession, their huge mouths adding very materially to the grand chorus of artillery fire.

By this time some of our field batteries with the army had managed to get in position, and returned the confederate shots about gun for gun. From our safe location the scene was a rather interesting one. The vivid flashes all along the river on both sides, and from our gunboats, two or more of which had been brought into action, lighting up the sky and surrounding country—the apparently endless succession of darkness and woods and fields and river with their lurid tints and murky shadows; the jets of fire passing and repassing through the air from one side of the stream to the other; the constant roar of guns which was redoubled by the echoes coming back from the surrounding low hills, that made me think at one time that a general attack was in progress along our front on the north as well as at our rear on the south; the shrieks of the shells, like those we imagine of lost souls, impressing with a sort of superstition in spite of our practical knowledge as to the causes—all these sights and sounds, and the sensations and imaginings they awakened, formed an exhibition at once costly and rare, to be witnessed by comparatively few people at long intervals of time.

It was evident that this attack by the enemy was intended to destroy our transports in the river rather than to damage the army directly; but the promptitude with which the lights on board the vessels were extinguished saved them by bewildering the confederate gunners and disturbing their range. After the first two or three shots the firing was remarkably wild.

The cannonading lasted perhaps an hour. When it had subsided partially I returned to camp, passing through that of contrabands on my way. The most of these poor people evidently thought their last day—or night—had arrived. From almost every tent that I passed there arose a prayer—from their heart of hearts I doubt not—the burden of which was:

"Lord, keep de bombshells above us!"

From the way the enemy's guns tossed their missiles—two or three hundred feet high—I am almost tempted to believe that their supplications were literally effective.

When I reached camp my expectation was that many of the horses and perhaps some of the men—though the latter were not tied fast like the former, and consequently able to run to shelter—were killed and wounded. Strange to say, not a single man of the Sixth Cavalry was injured, and but one horse, which had part of its head carried away by a shell and was killed. Our tent bore the mark of a shell, which had struck with the fuse side, leaving a perfectly shaped black impression upon the canvas, without cutting a thread. Another destroyed a cook's bed, but he was out.

The number of casualties from all this firing on our side was officially stated to be six or seven men; on that of the enemy it is unknown, but

191

probably less, owing to their scattered positions and meager numbers. One or two shots only took effect upon the transports, and the danger from these was very slight. The result of the whole affair may be briefly summed up as a great fight and an immense waste of ammunition.

As a precautionary measure, a battery of thirty-two pounder Parrott guns was installed in a small redoubt on the river bank south of our camp, and trained upon the opposite shore. At dark the command evacuated its quarters, and marched out upon the heights of Evlinton, about two miles north, and just inside our lines of defense, and bivouacked for the night. The scene from this elevated plateau on this night was certainly beautiful and suggestive. Above us the clear sky was full of twinkling stars; on the plains below us burned the campfires of eighty thousand men. On the bosom of the broad river rested a great fleet of boats, their forms dim and shadowy in the dull gloom, and beyond rose the wild woodlands. To the north of us we could only look into the dense forests and reflect upon the picture that we knew was there but which we could not see—one that partially was a counterpart of the one around us and visible, but the figures in which were governed by emotions and results the opposite to those of the figures in ours—the positive and negative poles of a sinister electricity, with the mutual properties of relentless destructiveness common to each. It was also painfully curious to reflect that, within the narrow bounds which circumscribed the two armies, there were gathered together a great host of men who, were they dressed in the same uniform, would be indistinguishable one from the other, and yet who, marked on the side by a blue film and on the other by a gray film, were ready to destroy each other without a thought of regret.

A cool, delightful breeze came up the river, and lulled us into a sound and refreshing sleep, from which we were not awakened by the guns of the enemy. I am sure the feeling of the entire command upon our return to our tents the next morning was one of regret, the delicious atmosphere on the heights being so much in contrast with the hot, poisonous air in the camp.

On the evening of the 3rd we again evacuated our quarters and rode out of camp in the delightful anticipation of another night of refreshing and undisturbed sleep on the heights, but in this we were sadly disappointed. Instead of following the road of the night before we marched up the river toward Haxall's Landing, and halted by the roadside, where we were obliged to "stand to horse" until daylight. At an early hour the command returned to camp, a very tired and disgusted body of men to whom the whole proceeding had very much the appearance of a cruel hoax. Another sweltering day was passed in feverish sleep or wretched wakefulness in those glowing tents.

On the same evening the regiment saddled up at the usual hour and marched some distance up the river, and then swung off on the road leading to White Oak swamp. On our way we passed near the camp of the One-Hundred-and-Second Pennsylvania Infantry and to our surprise learned that the division to which they were attached was also under orders to be ready to march on call. As we had now reached a point beyond the range of the guns of the enemy from the south side of the James, the preparatory order to that division confirmed a rumor which had been afloat during the earlier part of the evening; that a movement against the enemy opposite our left flank was intended. Questions addressed to the troops of other divisions encamped along the road revealed the fact that they also were under similar orders, and that the proposed advance, if made, was likely to be a general one.

Our march, which was a weary, monotonous movement over wretched roads and through wretched woods at one time, and across wretched wastes at another, continued, with more or less interruption for several hours. Finally, at perhaps one o'clock in the morning of August 5, there were indications that we would soon stop for the night.

We were riding along leisurely, many of the tired men reeling in their saddles from want of sleep, when there came upon the still damp air a voice so startlingly distinct that it seemed but a few rods away:

"Halt! Who goes there?"

A reply followed promptly:

"Not a friend, damn you!"

Bang!

As the echoes of the gun died away there arose a howl of pain, and in a few moments a private soldier belonging to the Eighth Illinois Cavalry[3]—which regiment, unknown to us, was in the advance—rode past us toward the rear, groaning over a wound in the leg.

A halt until daylight now occurred, the regiment remaining in the road in the order of march, the men dismounting and dropping down upon the ground in front of their horses where they stood, or leading

---

[3]   See Abner Hard, *History of the Eighth Illinois Cavalry Regiment, Illinois Volunteers, During the Great Rebellion*, Aurora, Illinois, privately published, 1868. It may be worth noting that the 8th Illinois Cavalry is frequently credited with opening the Battle of Gettysburg.

them off to one side to avoid being trampled upon, and falling asleep almost as soon as they touched the ground. In a few moments a casual observer might have been led to think that this shadowy column along that dark road was composed of riderless horses exclusively, from the entire absence of visible human beings. These hours of waiting in this sepulchral gloom were solemn ones to me. It was evident a struggle would begin at early dawn, the result of which no one could foresee, and that some of us at least who will it be?—would rest in gloomier shadows upon the setting of another sun. With these saddening thoughts I fell into an uneasy slumber.

It was still dark when the bugler sounded "to horse." The sleepy men sprang to their feet and clambered into their saddles, and in a few moments we were pushing forward at a rapid gait. In a short time we reached a spot from whence arose a sickening stench of dead bodies, and we then knew we were upon some battlefield.

Just as daylight was breaking in the east the sound of cannon was heard in our front, and a shell came crashing through the timber and burst over the left of the regiment. The bugler sounded the trot, and we moved rapidly down a hill for some distance, and then up another, and as we emerged from the woods I saw on the right side of the road a white frame house, now shattered and torn to pieces by shot and musket balls, with scarcely an inch of its weatherboarding that bore no scar, which I recognized as the one I had ridden past on my journey from White Oak swamp to Malvern Hill on the 30th of June. From this I knew where we were.

The confederates occupied the position held by our forces during the battle of July 1. This they had strengthened by a small earthwork, and seemed to hold the hill as a sort of outpost only, for purposes of observation, and numbered perhaps about five hundred men in all, most of whom were infantry, who were supported by four pieces of artillery. The Eighth Illinois Cavalry formed in close column to the right and rear of a strip of woods some distance from and in front of the white frame house, and which served as a screen; one of our light batteries dashed up and unlimbered to the left and rear of the Eighth, and opened a vigorous fire; while the Sixth Cavalry formed in close column in rear of the guns, with drawn sabres, to support them in case the enemy should make an effort to capture the pieces. Our forces having thus taken position, our battery kept at work with a will, though it seemed to me their fire lacked effect, as the enemy's battery was served with marked precision.

The point held by us was favorable to the capture of the enemy in case of the arrival of additional troops of ours to occupy the only outlet for the confederates, which was the road leading through the woods on the west, from which I had seen the battery operate upon the signal officer during the battle of Malvern Hill, and which at this moment was easily accessible to our soldiers. From the vigorous fight they were now making it was evident that they meant to hold the hill as long as possible, though isolated from their army—an additional circumstance in our favor, because it would give time in which to complete our movements.

It was with much mortification, therefore, that we beheld our infantry support, as the head of their column appeared advancing along the White Oak swamp road, file to the left instead of to the right, and deploy across the plain in full view of the enemy. This movement was a grave blunder for several reasons, among which I may mention the unnecessary exposure of the soldiers to the fire from the enemy's guns, the alarm given the confederates upon the display of such a large force, the failure to close the only outlet to their escape, and consequent barrenness of results of our expedition. As other troops appeared they took the same course, apparently being under the same supreme command.

The inevitable consequence followed after a short but vigorous defense, during which the enemy inflicted upon our forces serious loss, they evacuated the position and escaped along the road above mentioned toward Richmond, and left us nothing to repay our waste of strength except the empty redoubt and the consciousness that we had forced them, after the display on our part of a formidable force, to retreat upon their main army, and humiliation at the reflection of how easily we might have captured them all, with their guns. The fault of this mismanagement, it was subsequently stated, rested upon the shoulders of some general said to have been drunk at the time; but whether he was court-martialled and punished I know not.

My sensations during this action were by no means pleasant. To support a battery mounted, and posted in rear of the guns, and to receive the shots from one's enemy without an opportunity to reply, and when one in this quiescent position has plenty of opportunity to reflect upon his chances of having his head knocked off or his stomach torn out or an arm or leg carried away summarily, and without the soothing influences of anesthetics, and where, under the effects of one's religious education, he is led to ponder upon past misdeeds, and their bearing upon the weal or woe of a future existence, which he may soon be in a position to test literally, are, I submit, conditions not to be called desirable. However, here I was, and there was no visible help for it. I found myself, as the enemy's shells burst in the air in front and one and all around us, continually figuring up, in a sort of mathematical daze, the probable angle of flight from the trunk of the missile assumed by the pieces, and the likely load of damage to be sustained by the mass of human beings within their reach. Occasionally 1 would be aroused from this particular reverie by the shock of seeing a shot—or the effects, rather—tearing through a body of horses or men, as was the case in several instances, and during the terror thus inspired I would begin making all sorts of promises to be good in the future if only I was spared this once—promises, I am compelled by candor to confess, that have not been fulfilled and then I would relapse into that sort of mathematical daze again. As a matter of course the men sat with heads bowed low upon their horses' necks, their sense of danger prompting them to lessen to smallest possible fraction the exposed portion of their bodies. Sometimes one would hear an exclamation, apparently wrung from the inmost recesses of some soldier's heart, and breaking forth in an intense, savage sort of way:

"My God! Why don't they let us charge that battery?"

The question would run through one's mind so naturally that one would be led to think that he had himself spoken the words.

To add to the discomfort of our situation the powder smoke from our guns floated back upon us, and mingled with our breath, parching our throats until they seemed to be covered with scales. This intolerable thirst impelled me to ask permission to dismount and go down to a spring that bubbled out of the side of the hill just inside the woods—a few steps away from our ranks and directly in rear of the spot upon which was formed the squadrons of the Eighth Illinois Cavalry—to fill my canteen and this permission was granted with the annexed condition that I should take all the canteens of the company and fill them. This I at once proceeded to do, feeling considerably relieved at the prospect of being for a few moments, at least, out of the line of the enemy's fire.

I had been at the spring for a few moments, and was busily engaged in filling the canteens, when I heard a rustling among the branches of the trees above me, and on looking up my eyes rested upon a queer apparition. One of the horses belonging to the Eighth had been struck on the right foreleg, just below the knee, by a spent shot, which had broken the limb, and he was now walking down the hill towards the spring, reared up on his hind legs in his misery, no doubt trying in his blind way to end the pain of his wounded limb, the one part of which was hanging down helplessly at right angles with the other. As he thus walked his head was up among the branches of the trees. After a few moments the poor creature came down upon his uninjured foreleg, and stood perfectly still.

A short time after I had distributed the canteens to their owners and remounted my horse, and just as the firing had about ceased, an order came to detail a party of thirty men—three from each company—under charge of a sergeant, to go out along the White Oak swamp road and drive up the stragglers that had fallen out from our infantry ranks, as the enemy's cavalry was reported as about to make a demonstration in that locality and capture them. Upon this detail I had the fortune to serve.

Our mission was entirely successful. Scattered along the road for a distance of seven or eight miles, at intervals of from forty to sixty yards apart, sometimes singly, at others in groups of from two to half a dozen, some walking busily along swinging their muskets in a way that showed how well they were enjoying themselves, others cooking their breakfasts on piles of burning rails or sipping the coffee already made, and still more lying wrapped up in their blankets and oblivious to their war-like surroundings in their deep slumbers, we found and gathered up a force of twelve or fourteen hundred men.

It is the settled principle of infantry stragglers to hate cavalry patrols. It is no use to undertake to convince them that you are simply solicitous for their own and the country's good—you cannot disarm their innate dislike. We found this principle reaffirmed on the present occasion. In some instances entreaties and arguments availed nothing; they would not go on; and it was only when we applied, after all persuasion was bound to be in vain, the flats of our sabres with heavy hands to their backs and heads that they were reduced to a state of mind to be impressed with the manifold reasons urged why they should go on and rejoin their regiments.

There were points where the road ran along in full view of the confederate cavalry pickets, which were stretched in a line extending from north to south, and of course the danger of a raid under the circumstances was imminent. The enemy could not but be cognizant of the existing state of affairs, and if an attempt to capture our stragglers was not made, it must have resulted from carelessness or negligence on their part. Perhaps the confederate troops were absorbed by the threatened advance in force of our army on this moving from Malvern Hill towards Richmond to attend to a matter which, though successfully attempted, would prove of no utility in checking our onward march.

A little episode occurred on this occasion which fairly illustrated the alternate fortunes of war. Six confederate cavalrymen, belonging to a North Carolina regiment, surprised and captured three of our infantry stragglers. While the parties were discussing the terms of surrender, three others of our soldiers appeared upon the scene. The condition of affairs was reversed, and the confederates gracefully yielded up their arms. Of the latter they possessed nothing except sabres, and poor ones at that—which in a measure may account for their apparent docility.

Upon our return to the hill we found that the enemy had fled up the New Market road towards Richmond, and that our troops had gone in pursuit, and we followed on after them. About two miles farther we reached a spot that had been the scene of quite a skirmish, in which several on both sides had been killed and wounded. Just beyond this we came upon our command, which had relinquished the chase and was returning towards the hill with the Eighth Illinois and a battery. They reported that the enemy had entirely disappeared from our front.

At the point where the fight had occurred the Sixth Cavalry halted, with two guns, and threw out a strong picket force. Here we remained for some hours undisturbed by the confederates, but towards evening, although no firing was indulged in, our outposts as seen from the reserve manifested a curious restlessness, riding about from place to place, and peering in all directions. A sense of uneasiness seemed to fall upon both officers and men. Half or three-quarters of an hour before dark the first squadron—our carbineers—under the command of Lieutenant Curwen[4] or "Sabreur," as he was popularly known, from the peculiarity of his pronunciation of the word *sabre*, was sent forward again along the New Market road to reconnoitre. When they had reached a point just beyond our pickets, and where on the left of the road the country is open, while on the right a dense forest abuts upon it, the party was fired upon by a force of confederate infantry, which rose to their feet and delivered a full volley upon our unsuspecting men. The enemy's line stretched along the skirt of the forest, on the opposite side of a high, strong fence, parallel with the road, and was inaccessible to a charge of cavalry; but our carbineers, instead of breaking up under the fire of their opponents,

4 There seems to be a minor error here. The officer's name is 2nd Lieutenant Curwen B. McClellan, formerly a sergeant with the 2nd Cavalry, who was appointed 2nd Lieutenant upon the formation of the 6th Cavalry.

wheeled by fours to the right—a movement that brought them into a single rank facing the woods, and began a vigorous fusillade from their Sharp's rifles. The confederates remained but a moment longer, and then fled in the wildest disorder towards the interior of the forest, leaving their dead and wounded behind. Six men of the first squadron were killed during these few moments. Owing to the character of the country through which the enemy had retreated, pursuit by our brave fellows was out of the question, and they retired in good order upon the reserves.

The effect of this encounter was to render our men very vigilant that night, lest a second advance by the enemy should be attempted. The next morning the regiment was withdrawn to the foot of Malvern Hill, with the artillery, but a strong picket force was posted well out on the New Market road to avoid a surprise which all seemed to apprehend. Nearly all that day the enemy continued to maneuver along our front and on our right flank in a way that made us feel uncomfortable, to say the least, creating a feeling of dismal suspense as to his next step.

Towards evening our wagons came up and rations and forage were issued for man and beast. As several hours had passed since a confederate had been visible, a sense of security seemed to pervade the officers, and we were ordered to unsaddle and groom and feed our horses. This duty occupied perhaps an hour, and upon its conclusion the men set about preparing their coffee and pork, congratulating themselves upon the opportunity afforded them of procuring a hearty meal of these great luxuries, of which they had now been deprived for several days.

The forage had been unloaded in the wood a short distance from the foot of the hill, and there piled up, and the wagons returned to camp. Just before dark I repaired to this spot to ascertain if I could secure additional forage and, while in conversation with the quartermaster sergeant, was somewhat startled to see a soldier come dashing down the road, with his horse at a full gallop. The rider, pale and breathless, dropped from his white lips a brief communication without halting, the import of which was fully understood by us both, in these words:

"They are coming!"

As he disappeared, I ran first for my arms, then my saddle, and then for my pony, and had the satisfaction of finding myself ready before a majority of the regiment was aware of the approach of the enemy. The picket had galloped to headquarters, and notified the commanding officer, and in a moment the bugle sounded "boots and saddles, " and the first sergeants ran hither and thither supplementing that order by urging the men to promptness. In an incredibly short time the soldiers were mounted and in line.

A few irregular shots in the dark woods beyond us gave a warning of the presence of the confederates. It was rumored that they had moved in on the rear of the videttes and thus cut them off from the reserves—which they could easily do, as the videttes were posted at isolated points on the roads and fields, so far from each other that to slip through the woods around them without their knowledge would be an easy matter. The shots fired made one thing clearly evident—the enemy was far closer to us than the line of pickets established during the day, and this fact gave color to the rumor of flanking.

The first squadron—the heroes of the evening before—was sent forward to ascertain the exact condition of affairs, and pushed gaily up the road. They had disappeared but a few moments into the now dark woods when a tremendous volley of musketry fell upon our ears, startling from us the little sense of security we yet felt. The first squadron soon returned, having encountered the enemy in a rather curious manner. They were riding along, not dreaming of the presence of the confederates, when the first sergeant of Company B, seeing what looked to him like a pair of white pants standing by the roadside, asked:

"Who is that?"

The pair of white pants made a sudden side step to the right and the owner thereof called out:

"Ready!"

A long sheet of flame, running at right angles with the road and on each side of it, burst forth, followed by a tremendous crash. Several men toward the rear of the squadron fell, and the balance retired hastily from the spot in some confusion, but escaped without further difficulty. The squadron had been saved from annihilation by several providential circumstances. The night had fallen by this time, and in the woods it was intensely dark. The enemy's line ran across the road at right angles, and when his troops heard the preparatory command, without waiting longer, no doubt supposing our men to be directly before them, fired straight to the front. Our loss had been occasioned by a few random shots that flew off obliquely from the line of battle in the excitement of the confederates.

This affair confirmed the rumor that the enemy had outflanked our pickets, and marched his infantry under cover of the woods until they had reached to within a few rods of our position at the foot of the hill.

It was now evident that the confederates were maneuvering in heavy force along our front and stealthily feeling their way towards Malvern Hill. Whether the appearance of the first squadron should warn them of the presence of our troops and thus lead them to suspect that they might encounter serious obstacles should they continue to advance, remained to be seen.

Our regiment, with the exception of perhaps half a dozen men, was now entirely withdrawn from the woods, and took up a position some fifty or sixty yards from their edge. The men excepted were posted on the road just inside the line of timber and across the little wooden bridge, as an advance guard, while perhaps thirty yards in their rear the first squadron was formed as a support, with carbines cocked and at the advance, ready for action. The balance of the force sat upon their horses without a weapon drawn. Apparently for the purpose of reminding us that they were still there, the confederates fired a few irregular volleys at intervals which, however, did no damage to us.

I doubt if any enlisted member of the Sixth Cavalry fully understood the object had in view by the presiding genius in command when he ordered the regiment to occupy the position. I know that in military circles the Common Soldier is not expected to question the motives of his superior officer, but in this case the disposition of troops appeared to our limited minds so specially adapted to secure our defeat and annihilation that we could not help indulging in some comments in regard to it. It was such a case that, at the risk of being deemed prolix, I shall recapitulate:

The enemy's line, composed of infantry, was known to extend along our front for at least a quarter of a mile. His troops were so completely hidden from our sight by the intense darkness and the woods that they would not have been visible at a distance of fifty yards. They were completely sheltered from a cavalry charge by a ditch and a strong high fence that extended along the edge of the timber, the former of which could not be crossed in itself except by the wooden bridge where the road ran through the woods towards New Market. They were now so close that we could hear commands given in quite a low tone of voice.

Our regiment was formed in close column of squadrons upon the low flat bottom at the foot of Malvern Hill, not over six yards from the edge of the timber, mounted, and consequently the most exposed without a weapon drawn, and fully conscious of the difficulties that lay in our way in case of an assault, and impressed with the belief that an attack from the enemy would result in our total defeat.

As we sat on our horses that night, waiting with nerves strung for the fatal volley that was to greet us upon the further advance of the confederates, there was a solemn silence that showed how each man appreciated the deadly peril of his situation. This terrible expectation—the more terrible uncertainty of the fate in store for us—this dead silence—the black woods, which a curious superstition vested with an unknown horror—the entire absence of a visible support—all combined to condense into the hours of our exposure here more of oppressive agony than any it has been my lot to suffer.

It was understood that several dispatches, detailing the circumstances with which we were surrounded, had been sent to General Pleasanton, who seems to have been in command, but the only answer returned was that "we must hold the position at all hazards." While we were so hampered in our movements, and were not allowed the poor privilege of adopting proper means of defense, it does not appear how this order to "hold the position at all hazards" was to be carried out.

It is further understood that Captain Saunders, commanding the regiment, who was absent during the evening, joined us, and took upon himself the responsibility of moving the command from its perilous location to one where, in case of the enemy's advance, we should have had at least a chance to make ourselves felt before being defeated. The men came to the right about wheel by fours, marched up and over the sharp ridge in rear, and, when the last squadron was under shelter, halted, wheeled to the right about by fours again, dressed the lines, and awaited developments. This proceeding wrought a wonderful change in the minds of the men. From the depths of despair we had been lifted to the pinnacle of hope. From that moment Captain Saunders was the beloved of the Sixth Cavalry.

It was evident that the enemy had paused in his advance, for ample time for his appearance had long since passed. It is highly probable that the confederates feared an ambuscade, and concluded that discretion was the better part of valor.

My nerves were to be subjected to a still greater test. In the hurry to saddle up and get into position, our forage had been abandoned in the woods, and shortly after the command ascended the hill a detail of twelve men was made out of each company to go down and attempt to rescue it. On this detail, with my usual fortune, I was placed. The prospects of success were not flattering; it was believed that the enemy were still in the woods in close proximity to the forage, and were likely to fire upon us in case we were heard. It was, therefore, with many misgivings that I descended the hill into the woods with the rest of the squad. Scarcely a word was spoken, but my heart beat wildly in my bosom, as, with compressed lips, we rode over the ditch into the woods, the noise of the hoofs upon the bridge sounding wonderfully loud.

The grain was secured, each man taking a sack, and with elated spirits we hurried from the spot to our places in the ranks.

There was a great deal of speculation indulged in among the soldiers as to what the finale of the affair was to be. The majority of the men seemed to think a battle would begin at daylight, for the forces of the enemy indicated a determination on their part to attack us, while our troops occupied the hill in great numbers and were capable of making a stubborn resistance. With an anxious hearts the tired men lay down about one o'clock in front of their horses to rest, but not to sleep.

An hour later orders to mount were quietly passed around, and with scarcely a word the men vaulted into their saddles. A rumor was afloat that we were thus withdrawn to enable the gunboats to shell the woods in our front at dawn. When we marched across Malvern Hill, however, it was found that our infantry support had been sent on to their camp at Harrison's Landing, and that we were alone in our glory in the presence of the enemy. Shortly after daybreak we reached Haxall's Station, where some light batteries had taken position on a great open plain, with guns trained upon the woods from which emerged the road from Malvern Hill. Our squadron was deployed as skirmishers along the edge of the woods in front of the pieces, remaining in our saddles in line the entire day, expecting the confederates to continue their advance. They now occupied Malvern Hill in force, and received a few shells from one of our vessels-of-war lying just below them in the river. As the enemy showed no disposition to disturb us, two-thirds of our exhausted men were allowed to unsaddle and rest themselves and horses.

The regiment remained here several days. The men took pleasant baths in the river, had plenty of sleep, and sufficient food and forage for themselves and horses, and were soon transformed from a band of forlorn to one of joyous soldiers.

Rumors reached us that a general evacuation by our army of that portion of Virginia was in progress. This was a demoralizing discovery, for it was a clear confession of defeat. So long as the Army of the Potomac occupied the ground at Harrison's Landing there was some color given to the assertion that our retirement from the positions along the Chickahominy was merely a change of base—a title that gave a sort of effete military dignity to the operations of the fatal Seven Days. But now we were to be deprived of even this hollow compliment, unless the military genius of newspaper correspondents should devise some peculiar term which would take off the wire-edge of humiliation.

About the 12th of August orders came for our withdrawal from Hall's Station, and long before daylight on the following morning the regiment silently marched away. Our route lay along the Charles City road, made famous by the stubborn action between the enemy and the Pennsylvania Reserves, and skirting the outer line of the entrenchments of our army north of Harrison's Landing. How far we travelled I know not, but by and by the regiment seemed to have been broken up, and the fragments scattered all through the country, our squadron being assigned to picket a road said by citizens to cross the Chickahominy at Long Bridge. We found the territory assigned to our care full of the good things of this life, from a roasting ear to a turkey. It is safe to say that the men enjoyed themselves, although the duties imposed were very arduous, and were happy. None of our troops were in the vicinity, but the confederate pickets were reported at a point distant perhaps six miles, in the direction of White Oak swamp. We were obliged, however, to exercise the utmost vigilance to prevent a surprise, and "stood tn horse" every night. Before morning, in spite of the frequent rounds of the officers to keep the men awake, they would be found lying asleep in front of their horses, holding on to the bridles with a nervous clutch, and wide awake the moment any unusual noise was made.

About one o'clock, while in this condition, a shot was fired in close vicinity of the camp, followed immediately by the swift clatter of horses' hoofs upon one of the roads leading to the reserves. A loud shot was also heard. It was astonishing to see how quickly the men sprang into their saddles and dressed their lines. I had no recollection of putting my foot into the stirrup at all. Fortunately, the alarm proved to be a false one. The imagination of Weissenberger—he who defeated the gentlemanly Frolbin in battle at Camp Scott—who occupied a post on the road above mentioned, conjured up an enemy in the darkness, and after the enemy had thus been conjured up Weissenberger promptly fired upon it, and then fell back at a gallop with a yell.

On the evening of the 15th of August, if I remember aright, I sat on my pony picketing the road leading to Long Bridge at a point perhaps two miles from the reserves. McHarness was posted on the same road a mile further on towards the bridge. Bobby, as usual when alone, was remarkably restive, squealing and pawing, and making me tired in body by the constant squirming and twisting he indulged in, and impatient in mind at the noise he made—the latter, as a matter of course, might attract the disagreeable attention of confederates, if any should be in the vicinity. My exhortations with the uneasy pony proved in vain; so, out of all humor, I dismounted to procure a stick to chastise him. While hunting about for one my heart relented, for I loved the brute, and could not make up my mind to hurt him; so picking up a dry cornstalk I determined to admonish him with that. "He will think this is a club and be frightened," thought I, as I flourished it in a threatening manner. Then, continuing the demonstration, I made a savage blow at him, but the cornstalk broke off close by my hand, and did not touch him. He sprang to one side, and suddenly swelled up in a curious manner, and shook all over. I was sorry I had frightened him so much. "Poor fellow—his heart is almost broke!" I thought. Then I patted him on the head and neck:, and told him I was sorry, and he began to rub his head against me in the old way. When I came to mount the saddle turned, and I discovered that the girth had been broken when he had swelled up in that curious manner.

Here was a dilemma. I was on picket on a lonely road—supposed to be mounted, with my revolver in hand—with a broken girth, and no surcingle to substitute for it. While surveying the situation, and wondering what I should do, Corporal Donaldson, who had charge of our relief, came galloping up from the reserves, his usually smiling face bearing a look of concern now, ordered me to mount and dashed on past without another word. From the corporal's actions it was evident something was wrong; but there was no way to fasten my saddle, and nothing remained but to mount the pony's bare back.

Presently Donaldson and McHarness joined me, and fortunately the latter possessed a surcingle, which he loaned me. In a few moments I was all right again, so we hurried back to where we had left the reserves. The spot was deserted, but a man had been left to notify us of the route the squadron had taken, and to act as a guide. It was now very dark:, and we journeyed along at a gallop, reining up at last at the sturdy "Halt!" of Billy Barlow whom we found posted at a crossroad. He had instructions to conduct us off the main road through a dense forest, which was as dark as Erebus is said to be, in an easterly direction.

From Barlow we learned that the entire regiment was ahead of us, the squadrons all having been withdrawn from the roads they had been guarding.

We had galloped perhaps one and one half mile farther, over fallen timbers and through swamps, when our course was suddenly arrested by encountering the head of the regiment, which was returning to the main road. Owing to some misunderstanding, the column had been following the wrong route, and our poor, tired horses were obliged to traverse the abominable path the second time. After an hour's march along the main road we reached another that crossed the one we were following at right angles, and the regiment turned off to the left along it.

The scene was now one that fully illustrated the horror of war. On each side of this road great fires were burning, which had been built by our infantry forces on their retreat; fields of grain were trampled underfoot; fences torn down; barns pulled to pieces. This picture of desolation extended for miles.

I do not think I shall soon forget this ride. As soon as the regiment gained this road it took up the trot, which was kept, with but few intervals of rest, for some sixteen to eighteen miles. There was such a cloud of dust that at times one's front rank man would be entirely invisible, and it was almost impossible to breathe. Our poor horses suffered terribly, many of them being so much exhausted that their riders were obliged to use their spurs freely to keep them up.

Once a strange cavalryman made his appearance and announced that the confederates were close at hand, and we were obliged to halt near an old mill and form our column to resist an attack; but after waiting half an hour or more, the enemy not putting in an appearance, we again moved on our way.

There is something so terrible in covering the retreat of an army, especially if you are halted to resist your pursuers. You know that, if attacked, your fight will be an unsupported one; your brethren-in-arms are all leaving you; your sources of support are receding in the distance; it may be necessary to sacrifice you for the salvation of the army. I am sure we all experienced just such feelings as we stood at bay on that lonely road, waiting to receive the charge of an exultant foe, our weary horses panting for air, our bodies perspiring and grimy with dust, and our hearts nerved for a last effort.

About daylight the regiment halted on the bank of the Chickahominy, near its mouth. Here we found a pontoon bridge built across to the opposite side. All the troops had already passed on and the engineers were waiting for us, so that the bridge could be taken up as soon as we were safe. A battery of artillery was posted so as to cover our passage if necessary. After a few moments rest the men remounted, and in a short time were on the eastern bank, where preparations were made to go into camp.

The regiment remained here until the morning of the 18th. The time thus granted to rest was a great boon to both men and horses, and was well employed in bathing and washing our clothing, in filling our lank stomachs, and in sleeping.

I was awakened from my slumbers during the first night of our stay here by the screams of a woman, which continued perhaps five minutes, and seemed to come from the direction of a house standing some distance from camp. As it was over before I could comprehend the matter—a woman's voice pitched to such a key was an unusual thing to hear in these days—I did not venture to see what was wrong, and casually speculated upon it. Someone, perhaps, attempted to force an entrance into the house. It was in the midst of an infantry camp.

We struck our tents on the forenoon of the 18th, and continued our march by James City—a spot historical as the scene of operations of the first colony south of New England—to Williamsburg, and thence to Yorktown. Here we halted and pitched our tents.

With an inexpressible feeling of relief, only to be realized by a soldier after months of hardship and peril—a grateful sense of security—we laid aside our weapons of war.

The picket no longer shuddered on his lonely post; the soldier no longer slept the fitful slumber of expectant attack; no cannon nor musket shot broke the stillness of the balmy air; the bugle no longer sounded "to arms," but in musical camp calls. Beyond us lay the magnificent York, its clear waves breaking upon the shore like a lullaby. For once, since the days before our soldiering—and those days seemed an immense distance back in the vista of time—we felt—safe!

Our days here were spent in the ways of pleasantness and peace. We bathed every day, taking our horses with us, and learning them and their riders how to swim together—an exercise affording wonderful amusement. The sailors on the gunboats cheered us lustily as we disported in the water around them like so many dolphins.

Yorktown to Knoxville

Rumors reached us from Washington that the confederates were crowding General Pope back from his advanced position in Northern Virginia; that the presence of all our troops was required to save our capital; and finally that the Sixth Cavalry would soon be required to meet new dangers on other fields.

These rumors were verified in the course of a few days by the appearance of a large number of schooners in the river off Yorktown. About the latter part of August we were safely embarked, and started for Alexandria.

Our trip was devoid of interest, and we were glad when it came to a close. As the vessel drew near to Alexandria we found the Potomac crowded with transports loaded with troops. Owing to the poor facilities for landing we were not disembarked for twenty hours after our arrival. At last, to our great joy, we were relieved from our hampered quarters, and trod on solid earth again.

Grateful to our eyes, recalling thoughts of home and friends, rose the well remembered dome of the Capitol and steeples of the city of Washington. Since the time they had faded in the distance behind us, as we floated down the river in the last days of March, our banner had received its baptism of fire and blood. The brave spirits that had departed as inexperienced recruits now returned as veterans.

The change brought no rest for us; ere the shadows of evening fell upon the scene, boot and spurred, our horses full of new life and vigor, the column wended its way to the front, from whence the war of arms told of hot work for the Army of the Potomac.

Our route lay over broken country, past earthworks, through woods, and across ravines, the command finally emerging upon the road running through the village of Falls Church—the Leesburg Turnpike. We had met with few of our troops on the way; there were some engaged in working upon entrenchments, and a small number of others encamped on the slope of a hill; but nothing indicated the presence of the entire Army of the Potomac. At the village the regiment halted, except our squadron.

We had reached a point some four miles beyond Falls Church, and near Tyson's Corners, when a dip in the road permitted me to look over the heads of the men in front and far up the road. As I did so, my eyes caught sight of three mounted men, dressed in gray, sitting on their horses about half a mile off, on the pike beyond us. I was surprised at this; it had not occurred to me that the enemy were in such close proximity to the Potomac, and, were it not for the inevitable gray uniforms, I should have doubted it even now. But there they were; there was no mistake about that.

On the left of the road at this place there spread out an open field, on the opposite side of which a pine forest extended along for some distance. It soon became evident there were confederates in these woods—perhaps a few infantry pickets. Two or three of Company G men were sent to watch them, but Company G men were soon fully occupied in trying to dodge the annoying shots that flew out like angry hornets from the timber. They galloped backwards and forward across the field, holding themselves very low, and on the side of their horses opposite to the position occupied by the enemy. It was a rather comical picture after all.

The three cavalrymen, as we neared them, rode off to one side and disappeared in the woods. Some of Company L men—ten or twelve—advanced as skirmishers, going down the road at a trot. Company L, it should be stated in passing, possessed carbines—which our squadron did not—and had been on picket here the night before. It had, with C Company, been in Washington up till this time, but now joined us for the first time, making up the complete regiment of twelve companies or six squadrons.

Company L men had just disappeared from sight when some shots were heard in their direction, and they soon reappeared, halting in a sort of disorderly way every few rods, and firing nervously up the road. It was evident the confederates were following them, although they had not yet come into sight. Presently, however, as our men straggled down close to where we had formed in the road, facing the woods from which Company G men were being so much annoyed by those unseen foes, and were still halting and firing in every direction except at the enemy, in a

210

wild sort of way, there came into sight six of them. They halted when they saw us, and all except one turned off the road behind low scrub pines, by which they were hidden from us. The one that remained deliberately raised a long gun to his shoulder, after reining in his horse at a favorable angle across the pike, and took aim at our party, the Company L men having by this time reached a point in the road on our left flank. It will be remembered that we were facing the woods, our ranks running up and down the road; consequently the solitary confederate, from his position on our right flank, had to fire along our line. As he was fully half a mile or more away, it occurred to me that he was not likely to hit any one, and I smiled at his foolishness, of halting there to shoot. when he might have approached so much closer without danger to himself. In a moment there arose a puff of smoke from his gun, and a bullet zipped past, within an inch of our noses it seemed to me. He then rode behind the bushes, and another man took his place. It was with some misgiving that, after the marksmanship displayed by his fellow, I awaited the dreaded puff of smoke. There was a general crouching up in ranks just then, each man endeavoring to make himself smaller than the man on his right. The large fellows in the company suddenly became objects of sympathy as they tried to shrivel up their well-developed proportions.

The puff of smoke appeared at last. A curious fascination kept my eyes fixed upon that man and his gun, which was broken by a sharp "smack" sort of sound, that fell upon my ears simultaneously with the zip of the bullet, as though one struck a horse across the flank with a shingle, and I felt that something was hit. I looked across, and saw private Boynton, of Company G, still seated in his saddle, but with the upper part of his body lying prone upon his horse's neck, his head drooping low past the mane, and from his forehead a stream of blood running down upon the ground. His right arm swung limply down, while his left hung over the opposite side of his horse's neck.

Poor fellow! He had joined his company that day, having been in the hospital ever since we had left Camp East of Capitol in March, and these were the first confederates he had seen under arms. I remembered him as an easy-going, mild-mannered man, who used to look on at the stag dances and boxing exhibitions in the old barracks with an innocent smile.

I suppose the soldiers who took part in this little excursion will remember the apparently objectless wandering around, while matters were thus approaching a crisis, of a man who seemed to have command of this reconnoitering party, but upon whom I began to look as a sort of evil genius, and who was said to be a major of some Illinois regiment. This evil genius seemed to be adapted to the peaceful pursuits of the husbandman, rather than to the savage occupation of the soldier, as he rode about with his military cap pulled down over his ears, and his body crouched up in his saddle, and with his eyes fastened on a void in a sort of daze.

They will also remember how Captain Irwin Gregg[1]—a gentleman because he was a hero, and a hero because he was a gentleman promptly, after a due representation of the gravity of the situation failed to awaken the evil genius to a just sense of his responsibility, removed the squadron to a position where it should have an opportunity to defend itself, and how, when, under the captain's direction, our skirmishers were deployed across the fields, and the few reserves were formed in close column ready to repel attack in a proper manner, the confederate advance was checked until they pushed up a piece of artillery; and how, through all the subsequent movements, when it was necessary to exercise the greatest good judgment, in order to hold the enemy until we should receive aid, he so adroitly controlled his little force and kept them so well in hand, as to completely baffle the confederates in their attempt to overrun us; and how, at last, when we uncovered the battery that had taken position just outside the village of Falls Church, the skirmish ended in the complete repulse of our pursuers.

One Sunday morning, six years after this occurrence, I walked out from Washington with a friend to Falls Church, feeling an intense desire to revisit the scene of this encounter. The day was a bright and balmy one, and we sauntered leisurely along, provided with lunches and two bottles of wine. I felt strange in thus treading as an unarmed citizen the ground where, when last I looked upon these scenes, I rode in blue ranks, and carried a revolver and sabre. My eyes could recognize but few objects. The road looked strange, but the old hills were there. At the village tollgate we stopped and devoured our lunches, sitting under the shadow of some grand old locust trees. Three miles beyond we began to inquire of citizens about the fight, but some of them had recently moved into the neighborhood, and could give us no information as to the affair; finally however, we stopped at the residence of Mrs.

---

[1] Irvin Gregg was born in Huntington, Pennsylvania, and was appointed a captain in the 6th Cavalry upon its formation in May, 1861.

Mary Mills, and from her learned that it was still a mile further on. Two of her sons—one a cripple, apparently from a paralytic stroke, about twenty-three years old, and the other a smart, good looking boy of perhaps fourteen, whom I could not help liking for his efforts to assist us in recalling affairs of interest in that neighborhood during the memorable days of the war—accompanied us to the scene of the skirmish. A house stood on the right hand side of the road—which house I had not remembered seeing—and to this we repaired and young Mr. Mills introduced us and our objective to Mrs. Marye, a widow lady, who resided in the house for the past sixteen or eighteen years. From Mrs. Marye we learned many interesting particulars. She had witnessed the whole affair, standing out in her front yard, not over thirty steps from the road.

From her statement it appeared that Captain Brisbane, as he had given his name to her, commanding over two new companies, C and L, was in charge of the picket stationed at Tyson's Corner and over other roads, and kept his reserves in her yard. He had been on duty during the night before the fight, and up till the time we had arrived. She thinks from his actions that he was not sober—his comings and goings were rather eccentric.

When our men retired she saw two riderless horses dash by, and she ran down to the road. When she came in sight of the prostrate body of Boynton two confederates had dismounted and were by him, rifling his pockets. Upon her entreaty they lifted him to one side, so as to be out of the way of their advancing column. The only sign of life the solder gave after she saw him was the drawing up of his right leg. He had been struck by the bullet over the right eye. She picked up some letters that the confederates had taken from his pockets and thrown upon the ground, one of which seemed to have been sent him from his brother, who wrote a letter dated at Winchester, Virginia, and who was evidently also a Union soldier. The body lay exposed to the weather for three days. None of our troops came up after the confederates retired until the second day after the skirmish, when a squad of cavalry made their appearance, and to these she appealed to bury it. After some hesitation they assented, and were about to do so, when they became frightened at some imaginary danger, and mounted their horses and galloped off towards Washington.

She now proposed to perform the last sad rites herself, but was dissuaded by some of her neighbors; finally some colored men were induced to attend to it.

Another man, in Company L, was killed still further up the road towards Tyson's Corners. The name of this soldier she was unable to learn. He was buried by the same party that interred poor Boynton.

Some two years after the close of the war a squad belonging to the party sent out by the government to gather up the remains of United States soldiers, and transfer them to national cemeteries, passed by her house. She pointed out the graves, and gave them the letters so that Boynton might be identified; but from the careless way in which they were tossed into the wagon she thinks they were not likely to be distinguished from each other. It is supposed they were brought to Arlington, but I have not been able to find their graves.

Mrs. Marye had two sons, about the same age as those of Mrs. Mills. The eldest—a resolute-looking man, somewhat disfigured by the loss of an eye—had served the Union cause as a scout during the continuance of hostilities, rendering efficient aid on many occasions.

I was much gratified to find that so many of the people in this neighborhood had really been in sympathy with the government of the United States, although their exposed condition had rendered it necessary for them to maintain a discreet silence on the subject of the war.

We left the houses of Mrs. Marye and Mrs. Mills much pleased with hospitable treatment, and pushed homeward, halting once in a field under a shade tree, where the remnants of our lunch and wine were devoured. At nine o'clock that night our homes were reached, by one tired individual, I am sure, as we had walked over twenty-six miles since seven or eight o'clock that morning.

In the evening after the skirmish, about dark, our regiment took up its line of march towards Georgetown. Now came one of those peculiarly, disagreeable night movements, so fully appreciated by all soldiers who have experienced them—the slow-motioned, uneasy, continuously-halting, patience trying—I am really at a loss for a word suitable to express the utter detestation in which we used to hold it. It is sufficient to say, that we followed a large train of wagons nearly, the whole night.

Here, for the first time, we met with some of the men who had served under General Pope along the line of the Rappahannock. I could not help contrasting the appearance of these troops with those who had served on the peninsula under McClellan. Pope's men, though suffering terrible privations and hardships, had a robust, healthy look, while those of McClellan were wan and pale, and bore unmistakable traces of malaria in their sallow features, contracted in the miasmatic atmosphere along the Chickahominy and James rivers.

After crossing the aqueduct into Georgetown, about nine o'clock that evening, our drooping spirits were much inspired by the cordial reception given us by the Union people of that city. No one can fully appreciate, unless he has realized it, the unutterable sensation of joy that thrills the soldier when, after enduring hardships amid hostile peoples, he returns within his own lines, and is received with the encouraging smiles of women and children. This is his glory—the great reward—the need unalloyed by other and base considerations—the gratitude and love of those whom he has defended on the field, and for whom he has suffered indescribable privations and perils. It was the better appreciated by us because, from the hour we had left Washington until our return, with the single exception of that family before mentioned on the peninsula, we had not seen the sympathizing face of woman or child. Now the dear creatures looked really angelic, dressed in their light summer costumes, and full of joyous enthusiasm for the cause.

Although, since the days of our crude ideas about war, we had ceased to shout except during the fierce excitement of the charge, there now broke forth one long, loud, impetuous cheer, which better expressed than any words possibly could, the feelings of the regiment, and indicated that, if our patriotism had seemed to have died away under the long-continued presence of toil and peril, it was now fully revived again, and all the more reliable for past trials. In vain officers ran hither and thither to check the demonstration; they seemed hardly able, with all their love of order, to repress their own voices. The discipline of the United States army ceased for the moment to exist; the regulations were forgotten and courtsmartial lost their terrors.

I have thus dealt somewhat at length upon the scenes on this occasion for the reason that these moments were those rare occurrences, when I felt supremely happy. My blood yet tingles with the memoirs of that halcyon hour in the little city by the Potomac.

After passing through Georgetown we moved up the Tennallytown road, halting about midnight some miles from the city, and remaining until dawn. The men were very tired and hungry, and appropriated to their own use an immense quantity of green corn, which they ate raw, without any of the formalities of seasoning. I expected to be sick from the effect of my imprudence in the matter, but was greatly disappointed, feeling rather better than usual afterwards.

Our march up the Potomac was resumed at an early hour. The destination of the regiment was unknown, but it was rumored that the enemy was threatening Maryland and Pennsylvania with invasion.

I was detailed, with three or four others, under command of a sergeant of Company E, as a rearguard. Our duty was light, having simply to keep up the stragglers and prevent pillaging, remaining for this purpose always about three hundred yards behind the regiment. It is a pleasant relief to ride out of ranks and away from official presence, where the feeling of military restraint is lost, and a sense of freedom substituted.

The scenery along the river was grand in its wild picturesqueness—the rugged, rocky shore which bound the edges of an immensely magnified brook, rather than a river, which is always associated in my mind with a stream that flows with a steady, calm current, instead of dashing along from fall to channel and from channel to fall, a succession of cataracts and whirlpools—the great hills and hollows, curtained and fringed in fantastical order by woods, in the deep, mysterious recesses of which I could imagine curiously-shaped monsters, whose presence had been invoked by the spirit of civil war, and whose mission was one of destruction—the blue sky overhead, with its alternate drifts of dark and light clouds—all this was much in contrast with the low, level country we had left shortly before along the banks of the James and York.

In the afternoon the regiment reached the village of Darnestown, where it halted for several hours. The rearguard was stationed in a convenient locality, and the several members composing it charged with the duty of preserving order and preventing the soldiers from annoying citizens. The headquarters of the rearguard was located in the front yard of a cozy mansion, occupied by a pleasant-looking old gentleman, whom I would set down as a presbyterian, who made himself sociable but kept discreetly quiet upon the all-absorbing "question". His wife was a kind, motherly-looking old lady, who talked with us as if we were wayward boys who had run away from home without leave.

Two buxom, rosy-cheeked young ladies, one about twenty years old, the other perhaps sixteen, honored us with their presence and conversation. One—the older—represented the Union sentiment, while the other, who was possessed with an inimitable bantering faculty, was conveniently rebellious. As I was a young and susceptible creature, free-footed

216

from all engagements, as the reader will have seen, I was much pleased with the sprightly vivaciousness of the younger, rather than with the grave, sedate bearing of her sister, who, however, possessed the handsomer face. The sergeant in charge of our squad was also an admirer of ladies, and was not long in assuming to be my rival, having, besides, a good looking face and figure, and outranking me, so that he had matters pretty much his own way. I think, however, his rank was to my advantage for it turned the current of female sympathy towards me as the weaker party. He was a liberal man, for he might have sent me off on some detail—which he did not.

The rosy hours sped on, as they always do when rosy, rapidly until evening had stolen on us unawares, and with feelings of regret we heard the bugler at the regiment sound "to horse". Instead of passing on through, as we expected, the command countermarched and returned, moving off on the pike towards Rockville instead of on the road by which we had entered the village.

The younger lady, when she observed this retrograde movement, exclaimed, laughingly:

"Oh, I knew you were afraid! The confederates are at Poolesville, nine miles from here. I knew you would not dare to encounter them."

Both the sergeant and I endeavored to reply to this sally, but it was of no use; appearances were against us.

To the rearguard was assigned the duty of collecting the stragglers that remained behind, and compelling them to rejoin the column. All of our party, with one exception, mounted their horses and started off to execute this order; this exception was the writer. I will not say that the young lady's charming presence detained me; oh, no. I had something very intricate to adjust about my saddle; was remarkably particular about my coat-straps. As soon as my companions were out of sight, she darted into the house and immediately reappeared with four pies and two immense apples and gave them to me, with the remark:

"Take these, and don't say a rebel girl never gave you anything."

I was literally overwhelmed by this demonstration, and stammered out my thanks in an incoherent sort of way, and made awkward attempts to stow the provisions away where they might be unseen, but only succeeded in smashing the pies over a portion of my great coat.

"Good bye," she concluded, as the balance of the rearguard appeared returning from their patrol of the village; "If you see Stonewall Jackson, give him my love."

She then passed into the house, while I scrambled into the saddle, after several unsuccessful attempts, being unusually nervous.

In a few moments the squad, headed by the sergeant, approached the spot where I stood, keeping up the middle of the road. I saw that his face bore a vexed look, and he undoubtedly had seen the young lady leave me a moment before. Something must be done to conciliate him or he might put me under arrest, I thought. Then I rode up to him, with what I intended as a smile childlike and bland on my benevolent countenance, took out one of the apples, handed it to him, and said:

"She sent it, sir, with compliments."

"I am much obliged to her," he replied, the vexed look fading from his face instantly, and replaced by a smile. "She is a nice girl."

I took care to keep my pies concealed, however, thinking their display might jeopardize my case.

It was now growing dark. Some of the rearguard party, with that curious instinct of discovery only possessed by lovers of whisky—which instinct of discovery, curiously enough, only applies to stimulants and cannot be utilized as to anything else—had been indulging themselves to some extent, and were quite hilarious. By this time the regiment was probably half a mile ahead of us and out of sight; but as we came to the top of a long slope it was indistinctly seen in the distance halted at a creek, evidently for the purpose of watering the horses.

At this point two of our party halted, ostensibly for another purpose, but really to take an additional drink from a canteen. No attention was paid to their movements, and we left them there. In a few moments afterward, as we were riding down the long easy grade at a leisurely gait, we were suddenly startled by the sharp report of a pistol in our rear. It instantly occurred to me that the confederates had dashed up from Poolesville, and I gave a frightened glance back into the gathering gloom, just in time to see a flash and hear another report, followed by a hoarse yell and the clatter of horses' hoofs upon the macadamized road, apparently rushing down upon us as if to stimulate our actions; we heard the familiar zip of a bullet in the air not far away. Our gallant sergeant, instead of forming his men, and endeavoring to check the enemy, put spurs to his horse and galloped madly down the road towards the regiment, shouting, with considerable vigor:

"Cavalry coming!"

Another shot came, followed by a quick cry of pain in response, but this cry I could not locate. This completed our panic; we followed our leader's heroic example, at the imminent risk of breaking our necks among the huge boulders and innumerable gullies that lay in our way.

"Cavalry coming!"

This we shouted into the ears of the astonished men in the regiment as we swept on past them. Just then I became cognizant of the fact that our party in the stampede had been increased by a riderless horse, upon the saddle of which two plethoric saddle-bags bounced up and down like a pair of distended bladders. This animal we captured, and turned off the road into a field that extended up a rather steep hill at the top of which we found several batteries of artillery parked for the night. Everything now seemed to be quiet, so what was left of the rearguard—I could only find two men, and neither of them was the sergeant—put up for the night on a pile of hay we carried off from a huge stack. The captured horse was found to be a good one, and the plethoric saddle-bags full of eatables and medicine. After kindling a fire, making ourselves full of a quart of strong coffee apiece, roasting some pickled pork on the end of a stick, and frying some crackers in grease and sugar, and fastening and feeding and grooming our horses, we spread out our blankets on the hay and laid down. By this time the hillside was covered with men and horses of other regiments beside our own, and it was evident that if the enemy had made his appearance, he must have hastily retired without indulging in further demonstrations. There was a sort of mystery about the affair, however, that bothered my brain that night. Whose cry of agony had risen on the air? Whose horse was this? Where were our pickets? Revolving these various conundrums in my mind in a distracted sort of way, I fell asleep.

At daylight next morning we were aroused by the blare of many bugles. After a hearty breakfast this branch of the rearguard set out to find the other branch, and especially the main stem, which was the sergeant. I found Kelly,[2] of Company M, a member of our party, sitting under a tree on the opposite side of the road, eating crackers and drinking cold water freely. As he was one of the two men who had stopped to take a drink on the hill the evening before, it occurred to me that he ought to know something as to what had happened. I questioned him some, but he gave evasive answers, and seemed to have a mysterious dislike to conversing upon the subject. Stepping up close to him, I said:

[2] There were several Kelly's in the regiment and more than one assigned to Company M.

"Kelly, let me see your revolver."

He turned deadly pale, and slowly drew it forth. Three of the chambers were empty.

"How is this? Now, Kelly, you know all about it."

The man had been taken by surprise, and made a full statement. He said that his companion, after they had taken their drinks, insisted on remaining where they were, but to this he (Kelly) would not accede, and so left him. As he rode leisurely along, thinking of no danger, he heard the clattering of hoofs behind him, apparently at a full charge, and a yell. He now thought of the confederates, being somewhat confused in mind by frequent potations, and, jerking out his revolver, fired wildly back. At this moment the horseman dashed past him, and in his excitement Kelly had fired two more shots after him, not once thinking about the companion he had left behind on the road.

Kelly was much worried lest some of his shots had taken effect on his friend, but that individual finally turned up all right, though confessing that he had been terribly frightened and fully impressed with the belief that he had been shot at by the confederates. He had made a friendly charge upon Kelly, but thought the shots that greeted him came out of a cornfield near the road.

The conundrums that had puzzled me the night before continue to puzzle me yet, except, perhaps, as to the pickets. Whose cry of agony rose on the air? Whose horse was this?

We did not care to press these inquiries for the reason that it might lead to trouble for Kelly. At the instance of the main stem of our rearguard, whom we found at last under a tree, the necessity which had occasioned our detail having ceased to exist, our little party dispersed to their respective companies, separating with mutual good wishes.

The troops halted here for two days, for the double purpose, I suppose, of resting them and permitting the concentration of other portions of the army. Word came to us that the confederates were crossing the Potomac in great force at Poolesville, and moving out into Maryland and up towards Pennsylvania. It was also understood that a large body of our own troops occupied Harper's Ferry and the adjoining country, under the command of Colonel Miles, which was now completely cut off from succor on the east, but as the position was said to be naturally a strong one, and well fortified, it was hoped that he would be able to beat off his enemies.

On the morning of the third day the bugler sounded the now familiar call of "boots and saddles;" there was a hurried packing of clothes and rations; there was the usual ceremony of forming by companies, carefully dressing the lines, a breaking by fours to the front from the right, and the regiment, accompanied by several other bodies of cavalry and artillery, moved out on the road towards Poolesville, repassing through Darnestown on the way.

The young ladies, with their father and mother, were standing in their front yard, and recognized us. The eldest said nothing, but smiled; the other, to whom I had remarked, "You see we are back again, and not so bad scared after all," laughingly cried out:

"Give my love to Stonewall, as I told you, and divide your pies with him."

I longed to stop for a short time, but the column inexorably moved on, and carried me in the irresistible current.

About six miles from Darnestown the command came to a halt. Then there were ominous movements among the orderlies, who galloped to and fro, as if our very existence depended on them. One presently stopped at the head of our squadron, and conversed with its commanding officer, Captain Irvin Gregg, a few moments.

As the orderly rode off Captain Gregg, turning to the men, raised in his stirrups, and called out:

"Attention, fourth squadron! By twos—march!"

This command was immediately put in course of execution, and we found ourselves marching rapidly past the other troops toward the front. Presently we reached a point where the roads forked; our squadron moved off at a trot along the one on the right while the other portion of the command kept the other branch.

The day was a beautiful one. The rich fields of Western Maryland were now spread before us like a panorama—a strange contrast to the scenes of devastation which we had left within the limits of the Old Dominion. Low hills, clear streams, well-cultivated farms, herds of sleek cattle, droves of noble horses, great barns, comfortable houses, and ruddy women greeted our longing eyes. The latter, be it recorded, wore no doubtful smiles; there was the reflex of genuine sympathy with the cause in their beautiful eyes.

Our meditations upon the manifold blessings of peace, however, were not of long duration. Though we had forgotten war and its paraphernalia of horrors, in the grand scenery around us, we were destined to a rude awakening. Our dreams were broken by the sharp crack of a rifle,

221

which seemed to come from the crest of a low hill in our immediate front, the top of which was crowned by woods. Almost at the same instant the heavy report of a field gun came up from the southwest, followed at close intervals by others, until we knew that a full battery was engaged.

As we rode forward up the long slope, and turned our faces in the direction from whence came these peals of thunder, after attaining a commanding position, our eyes could take in the whole of the contested field. Large forces of our cavalry, supported by artillery, appeared deploying at a gallop across the broad plains, the batteries marching in the intervals of space between the mounted regiments. In their front, distant perhaps one and a half miles, swarming in dull gray masses, were the confederate battalions. From a slight eminence near their center a bluish white cloud, hanging like an impenetrable drapery, shut out from sight the guns that were actually sending their missiles into our lines.

The regularity with which the enemy kept up his artillery fire, and the numerous bodies of troops displayed in the fields, showed his determination to make a vigorous defense. There was one hopeful sign—we could see no infantry. It was evident that we had encountered the rearguard, and might possibly be able to dislodge them.

In the meantime one or two more rifle shots broke in upon our front. Captain Gregg halted his squadron, and rode forward alone to reconnoitre. He had scarcely passed from sight into the long wooded avenue before two more rifle shots, almost simultaneous, and apparently at the spot where he must at about that moment have arrived, were heard. Lieutenant McClain now hurried our party forward, evidently fearing that Captain had been shot—a misgiving in which I presume all the men shared. As we passed over the hill several more shots were heard, and a dense cloud of dust over the road just ahead indicated the close proximity of troops. Our squadron was marched off to the left hand side of the road, and formed in a charging column in the woods, with drawn sabres, and awaited further developments. We were not long kept in suspense. Suddenly the clatter of many hoofs was heard beyond us; wild shouts broke upon the air; out of that cloud of dust a body of mounted men, three or four hundred in number, burst past us on the road down the hill like a whirlwind. This body, upon whose flanks we were about to charge, proved to be our own soldiers. At the same moment, and as if by magic, in the edge of some woods that skirted a small field in our front, a piece of artillery was unlimbered, which opened and sent a shell

222

crashing through the trees in frightful proximity to our heads. The shell burst over the fugitives that were fleeing down the hill. Simultaneously with this a gray mass of cavalry came swarming through the wood on our left flank, perhaps one hundred yards away. This was too much for us; an attempt was made to retire in good order, but the men were so panic-stricken that they dashed headlong down the road from the direction in which we had come, closely following the fugitives that had preceded us.

Although our flight was a ludicrous one—and I doubt not it was, after all, the only thing that saved us from annihilation, as our squadron was entirely too weak to confront the enemy—there were instances of individual pluck that, had I the names of the soldiers, would deserve particular mention. One man—a member of the Third Indiana Cavalry, which regiment, by the way, was the one which had been driven back upon us—stopped in the road, and, declaring that he would not continue such a disgraceful scene, met the confederate charge single-handed. I am not aware of his fate.

It subsequently appeared that the Third Indiana had preceded us on this road without our knowledge, and hence our belief that they were confederates. They had intercepted the whole body of the enemy who were resisting our forces on the left, and, had they been properly supported with artillery and men, the result would have been the capture of the entire rearguard. The frantic attempts of the confederates to escape led to a sudden and overwhelming attack upon our men, which proved successful, though at a cost of several soldiers killed and wounded.

Captain Gregg rejoined us during our flight, and by his coolness inspired the men with courage and succeeded in checking the panic.

To me the most humiliating part of the affair was the laugh that greeted us as we swept in disorderly flight past a house from the lips of a woman who stood in the doorway looking at our party—not a laugh of triumph and satisfaction, but of genuine mirth, such as might be excited by any comical scene.

Our confusion was not of long duration; our men soon rallied, reformed, and pushed up the hill with an enthusiasm they had not displayed during the first advance. The enemy were again encountered a mile or two further on—the fighting on our left had suddenly ceased in the withdrawal of the confederates from the front of our men at that point, and their retreat along the road, which formed a junction with the one our party occupied at the spot where we had seen them mustering with the cannon and cavalry—and the Indiana men went to work with a vim that must have surprised them. In a few moments they broke up and retired in confusion, hotly pursued by our soldiers. Their success on the hill, however, enabled them to escape to their main army.

The pursuit continued for several miles, with frequent collisions and loss on both sides. The balance of our forces, whose front had thus been cleared by these operations, now joined us, and reported that they had encountered the enemy near Poolesville, close to the Potomac river, where they had made a short stand, but had retired suddenly and apparently without cause.

A small number of prisoners had been captured. Most of these were loud in their expressions of confidence as to the success of their new campaign—the invasion of the North.

"Before many days," said one," your people shall hear our guns in Baltimore city. They shall have a taste of the suffering in old Virginia. We expect to recruit our army by thousands in Maryland."

It was surprising how hopeful our soldiers were, after their rough handling on the peninsula and in front of Washington. They opposed the confederate assumption of victory with smiles of incredulity, and contented themselves with saying they were glad that this invasion had been attempted; it would stir up the people, and supply the national army with hosts of men, and the confederacy might lose more than it gained.

In a short time after the advance was resumed we came in sight of the peak of Sugar Loaf Mountain. It rose grandly in the distance, standing out in bold relief against the clear blue sky. All day long the command moved slowly toward it, the advance guard encountering the enemy every few miles, halting at evening, and bivouacking for the night in the woods by the roadside. At dawn the march was resumed, and continued until we had reached the immediate neighborhood of the mountain. Here we found a small village, called Barnesville.

During the preceding day the advance had met with some success; capturing a few men and horses and a cannon. Our men pushed the confederates through the village and up the side of the mountain, and, fearing they might return during the night, posted the captured gun, heavily charged with grape shot, upon the road in a commanding position, and trained so as to cover the approach by that route. Events proved that their precautions were well timed. That night, about twelve or one o'clock, the enemy, no doubt chagrined by the defeats he had sustained, resolved to surprise our men by a midnight attack. A large body of mounted confederates advanced close up to the position held by our advance guard in the village, along the pike, and then halted, dismounted, and hitched their horses to the fences on each side of the road. This done, they fell into ranks, and marched on foot towards Barnesville, where they had expected to encounter our pickets. These movements, however, were fully known to our soldiers, who were thoroughly prepared. The gun was sighted upon the almost indistinguishable mass of horses, instead of the men, and discharged. The effect was wonderful. The horses stampeded, dashing down the road with fence rails dangling to their halter straps and disappearing into the woods on the mountain side. Over one hundred confederates, astounded at this unlooked for reception, threw down their arms and surrendered, and were further surprised when they saw themselves in charge of not over half that number of Union soldiers. No further disturbances occurred during the night.

The next day after our arrival an attempt was made to continue our march over the mountain, but the confederates successfully resisted our advance, using their artillery at intervals upon our columns with some effect. The position held by them was a very strong one, upon which, owing to its abrupt elevation, our artillery could not be trained. This elevation also enabled them to detect any movement we might make, and thus prepare them to resist it. Another element of strength was the density of the forest, by which they were completely hidden from our sight. On the top of the mountain they had established a signal station where we could see the different flags waved at intervals during the entire day. Our loss did not exceed more than two or three men killed and wounded.

That afternoon a brigade of our infantry came up and took possession of the mountain, from which the enemy retired without further resistance, a part toward Frederick City and part toward Point of Rocks, near the Potomac. In the evening the Sixth Cavalry advanced towards the Monocacy.

I shall not soon forget our ride across the Sugar Loaf. The night was intensely dark; the road was simply a narrow path along which we had to ride, Indian fashion, by file. One side the mass of rock and earth rose steeply, an impenetrable wall; on the other we felt, though we could not see, that a gulf yawned, ready to receive us upon the slightest mis-step of our horses. Fortunately no accident occurred, and the command reached the opposite side of the mountain two or three hours before daylight.

The regiment halted here, and "stood to horse" until dawn. We were completely chilled through by our ride, and as we had eaten nothing since the morning before, our stomachs were complaining in an unpleasant way. Plenty of good strong coffee, backed up by roast pork and crackers made us forget our troubles, and the march was resumed about seven o'clock with light hearts. Near the Monocacy we passed through a small village, called Greenfield—if I remember aright—perhaps two or three miles from the foot of the Sugar Loaf. From Greenfield we advanced toward Point of Rocks meeting with no enemy and reaching that place in the afternoon.

Here, in the front yard of a humble house that stood inside the apex formed by the road leading along the river to Harper's Ferry and the Baltimore and Ohio Railway, we found a white woman and her little son, aged perhaps six years old, standing apparently waiting for us. The little fellow waved a small American flag upon our approach. The incident was so inspiriting that even we, soldiers of the regular army, usually prohibited from making demonstrations of applause, and disciplined to a perpetual silence, could not restrain ourselves, and burst out into wild hurrahs that resounded along the hills by the river side for miles.

The woman reported that large bodies of the enemy's infantry and artillery had passed up the river the day before our arrival, under command of a General Loring. From the conversation she had heard she supposed there were some fifteen thousand confederates. She feared that our forces at Harper's Ferry would be captured if not immediately relieved, as this army avowed its purpose to make the attempt, and seemed to be hopeful of success.

The advance guard pushed up on the road towards the Ferry, supported by a portion of the regiment and two pieces of artillery. Our battalion marched in rear of the guns. After we had travelled perhaps a mile it became apparent from the movements of the advance that something was the matter. The road at this point ascends the mountain through a heavy timber, and the position was just such a one as would likely to be chosen by an enemy to resist an invading force. Our skirmishers came scampering down the road out of the woods in apparent terror, and the supporting column, observing this, formed into line and then deployed to the right and left of the road, while the artillery hurriedly unlimbered to the front ready for immediate action. Our battalion formed on the right to support the pieces. We waited in anxious suspense, expecting every moment to see the familiar gray lines burst from the cover of the forest, and to hear the old yell of confederate troopers.

Time passed on, but they did not appear. Not a shot was fired. Presently, however, we heard a rattling sound as made by artillery coming down the road towards us at a gallop; the crisis was approaching; the gunners sprang to their pieces, and lanyards were held taut; our hearts beat wildly, and all eyes were fixed in a steady glare upon the edge of the woods at the point from which emerged the road.

Here was a fall from the sublime to the ridiculous. A venerable African, with protruding eyes and wearing a look of terror on his old face, came dashing into sight with a two-horse wagon instead of our lively confederate friends and a battery. There was an immediate collapse on our part, though it would be hard to tell who were the most frightened for the time being—the soldier or the citizen. This affair kept us laughing for months afterward, upon a mere allusion to its comical features.

The regiment halted here during the night. I was sent with Lewis to picket the railroad track two or three miles north towards the Monocacy, going on post the last time about three o'clock in the morning, and remaining there until eight o'clock. Our post was close to a house, and shortly after daylight the occupant, a farmer, brought us out some bread and butter and sweet milk, of which Lewis and I partook with great relish. The citizen then expressed the belief that Harper's Ferry would be taken, saying he had evidence that it was at that very moment surrounded by a large army of confederates.

When we were relieved and returned to the place the regiment had bivouacked the night before it had disappeared, having taken the road towards Jefferson, a few miles north of Harper's Ferry. Some cannonading to the westward could be heard, which increased in vigor as the hours rolled on. On our way we met Billy Barlow, who was carrying a dispatch to Point of Rocks, from whence it was to be sent to Washington by telegraph, notifying the authorities that Harper's Ferry had been attacked, and was now surrounded, and unless relieved would be likely to surrender. We caught up to the command not far from Jefferson. At this village a few confederates were found who retreated wildly before our men, the latter galloping into the place amid the cheers of the populace and the waving of Union banners.

Simultaneously with the arrival of our regiment a body of federal cavalry dashed in along a road from the northeast, closely followed by the advance of Burnside's infantry corps. By evening from twelve to fifteen thousand soldiers had arrived, and were bivouacked in and around the village—an inspiriting sight. The mountainsides that night were covered with innumerable campfires as far as the eye could see, and, unless the enemy should retire hastily, the indications were that he would be attacked by our forces in the morning.

We found the country around Jefferson teeming with an abundance of grain and fruit. Peaches grew wild along the roads, and formed our diet principally, with green corn, eggs, milk, and butter, and the best of bread. The beautiful September weather, the bracing mountain air, and the genial Unionism of the citizens, all combined to render us happy and contented, and was in striking contrast with our disagreeable recollections of the Peninsular campaign. We were almost glad the enemy had led us into this region.

Early on Sunday morning, September 14, the writer was detailed, with a dozen or fifteen others, to gather in corn for our horses. The whole country was alive, for the people had been aroused by the terrors and novelties of actual war in their midst. For two days the thunder of artillery had rolled over the mountain from the direction of Harper's Ferry, and still continued as vigorously as ever. From up the valley towards Middletown ominous sounds floated down, indicating that the hostile legions were rapidly closing on each other.

Religious services were in progress in the churches of Jefferson as we rode past, but the words of the sermon were drowned by that other sermon which was being uttered from iron throats towards the west and south. The congregation hastily retired to the tops of houses and other commanding positions to catch glimpses of the battle. A heavy cloud of smoke gathered along the valley, and large bodies of federal troops could be seen marshalling from all directions on the north, or arrayed in long lines of battle at the foot of South Mountain. New lines of smoke, bursting into existence high up the steep wooded slopes in front of the union lines revealed the position of the enemy. The picture, set in its frame of mountains and valley, with the golden sun shining upon it, with its moving figures and banks of bluish white smoke, was a grand one.

Of the result of this engagement I need not speak. All are familiar with the history of the battle of South Mountain and of the surrender of Harper's Ferry. Firing at the latter point seemed to cease about noon.

The next day, I think, several thousands of our troops reached our lines as paroled prisoners from Harper's Ferry, all with bitter curses on their lips at the treachery of Colonel Miles, who, they said, had sold them for a dollar per man.

I have no comments to make upon this affair, by which our country was deprived of the services of eleven thousand men at a time when the nation was in an agony of distress from other defeats, and when the cause seemed beset with infinite peril. The act will stand in history with an unenviable record attached.

On the 17th of September matters reached a crisis in Western Maryland, and the great battle of Antietam was fought. Our regiment took no part, having been detailed to assist in keeping open communication between the Army of the Potomac and Washington City. This service, though extremely arduous—requiring us to be almost constantly in the saddle—was exciting and invigorating.

Three days after the engagement we started to rejoin the main army crossing South Mountain at the scene of the action there. The marks of conflict were everywhere visible in the woods. The steep mountain side from whence the enemy had been driven by the steady and heroic advance of our infantry showed that our soldiers had lost none of their prowess by their misfortunes on other fields. At the Stone Bridge across Antietam creek, where Burnside's corps had such a terrible struggle, we found evidence of a sanguinary engagement. Four or five hundred new-made graves stretched in rows in the strip of narrow bottom skirting the stream. On the other side, where the enemy's lines were drawn up to contest the passage, the ground was strewn with broken muskets and accouterments. Farther on toward Sharpsburg burial parties were still engaged in interring the dead. In a narrow ravine below the road the dead body of a Union soldier was visible, all swelled and blackened by the three days of exposure to the sun, the belt around his waist cutting deep into the flesh. Many of the houses in the village were struck by the shots, but the damage done was less than could have been expected.

We found the Army of the Potomac encamped upon the north bank of the river, and on the ground where the right wing had been engaged, while the enemy mustered in force upon the opposite shore. During the day of our arrival there was sharp skirmishing between the hostile lines, resulting in some loss on our side.

Here the battle must have raged with great fury. The fields were covered with dead horses, broken small arms, dismounted cannon, bullets, shot, pieces of shell, new-made graves. Trees and fences and houses were torn to pieces as if by a storm of missiles. Here, too, the dead were being gathered in from out-of-the-way places, while from the many hospitals around a stream of bodies were constantly flowing to their last resting places, carried on stretchers by details of soldiers.

The most painful scenes, however, were at the hospitals, among the poor mangled creatures, who still lived and suffered through the long weary hours. I visited a barn occupied by the confederate wounded. All around the yard outside were scattered pieces of legs, arms, and flesh. Under a canvas that had been stretched from some poles to shade those beneath I found some eighteen or twenty badly wounded men. Two or three dead bodies were lying as they had been when they ceased to breathe. One poor creature was stretched upon his back, in the last agony; in his struggles, the straw had worked up across his face, and now, when he was no longer able to move, with each gasp it was settling deeper into his mouth. One young lieutenant from Alabama, who had his leg torn open by a grape-shot—which grape-shot he had picked up, and now displayed as a trophy—was talking to some of our men in quite a cheerful manner. While regretting the war in the abstract, he had felt it to be his duty, he said, to defend his native south.

I was astonished to see great squads of confederates wandering about through the woods beyond the hospital, carrying their muskets, and apparently feeling at home. I am free to say that I cannot understand it yet. If they were prisoners of war they were entrusted to a greater extent than was prudent, at least; if they were not, it was about time they were captured.

I left this scene of woe with a heart sickened with war and its innumerable horrors. The strange machines of the South, which had inaugurated this slaughter, was doubly strange for their persistence in it. Begun without a reason, and continued against reason, it presented a pitiable spectacle, wherein two great sections of a common country were arrayed one against the other in a mortal strife by the machinations of a few men, who all through the struggle had managed to keep from the front, and to hold the direction of affairs at the Confederate Capital.

The conduct of our soldiers at Antietam has always surprised me. Weary from long, tedious marches; so often defeated upon the fields of Virginia until their most sanguine friends believed them to be utterly exhausted; confronted by confident and numerous foes, who occupied their own chosen ground and were commanded by their most popular general, it is certainly a matter of surprise that our soldiers should have displayed the obstinacy and valor which they exhibited at this battle. Clearly enough, such an army was unconquerable. The world will hardly be able to furnish an example of superior courage and endurance under similar circumstances. The whole subsequent history of the Army of the Potomac is in keeping with the invincible character indelibly recorded upon the field of Antietam.

At this camp, just previous to marching, the portion of the regiment without carbines received them. This was a welcome epoch in our military life, though they added much to our burdens and discomforts upon the march. Heretofore we had been compelled either to retire before the enemy when attacked, or close in upon his troops with sabres in hand. This great disadvantage had more than once affected the morale of the soldiers of our regiment, although perhaps no actual defeat had been suffered in consequence of the absence of these weapons, and the demoralization was perhaps the dread of some future untoward encounter. The guns furnished were Sharp's breechloading rifles—a very serviceable piece. The government was now putting forth every effort to fully equip its troops, for the war, which by this time had deepened and broadened into a contest of fearful magnitude, rendered such action an imperative necessity.

A few solemn reflections crossed my mind during these days. We had been in service some fourteen months, and had almost two years yet to stay. The now almost endless succession of skirmishes and battles prospectively stretched off into the future, diminishing our hopes of ever seeing our homes again unless as maimed or diseased creatures—a burden to ourselves and all the world.

The past five months of our soldiering had been spent almost continuously under fire; our once powerful regiment had dwindled away until it was now but a mere skeleton of its former self; our dead were scattered over a vast area of country; our ranks had been relieved of all surplus material of men half-hearted in the cause who had deserted us when it became apparent that we were to be no holiday soldiers, and the remainder, though few in numbers, were equally brave and reliable.

The letters sent home, though written in no boastful spirit, were full of genuine pluck; a despairing word was never allowed to creep in. The sentiment—"the last man and the last dollar"—seemed to have become a sort of fixed idea in every mind. The crude, stiff figures of the first days in ranks had disappeared; the easy, careless bearing, the laughing eyes, the joyous spirit that cropped out in shouts when the bugles sounded "to horse" for the uncertain march; the gladness with which they welcomed the arduous duties of the picket, if only it was upon some new road and promised a change of scenes and adventures; the alacrity with which they seized their rifles and fell into line as if by instinct upon a threatened attack—all these peculiarities gave promise of a glorious and gallant future for American soldiers. No doubt these months of struggle were having a similar influence upon the men on the other side. I would not detract one jot or tittle from their prowess as soldiers; I rather am proud of it. They had already proven themselves foemen worthy of our steel. They, two, were Americans, and their ranks no doubt contained a less percentage of men uninterested in the success of their cause then ours of men uninterested in our cause. This was one of the great advantages the Confederacy had over the North. It cost them infinitely less to raise an army of reliable men than our government, for the reason that, once enlisted, their soldiers fought out the battle, while at least one-half of ours made it the study of their lives to avoid all conflicts they possibly could, hugging all opportunities to be sent to dismounted or convalescent camp, from which it required a strong arm to remove them, and then, as a last resort, deserting the flag. This, perhaps, was the best step for the country they could have taken; it did not add to their guilt, for they had already broken from the solemn obligations taken on enlistment, and were thus deserters of the meanest sort, living off the government they had so vitally injured.

Six days after the battle of Antietam the regiment unfurled its banners and turned its face once more towards Virginia. We found the whole Army of the Potomac under arms and moving, the long blue ranks creeping like a huge serpent over the mountains and down the valleys towards Harper's Ferry. As the country north of the river was entirely clear of the enemy, our march was undisturbed by hostile demonstrations, and conducted by easy stages, without advance guards or flankers.

At the Ferry General Sumner's corps had already pitched its tents behind the well-finished earthworks, while in its front the enemy's pickets were visible well out on the road towards Charlestown, of John Brown Memory.

We went into camp at the village of Knoxville, some two miles down the Potomac from Harper's Ferry, where our Sibley tents were pitched for the first time in several months.

Knoxville to Falmouth

The prospects of a few days of rest in camp, of which both men and horses stood so much in need, had an exhilarating effect upon all. The forges were put in operation, and the blacksmiths kept busily engaged in shoeing the animals—the pikes of Maryland had made sad havoc with those put on before we left the Peninsula—their ringing hammers sounding pleasantly, reminding one of the peaceful days of yore. Fresh arrivals of horses to remount our stragglers became of daily occurrence, and outfits of clothing and arms and ammunition to replace that which had become worthless from the wear and tear of the campaign.

My poor little Bobby, who had borne me upon his faithful legs with a cheerfulness that often put me to shame for my occasional fits of peevishness, was now about disabled. He had carried me over two hundred miles since last shod—most of the distance over macadamized roads and rocky paths; his shoes had long since dropped from his feet, and no opportunity during those days of constant fighting and marching presented itself to have them replaced; the hoofs were so worn that there were now no means of attaching a shoe to them until they had grown out again. When I rode him—which I did not unless when compelled to—it seemed to me that I could feel the pebbles on the earth press into my very heart as the sensitive little creature would limp and shriek in his agony. Upon the first opportunity, therefore, after much argument and coaxing, by which I managed to convince our first sergeant of the absolute necessity of such a change, I secured one of the new horses, and Bobby was condemned and turned over to the regimental quartermaster, to be sent to a corral and recruited up. Much as I regretted to part from him, it was pleasant to think there were prospects of easier times in store for my faithful little pony than roughing life in the field under a dragoon. My last adventure with him was marked by an event which demonstrated that it was no longer safe for me to depend upon him in an hour of danger. We were sent across the river at Harper's Ferry, early one morning, to drive in the enemy's pickets along the Charlestown road, in front of Sumner's corps, to ascertain if possible the location of the nearest considerable force of confederates in the Shenandoah valley. Of course this involved a fight, which duly occurred, the enemy making no resistance until the regiment had reached a point near Charlestown, their pickets retiring slowly without firing. Here they halted and delivered a few shots, succeeding in killing a member of D Company, which was deployed as skirmishers across the front of the regiment and well in advance, whose dead body was carried past us to the rear by a comrade, swung across the horse before him. The enemy soon after opened with artillery, displaying some strength, and our company was withdrawn from the regiment and deployed as skirmishers across the country on the left of the road, advancing rapidly towards a strip of timberland which stretched away to the eastward. On our route we were obliged to cross numerous fences and ravines and swamps, and at a gallop; and before long it became evident that my pony could not proceed much further. I fell behind in spite of my efforts to keep up, driven almost frantic by the orders of the sergeant in charge to keep in line. Bobby could not cross a fence where there was one rail above another, and so for ditches, I had to ride around them all. At last, while riding through a cornfield he came in contact with several stout stalks, and stopped altogether. I made no efforts to urge him further; I would rather have lost my right arm than injure him now by whip or spurs, and so, amid the hearty—or, perhaps, heartless laughs that greeted me I dismounted and led the exhausted creature to a brook, where he drank heavily, and then revived a little. Upon our return to camp I vigorously protested against ever being again compelled to risk my earthly existence in such a manner.

Bopenhagen captured a confederate lieutenant upon this occasion. That individual—the confederate lieutenant—was not cognizant of our presence in that quarter, and was riding along leisurely on a visit to some pickets he imagined were located in a field in that vicinity, when a sudden turn in the road brought him face to face with our able-bodied Dutch private, who, in a turn of another sort, brought his cocked carbine to bear upon the unfortunate lieutenant with such promptitude that that individual immediately held up his hand as a token of submission. Bopenhagen divested him of his accouterments and took him to the rear, where they met Lieutenant McClain marching at the head of the reserve, to whom Bopenhagen reported with his prisoner. The confederate asked Lieutenant McClain for an escort of equal rank with himself to convey him to his destination, asserting that this was one of the courtesies of war, but this request was denied, with the remark that in the estimation of our lieutenant a private in the Union army was of higher rank than any officer in the confederate service.

During these days an order was issued by the War Department permitting volunteers to enlist in the regular army for the balance of their terms of enlistment, and settling in full their accounts up to the date of their discharge from their old regiments. In consequence of this curious order there was a terrific rush from the volunteer infantry to the regular cavalry and artillery—two branches of service then popularly believed to be a sort of sinecure, if there be such a thing as a sinecure in a common soldier's life. The pressure for discharges from the abovementioned arm became so great that the volunteer officers, to check it, threw obstacles in the way, and many were the devices and schemes invented and resorted to by the men to carry out their desires. Their camp guards were instructed to allow no one outside certain established limits; the guards at the bridge across the Potomac would permit nobody across to our side of the river without a pass; threats were made and restrictions of all sorts were created; but all to no purpose. The men would slip out of camp and cross the river in some way known only to themselves, and take refuge in our camp. On one occasion, when our company was returning from picket duty along the Charlestown road, we were beset by about a hundred infantrymen who wanted to enlist in our regiment. Said they:

"If you want them, we can get you fifteen hundred men in as many minutes. We are tired of this sort of service."

Lieutenant McClain said he could not take so many as they offered to procure him in that short time; then, with mock severity of manner, he ordered them all under arrest, formed them in the road, placed the company around then, as guards, and marched them in triumph, across the bridge to camp, to their great delight.

The strength of the regiment was about doubled under this order, being reinforced by some five hundred and fifty men. However no actual benefit was derived from them for several months afterward, as they had yet to be mounted and drilled. When the next campaign began they were sent to Washington by rail, where they went into camp.

Some of the cunning ones took advantage of the discharges received from their commands to join the regulars by leaving for home, and never showing themselves at our camps. These, however, were very few in number.

Considering all the results of this order from the War Department, I doubt if they established either its wisdom or expediency. A few of the men thus recruited were good soldiers after they came to us, but a great majority proved to be the reverse, attempting all sorts of dodges to shirk their legitimate duties, some even resorting to the cruel device of driving nails into their horses feet to disable them. Apart from this, there were several months of time lost in preparing them for their new duties, at a time when the regiments, depleted by their absence could but sadly afford to lose them. A proper effort would have filled our ranks with entirely new material, which could have been made equally efficient in the same length of time, of undoubted patriotism, and without that dangerous knowledge of the modes of shirking duties and evading discipline so aptly displayed by many of these recruits.

My new horse was a complete contrast to Bobby—physically and mentally, if such an expression can be allowed as applied to animals. He was a tall, raw-boned, gaunt, long-eared, long-headed old fellow, equally insensible to voice and spur, of peaceable proclivities as to his four-footed companions; Bobby was a low, well-rounded pony that smote his enemies hip and thigh on every feasible opportunity. Instead of Bobby's cheerful, affectionate disposition, the new old fellow possessed a most melancholy temperament which found an unmistakable expression in that long, doleful face, and seemed to have no appreciation of friendship or good treatment. I may err somewhat in speaking of good treatment; the contrast between him and my dear pony was so great, and first I was so prejudiced against him that perhaps I did not extend to him the hearty affection I so lavishly bestowed on the other.

However, in the days that followed I learned to think well of this new old fellow, this sombre, long-headed, hard-trotting, coarse-haired old horse, for, if he did not prepossess me at first sight, he afterwards proved himself one of the most faithful, sure-footed, and trustworthy of his kind. By common consent he was named Bucephalus—for the paramount reason that he was unlike that celebrated animal in every particular.[1]

While camped at Knoxville we were frequently sent across the river

---

[1] Bucephalus, the horse of Alexander the Great, was called the Great War Horse.

at Harper's Ferry and out along the Charlestown road, to drive in the advanced posts of the enemy. On many of these occasions we would lose a man or two, and occasionally capture a prisoner. Though these adventures were painfully frequent, they were so trifling in comparison with the mightier events of the war as to be entirely overlooked by the newspapers, and though the gallantry displayed at times was really deserving of notice by the journalists attached to the army, affording us at least an acknowledgement of duties well-performed, with a corresponding encouragement, they still remain a part of the unwritten history of the Sixth Cavalry. The participants have the simple consolation of knowing that they fulfilled their obligations with conscientious fidelity.

In addition to these frequent forays, the details of companies for videttes along Sumner's front were heavy, bringing each one on duty about twice a week. This, however, was a pleasant relief from the discipline of the camp, which was now being strongly enforced, and was exceedingly distasteful.

On one of these occasions, when shadowy Todd, shadowy no longer, was my companion on post, occupying a knoll to the left of the Charlestown road some four miles from Harper's Ferry, we enjoyed a new feature of military excitement. Sergeant Croy had charge of the videttes at this point. Across the road, posted on another knoll perhaps two hundred yards distant from the one on which we were located, were two other men.

Todd had managed to start a fire early, and surreptitiously prepare our coffee, while I kept a sharp lookout both to front and rear—in the latter direction, lest some of our officers should approach unawares and catch him dismounted, for which offense, being a disobedience of orders, he might be severely punished—and we were just diving into our frugal breakfast, when we became conscious that our friends on the other knoll were uneasy about something. They kept dodging and peering about in a curious manner, their eyes being apparently fixed upon some object far up the road. This road, by the side of which Todd and I were located, a little further out from us turned abruptly to the left around a belt of timber that was dense enough to hide a body of troops approaching from the south until they should pass into sight around the bend. Presently our friends waved their hands to us, and we hastily dismounted, tightened our saddle girths, remounted, reined our horses back down the knoll so that nothing but our heads were visible from the road beyond, cocked our guns, and awaited the result. In a few moments a party of confederate calvary made its appearance, moving cautiously out from the cover of the woods. We gave an involuntary glance backwards to take a last look at the point where the fence was down, and through which we should be obliged to escape, to measure the distance and assure ourselves, and then with beating hearts raised our guns to fire. There is something about this thing of deliberately aiming at human beings when there is an absence of savage excitement, that makes one hesitate; he does not care to shoot; he has a recollection of the horror of deeds of blood he used to feel, long, long ago. It seems to him an actual crime. Thus I, at least, felt upon this occasion. Both of us hesitated, held apparently by the same reluctance.

This hesitation, perhaps, saved some trouble and misunderstanding from occurring. Just as we were about to pull our triggers the party halted, and displayed a white handkerchief on the end of a stick. We understood it all now. This party was on a peaceful mission, and we promptly lowered our carbines, feeling a great sense of relief.

Evans, who happened to be in the vicinity, galloped down and notified Sergeant Croy of the arrival of a flag of truce. That non-commissioned officer, with due formality, advanced beyond our lines a short distance, accompanied by a soldier, and halted. Two of the confederates rode out from the main body to meet him. After a brief conversation each party returned to their respective lines, and Croy sent a man to Sumner's headquarters for the adjutant general of the corps, to notify him of a party bearing a white flag, who desired to communicate with the commander-in-chief.

The confederates dismounted, and disposed of themselves in comfortable positions to await further proceedings. About an hour afterward a staff officer arrived and went out to meet them, and after a short conference we saw the whole party mount their horses, and, headed by this staff officer, riding leisurely down toward our lines, apparently in the most amicable of moods.

During that brief time which had elapsed between the first appearance of the flag of truce until now, Todd and I indulged in the most absurd speculation possible as to the import of the communication they desired to make. Perhaps the confederates were bearers of peace proposition, of proposals by General Lee to surrender, and then we began to feel homesick at the base thought of a cessation of the war. These surmises were all promptly terminated by the appearance directly in the rear of the party of confederates, of quite a number of federal prisoners, who proved to be members of the One Hundred and Eighteenth Pennsylvania Volunteers, and who had been captured two or three days after the battle of Antietem, in an attempt to effect a lodgement on the south side of the Potomac.

The whole party halted beside a house where, after a short delay, our soldiers were formally transferred to the authority of the United States. They gave three rousing cheers for the Stars and Stripes, to the great amusement of the confederates. After a very agreeable interview our party took up their line of march for corps headquarters, while the confederate cavalry—which, by the way, belonged to the Nineteenth Virginia regiment, as I understood—remounted their horses, and rode slowly back to their camp, and we were again unrelenting enemies.

During our encampment at Knoxville General J.E.B. Stuart made his second ride around the Army of the Potomac, with success, recrossing safely into Virginia at one of the fords near the mouth of the Monocacy. Our regiment, among others, was sent out to intercept him, and after a very fatiguing night march halted at two o'clock in the morning, on one of the roads leading towards Frederick City where the tired men dismounted, built small fires, cooked and ate some rations, and laid down to sleep. Evans and I found a delicious retreat across in a field among some very fine hay, of which there was a quantity ample for our horses and a bed for ourselves. The night was quite cool, and we were so exhausted, and the gentle warmth was so agreeable, that before we were aware of it we were both sound asleep, from which we did not awaken until late the next morning. We found our horses quietly grazing on the grass near us, but the regiment had disappeared. Somewhat alarmed we hastily cleaned our animals, saddled, mounted, and hurriedly followed the road along which we supposed they had departed.

After some questioning of citizens we finally learned that a mounted force had marched past their houses just before daylight along the road towards Frederick City, and on obtaining this clue pushed along after it, not doubting that it was the Sixth Cavalry. Some hours later the thunder of artillery broke upon our ears, apparently six or seven miles distant, and directly ahead. We now broke into a trot, and had proceeded perhaps two miles, when looking up the long straight road our eyes discovered a picket, which picket, from the uneasy way he shifted from one point to another, was evidently alarmed at something. He wore a blue uniform, but seemed to be shy of us, and for this reason we became suspicious that he was one of their wolves in sheep's clothing so often mentioned. He showed signs of firing, and Evans and I halted. Presently a sergeant and twelve men appeared, and after scrutinizing us sharply motioned us to advance. Our explanations proving satisfactory we were allowed to proceed. The name of the regiment to which this cautious vidette belonged was the First Maine Cavalry.

We found Frederick City wild with excitement. The enemy's cavalry were momentarily expected to make an attack, and as our mounted forces were so scattered about on the different roads it was feared they might be successful. Many persons applied to us for information, but we could give them none. We could only speculate upon probabilities. The artillery fire could still be heard but this was rapidly moving off in an easterly direction, indicating a sort of running fight, and the probability was that the enemy's troops would keep together if possible, and this made the hope of keeping them out of town brighter.

As the sounds were swinging around towards the Sugar Loaf mountain, we started out on the Buckeystown pike to intercept it, expecting to fall in with the regiment in that vicinity. Instead of this, however, we followed the advance of our forces, consisting of some volunteer cavalry, exchanging shots with the confederates, who had escaped across the Potomac in the vicinity of the Monocacy.

Upon consultation we came to the conclusion that our best plan would be to return to our camp at Knoxville, instead of making further efforts at finding the Sixth Cavalry, and wearing our horses out in a vain attempt to rejoin it. General Pleasanton was already returning from his fruitless chase after the confederates, and this movement on his part was first-class evidence that the raid was over.

To avoid the rough, hilly road through the country, we crossed to the lower bank of the canal at Point of Rocks, supposing that we would have no difficulty in finding numerous bridges at short intervals upon which to cross to the mainland in case of necessity, and travelled up the river.

I do not think I shall soon forget that night. Before we had gone far it became intensely dark. A terrific storm came up; the lightning blinded us by its dazzling vividness, and the thunder deafened us by its terrific crashing, followed by a thousand echoes from the hills on either side; the rain came down like a deluge. The path was along a narrow causeway, which at short intervals was cut through for outlets by which to drain the canal, and across these chasms narrow wooden bridges, rather unsubstantial, and without a protecting rail on either side, were built. Under these bridges we could hear the sound of rushing waters, and shuddered to think how a single false step by our horses would pitch us headlong into the inexorable currents. We were imprisoned on either side by water—the rushing river on the left, the still but no less dangerous canal on the right. As we rode along, with reins loosened to enable our horses to feel their way over the narrow path and crossing, we peered in vain for a bridge to take us over the canal to the mainland. Finally, after groping our way for many hours, we heard voices of men beyond us in the distance, sounding wonderfully plain in the humid air—the storm had ceased two hours before—and upon reaching them found were at Berlin. Here we were delighted to discern a bridge, upon which we crossed, and once more stood upon safe ground. Learning from some of the men that we were but a short distance from Knoxville, and anxious to reach camp as soon as possible, we continued our journey, very hungry, wet, and tired, up the hill, halting once at a house where we aroused the inmates to inquire the way. A colored man came to the door, apparently not much pleased, but a few decided remarks had the effect of bringing him to his senses, and he condescended to give us some directions. After riding a few miles further we reached a hamlet where two or three roads formed a junction, and we were somewhat puzzled to know which one to follow. We did not care to annoy anyone by rousing them to inquire; besides, our horses were much fatigued, and we had concluded to halt until daylight by some farmer's barn, where we could procure feed, and indulge ourselves with sleep; so we took a road leading off to the left—which, fortunately, afterwards proved to be the right one—and soon reached a locality that suited us. Here we unsaddled our animals and turned them loose to help themselves at a stack of hay, while we crawled into the barn, spread out our blankets upon some chaff, and soon fell asleep, from which we did not awaken until late the next morning.

When we came out of the barn door we found our horses lying on the ground enjoying themselves. The farmer was just coming down towards us from the house, evidently somewhat displeased with the liberties we had taken, but he was soon conciliated, and entered into a pleasant conversation with us. There were some potatoes in the barn and we still had some meat and coffee left, and we procured bread at the farm house, and were allowed liberty to cook at the kitchen fire; so we managed to have a very good breakfast.

The farmer gave us such explicit directions that we had no difficulty in finding Knoxville, which place we reached early in the forenoon. The regiment had not yet arrived, but came into camp late in the day. Old

Blue turned up alone, with a wounded forearm, declaring that he had fallen in with two of the enemy's scouts, with whom he had a fight, and from whom he had managed to escape after receiving the wound mentioned. There was a bullet hole through his wrist, that was certain. Many of the men doubted the truth of his story, however, and accounted for the wound in other ways. I am willing to believe him for reasons not necessary to mention.

A letter from the Common Soldier, dated at Harper's Ferry, September 28, 1862, shows that he was somewhat elated over the favorable operations in Maryland, and cheerful of the future. Among other things he mentions the exhilarating effects of the smiles of Maryland girls, sweet milk, green corn, peaches, good bread, eggs, butter, and pies, and has them so mixed up in his imagination that it is hard to tell which he appreciates most. He also records the fact that he has seen his friend Lieutenant Chill Hazard and Sergeant James M. Davis—he who came over to Camp East of Capital to tell him how "it went" at Dranesville—and that the latter had a hole cut through his cap by a confederate bullet at the second battle of Bull Run.

One morning, towards the latter part of October, orders were delivered to the men to prepare for an expedition with three days' rations. Shortly afterwards our squadrons filed out upon the road leading to Harper's Ferry where we crossed the river to the Virginia side, turned to the left and passed over the Shenandoah and moved down the Potomac around the base of the Loudon mountains. It was a wild, rugged country, and indescribably gloomy, dense woods growing among immense rocks, where it seemed strange that the trees could retain their hold in the shallow side. The narrow unfrequented road followed the foot of the hills one or two miles, and then mounted them by a series of short curves, until, almost before we were aware of it, we found ourselves well into the interior. Here the prospect was much more pleasant. The surroundings of well-tilled fields, comfortable houses, and capacious barns gave evidence of the thrift and well-directed affairs of the inhabitants. What was the more surprising and agreeable, the people greeted us with smiling faces,and showered upon us gifts of grapes, peaches, apples, and bread—substantial evidences of sympathy we had not expected to receive in Virginia.

When the command had passed beyond the pickets near Harper's Ferry an advance guard was sent forward as a precautionary measure, with instructions to halt just outside of Waterville. This part of the program was carried out, and when the regiment reached the outskirts of the village, after a momentary halt, it dashed through the streets on a charge. Three confederate officers, with their horses, were found and captured, to their great surprise.

One of these—a stout, red-headed young man—as our men dashed up, was standing on a porch talking to a young lady, who afterwards was known as his sister. His horse was hitched to the fence below the house. The lady clapped her hands and exclaimed:

"Bless the Lord! I knew they would come! I knew they would come!"

The officer did not seem to be so jubilant, especially when he found himself confronted by carbines, and saw his magnificent horse led to the rear in triumph; but he submitted gracefully, and surrendered up his arms. His sister said that she was adverse to his serving in the confederate army, from which he was then absent on leave, and about to return. When, a moment before our arrival, they had been conversing about his prospects, she was trying to persuade him to remain at home, and expressed the wish that "the Yankees might just then come and capture him." The words were scarcely out of her mouth before she heard the cheers, and saw the men in blue sweeping down around the hill into the village, and her desires were literally satisfied.

The same sympathy apparent all along the road was extended to us by the people of Waterville, who expressed joy at being visited by Union soldiers. We remained here fifteen or twenty minutes, enjoying their hospitality, and then advanced on Leesburg, a village said to be full of secessionists, some few miles further eastward.

The command reached a point perhaps two miles from Leesburg at dark, and halted for the night. Early next morning Todd and I started along a narrow path in the woods to find a spring from which to procure water for our coffee, and succeeded in finding one. Here we kindled a small fire, and proceeded with our culinary arrangements. While thus engaged the sound of a child's voice, singing a simple song, apparently some distance up the narrow path beyond the spring, broke upon our ears, and presently a little girl, clad in humble garments, came tripping gaily towards us. When she saw the two strange soldiers she seemed frightened for a moment, but regained her composure and reluctantly approached. After a short conversation she seemed to become assured, and took us to her home, a little cabin of two rooms, standing on a hillside a few rods from the spring. Here we found her sister, some three or four years older, making rye coffee.

We soon found that our youthful hostesses were inveterate rebels. Their hatred of Yankees was intense. In their conversation upon the effects of the war they displayed a precocity that was amazing, declaring that they could get along very well upon rye coffee without sugar. They told us, with evident relish, of the hanging of thirty men belonging to Captain Means' company of partisan rangers some time before, by confederates, and expressed their sorrow when we told them we had seen Captain Means about two months before, on the occasion of his escape.

After a very pleasant repast—for we had carried our coffee and meat and bread over to the cabin with us—we bade these precocious secessionists farewell, and rejoined the command.

Two or three companies dashed through Leesburg, but made no capture, and after an hour or two the whole force started on their return to the ferry, passing over a different road from the one on which we had advanced. That afternoon we reached Hillsborough, near the mountains, when a halt of perhaps an hour was made. This village we found full of handsome females, but, unlike those at Waterville, they sympathized with "the other side." At Hillsborough we learned that some confederate cavalry had surrounded a church in the neighborhood during divine service the Sunday before, and conscripted the male portion of the congregation.

That evening we moved out of Hillsborough along the base of the mountains towards Harper's Ferry and camped some two miles distant from the former place. Two of our party, who were out foraging, were captured by Captain Bob White's company of confederate partisans.[2]

Loudon County was the theater of many exciting events during the civil war. The people were pretty evenly divided, and each party being enthusiastic, raised troops for service in each army. The consequence was an unrelenting, merciless crusade upon each other, and mutual murder upon any occasion that presented itself. People were shot in their houses at night, unarmed, and in the presence of their families; outrages of all descriptions, which, in regularly organized armies, would have been met by prompt and severe punishment, were committed with impunity. Society was uprooted, and a reign of terror inaugurated.

The next day the command reached camp at Knoxville after a

[2]   Actually, it was Elijah White. See Frank M. Myers, *The Comanches: A History of White's Batallion, Virginia Cavalry, Laurel Brigade, Hampton Division, A.N.V., C.S.A.*, Baltimore, Kelly, Piet and Co., 1871. This book was reprinted in 1956 by the Continental Book Co., Marietta, Georgia.

fatiguing march, very glad that the excursion was over. On this expedition one Bradley, belonging to Company I, confiscated a stallion, which he found in a stable near Wheatland, and which was valued at nine hundred dollars. Months afterwards, while picketing the Rappahannock, a party of mounted confederates, who had learned that we were members of the Sixth United States Cavalry, inquired after Bradley. They were informed that he had deserted some months before. They then said it was, perhaps, as well for him that he had deserted, as, if he fell into their hands, he might expect death on account of the stealing of the horse at Wheatland. They had discovered the act and the name of the perpetrator in some way, and were evidently in a proper frame of mind to kill him.

Shortly after the Leesburg raid, one cold rainy morning we broke camp for the last time at Knoxville. As the command ascended a hill to the eastward of our old quarters, and came into sight of the Potomac at Berlin, long columns of cavalry, artillery, and infantry could be seen winding their way southward towards the river and over the hills beyond. It was now evident that a general advance had begun, and that, before long, we would be plunged into another earnest campaign; so, as the regiment passed over the pontoon bridge that had been thrown across at Berlin, and once more pressed the soil of Virginia, I could not help turning my head and taking a last look, and to bid farewell to the happy hills of old Maryland.

A long, dreary, weary march, with a constant rain pouring upon our devoted heads, and the roads trampled into a mass of mud by the troops, brought us to the vicinity of a place called Taylor's Tavern. There followed one of those miserable nights which the soldier occasionally experiences, and when it requires all the faith that he can summon to carry him through. The fields were flooded; the rain continued—a fine, permeating, misty rain, that worked its way through everything; we were benumbed with cold; no fires were allowed until late at night, and then they were limited to just enough to cook our coffee; you could not lie down, for the ground was like a pond. Some of the men, who were provided with rubber blankets they had captured at one place or another, improvised beds out of fence rails, and stretched upon them, covering themselves up with those blankets.

For myself, I thought I could freely give fifty dollars to rest with the hogs in the sty at my old home; but as the sty was not forthcoming, I adopted the next best thing, and crawled into a barn not far off, where, despite the cold and discomforts of my situation, I soon fell asleep, only awakening at about four o'clock, when the shrill notes of the bugle could be heard sounding "to horse."

After daybreak the command moved a few miles further into the interior, and then halted several days, to permit, as we supposed, the concentration of troops. Here we began to take our first lessons in foraging—General J.E.B. Stuart's raid into Pennsylvania, and the thieving propensities said to have been displayed by his soldiers on the occasions having roused a spirit of retaliation in the breasts of our men, who, up to this time, as a general thing, had fully paid for articles taken and used by them—and we were wont to sally out, in parties of three or four, at midnight, after the horses had been fully cared for, with our revolvers buckled on as a safeguard against possible contingencies, and hen-roosts, sheepyards, beehives, and other eatables known to the common soldier as luxuries on account of having long been deprived of them, suffered accordingly. These days found us full of spirit, and just beginning to realize the wild excitement of a dragoon's life during an actual campaign. Unheeded were the government rations, except the staple articles of salt, sugar, crackers, and coffee; and these became simply auxiliaries.

One of the favorite incidents of foraging was to go, after the spoils had been secured, to a cabin, arouse the inmates, and compel them to cook for us. As a general thing, the parties thus unceremoniously awakened would be greatly frightened, but after a while would become more assured by our conversation, although we would maintain a proper reserve as to our identity. It was customary, after satisfying our stomachs, and retaining sufficient for the morrow, to give the balance to the family, and to repay them with money for the trouble and annoyance incurred. In selecting subjects for these raids large frame houses were given a preference, for the reason that the plain and lowly cabins seemed to be but poorly able to suffer. Nothing was wasted; what we gave away sometimes was sufficient to keep the family to whom given at least a week.

As one instance of these adventures, and to show our general disposition towards these people, I will mention a foraging expedition made one night during our stay in this camp by Sergeant Croy and myself. We started out about eleven o'clock, very hungry, fully equipped to protect ourselves against capture, for a point which we thought had not yet been visited by our troops, and where the prospect of supply was deemed to be more favorable than usual. Accordingly, pushing out over the fields, we made our way, the uppermost idea in our heads being to avoid the public roads for fear of confederate patrols and pickets. The night was very dark, and we were compelled to feel our way very cautiously across the fields and through the woods and over the ravines we had to pass. After travelling perhaps two miles we found ourselves in the vicinity of a farm house, and on a fence close by, cozily perched for the night, were four large turkeys. Croy, who was ahead, turned quietly around, pointed to the luxurious objects, went through a few pantomime motions, and then slipped stealthily forward, and gently seized the feet of two, one in each hand, adroitly swung one to me, and the next moment we bounded rapidly from the spot. There was fluttering and a dog came bouncing after us, but did not follow far, and soon all was quiet again. We cut off the heads of our prizes, and began searching for a cabin where we might have these prepared for supper. At last, passing through a piece of timber-land that stretched across a rather wild-looking hollow, we discovered the faint outline of a small house. Thither we wended our way, crossing a low fence, and coming out upon a narrow path which seemed to lead directly down the hill to the house. This path stretched past a spring of water, and near this spring, deftly settled into the flowing stream was a box, covered by a neatly contrived lid, and upon this lid was placed a large stone to keep it closed.

Croy slowly stopped, removed the stone, raised the lid, looked in a moment, softly lowered the lid again, stretched to his full height, and, with his right forefinger, pointed solemnly at the box, as much as to say, "We will attend to you after a while." It contained, according to his account, a full assortment of milk and butter.

We now crept quietly towards the house. All was dark and still. Croy knocked sharply on the door, and presently a female voice, with a very perceptible tremor in it, called out:

"Who is there?"

"Friends," we replied.

There was some delay, a cautious moving about and presently a light flashed through the windows. The door was then hesitatingly opened, and the owner of the voice, a good looking white woman, appeared, holding in her hand a lighted candle. Her fright seemed to increase when she found herself confronted by two Yankee soldiers, but on our assuring her that we meant no harm to her, but simply wanted her to do some cooking for us, for which she should be paid, she seemed to recover her equanimity, and quietly asked us to come in and be seated.

She was a woman apparently about thirty-five years of age, with blue eyes, light hair, and a countenance which, though serene, yet bore some marks of sorrow and care. She had no companions except her child, four years old, and a bright little colored nurse the latter kept her sharp eyes fixed upon us with a resolute stare, as though she were determined to permit no misdemeanor on our part.

I confess to feeling somewhat taken aback by the kind and confidential reception extended to us by this lady. We had expected to find a colored family, by whom we always expected to be treated kindly, and to look over our abrupt ways; but to be thus received by an uprooted white lady at such an unseasonable hour was an experience absolutely amazing. We felt that, under the circumstances, we were put upon our good behavior.

After asking a few questions about the wood and water, Croy and I threw our plunder upon the outer door step, so that the blood would not soil the floor, and proceeded to bring in these necessary articles, and in a few moments we had an immense pot swung up in the old-fashioned fireplace, over a crackling blaze; and soon after, when the water had reached the scalding point, the turkeys were immersed, the feathers stripped off, the bodies dressed, and then turned over to our hostess for the delicate manipulations of her feminine hand.

During all this time our conversation seemed of the pleasantest character, a mutual interest having been developed in our personal histories. Hers was a sad narrative. The war had visited upon her its full share of suffering. Her husband, she said, was serving in Longstreet's corps, attached to the artillery, and she begged us to be considerate to him in case he fell into our hands. His name was Benjamin Franklin. Sometimes she was compelled to live for days at a time on cornmeal, but her cow proved a valuable assistance to her, furnishing her with milk and butter. She had not heard from her husband for more than a year. The poor families whose protectors were in the confederate army received assistance from a person appointed for that purpose by the State authorities, who distributed rations in much the same way they were doled out to their soldiers—each person thus authorized having charge of a district for which he was held responsible. If I remember aright, they were, in this instance, allowed one-half bushel of cornmeal per week. Sometimes, however, as during the presence of our troops, this allowance was entirely cut off, and then they were obliged to pick up something to eat as best they could, often being reduced to the point of actual starvation.

The little boy was a very intelligent lad, with large blue eyes. He seemed to regard us with feelings of apprehension, as if he realized that we were arrayed against his father in war, and all our efforts to induce him to be sociable were in vain. He clung to the little nurse with a firm hold, keeping those large, blue eyes fixed upon us with a peculiar glare.

By and by our feast was ready. The smoking turkeys, stewed to a tender mass, and redolent with a sweet savor, were deposited upon an immense plate; our crackers and coffee were produced and prepared—we never failed to take these along, as they were necessary auxiliaries; and the whole party sat around the festive board apparently in the most joyous mood, the little nurse being so far netted as to indulge in several hearty laughs. But the boy—he remained stolid through it all.

When our meal was over there yet remained one whole turkey, and most of the other. The latter we presented to our hostess, in addition to fifty cents in money—all the change we had in our possession. The whole turkey we concluded to retain for the morrow's rations.

It was about two o'clock in the morning when we were through. A pleasant good-bye passed between us as we left the house, and the door closed upon us—perhaps forever.

I touched Croy upon the shoulder as we passed the spring, and, imitating his former action, pointed silently towards the little pantry.

"I would rather lose my right arm," says Croy, with an emphasis that surprised me, "than to touch a single article after such a reception as we have just experienced."

"That is exactly how I feel," I responded.

We glided silently away, reaching camp in due time, spread our blankets upon the ground, stowed away our turkey, laid down and soon forgot our troubles in the sound slumber that followed.

On another night, shortly after this, a party, headed by Sergeant McMasters, went on a foraging expedition in the same neighborhood. In reconnoitering a barnyard they discovered chickens roosting in the top of an apple tree, and the young men, already feasting in anticipation on the delicate fowls, crossed the fence and moved on the coveted prey, which were so perched as to render climbing necessary. Their little programme, however, was broken by an unlooked-for event. A sudden yell, from the powerful lungs of a farmer, rose upon the midnight air, followed by the savage bark of at least more than one dog; some of the young men were prepared to swear there were a dozen. The foragers beat a hasty retreat, laughing at one another in their pell mell flight; but the dogs came so close that some one must halt and make a stand to cover the retrograde movement. Sergeant McMasters stopped at one corner of the barn, drew his revolver, posted himself on the defensive, and awaited the coming of the enemy.

He did not have to tarry long. The yelp of the dogs came nearer and nearer; the stentorian voice of the farmer could be heard urging them on to a bloody conquest; the rush of many feet came sweeping round the building, and Sergeant McMasters setting his teeth in desperation, fired as they turned past the corner of the barn. The dogs, frightened at the flash and report, fled; the farmer, who had rushed headlong to the spot, called out to the soldier for God's sake not to shoot him. In the confusion thus created, McMasters managed to slip off, and the young men all reached home in safety, though sadly disappointed in their anticipations of a luxurious meal.

The joke stirred up many a laugh afterwards, under circumstances when laughs required no ordinary stimulants to rouse them. No doubt that stalwart farmer has had his laugh over the adventure also, and will tell his children in after days about his defeat of the Yankee foragers.

The last foraging expedition made by Croy and me from this camp was eminently successful. We travelled perhaps a mile, keeping off the main road, but always remaining in sight of it, so that we might not lose our way, when we came in sight of an old fashioned mansion, in front of which swung a huge sign. Of course, this must be an inn. Croy proposed that we should visit it, and procure supper there. I assented, and we crossed over the fence into the road, and approached with cautious steps, lest we might encounter a confederate first. The coast however, was clear. After a series of knocks at the door, it was opened, and two buxom young ladies appeared, one of whom held a light.

"I see you keep a tavern here," said Croy; "We called to procure supper."

"Gentlemen," said one of the young ladies, "this is a house of private entertainment; we cannot accommodate you."

"Well, there is a sign up there—ain't this a tavern?"

"This is a house of private entertainment—that sign says so. We do not keep a public house."

Croy looked puzzled. The young ladies looked as though they thought the conversation better close here, and made a movement as if to shut the door.

"Pri—vate—enter—tain—ment," slowly drawled out Croy. "I am a sergeant—you are a Private, Davis; they must mean you."

"Well," said I, "let us go; if they won't entertain you they can't entertain me."

The sign did read "Private Entertainment," and I have ever since been puzzled to know what it meant.

We did not leave the premises, however, without paying a visit to the barnyard. A close scrutiny of the trees failed to show the presence of fowls, and we crawled into a corn crib. Here, visible against the sky through a crack, we saw numerous legs, four of which we quietly and carefully grasped, and made our way to camp with two nice fat pullets.

On the last day of October Company F was ordered in from picket for the usual inspection and muster for pay, with the balance of the regiment. This formality consisted in a close scrutiny of arms and accouterments, and the personal knowledge of the commanding officer of the regiment that the men on the muster rolls were actually present or duly accounted for at that particular date. To facilitate matters, and prevent mistakes, the men fell into ranks under arms, with carbines at the shoulder and then each man in succession, as his name was called, dropped his piece to an order.

On this particular occasion, as soon as the inspection and muster of the fourth squadron was completed, we were ordered out on a reconnaissance toward Snickersviile, near the base of the Blue Ridge mountains. The squadron moved slowly forth upon the road to the front. The weather was delicious, and our ride a pleasant one. At a house by the roadside, perhaps three miles from camp, I purchased a large roll of nice fresh butter, which, to make the rest of the men feel bad, I displayed to their envious eyes, and which, for safe keeping, I carefully packed away in my tin cup, and then snugly fastened the latter upon the canter of my saddle, mouth uppermost, so that, in case it became softened, the delicious oleaginous material should not be lost.

About five miles from camp we passed the videttes occupying the extreme outpost—two men, who stated that the enemy had a picket at Snickersville, some three miles distant. Accompanying the squadron was a man who seemed to be a guide, said to have been old resident of the neighborhood, dressed in a blue uniform, and who seemed to be well acquainted with the people.

As soon as we had passed the outpost an advance guard was sent forward about two hundred yards; the column proceeded at a cautious gate and a sharp lookout on both flanks was maintained.

As we rode over a low hill, perhaps a mile from the vidette, the column came in full view of a blacksmith shop, a school house, two dwellings, and a cabin, clustered tolerably close together, about three hundred yards distant. Between our party and the schoolhouse, and about a couple of rods from the latter, hitched to a fence and some trees, stood a dozen or more horses saddled and bridled, while lying scattered around under the shade of the timber were an equal number of confederate soldiers. They did not seem to notice us on the instant, but presently one of them gave a shout, and then there was a great scrambling for horses on their part.

With us there was also great excitement. The advance guard was ordered to charge, and eight men from the head of the column pushed out to support them. There was some delay in this movement, the men ordered out seeming to hesitate; but the whole squadron finally dashed down upon the frightened confederates, who were making frantic efforts to get away. By the time we reached the spot they were all mounted and off as hard as they could gallop, with one exception. One man fled through the woods, leaving his animal tied; and this animal Sergeant Walsh attempted to secure by springing off his own horse and letting it go—which it did—following the confederates in their headlong flight. By this piece of strategy, Sergeant Walsh captured a horse that could not get away, and lost his own.

There was some wild firing on our part, at the imminent risk of killing our own men, and one confederate was said to have been wounded; if he was, he escaped nevertheless. Six of our men dashed up to the door of the blacksmith shop and, thrusting their cocked carbines inside, ordered all the inmates out. In response there appeared two or three very young colored boys, scared until their faces resembled dry wood ashes, and an old white man who could scarcely speak from fright. What he did say was unintelligible to the writer of these recollections.

An incident of a thrilling character occurred during this brief affair. At a critical moment, as our men, from the momentum of the charge, were about closing on the confederates, a white woman, clasping under each arm a young child, sprang out of a house into the road in front of our horses, and gave utterance to a series of piercing shrieks. Our men momentarily reined up to keep from riding her down, and this brief check gave the confederates more time to escape. While we were compelled to admire the peculiar heroism of this woman, it was a serious disappointment to lose our prey.

At the height of the charge I saw Thomas' horse stumble and fall, apparently shot. The rider pitched headlong upon the pike, his face plowing up the ground, and when he raised up, the blood was flowing freely, giving it, with the dust, a rather frightful appearance. This occurred in front of the cabin. A colored woman stood in the door. Throwing up both hands she exclaimed:

"Oh, Lord! Oh, Lord! He'd killed! He's killed!"

Neither Thomas nor his horse, however, were seriously hurt.

The squadron remained here only a few moments. It was apprehended that the confederates, whose camp was visible about a mile further up the road, might make an attack upon us in force, and we were entirely too weak to think of inviting such an effort; so we turned our forces homeward and rode slowly from the spot.

As the column regained the crest of the hill I glanced back over my shoulder, feeling uneasy lest the enemy would come, and saw one of the confederates running on foot from a barn in which he had been concealed across towards the woods. I also noticed, away up the road towards the mountains, some thirty of their men, mounted, and mustered as though about to follow us, though they disappeared as we descended the hill, and were seen no more, and we were allowed to pursue our way to camp undisturbed.

In the excitement I had forgotten my butter. While riding homeward, discussing the rout at the blacksmith shop, I became conscious that the men in my rear were laughing at something about me. The joke was grimly apparent when, on looking around, I found that the tin cup had executed an imperfect somersault during the charge, and the delicious oleaginous material, assuming a liquid state, had meandered down the smoking flank of my Bucephalus, and was now entirely lost to me. I smiled faintly and gritted my teeth.

Sergeant Welsh, riding back on his captured animal, was the object of many jokes, which he acknowledged with a wry face.

On the next day, November 1, the army began its advance towards the Rappahannock. Our brigade did not leave its quarters until noon, although camp had been broken in the early morning. At that hour a brisk cannonade could be heard in a southern direction, which indicated that our troops had already met with resistance. Our column then filed out upon the road, and moved off at a trot towards the scene of action, arriving upon the field about three o'clock, where we found the first brigade of our cavalry division engaged with the enemy at a village called Union, holding their own, but unable to advance. The enemy's troops, consisting of cavalry and light artillery, appeared on the plains beyond the village in considerable force, while the skirmishers stretched across our front for fully half a mile. Their guns were served with remarkable activity and skill—far better than I had ever heretofore known them to be—and as the Sixth Cavalry rode into sight they sent us their iron compliments with a most unpleasant promptitude. I confess to feeling considerably relieved as we were hurried out of their sight behind a few houses and an old barn; but they seemed to trace us even here, for in a few moments their missiles came tearing through in a frightful manner. Fortunately our column was formed upon a depressed spot, and the shots flew over our heads with savage screams, and went crashing into the timber far to our rear. Our own artillery seemed to be actively served, but were unable to make any impression on the enemy.

An incident occurred during the action which, despite the terrors of our situation, provoked a hearty laugh among our men. A colored man—a servant to one of our officers—who had displayed his courage rather ostentatiously on this occasion, posted himself upon a fence at a point hitherto undisturbed by the enemy's fire, where he might have a fair view of the skirmish. Suddenly, as he stood smiling at the soldiers "ducking" at the shells, a shot from the confederate battery came hurtling through the air, struck the fence beneath him, and tumbled the occupant in an inglorious heap upon the ground. He sprang to his feet, looked wildly about for a moment, as if wondering what it was all about, and then, without waiting to pick up his cap, rushed frantically over towards the regiment, stopped, and began stuttering, and finally ran off to the rear out of sight. I have not seem him from that day to this.

Reinforcements continued to arrive during the afternoon. In the evening the enemy retired in good order toward the southwest, leaving a strong picket along our front. At dark our regiment marched into some woods on the left, and bivouacked for the night. A line of skirmishers, pushed up so close to the confederate videttes that they could converse together in an ordinary tone, protected our reserves. That evening foraging parties, Union and confederate, husked corn from the same field without disturbing each other.

While down at a spring, the next morning, to procure water, I met a citizen.

"What regiment do you belong to," he asked.

254

"Sixth United States Cavalry," I answered.

"Oh, I am glad to hear it. I never blame the regulars for fighting our people, for they could not help it, being already soldiers. But these volunteers, they enlisted to subjugate our people, and I don't like them."

When I explained to him that all had been enlisted since the war began, and for the specific object of destroying the confederacy, and that we were really twin-brothers of the gallant volunteers, he gave me a look of withering contempt and silently departed.

Our troops remained at Union throughout the next day. About nine o'clock in the morning a force of the enemy's cavalry, apparently about seven hundred strong, appeared on an open field probably two miles distant, and began maneuvering as if on parade. The ground occupied by them was so much lower than our position that we were afforded a fine view of all their movements. To spice their performance with a little excitement one of our three-inch rifled guns was immediately manned, carefully sighted, and a shell sent shrieking towards their column. It seemed to burst directly over their heads, and they scattered out like a swarm of ants, until their horses covered all the field. They soon closed up again, however, and aligned their ranks as before. Another shell, fired with greater precision, again scattered them. Yet no one seemed to be hurt. The reforming of ranks occupied a greater length of time, the men beginning to show signs of trepidation. A third shell seemed to explode in their very midst; the column became as a mass of ants again, now scattering and flying in every direction in hopeless disorder, appearing no more during the day.

Late on the morning of the 3rd our brigade took up its line of march southward, leaving Union to the sound of music by our superb band, and full of martial enthusiasm. As the last notes died away in the distance in our rear another sort of music, not so melodiously but more exciting, broke upon our ears from the front. Our advance guard encountered mounted confederates, who soon evinced a determination to savagely resist our progress. In a few moments they developed their artillery—three guns—which was admirably posted and handled with wonderful vigor and precision. One gun occupied a position in the road in our immediate front, another an eminence on the right, while the third was located on another eminence on the left. From these three points we were subjected to a galling fire. The gun in the center opened first, and sent a shot tearing through the timber over us; the one on the left followed, driving another shot directly into the head of our column, striking the ground and throwing up a huge cloud of earth, and rebounding away across the fields; then came a shot from the right, which struck the ground a dozen feet from the set of forms in which I was riding, covering us with dirt and bouncing with a wicked shriek diagonally through the column. Singular to say, although all the missiles were so remarkably well directed, not a man on horse was hurt. It so happened that, at the particular spot through which they passed, the men were somewhat scattered, and so escaped injury. The effect was demoralizing, but the soldiers soon rallied, closed up, and moved on.

McKibben, when the second shot struck in the head of the column, rode out of ranks and passed towards the squadron, exclaiming:

"Golly, it's hot here!"

A stern order from the first sergeant brought him back to his place, and perhaps prevented a stampede, of which McKibben's movement was an incipient beginning. A great weight seemed to crush us all until we could scarcely breathe. The least flinching on the part of those having control would have involved the entire command in an ignominious flight. The faces of the men were deadly white, with dull blue shades under their eyes, which gave them a curious expression.

It was clearly evident that our position was one of peculiar peril, and that our movements, to be effective, must be rapidly conducted. Captain Saunders commanded the regiment, and we knew he would bring us out all right—that was our immediate consolation. Close behind him was his fearless bugler, who, under whatever circumstances, never failed to sound the proper call. When at length we saw the captain turn to his bugler, and apparently give him some command, and the latter raised his yellow horn to his lips, to transmit it to the regiment, there was a vast sense of relief. The notes broke forth loud and shrill, sending a quiver of excitement through one like the shock of an electric battery.

"Forward—trot—gallop!"

Instantly a flush swept over the deadly white faces, and an expression of satisfaction took the place of the dread uncertainty and hesitation that had been visible a moment before. On dashed the regiment, plunging into the woods, down ravines, across lowcrested hills, followed by our ever faithful section of battery M, Second Artillery, while the enemy's guns, dreaded no longer, fired in wild confusion far to our rear. At length the head of the column wheeled sharply to the right and the regiment swept up the side of a low ridge and duly deployed in column of squadrons. halted and dressed the lines, and drew sabres. Our guns came up at a gallop, and in less time than it takes to write this they were in battery and blazing like two miniature volcanoes. We were now very close to the confederate battery. This soon opened upon us, but, though firing with great rapidity, lacked the deliberate precision which had marked its operations at the beginning of the contest. In a very few minutes our fire silenced and dislodged it, and the pieces were limbered up and precipitately retired, having checked our advance only a few moments.

Our line of skirmishers immediately pushed forward, supported by the entire brigade, and a sort of running fight ensued for some distance. It was apparent that the enemy were controlled by an officer well versed in cavalry tactics, and who fully understood how to cover a retreat; as soon as one section of artillery and its mounted supports were dislodged and retired, they uncovered another section and battalion a short distance in their rear, which would immediately take up the fight and resist our advance as long as possible. By this process every movement of ours was arrested and fiercely contested, so that every foot of ground for at least forty miles was fired over during those six days of skirmishing. If the retreat was well conducted, higher qualities were displayed by our commanding officer in directing the operations of the advance. The country afforded great facilities for defense, and many obstructions to aggressive movements, and these natural difficulties became really formidable when used to advantage by a wary foe.

When the enemy had been driven from two or three positions the command halted for the night, and after throwing out a strong force as pickets, the men were allowed to unsaddle and rest until morning.

Sometime after dark a party of us was detailed as foragers for corn. We rode out bareback for perhaps a mile, and finally found a field in which the corn had been "topped," and was now about ready for husking. I suppose when the farmer planted his corn he did not expect he would be put to so little trouble to have it husked. The hundreds of cavalrymen went through the field like a swarm of hungry locusts, and in a few moments the work was done, though, perhaps, not so thoroughly as farmers were wont to have it done—and yet, no doubt, too thoroughly for this particular farmer's comfort.

After our corn was secured, a few of us longed for a little amusement on our own account; so we rode down towards a spot where we could see the dim outlines of a house, and after the fence was carefully laid down we made a miniature cavalry charge into the yard. As we reined up in front of the door it was opened by a good-looking young lady, who, when she caught sight of the hateful blue, slammed it shut with a vigor that fully expressed her disgust. Presently there was a squealing among the chickens, which seemed to be in sore distress, in a coop at the end of the house. The door opened again, and out stepped the handsome young lady and the handsome young lady made the following eloquent remarks:

"Gentlemen—I know you are gentlemen—and if you are gentlemen, please let our chickens alone!"

Which eloquent remarks from the handsome young lady had the desired effect, and the men retired with a hearty laugh, without disturbing anything except her equanimity

The next day the advance began about nine o'clock. At the head of the column rode the gallant Sanders, mounted on a powerful black horse. He was a large, red-faced man—a cross-looking individual at all times. His cheek was disfigured by a large scar, and this added to his savage appearance when angered. A meerschaum pipe swung from his lips in an easy, careless manner. I have often thought that this pipe was of great service to the men. There was such a jaunty, saucy air about it that seemed to affect everybody around with something of the same qualities.

It is, perhaps, proper to mention that Captain Sanders was afterward mortally wounded in action in East Tennessee in 1864, whither he had been sent after his promotion to the rank of brigadier general of volunteers. He died with patriotic words upon his lips. His appointment to a cadetship at West Point when a young man was made through the influence of Jefferson Davis, then Secretary of War. Sanders was a native of Mississippi.

The enemy, after rather severe fighting, was dislodged from two or three positions, with some loss in killed and wounded. At one point, as we rode up to form in rear of our section, a squad of the enemy's skirmishers attacked our left flank, but a few carbiniers soon drove them off. After the third or fourth round by our pieces, a shot was sent through one of the caisson chests of the confederate battery, which instantly exploded, and the enemy fled in disarray. When we came up, although no dead bodies were to be found, the fence near by was covered with blood, and I picked up a gray cap, which was full of brains and red hair.

The confederates finally made a most determined stand near an old stone mill. Here they seemed to be reinforced by guns and men. The road upon which we advanced to the attack was very much exposed, and the gauntlet of fire through which the regiment had to pass before setting into position was intolerably annoying.

We managed, however, to get close up to the enemy's batteries without suffering much loss, and then our guns swung into position, and responded with well-directed shots to their fire. Our movement was well supported. In five minutes after we had been brought into action an additional battery, located on a knoll on our right and rear, perhaps half a mile distant, supported by infantry and another on our left and rear, sent their shells hurtling over our heads into the confederate lines, and added to our enthusiasm. The Eighth Illinois Cavalry was formed in close column on our left. Both regiments were partially sheltered by a depression in the ground, but occasional shots came very low and tore through the ranks, killing men and horses. At times the confederates used grape shot, the shrill whistle of which sent an ugly thrill through one's flesh. Fragments of shells could be heard going through the air with a sort of fluttering noise, clipping off the limbs of trees or pattering upon the sod and rocks.

The action continued until about dark, when the confederates withdrew from our front. Once during its progress the guns of our battery exhausted their ammunition, and the enemy, no longer disturbed by their fire, made it uncomfortably hot in our neighborhood. During this interval I noticed a little interview that occurred between the sergeant in charge of the section—a long-haired, long-whiskered man, who went about the pieces as coolly as any man would go about any other business—and one of the drivers. The parlance was unintelligible to me, but from subsequent events I suppose ammunition was wanted.

"Number six, go to the caisson driver, and tell him to drive up with the caisson," said the long-haired sergeant.

Number six seemed disposed to argue the matter. The sergeant made a savage jump towards him, exclaiming:

"Damn you, go, or I'll brain you!"

This demonstration had the desired effect, and number six hurried away. Presently a man drove up with a caisson, accompanied by number six, and the section was soon at work again.

The command halted here for the night. About dusk we were relieved from the advance by the first brigade, which marched after the enemy perhaps a mile, when it halted and established pickets. Our men were allowed to unsaddle and build fires, and in a short time the country was full of blazing lights.

A squad of four or five men belonging to Company F went out foraging about two o'clock that night. After groping their way some distance from camp, they reached what appeared to be the house of a well-to-do farmer, which seemed to be entirely deserted. An entrance was forced, and candles found and lighted. The family must have fled from the house in great haste, as all articles of furniture remained behind ready for housekeeping. After helping themselves to eatables, the men began exploring for liquors, and in the cellar was discovered a barrel of cider. Instantly all sorts of cups were brought into requisition, and the delicious fluid sipped amid mutual congratulations all around.

Private Kettleburger, who was one of the party, soon satisfied himself with cider, and, being of an exceedingly businesslike disposition, hunted up another candle and proceeded to explore the upper portions of the house. All through the building there were the same traces of instant desertion apparent. In one room in the upper story he discovered a bureau, the drawers of which he ransacked, and there found a large package of newly written letters, all of which were addressed to parties and places in the far south. Here was a prize, or rather, here were prizes. This was a confederate mail, and a legitimate capture as contraband of war.

Kettleburger, however, did not have so much appreciation of its military importance as he had of its probable monetary value. In this peculiar frame of mind he began to tear open the letters, in the hope of finding greenbacks, and had proceeded for a short time, without meeting with success, stopping now and then to read a little, when a single heavy step upon the floor behind him set his heart to jumping by its suddenness. He dropped the letter, snatched up the candle, and looked around.

If he was startled at the sound, the object that met his gaze was ten fold more frightening. Immediately in his front, attired in a dark suit, with a white slouch hat drawn tightly over his eyes, stood the stout figure of a man, whose face was partially hidden by that outlandish hat, and was further concealed by heavy black whiskers. His right arm was extended; his right hand grasped a revolver, and that revolver seemed to Kettleberger to look into his eyes with a curious fascinating power.

This vision was too much for Kettleburger. Instantly the candle dropped from his nerveless hand, and disappeared into utter darkness. Simultaneously there was a blinding flash, a stunning roar, and a heavy

260

trampling of feet. Up rushed Kettleburger's companions with their light. That individual was found standing in the middle of the floor, bare headed, with both hands lifted up, and contemplating vacancy in a sort of daze. Fortunately he was unhurt. The dropping of the candle had saved him. His enemy had disappeared, but in the wall over the bureau an ugly rent showed that this had been no unreal vision.

A singular part of the occurrence was the disappearance of Kettleburger's forage cap. It was nowhere to be found, but on the floor lay the odd white outlandish hat. The building was thoroughly searched, but no trace of anyone could be found. The men put the hat on Kettleburger's head, and the whole party left for camp, feeling a singular dread in connection with this mysterious affair. They kept quiet about the matter for awhile, but, upon my repeated questions about that hat to Kettleburger, he finally confidentially told me all the particulars.

The next day, after some skirmishing, the enemy made a stubborn stand at Upperville. The scene, as we rode upon the field, was a grand one. Our two brigades of cavalry, accompanied by two pieces of artillery, came up at a gallop, and marched, countermarched, deployed, threw out skirmishers, and formed lines and columns, all the while under a sharp fire from the enemy's artillery, over the broad, slightly rolling fields, like the movements of dancers in some immense dance. There were no mistakes; no confusion; each brigade, regiment, and squadron, with the sections of batteries assigned to them, swept into their respective positions with mathematical precision, and prepared for the contest with an unsurpassed coolness. In a few moments our miniature volcanoes were blazing all along the line, and the enemy's columns melted from sight like snow under the rays of a midsummer sun.

In half an hour the action was over, the confederates retiring hastily, one portion across the mountains towards Winchester, and the other upon the road leading southward along the eastern base of the Blue Ridge.

That night the command bivouacked in the woods east of Upperville. About dark the advance of Burnside's infantry came up, the general commanding establishing his headquarters near us. His troops occupied and held the gap in the mountains and guarded the village, while the cavalry were allowed to rest themselves and horses.

An incident occurred here, which showed the bond of sympathy existing between common soldiers of all arms, and how useless it was to attempt to establish arbitrary regulations among them. At the house of a wealthy Virginian, and consistent secessionist, a guard of several infantrymen, under charge of a sergeant, was posted, with instructions to permit no one to disturb anything about the premises. About midnight several of our men, who had noticed about two hundred boxes of honey in the yard, went down to secure some with which to sweeten an hour or two of campaign life, but were astonished to encounter the sergeant and his guard. A conference ensued between them, at the conclusion of which the sergeant said:

"Well, boys, my orders are to allow no one to enter these premises, but once in, I have no orders to keep you here."

"All right," was the response.

The sergeant dropped something upon the ground, and stooped to pick it up. The soldier on post made an about face to walk his beat, and in a moment our men were in the yard.

"How the devil did you fellows get in here?" exclaimed the sergeant with mock indignation, rising to his feet.

"Jumped over the fence," was the reply.

They then went down to the honey, and each man, securing a box, started for camp, the sergeant protesting that he had no orders to keep any one in the yard. That night our stock of luxuries was materially increased, and each man had as much honey as he could eat. It was really delicious.

I did not take part in this capture, being on a foraging expedition in another direction, accompanied by Evans and Manners, though I shared the honey after my return. Our party secured two ducks and two chickens. Finding a cabin, I went up and rapped loudly upon the door. A faint female voice answered, asking who was there.

"Friends," I responded. "Yankee soldiers."

"Please, gentlemen, don't come in. Mother is very sick."

"Oh, excuse us. We won't disturb you."

So off we went to another cabin. Here we were more successful, the inmates admitting us cheerfully. We found an old colored man, with a much younger woman—the latter admitting us—while out of a bed in the corner were the upraised heads of half a dozen bright-eyed children who surveyed us with a curious stare.

"We would like to have you do some cooking for us, Aunty," said I; "We have some poultry here."

"Very well, gentlemen," replied Aunty, "I will try to please you."

"Where is your wood pile? We will help you some."

The wood pile was around at the back part of the cabin, she said, and out we went and brought in several sticks of cordwood, and piled them up in the old fashioned fireplace. In a few moments a bright fire was blazing, and a great pot swinging upon a chain that hung pendant from a cross-bar in the chimney.

With us the adult colored people were all known as aunt or uncle, according to sex, while the younger portion were called sons and daughters. It seemed to afford them great pleasure to be so addressed.

The old fellow was the father of the woman, whose husband was at work on a distant farm, and only came home on Saturday nights. His appearance indicated his age to be at least eighty or ninety years, but he may have been much younger. He stated that he was one hundred and seventy years old. He was very garrulous, and seemed anxious to tell us the reminiscences of his boyhood; and although we felt no especial interest in his history, to please him, and thus contribute to the general good humor that prevailed, we encouraged him by approving grunts and nods. His daughter took hold of the work in hand in a way that showed she was master of the situation. In a few moments the water was hot enough to make the feathers yield, and after the fowls were cleaned the chickens were put in an old fashioned Dutch oven to bake, while the ducks were stewed in a pot. We had brought with us a haversack full of crackers, some of which, pounded up into fine particles, were transubstantiated into dressing for the chickens, while cornmeal was used to thicken the soup of the ducks.

Manners stretched out upon a bench, and was soon snoring. Evans and I sat and talked to the old man, whose tongue rattled until I imagined myself seated by some sort of a buzzing wheel, and caught myself dreaming. At length, when everything was ready, we roused Manners from his slumbers, and giving the old fellow the head of the table, placed his daughter on his right, and grandchildren, whom we prevailed upon the mother to be allowed to partake of this grand meal, on his left, while our party was ranged completely opposite. Aunty's best dishes came out—they were not so costly, but clean; a holiday was declared to exist; and amid a general rejoicing we ate one of the best meals I ever tasted.

It must have been two o'clock in the morning when we bade them goodbye. We parted from our friends with mutual good wishes, hoping the old man would live one hundred and seventy years longer. At camp we found the men still eating honey and crackers, and with us they generously shared. Owing to our hearty supper at the cabin, we did not so well appreciate it as we should if hungry, but tried to do it justice.

263

On the following day the advance was resumed, the first brigade leading off in the pursuit of the confederates who had followed the road running southward east of the Blue Ridge. Their pickets were soon encountered, and offered but slight resistance during the morning hours; but late in the day they began to manifest signs of uneasiness, and to struggle harder to resist our march. About eleven o'clock we passed Markham Station, near which a house was pointed out to us as the residence of Colonel Elzy, commanding the Seventh Virginia Cavalry, of the confederate army. Later in the day our brigade halted, after moving off the road into a field on the left, where the whole force was formed into columns of attack. Here we remained seated in our saddles for several hours, apparently awaiting some development by the enemy, who at this time was in force in front of the advance.

On the opposite side of the road there stood a large, old-fashioned frame house, amid some great apple trees. The yard was full of poultry, beehives, and other evidences of good living. A well—one with the "old oaken bucket"—was situated near the kitchen door. To this well a few thirsty soldiers strayed for water, carrying bundles of canteens to be filled for the use of comrades in the ranks.

An old lady—a good-natured looking personage, perhaps, when her features were in a state of repose—made her appearance at this moment. She was a rather fleshy woman, weighing, I should judge, some three hundred and fifty pounds. A flush of indignation overspread her dignified features as she beheld the "invaders," and she at once began to ventilate her opinions of Yankees in general and Yankee soldiers in particular.

"You are a set of vandals," said she; "You come down here to rob and persecute us; you slaughter our soldiers; you are thieves and murderers."

The men listened to her tirade with good-natured laughs, and occasionally prompted her with more expressive epithets than she had yet used. With each effort her excitement increased, and her shrill voice soon began to be heard by the entire brigade. Apparently amused by the scene, the officers sat upon their horses and watched the proceedings.

Presently a soldier picked up a fat hen, which began to squall, and after him rushed the old lady, now boiling over with indignation, flourishing a broom. The man let the chicken go, and ran off from her immediate presence in mock affright. Scarcely had this one dropped the fowl before another soldier, standing in her rear, snatched up another chicken, and on him turned the old lady, making similar demonstrations with her broom, with like success. This performance was repeated many times in rapid succession, the soldiers continuing to pick up and drop the chickens, while she ran first at one and then at another, sometimes getting in a pretty sharp stroke upon some unfortunate one's back, amid great laughs by his comrades. She soon began to show signs of physical exhaustion, but her spirit was yet undaunted. The scene by this time was highly ludicrous, and the hills rang with the shouts of laughter of the soldiers of the brigade. And old man, apparently her husband, who was her antipode as to flesh—a thin, cadaverous, dyspeptic-looking person—appeared once or twice at the door, and tried to coax her into the house, but she indignantly refused, and even threatened to apply the broom to his dilapidated back; so he shrank out of sight, and left her in charge of the field.

Finally, selecting one soldier from among her tormentors, who had made himself particularly annoying, she dashed after him with the broom, exhibiting a new vigor in her movements. Then began an exciting chase. Round and round the house they flew, the soldier barely keeping out of her way—though, if he had desired, he might easily have done so—so as to encourage her renewed effort, while she followed in pursuit, her fat face glowing a deep red from exertion and indignation, with the sweat meandering to her chin in more than one current. At last, suddenly changing his course, he led her, close behind him, through an avenue of beehives, and then, when both were fairly under headway, tipped over a couple of the hives on the right and left, and then darted like a deer through the open gates toward the brigade, leaving the angry and bewildered woman amid a cloud of infuriated bees.

This was too much for her. Blinded and in pain she ran shrieking into the house, disappearing behind the dilapidated old man, who had come to the doorway again, and who now seemed to have become transfixed to the spot by the events transpiring in the yard. He did not remain long in this state of daze, however; the bees aroused him to a condition of consciousness by their pointed attention—no pun intended—and he, too, disappeared, slamming the door wildly in his frantic efforts to shut it, and as it rebounded open again his dyspeptic heels were seen high in air, having met an obstruction in the shape of a chair, and which they had no time to avoid and were unable to get over.

The other soldiers in the yard, who, up to this time, had seemed to enjoy the amusement, now began to show signs of uneasiness, and were soon madly careening from the spot, beating themselves about the head and neck in a frightful manner, like a lot of lunatics just released from an asylum. One fellow made serious efforts at putting his head in an old tin bucket that was lying under one of the apple trees.

In the meantime it appeared that certain other soldiers, of a practical, matter-of-fact turn of mind, were all this time transacting business of a different character—engaged in rummaging bureau drawers and cupboards in search of valuables and eatables. One of these—Charlton, the "Pittsburg boy"—emerged at this juncture in hot haste from a side door, bearing in triumph a white sugar bowl, while close in his rear flew some article of furniture hurled by the hands of the indomitable old lady, who now reappeared and shrieked that the soldiers were robbing the house. As this was pushing matters too far, several officers galloped over to her relief, dismounted, and ran in to arrest the culprits. Charlton was ignominiously compelled to return with the sugar bowl, which he did with many signs of reluctance and dissatisfaction.

The dyspeptic old farmer met the officers at the door, and announced that there was at that moment a soldier in the garret loft stealing potatoes, and in company with one of them started up the stairs as a guide and to help make the arrest. It happened that there were two modes of access to the garret—at one end by means of a common ladder, and at the other by the regular stairway. The latter approach was occupied by the officer, who quickly ascended, while the farmer climbed up the ladder to head off the thief. This very original plan, however, proved worse than a failure. When the officer had reached the head of the staircase, and looked into the garret, he beheld the object of their search busily engaged in filling his haversack with potatoes. At almost the same moment the soldier saw the officer, and, dropping the haversack, made a rush for the ladder. He did not stop to climb down in the ordinary manner, but simply leaped feet foremost through the opening, and came in sudden and severe contact with the farmer, who, by this time, was something more than half way up the ladder. They both fell in a heap upon the floor, but the soldier instantly regained his feet and ran down the stairs in a twinkling, rushing wildly for the nearest open door, now closely pursued by the other officers. A new and formidable obstacle presented itself, however, in the person of the old lady, who suddenly interposed her three hundred and odd pounds of flesh between him and the outlet, and threw out ponderous arms to catch in their unwonted—or, rather, unwanted—embrace. Like several of the great men of whose lives we read, in this instance, at least, the soldier was determined to know no such word as fail. With a desperate bound he sprang against this obstruction, and on the next instance the pair rolled out of the door together, a mass of blue and white clothing mired together in great confusion, while arms and legs were striking out wildly in the air. The blue was soon extricated, however, and the soldier rushed for his horse, sprang in the saddle, and galloped to his company, while the old lady, after some effort, assisted by the officers, regained her feet and retired into the house, amid the yells and shouts of laughter that rose from the brigade.

It is likely this affair would have lost much of its mirth provoking qualities to the immediate participants by the application of sharp punishment, had not, at this particular juncture, orders been issued to advance; the shrill bugle sounded in quick succession the commands "to horse," and "forward," and circumstance was forgotten in the anticipation of the stirring events expected to immediately follow.

During all this time sharp skirmishing was in progress between the advance of the first brigade and the enemy's cavalry; the latter, however, now seemed to have given way, and our march was uninterrupted for several miles. The road ran along the side of a range of hills to the left, while on the right the rugged sides of the Blue Ridge arose abruptly against the cloudy sky, until they almost seemed to hang over us at places.

A couple of miles from the spot at which we had halted the command passed several dismounted men of E Company, Fifth Cavalry; these were convoying as tenderly as they could the bodies of three enlisted men and Lieutenant Ash, all terribly wounded, towards the rear. From them we learned that this officer with his company, consisting of some thirty men, had been the advance guard of the first brigade. They had kept perhaps a mile ahead of the column of support, and some distance beyond this point had encountered two squadrons of confederates, nearly two hundred strong, and supported by a section of artillery. Lieutenant Ash made a charge upon the enemy with his company, and, doubtless surprised by this sudden onslaught, and thinking, perhaps, that it was properly supported, the confederates fled in disorder along the road, leaving their two guns to the federals. The enemy presently discovered the true state of affairs, and returned the attack. After a sharp fight of some minutes our troops were badly defeated, and driven back upon the brigade, losing the artillery they had captured.

Lieutenant Ash had received five wounds in this conflict, but survived them. He was killed subsequently at the battle of Chancellorsville, where he led the charge of a brigade of infantry upon the works of the enemy. He was celebrated for his extraordinary fighting qualities. In appearance he reminded me strongly of an itinerant Methodist preacher. Small in stature, of delicate limb, a face beardless and deadly pale, with jet black hair and eyes, he presented a great contrast to the robust frames and swarthy faces of his military companions.

That night the brigade halted and bivouacked in the midst of a wild, hilly country, close to the base of the Blue Ridge. We were weary from continuous marching, and night marching, and devouring excitement of constant fighting, and sleep fell like a balm upon the nerves of the tired soldiers and their faithful horses.

Early next morning the advance was resumed. The confederates were soon encountered, and made a well-directed resistance to the march of our troops, and our movements were necessarily slow and cautious. As the day wore on it became evident that the enemy had been reinforced. Our skirmishers reported that the confederates had dismounted men posted in the thickets on the right of the road, who were using their rifles with effect upon our mounted and exposed soldiers. As we rode around a spur of a hill I glanced at our flankers, and caught sight of one of them just toppling backward over his animal's crupper, while the horse wheeled and dashed madly to the rear.

Our portion of the brigade did not take part in the action, except, perhaps, one or two companions were deployed as skirmishers, and exchanged shots with the enemy on the right. Towards noon the firing in front grew heavier, and dead and wounded men were being carried to the rear in considerable numbers.

About one o'clock the whole force was advanced, and operated as best they could in the wild, rough, thickly-wooded country. Our color bearer ignominiously failed in his duty, and was disgraced upon the spot. We found the enemy making a most determined stand, at a point called Barbour's Cross-roads, holding a strong position. Here the confederates had built barricades across the road, and had posted a battery on a commanding eminence, from which the shells were being thrown in the liveliest manner. Along the fences and among the timber the dismounted men spoken of were keeping up a rapid fusillade.

Upon the slope of the hill from which the confederate guns were firing, and in their immediate rear, were formed the squadrons that supported them. On the east a long line of gray mounted men stretched facing us just below the crest of the hill.

Our battery was at work but for some reason or other—some one said it was on account of a high wind that prevailed across the line of fire—the enemy could not be silenced.

The confederates held the cross-roads in force. This was the key of their position, and to their dislodgement from this point every effort was directed. They had their choice of roads upon which to retreat—along the road leading to Manassas Gap, or the other running eastward through Orleans. Owing to the nature of the ground, we could not operate on their flanks except with a few skirmishers.

The Eighth Illinois Cavalry pushed straight on for the battery, supported by the Eighth Pennsylvania Cavalry, under a most galling fire. The Illinois men charged upon and carried the barricades, while the Pennsylvanians gallantly met a column of the enemy, which was sent out for the apparent purpose of breaking in on the flank of the Eighth Illinois, and handsomely defeated them in a hand-to-hand fight. So energetically were all these movements conducted, and as bravely as they were executed, that the enemy, in a few moments retired in confusion from the field along the Manassas Gap road, barely escaping with their artillery, and leaving their dead and wounded behind.

At the barricade there occurred a single handed fight between a member of the Illinois regiment and a confederate, both mounted. The result was a dead Illinois horse and a dead confederate. As we rode past the quadruped and biped lay close to each other, with intermingling blood. Quite a number of dead were scattered around, showing how sanguinary had been this remarkably, brief struggle.

Our forces followed rapidly in pursuit of the retreating confederates. We found evidences of the disorder of their flight abundant everywhere, and especially at the point at which the rout had culminated. The road to Manassas Gap wound down around the low hill upon which their battery had been located, and crossed a small rivulet to another series of low hills. Just below the battery the road passed through a cut, the sides of which stood up almost perpendicular, and were some twelve or fourteen feet in height. How the enemy's cavalry passed through here may be imagined, from the fact that every, inch of space, apparently, from the top to the bottom, of the sides of this ravine bore the impress of horses' feet, showing that those on the flanks must have been literally upheld by the unfortunates in the center. The road was strewn with sabres, pistols, guns, hats, and other articles torn off in the fearful pressure. On the side of the road, near this point, ghastly and bloody, lay the body of a confederate sergeant, who had been killed by the last shot fired by our cannon.

Among the dead and wounded of the enemy, our officers recognized several persons who had been associated with them in former times in the regular army. One of these, whose leg had been torn off by a shell, was loud in his denunciations of his former comrades. While engaged in dressing his wound, the confederates began such a sharp fire upon that particular point that our surgeon was obliged to abandon him to his fate for a time.

This decisive defeat seemed to render the enemy incapable of further resistance in this section. One more day was spent in reconnoitering Manassas Gap, which it was said was held by Stonewall Jackson with twenty-five thousand men. It is probable there was some foundation for this rumor, as I noticed our officers seemed remarkably cautious in their movements in this vicinity.

From this point the command moved to Orleans, and halted for one or two days. Our foraging expeditions afforded an abundance of the best of living, and our adventures contained just enough of excitement to make one thoroughly enjoy the vicissitudes of a soldier's life. The inhabitants of this section were very bitter in their denunciations of the federal government, federal soldiers, and everything else connected with the United States, and for that reason our men felt under no obligation to practice self denial in the matter of subsistence when so much luxury was "lying around loose." In these midnight forays, so far as my knowledge extends, no personal violence was offered to the people, and no supplies taken except such as were needed to satisfy the wants of men and horses. When it was at all possible, a discrimination in favor of the poorer classes was made.

While it seems hard that whole communities should be stripped bare of necessaries of life, even during war time, in a hostile State, the experiences of this civil contest demonstrate that, to be successful, the invading party must after all, resort to such measures. War is not made for amusement. There is a sad earnestness about it which overshadows and holds in abeyance every kindly feeling that struggles to the surface on behalf of noncombatants in an enemy's country. It may be different in countries under monarchical forms of government, where the people have little or no interest in the conflict—where it is a matter of thrones;

but as in our war, where every individual, north and south, from the cradle to the grave, as it were, felt that they had something at stake—when each one's sense of honor would admit of no thought of submission—it was to take just so much fighting, just so much blood-shed, just so much hardship and suffering by the people at home and in the ranks, to bring either section to terms; and these horrors were together to form one sum—that of complete and utter exhaustion. The flag that had been so beautiful as an emblem of peace was to be for the time the sign of a scourge worse than the plagues of Egypt in the days of obdurate pharaoh.

The command reached the vicinity of the Rappahannock river about the 18th of November. The first snow storm of the season set in about this date, and the men, from the sudden change in the weather and their unprepared condition—we were still depended on our summer outfit—suffered much. On the day this storm occurred two squad-rons—Company F included—were sent out on a reconnaissance towards the Rappahannock. I grew so cold during that ride that my hands became numb and helpless, and my body shivered as with an ague fit. After proceeding several miles, and as the advance guard rode up the long wooded slope of a hill, they were fired upon by a confederate picket, and the bullet came whistling down past our column. What a change seemed to take place in the atmosphere at this moment. That single shot raised my blood from forty degrees fahrenheit to about two hundred, and sent it rushing through my veins like hot steam. The perspiration broke out all over my body, and trickled down my back and legs. The numbness of my fingers and toes had departed; I was no longer helpless.

When the column had reached the top of the hill, from which we obtained a view of the country beyond for several miles, I looked anxiously over the extended landscape for the enemy's troops. Nothing of a hostile character was to be seen. Perhaps a mile away there stretched across the fields what I supposed to be the posts of a fence, set preparatory to attaching the rails or boards; but as we came closer I was not so certain about it.

Our advance guard, consisting of a dozen or so men, trotted gaily down the road ahead of the squadron, and were fully half a mile beyond us. I still kept my eyes fixed upon the posts, for it began to creep into my mind that these were likely to become animated before long; and sure enough, as our advance began to ascend the hill, there was a visible movement along that row, and the posts changed to men with a suddenness that, despite the suspicion that had somewhat prepared me for the transformation, was absolutely startling.

This was a line of confederate infantry, deployed as skirmishers across the fields for perhaps half a mile. They began a brisk fusillade upon us at a distance of four or five hundred yards, but as our movements at this time were very rapid, few or none of their shots took effect. The head of the column wheeled off the road and took up a position under the cover of a low ridge, which served as a sort of shelter, though the left of the line—and the writer, with his usual fortune, was aggravatingly near the left file—was exposed. From this point a few of our men were sent out and deployed as skirmishers in front of the confederates, and a desultory fire was kept up without damage to either party for perhaps half an hour. One horse on our side happened to be shot in the foreshoulder—the only blood drawn. The enemy kept up to his line so well that it was evident a support was somewhere close at hand, which only awaited a favorable opportunity to open a serious fire upon us. Back of the skirmishers was a heavy forest, where it was likely that a strong force was posted.

I had borne myself up very cheerfully from the moment a fight seemed probable until now. A sense of dread, like the shadow of a cloud, fell upon my head as, upon raising my eyes to look over the field, they rested upon our evil genius—the Illinois major who had led us upon the enemy near Falls Church in the September previous. There was no mistaking him—the stooped shoulders, the forage cap pulled down over his ears, and the stupid glances of vacancy which so distinguished him upon that eventful occasion. Now, as then, he seemed to be in command of the party; and now, as then, he seemed to be utterly undecided as to what course he should pursue. First to one side of the hill, and then to the other, he jogged with a trotting gait upon his horse—it was hard to tell which trotted the most, the horse or the rider—gazing around with a sort of dazed stare which demonstrated that he saw nothing distinctly, he was the very personification of idiocy. How this utterly helpless individual came to be placed in command of so important a trust as that of a reconnaissance, which really demands an officer of discretion and acuteness, has always been a mystery to me.

Fortunately, our stay here was of short duration. Our squadrons were withdrawn by detail, each company halting alternately at given distances on the road to cover the retreat, the one in front of the enemy retiring to the rear of the others as soon as they were in position. As soon as they discerned this retrograde movement, the confederate skirmishers commenced advancing on the double-quick, yelling vociferously, and uttering epithets that, among a less disciplined party than ours, would have been understood to call for a fight. They informed us that we were damned Yankees, and intimated that our ancestors on the maternal side were female canines. Occasionally they would stop to load and shoot, and their bullets were really annoying. A few ran into a house in advance of the others, and began firing out of the door and lower and upper windows.

This occurred while our company was taking its turn as rear guard, being formed on the left hand side of the road as we faced the enemy, on the slope far up the hillside. My front rank man—I preferred the rear rank in these days of sabre charges—the diminutive Schilling—one of the party who bade such an affecting farewell to the German fair when we left Pittsburg—sat on his horse complacently contemplating the snowy landscape stretched out before him, upon which the gray imps were dancing up and down and shouting. Suddenly he gave utterance to an exclamation, and dropped forward upon his horse's neck, just as I had seen poor Boynton do at Falls Church, only this time I saw no blood. All eyes were turned upon the unfortunate Schilling. I congratulated myself upon my astuteness in selecting the rear rank; I might have suffered this sad fate, I thought.

One of his German friends, who rode beside him, tenderly put his arm around Schilling's body and raised it gently up. The little fellow was very pale, but he opened his eyes presently and looked around.

"Where are you hit?" sympathetically inquired a friend.

"I—I— don't know," was the response.

A close investigation revealed the fact that he had not been touched. A bullet, well nigh spent in force from its long flight, had fallen upon the buckle of the stirrup, and was there half split and sticking fast. This discovery possibly saved Schilling's life, as it broke up the hallucination under which he evidently labored; he had undoubtedly believed himself shot.

The confederates hurried matters on our side at this time by disclosing a piece of artillery, which they brought out of the woods in rear of their line of skirmishers, and throwing over two or three shells. These passed above our heads, and smashed through the tree tops, finally bursting half a mile beyond us.

However, our party escaped without sustaining further damage, and rejoined our regiment. We found the Sixth Cavalry encamped in a thick forest of small pines, the men enjoying themselves around rousing fires of fence rails, making their coffee and roasting great pieces of pickled pork upon the ends of sticks. When our frugal meals were over, we swept off the snow at places selected for our beds, gathered in pine branches and leaves and plenty of rails for night, went out after persimmons, which were now in good eating condition, and very plentiful, and made ourselves happy generally.

That night Wallace, Croy, Charlton, Evans, Old Blue, shadowy Todd, shadowy no longer, and I were grouped about a great roaring fire. After the usual number of stories had been told, and discussions settled, we rolled ourselves up in our blankets and slept soundly until morning, undisturbed except in one instance. We opened our eyes and found Wallace vigorously stamping upon the spot which had once been his couch, but which, being composed of dead pine boughs and leaves, and of course of a combustible nature, had by some means taken fire. The heat aroused Wallace, who sprang up in time to find his blanket sadly burned and useless as a covering.

There was a great laugh at Wallace's expense on this discovery. The Scotch face rivalled the glow of his great red whiskers in his anger, but beyond a muttered "damn"—an expression which, without prefix or affix was all that vexation could drive from his lips—he said nothing. Croy generously extended to him his hospitalities, which were accepted, and our party soon settled into its normal condition once more.

During these days of wild soldiering the men were addicted to playing practical jokes upon each other. Sometimes when a party would be lying asleep around the campfire, with their boots out and their bare feet stretched out towards the welcome coals, a comrade would move a blazing branch closer to the glistening soles. Presently the sleeper would move uneasily and draw up his pedal extremities. Then the branch would be moved closer, followed by a similar movement, and this programme would be followed up until the sleeper had gradually travelled over considerable ground.

When at last the sleeper awakened, he would look about him with a bewildered stare, until the laughs of his comrades brought him to a realization of the pranks that had been played upon him.

There was another mode of dealing with soldiers accustomed to sleep with their mouths open. A long train of paper would be made and laid, with one end in his mouth, and the other off some distance. The end farthest away would then be lighted, and the paper would burn gradually up towards his face, and presently awaken him with its light and heat. On such occasions it was a comical sight to observe the curious emotions displayed upon his face—the uncertainty for a time, and then the sudden consciousness that brought him to his feet with startling suddenness.

Sometimes, when the men were very tired, and were obliged to sleep with their boots on—especially after a day of intense excitement—in their weary slumbers they would sometimes thrust their feet into the fire, and literally burn their boots before they awakened. When at last aroused, a remarkable agility would be shown in pulling off those particular boots.

It was a common occurrence to have part of one's clothing set on fire by the showers of spark that were continuously flying from the huge fires of dry chestnut fence rails, and badly burned before one was aware of it. By such an accident as this, one of our men lost the entire tail of his great coat, and was obliged to go it "bob-tailed" for some time.

A day or two after this reconnaissance the regiment moved to the vicinity of Amissville, and encamped for several days. From this point to the Rappahannock river the distance was perhaps two or three miles. Our videttes were posted well out on all the roads, to guard against surprise. How judicious this precaution was subsequent events will demonstrate. In these days of military vicissitudes, the discipline that obliged us to fall in under arms at each roll-call, annoying as it might be, proved to be a measure of wisdom.

Our foraging expeditions from this camp were generally successful. Sheep, hogs, and chickens were laid under tribute and were gathered in nightly. The men grew healthy under this high living—which, however, was by no means of regular occurrence, as some days we were altogether without food—and their hearty shouts and boisterous mirth showed that, with all their trials and perils, there beat happy hearts within their bosoms.

I went out one night alone, desiring to replenish our larder with fresh meat, leaving Todd—that quiet individual and I were fast friends now, and "bunked" together—to take care of arms and horses. I strayed off from camp perhaps a mile, across fields and through woods, being careful to establish marks by which I should be able to find the way home again. By and by I came upon a flock of sheep, to which I gave chase. I was tolerably fleet of foot, and kept close to them, driving them into fence corners and over all sorts of obstructions. Finally one of them

made an effort to jump through a fence, but became fastened, and I caught it. Out came my knife, and I felt for its throat; while thus engaged, however, I felt its heart beat wildly against my leg.

"Poor old fellow!" thought I, "how hard it must be for even an animal to yield up its innocent life!"

I hesitated; I put down my hand and stroked its head; and then, returning my knife to my pocket, dismissed the sheep with my blessing.

Did the creature really understand me? It seemed loath to go away, and instead of appearing frightened followed me all around that field. Usually I am not of a superstitious temperament, but there was something about that animal that made me uneasy. It was bound to be about my legs, rubbing its head against me whenever I permitted it do so. At last curious thoughts came into my head. Those solitudes which surrounded me—the hour of the night—the groups of dead that I had seen on fields of battle now rising in imagination about me—that singular sheep and his singular actions—these facts and fictions, substances and shadows, were too much for me. I turned my face towards camp, and travelled faster than usual until I saw the lights of its myriad fires. The foraging expedition was a failure that night.

The last I saw of that sheep was after I had crossed the fence out of the field. I looked back after I had travelled about two rods, and there he was, mounted on his hind feet, and with his fore feet upon the upper rail, and his white head up in the air, and his eyes peering after me—at least I felt that they were. The picture was a ghostly one, and I did not stop to take the second glance.

One or two days after this we were ordered out a couple of miles towards the river, dismounted and with carbines, and posted in line of battle across the road and to the right and left of it. In front of us a line of skirmishers was established. This condition of affairs was maintained until evening, when we were marched back to camp. Although I could not discover the object of this expedition, it was evident an attack was expected, and we had been sent out to meet it.

The next morning I was detailed with Barlow and two or three others, to go with the company wagons and gather corn for our horses. About two miles from camp in the direction of the Rappahannock we found a field of unhusked corn. An hour's hard work filled the wagon, and it was started homeward. We were without arms, and riding our horses without saddle. The rest of the men went on, while I lingered behind, cogitating on many subjects, and in a peculiarly reflective mood,

277

wondering how the woman who had once been my Sarah Jane was getting along in her married life whether the war would soon be over—whether we were likely to have a fight this week—where we should go into winter quarters—whether I should ever see home again, &c.

My contemplations were somewhat disturbed by hearing a single rifle shot in the distance, sounding as though it were in the direction of the Rappahannock, and a mile away.

"There goes another hog," said I to myself, speaking aloud, supposing that some enterprising Yankee was endeavoring to secure fresh pork.

Shortly after there were two more shots, apparently much closer.

At this time I was dismounted, standing near a fence, while Bucephalus was grazing near by, with his long head poked under some branches.

"Ah!" I exclaimed, "more foragers, it seems."

The words had barely escaped my lips when there fell upon my ears fully half a dozen reports, fired in a wild, peculiarly irregular manner, which I understood far better than any alarm. The confederates must be driving in our pickets, and that very rapidly.

I ran for my horse, mounted, and galloped towards camp. The participants in the skirmish were hidden from my sight by the low crest of a hill, but I could now distinctly hear the rush of horses and the yells of the confederates on a charge. My route lay across fields, the fences of which had been torn down when we had brought our wagon for corn. I had left the road, and felt satisfied that, unless intercepted by flankers, there was little danger of meeting the enemy on my way. I galloped harder than ever as these thoughts flashed through my mind, and in a short time came in sight of camp. To my great astonishment it was entirely deserted, and a great fire was raging at the spot where our commissary stores had been deposited. The regiment was nowhere to be seen. From the way matters looked, it must have marched off in a wonderful hurry.

Before I left camp I had resolved myself into a laundress, and washed out a shirt and pair of drawers, and hung them upon some bushes to dry. They were there still, and I hastily put them on—I had but the one suit of underclothing. I found my saddle and arms where they had been left, and in a few moments was mounted and in search of the regiment. Two or three stragglers, who cared for the officers horses, and were known as "dog-robbers," were down by the edge of the woods gathering up some forage, and then, with chattering teeth and quivering limbs pointed spasmodically towards Little Washington, when I inquired the route the regiment had taken, and I rode rapidly after it.

As I galloped up the slope of a hill I saw a battery of artillery dash up to a commanding eminence above me, wheel, and unlimber, and prepare to open fire. It was enveloped in a mass of dust, and I was unable to distinguish the uniforms of the men, but felt satisfied they were federals. However, my error was soon made manifest. A white cloud of smoke rolled up, followed instantaneously by a stunning roar, and I heard the shot whizzing over my head, and saw the earth plowed up by it in one of the fields beyond our late camp.

I appreciated the situation in a moment. Wheeling my horse, I galloped from the vicinity in a direction opposite to that of the battery. On my way I overtook two women—one white, the other colored——hurrying across the fields in the same direction, on foot, bareheaded, and giving utterance to loud lamentations, as if their hearts would break.

"Which way did the United States troops go," I inquired, feeling somewhat uncertain whether or not I had better trust them.

They pointed toward a body of timber just ahead.

"Do you think the rebels will drive our people back?" asked the white woman, while both looked into my face anxiously.

"It looks like it just now," I responded; "yet I guess not very far."

I hurried away, glancing occasionally to the right and left lest I should ride into the enemy's ranks unawares, and was soon into the timber and through it. Here I found a confused mass of cavalry swarming over the fields towards and through Amissville, while a battery of artillery from the confederate side was hurling shot and shell into their ranks.

At Amissville a number of citizens were out watching our movements, and in the eyes of many there was a gleam of triumph.

"Why, where is you alls going?" asked one grayheaded, cadaverous old man, with a sarcastic grin on his wrinkled face.

"Oh, jist out here, so that your god damned old town will be between two fires, and be tored to pieces," said a lank chap from Illinois.

Just outside of Amissville I had the satisfaction of seeing two of our batteries unlimbering for action, and their supports forming in column in their rear, with drawn sabres. Across the fields to the right and left of the road other regiments were forming, and a line of skirmishers deploying across their front and on both flanks. A few moments later

279

our guns were thundering defiance to the enemy.

The action lasted but a few moments. Our troops easily repulsed the confederates, and captured some prisoners, among them the representatives of sixteen different regiments. This showed that their movement had been well supported. It was evidently a reconnaissance on their part to determine the exact location of our army.

After the enemy had retired our forces were withdrawn from Amissville, and marched to Waterloo Bridge, and from thence to Warrenton. The command reached the latter place late at night, and encamped—a very tired and hungry body of men. Rations were issued and devoured, and the soldiers lay down to rest with a blissful sense of security, for thousands of camp fires made the sky lurid for miles around us, and indicated that we were in the midst of the Army of the Potomac.

We remained at Warrenton one or two days. From here we advanced towards the Rappahannock on the road to Sulphur Springs, distant perhaps six or seven miles. After passing several infantry camps we reached the apparent limits of our lines, and skirmishers were deployed and advanced to feel the way to the river, and the command followed in close column with drawn sabres to support them in case of an emergency. Greatly to our surprise we found ourselves marching in this hostile array through the camps of a division of our infantry, who turned out in great numbers to see us, wondering what it all meant. A halt was ordered, when it was ascertained that our pickets were along the north bank of the river at the Sulphur Springs, and then our skirmishers were called in, our sabres returned to their sheaths, and the advance continued in column of fours, as on an ordinary march.

The regiment halted at Sulphur Springs for two or three days. A strong picket force was posted along the river for three or four miles, and the command remained under saddle during the first day and night. The confederate videttes were visible on the fields south of the river, and seemed to be more vigilant than usual.

This once famous resort presented a sad picture of the desolations of war in its ruined buildings and devastated fields. During General Pope's celebrated campaign some severe artillery fighting had taken place all along the river here, and completed the wreck.

The first night we remained here leaves no pleasant recollections in my memory. A heavy rainstorm came up, and drenched us to the skin. To add to our discomforts no fires were allowed; the ground was one mass of mud, and we could not lie down; we were compelled to wear our arms constantly. Once, about midnight, influenced by my sufferings, I took off my sword belt and hooked it on my saddle. Then I hunted up some rails and branches, and improvised a sort of bed.

I do not know whether I had fallen asleep or not. At all events, I heard the stern voice of Lieutenant Irving[3]—this officer was in charge of F Company at this time—ring out upon the night air:

"Sergeant Swartz—Sergeant Swartz!"

Sergeant Swartz appeared.

"Whose horse is this?"

"Private Davis second, sir," replied Swartz.

"Send Private Davis second here."

Swartz called me, and I crawled reluctantly from my roost.

"Is this your horse—are these your arms?" gruffly asked the lieutenant.

I acknowledged that they were mine.

"Well, sir, just put on your arms. If I catch you doing such a trick again, I will tie you up by the thumbs."

I was sadly hurt by this threat, but felt that I deserved it all. It was a breach of discipline on my part, in the face of the enemy—a requirement that all of us, from the highest to the lowest were morally obliged to fulfill, and I had no right to expect an exemption. In addition to this, my poor horse was bearing his share of suffering without the weight of my arms, and it was base in me to add to him my burden also.

The only thing I can plead in extenuation of my conduct on this occasion—or rather in extenuation of my thoughtlessness, for had the matter been fully reflected upon I should have reached a proper conclusion, I am sure, and would not have been guilty of such an action—is the personal agony I was then enduring, having stood around for some eight hours, trying to keep warm, and my overwhelming fatigue. Had the entire command followed my example, and a sudden night attack ensued, I shudder to think of the result.

It may safely be inferred that, during the remaining part of that night, I accepted the situation like the other soldiers, honestly, if not cheerfully.

When I recall, in these peaceful times, the exquisite agonies of these wet, dreary, cheerless nights, and the terrors of those days of horror and death, they seem to me like the uncertain experiences of evil dreams. I

[3] There would seem to be a confusion of names here. There is no Lieutenant Irving listed for the 6th Cavalry. There are, however, two lieutenants with the first name of Irving. The officer referred to may be one of these.

281

can scarcely believe that I was really an actor and a sufferer. I am wont to sit, on the long, cold winter evenings, before my cheerful fire, and to listen to the sweeping winds without, and to think of our lonely watches on other cold winter evenings along the banks of the windy Rappahannock. I half close my eyes, and then the dim distant hills beyond the river rise before me, and on the long slopes, perched on their horses on some knoll or at some crossroads, I see again the gray videttes. On our own side of the stream the old familiar forms maintain their weary vigils; the blue lines stretch over hill and lowland, over field and through forest—a host whose memory I treasure in my heart of heart with a reverence and a love that grows stronger with each succeeding year.

It is a comfort to me to be thus able to muster before my mind's eye those grim battalions. Materially I shall never see them again; they are gone forever, but their forms and faces are indelibly impressed upon my memory, and for this inestimable boon I am grateful.

I have never met, outside of the army, the pure, unselfish characters I found there. When a soldier divided his little all with a brother soldier, it was without hope of reward, without thought of future gain. It seems to me that the sort of communism that distinguishes the life in the army from that of civilians tends to develop a nobility of soul in this respect.

No man knows what the flag of his country means until he has followed it in war. He looks upon it before that event as simply a piece of bunting to be displayed upon certain occasions; but it is only when it marks the line of battle—when it leads the column of attack—when it floats out like an angry flame amid the clouds of sulphur smoke, and points the way to victory—that he truly appreciates the symbol of his country's sovereignty.

In the forenoon of the third day after our arrival at Sulphur Springs the confederates attacked our pickets and drove them back from the river. They then posted a battery upon a commanding eminence on the opposite bank, and opened a vigorous fire upon our camp, from which we were obliged to retire in haste and confusion.

This matter of having one's pickets driven in and camp assaulted is a rather lively experience, especially if made in earnest. First you hear two or three shots in the distance; then presently a volley; then at headquarters a bugler will appear, and, if there is time, he will sound "boots and saddles;" if there is no time to saddle, but a sufficient time to march out to meet the assault, he will sound "assembly," and the men will fall in on foot; if the enemy is then at camp limits, he will sound "to arms." In place of the severe quiet of a moment before all is confusion. There is a snatching up of arms, a slinging of saddles, a rapid manipulation of coat straps and saddlebags. In most instances there will be a mounting and marching out upon the parade ground without orders. Old soldiers, although to observe them you would think the whole thing is a confused muddle, will come out at the end of five minutes in a condition fit for a dress parade. Their figures know just where to go, and their movements will be timed so as to close the last buckle at the proper moment.

One of our batteries unlimbered on the sharp crest of a hill back some distance from the river, and we were marched up to support it. In a few moments our guns returned the enemy's fire, and for a while there was an exciting artillery duel. The command was so completely sheltered under the ridge that none of the enemy's shots took effect.

I confess I was rather glad we were driven from this miserable place. Our experiences here had been so distasteful that the men were utterly disgusted with the entire surroundings. To our mind, the occupation of Sulphur Springs by the confederates would have revenged us sufficiently.

A short time after the confederate artillery opened, they advanced a force under cover of its fire to cross the river. These were met by our skirmishers, who held them in check for some time, but were finally obliged to retire with some loss. The confederates then forded the Rappahannock, and pushed up the road toward Sulphur Springs.

Near the river, on a slight eminence, someone had run up the hind wheels of a wagon, and mounted upon it a small log, giving it at a distance a slight resemblance to a cannon trained upon the crossing place. When the enemy's skirmishers reached the spot, one of them was heard to exclaim, as he sat on his horse contemplating this counterfeit piece of artillery:

"Oh, what a gun!"

The confederates did not press up close to our line on the hill, but halted at a safe distance, apparently awaiting developments. Late in the afternoon our battery was withdrawn, and the whole command, except a strong rearguard, hurried away along a road running toward the east. We continued to march until late in the evening, and then bivouacked in an open field on the left of the road, where the detachment that had been left behind at Sulphur Springs rejoined us.

Although the men were very hungry and tired when they halted, the horses had yet to be fed and groomed, and their own suppers prepared. In these days the men were paired off, as a general thing, and while one attended to both their horses the other prepared their meal. In this instance my "bunk", the shadowy Todd, rode over to a cornfield and husked corn for our horses, while I attended to the "household" duties. When he returned I was busily engaged, and did not notice him; but presently I heard him call me. On looking up I saw that a sharp contest was going on between Todd and the little Dutchman, Draker—the latter making energetic efforts to wrest the corn from my quiet "bunky," to feed it to his querulous little sorrel.

It was evident that something must be done for the relief of Todd. He was not a pugilist, and the querulous little Dutchman was making rapid progress towards possessing himself of the feed. I sprang up and ran over, and Draker retired to his saddle, muttering a sort of jargon not understood by natives of the United States.

While Todd was feeding the horses Draker made another attempt to capture the coveted corn. I suppose the old fellow imagined he had some right to it, or he would not have made such efforts to secure the forage. I went to him and explained to him that he could not have the corn; that it was ours, and we intended to use it; that there was the field, and he could easily procure all he wished in a few moments. Instead of being pacified he became greatly enraged. That unknown language poured from his lips like a torrent of boulders rolling over jagged rocks. Presently he exclaimed, in broken English, gesticulating vigorously:

"I will get mine sabel."

Draker had a remarkably high opinion of his qualifications as a fencing master. The "sabel," as he called his sabre, was his stronghold. He never said he would shoot a man—he always proposed to slice him up with cold, keen steel. In this instance he reached over to his saddle. and jerked out of its scabbard that glittering weapon, and with many flourishes advanced upon me.

Todd saw him, and uttered a low cry. I did not think Draker would make any serious attack on me, but concluded to surprise the querulous little Dutchman by different tactics. I went quietly to my saddle, drew out my revolver, and brought it to bear upon his little body.

He did not seem to notice my movements, but came on. When within a couple of paces his eyes fell upon the pistol. The effect was marvelous. He suddenly stopped, and without a word went back to his saddle and returned his sword, took his nosebag, and trudged away after corn.

Somehow or other I never could harmonize with Draker. My feelings were and are of the kindliest sort towards him, but it seemed to me that the querulous little Dutchman was determined to misunderstand me. He would persist in declaring that I was subjecting him to ridicule—a matter that was never in my thoughts. To counteract this singular hallucination I abstained from saying anything to him or about him in his presence.

The next day our march was continued towards Falmouth. In the afternoon we passed the First Pennsylvania Cavalry, which was on duty in the vicinity of Deep Creek. As many of my friends and former schoolmates were attached to that regiment, I made efforts to see them, but was disappointed. The companies to which they belonged happened to be on post as videttes along the Rappahannock River.

That night the regiment bivouacked in a dense forest of pines near Hartwood Church, some twelve or fourteen miles from Fredericksburg. It was about dark when we halted, and after the horses were attended to, great fires were kindled all through the woods. The men were in the highest spirits, and made the forest resound with shout and song.

Bewildered by the myriads of fires blazing beneath him, the roar of voices, the swarms of men and horses, and blinded and suffocated by the cloud of smoke that was rapidly settling among the tops of pines where he was perched, a raccoon came wandering down the trunk of a tree, and was easily caught by one of our men—the smiling Simmers. That benignant individual tendered the writer a hindquarter, which was accepted, as I was very meat-hungry. I cooked it, but found that this was an easier job than to eat it. It had an ugly, wild, rank taste. However, after great effort I managed to devour the whole of this part of the animal, Todd very generously yielding to me his share—though I am inclined to think Todd was not altogether disinterested in this matter. His was a rather more delicate stomach than mine, and probably lacked the ability to retain within it this kind of sustenance.

On the following day the regiment reached the vicinity of Falmouth, and went into camp. We found Sumner's corps occupying the country on the north side of the Rappahannock, while the heights on the opposite side were covered by the camps of the confederates. Lying below us, on the broad bottoms south of the river, we could see the town of Fredericksburg, which was destined in a short time to be the theater of a most determined and bloody struggle.

Our campaign from the Potomac, at Berlin, Maryland, to the Rappahannock, at Falmouth, Virginia, had been one of varied experi-

285

ences. It had occupied a period of some twenty-two days, and, although not distinguished by any great battle, was made up of almost constant fighting and marching, during day and night, in sunshine and in storm. Our rations half of the time had been scanty, except when reinforced by our foraging excursions; our meals had been irregular, the men eating whenever an opportunity occurred; the excitement had been continuous and exhausting. Upon the whole, however, the men had borne up well, having by this time become enured to the hardships and dangers of campaign life. I suppose most of them had largely gained in weight. The old weary look that had characterized them when they left the Peninsula was no longer visible; it had been replaced by a cheerfulness that indicated how much they were enjoying their military career.

We were now one year and five months old as a regiment. We had received our baptism of fire at Williamsburg, in a hand-to-hand fight. Since then the Army of the Potomac had participated in many battles and skirmishes, and the losses in killed, wounded, and missing had already reached a fearful aggregate. Though often defeated through the incapacity and treachery of its generals, and wearied by long and often useless marches, though exposed to death at all times by violence and disease by the fever-stricken swamps of the Chickahominy and Bull Run and Antietam; through all this carnival of blood and horror it had borne itself with a demeanor worthy of an American army.

I have often felt that the Army of the Potomac resembled somewhat a splendid high-spirited horse, which had been inflicted by many incompetent riders, and most of the time by several at once. It would be ridden at a wonderful gallop, upon all sorts of obstructions, and just at the critical moment reined in with a savage jerk upon the lines of its stiff curb bridle. It was only when that skilled horseman, Grant, controlled its movements that it cleared with gigantic leaps the vast obstacles lying between Washington and Richmond, and brought the guns to bay at Appomattox.

The Fredericksburg Campaign

Now for the first time I learned that General McClellan had been relieved from the command of the Army of the Potomac, and that General Burnside was his successor. There was much excitement among the soldiers in consequence of this change, for without doubt the troops loved the retiring officer. Although I had lost much of my old faith in McClellan since the Antietam battle, I could not help feeling that his removal was a real loss, accomplished as it was at a critical juncture and under circumstances of a questionable character as to expediency. It seemed to me that it might have been consummated either before the movement commenced or when it ended at Falmouth; though from what I have since learned it seems that an immediate attack on Fredericksburg had been intended, and was only frustrated by the non-arrival of the necessary pontoons. As for myself, I was willing to serve for the cause under any commander, and felt it to be my duty to use my humble efforts to allay the excitement by calling to the attention of my comrades to the fact that we were not serving under the standard of any particular general, but the flag of our common country; that any other feeling was not worthy of an American heart; that our oaths were absolute, and could not be avoided under any circumstances without involving us in the crime of perjury. In a few days the excitement seemed to abate, and the grand old army was prepared to do its duty.

Our camp was established near the mouth of Potomac Creek, and here we rested for one or two days, improvising all sorts of shelter to protect us from the weather, for as yet no tents were issued. On the 22nd of November our company was ordered out to picket along the Rappahannock river at Hartwood Church, and we started early in the morning for that point. The route to our post led us through Falmouth and along the heights bordering the river on the northwest, and as we rode slowly

287

along, I took a good look at the enemy's camps on the opposite side. According to my estimate, formed from their extent and concentration. I supposed there were from forty to sixty thousand confederates in sight. Their infantry pickets were pushed close to the edge of the river, and from appearances it was evident that they intended to make a stand at this point. It occurred to me, from the topography of the position occupied by them—the range of heights starting from close to the river above Falmouth, and sweeping in a semi-circle off to the southeast, and running up to the river again below Fredericksburg, leaving that town in the center, and commanded by admirable positions for artillery along a line of from three to four miles—it could not have been better fitted for defense against an advance from the point occupied by our troops.

When we reached Hartwood Church our course suddenly changed to the left, leading towards the south. An advance guard of four men under Sergeant Bucton, was thrown forward to feel our way, and in this manner we moved down to what was afterwards known among us as the gold mine. Here we halted, while the advance reconnoitered towards the river. They followed a common bridle path down to the United States ford, coming in sight of the enemy's pickets on the opposite bank of the stream, which here was about the size of a common creek. Owing to the density of the pine forest at this point the men were within a few yards of the confederates before either party was mutually discovered. There were some twenty of the enemy here. Up among the trees a short distance from the bank their horses were standing hitched, along a road that left the ford and wound around up a shallow ravine between two small hills. On the top of one of the hills stood an old farm house.

When they saw our men the confederates ran from the bank and sprang into a dry millrace that extended along the stream, and now served as an entrenchment. One of them, who had been attending to a call of nature, gathered up his clothes and ran up the hill for dear life. Sergeant Bucton cried out to him to stop, saying that he was not coming across—that he was only going to establish a picket post, and would not fire on their men. The confederates then came up out of the millrace and resumed their position, and soon were on friendly terms with our pickets. A small boat on our side furnished additional means of communication, and quite a traffic soon sprang up in tobacco, papers, coffee, and other things. It was mutually agreed that no firing should take place without due notice first having been given by the aggressive party, so that the other might not be taken at a disadvantage. As a guarantee for the faithful observance of this treaty, it was further agreed that the weapons of the pickets should be left back in the woods at least thirty steps from the post, excepting their side arms—pistol and sword—which were to be retained.

The position occupied by each picket prevented them from seizing any one advancing from his rear, but admitted of the opposite party observing such approach; that is to say, the confederates could see some distance up the bridle path on our side, which the federals could not, and the federals could see up the road on the confederate side, which the confederates could not. For this reason the parties agreed to notify each other whenever any one was coming on their respective sides. Each one would call out "Relief coming," or "Officer coming," as the occasion might require, though the latter did not trouble us often.

I confess to feeling a little curious the first time I went on post on this day at the ford—it was such an odd thing to be so close to the confederates and on such friendly terms. Six men were on the bank on their side. The gray uniforms aroused in me an almost uncontrollable prejudice, which for a time I could scarcely conceal, and I suppose the confederates must have thought me an unsocial fellow, for they soon ceased talking to me and sat down to a game of cards. Their soiled suits of butternut pants, thrust into their boots, swarthy faces, covered with heavy growths of whiskers, slouch hats, and unpolished sword belts reminded me of the stories I had read of brigands. I wish I could have photographed that party as they sat there at their cards, in the shadow of those tall pines; it would have made a splendid statue group for the immortal Rogers.

Presently one of them looked over at me, and then glanced up the bridle path in my rear. He gave the understood signal.

"Officers coming."

In a few moments two strange men—one looked to me like an aid-de-camp, but the other like an orderly—came down through the woods to my post. They halted in the timber, and dismounted, the orderly taking charge of the horses, while the officer walked up to me. He was a very young man, of pleasant mien, but apparently of a strong nervous temperament, judging from the way he started as he caught sight of the confederates so close to him, and then looking at me as if asking an explanation.

"These are pickets, sir," I said, saluting him. "They will not shoot."

The party had stopped playing, laid down their cards, and were looking earnestly at us. They seemed to be apprehensive that an attack was to be made. Their close attention seemed to disturb the officer, for he remained only a moment, and then nervously walked back to the horses, saying, as he left me:

"You had better watch those fellows. They are not to be trusted."

"What did he want?" called out the confederate who had first observed him after he had gone.

"Oh, nothing—he seems to be inspecting our picket line," I responded.

The gold mine was quite a curiosity to me, as I had read such wonderful stories about those in California. Up till this day I had been entirely ignorant of the presence of the precious metal in Virginia, and was astonished when, seeing a singular sort of a mill located here, and asking a citizen about the matter, he informed me that it was used before the war grinding up rock to extract the gold therefrom. The mine and mill belonged to a New York company, but the latter had not been in operation since the commencement of hostilities, on account of the embargo on powder, which had to be used to blast the rock. I noticed in the mill two large burrs, apparently of cast iron, which had been used to grind up the stone. The rock was pulverized as fine as flour, after which it was put in a large furnace and heated, and then washed in long wooden troughs with corrugated bottoms. In a quantity of this ground rock I found numerous small globules of quicksilver, which seems to have been extensively used for some purpose in gold-washing. Of course, my ideas about the modus operandi were very crude, being gathered up from what I saw around the mill.

Partly for amusement, and partly for the purpose of having it to say on future occasions that I "had worked in the mines," I washed out some of the crushed rock in my tin cup. I kept adding stone dust and water, each time shaking it up and pouring off the muddy liquid, and in a short time had the satisfaction of beholding in the bottom of my cup a bright yellow film, drifting like minute waves on the leaden colored tin, but so delicate that a breath would stir it about. which I was moved to think was real gold.

The yield of this mine was stated to me to have been about four dollars per day to the hands. There were several other mines in the vicinity, or rather surface digging along a creek bottom, where men sometimes picked up small amounts of the precious metal.

Land was remarkably cheap, selling from two to five dollars per acre, according to location and improvements. The presence of gold did not seem to enhance its value. The improvements mentioned were mostly of a very superficial character—small cabins and brush fences.

On one of these days of picket duty, while off post, I took my carbine and strolled off in quest of a small pig, feeling within me a strong appetite for something of that nature. Taking a bypath I crossed beyond our lines unobserved, and after riding for some time emerged from the woods and found myself on the border of a poorly cultivated field, about the center of which stood a small one-story cabin. A few fowls were roving listlessly about the door, and near by, with its head hidden in a basket, a very delicate calf was making frantic efforts to eat out the bottom of the vessel, judging from appearances. A small dog made his advent on the scene, and barked vehemently at the sudden apparition of a federal soldier, in whom he seemed to recognize an enemy.

I dismounted and walked slowly up to a pair of bars in front of the cabin, and as I reached them a tall, sad-looking old lady made her appearance at the door, and quietly greeted me with a faint smile. By this time I had fully resolved to myself to disturb nothing about this place, for here there was no surplus of this world's goods visible; but I concluded to make a few purchases.

"Have you any bread to sell, Madam?" I asked.

"We have none—wish to the Lord we had," she replied.

Two little curly headed, black eyed girls came to the door and joined her, peeping out from behind her dress in a half frightened way.

"Have you any milk?" I inquired, anxious to buy something.

"We have not—wished to the Lord we had," came the answer in the same quiet, even tone.

Once more I asked, feeling nonplussed by her desolation.

"Have you any meat?"

"We have none—wished to the Lord we had," was the stereotyped reply.

I felt desperate, and turned to my horse for relief, pretending to fix something about the saddle, but in reality wondering what to ask for next. The old lady stood watching my movements intently, and the little girls still hiding themselves behind her dress.

By this time the poor little calf had also raised its head, and was looking at me, apparently waiting to see what I should want next, and wearing on his long face what I imagined to be an expression of—"you may have all you can find about here to eat." The little dog assumed a sitting posture, and also seemed to be thinking about the same thing.

Presently, somewhat to my relief, the steady gaze thus fixed upon me was attracted by another object. Coming out of the woods at the opposite extremity of the field, and approaching the house at a half running gait, with her jet black hair floating wildly down her back, and her every movement betokening the wildest excitement, appeared a woman. She was apparently about thirty years of age. My first impulse was to mount my horse and ride away, rather than to risk an encounter, for from her unnatural appearance I was impressed with the belief that she was insane. Before I could decide in the matter, however, she had reached the cabin, and walking straight up to me, without any preliminary remarks, caught hold of my carbine with an air of unpleasant familiarity.

Now, as I am constitutionally a cautious person, and as the aforesaid carbine was loaded with powder and ball, and as I looked into her—I had almost said fierce—black eyes, and began to conjecture what she might do with a Yankee soldier if allowed opportunity, I concluded that such opportunity should not be presented, especially with my own weapon, and deemed it wise to at least control the safe end of the gun myself; and as I had heard that the best way to deal with a lunatic was to exhibit no emotion of fear, I quietly held onto the breech while allowing her to examine it.

"What a pretty gun!" she exclaimed, after a moment's pause.

"Yes, ma'am," I said, "it is a nice gun."

Presently she released the carbine, and began toying with my horse, stroking his head, and talking in an incoherent way all the while. I looked hurriedly at the old woman in the door of the cabin, and saw that she was intently scrutinizing her companion, with an expression in which I imagined I could detect a mixture of wonderment and fear.

By and by the excited woman ceased her rapid, nervous movements, and began to talk in a more rational manner, and she soon began to tell me about something that had just happened in the road beyond the woods, but which was so decidedly mixed up that for the life of me I could not understand it. I noticed, however, that while she spoke of this event, whatever it was, her old excitement began to manifest itself again.

A short pause in her conversation enabled me to speak, and I improved the opportunity to attempt to cultivate her good graces, assuring her that mine was a peaceful errand; that I had come to the cabin for the purpose of purchasing some food, or to exchange coffee or salt meat for fresh meat; that I was really sorry that I had disturbed them, and that I should now return to my people. I flattered myself that this little speech would have some effect in allaying her excitement; I now flatter myself that it had that effect. Her whole demeanor underwent a change; she ceased to speak incoherently; her great black eyes softened; her features were transformed from their former harsh expression, the ridges on her forehead and around her mouth faded away, until she stood before me a really handsome woman.

"You must excuse me, sir," she said, "I was very angry. I see you are a gentleman, and have respect for us. This is my mother, and these are my children. My husband is in the confederate army, serving as a conscript. He was a strong Union man—voted against secession—and his neighbors knew it. After the war had been going on a short time they sent after him to join the army. This he refused to do. Then a party of men came after him. He was splitting wood in the yard, and they gave him barely time to kiss me and the children. He was conscripted for three months, they said, but he has been gone for over a year, and is not yet released. I saw him once since, when the confederate army was on its way to Pennsylvania. He passed here. I have not since heard of him, poor man."

She further told me that her name was Monroe. They had suffered a great deal since her husband had gone away. They had to cultivate a small piece of ground from which to raise enough corn upon which to subsist. They had managed to keep a few chickens, and some pigs, and this calf. Some of our troops had been that way early in the summer, and killed her pigs, and most of her chickens. The calf she had saved only after a resolute effort.

She was in the cabin one day, when she heard the calf bawl. One of her little girls ran in, and exclaimed:

"Oh mother—mother! A Yankee has got the calf!"

Out she rushed with a table knife. Sure enough, a federal soldier had the calf on his back, and was making pretty fast time towards the woods. She knew him—he had been there a few hours before, ostensibly for the purpose of purchasing some corn bread and eggs. He said he belonged to Company B, Thirteenth Massachusetts volunteer Infantry.

"Damn you, sir, drop that calf," she shouted, dashing after him, "or I will cut you to pieces."

Company B stopped short, apparently astonished. He dropped the calf and ran into the woods, and she saw him no more.

From the flash that seemed to burst out of her eyes as she told this, I am inclined to believe that she might slice one up if one made her angry.

After passing a pleasant half hour at the cabin, I mounted my horse and rode away to the reserves, after promising to return in the evening and take supper with them, and to bring some of our camp luxuries along.

I invited Sergeant McMasters to accompany me that evening, and he assented. We had gathered up quite a store of coffee, sugar, pickled pork, and crackers, and carried them along. We were cordially received at the little cabin, even the calf and dog seeming to take a kindly interest in us.

The old lady entertained us with her history and that of the neighborhood, while a goodly supper was being prepared by her daughter. We were thus promised a luxury we had not enjoyed for some time—a good meal prepared by womanly hands. The old lady said she was over fifty years old—had been born and bred in the neighborhood, and had never been ten miles from home.

Mrs. Monroe now explained the cause of her excitement when I had first seen her. Accompanied by her half-witted brother, she had started to go down to the gold mine to one of her relatives, and on the road encountered one of our pickets, whom we afterward ascertained was the festive Leonard.

Leonard had halted them, and stated that he had orders to arrest all males, and prevent them from passing to and fro across the line. He then drove the frightened idiot away at the point of his pistol, following him for some distance. and then returned to Mrs. Monroe, and made insulting proposals to her. She had resented this indignity, and started off, threatening to notify our officers of his conduct, and though Leonard followed her some distance, and threatened to kill her, she finally escaped home.

As she recounted the incidents connected with this adventure, her old incoherent manner began to return, and I hastened to change the subject, lest we should have a scene, and in this I was successful.

After enjoying a splendid supper, and conversing a long time, Sergeant McMasters and I returned to the reserves, reaching the bivouacking ground at a late hour. Our absence had been unnoticed, and we made our little bed under a tree, and laid down to sleep until my turn came to go on post.

Our picket duty, although quite severe, was much more preferable to us than the monotonous routine of camp life, and we were always glad when our detail came for that service. We had many little adventures that served to lighten our hearts and quicken the hours of our term of enlistment. As a specimen of the way in which the eccentric geniuses of the command were wont to amuse themselves I will relate a performance of Old Blue, as he afterwards informed me.

During one of the nights the company was in the vicinity of the gold mine, Old Blue, Evans, and Charlton—the "Pittsburg boy"—paid a visit to a farmhouse near the Rappahannock, some two miles from the reserves. Here they found a deserter from the confederate army, and a girl, the daughter of the farmer, whom this deserter was courting. In the simplicity of their loving natures the couple laid all their troubles before the trio of federals.

"You see," said the deserter, "I did not care to fight you alls. I don't know that I have anything to do with this war anyhow. They took me away by force, and I came home as soon as I could safely do so, when you alls came this way. I like this gal, and she likes me. We want to get married, but there's no preacher about these parts, and we can't go to Fredericksburg, for I would be arrested for desertion. What to do we don't know. I suppose I will have to run away from here without Jane, for they'll be after me I know. I have to keep hid through the day, and only crawl out at night."

"Well," says Evans, "if you want to be married, here's a preacher."

And he points to Old Blue, who suddenly looks pious.

"You don't say," exclaimed the deserter, looking at Stewart.

"Yes, I'm a preacher—a Methodist preacher," responds Old Blue.

"And kin you marry us?" inquired the girl.

"Certainly I can," says old Blue.

The twain looked at each other. The old farmer and his wife looked at each other. The federal trio looked at each other with solemn faces.

The girl's mother says, looking at her daughter:

"Now is your chance, Jane."

A brief consultation was held between the lovers in a low whisper. Presently they seemed to reach a conclusion, and said they were ready to be married.

I suppose that, at this juncture, any three men, except that particular federal trio, would have broken down; but to them there was no such word as fail. Old Blue joined the hands of the loving couple, and then undertook to say a prayer. There was some difficulty about this part of the programme, for it had been many a year since Old Blue had put up any sort of a petition; but he went over what he knew of the Lord's prayer, and "now I lay me down to sleep," and "there are four corners to my bed," etc., finally getting through, and the rest of the party responded "amen." Stewart had been at his sister's wedding, and he recollected that on that interesting occasion, something was said about "What God had joined asunder let no man put together," and then wound up with, "I pronounce you man and wife"—this with a great flourish. The wedding was consummated to the great joy of the whole party. The old farmer produced a bountiful supply of apple brandy, which soon confused the minds of the federal trio, but they managed to get back to the reserves all right. Stewart called on the couple some two weeks afterwards when on picket again. He found them enjoying their newly married life.

"I will have to go away from here," said the deserter. "Me and Jane think of going up to the north."

"Well, that's a good place," says Old Blue, "plenty of work up there now."

Innocent couple! May their lives have continued so innocent and happy.

During these days the enemy made no demonstration upon our line. From appearances, it seemed that both armies were well contented to prepare their winter quarters and rest after the bloody campaigns of the past summer. Letters began to come from home regularly now, cheering us with the plaudits of our loved ones, and newspapers, too, dropped among us, full of encouraging accounts of the rapid enlistment of troops, and of the gigantic preparations being made for the fierce struggles yet to come. As showing the feelings of the Common Soldier at this period of his military career, as well as his growing hope of reaching home safely once more, and the consequent pecuniary precautions for the future, I transcribe a letter dated November 28, 1862, at the mouth of the Potomac Creek, near Falmouth, Virginia:

Dear George—I received your letter containing the five dollars all right. I am very grateful for your kindness, and assure you that these home gifts, accompanied by such cheering words, indicating that I am not forgotten by those whom I esteem above all other earthly friends, will contribute to enable me to bear all the perils, and dangers, and sufferings of campaign life. I did not need the money when I received it, as Uncle Sam had already relieved the "pressure;"

but I have taken care of it, and have now some seventy dollars, which, with three months pay—thirty-six dollars—still due me from the government, make one hundred and six, and twenty in your possession, one hundred and twenty six—the full amount of all my earthly possessions. As soon as I get an opportunity I will send you the money to keep for me.

We returned yesterday from picket duty on the Rappahannock. The rebels were just across the river from us. All hands were jolly, but hungry, for we were two days without rations. The rebels paid us a visit, and some of our party went over to their side, and procured some tobacco.

The cold rains of November began about two weeks ago, and continued for six days without intermission. We haven't a particle of shelter, and are obliged to take things as they come.

Good bye. God bless you all. I hope I shall be spared to see you once more. Please write me as often as you can—you don't know how it cheers me up.

This period marks the beginning of my hope of passing safely "out of the valley of the shadow of death." I had escaped so far, and the idea was taking root in my mind that I should possibly live through the remainder of my three years. Still there were two summers before me, and the campaigns of the one we had just passed through warned me not to be too sanguine. The two sections were just getting well down to their work. All hopes of compromise had departed from both sides—it was mutually decided to fight it out to the bitter end. One flag or the other must be hauled down forever.

"If I can only get through next summer," I thought, "my chances are of a hopeful nature. We shall, perhaps, be down below the belly of the bottle by that time, and can make short work of the dregs."

On one of our excursions up the river on picket, after two days' duty, we were relieved quite unexpectedly by another company of our regiment, and returned to the camp near the mouth of Potomac Creek. Here fresh rations for the men were received, and a large amount of forage, both of which were eagerly appropriated. One of our men, Schumacher, the hero of the ride on the Peninsula, and of several incidents at Camp East of Capitol, was missing from rollcall that night and the next morning. Towards noon, however, his comical face appeared in camp. I inquired where he had been all night, and he related to me a peculiar adventure.

It seemed that Kettleburger and Schumacher were stationed together as videttes on one of the most advanced posts. Feeling somewhat

297

hungry, and not expecting to be relieved until the regular hour, it was proposed that Schumacher should ride out in quest of food while his companion should remain on post. During his absence the relief squad came around, and Kettleburger was obliged to turn over his orders to his successors and return to the company, and Schumacher, who remained absent more than an hour, was obliged to start for camp alone.

The distance from his post to camp must have been from twelve to fourteen miles. It was quite late when he started, and darkness and a storm overtook him simultaneously. A deserted church by the roadside presented an opportunity to secure shelter, and Schumacher, with the true instinct of a cavalryman, pushed open the door and led his horse into the sacred edifice; then, unsaddling the animal, and feeding him some oats in the nosebag, he made his own frugal meal on crackers and raw pork. After this he fastened the halterstrap to the leg of a bench, and began to search for a comfortable corner for himself. While thus engaged Schumacher became conscious of stepping on something soft, and, stooping down, he found what felt to him like an army blanket, and under the blanket the form of a human being. He was not startled by his discovery; some one had taken shelter here before him.

" I'll not disturb him, " thought the considerate Schumacher. "It will be cool enough for two blankets tonight, so I will get mine and throw it over us, and it will be warmer for both."

The German went over to his saddle, unbuckled the pommel and cantle straps, procured his great coat and blanket, and then groped his way back to the side of his sleeping comrade. Then he spread out the great coat to lie on, and the blanket over both, and crept in closer to his new friend. In a moment he was sound asleep.

The sun was shining brightly through the windows of the chapel when Schumacher awoke next morning. His horse was gnawing at the bench to which he was tied, and which he had upset during the night. The German arose, put on his blouse, and went over to his faithful beast and gave it the remainder of its feed and a slight grooming. He then took from his saddlebags the elements of a cup of coffee, and some crackers and raw pork, and started outside to kindle a fire to prepare his breakfast. As he passed out he glanced over to his bed to see if the strange comrade had awakened, but as yet he had not moved. He was lying on his left side, with his face toward the wall, and partially covered. A blue forage cap laid on the floor near his head. A musket stood leaning against the wall nearby, and on a bench was his belt with cartridge box and bayonet.

The German soon had the fire started, and the coffee and pork simmered with a sound that was pleasant to his ears. Around him was a dense woods, now clad in the solemn hues of autumn, and its wild solitude impressed him with an ill defined sense of dread. No person was to be seen. Schumacher remembered, however, that the federal infantry pickets were stationed within a mile of the church, and though he felt uneasy he had no fear of being captured by confederates. The uneasiness was of a superstitious order; a church alone in the woods is suggestive of cemeteries, though in this instance there was none. A sense of unutterable loneliness seems to pervade the very air.

A soldier's meal is soon prepared. Schumacher sipped his coffee and munched his hardtack and pork with his usual zest. When his frugal breakfast was finished, the thought occurred to him that it would be an act of courtesy in him to tender his companion a cup of hot coffee. He went into the church, and found the stranger still lying in the position in which he had left him. The German stopped a moment and muttered:

"He sleeps long. He must have been very tired."

Then he called him, but there was no answer. Then he went up and shook his foot with his toe, but the stranger did not stir. A vague terror seized Schumacher. He went to the man's head, and, catching hold of the blanket, began to turn it slowly down off the face. As he did so, his hand touched the soldier's brow; he dropped the cover and started back. That face was cold in death.

Without further ceremony Schumacher hurried from the church, mounted his horse, and galloped down the road to the point at which the infantry picket was located. The captain of the company on duty there, with one or two men, returned with the German to the chapel. The dead soldier proved to be a member of their company. He had complained of being sick for two or three days before, and had strolled off without notifying anyone of his intentions. By birth he was a Canadian, and had a mother living in that province. On his body there was found a gold watch and some fifty-six dollars in greenbacks. His late comrades took charge of the body, and the German returned to camp.

I shall not soon forget the grimaces on Schumacher's face as he told me of this adventure. He accompanied the narration with wild gestures as only a German can, and I seemed to see him in his agony of horror upon his discovery that the man was dead. Whether he was alive when Schumacher laid down beside him on the evening before is a question that cannot be decided in this world.

The details for picket duty fell upon us at very short intervals during these days. Our camp was removed from near the mouth of the Potomac Creek to a spot near army headquarters, and from here, provided with three days' rations, we would march for our post on the upper Rappahannock. The reserves were removed on each change of detail to some new locality, for the purpose, I suppose, of preventing the confederates from becoming too well acquainted with their whereabouts; but the videttes occupied their regular station. On most of these occasions I managed to call upon the Monroe family, and by them was always hospitably received. I felt a deep sympathy for this unfortunate people. They belonged to that class of uneducated southerners known before the war as "poor white trash;" they were now the innocent sufferers by a war in which they had no interest whatever. I found them full of strong prejudices, however, against the "abolitionists," whom they had learned to thoroughly hate. Mrs. Monroe asked me, once, in a serious mood, if Abraham Lincoln was a white man, and, upon my assuring her that he was, she said most of the people around the neighborhood believed he was a colored man. She was a great admirer of Stonewall Jackson, and asked me if I believed he was really a man. She seemed to think he was a god, sent to fight the battles of the south. Of course, I did my best to disabuse her mind of these popular errors—popular, because I presume they were shared generally by people of her class, of which she was doubtless a fair average specimen—but while she seemed willing to believe me as to statements of fact, she could not accede so readily to my assumptions that the south would be defeated in war.

My visits to her cabin were necessarily of an adventurous character, as she lived beyond our lines, and, owing to late stringent orders, I was compelled to postpone them until after dark. I usually had little difficulty, in finding my way, and in returning in good time to go on post as vidette. One night, however, I started about nine o'clock for the cabin, following my old route—a narrow by-path that led through the lines—and rode leisurely along for perhaps a mile. Suddenly, when least expecting it, I was startled by seeing the form of a mounted man loom up before me, faintly distinguishable in the darkness and under him a gray horse, and at hearing the sharp challenge, "Halt! Who goes there?" accompanied by the clicking of the hammer on a carbine.

"Friend," I answered promptly yet not feeling so sure about it.

"Advance, friend, and give the countersign," was the response.

300

It was easy enough for me to advance, but it was not so easy to give the countersign for the very simple reason that I did not know what it was. I had not been on post since before dark, and the countersign had not yet been entrusted to me. However, countersign or no countersign, I must advance, for these fellows on picket at night in an enemy's country are not to be trifled with, and as I cautiously rode up the soldier kept that dreadful gun pointed at my breast.

Fortunately for me he belonged to Company A, and of course was a sort of acquaintance of mine. He allowed me to pass when I told him I was going out to a post upon which two men of Company F were stationed. I rode on, feeling somewhat disconcerted by the occurrence, and wondering how all this was going to end. I had gone perhaps half a mile further, when I heard a stamping noise ahead, followed by the neighing of a horse, and far down the path the faint white of another gray horse was visible. I knew this, too, was a member of Company A, for that was our gray horse company. Feeling that he might not be so considerate as his fellow I had just left, and being completely nonplussed at the changes that had been made in stationing the videttes—none had been posted on this path before—I determined to return to our reserve post as the best means of escaping from my awkward and rather dangerous predicament. For this purpose I wheeled my horse's head into the woods on the left of the path, intending to pass the pickets I had just left by a detour, for I concluded that he might become suspicious of me for riding back and forth across the line at that hour of the night and hurried along as rapidly as circumstances would permit.

My ride through the woods was anything but agreeable. I was obliged to lie flat upon my horse's neck to keep the limbs of the trees from tearing me from the saddle. I felt no certainty about the matter, but pursued such a general course as I thought would bring me back to the path at the proper point, being careful to keep far enough off so that my movements might not be heard, else my troubles might increase rather than diminish. At last I reached a road that seemed to be the one that I had left. I felt confident that I had made my way around the picket, but, having become bewildered by my ride through the pines, I could not tell which direction to take. Finally I remembered that on leaving the road I had turned to the left from a front face, and consequently my proper route now was to the right; so, feeling quite encouraged once more, I wheeled my horse in that direction and rode merrily along. I had proceeded half a mile or so when the road I had been so hopefully following brought me squarely up to the gates of a farmhouse, and then ended.

This sudden extinction of my path thrilled me with terror. Where was I? I keenly-examined the surroundings, but could not remember ever having seen the place before. The conclusion forced itself upon my reluctant brain that I was completely lost. To add to my confusion, several dogs came rushing down from the farmhouse, barking furiously. I felt that it was necessary to beg away from this inhospitable spot, and so galloped back a few hundred yards.

Then I stopped to collect my thoughts. Here I was in a strange land, surrounded by a hostile people, to whom I dared not apply for relief, in danger of being shot at by our own pickets, and in peril of being court martialled if I did not reach the reserve post before my absence was noted. This was a dilemma of three horns, from either end of which the chances of my escape were decidedly slim. The night was already far advanced; my relief went on post at three o'clock in the morning, and if I were absent, arrest and trial on some direful charge would certainly be followed by dreadful results.

At last, feeling that something must be done, I said to my poor, old, despised horse—he of the long head and abominably hard trot, which had fallen into my possession as the successor of my affectionate Bobby at Knoxville, Maryland, some months before—

"Old fellow, upon you depends my fortune; go which way you will."

I loosened the reins and touched him with the spurs. He pricked up his long ears, and started forward quite briskly—a strange contrast with the plodding gait so usual to him—and had proceeded about one hundred yards when he stopped a moment as if to consider, and then wheeled short around to the left and pushed into the thick jungle of low pines that here lined the road.

"Oho! Is this where you are going?" I thought, supposing he would soon stop; but a few moments more showed that he had no intention of halting.

I threw the upper portion of my body along his neck just in time to save myself from being torn from the saddle by the dense and mated limbs as he plunged in among them. I felt that I was parting company from some portions of my blouse, but it was then too late to discover a remedy, and my situation was too grave a one to find fault about trifles. However, in a few moments we were through the worst portions of the chaparral, and presently came to an old road.

My horse seemed to have no hesitation as to which direction he should take. He wheeled to the right, and started off at a brisk trot, but as he jolted me so severely I was obliged to rein him down to a walk, and then patted him encouragingly on the neck as a sort of compensation for interfering with his manifest desire to adopt a greater rate of speed.

I do not know what he thought about this mark of affection. I had been vexed when he was given to me at Knoxville; my temper had been kept stirred up by jests of my companions ever since; on many occasions his hard, jolting trot had developed and aggravated the chronic pain in my side; all the feed I could get into him did not seem to make one rib the less to cease its glare from beneath his shaggy side. Altogether I fear I did not treat him in the considerate manner he deserved, although I was too conscientious to actually abuse him.

I now began to feel a strange confidence in this poor brute; it appeared to me that, if he had no objective point in view, he would not push forward with such decided vigor. Twice afterwards, only, on that ride, I was compelled to rein him up—first, when we came to where a tree which had been broken off some distance above the ground was lying across the road, and he attempted to pass beneath it, and I found there was no room for me, and so directed him around it; and next, when challenged by the vidette on post at the reserves, about half an hour later. A few hurried words satisfied the sentry, and I pushed on to Company F, just in time to avoid meeting with Lieutenant Brown, who had been aroused by the challenge, and was coming down out of the woods to see who had arrived.

I shall not soon forget the feeling of gratitude that glowed in my heart as I laid down to sleep that night. I had escaped out of an ugly sort of a difficulty by an extremely narrow margin, and through the sagacity of an animal I had always treated with a contemptible meanness. I fully resolved that this lesson should not be lost upon me hereafter, concluding that I should not risk my life and reputation as a good soldier by such expeditions—for although there was nothing dishonorable in my motives for visiting the Monroe family, having been led to these visits by my strong sympathy for their extreme desolation, I felt that circumstances might arise which should attach suspicions to them of a humiliating character.

From this hour forth I was a firm friend of the late despised Bucephalus. He had proved himself indeed worthy of the name he bore; for if he was not a well-proportioned, blooded war-horse, and did not bear upon his back one who held the destinies of a people in his hand, in his humbler sphere his duty was just as well performed, under circumstances infinitely more discouraging and thankless, as that of his famous predecessor.

On the 9th of December Company F was sent out to the gold mine on its usual detail for picket duty, to remain there until the 12th. On the night of the 10th, at eleven o'clock, I came off post, and was made to go on again at three o'clock in the morning. As soon as we had made a cup of coffee, Charlton, Evans, and I—Todd, my "bunky," was at camp. having been detailed for guard duty the morning we left—gathered up some pine boughs, had a nice rail fire to ourselves, spread our blankets together on the ground, and laid down "spoon fashion," for the night was quite cold, congratulating ourselves that we were so comfortable. We had scarcely dropped off into a refreshing slumber when the reserves were startled by the sharp report of a gun close at hand, and the vidette on post just up the road toward Hartwood Church came dashing back upon us and reported the appearance of a force of cavalry advancing towards him. He had challenged them, but received no answer, and fired into them.

In an instant all was confusion. We could hear loud shots up the road, as if by an enemy preparing to attack, and this added to the consternation. To make matters worse, some of the men had very indiscreetly, and in willful violation of orders, unsaddled their horses, and were now throwing them on in all sorts of shapes. Every moment we expected to hear the fierce yell of confederates on charge, and to be overwhelmed by a rush of troopers. Indeed, we were so utterly unprepared that a dozen determined men could have played sad havoc with our entire squadron.

I can scarcely tell how our trio mounted; but we were on our horses in an instant, and each one held under his arm a bundle of some sort, for we concluded to hold on to our goods as long as possible. Of course, if there was to be a fight all these things would have to be dropped.

Fortunately, however, the supposed enemy proved to be a regiment of New York Cavalry, which had been ordered out to relieve us. This seemed to us a curious procedure, their coming at such an hour when we did not expect to be relieved until the 12th, and there was much comment thereon among our men. Some of them were hurt by the shot from our picket, but they were somewhat startled by their reception, and felt disposed to return the fire, thinking that by some mistake they had been

304

led in among the Confederates.

This occurrence was another lesson to us, though the consequences might have been serious. For some time there had been a gradual relaxation of discipline in the companies, owing, perhaps, to their being alternately detached from the regiment and almost constantly on duty.

That night we took up our weary march for camp. When it was announced that we were to be relieved, we had hoped our squadron would be allowed to remain here until daylight; but it seemed that the orders were imperative, and demanded our immediate return to headquarters. By the time the men on the different posts were changed, and we were ready to march, it must have been at least one o'clock in the morning.

Many were the speculations as to the meaning of this affair indulged in while on our way to camp that morning. The men grumbled continuously as they rode, half asleep, over the rough corduroyed route, and were ready to quarrel upon the least provocation. The horses—poor creatures! How my very heart went out in pity for them—could hardly keep their feet on the turning, treacherous logs, often cursed, and spurred, and their tender mouths rent by the cruel curb bits until the blood flowed, because their riders were out of humor, and must have vengeance on something. Draker was conspicuous, as usual, for his ugly disposition. The irate German very much resembled a glass of his favorite foaming beer, wherein every bubble was a curse. The querulous little sorrel seemed to vie with its rider, and bit and kicked on the slightest of pretexts. Sergeant Wallace uttered his usual "damn" whenever his horse stumbled into a hole. My long-headed Bucephalus laid me under additional obligations, for he was more than usually careful on this occasion, and never made a misstep. There was the usual succession of "trots" and "walks"—an irregular gait, which was fearfully tiresome on both men and horses—during the ride.

The squadron reached Falmouth long before daylight. Though it was dark, we could see that the place wore a deserted look; that the camps and batteries which had crowned the heights above the town where we had gone on picket two days before now contained not a single man nor gun. All along the road, where the brigades and divisions of infantry had been quartered, not a sign of life was visible. Not even a fire could be seen in all the fields where there had been thousands flashing up a few days before.

What could all this mean? The question was often asked, but could not be answered. Surely our army had not retreated? I looked from the hill top towards Fredericksburg, but all was dark and still. On the heights beyond that town there burned the confederate campfires in their old positions. Dimly glimmering below us, stretching off into the distance until it faded entirely from sight, like a mystery, flowed the peaceful Rappahannock.

Too sleepy and tired to take much interest in anything, the column of weary men plodded along its way. A cold, keen wind came down from the northwest, and seemed to cut its way through our shivering bodies, until we were glad to brave the crest of naked hills and plunge into the ravines and forests of pines in the interior. At last, with a great feeling of relief, we saw the head of the column turn into camp among the tall Sibleys—these tents had been issued lately—and then filed along the picket rope.

Usually, when a company of men came into camp from any duty, it was customary for it to form before its quarters, align itself, and execute the formal movements pertaining to dismounting—a ceremony that occupied from beginning to end perhaps five minutes. In this instance the regulations governing in such cases were entirely disregarded, the men rushing in and unsaddling in a pell mell style.

Todd, my "bunky," requested me to crawl into his nice warm bed—an invitation I was not slow to accept, for I was very sleepy and cold. In a few moments I had forgotten our cheerless ride in the happy delusions of a sound slumber. I do not know how long it was, but it seemed as though I had just fallen asleep, when the camp was rudely aroused by the sound of a tremendous cannonade. Almost simultaneously we could hear the shrill notes of our bugles sounding "assembly," and the sleepy men rose tardily from their couches and crawled into the chilly December air. I am free to say that this was a moment of supreme trial. Being forced out of bed when one has been sound asleep, and driven into the cold air, is not conducive to enthusiasm—it disgusts the oldest veteran. There was no help for it in this instance, and the poor men fell into line, unanimously wishing they were safe at home again.

Off in the southwest the dull sky was lurid with the incessant flashes of guns, while the earth beneath our feet shook with their rapid detonations. It was still very dark—that peculiar thick darkness which precedes the dawn. The scene was one of fearful grandeur. Thus far we had been entirely ignorant of the movement on Fredericksburg, and had only a vague conception of something unusual in progress from the ominous silence in the old camps; but now the impression prevailed that the bombardment of that town had been begun. The excitement counteracted the agony of turning out somewhat, and raised a little excitement. There was much confusion among the men, owing to the scattered condition of the companies and their equipment, but by and by the horses were all saddled, and a cup of hot coffee with crackers and hastily broiled pork devoured. In half an hour after the first call the bugles sounded "to horse," and the first sergeants shouted "lead out." Then halter straps were hurriedly unfastened from the picket rope and slipped through, the ring on the left of the cantle, and the men led their horses into line and mounted.

Daylight was just beginning to glimmer over the eastern horizon as the regiment filed out of camp upon the road leading towards Fredericksburg. The roar of the cannonade still rolled up from the valley beyond us, and as we reached the heights overlooking the river the flames from burning buildings could be seen across in the town. We found a few sick stragglers in the old camps, and these reported that their respective regiments had gone to the front the evening before. Stretching across the broad bottoms far along the river, some in line and others massed, were the divisions of the Army of the Potomac. It had not retreated; the grand columns were again confronting the old foe, and were being led into a battle in which, though ultimately repulsed, they were to show a sublime heroism. The stars and stripes floated proudly over each battalion; the batteries in front of the town were blazing like volcanoes shrouded in a dense mass of smoke. A heavy fog hung over the whole valley.

The regiment halted and dismounted in rear of General Sumner's headquarters, a large mansion on a hill overlooking the valley and town, and known as the Lacy House. There was a signal station here, and the officers had a large field glass poised on a frame, and covering the field of battle, where one would sit and take observations and give orders to the soldiers who held the flag. Then there would follow a vigorous waving and a series of incomprehensible dips and halts.

Leaving the regiment after the fog had lifted—having come to a sort of tacit understanding with the first sergeant that I should keep within communicating distance, and at all events to come back early and report as to the visible condition of affairs—I rode slowly to the crest of a hill overlooking the whole field of action on the right. Here a scene inexpressibly grand broke upon my view. Far on my right, flowing out from between the abrupt heights beyond Falmouth, like a silver ribbon, came the narrow Rappahannock. On the south bank, posted upon an eminence, enveloped in a white cloud, from the midst of which there came flashes of lightning, thundered a confederate battery, its fire apparently directed towards the northeast. Further down the stream, on the north bank, and where the valley begins to widen, were formed large masses of our infantry, and still further below these, just in front of Fredericksburg, three or four of our batteries flamed incessantly, pouring their iron hail upon the deserted town. The road leading to the fury from the north was crowded by a pontoon train, which was moving slowly towards the river. On the opposite side of the stream lay the town, helpless under its scourging, partly on fire. Still further down the river, moving in ominous silence toward the south, stretched the lines of our army.

I turned, and tried to take in the whole picture at a glance. The broad, beautiful valley—the cloud-enveloped batteries—the river—the heights—the burning town—the pontoons—the marshalled hosts—the literal forests of steel—the waving banners—these formed a panorama worth ten years of life to behold. None of our troops at this point had effected a crossing, though they seemed to be vigorously at work endeavoring to lay the pontoons.

To obtain a better idea of the condition of affairs I rode down the hill to the ferry, where the work upon the bridge was in progress. Here there was much confusion. The confederate riflemen, hidden in basements and cellars and all sorts of places along the south bank, were making sad havoc, killing the mules and drivers as rapidly as the teams appeared on the shore—which they could easily do, as the river is quite narrow at this point. As a consequence, there was a perfect jamming of pontoon wagons, blocking up the approaches to the stream. The bridge had been laid about half way across, but until the enemy was dislodged from his position it was utterly impossible to extend it further. Along the river shore, under the bank, a line of our infantry skirmishers was posted, and on the bank above the batteries of artillery; and under cover of a combined fire of cannon and musketry the efforts to lay the bridges continued, but as soon as the men showed themselves at the outer end they were shot down by unseen foes.

I turned to the left from the road, and proceeded to the edge of the river bank close to the position occupied by a battery of the fifth Artillery, which was firing vigorously into the town. Here I was met by a soldier of the battery flourishing a sabre, who ordered me to take my horse to the rear, as the presence of a mounted man would attract the enemy's fire. Having no particular desire to become a target, I complied, and going back about one hundred yards found a post, to which, after dismounting, my horse was hitched. At the foot of the post some one had left about a peck of corn, and upon this Bucephalus made a vigorous attack, with brilliant prospects of achieving a victory. Then I returned to the river bank to watch operations.

The cloud of smoke over the town wore a deep red tinge, which I soon ascertained was brick dust, from the pulverizing shots that went crashing through the walls of the houses. The streets were entirely deserted, save at occasional intervals, when, like a herd of frightened rats, soldiers and citizens would scamper across or up them towards the rear of the town. Directly opposite to our battery, very close to the bank of the river, stood a frame house, one part of which was on fire. At a window in the second story of another portion of the building, apparently unconscious of all danger, stood two females, who waved white handkerchiefs to our men, and whose voices, whenever there was a lull in the storm, could be heard plainly:

"Why don't you come over? Come over."

They may have been Union women, or there may have been, lurking under the invitation, a very bitter sarcasm. Under the circumstances, when death seemed sure to follow any attempt to cross, it looked very much like a ghastly irony. Of the courage of these parties there can be no doubt. When at last the fire came to that part of the building they disappeared from the window, and a few moments later I saw them leave by the front door and walk slowly and proudly up the street, amid a shower of missiles, and disappear in the distance and smoke.

Sitting along the bank here, exhibiting a nonchalance that would have brought floods of tears to the eyes of the soldiers of Napoleon III at Sarbrucken,[1] were a squad of our drummer boys. They were singing in chorus some lively-tuned song, only snatches of which I could catch in the roar of the guns, and the only words of which I could remember—

"In Uncle Sam's service, so far away from home."

I could not help admiring these brave little fellows; their light hearted bearing would have been creditable to veterans.

I was soon joined by an enthusiastic cavalryman, who rode up and

---

[1] Napoleon III (1808-1873) emperor of France, waged a war against Prussia in 1870 in which Saubrucken was a major battle. France, without any allies, lost.

requested me to hold his horse while he crawled down the bank and took a shot at the confederates with his carbine. I respectfully declined, stating that I had one animal to attend to, and that circumstances might occur which would compel me to abandon that locality in a hurried manner. Determined not to be foiled in his patriotic object he called one of the drummer boys, to whom he handed the reins. Then he crawled down the bank out of sight, and perhaps did good execution with his gun. I was too much interested in the fight to notice the boy and the horse. The bombardment went on as usual, honey-combing the walls opposite. Presently the cavalryman reappeared up the bank.

"Where's that boy with my horse?"

I looked around in astonishment as he propounded this conundrum. The boy and animal were gone; the graceless scamp had undoubtedly stolen it from under my very eyes. The disconsolate soldier started to find the culprit, and the last I saw of him he was wandering around amid the smoke of the batteries, haunted, no doubt, by the vision of a general court-martial, and the loss of one hundred and twenty dollars of his pay on account of the criminal neglect that deprived him of his steed.

Sometime later a lull of some minutes occurred during the firing, during which a body of our troops marched down the road to the ferry, and filed to the left along the shore. Here they embarked in pontoon boats, each boat being supplied with several long poles, and prepared to cross the river. The excitement at this moment was intense. The batteries along the river were shotted, ready to support the movement. With bated breath I awaited the result. The prospect of their complete annihilation was painfully vivid. Each boat was crowded to its utmost capacity, the men all standing up. To be seriously wounded was equivalent to being drowned, for there was no room to fall on board.

At last the supreme moment arrived. The gunners sprang to their pieces; the lanyards were held taut; the cannoneers poised themselves in expectancy.

"fire!"

The word ran along the line; a stunning roar followed, as some thirty guns opened simultaneously. The horses attached to the battery beside which I stood—a herd of splendid jet black animals startled by the explosion, stampeded, and madly dashed off towards the heights in our rear.

A loud cheer arose along the shore. I looked down, and saw the boats push boldly out into the river. For some minutes the men were undisturbed, the savage fire from the guns no doubt compelling the enemy to keep under cover; presently, however, there came an irregular musketry fire, with much effect, but our men kept steadily on. As the boats reached the middle of the river the confederate fire grew suddenly heavier, coming in a sharp volley. Our troops swayed nervously, checked their boats, and stopped. This was the critical moment. Our batteries redoubled their energies. A faint cheer, that presently developed into a wild huzzah, arose from the men in the boats, and a final effort was made to reach the southern shore. When within twenty or thirty yards of it, they leaped overboard into the stream and swarmed out of the water and up the bank like a great blue wave. The struggle here was of short duration. In a few moments the enemy had retired, and I counted twenty-eight confederates and one drummer boy filing down the bank as prisoners of war.

A red-looking flag, visible all the morning, which clung closely to the mast upon which it depended, and was supposed to belong to the confederates, was torn down from a housetop a short distance up in the town from the river by some of our adventurous spirits. It proved to be the British colors over the English consulate, and was restored to its original position on the house.

This closed successfully one of the more courageous feats of the war. I afterwards learned that two regiments shared the honors on this occasion—the Seventh Michigan and Seventh Maine, if I am not mistaken. The crossing of a river under such a fire without doubt required more grim pluck than even that which made Napoleon I famous—the bridge of Lodi. There the men were carried over by the hot blood of a charge; here the process of poling across the stream in narrow boats was not a movement in which a fiery enthusiasm was available—it needed a combination of coolness and rigid determination.

The excitement among our soldiers on the north bank as their brothers pushed up into the town became almost uncontrollable. Immediately a very forest of planks could be seen moving steadily out upon the unfinished bridge. Thousands of strong arms were there ready to help complete the work, only too glad to succor their gallant comrades beyond the river. There was a steady rattle of lumber and shouts, and the bridge sprung across as if by magic. A few moments more and the forest of planks changed to a forest of steel, and armed men by thousands poured across in an uninterrupted stream, pushed up the streets and along the river bank to the right and left.

For the first time I saw General Burnside. He was sitting on his horse on the edge of the bank, looking upon the inspiriting scene. He must have felt proud of his soldiers on that day.

I felt a strong desire to visit the town, and see the effects of the bombardment. Presently I saw General Patrick, provost marshal general, with an escort of nine men of the Second Dragoons, ride down toward the bridge, and I fell in with the odd file and went along. As long as I formed a part of the escort of such a distinguished man I should not be troubled for a pass. The only misgiving I felt was that General Patrick might look around and notice a strange sheep in his flock, and send me to his abominable guardhouse. My curiosity was strong enough, however, to overwhelm all fear of consequences, and I rode on. The general did not seem to notice me, and I felt sure my fellow soldiers would not betray me.

By the time we had crossed the river I estimated that fully twelve thousand men were already within the limits of the town. We found guards posted at the corners of the streets running towards the rear of the place, to prevent the men from exposing themselves and attracting the fire of the confederates, who were known to be in great force somewhere in that direction, and the troops were masked and sheltered on the cross streets behind the squares of buildings. Pillaging was already going on quite extensively, but the appearance of the provost marshal general checked it somewhat, only to be renewed with redoubled vigor after he had passed along. At one place, in a small front yard, lay a dead cow, torn to pieces by a shot that had passed through the house. Few white residents could be seen, but squads of colored people, with faces gray with tears, began to creep out of cellars and other places in which they had sought shelter during the bombardment. Soldiers, clad in grotesque habiliments they had gathered out of houses, such as tall citizen's hats, or female bonnets and dresses, were parading here and there, amid the shouts of laughter of their comrades; but when some one called out "Patrick," these geniuses scrambled out of sight with astonishing agility.

At one of the guarded corners we came upon a sentry and a citizen man and woman. The former was warning them to go back; that he could not permit them to enter our lines; it was against his order. The parties seemed disposed to argue the matter, but when we came up the general put a termination to the controversy by peremptorily ordering them away, and flourishing over their heads a cowhide that he carried in his right hand. We followed them some distance up the street, which led

312

towards the rear of the town, ever and anon the general urging them on at a more rapid gait.

The town here was filled with a dense smoke, and one could see but a short distance ahead. We had passed several squares when I noticed one of our men, who had apparently ventured out here on a foraging expedition, suddenly spring behind a large tree just beyond us. At the next moment a shot was fired in our left and front. I labored under the impression that it was from our pickets, for I could not believe General Patrick would have risked such a trip beyond the federal lines; but a second shot, followed by a bullet whizzing past our little party, sadly disturbed that opinion. Then there came two or three more in quick succession, and these seemed to have made our precious bodies their objective point, fortunately missing us, but thoroughly demonstrating that we were among the philistines. Just then the general wheeled his horse to the rear, and we countermarched at a walk. This movement brought me in rear, to my great discomfort.

I possess one trait of which I am proud—which stands preeminent among all my weaknesses—and that is my decision of character. Had I been alone on this occasion, this particular trait would have been exemplified, for I would have decided to retire, and should not have stood upon the order of my going. As it was, however, I was compelled to stay with the squad until a more favorable opportunity presented itself. It would never do to bring the reproach of the Second Dragoons upon the name of the Sixth Cavalry, of which regiment I felt I was an humble representative; so I concluded to see the unpleasantness through to its end.

Soon after another volley of at least a half dozen shots came. We were now riding close to the sidewalk, and past a tall, closelybuilt broad fence, and the bullets tore through the planks, having evidently come diagonally across the street. My poor horse staggered sideways across the fence, and stopped, trembling in every limb. I felt certain he was shot, and visions of that general court martial and fine of one hundred and twenty dollars began to float in my imagination. I was there without orders, and of course if my animal was killed the fault laid with me, and I should be compelled to shoulder the loss.

This must have been a strategists movement on the part of Bucephalus, for he soon recovered himself, and an examination proved that he was uninjured. The ancient animal trotted into his place in the liveliest manner, and evinced a disposition to outstrip his fellow horses, but I held him in.

This last volley seemed to have a wholesome influence upon General Patrick, for he quickened his horse's pace to a sharp trot, and we hurried down the street. The few straggling shots that came afterwards flew wide of their mark. In a short time we had reached our lines in safety, and resumed our normal gait of observation.

I had now a serious notion of abandoning my self-imposed service on the general's staff, and return to the north bank of the river. My love of adventure, however, and a strong desire to have much to tell the men who were standing to horse near General Sumner's headquarters, impelled me to remain a while longer with the party.

Our little squad turned to the right, and followed for some distance a street that ran parallel with the river. A little way from the corner, at the door of a respectable looking house, we came upon a man and a horse. The man wore citizen's clothes, and I was under the impression that he was one of the sutlers attached to our army! The horse was literally loaded down with bed clothes, dresses, and other fabrics, and the man was still piling more on. He did not seem to notice us until we were in the street opposite. The general wheeled his horse and rode across, halting the party in citizen's clothes. Putting on a terrific frown—the general's face, in his calmest mood, is suggestive of all the horrors of the inquisition—he demanded, in tones of thunder:

"What the hell are you doing here?"

Had the citizen's death-warrant been read to him, I doubt if he would have shown greater trepidation. His knees smote together; his face turned scarlet and then ghastly white; his lips trembled so much that not a word could be understood. He glanced at the general and then at the horse.

"You damned pillager," roared Patrick, "take these things back where you got them."

He rode closer to the man, who promptly caught up an armload as ordered. As he did so, the cruel cowhide came down over his head and shoulders in a merciless shower of blows, and he screamed and begged for pity. When satisfied the general ceased to strike him, and, turning to his orderlies, ordered them to arrest the man and take him across the river to the provost marshal general's headquarters, and there have him confined, and this order was immediately put in course of execution. This performance was enough for me.

"What," thought I, "if that cranky cuss should discover that he has one more individual on his staff than belongs on it? Maybe that cowhide might find another victim."

As the orderly rode out of sight with his prisoner and the prisoner's horse, and the general proceeded on his way, I suddenly reined up, wheeled around a corner, and galloped back towards the bridge, much relieved to find that my movements had been unnoticed.

I had all along been impressed with the conviction that the confederates were only awaiting the concentration of our troops in masses in the town before they should open a fearful fire from their batteries on the hill. I felt painfully uneasy lest these apprehensions should be verified, and especially before I had recrossed the river. I felt satisfied that a well-directed and wellsustained cannonade of ten or twelve batteries upon the place, crowded as it was at this hour by Union soldiers, could not be otherwise than disastrous. When I reached the bridge I noticed that a guard had been posted there since I crossed, and also that the guard was permitting no one to pass to the north bank without authority. Here was another dilemma. Fortunately, however, a colonel and his orderly rode past me, and I fell in with the latter, knowing that now I would not be questioned by the guard. We rode across the river together, and, with a sigh of relief, I turned my horse's head towards Sumner's headquarters.

It was now quite late in the afternoon. As I rode up toward the hill I saw two of our companies marching down in the direction of the river. Apprehensive that the regiment had moved, I went up to the squadron and inquired, and was informed that the balance of the command was still on the hill. The men did not seem to know whither they were going. I told them if they crossed the river they would not proceed far before being disturbed. The result proved as I had predicted. They went into Fredericksburg, and pushed up one of the streets leading to the rear of the town, with an advance guard deployed across from curb to curb. In a few moments they were fired upon, and two of the horses were killed. The squadron then returned to the regiment.

I found the regiment standing to horse just as I had left it in the morning. My many adventures were related, and the belief expressed that our army would suffer defeat in this attack. The position occupied by the confederates was a remarkably strong one, and it seemed to me that our advance was to be made upon the point the easiest defended.

Just before dark the regiment mounted and rode back about a mile from headquarters, and halted for the night. After a hearty supper, and carefully grooming our steeds, very sleepy and tired after the weary days and nights we had just passed, the soldiers laid themselves down to rest in rear of their horses with their saddles for pillows. Unfortunately, our animals were all hitched on the same side of a post and rail fence. Sometime in the night, when we were all sound asleep, the horses became frightened, and stampeded, dashing back upon and over us like a whirlwind, with the huge fence rail still fast to their halterstraps and flying well up through the air. Of course this brought the men to their feet in a state of consternation, but, strange to say, not one was injured. The horses were finally gathered together, and fastened to stakes and bushes. Our rest, however, was sadly disturbed for the night.

Reveille sounded at dawn on the morning of the 12th, and the regiment marched early to its position at the Lacy House. A heavy fog hung over the valley, and obscured the field of operations, but by twelve o'clock this had cleared away, but little firing occurred during the day, both armies being apparently engaged in preparing for the great struggle that all felt was yet to come. It was stated that three other bridges had been thrown across the Rappahannock—two in front of the town, and one some three or four miles below—and that the whole army would be crossed to the south side before an attack in force would be made upon the enemy's works. For ten hours there was a constant stream of soldiers—infantry and artillery—flowing across on the pontoons, and filing up the bank and deploying and massing upon the broad fields and in Fredericksburg. Some desultory firing could be heard off towards the left, indicating that the confederates were resisting the establishment of our lines of attack. I estimated that some seventy thousand men were bivouacked at and around Fredericksburg by nightfall, while the left grand division, under General Franklin, reported to be some forty to fifty thousand strong, had crossed or was crossing at the lower bridge. General Burnside, however, as I see by his testimony before the Committee on the Conduct of the War[2], thinks he had, all told, about one hundred thousand men on the south side of the Rappahannock during the battle, which, of course, is a reliable statement.

A feeling of uneasiness—of misgiving as to the wisdom of this attack

[2] The Committee on the Conduct of the War was a joint Congressional committee created in December, 1861. Throughout the war it investigated various generals and campaigns and frequently criticized commanders and campaigns. Composed primarily of Radical Republicans, it has generated considerable historical debate on its purposes. it is believed by many to have been unduly critical of Union military commanders who were not passionately anti-slavery partisans.

on the enemy's works at this particular point—seemed to pervade the ranks of all the army, and found free expression. A feint had been made some twenty mlles down the river, intended to draw off a larger portion of the enemy's forces to protect his right flank, but this effort, even if successful, was completely neutralized by the great delay in getting across and attacking on our right and left center. I do not write this as being apparent now with all the light of history, or with the testimony of the chiefs of divisions and corps before us, but speak of the feeling that existed among the rank and file before the action began, on the memorable 13th of December. The Army of the Potomac fought that battle with the belief that it would be repulsed—a belief that of itself was sufficient to insure defeat in any other than an American army. It struggled against fate from a sheer sense of duty to the country—as a forlorn hope that goes to its death for the cause it represents. There was much yearning after McClellan, which was expressed in murmurs at times, but with all this not one disloyal word could be heard. It seemed to be felt that, although he would not effect more, he would risk less, than General Burnside.

Our regiment returned on the evening of the 12th to its bivouacking ground of the night before, and remained until next morning, when it assumed its old attitude at the Lacy House. The morning was foggy as usual—these days were remarkable for this peculiar feature—the country south of Fredericksburg being entirely obscured from our sight. About nine o'clock I rode down to the river and found bodies of our troops still crossing the bridges. Some cannonading began well out towards the left wing, and volleys of musketry soon rolled up like the rattle of an immense number of drums. I pushed on down the stream towards the railroad bridge, being too cautious to pass over into the town, as I was suspicious there would be warm work in that locality before night, and the recollection of the shots that flew so uncomfortably near me while on the Patrick raid inspired me with a wholesome fear. The fog had already begun to rise, and I could see our lines gradually extending across the open fields in front of the enemy's works. A light fusillade broke out to the left of the town, but soon ceased, and by the time I reached a position from which the field could be fairly seen the confederates had quieted down. At this moment but one gray soldier was visible to me—a sentry, who was posted just at the foot of the hill on the road leading up to Marye's house, and who walked his beat with military precision, apparently indifferent to the formidable lines that were forming across the plain in front of him. As the day grew clearer, and the heights and fortifications of the enemy developed into view, the scene became one of sublime grandeur. Our troops were moving rapidly into position, the confederate artillery now beginning to thunder from the height, a prelude to the fierce storm that was brewing, and to drop their scattering shots into columns that were marching up to deploy into lines of battle. The firing of Franklin's men grew heavier as the morning hours rolled on, showing that serious work was in progress far below Fredericksburg.

Close to the railroad I found the empty foundation of a house, and down the stone steps into this I led Bucephalus, where he might be secure from straggling shots that were already finding their way across to our side of the river. Here I anchored him to a large loose stone. Then proceeding on foot to an eminence close by, from which a good view of the operations could be had, I was fortunate enough to fall in with a brother cavalryman who possessed a spyglass, which he kindly invited me to share with him.

A large number of citizens, carpenters and other mechanics, who had been employed on the railroad at this point, were congregated on an adjoining eminence. Some siege pieces of artillery which were posted on a hill above us and to our left, began to fire upon the confederate lines. Our citizen friends were in high spirits, making many jocose remarks as the Union shells shrieked through the air past them, and burst over the enemy's works.

In the meantime our line of battle moved steadily forward. The confederates were still invisible, save the precise sentinel, who yet walked his post. With an intense feeling of anxiety we watched our troops approach the reddish wall that ran along the foot of the low hills in rear of the town, and behind which, unless it was evacuated, we knew were concealed the enemy's infantry. The space rapidly lessened between them; a spasmodic, irregular fire began along our line—an evidence of the nervous element in human nature—to which there was no response. Could it be possible that they had retired? The hope we began to feel was suddenly chilled when, quick as a flash of lightning, as our forces seemed to be almost up to the foot of the hill, a long narrow strip of white cloud leaped into sight above the edge of the reddish wall, followed by a fearful crash, and it seemed to me that every third man fell from our ranks. Simultaneously with this a cannonade opened from the redoubts all along the crest of hills, and the battle in front of our right wing had begun in earnest. The savage fire of musketry and artillery swept off towards the left, until the line engaged must have been at least two miles in length.

Never shall I forget that fearful afternoon.

One hour's fighting developed the policy of the confederates on this part of the line. Their infantry, which was well protected by the rifle-pits extending along the foot of the hill, kept up a murderous fusillade upon our exposed line of battle, while their artillery, from the commanding position of the crescent-shaped heights, was able to deliver a converging fire upon our reserves, which were massed upon the open plain to support the men at the front.

The guns of a battery of brass pieces, posted among some timber off on the heights eastward of the town, seemed to be served by experienced gunners, and were especially annoying and destructive to our troops, dropping their shells with wonderful precision into the blue masses in the fields below. The conduct of our soldiers during this trying ordeal was worthy of all praise. Although shattered and partially dispersed by this well-directed fire, without any means of replying to it, they would keep closing up constantly, and maintained their position throughout.

In the door of a small cabin, which stood on the heights a short distance to the left of Marye's house, close to a confederate redoubt, apparently serenely contemplating the struggle going on almost at her feet, sat a white woman all through the hours of that afternoon. Although she was on the wrong side of the line, I could not help thinking that in her veins there must flow some of the blood of 1776—that her courage must have descended to her from some matron of that patriotic period. No doubt her children will tell, in after years, how their mother looked on the bloody field of Fredericksburg.

The enemy's guns, from the position occupied by them, were obliged to deliver a plunging fire upon our troops. As the shots struck the earth they threw up great masses of dirt, thus giving to the scene something of the appearance of black water splashing into the air. There was a peculiar savageness about this effort that forcibly impressed spectators with unpleasant sensations.

The position occupied by our party was quite safe, although occasionally there would come a shot or a shell flying over our heads or bursting in the air in close proximity; and once in a while some musket balls reached us. The latter certainly never came from the confederate lines of battle. My belief is that either some of the enemy were concealed in the town, or they were random or accidental shots from our own men.

319

The whizzing of bullets on the field of battle, although it must have been one mile distant, could be heard distinctly, except when the cannonading grew heavy enough to drown it. The noise made by them was what I might call a many toned buzzing, from the gritty pe-o to the ragged zube. It was veritable death music.

Mounted men seemed to have their share of peril on the field of battle. I would occasionally see someone gallop along the line. apparently carrying orders or giving directions, and the next instant the horse would tumble to the ground, or dash away to the rear riderless.

When the shots from the enemy's cannon began to drop on our side of the river they created unpleasant sensations in the breasts of the citizen spectators. The latter did not appreciate this condition of affairs, and places of shelter came into sudden demand. Two large trees, which stood one at each end of the house foundation in which Bucephalus was anchored, were objects of an animated contest, and it was quite laughable to watch the comical struggle for their possession. Finally a compromise was effected, the ablest bodied individual crowding the others from the tree and hugging its trunk for dear life, while in the order of strength the others were ranged in a row behind, each one holding on to his fellow in front. Then the line behind each tree would make frantic efforts to keep the friendly shelter between it and the flying missiles—efforts that did not promise much success, for they flew in from each flank as well as from the front. A shot would come from the left, and then the line would swing off to the right; then one would come from the right, and the lines would swing off to the left. They clung to each other with an affectionate enthusiasm rarely exhibited by the male sex toward one another exclusively. As the firing became heavier their dilemma was correspondingly increased, the shells sometimes hurtling by from both sides at the same instant. For their benefit I repeated to them the artillery-man's saying:

"Bury yourself in the hole made by a shot—none will strike there again."

The maxim, however, did not seem to be appreciated. Presently they broke away en masse, and made very good time down the railroad track to the rear.

The mark of slaughter across the river increased in magnitude as the day wore on. I could see our troops plant their banners in the ground, and close up to them from the right and left as the ranks thinned out under the firestorm of lead that beat incessantly against them. The line of battle seemed to be renewed with fresh troops at hourly intervals; I counted six heavy lines that thus replaced each other during the day. Early in the afternoon, it was apparent that our men were unable to carry the heights, and further efforts seemed to me positively wicked, although an absolute withdrawal under the circumstances might have produced an actual panic, and thus lead to irretrievable disaster. Some of the confederate guns on our extreme right were already dropping their shot around the upper pontoon bridge, although with little or no effect. At all events, this bloody, despairing struggle must be kept up until nightfall to save, perhaps, the army.

But was there no hope from Franklin? During the forenoon the roar of guns on the left showed that he had attacked the enemy, but now there was an ominous silence in that direction. It was expected that he would break through the confederate line in his front, and swing around in rear of the heights beyond Fredericksburg, and thus force their abandonment; but the quiet mustering of large bodies of the enemy's infantry in full sight upon the crest showed that there was no pressure from any other quarter except upon our right.

In the afternoon, some of our light batteries galloped into position on the plains in rear of the town, and opened a vigorous fire upon the confederate line. The movement was boldly executed and the cannonade well-sustained, but barren of favorable results. One or two of them soon became disabled under the plunging fire from the redoubts above them.

In the evening our line retired a short distance, and then there followed a brief lull in the savage fighting which had raged for the past five or six hours. Presently I could see from six to ten thousand of our soldiers massing on the plain in the rear of Fredericksburg, evidently preparing for a last desperate effort to retrieve the failures of the day. Simultaneously with this movement the confederates, who seemed to divine the intention of our officers, began to push fresh troops down the slope into the works, and also deployed a line of infantry on the side of the hill a short distance above the rifle pits or stone wall. This formation would enable them to open two heavy lines of musketry fire and one of artillery upon the charging column when it should come within range.

Some of our field batteries opened sharply upon them, but these guns were soon silenced by the converging fire of the enemy's artillery. Just at dusk one column moved silently across the plain towards the heights. A short pause in the cannonade from the enemy's works followed; the confederates were evidently changing the bearing of their guns from our artillery to that mass of infantry. I held my breath in suspense. There was a huge black square blot—all individuality was lost to view in the evening shadows, yet the idols of nearly ten thousand households were gathered there—floating up against the hill. A wild cheer rang out upon the air; the huge black blot drifted forward with increased rapidity, and soon seemed to be close upon the stone wall. A single cannon belched forth a long sheet of flame from the crest of the heights, and the next instant the whole hillside, along a line of half a mile in extent, was ablaze with spluttering lights and great flashes of fire. No mortal troops could bear up against such a torrent of missiles. Our men gave way; the huge black blot broke into a thousand flying fragments; the confederate cannons and muskets thundered and cracked irregularly for a few moments, and then became comparatively quiet.

The battle was over for that day. It was clear that the cause had suffered a terrible reverse, and that our army occupied a position full of deadly peril. It had been defeated with heavy loss; a river was close upon its rear; a powerful and confident foe swarmed upon those heights which commanded almost its entire length and breadth. How will it end?

Sad and dispirited I remounted my horse and rode back to Sumner's headquarters. On my way, I passed numbers of our wounded, who had dragged their mutilated bodies across the river. Some of them were shedding tears over the final result of the unavailing struggle. The gloom of an unutterable despair seemed to have settled upon their spirits.

The men of the regiment had already heard of the defeat, and an unusual stillness prevailed among them. Todd was completely disheartened, but not disposed to give up the fight. As we rode back to the bivouacking field a shot from one of the enemy's siege guns came whizzing over our heads and fell away beyond. It must have been thrown fully four miles. That night, worn out by excitement, Todd and I went to bed supperless, and soon sank into a blessed oblivion.

To show the feelings of the Common Soldier at this stage of his military career, I transcribe a letter dated December 21, 1862, near Fredericksburg. It is inserted at this point because it refers particularly to the events just narrated, although written eight days afterwards;

Friend George: For the first time in two weeks a favorable opportunity presents itself for writing, and I shall endeavor to improve it.

I received yours while on picket duty, and felt gladdened by the kindly expressions it contained.

You have doubtless heard, ere this, of the great battle of Fredericksburg, which took place here on the 13th instant, and resulted in the repulse of our gallant army, with the loss of from ten to twelve thousand of the best young men of the country. I have no doubt this will cause a universal depression of the public mind, as well it may; but I trust that it will soon be relieved by the tidings of some great military victory.

I am sorry from the bottom of my heart that McClellan was relieved, for it is useless to deny that it caused a great deal of bad feeling among the rank and file of this army. McClellan had been kind to his men, and won them over to him by the tenderness he displayed toward the sick and wounded. I thought well of him as a man and a general, and although willing to fight for my country under any one placed over me, I should prefer him to any of the officers who have, so far, assumed command of the Potomac Army, or as mentioned in that connection.

I had a fair view of the action in front of our right wing and center. The enemy's position at these points was strongly fortified, and could not be carried. Our men acted throughout with the noblest bearing. The confederates were able to bring three lines to bear upon our men, and most fought under cover, while our troops were exposed upon an open plain. I saw whole brigades march up in splendid array, and in a short time they would be scattered like a lot of skirmishers. From right to left, I suppose the line of battle extended five or six miles. I do not think the enemy lost over three thousand men.

Please write often, as I feel cheered by all letters from home. I hope we will soon be able to bring this terrible war to a successful conclusion.

God knows our men are brave enough; but they need—a leader.

Throughout the 14th the hostile armies confronted each other in sullen silence, which was broken at intervals by light skirmishing—the lingering throbs of an expiring great conflict.

About noon our squadron was ordered up the river to resume our picket duties. As we rode over the heights, at Falmouth we could see the confederate and Union lines running parallel with each other far down the Rappahannock, our men stretched prone upon the earth to protect themselves from the unerring aim of the enemy's sharpshooters, who were picking off the absent-minded and restless individuals with painful frequency. Along the line of attack of the day previous were scattered the dead bodies of the braves who had fallen in the struggle. Beyond the crest of the hills, maneuvering on the tablelands, large numbers of the enemy's infantry were visible.

The squadron halted near Ballard's Dam and Bank's Ford, about midway from Falmouth to the United States or Richardson's Ford. The confederate pickets occupied the southern bank, and, though friendly enough, were unpleasantly sarcastic in their allusions to the recent engagement. They seemed to feel satisfied that they had obtained a substantial victory, and in our despondent mood we were not disposed to deny it. The line assigned to the squadron to be guarded was very long, and, to facilitate matters, Company F was divided up into squads of three men each, and these were posted at different points, with orders to relieve each other at the usual intervals of three hours. The other company was placed at a convenient spot from which to support the pickets when driven in, should such a contingency arise. A post was established at all the crossroads and fords, and stationed at short intervals on commanding eminences along the river.

This arrangement brought Evans, Old Blue, and myself on one post, under charge of Croy, at Ballard's Dam. Here we made ourselves comfortable, pleased at the prospect of escaping from official domination—that most detestable of all annoyances in the life of the common soldier.

Stewart and Evans were indomitable foragers. While I could not always justify their manner of conducting this sort of business, yet, when they brought in those delicious bits of mutton and veal and pork the temptation to partake overcame all scruples and was too strong to be resisted.

As an illustration of Stewart's practical character as a forager I will relate an incident. One afternoon, when he had become quite voracious from hunger, he stopped at a farmer's house and asked for food. The request was peremptorily refused. Old Blue walked up to the cupboard, threw open the doors, and proceeded to help himself. This audacious conduct aroused the indignation of the family, but they did not care to make a positive demonstration upon the intruder, as Stewart was a wild, ugly-looking fellow, very much resembling one of the aboriginals of this country, with a revolver and sabre swinging in ominous manner on his long lank frame. They had recourse to a negative stratagem they proposed to work upon his feelings in an indirect way. Complaints were made of the disposition of Union soldiers to rob and plunder houses, and thus leave poor families without anything upon which to subsist, and recited many soulharrowing instances that had come under their own immediate observation (looking hard at the animal feeding from their crib in the corner). The dogmatic Stewart, while cheerfully acquiescing in the remarks made with a most provoking complacency, and mentioning several soul-harrowing instances that had come under his immediate observation, kept slinging the edibles into his capacious mouth with a precision and frequency that was positively alarming, both of the elbows of his long arms somewhat resembling, in the regularity with which they worked, a pair of horizontal walking-beams. Old Blue usually had an excellent appetite—during the first days of our soldiering, at Camp Scott, he devoured the whole day's rations for breakfast—and on this occasion he fairly outdid himself. It is safe to assume that, as the family saw that long, lank, wide-mouthed, round-headed, high cheekboned, wicked-looking Yankee withdraw from their front, they experienced at least one delightful sensation—that of relief.

The genial, good-looking Evans was generally successful in his negotiations with the female portion for food, and never even faced a requisition. If refused, the suavity of manner displayed in his withdrawal frequently induced the obstreperous parties to call him back and load him down with edibles.

The next morning after our little party had entered upon the discharge of its duties at the dam, Evans and Old Blue sallied forth to procure some fresh meat, while I remained behind on post. They soon returned, bearing in triumph a half-grown sheep and a calf, which in due time were dressed and hung up to the limb of a tree. With a portion of this mutton we made an excellent breakfast, and after this was completed mutual congratulations were exchanged upon our having sufficient fresh meat for many subsequent meals.

A few moments after breakfast, however, much to our horror, Lieutenant Brown, commanding the squadron on this occasion, put in his appearance on the road above, evidently making a sort of grand round of inspection. There was no time to hide the forbidden commissary stores, and the officer, although very near-sighted, soon perceived it as Corporal Croy walked up to where he sat on his horse. After few questions as to the condition of affairs on this part of the line, and delivery of a number of instructions, Lieutenant Brown demanded:

"Where did that meat come from?"

Croy did not know, but called Evans.

"Got it from the engineer corps," said that genial individual. "A party of them came along here a while ago, who had more than they wanted, and they gave it to me."

The party mentioned as the engineer corps were some infantry on fatigue duty corduroying roads down by a mill about two miles from Ballard's Dam. The lieutenant would pass them on his route, and might have asked them if he chose to do so.

"Very well," said the lieutenant severely, "I will investigate this matter when I return from my tour of inspection."

We awaited his return with fear and trembling, but hid the calf in some brush close by, as he seemed to have noticed only the sheep. When he returned, however, the circumstances appeared to have been forgotten, as no reference whatever was made to it.

After this unexpected visit great care was taken to keep our commissary department invisible to the official eye.

While we were stationed here I partially made the acquaintance of an old gentleman who had formerly been an overseer or superintendent of one of the gold mines in Spottsylvania County, on the other side of the Rappahannock. I was much interested in his narratives of mining operations in this part of Virginia, which, up till about the time the war broke out, seemed to have been attended with favorable results, though, no doubt, under a more perfect system, the mines would have proved much more profitable. As an illustration of the manner in which the business was conducted under slave rule, I will append an incident belonging to a class of common occurrences in those days. A slave employed in one of the mines—a stout, intelligent mulatto—was detected one day in slipping something into his mouth. One of the overseers instantly charged him with stealing gold, and grappled him, while another forced him to open his mouth under the threats of death. An examination revealed a lump of pure gold, worth about ten dollars, which he had secreted. Severe punishments were invariably inflicted in all such instances.

These days on picket duty were happy ones for us. Here the discipline of the camp was forgotten, and monotonous routine of guard-mounting, fatigue police, and drill, existed only in memory. We were glad to assume a soldier's real responsibilities, for that looked like service, while the military ceremonies in camp smacked of a meaningless display much of which, while no doubt necessary to efficiency of discipline, yet always seemed to me to have nothing whatever to do with war, the business for which we mustered. I presume, however, that all these matters have been duly studied by those who have prepared our Army Regulations, and have a usefulness in their way; but a suspicion that official pride and pomposity were in many instances consulted rather than the exigencies of real service continually forces its disagreeable proportions into my susceptible mind in spite of all my well-meaning efforts to master it.

Thus, for instance, while such ceremonies as turning out the guard, saluting officers according to rank, standing to attention, etc., are insisted upon with the utmost particularity, target-practice—a real element of war—was rarely permitted, and then only under circumstances which stripped it of all excitement and evaluation. I cannot help feeling that many of the requirements of camp discipline must have been very humiliating to our proud volunteer soldiery, and did much to change them from brave, impulsive men into a sort of automaton; but, as the latter state is said to be necessary to the proper composition of armies as we are told in the old books—I suppose we had no reason to complain.

At the end of three days we were relieved, and returned to camp, this time locating our tents near the commanding general's headquarters. We found our army in its old position on the north bank of the Rappahannock, having crossed, we were told, on the night of the 15th of December. Our soldiers were in a bad condition, sadly demoralized, and many of them giving expression that shocked me—open menaces of mutiny. The prospects of the cause seemed to have grown suddenly dark under the shadow of recent events. To increase dissatisfaction our food was scanty and lacked variety, being the same old song of coffee, sugar, crackers, and pork. The newspapers that came to us were freighted with the stories of political excitement and uncertainty. The republican, or war element, seemed under a cloud, and the democrat, or peace-at-any-price party, were loud in their denunciations of the abolition crusades. Mr. Lincoln's preliminary proclamation, which in the September previous had notified the world that on the first day of the New Year all the slaves in certain insurgent states would be declared free unless such States returned to their allegiance to the government of the United States prior to that date—a proclamation which was a sort of compromise with slavery, and issued as an expedient—was about to be consummated.[3] This proclamation was a favorite theme of conversation among discontented soldiers, who were prompt to find any excuse for refusal to do their duty. I confess that I was not prepared for such a demonstration on the part of the government, although fully convinced that the measure

[3]   The Emancipation Proclamation was issued following the Battle of Antietam, on September 22, 1862, and was to take effect on January 1, 1863. As the memoirs note, it was a compromise. Abolitionists disliked it for it did not free all the slaves while Confederates were outraged at this tampering with their "peculiar institution." As Sidney Davis subsequently remarks, it was not popular with Union troops either. Many felt that the war was to save the Union, not to free the slaves.

was a righteous one; I feared that the great prejudice of the people might overcome their patriotism, and produce disastrous results. In the light of the history of the succeeding years, however, the hand of providence is visible in the shaping of the course of the government, and what was then looked upon as a matter of doubtful expediency is now regarded as a measure of consummate wisdom.

On the 24th of December, the squadron was sent up the river on picket, and the next morning I rode from camp to join the company—I had been on some duty during the previous day. As I passed up the heights beyond Falmouth a confederate infantry picket, who was posted on the river bank, hailed me.

"A Merry Christmas!"

He held up his canteen in full view a moment, and then took a drink. I responded with a military salute, and trotted away.

Two or three miles beyond this I met a German soldier. He, too, flourished a canteen, but in an uncertain sort of way.

"You fights mit Sigel?" he asked.

"I fights mit anybody who fights for de Union."

"Goot. Then you drinks mit me."

"Thank you friend, I never drink."

He looked at me with a curious expression on his honest Dutch countenance.

"Vell, vell, vell."

"Good bye, friend. A happy Christmas to you and your frau and kinder."

I rode away, but could still hear him repeating:

"Vell, vell, vell."

Just before I got out of sight I looked back. He was still standing where I had left him, slowly shaking his head in a mute astonishment at my refusal to drink, each shake saying, as plainly as words could speak:

"Vell, vell, vell."

About the 20th of January the Army of the Potomac made another movement, this time towards the fords on the Rappahannock river above Falmouth. Our company was then on picket near Bank's ford, and we received the first intimation of the contemplated campaign from the confederates opposed to us, who seemed to fully understand the whole programme. Large bodies of their troops marched to the crest of the hills running along the river in our front, and began to throw up defensive works and obstruct the roads leading from the different fords southward, in anticipation of the expected federal advance. All day and all night the din of busy preparations could be heard. On the evening of the second day they professed themselves ready to resist any attack. That night they held a grand ball at a farmhouse just across the river from our videttes, where the sound of music and dancing could be heard until nearly daylight.

As was usual whenever the Army of the Potomac began a movement, a great storm of rain came and deluged the land. On our way back to camp, after having been relieved, we met our troops on the march. They had literally been mired, the artillery and pontoon trains having sunk into the treacherous earth and become utterly immovable. Efforts were made to corduroy the roads. Over three thousand men were marching, or rather wading, along, each one carrying a fence rail as we passed. I was glad then that I was not an infantryman.

The story of Burnsides' "stick-in-the-mud"[4] is too well known for a recapitulation. It is sufficient to say that in a few days, after a fearful effort, the army was obliged to return to camp as best it could, leaving a great deal of material scattered through the country on the extreme right until the ground should harden; material was then brought inside our lines. Not a gun was fired during the movement.

The demoralization which had begun at Waterloo upon the removal of McClellan, and increased immeasurably on the bloody field of Fredericksburg, culminated during this trying ordeal. The threats of mutiny became more and more outspoken. There seemed to be a combination of private grievances in addition to the rough fortunes of war. Several months had elapsed since the army had been paid. Furloughs were unobtainable. Letters from home told doleful stories of the want and suffering among the families of the men. The prices of living were rising all over the land, and the pittance of thirteen dollars per month was not enough to keep the body and soul together of more than one person. Threats of desertion were openly made. These days were indeed dark ones for the Republic.

To show the hopes and fears and yearnings of the Common Soldier at this stage of his military career I transcribe extracts from letters dated at Camp of Sixth United States Cavalry, January 28, 1863:

[4] This is known as Burnside's "Mud March." After the defeat at Fredericksburg, Burnside decided to again attack the Confederates further up the Rappahannock at Bank's Ford. The movement of troops occurred between January 19-24, 1863 and was an unmitigated disaster due to the condition of the roads. Burnside eventually called off the movement.

Dear Friend: You will please excuse me for not writing to you sooner. The difficulty was in the lack of postage stamps—I had but one, which was used to send the last letter to George, and I expected to have you hear through him all the important news. Lately our duties and drills have been so constant and excessive that I have barely time to eat through the day, and our little pieces of candles shed such miserable light, and are so miserable unhandy that I have no heart to write of them.

I suppose this apology will be sufficient.

Although soldiering in these days seems to be unsafe and has brought many to untimely graves, it rather appears to agree with me. Since enlisting I have gained in flesh twenty pounds, and have changed somewhat in appearance. I now weight one hundred and fifty-eight pounds and have a respectable beard.

You know I will be twenty-two years of age in March.

I would like to come and see you once more, but I suppose I shall have to stay here until my time is out. I have seventeen months to serve yet; my nineteen months will be complete next week. It has been eighteen months since I was at home—a longer period of absence from it than I ever before passed.

I wonder if I will recognize the old place, and the dear faces I was once so glad to see? Or the voices that were once so familiar? Does the old farm look as it did a year and a half ago? I should be glad to live once more in the old stone house, where passed the happy hours of my boyhood. It seem like an odd word for me to use—"boyhood;" I am but a boy yet, in feeling, at least.

It seems to me that I have lived an age in these few brief months. Our parting at the mill by the riverside is pictured in my memory like a dream of long ago. I look at myself in a glass, and feel curious to know who the shadow is, for I cannot believe it to be myself, it is so odd-looking—and that beard!

What dogs, and horses, and cows, and men have you now on the farm? How is Little Jim—I suppose he is big Jim now—and Matty, with her bright blue eyes, and Kate, and Wallace, and Charley, and Mary, and Catherine and her children? Who helps you with the work in the kitchen? Did Joe Bentley go into the army? Have you the guinea pigs yet?

I should like to be at home to get some of your good coffee and bread. Since leaving you I have had to live on coffee without cream, hard bread, salt pork, and occasionally fresh beef, beans, boiled rice, and at times a few potatoes and onions. Those were government issue. I sometimes forage for luxuries.

I have been off duty but one day since enlisting with a bad cold. Tonight I have the tooth-ache, and the rascal must be pulled out.

Is my trunk, with its precious treasure of books, etc. all safe? I wish I could see father's likeness. I will get you a portrait of mine done up in "sojer" clothes, and send it to you—I have had none taken yet.

Has Hiram the old Bonesight yet? I have seen some chances for a good shot since I beheld the old gun. My rifle is a breech-loader, and will throw a bullet about a thousand yards, and can be loaded and fired with great rapidity. It is one of Sharp's guns.

It is raining hard tonight.

This letter was written to old Mrs. Samuels, the housekeeper at Bentley's. She had been a very mother to me since I had lost my own in 1845—not indeed by death, but by an indenture which separated us as effectually and as cruelly as death.

I found the original of this indenture among some old papers at Bentley's about twenty years after its execution, and have it now. As it is an odd sort of a document, and will read strangely in these days of enlightened and liberal public opinion, a copy is here transcribed. An inexorable necessity is the explanation of this curious transaction. It was the old story of marriage, intemperance, abuse, separation. My mother, homeless and friendless, gave me into hands she trusted would provide for me, went alone into the world to struggle for herself, and did not reappear for thirteen years.

Allegheny city, September 20, 1845

This article of agreement between Levi Bentley, of Washington County, State of Pennsylvania, of the one part, and Nancy Davis of Allegheny City, of the other part, witnesseth:

That the said Nancy agrees to give her son Sidney to the said Levi Bentley to raise until he shall be fit to go for a trade. He also agrees to feed and clothe the boy during the above period. Mr. Levi Bentley also agrees to give the mother Nancy Thirty-five dollars in cash this day, which she receipts for. It is distinctly understood by the parties that the said Levi shall have the sole control of the boy, without the interference of his mother Nancy, in consideration of the above thirty-five dollars.

In consideration of the above the parties have set their hands and seals the day and year above written.

Then follow the signatures of the parties to the instrument, attested by a witness, and a receipt for thirty-five dollars. On the back is an endorsement;

"Memorandum of an agreement between Levi Bentley and Nancy Davis in regard to the boy Sidney."

Although father lived at Bentley's, he exercised no claim over me as a parent, but allowed the indenture to have full effect. Levi spared my feelings in the matter, for I did not know of the existence of the document until the consummation of its terms.

It will be observed that mention is made in the letter to Mrs. Samuels of my having the tooth-ache, and there is, also, an intimation that the grinder must be pulled. Full of this determination I went over to Brooks—that little fellow was a sort of hospital steward now—and ordered him to extract the nuisance. It was to be the first event of the kind since I had grown up, and there was an uncertainty in my mind as to the amount of agony I was to endure. The tooth was a double one.

Brooks got out his instruments—it was his first effort at this sort of surgery—fastened on the grinder, cast his eyes heavenward, and gave a terrific jerk.

"Oh—oh!" says I.

Out came a tooth, but it was not *the* tooth—it was one without a speck—a beautiful specimen of ivory. I soon became aware of this fact.

"My Lord, Brooks! You have pulled the best tooth in my mouth," I exclaimed in an agonized voice.

The little fellow, although seldom exhibiting compassion for anything, seemed now to feel about as bad as I did. It was too late, however, to complain, and the obstreperous grinder was aching harder than ever. The instrument was again brought into requisition, and this time there was no difficulty in finding the right tooth, on account of the vacancy beside it. Brooks gave another tremendous jerk.

"Oh—oh," I howled.

Something cracked, and the aching suddenly ceased, but the tooth did not come out. I felt so comfortable after the cessation of agony that I did not think it worth while for him to try again. It was several days before I could shut my jaws together—the grinder stood a little above the rest—but after awhile it settled to its place, and felt like some foreign substance instead of one of my teeth. It never ached afterward, however.

My experience with Brooks did not impress me favorably with his qualifications as a dentist. He was, perhaps, a success so far as the administering of quinine was concerned. This mistake was always mentioned by him afterwards in terms of heartfelt regret—the only sorrow I ever heard him express.

The other letter of January 28, addressed to another person, is confined to a statement of the condition and feeling of the army at that time. An extract says:

George, I am actually beginning to lose hope. The army seems to be disheartened. Many of the soldiers express the belief that the negroes will go north and occupy their place in the workshops.[5] Large numbers of the married men receive letters from home describing the destitute conditions of their families. The army has not been paid for some six or eight months. There is a vast amount of sickness among the new troops, who, unaccustomed to the hardships of campaign life, sink under the fatigue, exposure, and anxieties to which they are subjected. Home sickness, and the change from the luxuries of the table to the coarse, common fare of the army, renders hundreds dispirited and dissatisfied. The democratic papers taunt them about "this abolition war", as they call it. The old soldiers curse and growl about politicians generally.

Events since the war have demonstrated how groundless were the fears that the colored people would leave their native south to supplant white labor in the workshops of the north. During a period when they were subjected to all sorts of indignity and abuse at the hands of lawless marauders, generally known as the Ku-Klux-Klan, they have clung to the land of their birth.

One day I went over in company with Willie Ferree, of the One-hundred and Second Pennsylvania to the camp of the One hundred Fortieth Pennsylvania Volunteers, a regiment of new troops, one company of which was from my neighborhood. Many of the members were old schoolmates of mine. As we were veterans by this time, and had smelt gunpowder on the field of battle, we strutted about quite proudly among the "recruits". They were just then trying to bring their stomachs into subjection—to contract these refractory members to the capacity of army rations, and discipline the organs of taste—with rather indifferent success. Their remarks about military diet reminded me vividly of the early days of our soldiering at Camp Scott, where the men of the Sixth Cavalry passed through the same trying ordeal. Just now the One hundred and Fortieth was patronizing the sutlers rather extensively.

Much of the sickness among the new troops could be traced to the vicious system of sutlers in the army. These arrogant cormorants, who, by some strange, inexplicable means, were allowed to locate themselves among the camps, constituted a monstrous evil, without a single redeeming feature. They obstructed the channels of transportation; they introduced unnecessary commodities of food which destroyed the relish for army fare, and vitiated the taste and sickened the consumers; they

[5]   This fear was widespread and was one of the causes of the draft riots in New York in 1863.

333

surreptitiously or otherwise brought poisonous liquors within reach of men who could not resist the temptation to drink and these went into the guard house as a consequence, and were often court martialled, and lost the money that should have been sent home to their suffering families; they charged exorbitant rates for the most trivial of articles; they were domineering in disposition over any common soldier who sought to deal with them. I speak of them as a class; there may have been exceptions.

Attached to the army is an extensive medical corps; this corps, after much scientific research and experiment, adopted a military ration, composed of substantial food, to be varied at stated intervals, and this ration is complete as to the actual wants of the soldier, and is demonstrated to be the healthiest diet that can be devised.[6] It is coarse and plain, but in time the soldier learns to relish it quite as much as the food he consumed at home. After the government has been to the expense of establishing and supporting this medical corps, and has adopted this wholesome ration, and the soldier, at the end of the months of self-denial, accustoms himself to the diet, a pompous citizen, whose interest in the matter is exclusively selfish, is let loose in camp, brings in his stock of sweet cakes, bad whiskey, and other trash, sometimes during war obstructing the transportation of men and material essential to its proper prosecution, deludes the army, pockets an immense sum as profit, demoralizes the soldier and disgusts him with army fare, overthrows all the sanitary regulations which the expensive medical corps establishes, disables vast numbers of men, and is, indirectly perhaps, but nevertheless, an ally of the enemy, if he does not happen to be a paid spy in his service. That is the sum of the effects of the sutler system.

At noon one day the squad in our Sibley were sitting eating their bean soup around the tripod of the tent pole. A gun was fired outside—a common occurrence, by the way, and one which seldom occasioned comment, for we were encamped in the midst of the army—and I jocosely remarked:

"There goes red-head!"

"Red-head" was a phrase used in the company, on account of the color of his hair, to designate Lieutenant Irwin, the officer that gave me the scolding during the night at Warrenton Sulphur Springs, when I hung my equipment upon my horse. He was much disliked for the savage way in which he enforced discipline, although it is but just to him to say that

---

[6]   The Medical Department was extensive but it had little to do with the adoption of rations.   That matter was handled by the Quartermaster Department.

I believe his motives were good. The above remark meant that some one had shot Lieutenant Irwin, though, of course, such an event was not seriously contemplated or desired by me.

A moment afterwards we became conscious that something unusual had happened in camp. There was a running of men in different directions, and confused shouts that we could not understand. In a few minutes it was announced that one of Company K's men had been shot and killed by a comrade. They had just returned from picket, and unsaddled, when these two men, who were "backups" began playfully chasing each other around and among the tents. The one in advance, in running past a tree against which leaned a carbine, hastily snatched up the gun, wheeled, brought it to his shoulder, levelled it at the other, and fired, the bullet entering his heart and killing him instantly. His horror-stricken comrade had forgotten that the gun had not yet been unloaded since coming in from picket, and was beside himself with sorrow at the untimely fate his beloved comrade had met at his hands. He was placed under arrest, but as the affair was the result of an accident the commanding officer ordered him to be released and returned to duty.

Strangely enough, the soldier killed was red-headed though the coincidence, if it can be called one, ended at this point. The red-head I had referred to is still living, and holds a commission as captain of cavalry.

Winter Quarters—Unhappy Days

As cold weather approached, the men began to devise means to make themselves comfortable. Our Sibleys were raised a couple of feet from the ground on split logs, these averaging six inches in diameter, cut short, sharpened at one end, driven into the ground with the "belly" or round side out, and with earth banked up against them on the outside. The effect of this elevation of the tents was to increase the standing room of the men—to enable them to rise to an erect position, and to add to the number of cubic feet of air per man. On the tripod was suspended a camp kettle, in the bottom and around the sides of which were punched holes to create a draught, and these kettles were thus improvised into stoves. The men were obligated to cut their wood very short on account of the small proportions of the kettle, and the fire had to be fed with fuel constantly in order to keep up a heat. The smoke ascended through an opening in the top of the Sibley, but the cloud hung heavy a few feet from the ground, and made the water come to one's eyes when one stood erect. As it was necessary to suspend the kettle or "stove" a few inches from the ground in order to obtain the proper draft, there was some difficulty experienced in warming, one's feet—we had to elevate first one and then the other, or rest both at once over a piece of cracker box or like article.

When a squad could not procure a camp kettle they resorted to other expedients. A mound several inches in height was raised under the tripod, and on this mound the fire was built, the elevation assisting the draught very materially.

About a dozen men occupied each Sibley. Although nominally two and two slept together, in reality there was but one bed for all, as they laid close together in a circle, with heads outward and feet grouped

337

around the tripod. This arrangement recognized the "bed clothes," and added to the comfort of all.

A sort of cap, with ropes attached, was fitted on the iron tip of the tent pole. This was used to cover the opening at the top of the Sibley to keep out rain, or could be left partially open to allow the smoke to escape, or shifted around as a guard against the wind when the haze was from a particular point of the compass. Altogether the arrangements were quite complete.

The horses were sheltered as much as circumstances would permit. A cordon of pine brush, densely packed together, was built around each company's stables, to break off the cold winds, and a sort of roof of the same material, supported by long poles served to protect them from the falling rain and snow. There was much sickness among the animals, mostly from glanders, and a sort of curious disease which affected the tongue, that member swelling and turning from a natural blue to bluish black color. When a horse became affected, it was sent to a corral, or sort of horse hospital, where it was duly attended by a veterinary surgeon. The latter was a citizen in this case, whose only claim to distinction, like many of his brother physicians to a different sort of animal, was his ability to look wise and say nothing.

The service now felt the need of properly educated veterinary surgeons and suffered a vast loss from this vital want. The experience in this respect so dearly bought during the existence of the war should be turned to account in these days of peace, when the opportunity to improve it is within reach. The government should establish a school for the education of persons in this particular department of medicine—it might be connected with West Point—or in some way foster such an institution. As it is, the subject seems to be comparatively unknown, and when a horse becomes sick it is put through the same haphazard course of treatment that is designated among men as "old woman cures"—no effort being made to study the different diseases to which these useful animals are subjected. The benefits of such a corps would not be confined to the army—they would extend beyond this organization to the millions employed in all the departments of industry. To use a homely but expressive phrase—"it would pay."

For the first time in the history of man, the rights of what is known as the animal creation have been recognized in law by the establishment and incorporation of societies for the prevention of cruelty to animals. This is a good beginning of a great work. Let its influence be extended beyond the mere prevention of cruelty to the study and prevention of diseases among animals, and especially among that class to which he owes so much—the horse.

On the 22nd of February a heavy snow storm visited the country around Fredericksburg and added somewhat to the discomforts of the army. As this was the anniversary of Washington's birthday, we had expected a sort of holiday, but the chilly blasts and driving snow obliged each of us as were fortunate enough to be off duty to keep under our frail shelters. The earth was not relieved of this disagreeable mantle for one or two weeks, the snow having attained a depth of some six or eight inches.

Two days after, I had a remarkable horseback ride—or, rather, the remarkable part of the ride was after I had been forced from the horse's back. A new animal had been assigned to me some days before—my old, faithful, long headed beast had taken the tongue disease, and when no longer able to eat hard oats and hay was sent to the horse hospital for treatment—with which I had not yet become fully acquainted. Being rather careless, on this occasion I rode it over to a brook with the balance of the company to water, without taking the precaution to put on a bridle, simply using the halter strap looped around his under jaw, Indian fashion. On our way we had to pass over a newly cleared field, where the stumps stood black-looking a few inches above the snow. My horse walked over this field to the watering-place quietly enough, drank the amount it desired, and then we started on our return. I was a little cautious of these black-looking stumps, and on passing one would gently press on the halter strap as a sort of guard against surprise. About half way back I passed quite a large one on my left side, and went through the same programme of slightly reining up, but the horse did not seem to be afraid, and just as the stump was partially behind us I slackened up my hold. At that instant my horse gave a sudden sidespring to the right, and then dashed off at full speed across the field towards camp. By the first movement I was thrown off my balance, and made a vain effort to regain his back. The halter strap had fallen from my left hand, and thus unchecked he almost flew through the air, every now and then giving me terrific jolts whenever one of his fore feet stepped on the dangling halter strap and savagely jerked down his head. I found I was slipping off in spite of my wild efforts, and by a desperate struggle I clasped him with a death grip around the neck, and just then, by one of those periodical jolts when the horse stepped on the strap, my arms were thrown forward

339

close up to its ears. Somehow or other my feet became also coupled around the animal's withers. The situation at that moment may be summed up thus: The frightened horse was dashing along with lightning like rapidity; I had swung completely around under its neck, and was hanging on with hands and feet uppermost and locked together on the top of the neck. I suppose the picture was a comical one to everybody except the rider, if at that instant I was a rider. I am sure I felt by no means humorous; I could not have laughed if I had tried. The final result of this curious adventure was something that I could not help regarding with an anxious solicitude. If the hold of my feet gave way, my legs would swing down under the animal's ponderous hoofs, and perhaps be broken in pieces; if that of my hands gave way, my head would swing down and, and meet a like fate. This was a true dilemma, substituting the alternatives for honors. I figured up the result of these two contingencies at a rate that would have made the author of the Lightning Calculator ashamed of himself. I also mentally repeated a sufficient number of passages from scripture and other religious books to make up a good-sized volume. I involuntarily went over in detail all of the bad deeds done in the body and made an indefinite number of promises never to do so again.

In the meantime, as if by instinct, I became aware of the rapid approach of a new and more terrible danger. We were nearing the woods, or rather where the woods had been before our going into camp here. Most of the trees were cut down, but the stumps were left standing two or three feet high from the ground. It occurred to me that when we came to this clearing the horse would be likely, in his mad affright, to dash against one of these stumps, in which event it would be my lot to come in contact first, and while this fact might save this beast from permanent injury it would be sad for my back. Besides, my grip was becoming more uncertain, and I should soon drop from sheer exhaustion anyhow.

Presently we came into this rough clearing like a whirlwind. I waited for the dreaded catastrophe with beating heart. My hold began to slip; my head swum, and then as my feet commenced to unlock, I closed my eyes. I knew now that the great problem was about to be solved. At that instant there was a sudden surge and jerk that tore me loose from the horse. I heard him utter a deep groan that startled me with its human--like sound, then found myself standing in a muddy road that ran through the clearing, squarely erect, unhurt, though slightly sick at my stomach.

340

A couple of yards away lay the horse on its back perfectly still.

Our course through the clearing had been at right angles with this road. When it was reached, the fore feet of the horse had gone down into the wagon rut, which was nearly twenty-four inches deep, from which they could not be extricated promptly enough, and as a consequence the animal turned a complete somersault. The fall stunned the horse somewhat, but I soon had it on its feet, and led it slowly down to the stable, having had a surfeit of equestrianism for that day.

This lesson was fully appreciated by me. I never turned out afterwards mounted without the proper bridle, and duly prepared for emergencies.

About this time Craven, who had been sick for some time, was discharged "by reason of disability," as the phrase goes. That peculiar German, Schumacher, also became disabled from an attack of rheumatism, was sent to the hospital, and took no end of medicine and applied no end of liniments to the party affected. This once cheerful spirit never seemed to recover from the shock it had sustained in the adventure with the dead man at Hartwood Church. In due time he was ordered to be discharged "by reason of disability." On the day of his departure for home several of his German friends accompanied him to the railroad station to see him off and bid him good bye. He rode down in an ambulance, and after much effort and assistance he was safely deposited on the train. When the cars started they waved their caps to him, and to their great surprise Schumacher suddenly sprang to his feet, ran out on the platform of the receding train, threw his crutches right and left, laughed loudly, and then disappeared inside. The fictive German had successfully assumed the role of an invalid to secure a release from the service, and I suppose was happy over the result. There is little doubt that the government was much the gainer in the end; an unwilling soldier is an expensive and useless soldier.

Shortly after Burnside's failure to cross the Upper Rappahannock he was relieved, and General Hooker assumed command of the Army of the Potomac. This change of officers relieved many saddened hearts. Hooker was popular among the soldiers on account of his military reputation. Whether or not overrated as to his abilities in the field, one thing soon became evident—on this occasion he seemed to understand what was needed to meet the emergency that was upon us. He inaugurated many reforms and corrected many abuses. A system of furloughs was established—so many men of a company, according to strength on muster, were allowed ten days' leave of absence at a time. The quality of food was changed, and issues of vegetables ordered, and bakeries established in the different camps to supply the men with fresh soft bread to take the place of "hard tack".

I was surprised at the great change for the better that seemed to have taken place—the cheerfulness that had superseded the old despondency. The men seemed to have become rejuvenated by some mysterious process. They forgot all their disasters, and grew buoyant with hope. The determination to carry on the war to a successful conclusion, which had almost disappeared during the last days of the Burnside control, came to the surface again stronger than ever.

The cavalry corps was reorganized and its strength vastly increased. It was during these days that Hooker gave utterance to that expression which, in spite of his former personal popularity, stirred up against him a dislike among the mounted of the army:

"He had never seen a dead cavalryman."

This remark, while it may have been literally true as to Hooker personally, was, to say the least, injudicious, and at once displayed a prejudice towards one portion of his command that, no matter how much he may have felt it, he should have studiously left concealed. It lowered that portion in the eyes of the others, encouraged open insults toward men who were unfortunate enough to wear the jackets with the orange stripes, supplied the courageous corps of newspaper correspondents with any amount of stock-in-trade criticism, and, coming as it did from the head of the army, obtained a currency and credit that worked incalculable mischief. In addition to this, it discouraged the class of soldiers to which it referred. To my mind, it was sufficient ground upon which to justify his immediate removal from a command for which subsequent events showed him entirely unfitted, and of which unfitness this silly expression was a sufficient evidence.

It must have been humiliating to General Hooker to read, in after years, of the exploits of this corps which he at that time openly professed to despise, under the leadership of gallant Phil. Sheridan. Though composed of a force not exceeding one-tenth of the entire army under his command, it captured ten times the number of battle flags and guns in open field fighting that the Army of the Potomac did in the campaign under his leadership, and vastly aided in those mighty efforts that closed the war. It fought infantry and cavalry, and, except in a few instances where met by overwhelming numbers, was always successful.

In this high defense of the cavalry corps not one word of reproach or derogation of the services of the other arms is intended. All honor to the hard-working infantry and gallant battery-men! We would not take a single leaf from your wreaths of victory! Through all the fierce struggle of the great war we were only too glad to count you as supporters and allies. Your flag was our flag, and we sought, to the best of our ability, obstructed and discouraged as we were by incompetency and prejudice, to uphold it under all circumstances. We hail you, brothers-in-arms, and accord you unstinted praise for your deeds of valor and endurance!

General Sheridan, in his report to the Committee on the Conduct of the War, has indirectly intimated that he met with this prejudice when he joined the Army of the Potomac, and speaks of the tendency to fritter away the strength of the corps in fruitless forays and useless picket duty. He announced as his policy a different course entirely; the men and horses were to be built up, as it were, in morale and physical ability; cavalry was to fight cavalry, and infantry to fight infantry. Pleasanton's testimony also conveys the impression that General Meade exhibited a strong feeling of contempt towards his mounted men and their officers during the days of the Gettysburg campaign.

I presume that, in proportion to the actual number of men in the field, deducting those on duty at the different headquarters, and on other details less dangerous, the number of casualties in the cavalry force would average fully as many as those of the other arms of the service. These occurred few at a time, but often and gradually wore down the regiments. The campaigns subsequent to the reorganization of the corps by Hooker demonstrated that the duties which had been exacted from a puny force of less than four thousand men, and for which they had received no commendation whatever, were fully sufficient to actively employ a corps numbering five times that number. Hooker was certainly entitled to our gratitude for vastly reinforcing us, and affording us a relief from our extremely arduous and thankless service.

Speaking alone of the experience of the Sixth Cavalry—and I suppose they were the same as those of other regiments—it may be mentioned that the men averaged, as to camp and stable guards, three days and nights in the week. In addition to this were the picketing and drills—the former averaging three days and nights per week, while the latter took up the balance of the time. Often each of the men were posted one or two miles from his fellows, and sometimes was not relieved for six or twelve hours. Our series of skirmishes, overshadowed as they were by the vast continuations of armies and operations throughout the country, were unrecorded, though the losses in killed and wounded during a given time would perhaps equal that of any infantry regiment during the same period. Thus, for instance, in the action at Williamsburg, thirty-one men were lost out of the battalion that fought, and in the Gettysburg campaign, fourteen months later, the loss ran up to three-fourths of the entire command, and over one-half of these were killed and wounded. Of the number of men actually with the command from Williamsburg to Gettysburg inclusive, over one-third were killed and wounded, or over three hundred men out of nine hundred. Of course, this is hardly a fair estimate, for it takes the highest number of men that were in the regiment for duty at any one time, and not the average.

In Sheridan's report of his campaign in the Shenandoah valley, he gives as his effective force at the commencement of that campaign, in round numbers, eighteen thousand infantry and three thousand five hundred cavalry. The losses of the cavalry force amounted to four hundred and fifty four killed and two thousand eight hundred and seventeen wounded; total three thousand two hundred and eighty-one. About the 6th or 7th of August, as appears from a dispatch sent to General Sheridan by General Grant, the cavalry was reinforced by five thousand mounted men, making the total number about eight thousand five hundred. It will thus be seen that nearly one half of this force was killed or wounded during the campaign from August 4th to October 19th. The number killed belonging to the infantry was fourteen hundred and sixty-five, and wounded eighty-nine hundred and eighty-six; total ten thousand four hundred and fifty. This arm was reinforced by Jones' division of the Nineteenth Corps about August 12, numbering probably six thousand men, though the actual strength is not given, bringing the total infantry force up to about twenty-four thousand. It will thus be seen that the losses of the cavalry corps were larger in proportion than that of the infantry in this celebrated campaign, although less than one-third of their loss was sustained in the actions known as battles in that campaign—the balance in skirmishes.

I have sometimes been led to doubt the existence of the great utility that has been attached by our military authorities to the sabre as an arm for mounted men, in these days of breech loading and repeating rifles and pistols. It is true that the history of European wars represent them to have been effective weapons, but that was before the improvement in firearms had reached such a state of perfection.

344

From the little I have seen I am not even convinced of the truth of European history on this point. For instance, there are seven different accounts of Napoleon's great cavalry fight at Eckinwald, and they all differ as to losses—ranging all the way from five thousand to twenty thousand. It is stated that the mounted troops were constantly engaged in a hand-to-hand fight for four hours in the darkness of the night. There is described the spectacle of a large body of cavalrymen belonging to different armies, thrown together in the fierce tumult of the charge, and, as a necessary consequence, totally disorganized, cutting and slashing promiscuously, as they must, for it is dark, and they cannot distinguish friend from foe—and this for four hours of time!

It was my lot to take part in four charges upon cavalry, in which the hostile troops were jammed in together close enough for the use of the sword, and on each occasion one or the other gave way in less than five or ten minutes. The party defeated fled as best it could, until it became clear of the other, and reorganized, and then, and not till then, was it ready to renew the contest. As long as it was running it was completely harmless so far as the sabre was concerned; the only men that kept up any resistance were those who managed to draw their revolvers. In all these hand-to-hand fights, the combatants would "double-team" on each other if they had an opportunity—that is, two or more men would attack one of their opponents—and the chivalrous object of the affair would degenerate into a simple exhibition of brute force. In these cases there was but little use for the victim to say that he surrendered; all he could do was to throw up both arms and protect his head as much as possible until his enemies became exhausted, or, better still, throw himself off his horse on the ground.

In all these instances but few men were badly hurt, and not more than two or three killed outright, with sabres. There were some ugly scalp wounds and bruises. The only man killed with a sabre of whom I am cognizant was a confederate. It occurred during the action at Williamsburg. I relate the case upon the authority of the soldier who did it, and of another who witnessed the deed. In the charge into the swamp, Leonard came upon a confederate who had been dismounted, and had sunk so deep in the mire that he could not extricate himself. He was quite an old man. His hat had fallen off, and his bald head was exposed. Leonard struck a cruel blow upon the top of his skull, from which the blood spouted up, but the man did not fall. As Leonard raised the sabre to strike again the confederate threw himself on his back to avoid the blow. Then Leonard leaned over on his horse and attempted to strike him, but the man caught hold of the sword, and in the struggle to hold it had his fingers terribly, cut. Leonard jerked it loose, and thrust it in the stomach of the confederate and thus killed him. This was not a fair fight.

There are many uses to which a mounted force would seem applicable. It may raid on an enemy's communications and supplies; patrol roads; be moved, during a battle, to different points with great rapidity; dismount and attack as infantry, or ride over a line and break it; snap in upon a battery, if its support is not too strong, and capture it. In all this the sabre is simply a burden. The most that may be claimed for this weapon is, perhaps, that its presence in the right hand keeps the men from shooting one another with their revolvers in the excitement of a charge. Assuredly, the number of men killed and wounded by it is insignificant and unworthy of notice.

As a general thing, the volunteers fastened their sabres to their saddles, and thus obviated one of the great objections—the dangling of the sheath against their legs when maneuvering dismounted. With us this was not permitted.

Our men always seemed to prefer fighting on foot, as infantry. It appeared like business, this aiming and shooting at one's enemy. If it is necessary, one can hug the ground or tree instead of sitting on one's horse, exposed to the storm of missiles.

However, the Common Soldier will leave the question to the consideration of the profession, simply putting on record his doubt as to whether the value of the sabre as a cavalry arm in these days of improved weapons is sufficient to justify its cost and the incumbrance it imposes on both men and horses.

Ambitious to send home a picture of myself, to let the folks see what we looked like in the field, I went over to the establishment of an artist who had located near army headquarters. Charlton, the "Pittsburgh boy", was there, having his horse and a very diminutive donkey with him. I have this picture now as a relic of old times on the Rappahannock. I am on Charlton's horse; Charlton is on the donkey; the donkey's ears are tied together to keep them steady; a slouch hat, coubled up on one side, and fastened with a brass eagle surmounts my noble brow; a sabre swings at my side; my, face shows slight symptoms of a beard. Altogether I think these two boys look more like brigands than soldiers.

The jovial Hamilton had his good-natured face sadly disfigured by the heels of Lieutenant Irwin's horse early in February. He had been over to see some friends in one of the infantry regiments and imbibed too much commissary whiskey. On his way home the animal became frightened and threw Hamilton back over its haunches, at the same instant kicking poor Samuel squarely, on the nose, knocking that appendage all out of shape, or rather, into the oddest kind of a shape.

One day, I went over, in company with one of my infantry friends, to the camp of Newton's division. Our route led us past a spot where the dead horses from the different cavalry and artillery camps were dragged for burial—a good sized field about a mile from headquarters. Some thirty or forty of the defunct animals were lying in a row, awaiting the arrival of the burial detail. We noticed a small party of men gathered about one of the brutes, and, prompted by an idle curiosity, walked over to see what they were doing. The horse, which was still breathing, appeared to be in the last stages of that loathsome disease, the glanders. His throat was cut, but the blood flowed very slowly from the wound. Two men were at work on its flank—they had cut open the skin and stripped it off for a space about eighteen or twenty inches square, and now sliced off great pieces of flesh as one would do when preparing it for cooking.

"What are you doing, boys?" we asked.

"Getting some meat," was the response.

My friend and I looked at one another in astonishment. Hooker had been in command for some time, and there were no complaints as to the quantity of food or its quality, so far as we had heard.

"What will you do with the meat—have you dogs?"

"No—we have no dogs; we are going to eat it."

We turned from the spot utterly disgusted. The men seemed in earnest about the matter. They spoke a broken dialect—either French or Italian. As we were going out of sight into the woods we glanced back. They were still cutting away at the flank of the horse. I had read stories of armies so reduced by hunger as to be driven to eating their horses, but here was a case where preference seemed to be given to that sort of dish.

"Well," said my friend, "who would have dreamed of the existence of such a band of wretches in this enlightened age and country? They could be court-martialled and condemned to bread and water for six months."

I confess that my feelings fully concurred in this sentence.

347

Captain Sanders left us during the winter, having been promoted to be brigadier general of volunteers, and the command of the regiment devolved upon Captain Cram. I do not think we were so happy under this officer as we were under the gallant Sanders. Captain Cram was a curious, capricious man, seeming to be most delighted when the men most feared him. A perfect reign of terror held sway over the guards. He would come down to the guardhouse at all hours of the night, sometimes wearing his sidearms and at other times without them, and then, in violation of all regulations, the guard and prisoners were obliged to turn out and fall into line—the latter in their bare feet and drawers—that he might be saluted according to rank. A little hatred towards him was developed throughout the entire regiment. Whenever a soldier had occasion to speak of him, his name was invariably coupled with uncomplimentary phrases. The universal desire was often thus briefly expressed, except for our religious:

"Damn Cram!"

Thus religious wore off the round edge of a curse:

"Darn Cram!"

The young man from the country, who still retained a wholesome fear of profanity, as inculcated by his conscientious parents, contented himself as follows:

"Gol darn Cram!"

All sorts of violent deaths and untimely ends were pictured as in store for the unfortunate Cram. Few of the men seemed to believe that he ever allowed himself to become sober while in command of the regiment that winter. Towards spring, when Major Starr was assigned to us, and took charge, poor Cram seemed to have dropped from the pinnacle of happiness to the depths of despair. Starr was a strict disciplinarian, and rigidly exercised it towards all—officers as well as men. In his presence Cram appeared heavily ill at ease. His trepidation was visible to everyone, and a smile was sure to pass along the line on such occasions. The major was rather liked for this uniform application to the high and low of the rules and articles of war.

The querulous little Dutchman, Draker, had a dispute with Rheol, another German, and it became necessary to resort to the code of honor to settle it. The weapon selected was sabres. Accompanied by a small party, they retired to an open space among some low, thick clustered pines, which effectually screened their operations from the official eye. Here they were placed in position close enough to reach one another with their sabres. From the way Draker swore and Rheol chattered one would have expected any amount of bloodshed.

At the proper moment time was called. The blades flashed in the air amid a series of strokes and thrusts, but the careful Dutchmen had retired from each other a sufficient distance to render these demonstrations perfectly harmless. It was no use to expostulate with the combatants, and urge them to close in on one another; they still swore and chattered and struck and thrust at one another at a safe distance.

In the course of an hour the duel was over and "nobody hurt." This was another of our funny reminiscences, that served to bring out a loud laugh whenever our stock of amusements ran short.

Everybody now seemed to develop a bitter feeling throughout the Army of the Potomac, under the management of General Hooker. I began to be hopeful that at last we had found the right man to lead our legions in the east. Fresh troops arrived almost daily from the north—an evidence that the people at home were coming to our relief. Although the losses of men in the new regiments for the first five or six months after reaching the front from sickness, death or desertion were immense comparatively—in some cases running twenty-five or thirty percent—our real effective force was rapidly augmented. A reaction from the old despondency appeared to have taken place, and the men began to speak lovingly of "fighting Joe." The cavalry corps, setting him an example he would have done well to imitate, smothered the wrath his careless words had stirred up and was prepared to do its whole duty to its government and flag.

Toward the latter part of February the Sixth Cavalry was relieved from picket duty on the right of the army and transferred for the same service on the left, along the lower Rappahannock. On the 25th, one company was detailed for this purpose. The day was quite cold, and the snow still covered the ground. A fine rain was falling, that penetrated our clothing like a sponge, and made the men very uncomfortable. The roads were in a horrible condition, the horses sinking and floundering at almost every step, throwing the mud into the air in a steady shower. We carried three days rations for the men and feed for our animals. The prospect of a pleasant time on duty was rather dim, but we felt certain of having shelter when we should reach our destination. A ride of several hours brought us far beyond the lines of our infantry camps. We crossed a small stream on our way, and one or two miles beyond this entered a forest. While marching through these woods a loud cheering broke upon our ears, apparently from men in our immediate front. As we had reason to believe that we were now far from the camp of our own troops, this yelling awakened in us grave apprehensions as to the presence of the enemy's troops; our destination and duty were not positively known so far, and the conclusions at which we had arrived were only the result of speculation. Presently the company emerged from the woods and rode up a slight eminence, from the crest of which an extended view could be obtained of the surrounding country. The Rappahannock river, narrow and tortuous, flowed upon our right hand, while beyond it, on the long gradually-rising slope that stretched off to the southward were the camps of several thousand men. A large party was assembled upon the broad fields, engaged in a snow-ball battle, and from these, full of the excitement of the gray arose the cheers we had heard. A glance was sufficient to show that they were confederates. These camps, as we afterwards learned, were occupied by a portion of Stonewall Jackson's corps—a brigade of North Carolinians—which had been stationed here to resist the advance of our army from their quarters. We found their infantry pickets scattered along the banks of the river, in some places protected by slight breastworks, while ours were mounted men, and completely exposed to attack, but a truce or tacit understanding not to shoot seemed to exist between the two parties. The river at some places was so narrow that little difficulty was experienced in conversing with each other. This, however, was strictly forbidden by the officers on both sides.

I do not think the members of Company F will soon forget their experiences on picket along the lower Rappahannock during those last days of February, 1863. An extraordinary precaution was manifested by Lieutenant Balder, on account of the mysteriously spiriting away and capture as we afterwards learned, of a whole company of Pennsylvania Cavalry from this very neighborhood a short time before our arrival. During the first day we huddled together in an old barn while off duty, but after nightfall the lieutenant marched us silently from this slight shelter to an open field about one mile away, where the reserve had to stand to horse all night. No fires were permitted. The fine rain still continued without intermission, and we were wet and numb from cold. The ground was covered several inches deep with slushy snow, upon which, if anywhere, we were compelled to lie down. Our line of picket posts extended along the river bank for a distance of two or more miles. The men were on three reliefs as on the regular camp guard detail, each relief riding beat for two hours and then off for four hours. Two hours of these four were consumed in changing the sentinels, and, as a consequence, the usual order of things was thus reversed—the men had only two hours in which to rest and sleep—if such a thing as sleep were possible under the circumstances. To keep ourselves absolutely out of the snow we gathered some brush and made a sort of bed. During daylight we were allowed to make a small fire to cook our coffee and meat, but when night came we were always moved away from the spot we had thus occupied, and new provision for a bed had to be made. This changing about was to mislead the enemy in case he should attempt our capture.

We had come out on picket for three days, but the creek rose, and completely cut us off from the army, and we were compelled to remain until it subsided, which occurred three days after our time was up. As a consequence, our rations gave out, and this added maliciously to our suffering. Often, after I had laid down, I sank into a sort of stupor rather than sleep, and when aroused my limbs would be perfectly numb and stiff from the wet and cold. If my readers would at all realize the Common Soldier's feelings at this time, let him imagine themselves in his place.

Our poor horses suffered terribly from being saddled so long, rode so hard, and so poorly fed as they were during the last three days. While on post they were ridden over their respective beats constantly, each beat connecting with another, so that the whole river front was securely guarded. Each sentinel was obliged to challenge each other sentinel, and everybody else who approached, and to ride with his carbine at an "advance," ready to fire on an instant's alarm.

How my thoughts wandered homeward during those long, long, suffering hours!

"They are asleep in their nice warm beds, without any one to disturb them, while I, poor boy, am exposed to this storm and cold and danger. No roof to shelter me, no fire to warm me, no bed to invite my benumbed body to rest. Well, be it so! I shall try and do my whole duty without murmuring. I guard their home, even if I am so far from them. May God help me to brave it all!"

There was an unspeakable comfort for me in the thought that I was actually protecting, while on this outpost by the river side, and in the presence of our common enemy, the loved ones on the old farm by the side of that other river in Pennsylvania. During the day, while on duty,

351

when there was no longer a necessity to ride our beats, I sat on my horse looking at the gray squads on the opposite shore, and humming almost constantly that sturdy air, "Joe Bowers." The weather cleared off towards the last, and those harbingers of spring, the robin red-breasts, made their appearance in great numbers along the banks among the bushes. In the afternoon the confederates had their dress parades in full view, amid the swelling music of their bands and the rolling of drums—an exhibition of great interest to us. Our men would criticize their marching and maneuvers with great particularity. It was with curious sensations that I looked upon those gray battalions, and reflected that they barred our progress toward the south so effectively, and that those strange flags were a constant defiance to our flag.

Relief came to us at last—a squadron was to take our place on picket, and our company wagon with rations for the men and food for the animals. As if to repay me for my sacrifices for home and friends, the soldier that brought our food also delivered to me two encouraging letters from the occupants of the old farm house. When our sentinels were all relieved the company was marched back from the river a short distance, where we cooked our pork rations, and indulged in a hearty meal, fed and groomed our horses, and made ourselves comfortable until the next morning. Then a light-hearted, cheerful lot of men rode leisurely back to their camp near army headquarters.

Extracts from a letter dated at Camp of Sixth Cavalry, March 4, 1863, will show the feelings of the Common Soldier at this stage of his military career:

Dear Friend: Your welcome letter reached me a few days ago while we were on picket on the Rappahannock river several miles below Fredericksburg. We were out six days, and experienced very severe weather, as it stormed and rained on us nearly the whole time, and we were without shelter. Fires were not allowed at night, for fear of attracting the enemy's attention and leading his troops to our location. Of course, sleep was about out of the question owing to the extreme wet and cold. Opposite our post was a confederate battery and a camp of North Carolina troops. During the first day of our picketing they turned out in a field and had a pitched battle with snow-balls. Every evening when it did not rain too hard, one of their brass bands regaled us with music, playing "Dixie's Land," and other confederate war tunes.

The river at this point is about two hundred yards wide. The pickets of both armies occupy the banks. We found the confederates friendly and disposed to argue the questions of difference between the sections, and at times the discussion would become quite animated. Whenever the zeal of the respective parties became too ardent, and were likely to lead to mutual embarrassments, the matter would be allowed to drop until the disputants cooled off somewhat. It was against the orders of both sides to converse at all.

Your letter suited me exactly. It was just what I wanted to get. I thought it might rain six months—I could brave it all, if only I could have assurance that I was kindly remembered at home.

I am sorry to hear that George is sick, and that you, too, are suffering from a bad cold. I hope you will both get well soon. I am also sorry to hear of Matty's death. She was the first baby I ever undertook to nurse.

In two days more I will be twenty-two years old. First year of manhood has been rather an eventful one, such as I little dreamed of living to see where I used to go to the old log school house on the hill. Then I never thought of the rude conflict of war. Amid my troubles with Hindman's dog, and the school teacher for being always late, and then ever-teasing Emmeline Thompson and meek little Esther Lyons, and other difficulties to numerous to mention, there was little room for reflections upon such sad contingencies as are thrust upon us today. It seems that almost every one of my old schoolmates is in some way affected by this cruel state of affairs. May it soon end!

I suppose I will always be a soldier. This life seems to agree with me, after all. My mind is relieved from that peculiar unrest from which I used to suffer while at home—that desire to wander. This is the result, I suppose, of the constant excitement of adventure we experience here. I might not be so well satisfied if the war were over and we were settled down to the irksome discipline of camp life. I might become weary enough of it then.

I must tell you that I have another horse. The long march from Harper's Ferry was severe upon Bucephalus, and I think caused him to be sick; so he was condemned and turned over to the quartermaster. Tell little Jim to send me a name for my new animal. Can't he write me a few lines in your next?

I am glad Congress has passed a conscript law.[1] It seems that the conflict has reached that point where the eccentricities of volunteering cannot be depended upon—the men may come, or they may not. Under this law they must come. The act gives the men in the field assurance that the struggle is to be continued—that there is to be no compromise on the basis of a violation of the integrity of the Union. It is to be fought out to the bitter end.

I think if members of the peace-at-any-price party were brought out here, and were shot at a few times by their friends over the river, they would be likely to have a change wrought in their minds in regard to the docility of southerners. So far as I can see, the authorities at Richmond proffer nothing that we can accept under any circumstances without surrendering the vital principles for which we have thus far contended.

---

[1]   This refers to the draft.

353

It is not pleasant to us to hear of the liberation heretofore shown deserters at the north. They should be driven to seek shelter elsewhere than in the land they have tried to betray. Our people might learn a lesson from the inhabitants of the south in this respect.

Sergeant Robert McMasters is going to try for a furlough under Hooker's new orders. If he succeeds I shall ask you to send back with him father's likeness. I desire to have it so much, for it seems an age since I saw him.

Yours, as of old,
Sid

The story about Hindman's dog, mentioned in the letter, is a peculiar one. When about six years old I was sent for the first time to school in the country. The old log hut in which we were sent to study was located about a mile from Bentley's, on Pollock's Hill. The path I followed on my way to school led me near Mr. Hindman's house. A large dog, very young in years, met me in the road on several occasions. I had seen John Hindman, a protege of the farmer above named, with his dinner basket full of nice pie and cake, and, as my dinner was made up of plain bread and butter I envied John's commissary stores very much, and began to concoct a plan whereby I might secure some of those good things on earth. Finally a scheme presented itself to my mind. I gave the dog my dinner, and then, by a mighty effort known only to children, broke into loud lamentations. Mrs. Hindman, a good natured, kind lady, came running out to see what was wrong.

"That dog took my dinner," I blubbered.

"Well, child, don't cry. I will replace it," said she.

I went into her house, and she put me up such a dinner, as she always gave John, or rather better, perhaps. I thanked her and trudged off, delighted with the result of my ruse, and, when out of sight of the house, took off the lid of the basket and feasted my eyes upon the stores of pie and cake therein deposited. I lived well for that day at least.

This plan was successfully carried out for several days. The dog soon learned to meet me, and was regularly at his post. It finally occurred to me that perhaps I was practicing this dodge too often, though Mrs. Hindman never hinted that she suspected anything.

"I will miss this morning, and do on my bread and butter," thought I.

On I trudged, without paying attention to the dog, which had met me as usual. If I had come to this conclusion the dog had reached another conclusion. When it discovered that I did not disgorge as was customary, the animal came of color and began to growl viciously. I became frightened and started to run. It sprang upon me, and caught my left wrist—the basket was in my left hand just enough to hurt and to leave blue spots upon the skin. I dropped the basket any set up a howl in earnest, the dog in the meanwhile, helping itself to my bread and butter.

This denouement led to my changing routes to the school house, in order to avoid that dog. Some twenty years afterward I wrote a letter to Mrs. Hindman, recalling the circumstances, and confessing my participation with the dog in the previous thefts of my school dinners, and apologizing for the deception.

About the 5th of March two of our Washington County friends, Mr. Peterson and Mr. Chester, came on from home to see their relatives in the Army of the Potomac. We were all glad to see these citizens—they were an actual curiosity. Of course, we were proud to show them the various conditions of a soldier's life in the field—our battalion in blue in their winter quarters, the guards, the pickets—cavalry, artillery, and infantry—and the confederate camp beyond the river. They left us with many good wishes, apparently delighted with their experiences, and doubtless full of pleasant reminiscences of their visit to the armed legions along the Rappahannock.

About the middle of March General Hooker, apparently determined to have a dead cavalryman, sent General Averill across the Rappahannock at Kelly's Ford with a force of mounted men. A hot skirmish ensued, furnishing several specimens of the curiosity sought for, and after sundry maneuvers, the object of which still lies hidden within the ponderous hair of Hooker, our troops were marched back to their camp. This action demonstrated even to the commanding general the fact that our mounted men were capable of effective work against the cavalries of the south when brought. It proved a successful beginning of a series of cavalry operations which were continued with equal success until the close of the war. It should be recollected, however, that Averill's force was equal in numbers on this occasion to the entire corps on the Peninsula.

Sergeant McMasters was the lucky recipient of a furlough on the 23rd of March. As he and I were from the same village, I was much gratified by his success, and took occasion to send some little trinkets, with some money, to my friends at home for safe keeping until I should return. Among my relics were a copy of John Moore's poems, which I had managed to carry with me all through the campaigns—I was somewhat romantic in those days—and the copy of Cleveland's Compendium of English Literature mentioned in a former chapter as the property of Miss Mayo of New Kent County, Virginia.

McMasters returned on the evening of the 2nd of April, while the company was on picket eight miles down the Rappahannock. He brought cheerful news from home, and, as if to fill my cup of happiness, a portrait of father. This picture was a faithful one, and the sitting was characteristic of the original. True to his eccentricities, he had assumed a position in which a long wooden horn, fabricated by himself while in one of his peculiar moods, occupied an unusual prominence. He was very hearty looking—much more so than I had reason to expect after the severe accident that had befallen him about one year previous. I was gratified to learn that he had, in accordance with his promise to me long before I had left home, controlled his appetite for strong drink, and had thus shown how much he appreciated his absent boy.

Our guard and picket duties fell heavy upon us as spring approached, but there was some compensation for this in the fact that time thus consumed passed more rapidly than if we had been idle, and our camp life was thus rendered less dull and monotonous. While off other duty our drills came in for a share of our attention. Of reviews there were but few. There was a grand one, however, in which nearly the entire army participated. The display was magnificent, the men looking hearty and cheerful, executing their maneuvers with a precision that showed a high state of discipline, yet with the peculiarly graceful nonchalance and dash that is so characteristic of American soldiers in the field. I felt, as I stood upon a hill overlooking the scene, an unutterable pride in the grand old Army of the Potomac, whose sturdy columns had covered themselves with glory amid the fearful trials through which they had passed during the last two years.

It was quite pleasant, during the cool, bracing mornings, to rise at dawn to the music of a thousand drums and bugles, which broke upon the ear with the roll and blare from all directions. There was something indescribably thrilling in the mellow artillery calls, the shrill "assembly" of the cavalry, and the barbaric clatter and rattle of infantry reveille, that sent the hot blood coursing through one's veins, and made one proud of his existence. When the first notes ring out, the grand old flag rises majestically on the staff, and shakes out its folds, tinted with the yellow sunshine that now glimmers across the eastern horizon like a golden billow, upon the breeze. The countless companies muster simultaneously in a hundred camps, the men answer to their names, and the lines break up and disappear as if by magic, the whole mass apparently actuated by a single impulse.

Our camp duties were the same as those imposed upon us at Bladensburg and Camp East of Capitol during the winter previous. From "retreat" until "tattoo" the time was spent as best suited the casts of the soldiers—most of the men engaged in "draw poker," a game that had developed wonderfully since the regiment entered the field. The religious element confined itself to "checkers," or other orthodox games. Others wrote letters, or discussed the experiences of the day or the probable duties of the morrow. It was noticeable that the great question of the time—the war—in its historical aspect, was seldom mentioned among the men. Military life seemed to have become a second nature, a regular business, and its duties were referred to as the duties of any ordinary avocation. The coming campaigns and consequent battles are, of course, regarded as unpleasant and dangerous episodes of this peculiar business pursuit, but these risks seemed to be regarded as the risks men usually incur in any other employment. The martial spirit we had been taught to believe existed in men, and which only needed a tap on the drum to arouse, proved to be a myth. It was regarded simply as a method of giving direction or instruction. The life we were leading, however, had one marked effect on the men. Their actions and dispositions seemed to be pervaded with a boyish spirit; they seldom spoke of the business transactions of civil life; questions that agitate communities, such as trade, finance, tariffs, reforms, religions, were rarely discussed. The oldest men in the company would scamper and chatter like so many school children.

Reading one evening the personal column of the *New York Herald*, it occurred to me that some amusement might be afforded by advertising there for a wife. I read some of these notices to our squad, and the result was, after an interchange of opinions, the formation of a joint stock company of four persons, myself among the number, with a paid in capital of one dollar, twenty-five cents apiece. We supposed that there would be at least one hundred answers to our advertisement, and of course, there would be no necessity of inserting more than one notice. It was agreed that the answers should be divided into equal numbers, if possible—the odd ones, if any, were sold to me for my services in writing the advertisement—and their assignment to stockbrokers determined by lot. All these arrangements were satisfactorily completed.

I wrote out the "personal," which, as near as I can remember, ran as follows:

A handsome young officer, worth fifty thousand dollars, wants a wife. Address No. 28 F Company Sixth United States Cavalry.

This advertisement, with five dollars, was duly sent by mail to the HERALD, and for the next few days the members of the joint stock company were on the qui vive as to the result. For some reason the newspaper man failed to visit our camp for perhaps a week, and we were unable to ascertain whether the notice had been inserted. The matter was kept a secret from the company outside of our squad, with the exception of Brown, who was then acting as first sergeant, and whom I thought it expedient to notify that I expected certain letters addressed to my company number, which I should thank him to deliver to me. Several days elapsed, and no answers came.

One morning, however, there was evidently some excitement in the first sergeant's tent, and shortly after one of the stockholders came to me in a state of great perturbation and privately told me that two letters, addressed to No. 28, had arrived; that Sergeant Brown had taken the liberty to open them and expose their contents to the company. When my informant had remonstrated with Brown as to the propriety of breaking seals on private letters, the latter used threatening language in regard to persons who would receive correspondence addressed to fictional names. At the close of this recital I went to see Sergeant Brown. On my inquiring whether there were letters for No. 28 he seemed somewhat embarrassed and ashamed of himself, and delivered them to me, declaring that he had entirely forgotten the notification I had given him that letters to such address would probably come. I merely said, in reply, that it was not customary to open letters received in the mail addressed to parties in the company and show their contents around camp. Those bore my military number, which was as valid as my full name, inasmuch as it marked all my equipment, and constituted my legal claim to such equipment, and no power could deprive me of them outside of the proper authority. Brown acknowledged this, and apologized, and I started for my tent, anxious to read the thoughts transcribed in these mysterious letters.

I have always felt a peculiar pleasure in contemplating an envelope, and speculating upon the unknown contents of the missive enclosed within. There is a sort of excitement aroused, akin somewhat to that experienced in a game of chance, in which the greater the uncertainty felt, the keener grows the interest. If it be from one's sweetheart, the question arises as to how the letter will begin—whether addressed to "my dear," or "my dearest," or whether it contains a notification that one's attentions were no longer desired; or whether she has been slyly married and now writes to tell one of the fact. If from home, whether we are well, what news from the neighborhood, and a thousand and one other speculations. In this case. there was a double interest, on account of the peculiarly infatuating subject of correspondence and the medium by which it had been opened.

One of these letters was written in a bantering, jovial spirit, and was, I half suspected, the work of a male hand. It stated that the author was worth $100,000 that she wore false teeth, false hair, had a glass eye, and was "sweet seventy" or more. The signature I have forgotten. The missive was dated at Staten Island, New York. Correspondence with a view to marriage was solicited.

The other letter was dated at Rhinebeck, New York, and was evidently genuine so far as sex was concerned. It stated that the writer answered the advertisement simply for the purpose of creating amusement, believing that the whole matter had been prompted by a spirit of pleasantry. If she were right in this conjecture, she would be happy to open such a correspondence. The note was so neatly written, and exhibited such modesty and grace, that I was prepossessed at once with a favorable opinion of the author, and specially pleaded with the other stockholders that this letter might be assigned to me. My request was granted, and I immediately framed a reply suitable to the occasion.

When an answer had been received, I felt it to be my duty to throw off the mask I had assumed as an officer, and to appear in my real character as a penniless soldier. I informed her that my object had been to secure some sort of amusement by which to while away the many hours of monotonous service. If she should feel disposed, after this confession, to honor me with her correspondence, I was sure the happiness it would afford would go far toward the accomplishment of the object in view, and place me under grateful obligations to her. To this she assented.

Thus a correspondence was established between us, to continue only during my term of enlistment, and with the complete understanding that nothing of a matrimonial character was to be discussed, from which I derived a great deal of pleasure during that long, dreary winter. The lady was a Catholic, and her communications were tinged with strong

359

religious convictions, with which, though a sort of barbarian, I could find no manner of fault. I am afraid, however, that the moral instructions had at most but a momentary influence on my wild young life. On one occasion, when I had written in regard to my straitened circumstances, and wondered what I should find to do when my term of service had expired, she informed me that her brother was a commission merchant in New York, and if I should think proper to come there he would find me employment.

These two letters were all that came in answer to our advertisement in the HERALD, so that our expectations of a multitude of different correspondents failed of realization. The joint stock company dissolved by mutual consent, and I was left in possession of its fruits. The letter from Staten Island was not answered, as I was under the impression that all was not exactly right with it, and did not care to be an object of fun for some unknown wag.

A young man whose name is borne upon the rolls of Company F as Charles Centre[2] was a member of the squad to which I was attached, and occupied the same Sibley tent during the winter of 1862-3. He was one of our infantry recruits, having joined us at Knoxville during the days allotted to members of volunteer organizations to enlist for the balance of their terms of service in the regular army. He represented himself as having belonged to one of the New York State regiments, the number of which I have forgotten. He also stated that he had at one time been employed as a scout by one of our generals in the valley of Virginia, and had passed through many adventures while on this duty. He further claimed that, prior to the war, he had been a member of a theatrical company, or was in some way attached to one of the theaters in New York city, and was a relative of a manager named Eddy. He seemed to be somewhat romantic, with a brain that literally overran with quotations from Shakespeare, negro minstrel dialogues, and songs, and stage slang. For some reason or other I felt from the first an uncontrollable dislike for Centre. I was under the impression that he was one of the hangers--around-theaters—a "supe"—and at best rather a suspicious customer. He was an inveterate borrower, possessing a peculiar faculty of approaching one when he desired money, and lacked promptitude about paying back at the proper time. What he did with his money was an inexplicable mystery; if he spent it for luxuries, he must have gone off to a corner by

[2]   Charles Centre, a native of Ohio, transferred to the 6th Cavalry on October 22, 1862, when he was 22 years old. He is reported to have deserted on May 11, 1863.

himself to enjoy them. There was a certain shrewdness, however, about the man that cropped out on many occasions. He would insinuate himself upon one just at the time one had some delicious bit of roast shoat or chicken, and suggested all sorts of divisions that might be made. Just then he was endowed with a wonderful faculty of remembering instances of meanness on the part of some one who, when he had something nice to eat, was too stingy to share it with a friend. In spite of my dislike for him, on these occasions I felt bound to yield a portion of my meal to Centre, his allusions to meanness being more than I could resist. He was a rare specimen of the genus bore.

While on picket duty along the upper Rappahannock, it was noticed by members of the company that Centre was never without some luxury, in the way of eatables, such as pies, cakes, butter, milk, eggs, and other articles not common to the commissary department of the United States Army. How he procured these was a subject of curiosity among the men. To one of his intimate friends—by, this it is to be understood one from whom he had borrowed money—he explained that they were given to him by two lady friends living in the neighborhood of Hartwood Church, with whom his personal appearance had, he thought, made an agreeable impression. He also confided to this friend the fact that they were endeavoring to induce him to desert to the confederates; they told him their brother was a member of the first Virginia Cavalry, to whom, should he leave our army and go through the lines, they would give him letters which should insure him a position of profit and safety at Richmond. He had promised them that he would avail himself of their offer at the earliest opportunity.

As Centre's reputation for truth and veracity was below par in the company, these statements were not credited, but were attributed to his great vanity as to his personal appearance, and for this reason were not reported to the commanding officer. Subsequent events, however, demonstrated that they had a real foundation.

In a letter dated April 4, 1863, the Common Soldier thus gave expression to his hopes and plans for the future—his dreams of living through the war were becoming more vivid and portentous as the months rolled on:

Dear friend: Robert McMasters arrived here safely on the night of April 2nd, while our company was out on picket eight miles from here, on the Lower Rappahannock. He gave me the things you sent me, and the note from George. I also received the letter you sent me containing the postage stamps. For all of which you are entitled to my sincere gratitude.

I am delighted to secure father's likeness. He looks well, and just as natural with that horn in his hand, as he did in the olden times. How my heart goes out toward the poor old man!

I am glad to hear that George is recovering from his recent illness. He should endeavor to procure a pass from the government, and pay this army a visit. I should do all I could to make him comfortable while here. A battle might take place while he was present with us, which he would then have an opportunity to see. At all events, his trip would repay him well. Not every generation will put on exhibition such a gigantic tragedy as we are now acting.

There are rumors of a conflict soon to occur. Of course, rough times are to be expected, as the summer is rapidly approaching, and we are not likely to be kept idle then. I confess I am somewhat tired of lying around this section, and would welcome anything that promises a change of scenery and duty. If an attack upon the enemy be made by our army, I suspect it will take place from some point up the river. Hooker will not be likely to follow the example of Burnside.

I have fifteen months more to serve. I expect to save a hundred dollars per year, and at my discharge will get one hundred dollars as bounty. So, if I live, I will have four hundred dollars with which to commence a citizen's life. I will then be twenty-three years of age. I must then go to hard work on some farm, and at twenty-five I must marry and settle down for life. This is the programme I have laid down for the future. My rambling life must end with my service. I will then have seen all I desire to see. My army life seems to have benefitted my health a great deal.

According to promise, I have christened my horse Jim Crackcorn, the name proposed by little Jim in his letter. I was glad to receive his tiny note—he writes quite plain .

So Hiram, wants to know if I recollect a certain stormy day in March, while we were at work on the top of the old hill at home, when the wind sent the snow whirling into our faces—when we sat around a huge fire of burning stumps and ate our dinner of boiled pork and potatoes. I think I do. I have often thought of it since, while eating my crackers and meat around our campfires during the stormy days of last November, or lay shivering upon the ground clad in no extra clothing save my overcoat. For a long time I have carried no blanket except my saddle blanket.

It seems to me I can stand almost any kind of weather now; exposure seems to have little effect. At one time I was so easily affected by the sight of human blood that a sight of it would make me deathly sick; now I am not so nervous in this respect.

The next time you write tell me how the men sit at the table. Who occupies the places of Benjamin and Levi? Does father still remain near the door? Have

362

the blackbirds come back to the cedar tree in the yard this spring? How does father's Fort Sumter stand the weather? I believe our regiment and M Battery Second Artillery could capture it, if the obstructions are not utterly insurmountable.

This is Easter Sunday—so I am told. I do not know how my informant found out, for I do not know one day from another. I wish I were home to help you eat eggs. It is very stormy—snowing and blowing. Our fire smokes badly, and brings water to one's eyes in spite of himself. My dinner of rice soup is ready, I understand.

James Barry was over to our camp this Thursday, but as I was away on duty he failed to see me. I was sadly disappointed.

McMasters says there was some inquiry as to how I bore the loss of my girl. You see I survive. There are others, no doubt.

My love to old schoolmates.

Father's "Fort Sumter" was a sort of cavern he had constructed, and which he had thus named. He had dug a causeway some thirty or forty feet into the side of a ravine, the sides of which were braced by upright posts five feet long and five or six inches in diameter. Pieces of timber placed close together across the top kept the earth from falling in. A rudely constructed fireplace by the centre of the hall was used when the weather became cold. The flue ran up and extended along under the surface of the ground for some distance, and in the soil on top of this, in early spring, he planted corn and potatoes, expecting the warmth to urge their growth. While I did not like to say so to him—it was a pet project of his, and any expression indicating a doubt as to the success of his scheme was sure to offend him—my belief was that the great labor expended in the construction of "Fort Sumter" was altogether useless, and the "fort" of no account, except as a curiosity.

Towards the middle of April there were many rumors afloat as to the immediate commencement of the spring campaign of the Army of the Potomac, but as the weather continued to be extremely unfavorable for military operations these rumors seemed to lack foundation in fact. A few days later, however, the cavalry began to concentrate on the right of our lines—a well understood sign of hot work soon to be commenced.

About the 25th the Sixth Cavalry broke camp and moved up the river towards and beyond Hartwood Church, where the regiment halted for the night. The morning and most of the day had been quite fair, but towards evening the sky was overcast with clouds, and during the night a heavy storm set in and deluged the county. It was the same old fatal sign for

363

the Army of the Potomac—a great storm upon the inauguration of a campaign—so easily recognized by the old soldiers of that organization.

My Jim Crackcorn had been lame for some time; he had travelled over the twenty or twenty-five miles of the march on the first day on three legs, and when "to horse" sounded on the morning of the second day and the advance was about to be resumed, I found that he could only use two—a very unpromising condition for hard service. Of course, further progress was out of the question. The first sergeant spoke to Lieutenant Balder about the matter, and then came to me, and advised that I should remain for the present with the train, which then was parked near a place called Morrisville.

About noon the command moved away. I had been further instructed, in case there was no improvement in the condition of my horse, to make my way back to camp if I could. As we were now some miles from our lines, and as the intervening country was swarming with guerrillas, the prospect of a trip through those lonely wilds, leading a crippled horse, with no companion save the poor animal in my charge, was far from being a pleasant one. The instances of capture and murder by these predatory knights of the double-barrelled shot guns was painfully frequent. Owing to the slow gait at which I should be compelled to move, I should be obliged to remain one night outside our lines. The citizens residing along the route were decidedly hostile—indeed, it was generally believed that they were the identical guerrillas above mentioned—and it would be injudicious to trust myself among them after dark; so the sad fact was realized that, in case the attempt to return was made, I must camp in some forest alone. Even then I might be watched and followed by some belligerent farmer, and opened upon at short range with charges of canister by his double barrelled artillery.

Acting under orders I resolved to set out with my crippled horse for dismounted camp, which, I learned, was located at or near Aquia Creek. With this determination I set out one morning very early on my return. The task for me was not an easy one. I had about thirty miles to go, over a miry road, through a lonely country imposted by guerrillas, with a crippled animal which could at best travel only about two miles an hour. However, I determined to do the best I could. Nearly all day I led my horse. leaving the main road in order to avoid the rebel cavalry. Not a solitary person met me save one or two colored men.

About four o'clock in the evening I was surprised and pleased to find myself in the vicinity of my old friends, the Monroes, near the gold mines. I went up quietly towards the cabin, and saw the old lady swinging one of her grandchildren, while her daughter was feeding a poor old gray horse. The latter looked up the road and saw me, and immediately betrayed great excitement, looking first at me, then at her horse, and then at me again. All at once I saw her regard me with a steady gaze, and in a moment later she came bounding towards the bars like a deer. Down came the rails in a trice, and, with a welcome that made my heart jump she helped me in with my crippled animal. The old lady also seemed delighted to see me, and it was some time before I could get a word in edgewise. Mrs. Monroe said that when she first saw me she did not recognize my face, though she knew I was a federal soldier, and she was much alarmed lest I would take away her horse, assuring me that I was the first Yankee that ever got to see it, as she had kept it completely hidden during the whole of the time our troops had occupied that section. I had intended to keep on and reach our picket lines that evening, supposing that they were only one or two miles further on, but the women pressed me so earnestly to remain for supper that I was compelled to do so. A right good meal was prepared, and, as I was very hungry, I enjoyed it very much.

I was much amused at the accounts of their sensations during the battle of Fredericksburg. The old lady said she was aroused before daylight by the thunder of artillery, and that she thought the world must be coming to an end. The younger one bantered me a little about the result of the battle, but I told her we would fill all Virginia with graves before our people would give up the contest. This frightful announcement seemed to have the desired effect, for she changed the subject. She had not yet heard from her husband, and thought he must have been killed. I asked if any southern soldiers had been in the neighborhood lately, and she said that on the day before a lieutenant of the Fourth Virginia Cavalry, with a small party of men, had been at the cabin. The lieutenant, she said, had stated that the Yankees were about to make another movement, and that fighting would probably result within the next two weeks. She also said that our pickets were at least twelve miles down the Rappahannock, and that I would not be able to reach them that night, and advised me to allow my horse to be put up and fed with her own, assuring me that I would be much safer with them than alone on the road that night. Feeling that I could trust them, as they had received many favors from me, and had always been treated in a respectful manner by me, I consented, and unsaddled and cleaned my poor crippled animal. After this duty had been satisfactorily performed, it was taken in charge by my hostess, who led it, with her old gray, into what would seem to a casual observer as a large brush heap, but which, in reality, was a stable, and both horses received a plentiful supply of oats, which I had taken the precaution to bring along with me from the train. The saddle was put in the lower part of the cupboard. with my weapons, where they would not be likely to attract observation in case visitors should come to the cabin that night.

It was about ten o'clock when, after spending a pleasant evening, Mrs. Monroe took me through the bushes to the cabin of an uncle of hers, whom she called Americus. From his ancient appearance, he might have been the veritable Americus Vespucius of history. A large, hale old fellow, with very long, white hair, and with the old Virginia dialect, he was altogether not entirely disagreeable. His tongue, however, rattled continuously, and it was still going when I went to sleep. I had made my bed on the floor with my horse blanket, as I had preferred to sleep by myself, although the old man insisted on my sharing his couch, in a manner which showed his sincerity.

My slumbers that night were often broken, as the least noise, from my nervous condition, was sufficient to waken me; for, although I felt no real alarm, I was always on the lookout for unwelcome visitors.

Early that morning I arose, washed myself, ate my breakfast, and started for camp, followed by the uttered well wishes of my southern friends. A long dangerous ride still extended before me, and I followed my old tactics of following bridle paths, with which, in this section, I was very well acquainted. Just below Bank's Ford I found several soldiers belonging to the engineer corps, who seemed to be at work on the roads. Feeling very thirsty and hungry—it was now about one o'clock in the afternoon—I rode up a hill to a house, where I found two old maids, and politely asked if they had any milk to sell. A look of indignation passed over their faces, and the oldest one replied curtly, "No, our cows have been feeding on garlic, and the milk tastes oniony."

I felt somewhat taken aback, but again inquired, "Have you any meat or bread you could sell me? I am quite hungry, and am willing to pay for all I get."

"We have neither meat nor bread to sell—hardly enough for ourselves," replied the eldest. "The Yankees have so stripped us that we are on the point of starvation," chimed in the other.

I expressed my sincere sympathy for them, and, determined to overcome their apparent dislike towards me, or to test their sincerity as to whether they would accommodate me with anything, I asked if they could give me a cup of water. They appeared somewhat nonplussed for a moment, when the elder said, "The spring is at the foot of that steep hill, and we are too weakly to carry it up to the house. The Yankees coaxed away our servants, and we are scarcely able to get along."

"Give me the bucket, and I'll bring you some," I said; and moving towards a water bucket—which, by the way, was even now better than half full—I poured the contents into a tub, and started down the hill before my bewildered friends could stop me. It did require some effort to bring water up that hill, and I could not blame then, if they did not relish the task. In a few moments I had returned, and, taking a cup, which I found sitting on a bush, I tendered each of the ladies a drink of cool, fresh water. To my surprise it was graciously and thankfully accepted. A great change had come over them; their frigidity had given place to a genial sunshine, and quivering smiles wreathed their old faces. The youngest disappeared, and in a few moments returned with a huge bowl of milk, which she tendered me.

"I thank you," I said, "but I cannot drink milk which tastes of garlic."

"I do not think there is much taste to it now," she replied. "We took the cows off that pasture sometime ago."

"Well, indeed," I said, feeling that I had the inside track now, "I really don't relish milk which has the slightest taste of garlic; it sickens me."

But she pushed the great bowl into my hands, and I was obliged to taste it, when, to my surprise, there was not the least perceptible odor of garlic about it. This was reinforced in another moment by the elder sister bringing me a huge piece of bread, covered with the nicest butter, and an immense piece of meat, which I was also compelled to take; and I confess my appetite was not disposed to allow me to refuse. A pleasant conversation on minor topics ensued, and after an hour's stay we parted on the best of terms. I note this circumstance more particularly due to what can be accomplished under difficulties.

I had several miles yet before me. My horse seemed a little better, but the poor brute could make but little headway. About three o'clock I saw, stretching across the fields in front, the infantry picket line of our army, with the sentries walking their beats with military precision. I pressed on, glad to once more find myself in the presence of friends.

367

When within thirty paces of a sentinel he suddenly faced me, brought up his gun to a "ready," and called out: "Halt, dismount, advance." I obeyed each of these commands mechanically, wondering what it all meant, and feeling not in the least disposed to question his proceeding. As I came up within two paces he again ordered me to halt, and, without a word more to me he turned his head to the rear and called out, "officer of the guard, post No. 6." I confess I did not altogether relish these proceedings, as they pointed towards an unpleasant consequence. I had no written order with me—nothing to show that I had authority to pass the lines—and I knew that, once under arrest, there was often great difficulty in getting released, unless I should happen to meet some officer with whom I was acquainted, and should interfere for me. As the soldier finished his call I looked in the same direction, and observed a squad of soldiers lounging around a small cabin. From their midst I saw an officer emerge, wearing the red sash over his shoulder—the insignia of the officer of the day—and walk rapidly towards us. In the interval I observed that the sentinel belonged to the One-hundred and twentieth New York Hunters, that he was a young, pleasant looking man, who evidently knew his duty and was determined to do it.

As soon as the officer reached us he looked inquiringly at me and the sentry reported that I had approached from outside of the line. Up to this time I had said nothing, knowing that it was useless to remonstrate with a sentinel, who had no discretion; but, when the officer began to question me, I gave him full answers, and hoped he would pass me in, but he did not seem disposed to do so. On the contrary, he ordered the sentinel to pass me along the picket line, with orders to take me over to headquarters. Then began a walk which proved a severe trial to my already tired limbs. From post to post each sentry passed me along, like so many fresh state horses, while the sweat poured down my cheeks. I knew it was no use to expostulate with those grim looking fellows; they were "on duty," and I felt I had better save my breath till I got to head-quarters. My arms were not taken from me, and I was allowed to lead my horse, or, rather, pull him along—a matter which required much effort, and added materially to my fatigue. However, in course of time headquarters was reached, which proved to be only headquarters for that regiment. Here I was searched, my private letters examined, and put through a strict examination. It now began to be apparent to me that I was suspected as a rebel spy. One officer—a captain—asked me what I was doing with blue clothes on? I retorted angrily, "What do you think

I ought to wear? I belong to Uncle Sam's army." But it was no go, and after a few moments rest I was sent under guard to brigade headquarters. This was established at a house on the road from Hartwood Church to Falmouth, probably five miles from the latter place. As the guard halted in front of the door an elderly, quick spoken, man, with a strong French dialect, came out, to whom the guard reported, and who, I understood, was adjutant general of that brigade. He also questioned me closely. During the course of the examination I still held my horse by the bridle; and observing that the curb chain of the bridle had been unhooked, I put my hand down to replace it. This action seemed to displease the adjutant, who, I suppose, thought I did not pay sufficient respect to him, and he thundered out, "Look at me, sir!" I quietly turned and looked him resolutely in the eyes, which made him still angrier, and without further conversation he turned me over to a sentry on post at one side of the house, turned on his heel, and went into the house.

I was glad to get an opportunity to rest, so the guard showed me where I might locate myself on a porch that ran along the back part of the house, and accordingly I unsaddled and hitched my horse, took off my accouterments, spread out my blanket, and laid down for a rest. I soon fell asleep, and was aroused about an hour afterwards by voices, and found that I was to have company in my confinement—another cavalryman, belonging, I think, to the Twelfth Pennsylvania. It was the old story—crippled horse, a long ride back to the lines through a perilous country, enlivened, in his case, by an encounter with guerrillas, who, being on foot, were not able to catch him, and who, he said, had their guns hidden in a brush heap, in order to deceive him. We got along right well together, his voluble tongue running constantly, while I felt somewhat superior to him because I had been longer in the army, and he was a volunteer, anyhow. However, I did not allow my pride to render me disagreeable at all, and our conversation was mutually interesting.

The great question, which might be answered in many ways, was our ultimate fate. We confidently argued that we could certainly soon be released and sent to camp. Just at dark two guards came to us, and informed us that they had orders to take us to Colonel Stevenson's headquarters over in the woods; the commanding officer, I think, of the One-hundred and Twentieth New York; so we were compelled to resaddle and plod our way over a most wretched road for probably three quarters of a mile. Colonel Stevenson, a suave, good-looking man, was found seated by a blazing log fire, surrounded by a number of officers, mostly Indianans, who were talking and singing in fine humor. The colonel received us kindly, heard our story, and remarked that we ought to be returned to go home to our camp unmolested, as it was all nonsense to keep us under arrest. He then said, "I shall have to keep you, as it is my orders—and those, you know, I cannot disobey; so go on over there and make yourselves comfortable for the night—and if the rebels attack us tonight I will call on you to make a cavalry charge on them."

This speech, being a hit at our forlorn looking horses, brought forth a general laugh from the crowd, in which we joined, and we unsaddled and made our rude bed by the side of a log in pretty good spirits, without being put under the restrictions of guard. The colonel ordered his servant to prepare supper for us, and did everything to make us comfortable. The other officers seemed to have a bottle, but their chief did not partake, and most of the time was grave and silent, as though realizing the responsibility resting upon him as commander of the pickets. My companion and I spent a very comfortable night, our tired bodies appreciating the opportunity of resting, while the heavy weight which had oppressed our spirits since our arrest was sensibly relieved by the encouraging words of Colonel Stevenson. Early next morning we were aroused by the drums rattling out the reveille, and groomed our horses and fed them with oats furnished by the colonel, and furnished ourselves with a good breakfast of fried pork and ham. About eight o'clock the colonel called us, and said that he was advised to send us to the provost marshal's headquarters, where, he had no doubt, we would soon be released and sent to dismounted camp. His servant escorted us, carrying no arms himself, but allowing us to retain our own, which was very desirable, as we did not wish to appear as prisoners while passing the infantry camps. However, for some reason or other it seemed to me that the soldiers suspected us, for two or three thousand men must have asked us what rebel regiment we belonged to, to all of which greetings we did not deign to reply. About noon we reached the headquarters of General Patrick.

Here I hoped we would be brought before the general, and, although I knew from my experience in his company at Fredericksburg that he was a very stern man, yet I hoped to be able to explain all to his satisfaction. and that he would release me and allow me to go on to dismounted camp. To my regret we did not get the central interview, a clerk only receiving us, who immediately turned us over to the guard, and we were thrust in among about four hundred rebel prisoners—the dirtiest, most disagreeable crowd I ever saw. I was struck by the personnel of these prisoners. Some must have been well on to ninety years old, and some were not more than twelve. A great many seemed to have been citizens, who had been arrested on suspicion of being spies, as well as I could glean from the conversation. One old chap came up to me, just after I came in, and said, "Well, how did you leave the army?"

"Which army?" I inquired, thinking that perhaps he mistook me for a confederate.

"Well, our army—Lee's army," he answered.

"Oh, you seem to be laboring under a misapprehension," I replied, somewhat loftily. "I don't muster on his rolls."

The old fellow immediately withdrew into a tent. In addition to the rebels, there were quite a number of men charged with desertion from our army confined here, waiting to be sent to their regiments.

The men confined in this camp were not treated with much consideration, so far as the necessities of life were concerned. No comforts were supplied; the prisoner was obliged to take his chances as to a tent, and to sleep on the wet ground in whatever clothing happened to be in his possession when arrested. Coffee and bread and meat—uncooked—were issued, but no wood with which to build a fire was furnished, so that the first article could not be made available for culinary purposes at all, and the meat we were obliged to devour raw.

On the next morning after our confinement my garrulous friend and I applied to the officer of the guard for permission to cleanse and feed our animals, which we ascertained were in the headquarters stables. The request was granted, and we sallied out under escort, much gratified to breathe pure air outside of the abominable camp. We found them well sheltered—in much better quarters than those we had just left—and regretted to be obliged to return.

The discipline of the regiment on guard here—The Eighth United States Infantry—surprised me with its perfection. The sentinels paced their beats with wonderful precision, each one reaching the end of his walk at the same instant, and then, making an "about face," returned to the opposite with the same exactitude of step! The effect of this was to render impossible any attempt, unobserved by the prisoners, to pass the line, because the backs of no two sentinels were turned to each other at the same instant. The officers were very strict, one could easily conclude, from seeing them pass through the camp, and from their dignified and unsocial bearing towards the men. They were regulars, and fully appreciated that understood requirement of the service that prohibits the officers from mingling among the common soldiers with familiarity. The routine of camp duty here must have been very irksome and monotonous. The men, however, seemed to be quite cheerful and contented with their lot, perhaps glad to escape the more rough and dangerous service at the front. Their clean uniforms, polished shoes and burnished buttons, and gleaming arms, were in great contrast with those of the overworked regiments of the surrounding divisions.

We were not without adventures in this miserable place. On the second night after our arrival here, about midnight, we were startled from our slumbers by one or two musket shots. In a moment there was great excitement in camp, but no one dared to put out his head to see what it was all about, as we were warned that in case we did so the sentinels would fire upon us. We presently learned, however, that one of the prisoners, watching for an opportunity, had suddenly sprung from one of the outside Sibley's, and dashed across the line in among the tents of the regiment, and was successful in making his escape. By taking this course among the tents of the Eighth Infantry he had forced the guards to be cautious about firing, as there was great danger of striking the wrong man, and as a consequence the shot had been directed into the air far above his head. The next day he was recaptured and returned to prison.

Many of our new soldiers, who had been at the front probably one or two months, found their way in to our camp, having in most instances been arrested while straying beyond the camp limits by the ever-watchful provost guards. It was amusing to hear these parties complain of their misfortune. Almost invariably they would protest that they were entirely innocent of criminal intent, and that it was the very first time they had ever been under arrest for any cause whatever. Pleasant voiced young men, who would not have seemed out of place as members of the Young Men's Christian Association, instead of an organization created for the cruel deeds of war, were here, lamenting the sad fate that brought them under the iron grasp of General Patrick. Others, older in the service, took matters more philosophically, and smoked their pipes and indulged in games of "draw poker" with a nonchalant air, that showed that the guardhouse possessed no terrors for them—was rather a shelter from the ugly details of camp duty.

372

Once my companion and I were detailed, in company with a confederate prisoner of war, to go out on fatigue duty. This meant that we should clean the guard's stable of its surplus manure. Our companion of the other army could not understand what he had to do with such business, but did not complain much, seeming to be rather pleased than otherwise to get out of camp. My friend, however, swore voluminously, if such an expression be correct, technically speaking. Indeed, that was about all he did; the most of the work was done by our confederate, who seemed to be at home with a pitchfork in his hand.

Squads of confederate prisoners came in daily, having been captured at different points by our cavalry, which, as we thus learned, were making their way across the country beyond the Rappahannock, on an extended raid. The news of their successful progress was exhilarating to me, for I was jealous of the fame of that arm of the service. I was sorry, however, that I was not along to participate in the fun, instead of being detained in this vile den.

On the evening of the third or fourth day after our incarceration here the sergeant of the guard called out my friend and I, and informed us that we were to be sent immediately to General Pleasonton's headquarters. Our horses and equipment were then returned to us. The ammunition had all been stolen; our sabres and revolvers were sadly rusted, having been neglected and exposed to the weather. The side leathers of our saddles were warped and crimped all out of shape, and the coat straps had been appropriated. We protested against these outrages, but met with no response; and so, after a fresh volley of oaths from my friend, we were sent to our destination under an armed escort, arriving at the headquarters of the cavalry corps soon after one o'clock.

Lieutenant Ward, formerly commanding our company was on duty here. To him I told my story, and requested that he should do something on my behalf. He promised to make every effort in his power to have me released and sent to the camp of the dismounted men of our brigade.

The guard house here was jammed full of prisoners. There was no room for us, and we were obliged to put up a "dog tent" to shelter us. Considering the limited facilities at our disposal, we made ourselves tolerably comfortable. That night, however, a great storm came up, and swept away our frail shelter, and we were obliged to stand shivering out in the deluging rain until daylight—a miserable, forlorn couple.

Early that morning my garrulous friend and I separated, and we have not met since. He was sent to the dismounted camp of the men of his brigade. I hope, if we happen to see each other again, in this life or the next, that it may not be under such trying circumstances.

Late in the day a mounted man, belonging to some New York regiment of cavalry, called for me, exhibited an order to the sergeant of the guard, took my belt and buckled it around him, slung my carbine over his shoulder, compelled me to mount my crippled steed, and then, gruffly ordering me to follow him, put spurs to his horse and galloped off down the muddy road. My animal was in no condition to travel so fast; he was still able to use but three legs, and the road was badly cut up with ruts and ravines, rendering a rapid gait an unsafe one to assume. Besides, I did not care to urge the poor brute along faster than it chose to travel; there was no visible necessity to do so.

In a few moments my escort was far ahead of me, and then, making this discovery, he halted, and with loud curses ordered me to hurry along. I made no reply, and went mechanically forward, without an effort to increase the speed. When we were together again he assumed a threatening attitude and tone, swore awhile, and then dashed off at a more rapid rate than before. I was wondering to myself what course to pursue with this domineering Hibernian, who evidently intended to humiliate the unfortunate individual under his charge as much as possible, when his horse's legs suddenly reversed themselves, and stood upward in the air, while my guard, entangled in his double set of arms, was buried in a mass of mud beneath. I did not quicken my pace. There was no movement of either horse or rider while I rode up; to all appearances both might have been dead for hours. I reined up beside them, and surveyed the scene. The Hibernian's head was visible, but covered with mud. A great debate arose within my mind at this juncture.

"I don't believe a prisoner is supposed to help his guard out of difficulty," I thought. "I am supposed to be utterly passive—to do nothing unless ordered."

By this time the guard began to move, and finally crawled out from beneath the head of his horse. When he regained his feet he gently raised the bridle reins, and the animal reassumed its wonted perpendicularity. Both horse and rider were clad in an armor of mud, and presented a pitiable spectacle. The man was evidently crestfallen, as the balance of our way was traversed at a moderate gait, and not a word spoken by either party. I could not help smiling as I looked upon the doleful pair as they preceded me along that miry highway.

I was in hopes of being released as soon as I should reach the dismounted men of my own regiment, and sent to my proper destination. In this, however, I was sadly disappointed. When we arrived at the camp, which was located near the mouth of Aquia Creek, my guard presented me to the commanding officer, Colonel Blake, of the first Cavalry—an old, querulous spoken man, known among the common soldiers as Grandmother Blake—and handed him a dispatch relating to my case, as I suppose.

"You are a pretty looking soldier," said the grandmother, adjusting a pair of gold spectacles upon her masculine nose, and surveying me from head to foot. His tone satisfied me that he felt himself master or mistress of the situation, and I did not reply, though feeling as if he would not be looking so bright and clean had he been "through the mill" that had been grinding me for the past week or so.

Then, turning to his orderly, he said:

"My compliments to the officer of the day, and say that I want a fifth of the guard sent down here."

The orderly disappeared, and I remained "standing to attention," holding my horse just at the door of the tent and surveying the interior and the animated figure of the old man, who, by the way, was dishabille. He dismissed my Hibernian friend, who remounted after leaving my arms, and rode away. The guards soon came—dismounted cavalryman of my own command—and I was at once thrust into our regimental guardhouse. With a feeling that for the present, at least, my weary, uncertain journey was at an end, I cast myself on the ground outside the Sibley and fell asleep in a few moments.

When I awoke, an hour afterward, the sun was fast sinking into the west. I was very hungry, and requested the sergeant of the guard to send a man with me down to the quarters of Company F, so that some arrangements might be made for my rations. Quite a number of our men were here, and they greeted me with a hearty laugh when they saw the predicament in which I was placed. I had never been under arrest while with the company, and was always looked upon as a sort of moralist, but the joke was on me this time.

Sergeant Becton rendered me all the aid in his power to make me comfortable. Sergeant Welsh hurried over to see Lieutenant McKinstry, of our regiment—he was officer of the day—and brought back encouraging words, which, however, I am obliged to say—owing no doubt to the shortness of that gentleman's memory—were not immediately realized.

After a hearty meal I lounged back to the guardhouse, and prepared to make my circumstances as easy as possible. I was somewhat nettled to find that, during my brief absence, my "dog tent" had been stolen; but the joy in my heart at being "at home" once more soon made me forgive the thief.

Later in the evening Sergeant Becton came up to see me. He was suffering from a wound received in a peculiar manner. About a week before the regiment marched, he had been indulging in commissary whisky, and while under its influence, after taking a smoke, thrust the pipe into his pocket, after the fire, as he supposed, had been extinguished. He was mistaken, however. Something warm in that vicinity soon brought him to a sense of realization of that fact. A frantic unbuttoning of pantaloons and drawers, and jerking up of shirt followed, but the cause of commotion was not removed until he was so badly burned about the groin and thigh as to be incapacitated from doing duty. Although the injury was quite severe, I could not help laughing at the droll circumstances.

There were several hundred dismounted men, belonging to our brigade, in camp here. Across on the hills opposite there were other camps of men attached to other brigades, and among them some of my Pennsylvania friends of the first Regiment of Cavalry from that State. The guard duty was quite severe, a detail being sent away to a place called Ibedam, which the men translated "You-be-damned;" and, in addition, a large force was sent down daily to the wharves to unload schooners of military stores, and others were out building entrenchments to guard against an attack by Stuart's confederate cavalry, as was said. There were but few prisoners in the guardhouse, and these had very easy times. Once a day we were sent over to sweep up the ground around our grandmother's quarters, and while doing this I fancied the old woman eyed my movements with a sort of malignant relish. No matter at what side of the tent I was working, she was sure to be there, apparently profoundly studying my movements. Her attentions disturbed me sadly, as it occurred to my troubled mind that she might want to marry me.

One day—I think the third or fourth after my arrival—Sergeant Welsh informed me that I need not be surprised if I were released from confinement and sent to headquarters for clerical duties. This intimation surprised me, but I hoped it might prove true; and, sure enough, early next morning I was sent for, and, in company with my usual armed

376

escort, made my appearance at the office of the adjutant general of the cavalry corps, which was located here. The chief clerk questioned me as to my ability to make out reports, inventories, and other documents; but as I was utterly inexperienced in such matters, I felt obliged to be cautious in reply. He soon showed, however, that he was determined to find something that I could do, and dismissed the guard, saying he had an order for my release; so once more I was a free man.

I thanked the clerk with a full heart, but he cut me short, and told me to repair to my quarters, and to report to him at nine o'clock the next morning, when he would show me what he wanted to have done.

Some time afterward I found out the source of my good fortune. Sergeant Welsh, during the brief interval of my confinement, had made persistent efforts on my behalf, and being a friend of the clerk, enlisted him in my cause; between them they managed to concoct a scheme and successfully consummate it, which resulted in my release and detail for duty at headquarters.

In obedience to orders, I was at the office next morning promptly at the appointed hour. The clerk told me he was not yet ready for me, and I went to my quarters for that day. As I was reported "on duty at headquarters," I escaped all company details. The laugh was on my side now, as the rest of the men were grumbling at their laborious duties; but I did not press the joke hard upon them.

On the morning of the third day I went to work on an inventory of camp and garrison equipage scattered around the post.

"Everything in this camp must be found, properly classified and recorded, and the record brought to me," said the clerk. "You will go to every tent, and make a personal examination, so that there shall be no mistake."

This man, whose name I have forgotten, was a peculiar sort of a fellow—thoroughly conversant with the duties of the office, kind-hearted, very nervous, but sadly given to drink. Although a private soldier, he seldom performed duty in the ranks, being generally employed as a clerk. I was much surprised one day at the apparent recklessness of temper exhibited by him. The adjutant—a second lieutenant of the Second Cavalry—was dissatisfied at some report that had been made out, and took occasion to say so. The clerk, apparently thinking that the officer had questioned his veracity, sprang to his feet, with flashing eyes and quivering lips.

"I am a common soldier, sir," he exclaimed, "but I allow no man to intimate that I lie!"

The lieutenant explained what he had meant, urging that he made no such insinuation, and the storm subsided as quickly as it had arisen. It was the first time I had ever seen a regular officer exhibit so much consideration for the feelings of an enlisted man under such circumstances. Usually the guardhouse would have had an additional occupant.

After successfully making up my inventory, I was employed each morning in filling out blank consolidated morning reports of brigades and the cavalry corps. This occupied about half an hour, and the balance of the day I was allowed to myself. From these reports I learned that the number of mounted men operating under General Hooker was something over sixteen thousand; the dismounted force belonging to the corps was over four thousand, who were now on duty at or near Aquia Creek. About three-fourths of the cavalry had gone on the raid under Generals Stoneman and Averill, while the balance, commanded by General Pleasanton, remained on duty with the army.

At headquarters, acting as a servant for the adjutant, and thus managing to get enough food to keep body and soul together, was a boy, aged twelve years, whose history had been quite eventful. Nearly two years before he had followed his father, a member of a New York volunteer infantry regiment, to the front. At Fair Oaks, standing close up to the ranks during that sanguinary afternoon of the 30th of May, he had seen his parent shot dead, and found himself an orphan. Although so young, and now without a protector or relative on earth—his mother had died when he was an infant—he would leave the army. He was anxious to be a soldier, especially a cavalryman, but the regulations would not accept so young a recruit; so he drifted about from regiment to regiment, until he came among the Second Dragoons.

Toward the latter part of June, 1863, while the army was enroute to Pennsylvania, I saw the little fellow riding in ranks, dressed in full uniform, and waving a sabre and revolver, holding up his head proudly as he saw me looking at him.

"I am a soldier now," he cried. "Don't you see my sword?"

His handsome, childish face, gleeful smile, the black eyes, and long curling raven locks, looked strangely out of place in that grim, dusty column.

I never saw him afterward.

The month of April passed away. News came to us that the army was mustering along the south side of the Rappahannock, and the rumor was soon verified by the sound of sharp cannonading toward the front. This increased in volume, and amid its thunders the peculiar crackling fire of small arms told plainer than words that the Army of the Potomac and the Army of Northern Virginia were again struggling together in deadly conflict.

The fighting lasted several days. During its progress—as supposed—I wrote a letter to my friends at home, from which I make the following extracts:

A battle of great fury has been going on for the past six days, between the armies of General Lee and General Hooker. Many thousands have already been killed and wounded on both sides. It is said to be still going on, although I have heard no firing today.

I trust our forces will be victorious. If they are, and follow up their triumph, it may end this terrible war.

Our cavalry, I understand, have passed around the rebel army, and destroyed the bridges between it and Richmond.

I wish George and father were here now; they could see war in earnest. It seems hard that men should deliberately butcher each other in this way as though some fearful insanity held sway over the entire nation. All around us nature is blooming, and the world looks so beautiful. The cannons roar in one direction, and the birds sing in another.

Last Monday was the anniversary of the first time I "smelt gunpowder" at Williamsburg. I have "smelt" as much as I care to since then. Among all my trials, however, I have thought of my friends at home, and felt sustained by their sympathy.

We had a pretty hard shower here last evening. A sharp thunder-storm puts me somewhat in mind of the firing of a battery of artillery. The flashes of lightning and stunning roars is as good an illustration of a battle as I want.

I have had a series of adventures since I last wrote to you—had to travel alone through the enemy's country a good many miles, on my return to dismounted camp from the raiders, was arrested by our pickets, and sent to the headquarters of the Provost Marshal General of the Army, thence to General Pleasanton's headquarters, and thence to this place, where I found our regimental dismounted men. Was under arrest here two days, owing to the neglect of our officers to have me released, as I was guilty of nothing, having returned by orders of Lieutenant Balder, on account of the disabled condition of my horse. Since then I have been enjoying the best times I have ever had since enlisting—plenty to eat and little to do.

Are the peach trees in blossom yet, or the honeysuckle blooming in the garden? I suppose the blackbirds are singing to you from the cedar tree every morning. I almost imagine I hear them now.

379

Tell Little Jim that his Jim Crackcorn is completely disabled. His left hind leg and right fore shoulder are badly sprained. It was done before he came to me, but did not affect him much until about one month ago, and during the last march, while leaping a ditch, he fell, and has been simply worthless ever since.

I hope to see you at home in fourteen months, if spared. Wouldn't I be glad to see you this spring? When I think of the beautiful river and hills it almost makes me homesick.

I am not sorry that I enlisted. I have learned a great lesson, and seen sights that not everyone sees. It is true, I have suffered some hardships, and run some risks, but so far God has dealt mercifully with me. I know I should not have been contented at home during all this turbulent period.

It will be observed that in the letter mention is made of the operations of our cavalry. It was written in the forenoon, under the shade of a tree some distance from camp, whither I had wandered to be away from its turmoil. I am puzzled now to know where I obtained that information. General Hooker, as I see by the report of the Committee on the Conduct of the War, received a dispatch from Abraham Lincoln, dated Washington, May 6, 11:40 a.m., giving substantially the same information, which was the first intimation he received of it, as he says. By that time he had withdrawn his army to the north bank of the Rappahannock. While I had heard from our cavalry, I was ignorant of this movement by our army, although only a few miles distant from it.

During the first days of May good news came from the front news that the enemy's forces were defeated. and falling back in a demoralized condition; that Stoneman's mounted men had torn up the railroad, destroyed bridges, and burned up a vast quantity of supplies between Lee and Richmond; that thousands of prisoners had been taken; that many deserters were coming into our lines. Our military wags were constantly reporting "dispatches per picket line," the tenor of which ran off into all sorts of extravagant and grotesque absurdities. Here is a sample, that ran as follows, as near as I can recollect:

Fredericksburg, May 4, 1863 Enemy totally routed. His men are in a starving condition. Just fifteen minutes since three rebels offered to surrender to one of our pickets if he would divide a cracker with them. A whole brigade subsequently came in and laid down their arms on the condition that a box of crackers should be distributed among them. They are now filing past this office along the railroad towards Aquia Creek. One of these men reported that if our forces could procure fifty boxes of crackers for distribution the entire Southern Confederacy would immediately surrender. Orders have been sent to Falmouth for the required number.

As time passed on, reports of further great victories came into camp, and large trains of supplies and bridge timber continued to move towards Fredericksburg. This was something tangible—a good sign. However, one day this movement of cars was reversed—they all began moving towards the Potomac. At first, we patched up and fabricated all sorts of stories in justification of this extraordinary maneuvering. There was a report that the enemy's cavalry was about to attempt one of his characteristic raids, and pounce down upon the landing at Aquia Creek, to destroy our stores located there. A gloomy foreboding seized my heart. Sure enough, there was soon told the same old story—the Army of the Potomac had been defeated again, and was retreating, having lost from seventeen to eighteen thousand men.

"Oh Lord! How Long?"

Our soldiers returned to their old camps around Falmouth, and thus ended General Hooker's grand fiasco—the most humiliating event of the whole war. An organization one hundred and twenty thousand strong, splendidly armed and equipped, and on its own chosen ground, was defeated and driven across the Rappahannock by a confederate force of half that number—very poorly supplied—one third of whom had to make a forced march of many miles to reach the scene of battle in time to cooperate with its brethren! I pass over this extraordinary scene. The commanding general had shown himself utterly incapable of managing the body of men under his control; his peculiar temperament developed into that of a common scold under the pressure of the discouraging events and keen criticism that met him from all sides, and at last led him to abandon the army in the presence of the mighty danger which menaced it in the fields of Maryland and Pennsylvania.

In the list of killed I saw the name of my friend on picket near Hartwood, Colonel Stevenson, of the One hundred and Twentieth New York. He had fallen at the head of his regiment. Did he feel the shadow of his impending fate that night, as he sat, communing with himself, by the blazing fire?

My old schoolmate, Willie Ferree, fell mortally wounded at Chancellorsville, and was left lying on the ground in the blazing timbers, never to be seen again. Nearly two years afterward I met his poor old mother at her home in Washington County. We two boys had been

381

inseparable in antebellum days, and now, as the old recollections swept into her mind, she burst into tears.

"My boy—my poor boy Willie!"

These words came from her lips in a very agony of despair. The scene was more than I could endure, and I hastily and perhaps awkwardly withdrew, with an intolerable swelling in my throat.

He had fallen on the 4th of May, the last day of the battleyear which opened upon him on the field of Williamsburg. Two months before this I met him for the last time, when we paid a visit together to our friends in the One hundred and Fortieth Pennsylvania, who were then deemed recruits. I had never seen him in such high spirits. His frank, open countenance, and laughing brown eyes wore an animated expression that betokened his happiest mood.

"We are veterans, ain't we, Sid? These fellows are only recruits," he said, pointing to Barclay, Hindman, Cady, and others of the One hundred and Fortieth. "Never mind, you will soon be initiated."

About a dozen of my companions in the prison camp at the Provost Marshal General's headquarters passed down the road towards Aquia Creek during the days of the battle, among them the chap that had been to all the armies in the field in search of his regiment. He recognized me as I stood by the roadside. They were chained together, under charge of a guard.

"Well, here we go again," he called out to me. "You just got away in time. We have been in awful luck since you left."

"In what way?" I inquired.

"Oh, chained together, and exposed to the storms."

He then went on to relate their experiences in detail. Some of them were ludicrous, though sadly trying to their collective patiences. For instance, all would be huddled around a fire, trying to keep warm, when a blast of wind would drive them first from one side to the other. At other times, during the night, when all would be lying asleep, one man would awaken and desire to go after a drink of water or on some other necessary errand. Then all the rest must be aroused and go along, the chain forming a tie much stronger than any ordinary friendship.

I accompanied the poor creatures a little way down the road, and then bade them farewell. Whatever may have been the full extent of their crimes, without doubt their punishment so far had been simply horrible. Dragged about from one guardhouse to another, exposed to all kinds of weather, often going whole days without food, handcuffed and shackled

382

like so many convicted felons, although there had as yet been no trial, theirs was a weary, monotonous round of existence, to which, in comparison, the march, the bivouac, and the battle were delights.

Under the surface of army life, unseen and unheralded amid the glare and bustle and pomp of war, there are dramas of real life constantly being enacted by the common soldiery that would be called startling if reproduced upon the stage. Take these prisoners, for instance, all wan and haggard as they were, clad in their diversified, tattered clothing, wearing their chains, and driven along a muddy highway, and thus present them before the footlights of a theater in the presence of our fashionable audiences, and I doubt if they could realize that such a scene had actually been presented within our own day and time, and inside the limits of our noble army. They would probably locate it back in the history of the dark ages, when absolutism held unquestioned sway over the earth. Such a picture is irreconcilable with our ideas of the civilization and enlightenment of the present Nineteenth Century.

On the 16th of May the regiment returned from the raid, and went into camp about two miles from that of our dismounted men. The next day I went over to "call on the boys." Men and horses were sadly worn out by their arduous duties, but the former were in high spirits and brim full of stories of incidents and adventure. Altogether they seemed to have greatly enjoyed their trip beyond the lines. For a short time I was apprehensive of a dislocated arm from the vigorous hand-shaking to which I was subjected, but we finally completed the task. Burly Todd, my old "bunky," was delighted with the success of the raid, and loud in his denunciations of Hooker. The festive Leonard felt compelled to tell me how successfully he had "played rebel," while out foraging one night, deluding some enthusiastic female secessionist, and receiving a vast amount of bread and pies, free of charge, as a token of her approbation.

Six men were missing from the company, one of whom, my theatrical friend Centre, undoubtedly having deliberately deserted to the enemy. He had managed his little scheme with consummate ability. Complaining of feeling unwell, he requested Dawson to "fall out," and accompany him to a farm house standing near the roadside, as he desired to procure some mustard. Dawson did so, and as they rode over towards the dwelling the regiment filed past out of sight. As they were in the midst of the enemy's country, Dawson felt a wholesome fear of confederate cavalry, and was anxious to rejoin the command; but Centre had so many stories to tell the people and lingered so long. that Dawson was obliged to leave him behind, and reached the regiment about a mile from where he had left it. Two or three weeks later a letter, written by one of our men who had been captured during the raid and paroled, was received by someone in the company, stating that he had seen Centre with the confederates, and that the latter informed him of his desertion, and that he had sold his horse and equipment for eight hundred and seventy-five dollars, and that he was going to Richmond, and have a position in the secret service of the Confederate Government.

The horse sold by Centre was the one assigned to Sergeant Becton, but which, as the latter had not been able to do duty because of his late wound, was allotted temporarily to Centre. For several days the sergeant was savage over the loss of his animal, and vowed vengeance on Centre if an opportunity should at any time be afforded.

The cavalry had done good service on this raid, by the wholesale destruction of bridges, railroad and military stores, and, though their efforts had been mentioned with a contemptuous sneer by the "hero" of Chancellorsville, words of hearty commendation were written by President Lincoln. On reaching the Rappahannok on their return, that river was found to be unfordable, recent rains having added vastly to the volume of water between the banks. As our main army had been defeated and driven from Chancellorsville, and recrossed to the north side about ten days before, leaving the entire confederate army free to destroy them at will, the situation was not reassuring for the corps. General Hooker seems to have thought it scarcely worth while to make the slightest demonstration in their behalf. About six thousand horses, according to the report of General Pleasanton, two or three weeks later, on assuming command of the cavalry, were disabled by the severe marching, leaving the corps in a condition of utter exhaustion. This, added to the loss of nearly eighteen thousand men in battle, makes the Chancellorsville campaign a rather dear experiment.

Speaking of the losses in horses reminds me of a saying that obtained some currency in the army. A quartermaster, whose name I do not recollect hearing, was reported to have declared that it was nothing to lose a man, but a serious matter to lose a horse; a man costs two dollars, but a horse one hundred and twenty dollars. There was a peculiarity about this remark that had a curious effect on the men—a volume of expletives was sure to follow its recital.

I find a letter dated "Hooker's Army, Stafford County, Virginia, May

17, 1863," from which the following extracts are quoted as apropos to these memoirs:

Dear Friend:

I received your letter this morning containing the postage stamps, for which you have my sincere thanks.

I am well, and in good spirits. Your letter made me feel glorious.

I have just been over to see the boys in the regiment, who have returned from the raid. Though worn out from fatigue and from want of sleep, and dusty and greasy, they are just full of fun. They seem to imagine that the enemy's cavalry is nothing now —they were victorious in every encounter. I was so glad to see them and—well, my arm aches yet. I love these noble fellows; they are the best men in existence.

Everything is quiet here now. I am having the easiest of times! We catch some fish, and they taste delicious to my United States palate. The weather is nice and warm.

I am sorry to say our arms have sustained another humiliating defeat. No doubt the papers have told you all ere this. I did not see the battle. Aaron Conlin has been wounded. Lindsey Cady says he don't like the way the rebels pitch their waste lead around.

Within a week or ten days after the cavalry returned from the raid, the dismounted corps was broken up and the men ordered to join their respective commands. It was a positive relief to me to return to the old routine duty, the holidays at headquarters were growing sadly monotonous. There was entirely too much opportunity afforded to reflect on the long months yet to serve, and the probable phases and results of the gigantic struggle in which we were engaged. Though never seriously doubting our ultimate success, the disasters of the past warned me that there was yet hard and heavy work for the government and its soldiers.

385

The Severest Cavalry Fight of the War

About the 1st of June there began to occur ominous movements of troops necessitated by threatening demonstrations of the enemy, who, since the defeat of our army at Chancellorsville, were becoming bold and active. Our regiment took up its line of march for Dumfries, passing Stafford Courthouse on the route, halting at the former place one or two days. I could not help admiring the old village and its surrounding scenery, the latter now dressed in the rich green foliage of mid spring. From reports, however, this supposed paradise was a very Hades for Union soldiers, owing to frequent assassinations on picket. Evans was posted alone on the road about a mile distant from camp, beside a large oak tree. As a pleasant reminder of his duty as a vigilant guard, there were constantly before his eyes a dozen or so large gashes in the body of this tree, made by musket balls, and beside it the loose red earth of two or three new-made mounds gave emphasis to these comfortable tokens. Evans said he could not manage to get his customary nap while picketing here—a matter that greatly grieved him. None of our men, however, were disturbed during their stay at Dumfries.

After receiving a supply of forage, which seemed to have been brought up a sort of bayou on small schooners, the command marched from Dumfries, heading towards the west or southwest. It halted shortly after nightfall, and bivouacked in a dense forest of pines. My turn came to go on guard, and my post was located two or three hundred yards from the regiment, where, alone and dismounted, I was expected to keep watch over the lives of my brethren-in-arms. I walked my beat for several hours—owing to a heavy detail of videttes for picketing the roads in the vicinity, the camp guards were few in number, and each relief was booked for six hours on post—keeping time to an imaginary drum with great precision, but towards the last my limbs became very tired, and my eyes began to be intolerably heavy.

"I will just sit down with my back against this tree," I thought. "I can see just as well, even better, than when standing. Besides, no one can then hear me walking, and that will be a consideration."

How sensible this conclusion seemed—how overwhelming was the argument used to reach such a conclusion, under the seductive influences of my tired legs and heavy eyes! It seemed beyond my power to resist it, and so, locating myself as described, with my carbine lying across my lap, grasped with both hands, ready for instant use, I peered all around me into the thick darkness. There was an unbroken silence, save at intervals, when a dismal cry rose up from some discontented mule at the train, and broke its discordant notes upon the humid air.

I do not know how long I sat there. Unconsciously the scene changed. Instead of those dark woods there was broad daylight, and around me stretched a beautiful landscape. Across the fields and along numerous roads there swarmed thousands of soldiers carrying their arms at a right shoulder shift, and marching jauntily by with smiling faces. Then came squadrons of cavalry, batteries of artillery, and trains of wagons. Oddly enough, there was no sound of feet, no rumble of wheels—a dead silence made me think these were phantoms. Then another change came. I was at home by the dear old river, shaking the hands of my loved ones. Yes these were there father, Levi, Mrs. Samuels, Hiram, and poor Sam. Wilson—the latter without an enemy save himself. Still another change. I am going to school for the first time out at the old log cabin beyond Pollock's Hill. I enter, a little timid at the array of big boys and rosy-cheeked girls, and announce my name to the teacher. I cannot keep my eyes off those girls. Violet Patten greets me with a sympathetic smile, and I feel my young heart flowing out toward her. Then the rule is tapped, and we all rush out towards the playground under the old beech tree and—

Crack—crack—crack! I leap to my feet and look with an intense stare into the thick darkness. Crack—crack—crack! Not loud now—only just discernible to my ear, though at first they had sounded by my startled imagination like musket shots. They were but the breaking of twigs, as some one was cautiously feeling his way along through the woods a few yards beyond me. Then I heard the light rattle of a sabre. My gun was cocked and leveled in an instant.

"Halt! Who goes there?"

"Officer of the guard," was the prompt reply.

I recognized the voice of Lieutenant Balder, now in charge of

Company F—a Prussian, a rigid disciplinarian, who was never known to overlook a military fault. During the few moments that followed curious thoughts swept through my brain with the rapidity of lightning. Intuitively it occurred to me that he had seen my movements, and knew that I had been asleep. A court martial and death sentence was already convened and passed upon me. Yet I could save myself. He was outside my beat; I can shoot him, and report that I supposed him to be a prowling confederate. I press hard upon the trigger as this desperate phase of thought developed.

The lieutenant seemed to understand me. With a voice in which there was not the least trace of harshness he said:

"You should not have so exposed your comrades by sitting down and going to sleep. The safety of the army depends upon the guards. Try and do better hereafter. Duty requires you to be more careful."

The remarkable softness of language, so unnatural to him disarmed my fears; the allusion to my comrades and the army made me thoroughly ashamed of myself; the closing sentences became a resolve within my inmost heart ere they had been finished by his lips. My carbine came down, and the officer passed on his rounds.

After all, that delicious dream of home and school days was worthy of my fright, though my sense of a duty neglected wounded me grievously. The balance of my time was properly spent, and about one o'clock my relief came and I returned to the reserve, where, stretched upon my blanket, I was soon fast asleep.

The next morning the regiment resumed its march. As was the usual custom, the sentries were the last to leave, and followed on as a reserve to keep up the stragglers. Just as we were ready to mount our horses Lieutenant Balder rode up to Sergeant Wallace, the noncommissioned officer in charge of the guard, and directed him to take my arms from me, and place me under arrest, until he should have an opportunity to prepare charges against me for going to sleep while on post in front of the enemy.

The magnitude of this charge startled me, but my fears were moderated or neutralized by a sense of deep humiliation at being put under arrest for the first time in my company. However, there was no effective appeal that could be made in my behalf.

In the course of two or three days the command reached the vicinity of Catlett's station, on the railroad running from Alexandria to Richmond, a few miles from the Rappahannock river. Here I was released from confinement, and returned to duty, not, however, without gloomy forebodings as to the future, for instances in which men had thus been treated during the progress of a campaign, and afterwards arrested and tried, were becoming unpleasantly common in the army. To give color to my uneasiness there arose memories of Lieutenant Balder's unforgiving disposition—or, perhaps, it was, after all, a sense of duty on his part—in other cases, which were, at least, strong presumptive evidences of the line of action he would probably pursue in regard to my case.

The next day after being released I was again detailed for guard. My beat this time was one similar in some respects to that of a few days before—located in the woods a short distance from camp, and the sentry dismounted. This time I was determined to keep awake at all hazards. Two hours on post and four hours off—the usual number—fell to my lot on this occasion. I went on beat at ten o'clock, to come off at twelve. About eleven o'clock there arose a sudden commotion near the sutler's quarters. Loud shouts, followed by several pistol shots, and then a sudden "falling in" of companies, caused me to think that the enemy, by some species of stratagem, was already in the midst of the camp. I sprang to a tree, being somewhat uncertain which way to face, and cocked my gun. The uproar quieted down almost as soon as it had arisen and in a few moments no one would have imagined that anything had been the matter. I was completely nonplussed.

The mystery was explained when, an hour later, I was relieved and returned to the reserve. Some members of Company H, who had procured a supply of commissary whisky by some means, and imbibed freely, took into their heads to have some sport, and for this purpose carried out their revolvers and began firing into the sutler's wagon, to the great discomfort of a colored man who slept therein. The latter party jumped out and ran away, yelling vociferously amid the shouts of the revellers. The only damage done by the bullets was to a mule tied to one of the wheels, which was shot through the neck. The escape of the teamster was almost miraculous, as the bed of the wagon was perforated with balls. The crazy soldiers did not seem to realize the damage that might have been done in consequence of their mad prank, in the confusion and excitement of the troops in camp, many of whom supposed it was an attack by confederates. Among men less disciplined it is probable that an indiscriminate fight would have taken place before quiet could have been restored. I am not aware that the parties were punished.

390

Late on the afternoon of the 8th of June our brigade was ordered out, and marched southward towards the Rappahannock. On our way we passed detachments of infantry from two or three different corps, who seemed to be supporting our movement. Some time after dark the command halted behind a dense forest, on the northern slope of a hill, where orders were given to "stand to horse." Fires were not allowed for some hours, until our brethren of the volunteers took the initiative and kindled theirs, after which we were permitted to participate. It was clear enough that the enemy was not far distant, and reflections on the coming morn were fraught with some solicitude. One by one the men had driven stakes into the ground, or sought out bushes, until the whole party had managed to tie their horses to something, and crouched down upon the ground to sleep. Long before daylight the soldiers were aroused, and, after a short interval, during which most of us had managed to cook our coffee, there was a silent mounting by squadrons, and filing out upon the road, the advance was resumed. We had not proceeded far before the sharp crack of a gun fell upon the morning air, startling the hearts of the weary troopers. The jests and murmurs that had been heard up to this moment suddenly ceased. The men glanced meaningfully into each other's faces. The dull gray of the dawn gave a weird shadowy appearance to the landscape and those morning figures. Other shots were heard, then shouts, and the swift clatter of horses' hoofs upon a hard road. Just as our regiment mounted the crest of a hill, looking down beyond we could see the advance guard of our troops dash boldly across the Rappahannock by single file, the sprays of flying water in the air about them, while a number of dismounted confederates were leaving some slight earthworks along the opposite bank and making terrific but vain efforts to escape up the long slope stretching towards the south.

Owing to the difficulty in crossing, it was perhaps ten minutes before the brigade was over and formed, ready for action, on the fields stretching to the right and left of the common roadway that ran up towards the crest of the low hills south of the river. Skirmishers were immediately thrown forward, the whole force promptly supporting them, and the advance continued with but little opposition for perhaps one mile from the ford. About halfway up the slope we rode past an old-fashion-ed farm house, and near it, partially covered by an army blanket, lying prone upon his back, was the dead body of one of our officers, from whose death wound the warm blood of life still dripped over his dark blue uniform. I shall never forget the sudden chill the sight of this

391

object sent through my frame. Instinctively my eyes looked up towards the sun, which was just now rising over the dark green forests off to the east, and involuntarily ejaculated, in an agony of fear:

"Oh, if I can only live till sunset!"

The sharp crack of rifles in our front told how our men were steadily pressing upon the foe. This beginning so early showed that serious work was anticipated—perhaps it was the prelude to a pitched battle between the main opposing armies. Just where the road ran through a strip of woods we passed the writhing form of a dying confederate cavalryman. He was lying on his back; his arms and legs were moving with nervous twitching; from a wound in the neck the blood was flowing in irregular spurts; his eyes and mouth were wide open, but full of sand which had been dashed into them by the hoofs of the passing horses, and with each gasp it settled further and further into his throat.

"Poor soul!" I thought. "What a blessing it is that those near and dear to him cannot see him in his last terrible agony."

A little further on the regiment halted a moment until the fence on the left of the road was torn down, and then marched into the field and formed into columns of squadrons in front of some timber. The enemy had disappeared into these woods. A battery of light artillery—E Company of the Fourth United States, with four guns—came up in our rear.

There was now a halt for a few moments, and a rapid alignment of squadrons. With a sigh of relief I looked around me, wondering what was to come next. A courier galloped up to the head of the column, and spoke some words to Captain Cram. All eyes were bent upon them as they held their brief interview. Then the soldier rode rapidly away, the officer wheeled the head of his horse towards the regiment, and, though we could not distinguish the words, as if by instinct the men seemed to understand it all, and the next instant there was a gleam of steel in the air and a rattle of sabres as they were swept from their sheaths. The command then moved into the woods in front with its old time bearing.

Owing to the obstacles presented at every step the men became scattered somewhat, but seemed to preserve their organization and alignment. presently I could see the first light of the open fields beyond break through the timber, and at the same instant we were met by a scattering fire of small arms from a line of confederate skirmishers. Then the clear notes of our bugle, sounding the charge, broke upon our ears, and the regiment dashed wildly forward. My horse was still very lame, and ran against a tree severely bruising my leg, but I managed to cling to him. In the tumult that followed I have a vivid recollection of several scenes that were of a startling character. There was Lieutenant Stoll, once my first sergeant at Bladensburg, but now commissioned and attached to Company I, vigorously shooting at a tall, hatless man in gray, who was dismounted, and ran, bent half over, with both hands pressed against his temples, towards the enemy's lines, trying to escape. Although Stoll had the muzzle of his pistol close against the back of his victim, and must have at least wounded him, he was still on his feet as I passed. As we left the timber I could see a gray line across our front, and to the left of this a battery of artillery, which was now thundering and vomiting grapeshot upon us. Next my eyes took in a view of men and horses tumbling into a ravine just in front, and I had barely time to rein up my own animal to save myself from a like fate. I am still puzzled to know where our men went to so suddenly; they seemed to me to go up in a cloud of dust and smoke under the storm of bullets, and in a moment I found myself all alone, save the helpless fellows in the ditch, on a lame horse, within ten paces of the confederates. I did not realize the deadly peril of my situation, but felt perfectly cool, shook my sabre at our foes, and then wheeled and rode back into the woods at a trot. Just then the confederates began to yell, and I knew they were preparing to follow up their success by a charge. A storm of twigs, cut off by their heavy firing, were fluttering to earth. I could hear the rushing of squadrons and shouts of men through the woods to the westward, and then knew that ours was not the only force that was hotly engaged.

Just then I came upon crazy Miller, who was dismounted, holding hard to the bridle of his horse, which was dancing about in a vivacious though unpleasant way.

"What's the matter, Miller?" I inquired.

"I am badly wounded," was the reply. "Can't you help me out?"

"Yes, you must get out of this; the rebels are about to come down."

I took hold of the reins of the refractory animal, while Miller, who was holding up well, seized the cantle of my saddle, and, thus supporting himself, managed to walk quite rapidly.

"I am hit by a shell," said Miller.

"Whereabouts," I asked, looking for a mark of the terrible missile.

"In the back—gone clear through me."

I was astounded at the idea of a man with such a wound being still alive.

"Oh, no you ain't—let me see."

We halted a moment. He turned his back towards me. A small round hole, with an edging of crimson, appeared about the center of the back of his blouse, apparently having been cut by the bullet from a revolver. Then, opening his shirt bosom, I saw an extra teat, about an inch below his left nipple, projecting outward perhaps half an inch, that proved to be the conical point of the ball, which was lying just under the skin.

I am puzzled to know where Miller's heart was when that bullet went through, unless, like my own, it had jumped into his throat at the beginning of the fight, and had not yet fallen to its normal position.

By some means or other we managed to get back to the spot from which we had started in the field beyond the woods. A brief survey of matters here were not assuring to us. The Sixth Cavalry, now totally disorganized, were rallying about Lieutenant Ward to the number of perhaps one hundred men. His clear, shrill voice could be distinctly heard above the uproar, calling his company together. Just behind him, plainly visible to us, but hidden from Ward and his men by a narrow strip of timber that projected from the scene of our attack in a semicircle beyond him, a confederate regiment, numbering several hundred men—the Ninth Virginia, as I afterwards learned—was driving before it the broken columns of the First United States Cavalry by a furious charge. The men of the first had ceased all semblance of resistance, and were going pell mell towards the ford, while the confederates were close upon them, firing with their revolvers. Behind us the four pieces of E Company were going into position on a little knoll, the gunners endeavoring to train them upon the Ninth Virginia, but apparently so excited as to be incapable of doing anything in a proper manner.

A single glance at this portion of the scene impressed me with one important fact. We were in a direct line between the cannons and confederates, and, if those pieces were discharged, Miller and I were likely to be blown into midair.

"By George, Miller," I exclaimed, "we must get out of this."

During the brief time we had stopped here Miller was pouring out his vials of wrath upon the enemy in broken English—he was a German—seeming to have forgotten his dangerous wound in the fierce anger that possessed him. Half dragging him between two of the pieces, just as they opened fire, fairly staggering in my saddle as the whizzing missiles went by, I had the satisfaction to find ourselves safe from this

394

new danger. I glanced back to see the effect. The shells went wild, bursting in the air above and beyond the mark. It was a splendid chance for cool, collected gunners, that gray mass of men, not one or two hundred yards distant, but these panic-stricken fellows appeared helplessly incompetent, though the officer in command did his best to control them.

Just then Lieutenant Ward, with his handful of men, marched around the point of timber. He found himself almost directly in the rear of the Ninth Virginia, as it had passed his position, and promptly charged it, the men cheering wildly as they swept forward. It was a curious scene—this small body so boldly attacking a large force that was at this moment driving from their front quite a strong regiment; but the movement was successful. The confederates halted a moment, gave a startled look backward, and then their regiment broke up and fled by a detour westward to the rear.

"From the noise you men made," said a member of the Ninth Virginia who had participated in this action, to me, several months afterward, "we thought it was a whole brigade coming out of those woods."

Our men now rallied, and, amid great cheering, drove the enemy from that portion of the field. The plucky Miller tried to set up a yell, but, after a faithful effort, was obliged to give it up. Apprehensive that he would soon become so weak as to be unable to walk at all, I begged him to come on to the hospital and have his wound immediately attended. McKibben, who was now attached to the surgeon's staff, made his appearance, and agreed to assist in getting the wounded man to his destination.

At a spring of water near the farm house we passed a tall, savage--looking confederate, who, though he must have been a prisoner, still wore his arms. His long red hair and flaming whiskers, heavy eye--brows, and muscular frame made up a formidable object, of which I should have felt shy if alone.

With considerable difficulty we managed to get Miller across the Rappahannock. He delivered his last message to me to send to his sister, giving instructions about some little property that he possessed some-where, but I was so much affected that her name and address, and the particular points of his communication, were forgotten, or, rather, perhaps, fell upon unheeding ears. At the hospital we found some of our wounded already in, Lieutenants Wade and Madden among the number.

There was blood on Wade's face. Madden was shot in the body, and seemed badly injured, suffering much pain. Both of these officers, however, recovered and rejoined their commands within a few months.

As I bade Miller farewell he tendered me his horse—a token of the highest esteem, perhaps, that a dragoon can give as a mark of his gratitude for my assistance in his hour of peril.

"Take good care of him—he's ugly, I know, but treat him kindly."

Miller was a curious fellow—full of odd whims that earned him the sobriquet of "Crazy Miller," in contradistinction from "Chany Miller," and "Paddy Miller," two other members of the company. He had already passed five or six years of his life in the service, coming to us on a transfer from the Fourth United States Cavalry. Although choosing the hard and almost unrecognized sphere of the common soldier, there beat in his breast a heart just as full of unselfish patriotism as any in the land.

His horse—an iron-gray beast, clumsy and ungainly in its actions—had an uncomfortable penchant for standing on its hind feet when laboring under the least excitement. Still, it was a preferable animal to my own, which had fallen into a chronic condition of lameness, and was no longer reliable as a battle-steed. Under these circumstances I mounted the iron-gray and led Jim Crackcorn back to the scene of the engagement at Brandy Station.

On account of the uncertainty of the situation when I reached the ford, on my return, it was deemed advisable for me to remain with the infantry bivouacked on the north side of the river, burdened as I was with a led horse and a double set of accouterments. Although the cavalry had driven the enemy in their front southward, there appeared, at short intervals, bands of confederates on each flank, sometimes coming quite close to the river, and in many instances firing on our skirmishers thrown out to protect the ford. Shortly before my arrival some infantry, stationed on the left, and supported by two pieces of artillery, had suddenly been attacked and lost their guns. On the right the confederates pushed up a battery on an eminence which commanded the ford, and at the same time a line of their skirmishers advanced and attacked our men. For a short period the fusillade was quite brisk, though, on account of the great distance the combatants maintained from each other, I don't think any one was injured on either side. The scene, though harmless in effect, was quite interesting from our side of the river. Little puffs of dust showed where the bullets struck in rear of our line, demonstrating it to be within range, and giving zest to the excitement.

The confederates finally withdrew from the flanks, and about one o'clock I remounted and crossed the river to find the regiment. On reaching the woods which had been the scene of the fighting in the morning a strong sense of curiosity impelled me to visit the ground upon which our charge and fearful repulse had taken place. A little way in the woods a sight met my eyes that stirred up the bile of covetousness within me to an alarming extent. A large, jet-black stallion, carrying a splendid set of equipment, with revolver holsters on the cantle of the brass-mounted saddle, stood nipping the tops of bushes, without a solitary visible guardian.

"Golly! Here's a prize," thought I. "I must secure him."

I am sorry to say that my selfish nature here thoroughly asserted itself. Even now I had forgotten Miller's last gift, which the amenities of cavalry life required me to accept, and already pictured myself as mounted on the black stallion, with my brassmounted saddle and double holsters and two revolvers. On my approaching the animal, however, a man dressed in the uniform of a colonel of infantry, rose from among some bushes, and crossed over to it with an unmistakable air of ownership. Thus I was saved from committing a grave breach of trust.

I had almost reached the edge of the woods from which our charge began, when a sharp fusillade of small arms in that direction broke upon my ears, evidently quite close at hand. It then occurred to me that perhaps I had explored just far enough in that direction, and so returned to the spot where the guns of the Fourth Artillery went into position in the morning.

The common roadway leading from the ford southward, along which our advance had been made several hours before, seemed to present a feasible route by which to find the regiment. It led across to a small brook, and then up a long slope towards the southwest, past a farm house and barn, and beyond across the crest of a low hill. To this road I made my way, crossing several fields and tearing down many fences in order to attain it by a "short cut." In about half an hour I had reached the farm house, and from there made a brief survey of the surroundings.

Up the shallow valley down which meandered the stream that crossed the road below me I could see a small body of Cavalry. They were marching slowly towards the river, with that peculiarity of movement which characterizes a well-managed retreat in the presence of an enemy. As they came closer the line of skirmishers covering the movement became visible on the crest of the hill over which they had retired, the men falling back slowly, and halting every few steps and firing toward the rear. Then as these in turn had passed well down the hill the confederate line appeared in their wake, viciously pressing forward in a manner that showed the enemy's strong belief in his ability to drive our men.

The intense excitement I felt in this scene almost proved fatal to my earthly existence. I was suddenly surprised by the report of a gun on the ridge above me, followed by the whistling of a bullet in close proximity, and on looking up saw in dismay that the enemy's mounted skirmishers had appeared at the edge of some timber that stretched northward toward the river, being apparently a prolongation of the line advancing from the southwest. About the same instant I discovered that the body of cavalry retreating down the valley was the Sixth United States, endeavoring to disentangle itself from the meshes of a relentless foe. Acting on my first impulse—there was no time to discuss matters—I started as fast as I could urge my horse across the fields toward the regiment, supposing I could join it by throwing down the only fence that was visible between us. Another obstacle, however, of a much more formidable character, stretched across my path. This a ditch—deep, wide, impassable. No way of escape appeared, except by the road past the farm house and barn. This avenue was now almost in possession of the confederates, but I felt that an effort must be made to escape. Turning my horses' heads in that direction and lying close to the neck of the iron-gray I put spurs to its flanks and dashed forward as fast as possible. Jim Crackcorn seemed to realize the difficulties in our way, and did his best to keep up, his three tolerably sound legs swinging under his walnut-colored body with a vengeance. Just before we reached the barn I heard some of the confederates shout to me to halt, mingled with certain epithets known to soldiers who have served during the late war. I did not care to look up, lest I should lose courage, but "went it blind," digging my spurs still deeper into the flanks of the iron-gray, and tugging for dear life at the walnut-colored stud behind me. As we passed the barn several shots were fired, and I could hear the bullets go crashing through its weather-boarding in a way that was painfully suggestive of a funeral with the honors of war. None of these missiles took effect, and in an instant more we were going down the road toward the ford at a pell mell speed, and were soon out of danger.

I have since thought what a comical picture I must have presented on this occasion, lying flat upon the neck of one horse, and pulling another lame one along, as it were, by the reins, with those gray devils after me with their tantalizing rifles.

When I found myself at a safe distance I looked up the valley to see what was to be the fate of the regiment. It had halted, and showing fight by forming in squadrons on the slope and facing the enemy, while two guns were galloping up to their support. These soon unlimbered and opened fire, and the advance of the confederates was effectually checked. They did not again resume the offensive, apparently contented with watching the movements of our troops from a safe distance.

A few moments later I had rejoined the regiment, and received the approval of Lieutenant Balder for my action towards Miller and care of his horse and equipment.

It was now about five o'clock in the evening. Our forces returned to the north bank of the Rappahannock, and the movement of the day, which proved to be merely a "reconnaissance in force," as it is called in military parlance, to break up certain designs of the enemy by scattering his host to the four winds, ended, having been conducted, in the main, with entire success to our arms.

The action at Brandy Station, as it is called, was perhaps the severest cavalry fight of the war, in which any considerable number of mounted men were engaged. Including both sides, it is safe to assume there were from fifteen to eighteen thousand. The fighting in some instances was hand to hand, while in others there was heavy firing at close range.

The losses of the Sixth Cavalry during the day amounted to about one-fourth of the number in action or nearly one hundred men. Excepting the repulse early in the morning, it met with no defeat, but drove its foes some miles upon their infantry, and only retired under orders when the object of the expedition had been attained.

In speaking thus specially of my own regiment, no invidious distinction is sought to be made as to the balance of the brigade or division, or our coadjutants of the infantry and artillery. Each body in its allotted sphere *did its duty*—the glory of American soldiery. The two instances of failure on the part of other troops—the loss of guns by the infantry on the left, and the excitement and subsequent incompetence of the men of E Company, Fourth United States Artillery in the morning—are so effectually offset by our own repulse at the opening of the fight as to leave no ground for self-praise.

Instances of personal daring, or heroic endurance and sacrifice, of startling tragedy were not wanting in this engagement, and furnished themes of conversation among the survivors for many days afterward. There was little Ward, killed while leading the delicate details of successful retreat; there was Stoll, shot through the head while riding down the hill in rear of his company as I had seen them before leaving the barn. The ball had gone in at the back part of the head and passed out at the end of the nose. When he fell, one of his company rode back to help him. He was perfectly conscious, and said, in response to the tender of assistance—

"Go on, never mind me."

Strange as it may seem, Stoll lived several months afterward. He was taken captive and sent to Libby prison, and subjected to the hideous treatment common to that locality, and, in better hands, might have recovered entirely. The night before his death, true to his wild instincts, which had more than once made me afraid of him while company clerk at Bladensburg, he played a game of "seven up" with a brother officer.

Then there was Viall, of Company F—a lively, cheerful soldier from the west—who was killed late in the afternoon. The circumstances of this event were especially painful. The command, taking a favorable opportunity during a short lull in the action, were watering their horses "by company." A confederate battery, located on a distant eminence, was firing at intervals at the group collected near the brook, but up to this time had injured no one. When Company F went down, owing to the small compass of the pond, the first two or three sets of fours allowed their animals to drink, and then rode off to one side and fell into ranks. Viall, who was always a butt for the wags of the Company, and who invariably took their jokes good humoredly, was standing a short distance apart from the rest, allowing his horse to graze. Just then a puff of smoke from the confederate battery showed that something might be expected presently from that quarter. The shot fell short, struck the ground, and ricochetted high into the air, being plainly visible in its flight. Some of the men, as if by intuition, called to Viall to "look out." Poor Viall, apparently supposing it was the usual joke, raised his laughing face. At that instant the cruel shot fell, striking him between the eyes and carrying off the upper part of his head.

From the ranks I missed the stalwart form of our Scotch first sergeant, Wallace, who had disappeared in the charge of the morning. Sergeant Welsh, my friend at dismounted camp, was gone. Paddy Miller, the good-natured brave boy that came to us from the Twenty--

eighth Pennsylvania Infantry, had plunged single-handed into the midst of a confederate regiment, and was missing. What a command a thousand just such men would have made! Tractable, tenderhearted, sanguine, whose will rose with each new demand made upon his patriotism and courage, he was a very hero under all circumstances. Our quiet Swiss comrade had fallen, a bullet through his heart, making a cruel though not fatal wound. He was fortunate enough to escape capture.

The command bivouacked for the night near the ford, and returned to its camp near Catlett's Station on the next day. On the 13th, late in the afternoon, we were again in the saddle, and moving, as near as I could determine, in a northwesterly direction. A long night march ensued—one of those peculiarly spasmodic movements, "forward and halt, forward and halt," which satisfies the experienced soldier that he is either in the wake of a train of wagons or a battery of artillery, but most likely the former. The halts are just long enough to permit one to become sound asleep where one drops down in one's tracks, and the "forwards" are just long enough to half waken one. Between them they make up the most miserable of campaign experiences.

By and by there was a longer stoppage than usual, perhaps two hours in duration. Then the bugle roused the tired men, and the regiment moved rapidly forward. The road was in a terrible condition, having been cut up by wagons and artillery until it had now become almost impassable. We soon passed a battery standing in the road. One of the guns had upset and rolled down the hill, and the men were all gathered around trying to get it into place again. The poor fellows looked weary, covered from head to foot with mud, but they worked away quite cheerfully, occasionally breaking out with a song. I thanked my stars, as we rode by, that I did not belong to the artillery service.

All night long the regiment continued on its weary march. As the gray dawn came it revealed the outlines of the Bull Run mountains on the left hand, and we soon found ourselves in the vicinity of Thoroughfare Gap, through which, early in the forenoon, one of our battalions was sent to reconnoitre and picket.

Our company was designated as the skirmishing party, and, with carbines loaded and carried at an "advance," we trotted off to the front quite gaily. I shall not soon forget the feeling of awe, mingled with an undefinable dread, that came over me in spite of myself as we rode through the great portals of this wonderful gap. From the open country

401

we passed into the midst of a wild, rocky chasm, the sides of which were almost perpendicular to a great height. In a stream of clear water that meandered among the huge boulders both men and horses halted to quench their thirst and fill canteens. As I looked up those vast precipices, shaggy with dense forests, and reflected how easily our band of twenty or thirty men, separated by a mile or more from our people, might be drawn into an ambuscade and hopelessly cut off from all succor, I found my courage on the wane. This reflection, however, was a somewhat disjointed one, for, with the rattling of sabres, the sharp clatter of horses' hoofs over the stony road, and the severe jolting to which one is subjected while riding at the trot in a column, kept my mind in such a state of desperate distraction that unity of thought was utterly impossible.

The deep silence that pervaded our ranks showed that this feeling of awe and dread were common enough among the men. But few words were spoken, and these were usually of the grumbling, extorted sort, as when one trooper rode upon the heels of his front-rank man, and had a curse hurled at him for his stupidity, or when his horse made a desperate clutch with his teeth at the nose bag or forage sack, with their precious freight of oats or corn, and from which he refused to part until the piece clamped between his strong jaws came out.

finally, on passing some old buildings—a mill if I remember aright—the extreme advance guard, thrown forward some two hundred yards from us, after passing around a bend in the road, suddenly halted, and one of their number galloped back to the company. He reported that a small number of men were clustered about a cabin on the hillside about half a mile beyond them, whom he supposed were confederates. The advance was continued; when passing this slight curb in the road we were brought into full view of the opening of the gap, the chasm widening into a pretty valley. The cabin and the soldiers were plainly visible, the latter apparently trying to shelter themselves from something. To our astonishment and relief these were men of our own Company D, who had been sent out long before us, and whose presence there, by some mismanagement, had not been reported. By a fortunate recognition, however, we were saved from committing one of the common blunders of this war—that of firing on our own men.

On the western side of the Bull Run range the gap debouches into two small valleys, one to the right and the other to the left of a hill from three to five hundred feet in height. Through one of these valleys the railroad winds its way toward Salem or White plains, if I am not mistaken. A common road extends through the other towards the southwest. The D Company men, after a short consultation, advanced on these roads, a line of skirmishers stretching across the bifurcating hill connecting the two parties. Owing to the continual divergence of these highways the spaces between the files of skirmishers became wider at every step, until the men were no longer able to properly cooperate. Company F supported the advance, a part following on each road.

Suddenly the report of a rifle startled the sleepy troops, and two men, in citizen's dress, mounted on remarkably fast horses, appeared dashing up the hill between the skirmishers and their support in rear. These fellows had evidently been concealed in the woods or tall corn as our men passed by in the first instance. They galloped after one of our soldiers, who, finding himself thus cut off from the reserves, made an effort to escape by the Salem road towards the west. In order to reach this road he was obliged to veer his course to the right down a steep hill—a spot that perhaps rivaled the "Hundred steps" of Israel Putnam. A stone fence about four feet high skirted the edge of the field bordering on this road, which here was cut into the side of the hill, making a clear fall of perhaps fifteen feet from the top of the wall to the ground below. This was a desperate leap for horse and rider, but there was no hesitation on the part of either. The confederates shouted a halt, and then fired a second shot just as the pursued was high in the air over the road. The rider dropped lifeless upon the hard pike, having been instantly killed by the bullet. The two men halted an instant to look at the quivering body, and then galloped off towards Salem.

Poor Owen! Six years afterwards, upon the occasion of decorating the graves in the quiet cemetery at Arlington, I found his last resting place, and with a mournful pride placed upon the spot a wreath of blood-red roses. On the plain white wooden headboard, painted in black letters, appeared this inscription:

A. 256. Removed August 10, 1866, from S.C. Stone's farm, near Thoroughfare Gap, N.B. Owens, private Sixth United States Cavalry. Died June 14, 1863.[1]

The killing of Owens under these circumstances greatly exasperated

---

[1]   N.B. Owen's grave may yet be visited. The wooden headboard has been replaced by a stone marker.

our men. From some other people living in the vicinity we learned that the confederates were the sons of an old farmer, whose house was located on top of the hill on which the occurrence took place. A detail of a dozen men, myself among the number, was sent up with the hope of capturing them if they should happen to be present, Lieutenant Balder conjecturing that in the meantime they might have recently returned and been concealed about the premises. We dismounted, quietly deployed through some tall corn growing in an adjoining field, and surrounded the dwelling and out houses, but the search proved fruitless. An old man and some females were the occupants, who denied all knowledge of the affair or the parties concerned, and were not disposed to be communicative on any subject.

By the roadside just beyond the place where Owens fell stood a farm house, in which resided a good looking widow lady, though her hair was of that bright red color seldom commended by the poets. Some of our men were foolish enough to charge her with complicity in the affair, but beyond seeing the occurrence, she declared her innocence, asserting, however, incidentally, her entire sympathy with the cause of the Southern Confederacy.

Some time later in the day Kettleberger, who, in company with Manness, occupied a post on the side of the mountain south of the railroad, observed two suspicious looking persons lurking in the woods in his front three or four hundred yards distant, and fired upon them. They hastily retreated. There is little doubt that these were the parties that had killed Owens, perhaps in search of an opportunity to assassinate another "Yankee."

The command remained at Thoroughfare Gap two days, on picket duty. The wild, picturesque scenery of this region reminded me of other wild, picturesque sceneries in Pennsylvania, and, by half closing my eyes, I could almost imagine myself back among the old surroundings of the days of my boyhood. Abundance of food both for man and beast could be produced with little trouble, and added to our enjoyments. Somehow or other, however, during the whole time we remained, I could feel an indescribable dread constantly creeping over me of a sudden attack and defeat—a sense of loneliness and impending disaster.

On the afternoon of the second day I was posted alone on an eminence that commanded quite an extended view toward the west. At sunset, while contemplating the dying glories of the day, my attention was attracted towards a party of horsemen riding up the slope of a hill beyond me, perhaps half a mile distant. Upon reaching the crest they halted, and seemed to regard me with some curiosity.

Just then two young ladies came over to me from a house close by, and took a look at the cavaliers. They reported them to be Mosby and some of his followers. In ten minutes or so the confederates slowly rode down the hill out of sight, and appeared no more. It may be truthfully inferred that I was watchful during the remaining portion of my time on duty.

Late that evening the pickets were called in, and we returned through the gap and marched to the vicinity of Manassas Junction, reaching our destination, after a weary night march, at early dawn. We found the whole army concentrating along the east side of the mountains, and moving in a northerly direction. The command halted on the banks of Bull Run, remaining there some thirty-six hours, the men in the meantime replenishing their cadaverous haversacks and forage sacks, thoroughly cleansing themselves and horses of the grimy dust by plunging into the stream, and making everything ready for the rough days we now foresaw were soon to dawn upon the Army of the Potomac.

Sergeant Iverson, the "cook's police," who was with the trains, reported meeting with Center the day before our arrival, riding about among the wagons. Being unaware of the latter's desertion, he greeted him cordially, but to Iverson's astonishment, Center refused to be recognized, put spurs to his horse, and galloped away. It was supposed he was acting the part of a spy, though I am under the impression that the case was really one of mistaken identity on the part of Iverson.

Toward Gettysburg—Untimely Capture

On the 17th of June we were again in the saddle and moving towards the Blue Ridge mountains, marching slowly during the day, and halting for the night a short distance east of Aldie. The next morning the advance was resumed, and continued some miles beyond the village. Beginning at this place, and extending perhaps two miles, torn down fences, scattered equipment, dead horses, shattered trees, and new made graves testified that a sharp skirmish must have taken place quite recently, although we had not heard of its occurrence. It subsequently transpired that the First Massachusetts Cavalry and several other mounted regiments had driven the enemy from this position toward the west a day or two before our arrival.

During our advance a small party of confederate pickets were encountered on the road occupying a commanding eminence, who, however, retired without firing a gun, keeping us under their eyes in the meantime. About one and a half miles on they were joined by some thirty more, and posted themselves along the edge of a strip of timber skirting the road on the left hand side. No disposition to attack them was manifested by our officers. We halted perhaps fifteen or twenty minutes, and then moved off on another road leading toward the south, leaving a picket to watch the movements of the enemy. After proceeding about a mile on this road the command halted for several hours.

About one or two o'clock in the afternoon the bugle sounded "to horse," and the movement southward was continued at a slow pace. We had proceeded but a short distance when we heard the reports of small arms in our rear, which sent an uneasy thrill through my nerves, but our officers did not seem to notice the shot.

My apprehension was that the confederate pickets, emboldened by our movement from the hill, were advancing to drive off ours and retake possession of it; but this illusion was soon dispelled by the sound of the

407

firing approaching much closer, and the increasing rapidity of the detonations.

The regiment marched at a walk down around some low hills and across a small stream, and then up a long ascent. As we crossed the creek the cooks, servants, "dog robbers," with their pack mules and led horses, who were marching in rear of the command, came dashing down after us in a panic. At this moment we were passing a farmhouse, on the portico of which stood several buxom, good-looking young ladies, who seemed to be much amused by the nondescript mass of men, horses, mules and camp kettles surging wildly behind us. At this point the commanding officer, seeming at last to realize that we were really seriously attacked, cast anxious glances back at the fugitives, and then the commands "trot" and "gallop" came in quick succession from the bugle, and in a moment we were dashing forward around a short bend in the creek and up the hill. Presently we had passed out of the timber, and were abreast of some open fields. A halt was ordered, fifty or sixty men promptly dismounted and upset several panels of fence, and through this gap the torrent of men and horses poured, swept down over a ridge, formed squadrons, troopers dismounted, dashed back to the ridge with carbines in hand, deployed, moved a hundred yards further to the front, and aligned themselves along a stone fence that commanded the approach from there, all in less time than it takes to write this description. A battery of horse artillery, of four guns, galloped into position, two pieces on one knoll near the road, and two on another knoll on the opposite side of the field.

When our line was within thirty or forty paces of the stone fence the fugitives came pell mell out of the woods up the road, with the confederates close upon their heels and using their revolvers. The latter party instantly deployed along our front and opened fire. We promptly responded with our carbines and battery, and in less than two minutes the enemy disappeared in the woods and returned no more. A few of them, who were dismounted, lingered behind some stone fences and a large brick house beyond our right flank, keeping up an irregular fire, but soon scampered off, not, however, until a shell from one of our pieces had been "plumped" into the house, and then exploded with disastrous effects upon the internal arrangements. I am not aware that any of the inmates were injured. But one of our men was injured in this affair, and he was shot in the back and badly wounded by one our sergeants for acting in a cowardly manner, at the beginning of the skirmish.

The command garrisoned the stone wall until dark. Just after the skirmish had taken place our attention was attracted by the assembling of a large force on the top of a hill perhaps a mile distant, who, in the first instance were supposed to be confederates; but to our great relief this conjecture was found to be untrue. The men belonged to Gregg's command.

About one-third of the regiment was detailed for picket duty during the night, while the remainder were sent back behind the ridge and ordered to "stand to horse," ready to support the pickets. About ten o'clock a tremendous rain storm came up, and deluged the field. Then we were marched up to the top of the ridge. The rain pelted into our faces, and the horses, in spite of all we could do, would wheel in ranks to protect their heads, leaving us in utter confusion. At last the storm ceased, and the lines were reformed. Although the order to "stand to horse" had not been countermanded, both men and officers gradually made themselves as comfortable as possible, the former lying down in front of their animals and holding the bridle reins.

To secure my horse properly—I had already felt my hold loosening while half asleep—the reins were looped around my wrist. Where I was lying the water was about four inches deep. At first my soaked clothes had chilled me, but this gave way gradually to a pleasant warmth, and I soon fell asleep. Presently I was aroused by a tremendous jerk upon my arm, and awoke to the consciousness that I had been unceremoniously moved several feet. The iron-gray had been frightened at something, and sprang backwards, landing his hind feet in rather close proximity to Christian Draker's head.

"Got for dam," shouted the querulous little Dutchman, jumping to his feet, "What for you do dat?"

Another nap was broken by the same unceremonious means, and brought forth a fresh volley of indignation from Draker. It was certainly very provoking to one's disposition to be thus disturbed. Afterwards, however, the iron-gray was more courteous, and I slept quite soundly until daylight.

The sky was clear and beautiful when the men were aroused by the reveille, and this serenity of the elements, with the floating aroma of boiling coffee, the crackling and flavor of the roasting pickled pork, soon made all of us forget the trial of the previous night.

Charlton, Evans, Old Blue, and myself, were around a pile of burning rails, on the cheerful coals of which were our tin-cups, half full of water for the coffee, while from sticks, on the sharp points of which large slices of meat hung and dropped great globules of grease into the flames, were poised with affectionate care by four right hands. Our stocks of provisions were running low; there was just coffee enough for a good strong cup apiece, which we sadly needed after our exposure and excitement—a state of affairs that any member of the army in those days will instantly and fully appreciate.

"Water boiling!" shouts Stewart!

The four right hands poising with affectionate care the four sticks and their precious burdens, cautiously laid them down upon the unburned ends of the rails. Then each individual went to his saddle-bags, and from the depths thereof brought forth other kinds of vats, containing the ground coffee and sugar. A spoonful of sugar was then put into each cup, and the cadaverous bags of coffee afterward emptied of their contents. With lively satisfaction we watched the simmering water and its precious film of dark brown, as the little bubbles rose and broke around the edges of the little pails.

Just then a commotion among the horses, which were diving into their nosebags for their oats, attracted our attention. A lively contest was going on between Draker's querulous little sorrel and another horse for the possession of the same bag, which had slipped off one of their long heads. Draker, who was behind us at another fire, superintending his own breakfast, sprang to the relief of the sorrel. Alas for human hopes! His foot struck one of the projecting ends of the rails of our fire, and in an instant our four cups, with their precious contents, were upside down in the red coals!

The blank dismay that settled upon our faces may be imagined, but not described. Then came a burst of expletives, which were mercilessly hurled at the head of the querulous little Dutchman, but he heeded them not—the sorrel, the apple of his Teutonic eye, was suffering a defeat, and our lesser misfortunes were invisible. However, there was no help for the matter, and we were obliged to content ourselves with cold water.

About nine o'clock the bugles sounded "boots and saddles," and half an hour later the regiment was again on the road. The general direction of our movement was towards the west. We had proceeded but a little distance when the sound of cannonades broke upon our ears, the guns seeming to be six or seven miles away. The shots were at rather long, irregular intervals, and seemed to recede, as though but little resistance was being made by the enemy. Presently we reached the crest of a high hill, from which there was quite an extended view of the surrounding country. To our surprise there appeared, on the top of another hill one-fourth of a mile distant, a solitary confederate picket, mounted on a tall bay horse, who seemed to be watching our movement. The horse was quietly plucking the grass, with the reins hanging loosely on its neck, as though its rider apprehended no danger.

The road wound down around the hill to a small stream, and across this and up the side of the opposite hill on which this picket was established. The command moved very slowly at this point, while a small part trotted ahead, crossed the creek, deployed, and moved rapidly towards the picket. Owing to the position he occupied these men could not be seen by him, and he still sat there in blissful ignorance of the ugly surprise in store for him. As the line approached him the interest of the regiment in the denouement became painfully intense. I can see the picture yet—the man in gray, with bowed head, the browsing horse, the scattered men in blue with poised carbines closing in upon him.

Will they kill him? Will they capture him? Men shot down in the heat of battle are but little noticed, and awaken scarcely a pang of pity. The deliberate attack on an unconscious human being, however, is quite another thing. Half the men hope he may escape.

Suddenly his faithful steed throws up his head with a snort, looking in wild dismay upon the swarming troopers an instant, and then, as if by instinct, dashes madly to the rear. A dozen carbines crack, but their shots are harmless. Horse and rider disappear in the thick woods that skirt the field on the opposite side. Then I hear sighs of relief all around me.

The regiment moved rapidly down the hill, crossed the creek, and broke into a sharp trot up the ascent of the road that here ran through a dense forest. When about half way up a carbine was accidentally discharged in the ranks by Corporal Slatter, the bullet passing through his right foot, inflicting a severe wound, and the half-fainting man rode out to one side and was placed in charge of the surgeon. About half a mile beyond this a halt was sounded and the regiment was counter-marched back to the creek. Another road, leading almost due north, was found, and upon this new route the advance continued at a rapid gait. The country became more open as we proceeded, the low, undulating hills, dotted with pleasant-looking dwellings forming a pleasing landscape picture. Then came another halt for a few minutes. During the balance of the day, until four o'clock in the afternoon, our progress was quite slow, the stoppings occurring every few steps.

All this time a desultory cannonading had been kept up in the distance, but we could not see the contesting forces. We had followed the sound of conflict, which, like a will-o-the-wisp, seemed to keep just so far away—and I suppose in our heart of hearts we hoped the will-o-the-wisp characteristic might be indefinitely prolonged. As the day wore on, however, we came to tangible evidences of skirmishes—torn down fences, shattered trees, dead horses and dead men, and occasionally captured guns and caissons. Then we begun to smell traces of sulphur in the air, and a curious haze was visible in the little valleys and among the trees.

By and by the regiment took up the trot, and then the gallop, continuing the latter gait for two or three miles, when, on emerging from a narrow valley through which the road led to the top of quite a level plateau we suddenly found ourselves face to face with the confederates, and within one or two miles of Upperville, on exactly the same field on which the struggle of the year before had occurred.

The picture then presented was an interesting one. Fully six thousand confederates and several batteries of light artillery were drawn up to resist the advance of our troops. Their line was crescent shaped with the convex front toward us, their left resting near the base of the Blue Ridge, some two miles distant, and sweeping around towards the south, crossing the road to Upperville at right angles their extreme right located in some timber two hundred yards distant from the highway turning out to a line of flankers beyond this point. Directly in front of the enemy's line was our own, the formation being similar to theirs, excepting that ours was a concave line that accommodated itself to the convex formation in its front. Skirmishers met skirmishers, company met company, regiment met regiment, battery met battery, at all points along this line of two miles. The distance between the opposing bodies varied from two hundred to five hundred yards, according to the formation of the intervening ground. Thus the hostile battalions of gray and blue were ranged as we came upon the field, with banners and guidons waving, bugles sounding and artillery roaring a prelude to closer and hotter work.

As our regiment rode upon the field it formed into column of squadrons on the right of the road and about one hundred yards distant, and halted for orders. Occupying the road to our left and front there was another mounted regiment, also in column, with sabres drawn and ready to charge. At its head there rode an officer said by some one to have

412

been General Kilpatrick. Directly in its front, perhaps two hundred yards distant, drawn up across the road, was a body of mounted confederates, some sixty in number.

The first squadron of the federal regiment moved to the front and dashed down upon the enemy with loud cheers. The latter, without any effort at resistance, immediately broke up and fled beyond the woods, the pursued and pursuers disappearing behind the curtain of trees.

Before coming on the field we had been ordered by Major Starr not to cheer under any circumstances; to preserve perfect quiet, that the bugle notes and commands might be properly understood. This positive order prevented us from any elated shouting over the result of this effort of our volunteer comrades, and saved us, as a consequence, from a corresponding degree of humiliation when, a moment later, our men were hurled back from the forest by the enemy, who, in a counter-- charge, drove them clear up against the balance of the regiment supporting them. The confederates appeared to number about one hundred men.

The regiment now assumed the offensive, sweeping down the road and brushing the few confederates from sight behind the same curtain of trees. It would have been hell had the similarity between the charge of the first squadron and the charge of the regiment ended here; but it did not. A moment after their disappearance there arose a tremendous yell, and back came the federal column in great disorder, while jammed in upon their rear were several hundred confederates, who seemed to be having matters entirely their own way. The curious herd of blue and gray swarmed down the road past us to our rear for at least two hundred yards, when the confederates extricated themselves and rode leisurely back towards Upperville.

During all this time there was presented the singular spectacle of the Sixth United States Cavalry remaining in its position on the right of the road, looking upon the scene in much the character of a disinterested body without a sword drawn. This time the men were anxious, and would gladly have pushed into the fight, especially when the confederates, in their mad chase after the federals, had so completely exposed themselves to an attack upon their left flank and rear, and could, by a determined effort, have nearly all been cut off from their main forces and captured; but the military eye of the commanding officer either did not see or could not comprehend the demands of the situation, and thus fixed upon the fair escutcheon of the regiment the foulest, blackest of stains, that of refusing to go to the rescue of a kindred organization when so sorely pressed by a merciless foe.

Before reaching the woods the confederates halted, and presently formed in column on the left of the road, evidently determined to hold their position. At this juncture General Pleasanton rode up to Major Starr, with whom he held a short consultation, gesticulating wildly all the while. It was said that he was denouncing the major for disobedience of orders—that the latter, when the enemy had exhausted their strength upon the advance of our troops, was to have attacked vigorously.

As soon as General Pleasanton rode away our regiment wheeled by fours to the left and marched, with drawn sabres, across to the opposite side of the road—a movement that brought up immediately in front of the confederates, who were perhaps one hundred and fifty yards distant. I suppose the strength of the two bodies were nearly equal, but the formation of the enemy gave them an advantage—their front was shorter but their column much deeper than ours. Between us there was a partially dismantled fence, and just beyond it a narrow strip of marshy grass. It is to be noted, also, that these obstacles were much nearer to us than the confederates. I am this particular, because these points are needed to fully explain the results that followed our change of position.

Our squadrons were aligned with a faultless nicety; the officers took their places; the bugle sounded, in quick succession, certain clear, shrill notes.

"Forward—trot—gallop—charge!"

In the same regular succession these calls are obeyed. The sabres flash above the heads of the men. In an instant the troopers have forgotten that they are regulars, and the command of the morning is lost in the thrill of excitement. Then arose one long, loud, spontaneous cheer.

The enemy displayed no want of spirit on this occasion. Before we were fairly under way they advanced boldly to meet us. The long hard ride of the last hour had wearied our steeds; the halfdismantled fence and the strip of marshy ground checked our momentum. A moment later I became conscious that the enemy's column had struck us, and had completely carried off the whole left of our shallow formation, while the right, in which I was riding, exhausted itself against nothing, like a shot sent into space. Then I found myself immediately in front of the timber, and just inside the first line of trees there stood another confederate regiment, with drawn sabres. I was within twenty paces of these men before I could check my horse. Then I drew my revolver and fired two shots at them, when they began advancing, and it occurred to me that I had better leave that locality.

I will tell the reader just here, with a feeling of perhaps commendable pride, that I had fully resolved to distinguish myself in this action and, if possible, gain honorable mention. I will tell him, further, that in this there was not the least desire or ambition to "rise from the ranks," as it is called—to secure a commission; all that was wanted was a good word to send home to father and friends. To my mind the ranks were the fittest place for me. I will tell him, further, that this effort to secure recognition utterly failed, for the reason, I suppose, that our officers were too busily engaged at that particular juncture to notice a common soldier with any degree of particularity, and, what is more likely the true state of the case, I did no service worthy of such special mention, as distinguished from my comrades. Their gallant conduct on this occasion of peculiar misfortunes left little room for any notice of especial bravery by our soldiers.

I am not exactly certain how I got away; I only know that I caught sight of a cloud of yelling gray wolves swarming out of the woods; that I found myself in a crowd of eight or ten other men, who all leaped through a narrow break in the fence at once, and that fully one-half of these were confederates; that there was a sort of promiscuous hammering going on, enlivened by expressions of billingsgate that reminded me of a common street fight rather than a dignified battle; that there was one smiling red-headed confederate, who was trying to hit Bemis on the head, but that party threw up his hands and carbine and received the strokes on his arms; that Sergeant Croy, himself red-headed, struck the smiling red-headed confederate across his benignant face, and dismounted him; that by and by we got clear of the devils and assembled our broken battalions on one side of the open field, while the confederates quietly marched back and reformed on the opposite side.

Our men fell into line without regard to companies, and charged again, but were easily repulsed, making no impression whatever upon the solid mass of men in their front. A third time they rallied, and saucily formed within one hundred yards of the column of confederates, who, even with their prestige of success, did not seem disposed to attack us.

The two bodies of men remained glaring upon each other for a few moments, reminding one of the old saying, "one is afraid and the other dare not." It looked odd to me to see the hostile banners so close to each other, and upheld by armed men, and yet no struggle in progress. Theirs was a plain battle flag, of common bunting—the Southern Cross. Ours was of silk, dark blue field, eagle and shield, and bordered with a long golden fringe.

At this critical juncture we were surprised and pleased to see fresh regiments of our brigade sweep proudly upon the field and deploy into column of squadrons in our rear, with flashing sabres. We were not going to give this fight up yet. A battery of light artillery galloped up to one side, and instantly unlimbered. Our band trotted up to the right of our regiment, and struck up the tune of "Yankee Doodle"—though it seemed to me that was an odd jumble of notes.

Some one called out:

"Dismount—prepare to fight on foot!"

There was a sudden emptying of saddles, and springing into line in front of the horses. An instant later there was a cracking of carbines, emphasized with the thunder of our cannons, the shots throwing up great clods of dirt in our immediate front. The enemy immediately retired, keeping in very good order, finally disappearing beyond the woods. As by this time our troops had driven the enemy's left wing, and gained the road beyond Upperville, these men, who were known as the Jeff Davis Legion, were obliged to make a detour toward the south in order to reach their lines.

When the confederates began to retire we deployed skirmishers and pressed forward after them. I was on the extreme left of the line, the prolongation of which threw me away off towards a house and outbuildings. Perhaps one-fourth of the men went up the main road. Our advance was quite rapid until we reached a stone fence, which was a desirable position to hold in case of another attempted advance by the enemy. When our men had secured this fence, I found myself near a large stone spring-house, in which a slight noise attracted my attention.

"Here," thought I, "is a chance to distinguish myself. Perhaps I may be able to capture a prisoner in this building."

With heavy tread, and at the same time rattling my sabre upon the stone wall, so that the sound might have a moral effect upon the inmates, I strode up to the door.

"Who's in here?" I called out, with an awful voice.

For a moment there was a dead silence and then a very weak, scared voice replied: "It's us."

"Open this door, or it may be worse for you."

416

The door opened and out stepped three females—an old lady, one apparently her daughter, and the other a mere child of perhaps ten years. I confess feeling somewhat ashamed at this ludicrous denouement to my second effort at distinguishing myself. I could hardly parade these as prisoners.

"Oh, we are frightened to death," exclaimed the oldest young lady.

"Don't be afraid, ma'am," said I; "We are only having a Fourth-of--July celebration out here."

Where the laugh is to be expected in this heavy joke is not exactly clear to my mind; but perhaps some benefit resulted from it, as my captives seemed to be reassured, and began quite a lively conversation. The oldest young lady was loud in her praises of the gallantry of the southern troops; but on my mentioning that they had rapidly retired from the field she grew somewhat sullen, and said no more.

The shrill notes of our bugle, sounding the recall for the skirmishers, broke upon our ears, and the tired men began to scamper as fast as possible back to the led horses. By this time the entire brigade had assembled upon the field, and our spirits rose as our eyes fell upon the serried ranks and flashing sabres.

A survey of the field at this moment was worth ten years of one's life. The entire line of the enemy was in full retreat towards Ashby's Gap, and close upon them followed the men in blue, the skirmishers keeping up a spiteful fire upon each other, and sending up cheers of victory and defiance.

The sun hung low in the west; the solemn mountains stood out in bold relief against the clear sky; the atmosphere was hazy with the smoke of guns. The dull gray masses sluggishly disappeared in the deepening shadows, like some huge, undefined, supernatural thing of evil. Ever and anon came back the roar of some adventurous group, which had dashed up close to the enemy's lines, and clung to it with a vengeful pertinacity, hurling its deadly hail upon the now harmless and defeated foe.

The commands pushed on through Upperville and westward towards the gap in the mountains. The people of the village peered out from behind window shutters and half-opened doors, like frightened children, watching the cavalrymen as they clattered carelessly down the road. As usual Evans and Old Blue were foraging among the houses for edibles. The former afterward told me about how he besieged a cellar, and captured two women and a flock of geese which had then sought refuge

417

from the wily Yankees.

The road, at a point perhaps a mile west of Upperville, was the scene of a savage hand-to-hand fight between our advance guard and the enemy's rear, which was here brought to bay. After a brief struggle the latter retired into the mountains, and our soldiers took up a position to the right of the road, where they were supported by a battery of horse artillery.

The Sixth Cavalry, after advancing within a few hundred yards of the confederate line, turned into the fields on the left of the road, deployed into column of squadrons, threw out skirmishers, and pushed close up to the crest of a hill or outlying spur of the mountains and halted. A confederate battery was here posted, masked by dense bushes, but this was ominously silent for the time. In a few moments the command was ordered to retire from this position, and, wheeling by fours to the rear, started at a brisk trot down the hill and across the road to the right, where it took post to support a battery. This movement was barely commenced when the confederates, no doubt chagrined at their failure to entrap us, opened with a savage cannonade from the concealed battery, the plunging shot tearing up great clouds of earth all about us, but, fortunately, doing no harm.

There is probably no greater ordeal through which soldiers are obliged to pass than in this matter of trotting down a steep hill with their backs to the foe, with a vicious battery pounding away after them. There was some confusion on this occasion, but the men managed to keep their places tolerably well. The fact that we were retiring under fire was very humiliating because it gave us the appearance of a defeated regiment in the eyes of our brethren-in-arms on other portions of the field; and some newspaper correspondent made a special effort, in a letter describing the affair, to ridicule us mercilessly as "running regulars."

Away off up in the gap, distant perhaps two miles, the confederates had a large gun, said to be a twenty-pounder that they had taken from Harper's Ferry. This piece they commenced to use with great deliberation and precision upon our columns. Our three-inch rifles did their best to silence the monster, but in vain, owing to the great elevation. With terrible regularity the huge shells burst in the air about our devoted heads, the pieces shrieking viciously in their flight.

"Limber up!"

A slight shudder ran over me as I heard these ominous words. Our favorite battery had for once in its experience been overmatched. The men sullenly went about their work, and in a few moments the pieces were on their way to the rear, while the supporting column filed slowly after them over the rough ground. In this instance the discipline of the men showed to a wonderful advantage.

A curious scene presented itself as our faces were turned toward the rear. The broad pike towards Upperville was literally packed for miles with mounted men, one half of whom were advancing and the other half retiring. Of course a dead-lock was the result, and the entire force was threatened with inextricable confusion.

The infernal gun in the gap kept up its monotonous roaring. The shells seemed to have been filled with bullets, for there were whistling noises in the air after each explosion in addition to the peculiar screams of jagged pieces. When at last we had reached the pike, and the huge mass of men were in motion toward the rear, its fire was directed upon the retreating column. The road was fringed with trees on each side, and when a shell would burst over our devoted heads there would be a shower of leaves and limbs on both flanks. In all these terrible moments there were brief intervals of relief after each explosion, if one found himself still unhurt, that must be experienced to be appreciated by the soldier. I thought we were never to get beyond the reach of the devil. From its elevated position it was enabled to send its missiles some four miles, while the long straight turnpike gave the gunners the range with wonderful precision.

The command bivouacked at Upperville for the night. Our company was sent off to picket the roads some two miles southeast of the village where we had a very pleasant time.

The men were pretty thoroughly disgusted with the affair of the 19th of June. Major Starr, to whose want of judgment and feeble efforts on this occasion the defeats were properly chargeable, took an early opportunity to deliver the regiment a lecture, in the presence of the Second Cavalry, in which he charged the Sixth with cowardice during the first part of the conflict. Of course, this was resented, and, in a less-disciplined body of men, might have led to difficulties. The murmurs were not loud, but deep, and the fervent longing for the return to the command of Captain Sanders, or Major Gregg, of the old gallant days of 1862, found expression on the march, and picket, and around the bivouac fires, where no commissioned officer was present to check their confidential utterances, and the privacy which was duly protected by the freemasonry of the common soldier.

419

The government made one of its characteristic mistakes in assigning Major Starr to the command of a cavalry regiment in time of war. He was too old for such service, wanting in the dash and decision so necessary as a trait in one who has the control of such an organization during such a period. As an officer of infantry, or to take charge of a post which was expected to be besieged, and which it was desirous should be defended to the last extremity, I think he was just the man. With Starr at Harper's Ferry in September, 1862, we would have been ahead at least eleven thousand men. With its usual appreciation of the eternal fitness of things, however, the administration had located him just where he almost paralyzed the efforts of three hundred soldiers.

The resonances of Starr in the ways and means of inflicting degrading punishments upon the members of the command seemed to be unlimited as to number and variety. His favorite method, however, was to place the culprit astride a fence, tie his feet together below, his hands behind his back, and surmount his head with a nose-bag. This original feature, which an anxious and appreciating command was desirous of perpetuating for the plaudits of coming generations, won for Starr the appellation of "Old Nosebag."

There was one feature in Starr's administration, however, that in a measure compensated the men for their suffering and humiliation. This was the poorly concealed terror and hate with which he was regarded by the subordinate commissioned officers of the regiment. Cram, who was now the senior captain present, especially seemed to be an object of Starr's terrific disciplinarian efforts; and his manifest trepidation whenever the cold blue eyes of his senior were turned upon him was inexpressibly gratifying to those who had been subject to Cram's caprices at the camp near Hooker's headquarters some months previous.

The regiment returned to Aldie on the evening of the 20th, and halted on the scene of the struggle of the Massachusetts and Pennsylvania cavalrymen. An advance by the enemy from the west seemed to be expected, as a section of artillery was unlimbered and trained down the road towards Upperville, and this we were obliged to support, "standing to horse" with tightened girths during the night.

The next day we left Aldie by the Leesburg road. This thoroughfare was jammed with infantry, cavalry, artillery, and wagons, and our progress was of that peculiar irregularity and monotony which every soldier will recognize as madly demoralizing. Late in the evening we passed what was pointed out as the Monroe homestead, but I was unable to examine the place.[1]

About midnight the command reached Leesburg. A dead silence reigned among the villagers as we rode through, and by an intuition we had long since learned to trust we knew they were intensely hostile to federal soldiers.

A mile beyond the place the regiment filed off the road into a meadow and halted, the men dismounted from their weary steeds, tethered them to all sorts of substantial things, and threw themselves upon the ground to rest. The gray dawn of the following morning revealed a now familiar but picturesque scene. Scattered over the surface of the earth, in the irregular manner that reminds one of the dead on the field of battle, lay the sleeping soldiers. Here and there a loose horse picks his steps carefully among them, and crops the trampled green grass. Some of the animals are stretched out flat on their sides, as lifeless looking as their riders. Here and there a man reposes with his head on the neck of his prostrate steed as on a pillow. Amid all this apparent confusion,however, there is instinctively a sort of order preserved, which is instantaneously developed when the bugle sounds the reveille.

Our march was resumed late in the forenoon, and in a short time the command had reached the south bank of the Potomac river. Here we found a pontoon bridge, across which the army was hurriedly crossing. The regiment halted perhaps an hour, to await its opportunity to cross.

The First Pennsylvania Cavalry were also here, and I met some of my old schoolmates, Barry among them, with whom I spent a happy resume of our common boyhood. They were gallant fellows, whose devotion to their government was of that stable character which makes an army absolutely invincible. With a cheerful farewell, as their command received orders to march, they galloped away to rejoin it.

About two months and a half after this Barry was shot and killed while on picket duty near Warrenton, Virginia, by members of that partisan organization known during the war as guerrillas. Thus died a faithful soldier.

The Sixth Cavalry crossed later in the evening, and advanced perhaps a mile from the river, and bivouacked for the night. The horses were now unsaddled and thoroughly groomed for the first time in many days, to their great and apparent comfort, to which they gave expression by rolling half a dozen times within an hour. Then came the feeding, and

---

[1] The Monroe homestead, in Loudon County, Virginia, is currently privately owned but it is opened to visitors from time to time.

421

such rearing, and squealing, and snapping followed, making a very lively scene for a short time.

The next day our march was resumed towards the Monocacy. We were still in rear of wagon trains, and the day's progress was slow and uncertain, and grimly monotonous. The movement was continued until far into the night. Draker, the querulous little Dutchman, who rode in the ranks just in front of me, was in an unusually savage mood, and vented his rage upon the flanks of the little sorrel, while the animal executed a war dance in many different directions at once, to the great inconvenience of his fellow-horses. Among others I expostulated with Draker, and to this he responded by drawing his sabre and making a lunge in my immediate direction. The instinct of self-preservation is, naturally, pretty sharp in me, and upon the impulse of the moment, fearing he might drive the blade into my eye, I involuntarily swung my carbine in a sort of overhand manner, the blow falling upon the wrist of his bridle-arm. Just at this juncture Lieutenant Balder, hearing the disturbance, rode up, and seeing Draker with the sabre drawn, struck him across the back with the flat of his sword. The poor old fellow, mortified by the unexpected results of his frantic display, subsided from further exhibitions for that night.

The command bivouacked near the Sugar Loaf mountain, close to the scene of its skirmish the year before.

Early in the morning the advance was continued towards Frederick City, by a long detour, however, to the south and west of that place. A large number of men belonging to the command had procured liquor, which they had instinctively discovered among the farm houses—Draker, Old Blue, Charleston, Leonard, Kelsy, Brooks, and Powell, among the number—and for a time they kept up a great excitement in the columns. Charleston labored under a sort of hallucination that every citizen farmer we passed working in the field was a confederate picket, and wanted to "drive him in," bringing his loaded rifle to bear upon him. It required our best exertions to prevent the crazy fellow from firing on the object of his wrath.

Powell quarreled with Kelsey about the division of the contents of a canteen, and made threatening demonstrations upon the latter, who drew his revolver in defense. A short struggle followed, Powell seizing the pistol by the barrel and endeavoring to twist it from Kelsey's hand. In the melee it was accidentally discharged. A blanket, rolled up tightly and strapped upon the pommel of Powell's saddle, saved that individual

422

from an ugly wound in the hips, the ball lodging within the folds. The parties were separated by Sergeant Bucton, who disarmed Kelsey, dismounted him, tied his hands behind his back, and ordered him to follow on foot. Powell, the real aggressor, the brawny, meddlesome fellow who had stricken down Little McKeefery with the heavy curb bridle at Camp East of Capitol; who had knocked Chaney Miller, also a small man, senseless; whose brutal instincts made him an object of abhorrence generally, escaped, as usual, without punishment. After the excitement had died out, and we had proceeded perhaps half a mile, Powell quietly dropped out of ranks, rode to the rear of the column, and, drawing his sabre, made a savage attack on Kelsey. The latter managed to escape the blows by dodging, receiving several strokes upon his back, however, Lieutenant Balder rescued him from his perilous position, and the lucky Powell, without a word of censure, was ordered to his place in ranks.

By the time the command reached Frederick City, nearly all the drunken soldiers had fallen out of the column and disappeared. This demoralization was not confined to the Sixth Cavalry. Never, on any previous march, had I seen so many straggling, inebriated men. The fields by the roadside and the streets of the city were full of them. They swarmed in upon the houses of citizens like demonic locusts, and swung their deadly weapons about with a carelessness of manner that was appalling. In my estimation the number of men thus lost to the campaign was from 6,000 to 8,000.

At this time the locality of the confederate forces was unknown to the common soldiers of the army, and, as subsequent events proved, to perhaps every one else, except, perhaps, General Robert E. Lee. There were plenty of rumors, however, the most plausible of which—at least, the one most persistently indulged in—was that the enemy's columns were well on their way into Pennsylvania. Occasionally we managed to get a newspaper, but a perusal of the telegraphic dispatches from the seat of war only served to mystify one. If one-third of those accounts were correct, there must have been at least half a million confederates scattered over the one thousand square miles of which Hagerstown formed the center.

One thing seemed certain; blood had flown within the limits of the old commonwealth quite a distance west of the state line.

The prospect of a campaign in a free state roused the enthusiasm of the men to the highest pitch. They felt that were about to meet the Army of Northern Virginia on their own ground, instead of the ill-fated fields south of the Potomac. They felt, too, that something like a threatened invasion was a public necessity to reverse the northern people to a sense of their danger and duty, and oblige them to fill up the depleted ranks of the federal armies. It was believed that the disadvantages of the invasion would be of temporary character, while the defeat of Lee at a point so distant from his base, if properly supplemented by persistent fighting and a vigorous employment of our mounted men, might be rendered decisive and fatal to the confederacy. I use the words "defeat of Lee," for I do not think that one man out of a hundred in the Potomac Army dreamed of a different result. Each one seemed to think that a glorious opportunity was at hand to close triumphantly the weary war.

Day after day our scattered battalions poured along the roads converging upon Frederick City from the east and southeast, and through and beyond the town towards Pennsylvania. At the top of a range of mountains a short distance west of Frederick we met the German division of the Eleventh Corps. They were singing one of the songs of the fatherland, and keeping step to the music. As these sturdy notes swelled up from myriad of throats I felt my very blood thrill with delight.

From my observations of these few days I concluded that our infantry forces numbered about sixty thousand fighting men. The cavalry horses were pretty badly used up—perhaps not over eight thousand sabres could be relied upon for campaign service. The artillery I could not estimate with any degree of certainty, as the corps was much broken up and scattered among the trains. General Meade, in his testimony before the Committee on the Conduct of the War, thinks his army was about ninety thousand strong at this period. If he had subtracted six or eight thousand as stragglers, for which I see he makes no allowance, I think the figures would have been nearer the real number. Speaking of the cavalry, I cannot help recall the terrible trials of our poor horses during these historic days. For two months they had been under the saddle almost constantly, both night and day, marching and countermarching and picketing, occasionally for days without food, until in their ferocious hunger they bit at food, or clothing, or ate off each other's manes and tails. It was amusing though, perhaps, just a little melancholy to the unfortunate owner thereof, to see our animal snap vigorously at a haversack within their reach. No inducement seemed strong enough to separate those jaws, and generally the precious sack was rent in twain, and the contents scattered broadcast upon the dusty pike, before they opened.

I could not understand the conduct of the authorities during this campaign. After we had left the famished country south of the Potomac, and entered the well-stocked fields of Maryland, where every man had a right to expect the animals would be supplied with food, strict orders were issued to prevent foraging, and but very little grain or hay was allowed us. Most of the men, however—and I deem it should be recorded to their honor, even if the act was contrary to the Regulations—stole out at nights and secured something for their four-footed companions.

On the night of the 30th of June the regiment bivouacked near Mechanicstown, Maryland. After our customary evening duties were ended, Sergeant McMasters and I strolled out of camp in quest of pen, ink, and paper, to send a hastily written note home to friends and report our respective conditions. Our attention was attracted to a pretty little cottage perhaps a quarter of a mile from the field in which the command had bivouacked. Here we were warmly welcomed by the entire family, consisting of a man, wife, and three bright-eyed children. The oldest daughter gave us her copy-book there was no letter-paper in the house they said—and upon its leaves we transcribed our simple words. The Common Soldier, to place it upon record as a memento of that memorable epoch in his military life, copies the brief letter below:

Mechanicstown, Md., June 30, 1863
Dear Friend: As it has been some time since I wrote to you, owing to the active operations of the army, and as there has been a good deal of fighting among the cavalry, I thought proper to write and let you know that I am still alive and well, and in the good state of Maryland, only some seven miles from the Pennsylvania State line. I believe I last wrote from Catlett's Station, on the Orange and Alexandria railroad, in Virginia. Just after mailing that letter we were ordered to cross the Rappahannock river at Beverly Ford, where a fight was in progress, and went into action in a charge through a dense wood, on Jones' brigade of North Carolina cavalry, and tumbled head over heels into a ditch, while the enemy, who were just beyond a few paces, well protected by barricades of fence-rails, kept up a steady fire on our column from their revolvers. Our ranks returned much thinner than they had advanced, and the men were nonplussed at their hot reception. This engagement lasted all day, and perhaps it ended successfully for our forces. The command recrossed the river in the evening, and formed a new camp. In the afternoon of the next day we started again, and marched all night, reaching Thoroughfare Gap early in the morning. This gap is in the Bull Run range of mountains, and is a wild, gloomy place. We remained here two days, marching at dusk on the evening of

the second, travelling all night. At dawn the command halted at Manassas Junction. Stayed here one day and night, and then went to Aldie. From Aldie we advanced to Middleburg, where Pleasanton was fighting Stuart. Went into action in the afternoon at Upperville by charging across a swampy field upon a column of the enemy, which came out boldly to meet us with sabres flashing and battle-flags waving defiantly. After considerable effort the confederates were driven from the field. Remained at Upperville one night, and then returned to Aldie. At Aldie one night, and then away to the Potomac, crossing that stream two days later. With but few adventures we have reached our present locality, consuming ten days on the road from the river. So here we are, jolly as pigs, and every bit as dirty. I only got my shoes off one night in two weeks.

I am much pleased with the Maryland people. They have treated us with the greatest respect; the very air seems warm with kindness. The poor boys have so long been exposed to the hateful, spiteful glances of the Virginians that a little display of consideration almost sets them crazy.

The country here is splendid. The women are very handsome and well educated. The men seem to be very enterprising. The dwellings give evidence of good taste and neatness on the part of the occupants.

Well, good bye. I write this in the house of a very friendly family, who are entitled to my warmest thanks.

I hope we will go on to Pennsylvania. If I fall, I want to go down within the limits of the dear old Commonwealth.

During the 1st of July firing could be heard off toward the northwest, and word came that a battle was being fought at a point somewhere beyond Emmitsburg. Infantry passed camp at intervals during the day and until late at night, headed in the direction of the cannonading. On the morning of the 2nd the command resumed its march, and reached Emmitsburg in the afternoon. During the advance one of our new officers, whose name I do not recollect—a young, inexperienced fellow—accidentally discharged his revolver, and was promptly put under arrest by Major Starr. The great confusion depicted upon his countenance was a source of wonderful amusement to the rough men in the ranks.

While at Emmitsburg it was rumored that the enemy's cavalry pickets were interposed between us and the left wing of our army, holding a point called Union Bridge. From the precautions that seemed to be taken it was evident that we were in the presence of the enemy, and the exact situation of affairs was by no means clear to our minds. The cannonading in the northwest continued today, and at intervals rattling volleys of musketry broke upon our ears.

426

Early on the morning of the 3rd a detail of thirty picked men started off on an unknown mission—rumored to be for the purpose of opening communication with our forces by dislodging the confederate pickets at Union Bridge.

I was on duty this morning at Merritt's headquarters. This officer had just been assigned to the command of the brigade. He was a pleasant, handsome young fellow, wearing his rank with easy grace, and apparently possessing just the temperament for a cavalryman.

Towards noon the Sixth Cavalry received orders to assemble mounted for duty at headquarters, and a few moments later we were in motion towards the front. As the command filed out of the field into the road, I noticed, riding at the side of Major Starr, a strange man. He seemed to be a citizen, perhaps a farmer, coarsely dressed, and mounted on a common working horse. The man seemed to be somewhat excited, emphasizing his conversation by gestures with a rawhide which he held in his right hand. Starr looked as gloomy as usual, not in the least partaking of the stranger's animation.

Our route extended across a stream of water and towards the mountains. We had not proceeded more than a mile, perhaps, when two rifle shots startled us by their close proximity. These must have been from scouts, as they precipitately retired towards the mountains. The command halted a moment only, and then resumed its advance.

The regiment numbered at this time not over three hundred fighting men present for duty and was consolidated into three squadrons. About ten percent of the force had straggled off on a drunken spree near Frederick City, and had not yet reappeared.

It seemed that the farmer-like citizen riding beside our major was to be our guide during this expedition. It was said that he had come in from Fairfield, or Millerstown, in Adams County, Pennsylvania, distant six or seven miles, and reported that a confederate wagon train was at that village, foraging for flour and other provisions among the citizens. The force guarding this train was supposed to number one hundred men.

For some distance our route extended over a rather rough country. Two boys met us in the woods, who stated that the confederates had been along that road in the morning.

Presently the road descended into a valley, and just here we caught sight of a gray horseman dashing with the speed of the wind along a road on our left, which seemed to run parallel with the one upon which we were marching, and nearly a mile distant. He was headed towards

Fairfield, and was evidently an outrider of the enemy. He soon disappeared. On another road, away off on the side of the mountain south of us appeared a small squad of dismounted men, but whether these were soldiers or citizens we could not tell.

At this juncture Company F was ordered to the front as skirmishers, and we rode gaily forward at a brisk trot, carrying our loaded carbines at an "advance." The major and the balance of the command were soon lost to our view in the rear. In a short time we rode into Fairfield. The village presented a scene of confusion. No male citizens were visible, but a throng of females swarmed into the road around us, in a state of intense excitement, and manifesting great joy at our timely arrival. They stated that a train of eight wagons, loaded with supplies they had taken, had just left, and at that moment must be within a mile of the village.

The scene at this juncture must have been an amusing one to an appreciative observer. The women, with their white faces alternating between a laugh and cry, and with hair dishevelled, crowding about the horses, and a squad of armed soldiers, who were now roused into a fierce enthusiasm, fairly roaring with impatience during the few moments we were here delayed, formed a rare picture. The men had passed beyond the control of strict Lieutenant Bayer who, when he was sure that a stampede after the train was imminent, led off at a trot, driving the most boisterous of the spirits into the ranks by a free use of his sabre.

After proceeding some distance we came to a small schoolhouse, and just beyond this the road was intersected by another from the south. A momentary halt was ordered here. Lieutenant Balder was evidently puzzled as to which of the routes he would take, but presently he turned his horse's head to the left, and we followed him. An advance guard of four men, under Sergeant Brown, had been thrown forward, had continued straight ahead; but these turned back as soon as they discovered our change of course, and followed us at a brisk trot.

A short distance down this road we came to a comfortable-looking farm house, in the yard of which stood a heavily-built man of perhaps forty or fifty years of age. He showed signs of beating a hasty retreat, but a sharp call from Balder brought him down to the road, though with curious steps.

"Have you seen any rebels about here lately?" said Balder.

The citizen looked at us a moment as though debating in his mind what sort of answer he should make, evidently by no means certain that we were not confederates, who were trying to entrap him. The question was repeated.

"Six passed here a few minutes ago."

"What direction did they take?"

"Out that way, and up the road towards Cashtown."

It transpired that this was the road we had just left.

"You had better be careful, Captain," said the citizen. "There are many of them about here just now."

Lieutenant Balder contemplated the man a few moments, and then said, in his harshest voice:

"Is this Pennsylvania?"

"Yes, sir."

"And you farmers of Pennsylvania allow six rebels to ride unmolested about your state, and rob you just as they have a mind to?"

The man did not seem to relish this sally, and muttered out an unintelligible reply.

We galloped back to the main road, Brown and his men keeping ahead of us perhaps two hundred yards. In a short time we saw the advance guard suddenly stop on the top of a low ridge that crossed the road, and a moment later Kettleberger dashed back to us and reported the train just ahead.

"Tell Sergeant Brown to open the fight," said Balder.

Back galloped Kettleberger to Brown.

A portion of the men here dismounted, and tore down the fences on both sides of the road, that the men might deploy into line for action. Just in our rear, and on the right of the road stood a neat stone house, surrounded by fruit trees. A ripe field of wheat, and several of timothy full grown, extended around us. The fences were built with split rails, and were tall and strong.

We pushed into the field on the left of the road, and scattered out as skirmishers towards the low ridge before mentioned. Kettleberger came back just then, and said something to Balder, who angrily exclaimed:

"Tell him to open the fight—open the fight!"

Back galloped Kettleberger to Brown.

When he reported to the sergeant the latter did one of the oddest things on record. Deliberately dismounting, he crept into a fence corner, rested his carbine on a rail, and fired up the road.

At this instant we reached the crest of the low ridge, and from this point I cast a glance—a hasty glance—up the valley. There stood our prize, the wagons, distant something over a hundred yards, and along the road, apparently as a guard, were scattered some forty or fifty men.

As our line swept into sight these soldiers scampered away up the road, leaving the wagons to take care of themselves. Old Blue raised his carbine to his shoulder and fired, and a moment later shots rang out along our whole line. As my gun cracked the iron-gray reared up on his hind legs, and walked forward a short distance. I did not dare to touch the reins, as he might thus be thrown backwards; and all I could do was to lean up against his neck. A few moments were sufficient to satisfy me that I had better dismount; so, swinging out of the saddle, I threw loose the reins, angrily exclaiming:

"Go to the Devil!"

I do not know that he took my advice in a literal sense; he wheeled, however, and dashed towards the rear over the ridge, and the last glimpse I caught of him his hind feet were swinging high in the air.

I now turned towards the enemy. In the brief interval that had elapsed they had mustered with mysterious rapidity in great numbers on the road a short distance beyond the wagons, and showed unmistakable signs of an intention to rally to its defense. Our little force began to slowly fall back behind the ridge before this threatening array, firing rapidly, yet with commendable coolness. The balance of the regiment was not yet in sight. Company L had arrived, numbering twelve or fifteen men, making our whole force upon the ground some thirty-six or forty men. Company L, which was a short distance in the rear, dismounted and deployed in the meadow to the right of the road, while Company F took position under shelter of the ridge, and kept up a brisk fusillade upon the confederates.

A sudden gleaming of steel in the gray mass showed that they were preparing to charge, and a moment later they began moving down upon us. It was too late for me to retreat; the spot where I stood was too much exposed to attack, so I ran forward down the hill to an apple tree of large dimensions, and sheltered myself behind its huge trunk. I had reloaded my carbine and as the confederates came within range I dropped down upon one knee and opened fire.

I shall never forget my sensations during the brief time occupied by these events. The excitement that had thrilled through my veins at the beginning of the action passed entirely away, and a sort of rigid steadiness took possession of me. I had ample time, it seemed to me, to reflect upon my duty; yet it was with just a little effort that I took deliberate aim upon that mass of human beings. A prickly feeling crept up my spinal column, akin, perhaps, to the phenomena known as the raising of the hair on the back of an excited dog. I was quite secure for the time being, as the enemy were coming down with drawn sabres, and the road was inclosed on both sides with a high, strongly-built rail fence. The spot I occupied overlooked the road for over half a mile. Never before had I so fully realized the glory of battle. The confederates came within thirty paces of where I was hiding and then suddenly staggered under the crackling fire that greeted them from our skirmishers. My gun was working with the regularity of clock-work; my aim was carefully taken upon the center of the moving column, and at about the waist belt of the men, so as to disable either a horse or rider. A bugler, who carried, as I noticed, a copper instrument, began to sound the charge again, but the force of his regiment was thoroughly spent. Little whirlpools of men and horses appeared from one end of the column to the other, some wheeling to the rear and some to the front, alternately; and then it broke into fragments, and dashed pell mell to the rear, away up the road out of sight.

Here was an instructive scene for our military men. This confederate force, the Seventh Virginia Cavalry, Ashby's pet regiment, composed of really good and well-trained soldiers, charging with drawn sabres, were defeated and repulsed with a loss of sixty or seventy men by thirty-six or forty active carbineers, who were partially protected by fences and a ridge. Of course, it was not a "well-regulated" fight, but a cruel, close one, where every shot from determined men told upon their opponents, who were thus jammed up between two fences, and literally harmless.

As the confederates retired our men came dashing back over the ridge in hot pursuit, cheering vociferously. I also set up a yell that seemed to rise from my very toes. There was a momentary halt just below me to tear down the fence. Old Blue rode up and congratulated me, "for," said he, "when your horse came back riderless we thought you were gone." Lieutenant Balder ordered me to find the iron-gray and remount him. This requirement placed me in a quandary, for the animal was nowhere to be seen, and, besides, I could not very well fight on a horse that walked upright on his hind legs. Just then I discovered the L Company men deploying as dismounted skirmishers across the meadow on the right of the lane, and I crossed over and fell into line with them. Just as I passed into the field the remainder of the command marched upon the scene of conflict, with drawn sabres; the citizen, however, was no longer visible by the side of the major.

The charge of the enemy had enabled them to get their wagons away, and the road was now clear in our front. In a short time, however, I saw the gray masses mustering rapidly in the road far above, and a few moments later they came swarming towards us, driving our slender line of mounted skirmishers before them. Intuitively I looked back to see if we were supported, and beheld nothing but a mule with a cracker-box on his back.

The confederates were now close upon us, crowding in upon our men in the road, sabre in hand. A line of flankers extended well out from each side, and swung clear around our short line. Two pieces of artillery also appeared in the fields on the left. In rear of the cavalry marched a body of perhaps four hundred dismounted men.

All this scene I seemed to take in at a glance. It was evident that the Sixth Cavalry had its hands full for once, unless promptly aided by other troops.

A terrible struggle soon ensued in the narrow lane, the two bodies meeting in a hand-to-hand fight. As our men could present as much front as the enemy at this point they were enabled to hold them at bay for a short time. The artillery opened, but did no damage, owing, perhaps, to the intense excitement of the gunners. The flankers on the right and left pressed close in upon the devoted band, keeping up a rapid fire, to which our few skirmishers responded, but were not able to beat them back. At length our troops began to give way in the land, and were carried along pell mell by the heavy column of the confederates, the parties disappearing in a cloud of dust in the distance towards Fairfield.

Nothing remained for our little dismounted party but resistance to the bitter end. A brisk fire was kept up on all sides, directed mostly upon people who attempted to tear down fences and thus reach us. This was successful for a short time. Lieutenant Paulding rode up and said he had brought the major's orders for us to retire.

"Well, if we do," said one soldier bitterly, "he will probably accuse us of cowardice, as at Upperville."

The enemy succeeded in forcing the fence, and now swarmed across the field upon us. Our hour had evidently arrived. I had a new carbine, and, to prevent it from falling into the hands of the confederates, it was hidden in the grass. Then, drawing my revolver, I took post beside a small locust tree close to the fence, awaiting the arrival of four men who were advancing by file towards me, and whose eyes were evidently upon me. The fence was partially down in one spot directly between us, and this corner I proposed to defend. To deceive them, I leaned against the tree as if hurt, with my head bowed and my pistol hanging in my right hand. As they reached the fence the foremost man called out:

"Take off those belts!"

Without a word I levelled my weapon upon him. To my great surprise, instead of firing upon me, although they had pistols in their hands, the whole four wheeled their horses' heads to the left and swung over Indian fashion behind their necks for shelter. I took deliberate aim upon the thigh of the leader, but the cap merely snapped. I did not lower my pistol, but pulled the hammer back with my thumb. The men gave a frightened glance across their horses' necks, and then dropped again, as they saw the dreaded weapon still poised.

I do not know how the matter would have ended if my weapon had discharged. As it was, owing to the major's wonderful discipline, we were obliged to carry our revolvers for weeks at a time, during all sorts of weather, without emptying and reloading; and now the caps and cartridges were worthless. All the caps snapped.

"All over," and I dropped my pistol, and raised my cap in my right hand.

"Come across the fence, and give up your arms," said a young fellow of about nineteen or twenty years of age; who seemed to be a sort of leader of the party.

I did as directed, and, taking off my belt, to which was attached my sword and revolver—the latter fastened by a lanyard stood before them a prisoner of war.

Wallace, a little fellow of Company L, who had fought by my side during the latter part of the action, was making off as fast as his legs could go along the fence some thirty yards away. He had fired one shot at these men with his carbine when they were quite close, but without effect. They ordered him to halt, and the little Pennsylvanian had to obey, and he came over and joined me.

There was something about the affair that aroused my sense of the ludicrous in spite of myself. I felt that I must be a comical looking chap just then, and, thinking of this, I began laughing. Then our old bantering mood came over me, and I asked the youngest "brave:"

"Well, how did you like your job today?"

"Hot—very hot," he responded. "The toughest time we have had this year."

My captors were not remarkable for their military bearing. They reminded me of four farmers who had just left their plow and put on armor. The young fellow was especially conspicuous for the prominence with which his upper front teeth were displayed. They were members of the Sixth Virginia Cavalry, if I remember aright. However, I do not think little Wallace and I could have fallen into much better hands, for they were very civil fellows.

During this brief delay the few of our men who were yet free were keeping up a sharp resistance. As our captors were marching us off three federal cavalryman opened fire upon them, the bullets coming uncomfortably close to us, and they abandoned us and ran off a short distance. The federals were immediately afterward driven off by other confederates, and our escort returned, obliging us to grasp the cantles of their saddles and run as fast as we could to keep up with them. As we were already pretty thoroughly exhausted by our rapid movements during the action, this requirement was rather severe. However, as the firing ceased before we ran far, they allowed us to walk; and, panting for breath with great rivulets of sweat running down our backs and dusty faces, we made our way to the confederate rear.

By this time we were joined by other parties of prisoners, and all over the field we could see squads of them, under guard, coming in, some hatless, some wounded and bloody, some laughing, and some swearing. A little fellow, the blacksmith of Company I, remarkable for the length of his nose, came up, cursing furiously, and holding that organ with his left hand, while the blood flowed freely down his wrist. A sabre blow had descended upon it about one inch from the outer end, cutting it off completely, save just a thin strip of flesh next the upper lip, so that it hung pendant therefrom. I could not forbear laughing at him. He related with great gusto how he had killed the man that struck him, and was satisfied that far at least. A handkerchief was supplied, and the nose adjusted and bound to its place. In a few days it had healed up completely, leaving a neat little scar to mark the spot.

A confederate cavalry regiment met us a short distance from the spot of our capture, marching in column of squadrons, with drawn sabres. From behind them a savage-looking fellow rode out to meet us, and drew his revolver upon the head of an innocent German belonging to our Company A, who had joined us, exclaiming:

"Damn you, how many men have you got back there?"

The innocent German was too much frightened to speak at all. The question was repeated, with the additional remark that he would have a hole in his head if he did not answer.

"Come, come, that will do," said the young leader of our escort. "If you want to shoot Yankees the proper place to do it as at the front. These are my prisoners."

One of our men, whose quick-witted answer may have saved the Sixth Regiment from utter extermination, called out:

"There is a division of infantry just back there."

The confederates then rode away.

Our party now crossed over to the road along which quite a strong force of confederate cavalry was yet marching. These were the brigades of Generals Jones and Robinson, as we understood, and numbered in all some three or four thousand men. Of course, unsupported as our three hundred soldiers were—there could not have been any federal troops within six or eight miles of us—their defeat was only a question of time.

Quite a number of dead and wounded confederates were scattered over the fields and in the road. My eye rested involuntarily upon one man, attracted by some strange fascination. He was lying on his stomach, partially raised up on his elbows, while from his breast a steady stream of blood was flowing. His ghastly face was turned towards me, and his eyes regarded me with glaring intensity, so full of defiant, disdainful expression. Could it be that my bullet had stricken him down, and that, by some mysterious intuition, he had tracked me out? I shall never forget that picture.

A short distance from the scene of conflict we stopped at a house by the roadside to procure water. Here, lying on the grass under an apple tree, attended by McKibben, we found Lieutenant Chaffee, with a neatly cut crimson edged hole in his blue pantaloons over the front part of his thigh. He was quite cheerful.

At another house, perhaps half a mile further on, our party was turned over to the regular guard, and were marched into the yard among the other prisoners. Many of our wounded were here, some of whom were badly injured by sabre cuts and pistol shots. The carpenter of Company G was stretched out upon the grass, with a terrible gash across his head, five or six inches long. The occupants of the house, a man, wife, and two buxom daughters, were exerting themselves to the utmost to bind up wounds and otherwise care for the men. All their bedding must have been sacrificed for this purpose. Wash tubs full of bloody water stood about the yard, and strips of crimson cloth were scattered over the grass.

Our guards must have been of the refuse material of the confederate army. They were generally old, dilapidated looking fellows, armed only with sabres. It was useless to ask any favors of them; they seemed utterly ignorant of the courtesies due a prisoner of war.

I accidentally overheard a conversation between a man claiming to be a quartermaster in the confederate army and some of the prisoners which put a new phase upon our adventure. He stated that the train we had attempted to capture was sent out as a decoy, and that the farmer-like citizen who had visited us at Emmitsburg was really a spy. It seemed that we had overtaken the wagons too soon for the full accomplishment of their design; if the train had succeeded in getting along half a mile further we should have been thoroughly entrapped. As it was they were obliged to come out from their concealment and fight us to save it from destruction. The sequel will show that the farmer-like citizen, in due time, appropriately suffered the fate assigned by the articles of war to persons of his class.

Sometime in the evening the prisoners were ordered to fall into ranks, and then, bidding farewell to our generous friends at the house, we took up our march towards Cashtown. The men were much depressed in spirits at their situation, but bore up bravely.

Nearly all day we had heard the roar of guns off towards the northwest, which showed that bloody work was in progress somewhere; but the results were unknown. As we marched, however, we began to meet small squads of wounded confederates, trains of wagons, and disabled artillery, all moving in the direction of the Potomac. Every moment seemed to add to their number until the road was blocked by them, and a peculiar disorder manifested itself in their movements that attracted my attention.

"How is this?" I ventured to ask one of our cavalry guards. "Your men seem to be making for Virginia. Are they retreating?"

"Oh no," he said with a laugh; "our army is only changing position. Your troops have been badly whipped. We have already captured seventeen thousand prisoners."

"Well," said I, "of course I do not know how it is with your folks; but they look now as our people do when they are retreating."

"Oh, no; no retreat; only changing position."

Shortly before dark we halted in a meadow, and guards were established around us. The ground was quite low at this spot. On one side, along a belt of timber, a confederate infantry brigade was in position, and on the other the cavalry division that had participated in our fight, and a wagon train. It must have been quite close to the battle-field, for the musketry, which was yet crashing spasmodically, seemed to be just ahead. A constant stream of wounded men was flowing out of the woods to the rear.

A common sulky, drawn and pushed by several men, passed us as we came up to the meadows. In it, sitting upright with great effort, apparently, was an officer. His head was drooping upon his breast. Long yellow hair hung in girlish ringlets upon his shoulder. This, I was informed, was Major General Anderson. He had been shot in the body.

The night was a long weary, hungry one to most of us. My mind was full of conflicting emotions that drove off sleep in spite of the great fatigue I had endured. Everything except the light clothing upon my body was gone—haversack, canteen, letters, and diary. The confederates assured us that they made every effort to procure us food, visiting the neighboring farmers, stating to them that the supplies were wanted for federal prisoners, but that in all cases it was refused.

I had promised myself, a day or two previous to this, two specific pleasures should I cross the Pennsylvania state line: I should ride out of ranks and shake hands with the first citizen of the commonwealth we met beyond the border, and celebrate the coming fourth of July by an old-fashioned patriotic dinner at some farm house. Both of these propositions, I am compelled to say, were totally defeated. I had no opportunity to shake hands with anybody, and I had neither breakfast, dinner, nor supper on that eventful anniversary of our country's independence.

A heavy shower came up during the night, almost flooding the low ground upon which the prisoners were bivouacked, and added to our discomfort. For the first time in our military career officers and enlisted men were "equals before the law." There was no "standing to attention" nor touching the visor of the cap when any of these superiors approached, and they seemed very well satisfied to secure a seat on a rail unrecognized among us beside our fire. I must do them the justice, however, to say that they did not ask any advantages over us. The ugly, absurd requirements of the Army regulations, which places officers and men in a condition of constant hostile antagonism, and engenders a feeling of chronic hatred towards superiors on the one hand, and contempt towards inferiors on the other were for the present suspended.

437

Grim jokes about "cordwood brigades," "Company Q," and "put a nosebag on him" were occasionally heard, but there was no absolute disrespect shown. Even Cram, with all the different phases a common hate had assumed toward him, escaped insult.

Our loss in officers during the action was out of all proportion to the loss of enlisted men. Starr was wounded and a prisoner; Chaffee had been shot, Balder was dead, Cram, Paulding and our new lieutenant were prisoners. But one, Lieutenant Carpenter, managed to escape. Claflin, who had charge of the thirty men sent off on special duty on the morning of July 3rd, was not a participant in the action.

Of enlisted men I think there were killed, wounded, and captured about one hundred and ninety men out of some three hundred on the ground. Perhaps one hundred or more of these were dead and injured. Charlton, the "Pittsburg boy," and shadowy Todd, shadowy no more, lost some blood on the field. McMasters managed to hide himself away for several days, during which time he was fed by some of the farmers' daughters in the vicinity, and finally escaped. Dawson and Thomas got away, but fell among Stuart's cavalry a few days after and were captured.

Early on the morning of the 4th we were startled by the sharp rattle of musketry just over in the strip of woods held by the confederate infantry brigade, and the whistling of bullets over our heads. A sharp cry arose from the wagon train on the opposite side of our Camp, where some of the balls struck in among the mules, killing one or two and startling the courageous drivers. It transpired, however, that the infantry men were simply discharging their pieces to clean them, some of the more careless firing in our direction.

On To Richmond as a Prisoner

It was a dreary Fourth-of-July to our little band. Most of us had been without food for twenty- four hours. A dismal rain set in and continued most of the day, from which our thin clothing was no protection.

The guards here were mostly young boys, some apparently not over fifteen years of age. The confederates were evidently utilizing their entire population.

I saw the young man to whom I had given my sword sitting on his horse just outside camp this morning, and called to him. He recognized me, and came over to the line.

"Well, how did you get along after you left us yesterday," said I.

"Oh, had another fight down there," he replied. "I used your revolver." He was wearing the arms taken from me and seemed quite proud of them.

In the afternoon the prisoners were ordered into the road again. We were marched in an apparently northwestern direction, and passed through a hamlet which someone said was Cashtown. About dusk our party reached the main body of prisoners captured during the battle, whom we found camped by the roadside, and guarded by the remnants of Pickett's division of Virginians. Some thirty-three hundred of our men were here, all told. About all the information I could get out of them was that a battle had been fought at and around Gettysburg, but the final result was unknown. During the night, however, all doubts on the subject were removed. In the evening the road was crowded with troops headed towards Virginia, and for a time they were very orderly; but as the night wore on the scene became tumultuous, great masses of yelling soldiers and teamsters, braying mules, and rumbling wagons and artillery flowing past our camp like a torrent. The whole confederate army appeared to be moving. The campaign that was to be made in the northern states, and which to the hearts of the southern people had promised so much, was evidently a failure.

I asked one of our guards how many prisoners he thought were here, and he replied, "at least ten thousand." Such was southern extravagance.

Pickett's division had been badly used up in the battle. Three thousand men remained out of the eight thousand engaged. A good deal of dissatisfaction was manifested among them in regard to the North Carolina troops, who, they alleged, failed to support them.

The battle of Gettysburg was perhaps the most remarkable action of the war. Portions of the hostile forces met near the town by accident, and became engaged in a conflict which finally drew almost the entire mass of both armies into a bloody vortex at and around Cemetery and Culp's Hills. Not more than one hundred and forty thousand men took an active part, and yet the aggregate loss in killed and wounded footed up about forty-seven thousand—an unprecedented percentage. Of this the federal casualties numbered something over sixteen thousand, while that of the confederates exceeded four thousand six hundred killed and nearly twenty-six thousand wounded. This great disparity of losses arose from the exposure of the enemy's columns during the terrific assault made on the federal lines on the afternoon of the 3rd of July. Although the two armies confronted each other during three days, the time consumed by actual fighting did not, I think, extend over a period of time greater than twelve hours. It was a series of spasmodic efforts rather than a deliberately conducted battle.

Judging from the appearance of affairs on the road between Cashtown and Fairfield on the afternoon of the third, I have been impressed with the belief that the assault by Pickett's men was really an effort intended to cover the withdrawal of Lee's trains and wounded, preparatory to the retreat of his entire army into Virginia. The two movements seem to have been in the process of execution almost simultaneously.

On the 5th the prisoners were brought out of the woods to the road, and marched southward with the retreating hosts. A few hours later we reached Fairfield, and here found, scattered along the valley, fully forty thousand confederates. The village seemed to be almost utterly deserted. I overheard two young men, evidently citizens of Richmond—one an artilleryman, and the other attached to the infantry—conversing about the campaign and battle during a short halt here. The latter repeated with a trembling voice over a long list of names of their mutual schoolmates and acquaintances who had fallen. The slaughter had been terrific, he said.

I endeavored to form an estimate of the strength of the confederate army, but was unable to obtain any satisfactory results. One officer mentioned eighty-two thousand troops—I understood him to say infantry, but may have been mistaken. My friend Callaghan, then a member of A.P. Hill's corps, says there were nine divisions of infantry, averaging not over eight thousand men each. In addition to this was the cavalry, perhaps six or eight thousand strong. Counting the total force of the three arms of the service with the odds and ends which had been scattered through Western Virginia and were now called in to assist in various ways, it is probable that the entire number of men at Lee's disposal during the campaign was not over ninety thousand. Of this host the loss, in killed, wounded, and prisoners, must have been at least thirty-eight thousand soldiers.

In the afternoon we were marched up into the mountains through Fairfield pass, and again halted by the roadside to allow a portion of the confederate army to pass. Here the sound of cannonading broke upon our ears from far up the valley, and two or three miles away we could easily distinguish bodies of cavalry approaching. The confederates who yet remained a short distance above Fairfield took up a position to resist the advance of our troops. As the firing soon closed I suppose it was only a reconnoitering party.

It was amusing to listen to the bantering remarks of the common soldiers of each army during this encounter.

"Why, here come those damned Yanks!" exclaimed a prisoner, with mock surprise. "Can't we never get clear of them?"

"Guess they'll not disturb you." growls a gray back.

"Wonder where all the Yanks come from, anyhow," says another.

"Don't know where they comes from—knows where they'll go to if they ain't careful—to hell!" growls gray back.

With all their efforts to conceal it, there was an expression of gloom upon the faces of many of the men which showed that they felt all the chagrin attending the defeat of a high-spirited army.

I doubt if there would have been much wisdom in attacking in force the confederate rear at this mountain pass. A body of fifteen thousand men here ought to hold at bay fully three times their number, protected as they were by the character of the country from flanking operations.

Today I saw, for the first time, the commander-in-chief of the confederate army, General Lee. During the cannonading he rode up, in company with General Ewell, to a commanding eminence near the prisoners, and looked earnestly up the valley at the federal column. After this the two officers dismounted and sat down in the shade of a small tree, and partook of the hard fare of the common soldier.

I had fancied Lee to be a much younger looking man than he appeared to me on this occasion. It was difficult to see, in the tall, plainly-dressed, pleasant-looking, gray-haired man the attributes of the chieftain, whose name should stand highest upon the military roll of the confederacy.

Ewell, with his long curly hair, which gave him a sort of dashing appearance, clean cut features, and elastic tread, looked as though he might be depended upon under all circumstances.

A long weary night followed this day of intense excitement, and it seemed as though our tired limbs could barely carry us over the mountains. We were now in the midst of Longstreet's corps. At times the road was literally jammed with wagons, artillery, cavalry, and infantry, the latter being obliged to take to the woods to protect themselves from being crushed by the two former. The guards utterly exhausted by their excessively arduous duties, and about half the time, in the confusion of the darkness, they mingled with the prisoners in an almost inextricable mass. Quite a number of prisoners escaped during these periods of disorganization by stealing up or down the mountain side, as opportunity offered. Every few minutes there was a halt, and then, as if by common consent, both federal and confederate would drop on the spot, almost asleep before they touched the ground with their bodies. Most of us had not touched food for two days. As the night wore on a cool breeze rose that cut through our scanty clothing with the keenness of a knife, adding materially to our sufferings.

Shortly before daylight we halted near a place called the Mountain House, and remained until late-in the forenoon. It was rumored that we were to be paroled here, and returned to our lines. This caused a general feeling of joy among the prisoners, who had by this time become thoroughly satisfied with their experiences under the flag of the confederacy. Some of the officers warned the men that such an arrangement would not be recognized by the federal government, as a parole, to be binding, obliged the confederates to deliver the men either at Vicksburg or City Point. In addition it was urged that, if we accepted a parole, and were turned loose, the enemy would be released from all care over us, and the men engaged in guarding us would then be available for operations against our army. As the campaign promised to be a decisive one, it was our duty to make ourselves as burdensome as possible, and thus assist our comrades-in-arms on the other side of the line. The matter was thoroughly discussed, and the prisoners almost unanimously resolved to refuse the parole, if offered.

It was reported today that our cavalry had intercepted the confederates on the road some miles beyond the Mountain House, and captured many prisoners, and destroyed some three hundred wagons. The action was said to have occurred last night. The prisoners became exuberant over this manifestation of activity on the part of our pursuing army, and cheered vociferously.

It is said that misfortunes never come singly; today the proverb was reversed—good fortunes flowed in upon us like a river. Rations of flour and meat were distributed among the famished men, and soon hundreds of little fires were flashing up here and there, surmounted by nearly every sort of cooking utensil and all jealously watched by hundreds of hungry eyes.

An hour later we were on the road again. A few miles from the Mountain House we began to find evidences of the raid of the night before. The road ran along the steep mountain side for perhaps a mile, and was skirted by a heavy forest. Our troopers had broke in upon the startled teamsters like a whirlwind, here and there wheeling a wagon across the road, and thus effectually blockading the entire train. A number, with mules attached, had been hurled over the precipices below, and were dashed to pieces on the rocks. The spokes of the wheels of others were chopped, and thus rendered unserviceable. The ground was strewn with broken muskets for miles. These arms belonged to the confederate wounded, and had been in the wagons.

Our men were quite jubilant over the affair, and indulged in many sarcastic remarks in the hearing of their brethren in gray. The latter controlled their tempers with good grace under the trying ordeal.

In the afternoon we were marched off into a field to the right of the road and then halted, in order to allow the passage of a large body of troops that were being hurried southward. These were some of Longstreet's men, and with them rode that officer, dressed like an old farmer, with a very unmilitary cap drawn down on the back portion of his head. The confederates seemed to regard him with especial favor, and pointed him out to us on every occasion of his appearance.

While here a confederate brass band—the first I had seen since captured—marched up, vigorously playing *Dixie's Land*. The men in gray greeted the notes with wild cheers, while the prisoners groaned. Then suddenly, as the musicians came opposite us, *Dixie* was absorbed by *Yankee Doodle* and the prisoners cheered while the confederates groaned. This little episode stirred up a mutual good feeling between captors and captives.

This afternoon we passed through a village named, I think, Waynesborough, just inside the Pennsylvania State Line. The place seemed to be almost entirely deserted. We were kept going all night, crossing into Maryland, and headed towards Hagerstown. Just at dawn a halt of a few hours was made, and in a very short time nearly the entire party of prisoners and guards were scattered, sound asleep, along the pike. Sergeant Croy and I, feeling our grievous want of something for the inner man, went over to a farm house near the roadside. It was deserted. We roamed through the rooms, found them all well furnished, and then descended to the pantry. This was pretty well stripped of provisions, but a small crock of lard, a little flour, a tin cup, and a light skillet rewarded us for our efforts. To improvise a pail for the crock we tore some muslin in strips, tying one around it near the rim, and to this attaching the two loose ends of another. It occurred to us that, by strict economy, using it only when we could procure no meat, this lard would prove very serviceable, and last a long time.

We built a fire by the roadside with some fence rails, and made some porridge of flour and water, which we seasoned with a little salt, and added just enough of lard as a substitute for the flavor of meat. This, to one in our condition, was quite a respectable meal. Then we laid down, first carefully concealing our supplies, and soon fell into a profound slumber.

Some time during the forenoon we were aroused by the guards, and resumed our march. Just outside of Hagerstown a party of young ladies, standing on the portico of a brick house, were unusually facetious in their remarks about the "Yankees." In the town, however, we were rewarded by the bright smiles of "OUR girls." I was astonished at the outspoken Union sentiment of the citizens here, filled, as the streets were, with armed confederates. The prisoners became quite boisterous over their reception, and some of them were rather abusive in language, which was not at all well received. One man, more valorous than discreet, called our guards "damned whelps." This roused the anger of a lieutenant, who stepped up to him, and said:

"Sir, you are a prisoner of war, and I respect you as such, but I shall not allow you to abuse us in that manner."

The federal thereupon became silent.

We halted a short time upon one of the streets. On the sidewalk just across from where I was resting myself, stood two little boys, not over seven or eight years of age, who were silently and earnestly contemplating the prisoners. Suddenly one turned to the other, and ejaculated, as the tears rushed into his eyes, and his little hands became clenched:

"Damned rebels!"

I suspect that this was the first time he had ever sworn, from the peculiar manner in which he jerked it out.

Behind them stood a guard, leaning on his musket. He, too, heard the remark, and looked at the twain with a visible expression of astonishment upon his features, but said nothing. I confess my surprise at the idea of such little fellows having so great an interest in the contest, and taking sides with so much feeling.

Just beyond Hagerstown we found evidences of a sharp cavalry skirmish. The dead bodies of our soldiers were scattered along the road and over the fields for one or two miles, and every one of them was stripped entirely naked. It was a sad sight, those ghastly corpses lying uncovered under the rays of that burning July sun. Here a poor fellow was stretched in a fence corner by the roadside, swollen and discolored, the black blood all over his face and in his hair. Here a boyish face seemed to look at one with his half open eyes, while from his parted lips the foam was slowly dripping; there was a strong man, with heavy black whiskers, with a handful of earth clenched convulsively.

Oh, the hateful horrors of war!

The guards seemed to take much interest in calling our attention to our dead comrades, and dwelt with disgusting earnestness upon the peculiarity of the different wounds. I could not refrain from expressing, to one of them, my astonishment at their want of feeling. He became silent under the rebuke, and shortly after I saw him urging others to desist.

When within a short distance of Williamsport the prisoners were marched into a clover field, and halted. Rations of fresh meat and flour were issued to us, for the first time since we left the Mountain House. Croy and I made up a sort of pancake mixture with water and flour and lard, and partook heartily thereof, regardless of the envious glances of our fellow prisoners.

Shortly after our arrival, two of Company A men managed to get up a fight, and for a short time created some excitement. They were too weak to damage each other much, and the affair soon closed, to the infinite disgust of the pugilistic element.

It was amusing to observe the ungracious manner in which the men secreted their supplies of food. Generally the meat was all eaten as soon as issued and thus secured, while the flour that remained was rolled up in a blanket and carefully placed under the proprietor's head when he proposed to sleep. Others stowed it away in the toes of their shoes, while some kept portions of it in each pocket. Foragers were constantly prowling about, seeking that which they could devour, and nothing of a digestive character escaped their lynx-eyed investigations. Once I discovered one of these bummers coolly raising the head of a sleeping federal, abstract the bag of flour, and then gently lower the unconscious poll to its resting place.

The next day after our arrival near Williamsport, while enjoying a siesta under the shade of a delicate shrub, I was aroused by the announcement that another party of federal prisoners was approaching from the direction of Hagerstown. There were about sixty or seventy of them. At the head of the squad I beheld the tall form of the handsome Donaldson, and just behind him the shadowy Todd that was—the latter with one of his arms in a sling. Dawson and Werner were there too, looking disconsolately at their fellow prisoners in the field. There was something about our meeting under such circumstances that touched our sense of the ludicrous, and many were the bantering jests exchanged over the situation. Todd's face bore an expression of suffering that roused my sympathies. He was much worried that mortification (gangrene) might set in from his exposure to the hot sun and the want of proper care. A revolver bullet had passed through the fleshy part of the forearm, fortunately touching no bones, however. As often as opportunity was afforded, cold water was applied, to keep down inflammation. He had been shot in the action at Fairfield on the 3rd of July, but succeeded in concealing himself in the tall grass all afternoon and night. On the 4th he was discovered and captured, and since then had some pretty rough experiences.

Donaldson had been captured in a fight near Funkstown, Maryland, on the 5th of July. From him I learned that Evans, the daring, bright-eyed boy—the life of company F—was dead, killed during that encounter

446

by a confederate bullet.

Judging from Donaldson's statement the action at Funkstown possessed some queer though cruel characteristics. The small disorganized body that now represented the once powerful Sixth Regiment was sent, under command of Lieutenant Claflin, on a reconnaissance along the road towards the village. None of the enemy's pickets were encountered; the first warning our men received of the proximity of confederates was when they rode into the presence of several thousand men encamped just outside of Funkstown. The enemy instantly made preparations to receive an attack, a large body of cavalry mustering in an open field by the roadside, while a battery of artillery hurried into position as a support. Claflin, who had ridden to the front among his skirmishers, was almost immediately thereafter wounded in the shoulder, and obliged to retire. As he rode past the main body to the rear he turned over the command to Lieutenant Carpenter, remarking, at the same moment, that the confederates were about to advance by a charge, and giving Carpenter instructions to form the regiment into two reliefs to cover his retreat—the first line to be thrown across the road at the spot now occupied, and the second to take up a like position some distance in their rear; the first to open with a volley upon the head of the charging column as soon as it appeared, to check it, and then to retire behind the second line and reform, while the second delivered its fire in the same manner; the retreat to be thus continued until the federal lines were reached. Carpenter obeyed just enough of these instructions to aid materially in the destruction of his command. The two reliefs were formed, and then, as the head of the enemy's column came within short range, instead of distinctly giving the command to fire, he wheeled his horse to the rear, shouted something unintelligible, and disappeared down the road.

This sealed the fate of the regiment. The semblance of formation which up to this time had been presented was utterly broken up; and what, by skillful management, might have been a creditable retreat, became a terrible rout. The first squad dashed through the ranks of the second like a whirlwind, and then the whole body surged down the road in the wildest disarray, followed by a yelling and exultant foe. A high narrow bridge spanned a small stream some distance from the spot where the disorder began, and as the affrighted men and horses swarmed upon it numbers were crowded off over the side, and fell headlong into the water below. The confederates kept up their pursuit for several miles, shooting and sabreing our men. An abrupt close, however, was brought to the affair. The Sixth Pennsylvania Cavalry suddenly appeared upon the scene. This gallant organization at once took up the fight, and in a few moments were hurling the enemy back over the road along which they had advanced, thus relieving our men from a very ugly difficulty.

During the first part of the action the boy Evans, disdaining to run, rode out and met the enemy single-handed, and was immediately shot down. Donaldson afterwards found the body and buried it.

Of course, the party responsible for this disaster was promptly cashiered in disgrace from the army. Was he? The army register will show that he was promoted not long after this affair. The government is not in the habit of dismissing officers who could point to hereditary greatness or influence.

Many of the common soldiers will remember the crude dignity which Carpenter displayed at Camp near Westover, where he joined the command as an enlisted man, and how they resented it; how, too, he was suddenly transformed into a noncommissioned and then a commissioned officer, and placed over brave and experienced soldiers, to their infinite disgust. As explanatory of these astounding performances, it was stated that he bore some sort of relationship to General Dix.

In Donaldson's pocket there was a letter for me, from Frank Reeder, an old schoolmate of mine, which the handsome corporal had received on the day preceding his capture, little dreaming that he would so soon have an opportunity of delivering it in person. Perhaps it was the only incident of the kind during the war.

Poor Bayar was with the party. This quiet, inoffensive German, who had been detailed as hostler for Lieutenant Balder for some time, was with the company at Fairfield, but unarmed and in charge of this officer's led horse and riding his own. When the command gave way he had attempted to escape with the horse, and, as he dashed past Major Starr, the latter struck him a savage blow with his sabre across the skull, making a fearful gash. Being obliged to march with the rest of the prisoners, under a burning July sky, his wound became terribly aggravated as a consequence. The last time I saw him he was delirious with pain; and the gash was reeking with vermin. I am not informed as to his subsequent fate.

Dawson and Werner managed to escape during the rout at Funkstown by riding away on a by-road, but fell in with some confederate cavalry who were filing along the lines of our army. Dawson was brought before General J.E.B. Stuart, and closely questioned as to the number and disposition of the federal forces, but confessed himself as possessing little or no knowledge on that subject.

Lieutenant Balder was dead. He had displayed great gallantry during the action at Fairfield, exerting himself to the utmost to keep the men up to their work, and only retiring when it became unmistakably evident that everything was lost. The enemy were already in possession of the country between the scene of the encounter and the village, and as he rode to the rear he came upon a number of them drawn up across the road to intercept the federals who should attempt to escape. These men ordered Lieutenant Balder to halt and surrender. Without a word he put spurs to his horse, and, sabre in hand, he dashed straight in upon them. They broke to the right and left to allow him to pass, and then fired upon him, inflicting mortal wounds. He managed, however, to cling to his horse until he reached the village, where an old man and woman assisted him into a chair on a porch. When Donaldson came up he found him sitting upright, by the citizen, his face already pale and his eyes closed.

"Are you hurt, lieutenant?" asked the corporal.

Balder's ruling passion—military discipline—was strong in death. He did not forget to mention Donaldson's rank

"Corporal," said he, without a quaver in his voice, "tell the men to save themselves."

In a few moments he ceased to breathe.

Charlton, the "Pittsburg boy," the boon companion of Old Blue and the poor boy Evans, was among the wounded at Fairfield. Early in the action, while our men were driving the confederates, he was riding down along a fence toward a crossing, when a party made their appearance on our left flank. He partially turned in his saddle and fired at them, when, at that instant, he was pierced by a bullet in the left side, the missile passing downward through his body and lodging just inside the right hip joint, inflicting a terrible wound. Though the shock was a fearful one his presence of mind did not forsake him. Knowing that he would soon fall from weakness, and dreading to be thrown from his horse, and perhaps dragged by the feet, he dismounted and released his animal. Unfortunately, as he swung off its back he fell across the fence, striking on his left side, and breaking three of his ribs. He was utterly unable to raise himself up, and so here, with head swinging down on one side and feet on the other, and the blood streaming from his wound, poor Joe hung until Schilling came along and released him from his uncomfortable

449

position. With some effort Schilling managed to carry him to a farm house, and there left him.

A severe trial still awaited the "Pittsburg boy." In the same room there were about a dozen other wounded men, several of whom died in a few hours. As Frobin was the only person to attend to them, the dead remained where they lay. Charlton was propped up in a sitting position with pillows, and was obliged to remain in this uncomfortable position for five days and nights, suffering the most excruciating torments.

Subsequently he was removed to the house of an old, warmhearted, patriotic farmer, and there, under the kindest of treatment and constant watching of the family, and especially of Betsy—a buxom daughter of about eighteen—his strong constitution brought him up out of the shadowy valley. Joe soon became a favorite at the farm house. The warm-hearted, patriotic old man wanted him for a son-in-law; Betsy wanted him for a husband; and he expressed his willingness to accede to their wishes. As a consequence the ground for a new dwelling was staked off, and all necessary preparations made for its immediate erection.

Now, I should be glad to chronicle a proper sequel to this highly romantic beginning, but as a rigid adherer to the truth, I am compelled to record a different one. With his returning strength came back his overweening love of adventure; he grew homesick for the regiment and "the boys;" and, while thanking them all for their great kindness in caring for him, he turned his back upon Betsy and the new house, murmuring, "not for Joe."

Donaldson informed me, among other things, that the misfortune which befell the regiment at Fairfield was attributable to the efforts of a rebel spy, named Richardson, the farmer-like individual who had acted as guide during our march from Emmitsburg, and who had so hastily disappeared when the firing began; and that the train we had assaulted beyond the village was a decoy to lead our too confiding farmer into the toils of the confederates. This remark recalled to my mind the one that fell from the lips of the quartermaster of that train on the afternoon of that memorable day.

Richardson was subsequently captured by the pickets of the Fifth Cavalry, if I remember aright, and brought before General Buford. The evidence against him was conclusive.

"You have three minutes to pray," said Buford.

From the limb of a tree in a large field near Frederick City, dangling

450

on the end of a lariat rope, the body swung for several days—a ghastly warning to that class of warriors who find it profitable though dangerous to lurk and operate within the lines of an enemy.

During the days of our encampment near Williamsport the prisoners strongly indulged in the hope that the campaign now in progress would culminate in the utter destruction of the confederate Army of Northern Virginia. Several circumstances seemed to justify this expectation. Judging from the pell-mell character of the retreat—the apparently disorganized masses that streamed from Gettysburg to Williamsport—the entire lack of discipline among the men, as it seemed to federal eyes; the impassable condition of the Potomac, owing to the destruction of the pontoon bridge by our cavalry and the floods that swept down from the upper country; the immense losses in men and material which they must have suffered, and their inability to replace them; the circumscribing by federal lines of the area of the food supplying section; the tremendous efforts we felt sure our government was making to follow up its success—these manifest advantages roused in the breast of every captive a conviction that the decisive campaign of the rebellion was about to close.

But it was an idle delusion. The greatest battle, the greatest victory, and the grandest opportunity of the war slipped from the grasp of the authorities at Washington, by whose fault is unknown.

Some facts are apparent to the most casual observer. The battle of Gettysburg was fought by the army of the Potomac virtually without a commander-in-chief; so long as this condition of affairs existed, it was successful; and its success died away just in the proportion that the influence of the commander-in-chief became potent.

The confederate army mustered along the banks of the Potomac from forty-eight to seventy-two hours after its repulse on July 3 at Cemetery Hill; our army was not fully in position near Williamsport until the 12th, and yet the men say they were marching in some direction or other most of the time, meeting with scarcely any resistance.

To the coming historian, in whose impartiality the causes and effects of this great military muddle are to be balanced, and who shall accord praise or censure to each participant therein according to his work, I leave the subject.

On the morning of the 11th or 12th of July the prisoners were marched down through Williamsport to the banks of the Potomac, and prepared to cross. The people of the town treated us with marked courtesy as we passed through the streets, throwing us bread, and secretly taking charge of many letters to friends at the North. Owing to want of materials for transcribing, I was not able to take advantage of this opportunity. In justice to our guards, it should be stated that they placed the fewest obstacles in the way of this intercourse.

We found the river here the scene of great excitement and bustle. A number of small flat-bottomed boats had been collected, and a ferry improvised, and stores and prisoners were rapidly crossing.

I met here a Pennsylvanian—a robust, handsome fellow—who had been in the enemy's cavalry service for the past two years. He knew of no reason in particular why he would fight on this side of the line, save, possibly, that he did not like the abolitionists. He was pleased with his wild, adventurous life, however, and proposed to remain until the end.

Above the landing a tall, lank horse was floundering about in the canal, into which it had fallen, while a tall, lank confederate cavalryman, clad in the dullest of butternut, was making frantic efforts for its rescue. As I was hurried into one of the small boats at this juncture I am unable to record the result.

On the south bank of the Potomac we found Imboden and his brigade, consisting of some cavalry, Virginia infantry, and the remnant of the Washington Artillery, of New Orleans, left from the Chancellorsville campaign—four guns.

The prisoners, after all had been brought over, were marched out a short distance on the Martinsburg road, and turned into an open field for the night, surrounded by a guard of mounted and dismounted men. Just before dark rations of flour and meat were issued.

That man was fortunate, who, urged on by his voracious appetite, cooked and devoured his entire allowance at once; though under other circumstances he would have been called improvident. In a corresponding measure, that man was unfortunate who, with great self-denial, had systematically divided, his allowance into parts equal in number to the days it was to sustain him; though under other circumstances he would have been called provident. The raiders, stealthy as a flock of Norway rats, and just as vicious when caught, made sad havoc with the supplies of the latter class of individuals in the night.

It seemed to me that, had I have been brought into Old Virginia blindfolded, I should have recognized the locality. There was a sort of malign influence pervading the atmosphere that made itself felt in my bones.

Early in the forenoon the prisoners were marched out into the road, counted off into squads of hundreds, and started southward. Here I saw General Imboden for the first time. His appearance did not impress me as that of a military man; it reminded me more of a country storekeeper than that of a soldier. Rather small of stature, with a pleasant voice, unostentatious in manner, it was evident that he would not be a harsh man under whom to serve.

A peculiar feature of our procession was a man called Colonel Jones, said to be in command of one of Imboden's regiments—a heavy, coarse-looking fellow. One of the objects of his life seemed to be discussion. He displayed great uneasiness when not arguing political questions. Discussion was his normal condition. While with the prisoners he sought to impress them with the process of the confederate army, and the great wickedness of the northern people in seeking to coerce the southern people into a hated union. When one of our men ventured to suggest the different views our side held of that question, his response was, invariably, with that negro dialect so common during those days south of Mason's and Dixon's line—

"Tut—tut- tut! You all's are fanatics!"

Then he would tell again the old story.

Just outside of Martinsburg the prisoners were halted for a short time, and given a chance to rest. When the march was resumed the men were ordered into two ranks instead of four, thus doubling the length of the column. There was speculation among us as to the cause of this change in formation, but a conclusion was finally reached that it was for the purpose of impressing the Martinsburg people with an idea of our great numbers.

I was astonished at the sympathy displayed by the people of the village towards us. No one, in my opinion, can better appreciate such sympathy than a poor, tired, hungry, humiliated prisoner of war. When we came within reach of its influence it was a wondrous phenomenon, the sudden lighting up of sad eyes and quickening of laggard steps. These kindly feelings towards us found expression in a more substantial way; hundreds of loaves of bread were showered upon us. The guards, however, soon checked this demonstration.

An officer came up to the guard near me, and thus instructed him:

"If those people persist in this, cut them down on the spot."

Almost immediately after these orders were issued I saw a cavalryman beat one of our men over the head with his sabre while venturing out of the ranks for a loaf of bread that a lady was holding out to him.

453

Just before leaving the place a woman stood by the side of the street, occasionally uttering encouraging words to the prisoners. A confederate officer rode up to her, and said:

"Madam, these men would rather have your bread than your sympathy."

"Well," she replied, "they are welcome to that, too."

Into a house she ran, and a moment later reappeared with a huge basket full. Alas! for the chivalry of that officer. He drove her away with it, and thus deprived some of us of its coveted contents.

This was about the first expression of that capricious cruelty which subsequently embittered our prison experiences. Heretofore, while among the real fighting men of the Army of Northern Virginia, our treatment was as good as could have been expected—was honorable; but now a change of policy seemed to have taken place, so sharply defined as to be unmistakable, the manifestations increasing with every mile of our progress southward, until they culminated on Belle Isle.

At the outskirts of the village we passed a neat little cottage, standing on the left of the road, and some little distance from it. In the front yard, beside the low paling fence that extended along the turnpike, stood a sad looking lady, with a little girl and boy—the former perhaps six years old, and the latter about four. The girl was beside her mother, clinging to her dress, and looking shyly at the torrent of dusty men flowing by, while the boy was standing upon the flat top of the gate post, steadied on his feet by maternal hands.

"God bleth the blue-coaths! God bleth the blue-coaths!"

The lisping voice came up strong enough from his little throat, and earnest enough, too. There was no mistaking his sincerity. The guards and their prisoners looked in surprise upon the diminutive loyalist, who swung himself backward in his enthusiastic efforts.

"Hurrah! God bleth the blue-coaths!"

"Hurrah for the Union!" shouted the federals.

"Hurrah for Jeff Davis!" yelled the confederates.

The little fellow still kept up his ringing cry as long as we remained in sight, thrilling our hearts with its unutterable fervor.

Further on we passed a small, withered, weather-beaten old Irish woman, standing in the door of the proverbial shanty, and surrounded by scores of pigs, chickens, and ducks.

"God bless ye, poor boys," she exclaimed; "keep up a brave heart—ye'll all be recaptured soon!"

She, too, was received by a "hurrah for Jeff Davis," but the old lady held her ground, while a feeble shout from our men went up to encourage her. This demonstration of loyalty from one of her nationality surprised me, as I had understood that all of this class south of the Potomac were sympathizers with the confederacy on account of their known hostility to the negro.

We camped for the night just south of Martinsburg, having travelled about twelve miles today. Early next morning the prisoners were hurried into the road and began their journey. Very few of us had anything left from the rations issued by the riverside, and the order to move fell upon unwilling ears. The sun was terribly hot throughout the day, and our march was a dreary, monotonous one.

At midnight we were turned off the road into a field like a herd of cattle. As no rations were forthcoming, the prisoners were not put to any trouble by having to cook their supplies. There was no time lost in finding soft places on the ground, the exhausted men dropping down just where they halted. A heavy, chilling rainstorm had arisen about four o'clock in the afternoon, and added to our trials. As we were now in a confederate state, and under a guard of Virginians, there was no burning of fence rails permitted, and we were thus deprived of fire beside which to dry and warm ourselves. I think we had travelled about twenty-two miles today.

About two o'clock in the morning we were aroused for rations. These were extremely light—about a pint of raw flour and perhaps half a pound of meat per man—and I devoured mine on the spot, concluding to trust in providence for more in the future. A full stomach, in my case, is always conducive to sleep, and in this instance it seemed especially to stupefy me. With my body stretched in a shallow gutter, and my head on a limestone, I became oblivious to all surroundings.

Early in the morning the march was resumed, and in a short time the column filed by twos as at Martinsburg into one of the streets of Winchester for several hours. Quite a crowd of citizens gathered about the cavalcade, and attempted to open a trade in money with the prisoners, offering three dollars in confederate currency for greenbacks. As a pretext they urged that the federal troops would soon be in the valley again, when greenbacks could be used, while, as we would be at Richmond, the other sort of money would answer our purpose. Quite a number of our men accepted the tempting inducement, and exchanged. I had some eighty dollars but concluded to retain it. The wisdom of this course was afterwards fully established.

There was evidently little sympathy for the Union cause here. The contrast between our treatment here and at Martinsburg was so strongly marked as to be recognized instantly. A perfect fusillade of bantering remarks was kept up between the captives and spectators.

"How's Gettysburg?" a citizen would shout as he walked past

"Well, I guess we made our mark there," would be the deliberately spoken reply from some cool federal.

Our entire want of news from the battlefield gave them the advantage over us, for, although feeling that the confederate army had been defeated, we could not state definite results.

Shortly after the column halted I noticed a newsboy, with papers under his arm, coming down the sidewalk, and immediately hailed him with—

"What papers have you?"

"Richmond dailies," was the reply.

"All right. Bring me one."

He hesitated a moment, and then came. They were twenty-five cents apiece. The price was rather startling—the paper was but half a sheet—but I do not think I ever regretted the purchase.

Glancing hastily at the date, and then for the telegraphic dispatches, my eyes were transfixed by the announcement that Vicksburg had surrendered on the 4th of July!

During the preceding day the guards had volunteered the information that Grant had been driven from the front of that stronghold with frightful loss, his entire army being scattered in a totally disorganized condition all along the Mississippi River.

A little group of prisoners had gathered about me and as I finished reading the short dispatch announcing the surrender it spread throughout the entire column like wild-fire.

"How's Gettysburg?" yells a citizen.

"How's Vicksburg?" howls back an excited federal.

We feel that the laugh is on our side now.

The confederates proposed not to believe the dispatch, but they could not altogether conceal their chagrin. The newspaper editors were voted to be a lot of consummate liars.

The account of the operations in Pennsylvania was especially interesting to us. The paper contained a correction of a former dispatch, by which it appeared that the telegraph reported the capture by the confederates of 40,000 prisoners when it should have been 4,000—one cypher too many. Lee's losses were stated to be about 38,000 men. Evidently the past ten days had put an entirely new phase upon the war.

We left Winchester about nine o'clock, and reached Strasburg late in the afternoon. On the way we passed a confederate pontoon train which was headed towards the Potomac.

Some of our men called out:

"There goes another prize for our cavalry!"

I understood, subsequently, that the boats were actually captured by our raiders, who came across the Blue Ridge somewhere in the vicinity of Snicker's Gap.

As was customary, the column fell into two ranks, just outside of Strasburg and with that formation filed down the street. When about halfway through the town I noticed a young lady standing on the sidewalk, eyeing us very closely. Suddenly she darted through the line of guards, threw her arms about the neck of a prisoner, and kissed him passionately. The confederates immediately rushed in and separated the twain by force, the lady looking daggers at them as she retired into a house.

"I would that I had been him," murmured a little fellow by my side. I suppose this was the individual wish of the thirty-seven hundred men in the line that afternoon.

It was stated that the recipient of this unexpected and highly romantic demonstration was a member of one of the Union Maryland regiments, and that the lady was his betrothed. I should be glad to know that "when this cruel war was over" he met his darling under other and happier circumstances.

The column halted about a mile south of Strasburg in a strip of timber on the left of the road. It was quite dark now, and, weary from long marching under the rays of the burning July sun, I dropped on the ground to sleep just where I had stopped. To cool my body I had thrown open my pants and blouse and pulled up my shirt. Suddenly I was awakened by something that felt cold and slimy crawling slowly over my naked stomach. My first impulse was to throw it off, but remembering that Pierce, who was lying beside me, was a sort of practical joker, and supposing that he had procured a damp and decayed limb and stripped off the bark to make it feel cold and slippery and applied it to frighten me, I proceeded to remove the object with some deliberation. The darkness was intense and I could distinguish nothing.

Cautiously laying my hand down, so that Pierce would not have a laugh at my expense, I grasped the intruder. As I clenched it a vigorous squirming revealed the true state of affairs. The supposed stick was a huge snake, which, doubtless, had been disturbed by the many feet around him, and was trying to escape. I was up in an instant.

"Snake!"

I could scarcely articulate the word, but it seemed to be thoroughly understood by those concerned. The agility with which the crowd around me rose to their feet, and stamped, was surprising. Of the fate of his snakeship I am uninformed. It is to be presumed that, so far as the scare was concerned, the scale was pretty evenly balanced as between the reptile and the prisoners in that part of the camp.

In looking—or rather feeling—around for a better location, my attention was attracted by a constant coming and going among the prisoners, and I discovered that a fountain of water was the attraction. I think it was called the Shawnee Spring—a magnificent well, sufficient for the supply of quite a city. After quenching my thirst with its precious waters, I stretched myself out by the foot of a tree, and soon forgot my many tribulations.

The drums of our guards roused us early next morning, but it was quite late in the forenoon before our journey was resumed. We had expected to receive rations here, as promised by the confederates, but none were issued. Some of the guards very ostentatiously displayed bread, and thus taunted our hungry stomachs, apparently from pure malevolence. I had eaten my last meal beyond Winchester some thirty-six hours previous, and began to feel the cravings of the inner man in a way that was unmistakable; and the order to march certainly fell upon unwilling ears so far as I was concerned. As there was no help for it, however, I plucked up courage, managed to get to the head of the column—this was the easiest place to march, as all soldiers know—and then maintained my position until the cavalcade halted at Woodstock—a distance of some twelve miles, I think, from Strasburg.

I should mention that just outside of Woodstock we met the only reinforcements, probably, that Lee received from the south for at least twenty days after his defeat at Gettysburg—some fifteen hundred or two thousand men. They greeted us with confederate war songs as the two bodies of blue and gray passed each other, while our men responded with the *Star-spangled Banner*. The bantering greetings exchanged were accepted in a friendly spirit by both parties.

458

We left Woodstock about eight o'clock next morning, a hungry, humiliated, growling crowd. A thunderstorm had arisen the evening before, from which our clothing was still wet. A creek, much swollen by the rain, crossed the road, and this we were obliged to ford, the water reaching up to our waists. This adventure nearly ruined me, financially, as the greenbacks in my pocket-book became saturated with water, and I forgot all about them until after our arrival at Mount Jackson two days afterwards. Then the notes were all moldy, the paper beginning to show signs of decomposition; but I carefully smoothed out the wrinkles and dried them in the sun.

About noon the cavalcade reached Edinburg, some nine miles from Woodstock, and kept on to Mount Jackson, seven miles further, encamping at the latter place at five o'clock in the evening.

During the march this afternoon one of the prisoners, exhausted from extreme thirst, knelt down beside a brook to drink. One of the guards, an ignorant, vicious fellow, drew up his musket to shoot him. Croy, who came up at the instant, stepped over to the guard, shook his fist in his face, and said:

"Damn you, if you fire that gun we will tear you in pieces!"

The fellow looked at him in astonishment, lowered his musket, growled out a few angry oaths, resumed his place in the line, and moved on, as though he had been ordered to do so by one of his own officers.

A discussion sprang up between a prisoner, of Pennsylvania, and a guard, of Virginia, the question being upon the comparative productiveness of their respective states. After much was said, pro and con, the Virginian put in the following clincher:

"Well, I know all about your state; I looked on a map, once, and seed your state; and the soil was as poor could be—wouldn't raise nothin'."

His opponent wilted.

We passed another hungry night at Mount Jackson. I had eaten nothing since leaving Winchester except a piece of fly blown meat which had turned the delicate stomach of one of our citizen prisoners, and which he had earnestly contemplated throwing away; it was certainly unpalatable, but I kept it down.

Speaking of our citizen prisoners, I should, perhaps, explain that they were, as a general thing, farmers who had been gathered in from their homes in Pennsylvania by the confederates for some unexplained purpose, thrown in among the military prisoners, and with the latter doomed to a long march and longer imprisonment at Richmond. Most

459

of them were of that quiet, unoffending class known as Pennsylvania Germans, and submitted to their hard and uncertain destiny with the resignation of real soldiers. There were, I think, about one hundred and fifty of them.

The next morning rations of flour and meat were issued, to last two days. I made my flour all into "slapjacks," cooked all my meat, and devoured the entire two days allowance, determined that if I must die it should be with a full stomach. Then I laid down in a fence corner, and slept several hours.

We remained at Mount Jackson until the next day, and then set out for New Market, distant seventeen miles, reaching the latter place early in the evening. Here more rations were issued.

Remained at New Market all night, resting well, and marched next day to Harrisonburg, a distance of thirteen miles, where we encamped for the night, and received more rations.

I am thus particular to mention the times and seasons of the issuing of food, for these manna showers were matters of a dominant interest to all of us prisoners. During a portion of the time the bread market was brisk, a loaf commanding as high as five dollars, and often could not be procured at any price.

The next morning we were informed that the track to Richmond was open and our journey would be continued on the cars. This was good news, for marching on foot two or three days at a time is a rather trying ordeal.

The next morning the prisoners were transferred to another field, where they were stripped of everything except just what they had on their bodies. Fortunately Croy had sold his overcoat a few days previous to our arrival for a large sum in confederate money. I had nothing to lose, and was spared this trial. Curses both loud and deep came up from the hearts of the captives at this unexpected outrage.

The reason assigned by the confederates for this wholesale denudation of unarmed men was their utter lack of clothing and blankets. They complained of the activity of our blockade squadron, which, as they alleged, obliged them to resort to all sorts of plans to secure the necessary supplies for the approaching winter. While this was no doubt satisfactory to them it was very aggravating to us.

A large number of confederate prisoners were confined here, many of them wearing ball and chain, and serving out various terms for desertion and other offenses.

Quite a number of persons quietly made themselves known to us as Unionists, and gave substantial aid whenever the strict surveillance of the guards could be successfully eluded. From their accounts of the position they occupied, always watched, always suspected by their neighbors, and liable to conscription or imprisonment, I learned to appreciate the nerve and tact it required to people possessing such sentiments to remain within the confederate lines with their wives and little ones.

Seven or eight hundred men per day were shipped for Richmond on open cars. I was anxious to get to our final destination, but, owing to a general rush for the train, was crowded out for several days. Todd, McKibben, Old Blue, and several others of Company F managed to get away on the first day after our arrival, and were paroled and sent north before the week was out. Finally, on the Friday following our arrival, I think, my turn came. By vigorous efforts I managed to squeeze myself on board. The flat cars were so crowded that but half of the men, perhaps, could sit down at once. As there were no seats, we were obliged to resort to our "bunkies."

I do not think I shall forget that ride to Richmond during my existence in this life. The train moved, as near as I can judge, at the rate of about ten miles per hour. The sun was fairly blazing in a cloudless sky. For the first few miles the novelty of the ride stirred up our spirits; but the journey soon became a monotonous one, and the utter impossibility of one's resting oneself when tired of standing added to one's agony. Stoppages were so frequent that the expressed doubt as to our reaching Richmond before the month was ended seemed not to be so extravagant after all. The men began to suffer from want of water, and, although, we ran along the mountain side, and saw the clear crystal streams come dashing down almost within reach of our hands, we could not quench our consuming thirst. The harvesters were busy in the meadows; the farm houses in the distance reminded me of the contented days of "auld lang syne;" the cattle in the fields raised their heads to look at the supremely wretched tatterdemalions who boarded the black cars like so many bunches of flies, and as I looked on in my despairing soul it seemed as if we were to be forever isolated from all this happy world.

It had been quite late in the day before the train left Staunton, and, owing to the slow rate of speed, and the numerous stoppages, we had not travelled many miles before evening came upon us. A long dreary night followed. The train stopped at some unknown place for many hours, and the weary men huddled down as best they could, some on the ground and

461

some on the train, and slumbered as best they could under the circumstances.

At last the dawn came, and the train rumbled on toward its destination. The morning brought with it a certain sense of freshness that was grateful to our fatigued spirits. Afar off I could hear the still crow of feathered denizens of the barnyards, and it seemed to me that I could detect a sort of triumph in their notes that they dared not exhibit in other days, when our battalions swarmed along the Rappahannock.

Late in the morning we passed a station at which stood a solitary house. The platform was close to the track, and on it stood a bevy of ladies, and a little girl of perhaps eight years. The latter had a small confederate flag. By direction of the older-persons of the part, I suppose, she brought this banner to the edge of the platform, and waved it over the heads of the prisoners. A heavy fire of tobacco juice was directed upon its folds, when it was hastily withdrawn, with many expressions of profound disgust from the ladies, who, a moment before, had smiled at the humiliation they were about to inflict upon the hated "Yankees."

At another station the cars were surrounded by "snack" vendors, who asked one dollar apiece for very small and very bilious looking pies. Croy thought of the proceeds of the sale of his overcoat, and relying upon this financial basis bargained for two of these very small and very bilious looking articles. One he handed down to me, where I was sitting in a crowded position on the bottom of the car, and the other he proceeded to devour leisurely. It was pretended that the pies contained apples, but I think there was some mistake about it. A careful analysis disclosed not the faintest trace of sugar or "shortening" within them.

After the train started Croy informed me confidentially that his finances were not in the least diminished by the purchases from which I inferred he had not paid for the articles.

Which was very wrong of Croy!

The monotony of our ride today was somewhat relieved by the glorious scenery along the road, especially as we came into Charlottesville, and beheld the grand outlines of the mountains above Monticello, the University of Virginia, and the beautiful Rivanna. We stopped at Charlottesville a short time, and then steamed on to Gordonsville, where another delay occurred. At the latter place a small boy came up to the car, and thus accosted me:

"I say, have you heard the news from New York City?"

"I have heard nothing lately," I replied. "What is it?"

He struck an attitude, and then said:

"Oh, they've had a riot there—they've resisted the draft."

"Indeed, well what then?"

"And the United States have been obliged to suspend it—can't enforce it."

I could not help admiring the precocity of this youth, though the information he gave was having an unpleasant effect on my nerves.

"Oh, I guess there's a mistake about that. It's only one of your stories to keep up your courage," I replied.

"No, sir," was the rejoinder, "it's the truth. The people are bound to stop this war."

I confess to feeling a sense of relief when the train started just then, for this youth was evidently too well "posted" for me.

During the day I came in possession of some Fluvanna County scrip, which was used as currency within its limits, though worthless outside. From this it was evident that the finances of the Southern Confederacy were in a terribly muddled condition.

The ride from Gordonsville to Richmond was devoid of interest. I remember that it grew dark soon after we left the former town, and that there seemed to be an endless monotony of pine forests and lonely fields. But few words were spoken that night. The men were utterly exhausted from want of food and water and being crowded together so long without a chance to straighten their limbs in sleep. I managed to secure a seat on the end of a car beside one of the guards—a tall, lean, lank man, forty-five or fifty years of age, with long reddish hair and whiskers—and was as comfortable as circumstances would permit. About midnight I felt the guard lean heavily upon me, and from his hand slipped the dreaded musket. As it fell I seized it, and thus prevented its loss. The man was sound asleep. My first impulse, now that I had an enemy in my power, was to push him off suddenly between the cars, and have him crushed to death; but it occurred to me that such an act would simply constitute a cowardly murder; then the vision of a family in tears rose vividly before me.

I awakened him, gave him his gun, and cautioned him playfully as to his duty as a soldier. He seemed very grateful, and said he was completely worn out from fatigue. For a few moments he sat up, and then settled back again sound asleep, and I once more caught the gun as it fell. I allowed him to sleep until we reached Richmond, just before

463

dawn, when I aroused him. A few moments later Imboden's men were relieved by other soldiers, who fell into line around the train as soon as it stopped in the street.

As I raised from my sitting position I was seized with a terrible pain in my stomach, and fairly twisted in agony. Fortunately it lasted but a few moments, though to me the time seemed an age.

«««««««««««««««««««««««««««««««««««««»»»»»»»»»»»»»»»»»»»»»»»»»»»»»»

464

Life in Prison on Belle Isle

At dawn the prisoners were marched from the train to the sidewalk, and thence to the vicinity of Castle Thunder,[1] where they were halted for half an hour. While passing down the street the steady "click-clack" of a steam printing-press broke upon my ears, and reminded me of the old days at the *Dispatch* office, in Pittsburgh.

"Wonder if I shall ever see the typos again?"

Our eyes fell upon a scene at Castle Thunder that startled us by its horrible significance, foreshadowing the fate that awaited the loyalists who fell into confederate hands. At all the windows, peering through the iron lattice-work like so many crated beasts, were ghastly female faces, and white bony hands were outstretched and beckoning to us.

"Look on us soldiers of the federal army, and see for yourselves an exhibition of rebel hate. We are union people of East Tennessee.[2] We have been confined here for nineteen months, starved and maltreated as though we were beasts of prey. They have promised us our liberty if we would swear allegiance to their unholy cause, but we despised their overtures. We shall rather leave our bones in these dungeons than bow the knee to their detested flag."

These words fell from the lips of a woman, whose dark eyes, jet black, tangled hair, and pallid bony face made up a weird picture as it appeared behind the bars. Her voice was clear and thrilling, and each syllable was enunciated with startling distinctness. As she ceased to speak from the window, her form withdrew, and a moment later I saw

---

[1]   Castle Thunder, a converted tobacco warehouse, was used to confine political prisoners and persons suspected of being spies.

[2]   East Tennessee was an area staunchly supportive of the Union. Union sentiment was, in many Confederate eyes, tantamount to treason.

her pacing back and forth across the room in which she was confined. Cheers arose from the prisoners in honor of the fidelity of these unfortunates to the Union.

The guard now hurried us away, and a few moments later we were clambering up the stairs of an old building which, judging from the piles of stems in the different corners of the rooms, must at one time have been used for storing up tobacco. Our party was thrust into a large hall in the second story, and as we passed through the door each man received a piece of bread and meat—a very acceptable gift. Securing the most eligible locality to be found, away in a corner where there was little danger of being trampled upon, I stretched out upon the floor and soon was sound asleep.

"Fall in!—fall in !—fall in, here!"

There was something familiar about that voice. As I stepped into my place in ranks my astonished eyes looked upon the dramatic Center, who had deserted the company early in the spring. He paced up and down the line as though he were treading the boards of a stage. The prisoners of Company F gathered together with one accord, and discussed matters with language more forcible than refined. However, Center evidently had the advantage of us at present.

It soon became apparent that the specific object of this sudden mustering was to search the prisoners for money and valuables. Three others, beside Center, conducted the business. They went through the performance with the adroitness of professional pickpockets. The Company F men, headed by Dawson, joined the line which Center was searching, so they might obtain a good look at him.

When he reached them he appeared surprised for a moment, and then, regaining his self-possession, held out his right hand, saying laughingly, as he did so:

"Why boys, you here? How are you?"

The proffered hand was not taken. Dawson, whose face was fairly white with anger, responded:

"Well, Center, don't you feel like a damned traitor?!"

Center turned crimson, and then pale.

"Be careful, for I have power here."

Then recovering himself, he said to Company F men:

"Pass on, boys; I don't want your money."

Thus we escaped the fate which befell our less fortunate comrades among the prisoners.

Although the circumstance was not a legitimate one for diversion, I could not help feeling amused at the efforts made by an old German to save his greenbacks. Center was trying to persuade him to hand over his valuables, but without avail.

"By damn, what for you want my money? Dash is not ter way mit ter Union army."

Center said he understood that, but must do his duty, and should feel obliged to have him fork over without delay. The German still resisted, and Center called the guard for assistance. Between the two they swung up the offending man by the thumbs to a post. Forty-six dollars and a silver watch constituted the sum of the spoils found on the person of the Teuton, whose tears and oaths flowed freely as he beheld his all in the clutches of the robbers. A few moments later he was released, and paced up and down the room like one frantic with woe.

Shortly after the searching of the prisoners was completed we were ordered to fall in, and soon after marched over to the historic shore of Belle Isle.[3] Here we found some three thousand prisoners, and among them the men who had preceded us from Staunton. A large squad of these were paroled on the day of our arrival, and sent north. Several of Company F were of the fortunate number. I sent word to father and friends by McKibben, not deeming it necessary to write, fully expecting to be sent off to the same destination in a day two. The departing prisoners bequeathed to us all the bits of clothing and mess fixtures they had managed to smuggle into camp, bade us good bye and a happy return to our lines, and disappeared up the road leading to the bridge across the James River.

Ah! It was a happy return to us when it came, months afterward. But for hundreds who laughed loudest on that morning it was never realized in the flesh.

The camp of the prisoners was located on a narrow strip of bottom land nearly opposite the city of Richmond, and enclosed, I think, about three acres of ground in a square plot. It was laid out regularly, with streets crossing each other at right angles, and contained for its size a full complement of Sibley tents. An embankment about five feet in height, with a ditch of corresponding depth outside, surrounded the camp. Along the side next to the river there were several shallow wells dug, and braced up with headless boards, and from these we procured

---

[3]   Belle Isle, an island in the James river, was used to confine captured Union enlisted men.

467

the necessary water. Two entrances led into the enclosure—one from the west and the other from the north side. The sinks were built outside and north of the camp, over the water in the river, perhaps thirty feet from shore, and were reached by means of narrow plank footwalks. The cookhouse and commissary department were located outside of the enclosure and along the west front. The cemetery was a short distance up the river from the camp. The hospital stood near the cookhouse. The infantry guards were quartered near the commissary department, while, located on elevated ground a hundred yards south of us, was a battery of artillery, whose brazen throats looked down upon the mob of unarmed men in blue day and night.

The guards pointed out to us several objects of interest on the Richmond side of the river. There was the State House, over which floated the flag of Virginia, indicating that the legislature was then in session. Some distance to the left they showed us the residence of the President of the Confederate States of America. Near the river was the celebrated Tredegar Iron Works, busy night and day multiplying confederate cannon.[4] Up the river a short distance was the arsenal, where hundreds of women were busy manufacturing confederate cartridges. Near the high bridge, and at its island end, was a cotton factory, weaving confederate dry goods. A mile or so above the city were coal mines, out of which men were busily bringing the fuel which was to generate the steam to keep in motion confederate engines. Everywhere the energies of a determined people were in active operation continuing and executing the corollaries and preliminaries of a great war. Their every faculty was made subordinate to that one particular end.

Richmond looked rather pretty from our point of view, with its gardens and tasteful villas. There was, however, a peculiar grimy tint to the picture which showed that the people universally were not cultivating the fine arts. The air was smoky and at times dusty. The roll of drums came over the river from all quarters during the still evenings, making one think of a besieged city.

A sort of organization into squads was established among the prisoners, to facilitate the distribution of food. In each squad there were about ninety men, under charge of a sergeant, as a general thing, and these ninety were counted off into five divisions, each of which was also commanded by a non-commissioned officer. When rations were

---

[4] Tredegar Iron Works provided the Confederate Army with roughly fifty percent of the artillery used during the war.

issued—at ten o'clock in the morning and four o'clock in the after-noon—the sergeant in charge of each ninety, with a detail of one man from each of his smaller squads, marched out to the cookhouse and received the allowance assigned to his detachment and carried it inside the camp to his quarters. Then it was divided prorata among the five non-commissioned officers in charge of the smaller squads according to the number of men in each.

The most particular care had to be taken to distribute the food in an impartial manner among the men. The modus operandi was about as follows: first, the meat and bread were carefully divided into a number of pieces corresponding to the members of the squad, and, if soup were issued, a similar division of it was made. Upon each piece of meat a pinch of salt was deposited. When all was arranged one man, holding in his hand a paper containing the names of the men, would step off a few paces, turn his back to the food, and await orders. Another man would then place his hand upon a ration, and call out:

"Whose ration is this?"

The man holding the list, ignorant of the character of the food as to quantity or quality, would select at random some name on the list, and call it out aloud, and the man thus named would step forward and secure it. By this means fairness was exhibited to each person.

During all this ceremony a peculiar excitement seemed to unite the nerves of the men—somewhat akin, I suppose, to that of the holder of a lottery ticket, for which he has expended his last dollar, during a drawing. They would crowd up close to the food, and watch with unblinking, jealous eyes the precious bits as never man has watched his gold. If one secured a piece which seemed to contain a few crumbs more than another an uproar was sure to follow, and he would be thoroughly hated for the balance of the day.

The allowance of meat to each squad was about eleven pounds, bones included, just as it came from the butcher; and I often fancied that these must be of a peculiar breed of cattle from the amount of ribs they seemed to contain. A double loaf of bread was issued to each eight men. This was issued in the morning. In the evening the men were served a weak soup made out of the boiling water of the beef in the morning and what was called cow-peas—a dark, thick, tough-skinned, but very palatable bean—and the usual allowance of bread.

Though the exhibition was rather a pitiable one, it was amusing to watch the men, as the ration hour approached, collecting in front of the gateway leading to the cookhouse, and crowding over one another to catch a glimpse with their ravenous eyes of the coveted treasures, and eagerly discussing the quantity and quality of food about to be issued. Sometimes, the ragged mass in front of the gate would become so great that the authorities, to prevent, perhaps, a raid upon the commissary department, would order a bayonet charge upon it by the guards. Then the panic-stricken crowd would roll back over every obstruction with irresistible force, trampling under foot tents or men that happened to be in the way. One personal experience satisfied the writer that his better policy was to keep out of the track of that peculiar avalanche.

The avenue that ran from the western gate across the camp presented from day to day a curious scene. Little bazaars, at which were exposed for sale all sorts of trinkets, principally made of bone, stretched from one end to the other. At intervals, sitting cross-legged upon the sand, watching for victims like a spider for a fly, with bits of canvas upon which from one to six figures were painted lying beside them, and toying with a box of dice, were the proprietors of "chuck-luck" banks. A pale emaciated fellow came up, put down a bone ring upon a figure against one in the banker's possession; the dice rattle, and nine times out of ten the banker sweeps it off into his pile of trinkets. The stakes played for were generally pieces of bone, little notions, and sometimes pieces of bread. The latter indicated a state of great desperation on the part of the players. Money was seldom displayed, as there were too many ready hands to clutch the coveted greenbacks on the first opportunity. At times a large number of men would crowd about a "chuck-luck" bank, and become completely absorbed in the game. A monotonous refrain, "chuck-luck—chuck-luck—the more you put down the less you take up," grated one's ears on these occasions, and graphically expressed what many of the professionals will remember as being entirely true. Outside of creating some amusement, and thus preventing an intolerable ennui, there was little or no actual profit to bankers or bettors here.

Some "chuck-luck" playing of an extraordinary character came under my notice some two years later, while serving in Hancock's infantry, which I will put on record here. The corps was then in camp on the heights above Giesborough Landing, below Washington—old Camp Stoneman. The men had just received their bounties, and, as usual under such circumstances, gambling was in progress day and night. Idema and McCullough, two young Michiganders, belonging to the company to which I was attached, organized between them a "chuck-luck" bank.

They procured a large dry goods box, upon the bottom of which the proper figures were painted. For a short time they lost money; but presently the tide turned and Uncle Sam's currency flowed in upon them like a river. During this latter phase McCullough was seldom seen; his partner, Idema, generally excusing his absence on some pretext or other.

The wonderful fortune of the bank, however, was destined to a rude termination. A bettor, one fine day, becoming dissatisfied with his losses, and remarking that he thought he would see what was under that box, attempted to tip it over towards Idema. The latter, catching up his side of the box hurled it over upon the suspicious fellow, when lo! out from under it sprang the missing McCullough, and then the bankers made wonderful time towards the quarters of the company, followed by a swarming mass of victims. Their escape from a severe thrashing was by sheer good fortune.

It transpired that a small knot in the bottom of the box had been loosened, and into the loose side of this a nail was driven. When McCullough was under the box Idema would drag the dice upon this knot and hold while the former, hearing the figures called out, would lower the knot, and fix the dice to suit, and replace it.

The modes to which the prisoners resorted in hiding their greenbacks would have been amusing had the danger of their loss been less serious. One was obliged to be on his guard against both foe and apparent friend. I remember one old fellow, belonging to the New York volunteers, who took off the caps of the five brass buttons attached to his coat—they were rather larger than the regulation buttons—deftly inserted in each a note of large denomination, and replaced the caps. I understood the five notes aggregated three hundred and fifty dollars. Foolishly enough, he boasted of his sharp scheme to some of his fellows. One evening, shortly after dusk, he was standing in a dense crowd on the main street, when suddenly he felt a hand grasp him by the throat, and in an instant the entire breast of his coat was torn off, with all the buttons. Before the poor old chap could recover himself, the perpetrator of the robbery disappeared in the mass of men, and was never afterward discovered.

Great ingenuity was displayed in the manufacture of trinkets of bone by some of the prisoners. A young fellow from northern Virginia, among whose personal peculiarities were carefully cultivated long nails on his little fingers, seemed especially apt with his penknife in this respect. He wrought out a small finger ring, the set of which was a wreath and from this wreath, swinging by their hands, facing outward,

471

were well-executed figures of a boy and girl. He also displayed as the hook of a watch chain a coiled serpent, splendidly executed, also of bone. It must have taken many tedious hours to work out such elegant specimens of skill with the simple tools in his possession.

Reading matter in our camp was extremely limited. The works in my possession were Mrs. Hale's cookbook, the especial presence in this particular place, where I found it, I cannot account for, unless it was thrust in upon us by some agent of his satanic majesty, and the New Testament. The first named volume was a source of inexpressible agony to me, and yet it possessed a peculiar fascination which prevented me from hurling it into the river. Day after day I went through its pages, poring over the recipes for delicious condiments, while within me an everlasting hunger seemed to be gnawing at my very vitals. Occasionally I would read aloud to the squad in the tent, and thus arouse the public indignation to such a pitch that my ejectment usually followed. It was a cruel amusement to me, of course, but I think after all the effect was beneficial, for it called us out of the torpid state of supreme indifference into which we sometimes relapsed, and renewed the latent fires of physical life.

As time passed on, and the prisoners grew weaker and weaker under their privations, there became developed in them a sort of pettishness that was peculiarly annoying. It found vent in frivolous arguments and contentions over the most trifling of differences, which were too pitiable to be ludicrous, demonstrating the susceptibility of the human mind to the influences of its surroundings.

In our dreary, monotonous existence Sunday formed a sort of epoch, for on that day it was customary to count the prisoners. This was done by marching the men outside of camp, and then passing them in one by one. It was always a disagreeable task, usually occupying two or three hours, and keeping one in ranks in the hot sun for that period of time. On one of these occasions a couple of prisoners became engaged in a quarrel, amounting to nothing in fact, but one of the guards, anxious no doubt to "kill his man," promptly fired into that mass of four thousand creatures. Strange to say no one was injured. He immediately reloaded his piece, but by that time all was quiet, and he was thus deprived of a second opportunity to "distinguish" himself.

One day we were hurriedly marched out of camp, and formed in column as on parade. This unusual proceeding stimulated the speculative faculties of the prisoners, and rumors multiplied with wonderful rapidity.

Some said we were to be taken further south; others that we were to be paroled; others that our cavalry were about coming into Richmond, and so on ad infinitum. The parole theory seemed to have the most foundation, for it was observed that, shortly after our assembling, a file of guards would take two or three men at a time, and with them pass out of sight into a large wall tent that had been pitched near us for this special purpose apparently, and that these prisoners would shortly reappear on the opposite side of the tent and march straight back into camp. To dispose this theory, however, there were one or two circumstances that I could not help noticing. The men that left the tent looked rather lugubrious, and had a strange deafness to calls for information on the subject, and retired to their respective tents in camp without deigning to look around.

What could it mean? A grave suspicion suddenly entered my mind. Seeking Croy, I imparted it to the sergeant.

"By golly, I believe those fellows are robbing our people!"

He took the hint instantly. Possessing now no valuables himself, he kindly volunteered to push ahead and fathom the mystery, and then give back a sign that I might be forewarned in time to save my few dollars.

I watched anxiously for his reappearance on the opposite side of the tent, and soon saw his red head emerge, his face wearing his usual innocent smile. On stepping a few paces from the door he carelessly swung half about on his heel, and dropped his right hand upon his pocket. This was our signal, and my suspicion proved to be correct as to the mystery of that tent. The confederates were again searching the prisoners for their money.

I crept into the crowd, and, sitting flat upon the earth, took my greenbacks from my pocket and pushed them down between the "reinforcement"—a sort of outside lining attached to dragoon pantaloons, extending from the seat down the inside of each leg to add to their wearing capacity—and the inner lining, clear to my foot, and then smeared the outside with mud for several inches above. When my turn came the dainty clerk declined to soil his soft white hands with the mud, so that the vital spot remained untouched, and in a few moments, after answering some questions, I was allowed to depart in peace. As I left the tent I saw a tall black hat full of greenback sitting on a stand at one side, made up of the pittances of the private soldiers the confederate authorities had confiscated.

On meeting in camp Croy and I exchanged congratulations upon the success of our plan.

As the prospects of retaining my money were becoming less promising daily, I concluded that it would be better to divide it among such of the men of Company F as were penniless, and who were sorely in need of it, and who, if we managed to rejoin our command some day, could then repay me. This proposition was joyfully accepted by the parties interested, and three of my four twenty dollar bills were thus distributed.

The confederate officer in charge of Belle Island at this time was Lieutenant Bosseaux—a handsome, good-natured man whose trials must have been severe at times. It seemed to me that the sympathetic soul which was obliged by his duty to look after the wants of four thousand starving men, without being able to supply them, was indeed to be pitied. Next in command was Sergeant Hyatt, a tall man with light hair. Then there was a repulsive-looking fellow, blind of an eye, who was said to be from Baltimore, and whose countenance betrayed a viciousness of heart that ought have consigned him to a penitentiary. His name I do not remember, though I think his first cognomen was Martin. He wore the clothing of a citizen, and will be remembered by the prisoners for his extreme brutality. Sergeant Hyatt was also unnecessarily cruel, beating the men over their heads with a club on the slightest provocation, and at times "bucking and gagging" them, and leaving them for hours at a time lying out under the fierce rays of that blazing August sun.

It was said that Hyatt, in addition to his many other duties, was a sort of spy upon the confederate guards, to prevent their trading with the prisoners. This kind of business, however, under the darkness of night, developed into wonderful proportions. It proved very profitable to the confederates, the price of bread ranging from one to two dollars per loaf, and that of pies from two to four dollars per dozen. The bread was tolerably good, but the pies were fearfully if not wonderfully made. Composed of flour, water, and dried apples—very simple ingredients, to be sure without a vestige of what is known as "shortening," it required some courage to approach them, though hunger, unlike conscience, makes heroes of us all in an attack on supposed eatables.

In these hidden dealings the guards possessed many advantages over the prisoners. The latter were obliged to throw their pocketbooks, containing the money, over the parapet, and depend upon the integrity of the guards for the return of the proper amount of change, if any were due or bread or equivalent in pies, as desired. The food was usually put

474

in a haversack by the guard, and tossed over to the prisoner, who emptied it out and threw it back. To add to the excitements attending the business, the confederates sometimes kept the money without giving anything in return. It was useless to complain about the latter outrage, because the authorities seemed to encourage rather than punish their authors. Sometimes the individual, instead of receiving the coveted greenback, was "bucked and gagged" and deposited on the ground near the cookhouse, to repent at his leisure. Of course, to guard against such accidents all sorts of promises and oaths were required from the guards, without mental reservation in waiving their eternal salvation in case of deception.

The prisoners were not always to be beaten in the desperate struggle for food. Many ingenious methods were devised to secure supplies, which, if they will not bear the scrutiny of self-styled rigid moralists, I doubt not are fully justified by him who went into the cornfield on a Sabbath day some eighteen hundred years ago and plucked the ears of grain for himself and disciples. One plan was to take a one dollar or two dollar note, and affix beside the figure a cypher of dingy white paper, thus adding a tremendous percentage to its value in the darkness of the following night. As soon, however, as the guards discovered these counterfeit bills they retaliated with a vengeance. To illustrate one of their methods of revenge I will recount a proceeding I witnessed one midnight just outside my tent. The parties belonging to our side were two prisoners who, however, proved equal to the enigma. One of them crawled on his stomach close under the parapet, entirely concealed from the view of the guard, while the other advanced boldly to bargain for the bread. It transpired that this particular sentry had been imposed upon by a federal the evening before, and chose to revenge himself on a Yankee rather than run the risk of a second loss. The following dialogue took place as soon as our man took position beside the parapet:

"Hey, guard," said the federal, in a low voice.

The sentry stopped on his beat, and gruffly demanded:

"What do you want?"

"Want to buy bread. Got any?"

"Have you got money?"—after a slight pause.

"Certainly."

"How much?"

"Twenty dollars."

"Hold it up—let me see it."

The prisoner raised his hand, with the note hanging between his fingers, while the guard stooped down so as to bring it between him and the sky. Then rising up, and suddenly bringing his gun up to his shoulder and bearing directly upon the prisoner, he roared out:

"Now, damn you, stand perfectly still, or you are a dead man. Officer of the guard, post number seven!"

The officer and a file of men came upon the scene, and ordered the prisoner to come directly across the parapet, but as he did so he let the note drop from between his fingers to his partner, who secured it and crawled off to his tent like a monster serpent. The other federal was taken to the guard tent, and carefully searched, but, of course, without avail, and he was sent back to camp, while the guard was promptly lectured for rousing the officer from his slumbers without cause.

This sort of sharp practice on the part of the prisoners finally exhausted the patience of the guards, and a truce was tacitly established, under which trading went on satisfactorily for a time. Judging from the thriving business one lad did on the outside of the parapet one night, I estimated his receipts at four or five hundred dollars in the period from midnight till just before dawn.

In time the bills of small denominations among the prisoners were exhausted by the constant drain upon them in this surreptitious trading. As the guards were never known to return differences in change one did not care to place any more money in their possession than one could help. One Gavitt, a member of the First New York Artillery, captured at Gettysburg, and who was detailed by the confederates on duty in the commissary department, established a sort of brokerage business, which proved very profitable to him, if not the prisoners. He possessed facilities for procuring currency in his trips over to Richmond on matters connected with the commissary stores. The rate of exchange which he established was ten percent discount on all sums. In addition to other peculiar methods, he managed to give notes that required to be again changed, and thus reaped greater profits. For instance, if one had a twenty dollar note for which he desired bills of a smaller denomination, Gavitt would give him eighteen dollars—discounting two dollars—a ten, a five, a two, and a one dollar note, and by this means the victim was obliged to have the five and ten broken in due time, at the same rate of discount. Judging from the extent of this man's operations, he must have acquired a large sum of money through these means. Of course, he was severely denounced by the prisoners for thus taking advantage of their

476

cruel necessities, and threats of vengeance were freely made, which were to be duly executed when the revolutions of the wheel of fortune should place him in the hands of his victims beyond the federal lines. How well these vows were kept subsequent events will show.

At the time of our arrival on Belle Island that post was unmarked by a flag; but shortly afterward the confederates took steps to raise one. For this purpose they trimmed off the branches of a tall dead tree near the cookhouse, and increased the altitude by splicing to the top a long pole. Some difficulty occurred about the halyards, which could not be arranged without some one climbing to the upper extremity of the staff, but none of the guards seemed willing to hazard their lives by such an effort. finally the confederates called on the prisoners to furnish a volunteer for the purpose, promising as an inducement a loaf of bread. Of course, this offer was indignantly rejected; but presently one man, apparently of Spanish origin, ventured to accept the proposition, and after perhaps an hour's work successfully ran up the confederate flag. He then received the promised bread, and returned into camp. A crowd of infuriated prisoners immediately assaulted him, and, had not the guards rushed in and checked the disturbance, it is probable he would have been killed. He was then permitted to remain outside of the camp with other detailed men, and no doubt, when he came to sum up the results, was rather glad than otherwise that he had performed the service for the confederates.

While I shared the general feeling of humiliation that one of our soldiers should so far forget his honor as to deliberately hoist the banner of our common enemy over his fellow-captives, yet, taking into consideration the tremendous temptation which a loaf of bread at that time constituted, and the fact that some other method, had this failed, would have been adopted to attain the same end, I concluded to give the Spaniard the benefit of a charitable doubt at least. Of course, the injury was more fancied than real.

The flag was an odd-looking one with its white and red stars and cross and blue background and long plain white fly. Thereafter at reveille and retreat it was raised and lowered with appropriate ceremonies.

I was rather more fortunate than some of my comrades on the island in one very important respect. Some of Company F men were detailed to duty in what was designated as a fatigue police among the prisoners, for which service they received double rations. With one of these,

477

named Thom—a Michigander—I made an arrangement by which I received a stated amount of food daily at a specified rate. By these means I managed to keep myself tolerably comfortable as compared with others. Before this opportunity was presented, however, I had lost about all the flesh there was to spare from my bones. My hip joints had worked their way to the surface of the skin, and annoyed me with pain while reclined on either side. My hours of slumber were full of dreams, and the burden of these visions was food—food! I was always sitting down to tables that groaned under the choicest of viands, and, although I appeared to partake freely of these, I never seemed to be surfeited. Generally these feasts were at the old boarding house on Third Street, Pittsburgh, with the kind, motherly face of Mrs. Cook beaming on me from the opposite side of the table. When morning dawned, and my fearful sleep was over, an everlasting hunger was upon me, from which there was no escape. My breakfast was just sufficient in quantity to increase its intensity. I closed the meal with a groan that came up involuntarily from my inmost soul. As a sort of self deception, I usually broke up my allowance of bread into the old skillet—the relic of the house in Maryland, which I had carried all those long, hungry miles—and poured upon it a pint of water. By this means the bread was increased to double its size and weight, and actually seemed more satisfactory.

To add to the discouragements of our situation, it was announced that the federal authorities had concluded to make no more exchanges. The reason for this decision, as we were told, was on account of the refusal by the confederate government to recognize the military status of armed colored men in the service of the United States. No doubt the story was very highly colored as it came to us from the guards, whose efforts to make us miserable betrayed the wonderful genius they possessed in creating cruel surprises of this sort. The prospect of a prolonged and indefinite sojourn on the island stretched out as a gloomy certainty. While we did not, could not believe that our government thus intended to abandon us utterly to our dismal fate, yet it was clearly evident that something had gone wrong, because the usual paroling had ceased for a time.

Often our sufferings were increased by the actions of the more inconsiderate of our own men, who, to gratify a useless stubbornness of disposition, would violate prison regulations, and thus bring down upon the devoted heads of the whole party the vengeance of our captors. To secure the real culprits it was usual to stop the food supply of the camp to oblige the men to betray them. Of course, there was no alternative.

Owing to the desperate condition of mind into which an intense hunger had driven the prisoners it was no longer safe for one to be seen away from one's friends with anything of an edible character in his possession; hundreds of eyes, glittering with ravenous light, would fasten upon it as though bewitched by some wonderful vision, and the prospect of an assault upon the bearer would loom up with a painful vividness. If one wanted to trade with the sentinels during the night, it was necessary to take along a body guard of five or six men, to protect one from the wolfish stomachs that were sure to lie in wait at every corner. That organ had become the personal pronoun; it had absorbed the whole man; the brain, legs, arms, jaws, and other members had become mere subordinates to do its imperious bidding. It was the absolute monarch to whose beckoning all other faculties yielded an unquestioning obedience.

Happening to stand one evening near the eastern parapet my attention was attracted to a prisoner and one of the guards. It was the usual trading conversation, carried on in a low tone, and soon ceased, and the preparations to complete the bargain began. The federal threw over his pocket-book; a haversack was tossed across the parapet in return, when suddenly a tall dark form sprang up from the ground nearby, rushed upon the expectant trader, knocked him over, caught the haversack "on the fly," and dashed off towards the interior of the camp. But he was destined to meet with disaster; almost as soon as he had wheeled around four or five of the trader's friends were upon him, and he was forced to drop his booty.

One day a party of some forty sailors, belonging to one of the blockading vessels guarding the southern coast, who had been captured by the confederates during our expedition into the mainland, were marched into camp. They were all stout fellows, and their brawny forms and full faces were in marked contrast with their brothers-in-arms of the land service. Contrary to the notions I had formed of the generous character of American sailors, these men looked upon the ghastly mob with hostile contempt. They were favorites with the confederates, who gave them double the allowances of food that were distributed to the soldiers. In a short time the sailors became aggressive; armed with short clubs, and duly organized, they would make raids upon harmless individuals, and rob them of food and valuables. In this they seemed to be encouraged by the guards, who never, so far as I could observe, made any effort to check them. As the prisoners were weak and utterly discouraged no effort was made to resist the encroachments of these men, and their operations were continued with impunity during the whole time of their confinement with us.

One of the peculiar annoyances to which from time to time we were subjected was one of a character that, in consideration of the circumstances by which we were surrendered, might be designated as despicably mean. At intervals certain members of the guard, by way of amusement, would stand outside of the parapet, and, calling out the "Yankees," throw pieces of bread high up in the air so that they would fall among the prisoners, and then enjoy the scene of terrific scrambling and fighting over the crusts that was sure to ensue. Hundreds of men would surge and struggle and yell in their mad, incoherent way—a pitiful sight to one whose soul was susceptible of kind impulses. When the bread supply should be exhausted these men managed to keep up their sport a little while longer by tossing over small pine blocks, freshly sawed, which bore a resemblance to the food, and seemed to highly relish the chagrin of the man who, after desperately fighting for its possession, should look at his worthless prize with ill concealed disgust.

It is sad to look upon these terrible days. In them there was no respect shown to special friends. The impecunious stomach compelled the sacrifice of all sentiments of affection in the fierce struggle for existence.

With their ragged and dirty clothing, swarming with vermin, their gaunt frames, their long, bony fingers, opening and shutting convulsively, their matted hair falling over wan faces, sunken eyes which gleamed with an eager, hungry light that is indescribable, the prisoners on Belle Isle presented a pitiable picture. Though so garrulous and fault-finding toward one another; though they no longer possessed a flag or a country, and were apparently entirely abandoned by their race to a fate the most cruel of all others to a high spirited soldier; huddled in wild disorder within their crowded domain; counting each morning the ominous blanket stretchers that passed the western gate and the red boxes that came on the flat boat from the city—with all these discouragements and sad prospects their patriotic fervor never flagged in its manifestations. Listening to the conversations among them, as they crowded about on the sand, one would never hear a word that indicated regret as to their joining the army or a desire to see the confederate cause triumph over the one which they had espoused.

These red boxes—coffins—became objects of much interest to a class of men among the prisoners. These peculiar fellows would rise early in the morning, and range themselves along the parapet on the west side of camp, and wait patiently for the arrival of the flat; when this occurred, they would carefully count the coffins as they were piled up beside the tent in which was deposited our dead, and then hurry off to their respective tents, and report, with much gusto, so many "red boxes out there!"

No fear of encountering the "grim monster" was manifested. It seemed to me that, in the peculiarly exhausting process to which we were subjected, a sort of compensation was vouchsafed us by our considerate mother, Dame Nature, in that our loss of life diminished in just the proportion that our energies dwindled, so that, by the time the end was at hand, the victim slept his life away in unconscious ease. Of course, there were some exceptions; occasionally men died from cramps in the stomach, or other painful causes, and suffered terribly.

Perhaps one of the saddest scenes within my recollection of those fearful days, and one, too, which demonstrated the utter demoralization which this carnival of death and suffering was making in the hearts of the prisoners, occurred one evening about the last of August or the early part of September. In a tent adjoining the one occupied by our squad, stretched upon his bed of sand a young man, a member of the One-hundred and Ninth Ohio Volunteers, was dying. He was in great agony, uttering groans that went to my inmost soul. Mingled with these I could hear the querulous oaths of his companions as they quarrelled over the division of the rations of which he could no longer partake. The quantity was too small to divide among the dozen or so men who occupied the tent, and hence the dissatisfaction manifested. Until nine or ten o'clock that night these groans of the dying man rang in my ears, weaker and weaker during each successive hour, and finally ceasing with his last breath.

There was something about this affair that filled my heart with indescribable horror. Dying in prison, far away from the old homestead, surrounded by comrades in whom the terrible privations of Belle Island had apparently quenched away every sentiment of sympathy, hidden, indeed, by the friendly darkness, from the silly stare of the curious—one blessing—it was a sad, sad thought.

The water for the use of the prisoners was procured by digging down in the ground four or five feet and inserting in this well, to prevent the sand from washing it, headless barrels or casks. It was river water, which found its way through the gravelly formation, and was quite good, save for a fine, glittering black sand with which it was impregnated, that aggravated the diarrhea that prevailed to an alarming extent among the men during this period, and thus added to their sufferings.

The sinks attached to the camp were built on the river shore, perhaps twenty or more feet out from the edge of the water. An arrangement consisting of a narrow platform resting upon a few stakes driven into the soft sand, a pole forming the seat, and two or three ordinary planks leading from the shore to the platform, comprised the entire structure. Several large trees, growing upon the bank, threw their grateful shadows over the spot, as though in pity for the poor, sick creatures that constantly thronged here. Sometimes a prisoner would totter down to the planks, and, blinded by weakness, deliberately walk overboard into the river. Fortunately the water was quite shallow here—two or three feet deep, perhaps.

For a short time after our arrival upon the island the prisoners were allowed to visit the sink during any hour in the day or night, under charge of a guard, but, upon the pretext—and it may have been a valid one—that some of our men had abused this privilege, and attempted to escape, it was abolished, except from reveille till retreat.

The effect of this regulation was sickening. Every night the entire camp was flooded with excrement, which could not be removed by the fatigue party until late in the morning. For fully ten hours the atmosphere was thus burdened with noisome gases. This added greatly to increase the ravages of disease.

When sick call sounded in the morning a vast crowd would collect in front of the western gate in the vain hope of being sent to some hospital where they surmised more food might be secured, or perhaps they might be paroled. As a consequence, those really in need of treatment could not see the medical authorities at all. Medicine was said to be extremely scarce.

Funerals were getting to be frequent. Each morning a detail went around among the tents and gathered up the bodies of those who died during the night. Quite a number of bodies could be seen daily, lying side by side upon the plank floor just outside of the hospital tent, with blankets covering them from human gaze.

I remember, one Sunday, while we were marching out of camp to receive our usual counting, that I looked at the dozen or so of bodies that were stretched upon this platform. The hot sun was fairly blazing down upon them. They were entirely covered with blankets. One man was still alive, and as he laid on his back and opened wide his mouth in gasping for breath, I could distinctly see the blanket settle between his jaws.

Who shall tell of the unutterable agony of that dying soldier, suffocating gradually under a burning sky, crowded by the dead bodies of his comrades?

For a short time after our arrival on the island the prisoners were permitted, under guard, and in small squads, to visit the river for bathing and cleansing their clothing; but, owing to the attempt of one of them to escape, this privilege also was denied us. He swam off towards the Richmond side, but was captured and incarcerated in a dungeon in Castle Thunder for a couple of weeks, and compelled to be contented with bread and water in limited quantities.

The efforts on the part of the confederate authorities to secure the money in the hands of the prisoners were continued during the months I remained on the island. The most important business, after securing one's rations, was to keep one's greenbacks in one's own possession. The camp seemed to swarm with spies. Thinking himself safe, the possessor of currency would suddenly be surprised at times by a guard, and marched out and searched. What ultimately became of the money so taken remains to me a mystery, which may, perhaps, be understood on the last day. The reason assigned for thus depriving us was that it found its way, through our surreptitious trading into the possession of the guards, and thus became an inducement to desertion.

Great formality was observed on these occasions. They would take your name, company and regiment, and money, and the first three items would be duly entered in a book, while the latter was deposited in some one else's pocket book, and the prisoner coolly informed that he would receive it again on reaching the lines of the United States, but that any soldier did so receive it I have never heard. As a precautionary measure, believing themselves its more rightful custodians, the prisoners kept their money secreted in all sorts of unheard-of places.

On our arrival in Richmond the men were besieged to exchange greenbacks for confederate notes at the rate of three dollars of the latter for one of the former. They soon discovered that this was a bad speculation, for no one would take confederate notes from us under any consideration, apparently attaching but little value to them, or else fearing counterfeits, as it was then known that federal soldiers were well supplied with a large amount of excellent facsimiles of southern currency. The rates of exchange advanced rapidly, reaching thirteen dollars for one, offered without success.

One day, while sauntering up and down one of the camp avenues, cogitating on my misfortunes and wondering how and when they would end, I met a soldier coming in an opposite direction, with whom I exchanged glances, and passed. A moment later I heard a voice—

"Sid!"

Turning back, and looking steadily into his eyes, I recognized Joseph Laurence Moore, an old friend with whom I had parted in Monongahela City three years before. He was greatly changed in appearance.

"Glad to see you, Joe, but sorry for the circumstances under which we meet."

We had a long talk together about ante-bellum days and other scenes by the old river far away, and almost forgot our dilapidated stomachs and miserable surroundings. I found him full of patriotism, and hopeful of the success of the cause.

There were tents enough to shelter about one-half of the four thousand prisoners confined to the island, by crowding from sixteen to eighteen men in a tent. The other two thousand were exposed to the elements. The days were fearfully hot, and the nights damp and chilly. During the latter period the emaciated creatures were compelled to walk about constantly to keep their blood in circulation, and throughout the former they slept upon the burning sand. Often I have seen men thus lying upon their faces, half buried in the dust—how they breathed I know not—and fearing them dead would shake them, receiving for my solicitude a sleepy, stupid curse for disturbing them.

One day, while lying in my tent half asleep, the report of a musket startled me from my reveries. Instantly there was a great commotion among the prisoners, and, hurrying outside, I found a large crowd surging along the main street toward the eastern end of the enclosure. At the battery on the hill just above us the confederate cannoneers were thronging about their pieces, as if intending to open upon our devoted heads. The infantry guards were falling into line under arms, ready for action, some of them hurriedly deploying in front of the point toward which the crowd of prisoners was moving. Fortunately the captives discovered these hostile movements in time, and scattered to their quarters, doubtless saving many of their lives and limbs.

The cause of the excitement was soon apparent. A man named John Donnelly, if I remember aright, from Philadelphia, attached to one of the Pennsylvania regiments, arrived in camp on the day above named, and, sick at heart, stood at the eastern parapet, resting one foot upon the embankment, with his head bowed upon his hands, reflecting no doubt upon the horrors of his situation. The guard, whose beat extended along the ditch outside, called out to Donnelly to take his foot down, but the order seems to have fallen on heedless ears. Perhaps the prisoner, absorbed with bitter thoughts, failed to catch the words. Then the guard began cursing, and Donnelly looked up. The musket was already at the shoulder, and trained upon his heart.

"I did not hear you," said Donnelly.

The gun cracked, and the prisoner fell dead, the ball passing through his body and wounding one or two other men who were lying in a tent behind him. The guard coolly proceeded to reload his piece, and then walked his beat as though nothing had happened. Some of the prisoners lifted the body across the street, so that the confederates might look upon the face of the dead, and realize the fullness of the ignominy of the uncalled for deed. In half an hour it was removed to its last resting place and comparative quiet reigned in camp. One or two arrests were made of impulsive captives whose tongues were uncontrollable, but I believe they were soon returned to their old quarters.

By bribing one of our men who was employed on the ferry between the camp and the city, I was daily supplied with the Richmond papers, and thus managed to keep abreast with the progress of events in the outer world. Allowing much for the boastfulness of the southern press—a characteristic of those stirring times—and by sifting and culling their contents, and balancing accounts, the actual state of affairs was developed. Thus my mental condition was stimulated to some extent, and kept in a state of healthful activity—a blessed relief, that to be realized only needs to be experienced.

Early one morning the stillness was broken by loud cheers in the city, indicating that some unusual event had occurred. Presently a railroad train, loaded with confederate troops, made its appearance on the high bridge, and crossed to the south side. This was followed by another, and another, and another, until it was clearly evident that the confederacy was making some movement of a serious character. Among the prisoners there was a wonderful variety of opinion expressed as to its meaning. You could clearly discern, from the views of particular individuals, the mental peculiarities of each. My sanguine friends would declare that the rebel capital was being evacuated, and would soon be in the hands of the government; which view found a ready combatant in the person of morbid temperament, who would aver that some disaster to the federal arms was impending, and clinch his argument by pointing to the fact that in exhibiting so much enthusiasm the Richmond people knocked the bottom out of the evacuation theory. The guards were reticent upon the subject, but, by asking a series of questions, and making provoking assumptions of all sorts, I managed to discover that the troops belonged to Longstreet's corps. This was, perhaps, all that was known by those not high in authority.

To some noble souls among the captives, this movement of troops seemed of sufficient importance to justify an effort to escape from their bondage, and carry to our government information in regard to it. Some thirty men, by some means, contrived to get away, most of whom, however, were recaptured, but I have been told that a few managed to reach the federal lines in safety. One unfortunate man, who had, by traveling at night, and after suffering almost incredibly from hunger and exposure, almost reached the Union army, which was then in the vicinity of Culpepper Courthouse, was recaptured by a confederate cavalry patrol, and sent, in charge of a mounted man to some camp. Soon after the prisoner was observed to become very lame, and requested permission to use a staff, which was granted; but, at a moment when the attention of his escort was attracted in another direction, he felled him from his horse by a tremendous blow upon the head, and beat out his brains. Then, mounting the horse, the captive made another effort to escape, but rode directly into the midst of some confederate infantry, and easily fell a prey. He was sent back to Richmond, thrust into a dungeon, and there allowed ample leisure to ruminate upon the mutability of human affairs.

We did not have long to wait for news from the troops that had gone from Richmond. A day or two afterwards, noticing a telegraphic dispatch in one of the papers that an accident had occurred on one of the railroads leading through Georgia in which a number of troops were injured—who were spoken of as belonging to Longstreet's corps—and learning from other dispatches that the army of Rosecrantz was in motion in Tennessee, it was quite easy to divine their actual destination. The southern victory at Chicamauga was the result.

486

The prisoners now expected a movement by the Army of the Potomac upon Richmond, and speculation prevailed as to the promise of a successful campaign. Then it was said that our columns were actually in motion, and the prisoners eagerly listened, day after day, for the sound of cannon beyond the city; but they were doomed to disappointment. The inactivity of Meade was the subject of unfavorable comment, but, of course, men under such circumstances could not be expected to know much about the real condition of affairs.

About two o'clock one morning, while I was lying awake in my tent, fully absorbed in the contemplation of my surroundings, and wondering whether I should ever again see my old house, or escape from the torments of this everlasting hunger, the shrill voice of one of our guards broke upon my ears.

"Halt—halt—halt!"

The command spoken at short intervals was supplemented by the crack of a musket.

"For God's sake, don't shoot him!"

The words were scarcely spoken when another shot fell.

"My God—my God—my God!"

It was a piteous, pleading wail, so deep, so full of agony, that it yet rings in my ears. For several minutes it continued, growing weaker and fainter at each repetition, dying away to a husky whisper at the last, and then ceasing altogether. Though unable to see the victim, I knew that some poor soul had been ushered into eternity.

When the first flush of dawn began to make objects visible I crept softly from my couch of sand, and peeped over the parapet at the point from which the sounds had proceeded.

My eyes soon rested upon the bloody scene. The dead body of one of our comrades was lying upon its side, the knees drawn up to the chin, and the hands clenched, and the face wearing an expression of unutterable agony. He had been suffering from sunstroke since about the time of capture at Gettysburg, which seems to have affected his mind, and wandered out at the gate leading to the sink. The guards who should have prevented his exit were away from their posts at the moment, and failed to observe him. Then followed the universal challenge and death shots—the last one, which resulted fatally, having been entirely unnecessary, as he was then returning to the camp, as the wound conclusively showed, entering the pit of the stomach from the front.

The guard, a young, beardless boy, walked his beat rather proudly

487

that day, as though conscious of having performed a brave act. The body remained where it had fallen for several hours afterward, as a warning to the rest of us; but at ten o'clock a party of prisoners were ordered out to bury it, and it was deposited in the cemetery of the camp.

Fresh complications were reported as having arisen between the federal and confederate authorities upon the subject of the exchange of prisoners. From the Richmond papers we learned that Spencer Kellogg, one of our scouts, had been condemned to suffer death as a spy, and that the federal government was holding a confederate prisoner as a hostage. To retaliate for this, it was said, other federals would be seized, and, as if to give emphasis to the rumor, the guards came quietly into camp one day, and marched out a captive, without a word of explanation as to the cause or their intentions. However, as I subsequently learned, the man was claimed as a deserter from the confederate army and was never a member of a federal regiment.

The confederate authorities seem to have been accustomed to test their new cannon at a point just opposite our camp, and a short distance from the Tredegar Iron Works. During one of these occasions—probably owing to the awkwardness of the cannoneers the shells from the gun burst almost directly over our heads, fortunately, however, without injury to any one. The guards were panic-stricken, scampering hither and thither in a bewildered way, many of the sentries abandoning their posts around the prisoners. The scene was rather amusing to think about after the danger was over. For some time the captives annoyed their enemies by allusions to the incidents of the scene, complacently assuming that the latter were merely "homeguards," who were courageous only in the presence of unarmed men, upon whom they were prepared to open fire on the slightest provocation, and whose weakness in body alone rendered them liable to insult and injury.

It should be stated, perhaps, that the confederate command here seemed to be composed of Richmond youths and conscripts from North Carolina—the latter generally old men. The former were young, thoughtless fellows—the patrons, I should judge, of yellow-back literature, who would improve an opportunity for a shot at a "Yankee," while the conscripts were ignorant and bigoted, hating us much and despising the confederate service more, and deserting whenever a chance presented itself. I cannot say that there was any choice between these two classes.

The sentries called the hours from tattoo to reveille. The dialect of

488

the North Carolinians was prominent on these occasions, and amusing to the prisoners. For example—

"Post number fo'; all's well."

The object of these calls—and the custom was not confined to the confederate army—was to prevent the sentinels from sleeping on post. As a rule, the practice is enforced only in camp and garrison.

Amid all their sufferings and privations, the humorous element among the prisoners was constantly asserting itself. It mattered little whether the joke was upon friend or foe. The sense of the ridiculous seemed to have become keener under the horrors of the situation. It is true, the utterances were just slightly hysterical, and a rather melancholy lot of wrinkles puckered up the ghastly face, but the sorrowful combination of noise and countenances presented all the phenomena of a genuine laugh, and did much to buoy the subject above his misfortune.

The loathsome vermin that infested our bodies furnished us with abundant employment during our sojourn on the island, and seemed to develop the latent military genius among us as well. The system of attack on these carnivorous wretches, though not at all times elaborate, was generally effective; and, in justice to the heroism of the diminutive creatures, it may be truly said that they were extremely aggressive in their nature, and never awaited our advance. Woe to the man who did not wage unrelenting war upon them! His skin would soon be punctured with innumerable holes, and his body would constantly writhe in pitiful restlessness. It was customary to count our dead enemies in these Lilliputian engagements, grouping them into the various organizations known to military men, and designating as commanding officers those of the most imposing form. The man who did not slaughter his five hundred per day was of little consequence.

In these wars the ants that inhabited the sandy wastes of our camp were our faithful allies. These could be seen, at all hours of the day, carrying off their ponderous victims to their innumerable little tunnels, with a facility that demonstrated their perfect adaptation to that sort of business. With a little effort of the imagination, one could suppose a vast traffic among the insect denizens below us—a sort of commerce in livestock. Perhaps they were packed away for some future famine in the world of ants.

A toad made its home in our tent, not a bit afraid of us, and apparently feeling itself our social equal. It feasted upon the flies that thronged the camp, and thus made itself useful, though, of course, limited in its capacity. As those gray flies which abound along the James river are perfect in their methods of torment—I had discovered that in other days at Harrison's Landing the toad's efforts were duly appreciated.

It was strange to observe, during much of the period of our confinement, how, from want of other attractions or occupations, the minds of the men became interested in the smallest of things. I found myself studying the lives of the insect world about me, the peculiar adaptation of its denizens to their sphere of existence, and the marvelous intelligence they displayed in all their operations. So far as I could discover, they fulfilled their destiny as completely as the highest of us.

Sitting, this pleasant May evening, in my own house, jotting down these memories of Belle Isle, now the possessor of a beautiful family, with a larder amply stored with substantial provisions, a bed which, though in no sense downy, is clean and comfortable, in a peaceful land, while within sight of my window bands of soldiercitizens are decorating with the flowers of spring the graves of their fallen comrades, the sweet, solemn strains of their music floating in upon my ear, I cannot realize that I ever dwelt amid the horrors of that camp beside the James. The recollection of them seems like that of a hideous nightmare, the offspring of a fever—a delirium. But the pictures are indelibly impressed within my brain. The haggard faces throng about me with their pitiful expression of mingled hunger and horror, and the low voices complain of the neglect of the government that they had served so faithfully; and the thin arms are forever outstretched in mute appeal.

A citizen of Tennessee, apparently about sixty-five or seventy years of age, who had passed nearly two years in various prisons in the south on account of his bold avowal of Union sentiments, was brought upon the island about the first of September, and thenceforward shared our common hardship. From all that I could learn, the change was for him an improvement of condition. During all the long months of his captivity he had been the object of an unrelenting persecution; he had not even the feeble protection of the status of a prisoner of war to shelter him; he occupied the anomalous position of a citizen of the United States by choice and of the Southern Confederacy by compulsion, and was without the shield of either. He had borne up wonderfully amid all his trials, and was as defiant as of old. He was a fine-looking old man,

490

possessing a frank, open countenance, a pair of dark eyes arched by heavy brows, a mass of black and gray hair falling down upon his broad shoulders, and firmly set jaws. He had but few words to say in regard to the war and its results, but these were to the point.

"Never give up-the ship," he would exclaim, "our flag shall yet float over every inch of southern soil."

His brief speeches inspired the prisoners with new life and fresh patriotism, imbuing them with his own heroic purposes.

We had signed our paroles a day or two after our arrival on the island. These were printed in blank on the tops of pages of writing paper, and beneath them we were expected to sign our respective names, companies, and regiments. As near as I can remember, our obligations read about in this wise:

"We, the undersigned prisoners of war, do hereby solemnly pledge our honor not to take up arms against the Confederate States of America or to do any military duty whatever in the service of the United States until duly exchanged."

Our hearts had been gladdened at the bright prospects of an early release, but the days had lengthened into weeks, the weeks into months, and the hour of our deliverance seemed as distant as ever. The bewildering dispute between the authorities was just as mysterious as ever. About the last week in September, however, the camp was thrown into a state of feverish excitement by the news that on the succeeding day several hundred prisoners were to be paroled and sent to Annapolis. It was understood that the sick and wounded were to be the first re-leased—an announcement that affected the health of the camp very materially. The number of cases rapidly multiplied, as the increase of elongated visages testified. Gavitt, the broker, was reported as doing a heavy business in getting names for the first batch to be sent away, charging ten or fifteen dollars per head for the privilege.

The rumor of the pending parole, which had been too glorious for belief, was verified at the proper time by the marching away of six or seven hundred men towards Richmond. Another squad was announced to follow on the morrow. The excitement among the men grew to be terrific; the whole night long there was but one subject of conversa-tion—the absorbing question of a release from captivity. My old house was constantly before my eyes, but there was ever present a dread that some unforeseen mishap would dash my dreams to the earth.

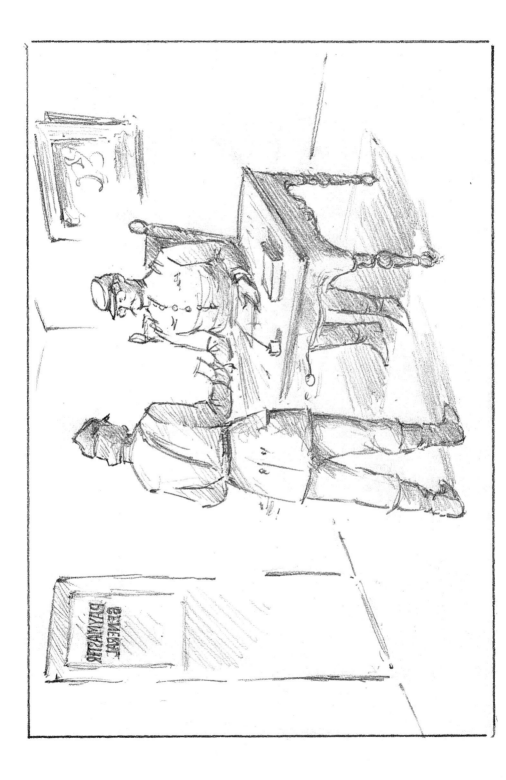

Parole and French Leave—Final Notes

On the 29th of September, 1863, six or seven hundred men—the writer of this included in the number—were marched out of the hated enclosure for the last time, and signed a new parole. By the merest good fortune, like the shuffling of a pack of cards, the paper on which my name was inscribed came uppermost toward the latter part of the performance while the roll was being called, although I had been about the last to sign, while thirty or forty others were left behind who had preceded me. My fortune, however, was their misfortune, though I was in no way responsible for the change.

There was an unaccountable delay in marching us away; a portion were moved up the road leading to the bridge, and the balance of us remained standing in front of the cookhouse. My heart came into my throat as I perceived this, and I dared not ask the guard in relation to the matter, lest he should say that we were to be taken back into camp. Finally, one of our squad, bolder than the others, ventured to inquire of Lieutenant Bosseaux if we were to remain.

"No; you are to go to City Point."

What a blessed relief!

While standing in line, looking back upon the poor starved wretches that gazed after us, I discovered myself to be carefully scrutinized by one of the prisoners who had, that morning, arrived from the battlefield of Chicamauga. He was of medium size, with dark eyes, and wore huge whiskers. When he caught my attention he called out:

"Are you not from Washington County, Pennsylvania?"

At that instant I recognized the familiar expression of an old schoolmate, despite the cloud of hair that shadowed the once smooth face. Seven years had elapsed since he had left our village to go south, and now he was in the service of the United States, a member of the

First Kentucky Infantry. There was but little opportunity to converse together, as, in a few moments, we were on our journey toward the Mecca of Union prisoners, City Point, followed by the longing glances of those comrades left behind. All were happy in the prospect of an early release; but alas! for human expectations, not another parole was made for five months afterward. The poor boys were sent to Andersonville where they suffered torments infinitely surpassing those at Belle Isle, but few—and those totally shattered in health and spirits—reaching their homes. Of the five men of Company F left behind on this occasion, two died, Jewell and Kettleberger.

With light hearts we took a long, lingering look upon our late prison, and bade it farewell. As we marched past the cotton factory near the bridge, the female employees honored us with a variety of slang expressions, but we were too much elated with our prospects to pay any attention to them. Arriving at the depot at last, and clambering into the cars that were to take us to Petersburg, the prisoners devoted a few moments to getting their breath, and then, as the train moved slowly away from the city. they pronounced the following benediction upon that particular portion of the Southern Confederacy:

"Woe unto you, Virginia, when we return within the borders!"

The guards at the train were a clever set of fellows. One of them, in charge of the cars in which our squad was domiciled, did quite a thriving business in retailing a liquid he was pleased to call apple brandy, but which I am afraid, bore slight resemblance to that celebrated product. A very small quantity seemed necessary to throw the subject into a condition of profound bewilderment, which, after all, was about all that was desired.

The prisoners disembarked from the cars at Petersburg, and took others for City Point. Little did we think, as we looked upon this portion of the Old Dominion, that here was to be the culminating point of the great war—that here our invincible legions were to bring to bay at last the cohorts of Lee, and receive their capitulation.

One of our guards, desiring to desert the confederate service, borrowed a suit of clothes from one of a party of sailors who were among our number, and succeeded in eluding the notice of his late comrades and escaped to the flag of truce boat. Taking into consideration its consequences, this feat, for boldness of design and adroitness of execution, certainly has few equals on record.

As the confederates had taken up about one mile of the track at the

494

City Point end, to repair other roads of more consequence to them, we were obliged to walk that distance—quite a task to our exhausted limbs.

The steamer "New York" awaited our arrival at the Point. Quite a large number of confederate prisoners were on board, whose well-rounded limbs contrasted curiously with the emaciated forms upon the shore. The Stars and Stripes floated from the jack-staff of the vessel, and on the river bank, over a wall tent, the Southern Cross shook out its defiant folds. Some one proposed three cheers for our flag, but the effort was a complete failure, the enthusiastic soldier who led in the movement being the only one whose voice was apparent, and he failed at the second hurrah. The days of suffering at Belle Isle seemed to have destroyed the enthusiasm of the men. With the confederates, the case was quite different. They fairly roared for the confederacy, Jeff Davis, and their colors.

There was some delay in completing the preliminaries, the money the confederates had taken from our men being, apparently, the subject of much dispute. During the controversy, the confederates were not permitted to disembark, and the Union prisoners were kept ashore. There was yet a latent dread within me that some untoward event would send us back to the dreaded island, which was not entirely dispelled until we were safely on board and steaming down the river.

Then came demonstrative importunities for food. It was promised us we were to have a "good square meal of coffee, meat, and bread." How our hearts thrilled at the announcement—"coffee, meat, and bread!" Just think of it!

Presently the commissary department made its appearance, bearing in its myriad arms huge boxes of soft bread and raw pork. Then there was a charge made by six hundred hungry Yankee soldiers, before which the glories of the immortal band at Balaklava pale into insignificance, amid the clamor and chatter of hollow voices that reminded one of his young ideas of pandemonium.

There was some disappointment manifested at finding the pork raw, for which the commissary department duly apologized, saying that there were no facilities for cooking on board the steamer, and as the prisoners were too hungry to deliberate long about the matter, there was soon a general plowing of teeth into the great mass of fat and bread. But the coffee—where was it? The question was often asked, but not answered in a satisfactory manner. The same reply—no facilities for cooking—came to us, and we were obliged to dispense with the delicious beverage.

495

There was a wonderful tact displayed by some in "skirmishing" for extra rations ("doubling" on the commissary that is) by falling into line the second time, and reappearing at the box, and when the individual who presided there ventured to express any suspicion about the matter, the subject would solemnly aver his entire honesty in the manner. One man succeeded in stealing five rations, ate them all without stopping, and paid the penalty of his indiscretion by dying on the spot.

Many of the incidents were ludicrous in the extreme, had they not been so shocking to the moral sensibilities, and one did not know whether to laugh or cry. But the wild excitement soon exhausted the poor weak creatures, and the decks became blocked with prostrate bodies of sleeping men, whose dreams were doubtless an improvement on those of a previous week.

In the evening, the steamer anchored in Hampton Roads, and remained until the morning of the 30th of September. Sometime during the day we arrived at Annapolis. Ten of our party died during the passage. Many were sick from excessive eating.

For the first time in my life I felt really ashamed of my appearance when, as we marched up the streets of Annapolis to the barracks, I contrasted my filthy, ragged condition with that of the soldiers and citizens of that ancient borough, and kept my eyes upon the ground during the entire period. My entire wardrobe consisted of a fatigue cap, tattered check shirt and blouse, pants, and pair of shoes, the uppers of which only remained, the soles having long before disappeared. My hair had not been combed for months, and was long and hung in matted locks upon my shoulders. My skin was rimy with sand; my hip joints had worn their way almost through the flesh, which was black with bruises.

The prisoners were marched down to the river side beyond the town, furnished with soap, ordered to strip off their clothing, and thoroughly cleanse themselves of filth and vermin. It occurred to me to put my pocket book, which contained a small sum of money, under one of my shoes. I had brought from Richmond, as a relic, a copy of the *Dispatch* newspaper, which was in the pocket of my blouse. We had scarcely got into the water before all of our clothing mysteriously disappeared, much to our dismay; but it was replaced by new outfits, thanks to the kindness of our Uncle Samuel. My old shoes, fortunately, were too dilapidated to attract the attention of the police detail, and thus, by the merest chance, my pocket book was safe.

My trials with that piece of rosin soap were terrific; being inexperienced in salt-water bathing, I was disgusted at my failure to secure a good, smooth lather. My hair was full of the soap, but on the application of water it became stiff and turgid like a brush immersed in white lead. After a great many efforts I gave the whole matter up, came out, put on my new clothing, and made my way to the barracks, wondering whether anybody else's experience was identical with mine, and too much ashamed of my ignorance to ask for information. Another effort with my hair was made by applying soft water, and with success; and I was thus rescued from any awkward dilemma. In my future ablutions in salt water, I carefully avoided the application of soap of that description, remembering that bath at the mouth of the Severn river.

Perhaps we were just a little disappointed with our supper that evening. It consisted of dry bread and coffee, the latter rather weak, and of a peculiar flavor. If it was a failure in one sense, it was a success in another. The six hundred paroled prisoners were somewhat curiously affected, and slept but little that night. An angry multitude thronged about a rather retired spot, with curses loud and deep. It seemed that the beverage had been adulterated with some powerful purgative, for medicinal purposes, by the officers of that branch of service which is distinguished by green sashes. We were informed that the object of this wholesale prescription was to counteract the injurious effects of the radical change in our diet.

After waiting patiently for a couple of days for a more pretentious bill of fare, without gratification (we were having bread and coffee for breakfast and supper, and thin rice soup for dinner) I concluded to have a feast at my own expense; so, strolling into Annapolis during the forenoon, I invested in four pounds of ham, and two dozens of eggs, and one pound of butter. Thus provided I returned to my quarters, and hunted up Dawson, Thomas, and one other member of Company F, whose name I do not now remember, but I know there were four of us; and after detailing Dawson as cook for the occasion—he was acquainted down at the barrack kitchen, he said—the rest of us laid down upon our bunks to await his call, and to mentally anticipate the grand treat that was pending for our little party. For once we were going to have all we could eat, and that, too, of the old and renowned dish of ham and eggs. The triplet could talk of nothing else, and looked with disdain upon the regular preparations for dinner. The old days of everlasting hunger on Belle Isle were at an end; a new era of plenty was about to dawn upon our lives, to be inaugurated with the present meal of ham and eggs.

497

We began to think, after a time, that Dawson was rather long in preparing the delicious dish—what had become of him?

"Who knows," remarked one, "perhaps he has appropriated the whole dish to himself?"

A horrible suspicion, to be sure; and immediately Thomas was detailed and sent out to hunt up the missing cook. Another long period of time passed, and still no sign of either dinner or Dawson or Thomas.

"Who knows," remarked my remaining friend, "perhaps they have gone halves."

Another horrible suspicion; so we both started for the cookhouse in a frantic condition of mind. To our great relief we found everything safe, and progressing rapidly to a satisfactory conclusion. The delay was promptly explained—the fire had been occupied by the presiding genius of the pots and pans, and Dawson had been obliged to await an opportunity. We were so delighted with the sight of crackling ham and eggs, and the delicious odor that greeted our olfactories, that it was unanimously decided to remain until the preparation was complete. Then in great state, the victuals were carried to the barracks, amid the envious remarks and sinister smiles of our less fortunate comrades.

I suppose that, since the days of Adam, there never was a meal eaten with such wonderful satisfaction, and with such a feeling of gratitude, than was this repast of ham and eggs. Our thoughts reverted, involuntarily, to the poor boys we had left behind on that island in the James—Kettleberger, Schilling, Jewell, and Manness of Company F—and we longed to share with them our luxuries.

Our joy was destined to be of short duration. Thomas, soon after dinner, complained of a pain in his stomach; Dawson echoed with a similar remark; so did our other companion; so did I. In a short time four persons might have been writhing and twisting in their "bunks" with expressions on their faces of mortal pain. Our luxury was followed by a fearful retribution; the ham and eggs were too strong for our weak stomachs, and for two hours we were in agony. Fortunately, no fatal result ensued, though we learned a wholesome lesson by that experience.

There was but little discipline maintained at College Green Barracks. The paroled men were allowed as much liberty by the commanding officer, Colonel Chamberlain, as was consistent with their welfare, and all the comforts which a soldier could reasonably demand were provided for them. The guards were a fine body of men, considerate, to a fault, of our desires. We were allowed the liberty of the city at all hours between reveille and tattoo, and many a happy stroll I enjoyed around its quaint precincts.

I had written home immediately after my arrival at Annapolis, notifying father and friends of my safe arrival within the federal lines. In a few days an answer came, the first tidings I had received from the old farmhouse in four long months. All were reported well. The letter said I had been looked upon as dead, as my last note was written just on the eve of the battle of Gettysburg, and I had not been heard from until now. Father, it also said, had given vent to his satisfaction at the news of my safety in his own peculiar way, sitting up all night, and blowing upon a long horn he had wrought out of wood and clay, varying this exercise at intervals by singing Welsh hymns. He had been very despondent at times, avoiding company, and retiring to the woods for days, maintaining a sort of hermit existence. I had, two days after our arrival at Richmond, sent word home of my whereabouts and condition by McKibben, who had then been paroled and sent north; but for some reason or other this news was concealed from father, although he had walked over to the McKibben farm, a distance of several miles, to ascertain the truth of what had reached him as a mere rumor.

Poor old man! When the war closed, and I had returned to civil life, and married, and, in pursuance of a plan marked out in the long ago, took him into my own home, often I have felt the tears coming into my eyes as I sat and listened to his story of that dark time.

We remained at College Green Barracks about two weeks. From thence we were removed to Camp Parole, distant perhaps two miles from Annapolis. Several thousand men had been paroled a short time previous to our arrival, a part of whom had not yet been sent to their respective commands, but in a few days all were gone. At this place even better accommodations were provided for us, and less discipline exercised, than at College Green. The men went and came entirely as they pleased, attending a sort of roll-call, merely as a precautionary measure, to secure a certain number of rations. Many went home on what was known as a "French furlough"—that is, without formal leave of the officer in charge of the camp. When they returned they came unquestioned, and tacitly were not deemed to have violated orders. But one point was to be observed—avoid the detectives that swarmed throughout the land, whose fees, when an arrest was made, amounted to thirty dollars, and this came out of the pocket of the soldier apprehended.

I confess these opportunities to get home completely demoralized me. Although I had but six months longer to serve, that brief period seemed to me like an age. The dull, unexciting life at Camp Parole aggravated the matter. For a time, the dread of being arrested as a deserter deterred me from attempting to reach home, but finally a curious circumstance ended my indecision.

One day a package, addressed to Dawson, came through the mails. On breaking the seal, it was found to contain a number of blank furloughs. Whence they came, or who sent them, was a profound mystery. No name was there to serve as a clue to the donor. Dawson solemnly affirmed that he knew no more about them than I did. The envelope was postmarked at Washington, and that was as far as we could trace them.

We had heard, incidentally, of persons in the camp who could fill out a furlough in the most approved style, and sign thereto the name of the commanding officer in such an admirable manner that even that functionary was obliged to consult his record to ascertain whether it were genuine; and, after due deliberation, we sought out one of these parties. He was very reticent about the matter; said he might be sent to the penitentiary if discovered; charged a fee of ten dollars for the service; but finally agreed, if we would give him the remaining blanks, to complete ours in consideration of the said blanks.

These forged furloughs were only of use to deceive detectives at a distance from Annapolis. Here there was no need of a leave of absence of any sort, the men possessing complete liberty. For some reason or other, paroled prisoners were not permitted to have furloughs by the War Department at Washington—it was alleged, by some, that this was because, under the obligation of our paroles, we were not subject to the military authority of the United States, but, in a limited sense, to that of the Confederate states. However that may be, it is enough to say that upon the noted point, confusion reigned supreme in Annapolis, and this was not dispelled by any official action until some months after our arrival.

I have mentioned thus particularly the circumstances surrounding the case, to justify the course pursued by Dawson and myself in this connection. It was a matter in which the government was in no way interested, and could in no way become interested, unless appealed to by Colonel Chamberlain, whose name was, perhaps, used without his

500

consent. I say "perhaps without his consent" for the reason that there is some doubt on this point; although it had become a notorious fact that his name was duly signed to all sorts of absences with leave by other pens than his own, he gave us no sign, by order or otherwise, that he objected to the proceeding. The matter was regarded as a huge farce by the prisoners of war, involving nothing of consequence at best, being, save for the detective element abroad, entirely superfluous. There was no intent to actually defraud the government out of one day of legitimate service, or Colonel Chamberlain of his authority, if he really possessed any, over the bodies of men whose obligations to the United States were, for the time, canceled by the exigencies of war. If there were well-- established principles governing in the matter, it was due to those interested that they should have been notified in an official manner of such principles.

In one respect the absence of a prisoner of war from Camp Parole was a positive benefit to the government—he, of course, forfeited his rations.

Not one of the thousands of absentees had, on their return, suffered the infliction of any punishment, or received one word of censure. This was evidence of virtual permission to go and come at will. If a guard does not halt you when you attempt to pass across his line of march, it is evidence of no orders to halt you, and you are not expected to run to the commanding officer's quarters to ascertain whether or not the guard has such orders.

On receiving our "furloughs," which were properly made out if improperly signed and were liberal to ourselves—the document stating on its face that we had a leave of absence until duly exchanged—Dawson and I selected an evening during which to start for home. As we did not know what instructions the guards and detectives on the cars from Annapolis to the junction might have, as a precautionary measure we concluded to walk to Baltimore and take the Pennsylvania Central railroad for Pittsburg.

The journey from Camp Parole to Baltimore—a distance of about thirty miles—was one that taxed to the utmost our powers of endurance. The night was very dark; the route lay through the loneliest of woods; the sand was several inches deep, and gave beneath our feet like snow; we were yet much weaker than we had supposed. The hope of seeing home and friends buoyed us up wonderfully, however, and was all that sustained our drooping spirits. Many times we were in doubt as to the

501

true road at the numerous intersections, and were obliged to rouse the farmers from their slumbers to ascertain the needed information, to their evident disgust.

From six o'clock till twelve we had averaged a little over three miles per hour. There were symptoms of rain, and we crawled through the window into a little frame church that we found by the roadside. As with country chapels, there is usually associated a graveyard. I felt something akin to awe stealing over me as I peered about in the thick darkness. Every cautious step we took sounded unusually loud and hollow. We conversed in whispers. The rain came down heavily upon the roof, and kept us prisoners. An occasional thump on the floor beneath startled us several times, but, fortunately, we made the discovery that a number of hogs, which also had sought shelter there, were the authors of the disturbances. We realized that there was a relief in the association with animals in such a weird place, and Dawson, perhaps the least nervous of the two men, saying he proposed to make himself comfortable, stretched out upon one of the low benches and composed himself for a short sleep. I selected another just in front of him, and did likewise, and soon two weary runaway soldiers forgot their woes through the seductive influences of "tired Nature's sweet restorer," etc.

While thus sleeping I had a peculiar dream. I seemed to be present at a discussion of the slavery question between a Bishop Potter and a Dr. Chandler—those were the names, but I do not know whether there ever were two such persons—the bishop for, the doctor against the institution. Each produced numerous quotations from the bible in support of his side of the question. All at once I became conscious of something wrong; the bench on which I reposed gradually pitched forward, and deposited me upon the floor. The fall fully aroused me, and partially awakened Dawson. My suspicion was that Dawson had perpetrated a joke, but he solemnly assured me that such was not the case.

After reflecting with some curiosity upon the vision and its interruption, I laid down on the bench again. The dream returned with its identical discussion and personages, and the bench repeated the freak of depositing me on the floor. I arose much more puzzled than before. Dawson complained that his slumber was sadly disturbed by my mischievous pranks; I reiterated my charges with some warmth, and he, as warmly, declared his innocence.

Of course, I ought to have laid down the third time and had the third experience of the dream and its denouement, but I did not. The rain had ceased, and, anxious to reach Baltimore early in the morning, we crawled out of the window through which we had entered, carefully closed the shutters, and picked our way to the road. Thereupon arose two important questions: which way had we come, or which way were we to go? The settlement of one involved the settlement of the other, but as we could not definitely recollect the relative position of the church to the road where we had entered the sacred inclosure, there was no way of settling either. Fortunately a dim light, glimmering through the trees at a short distance, led us to a stable, where some men were at work feeding and grooming their horses. They received us rather gruffly, but one of them finally came with us and gave the proper directions, in a tone of voice, however, which clearly showed that he did not like us so near his premises. From him we learned that it was about four o'clock.

We trudged along quite cheerfully, feeling rather stiff in our limbs, but generally refreshed, beguiling the gloomy hours by telling each other whom we expected to see at home, and what pleasant times we should have there. Dawson was blessed with a sweetheart; I had none, since I buried Sarah Jane's picture two years before at Bladensburg. I felt lonely in this respect, and appreciated his superior condition in this regard; and I will do him the justice to say that, judging from the way in which he enlarged upon the fact of his affectional possession, he seemed to fully appreciate that superiority himself. As I looked upon that handsome face and form, and remembered his loving nature, I fondly hoped that all the pictures he had drawn would prove real and enduring ones.

Daylight came upon us at last, and seeing the blue smoke curling up from the chimney of a little cabin by the wayside, we stepped over to the door, and inquired if breakfast might be furnished us. The occupant, an old colored woman—the other portion of its inhabitants were already away at their work—kindly invited us in, saying she would do the best she could for our accommodation. The traditional corn and bacon was set forth upon a rickety old table, and, as our appetites were quite keen, the meal was relished very well.

According to her statements, the colored people of that section must have experienced rather hard times from the war—subject to almost as many annoyances as were the white people of the free states under the drafting regulations. The United States authorities, she said, "jest came by and took every male nigger they could lay their hands on." I could not ascertain that this had been accomplished under the regulations of the conscript laws, or whether there had been a press gang at work who were determined that Maryland's quota of national soldiers should be filled at all hazards. Since that time, however, I have ascertained there were some very peculiar practices in vogue, in that benighted region, in which the inequality of the proportion of black and white conscripts was plainly discernible.

After paying Aunty for her trouble, we bade her good bye and resumed our journey. By this time our limbs were very tired and stiff, but we struggled on, rapidly diminishing the distance to Baltimore. A carriage, containing two men, met us during the morning. The occupants eyed us rather attentively as they drew near, so I was partly prepared to see it halt as it drove up.

"Good morning, boys; you are off early?" said one of the men, a small man, with keen, snapping black eyes.

"Yes, sir; we are on our way home, and are anxious to reach it as soon as possible."

"Well," said the small man with snapping black eyes, casting a glance full of meaning at his companion, who met it with another, "I must do my duty, boys. Have you leaves of absence?"

"Yes, sir," and we promptly produced the "documents." These he took, scrutinized carefully, and then returned.

"I guess I will have to let you go," he said, "I had hoped to get you to work on my farm, but as you are going home I suppose I must procure some one else."

"Yes," chimed in his companion, "some one else."

The carriage was then driven rapidly away.

"Well," said Dawson, after it was at a safe distance, "these papers have a useful purpose already."

Feeling somewhat jubilant over our success, we trudged along at a tolerably rapid pace. The houses appeared at shorter intervals along the roadside, indicating that we were near our present destination. By and by, as we reached the crest of a hill, the steeples of Baltimore burst upon our delighted vision; and then a perfect maze of houses and streets and vessels and water as far as the eye could see. The prospect was a magnificent one.

At a little store by the roadside, we stopped to procure refreshments. The keeper, noticing our uniforms, inquired:

"From Camp Parole?"

"Yes, sir."

"How did you pass Lee?"

"Who?" thinking, in a vague sort of way, that he referred to the commanding general of the Army of Northern Virginia.

"Why, Lee, the enrolling officer? Did you not meet two men in a carriage up the road?"

We saw how matters stood now. Then we related the circumstances of our adventure, and said that he wanted us to go on his farm and work for him.

"Him wanting to take you to his farm, not much," said the shopman, with a look of disdain. "He wanted to take you to Fort McHenry, and get his thirty dollars apiece."

We casually mentioned that we possessed "documents" that were talismanic in their effect upon that class of people.

We now pushed down the hill to Light Street bridge, hurried over that structure, took a street car for the Northern Central depot, where, after a bewildering transfer, we were finally safely landed. To our great relief, we were just in time for a train.

"Furloughs, sir," said the clerk, and the "documents" were produced.

He took them, stamped them with a sort of press, and passed them back to us with our tickets. At the door of the car on which we were to take passage, stood an armed guard.

"Passes," said the soldier, bringing his musket down.

The "documents" were again produced, examined closely, and returned, with the reply:

"You may pass on."

After all, it was a relief to us to find the train in motion a few moments later. Though so far we had been completely successful, there was just a tantalizing dread of failure from some undefined cause, which should deprive us of the privilege of reaching home. We could think of nothing else. I wondered how my friends would receive me, and whether I should be known; I had left home a beardless boy, delicate and pale from the confinement, incident to the life of a compositor, on a morning newspaper; now I was bronzed by the sun, and, though I shaved regularly, the black stubs of whiskers extended from my eyes to my throat, and gave me an old look. I could scarcely realize that I should see home again, for when leaving I was fully satisfied I would be killed.

By and by the excitement wore off, and, thoroughly exhausted in mind and body, we both fell asleep, with our heads reclining on the end of the seat.

We separated at Pittsburg—Dawson going to his home in the ninth ward, and I hurrying to my old boarding house at 151 Third Street. Here, a warm welcome was extended to me.

As the river was now closed with ice, I concluded to walk home across the country—the distance was about sixteen miles—and early next morning started upon my journey. From the crest of Coal Hill, I surveyed the city and frozen river. Ten or twelve years before I stood upon the same spot, a little boy, and gazed over the same region, but on different scenery. What a vast change those years had made! Looking back upon that time, it seemed to have belonged to a past century. Then the vast factories were turning out the peaceful implements of agriculture and commerce; now the war monopolized their work, and vast numbers of cannons and swords came into existence.

A few miles from Noblestown I met the first familiar face from my old home—W. W. Thompson, a schoolmate, now grown to manhood and married. He was driving into Pittsburg with farm produce. Beyond Whitehall I met another old friend, Mr. William Curry. As the scenery became more and more familiar, my excitement increased; my feet swung forward with scarcely an effort on my part, it seemed. When within four miles of Bentley's, I suddenly became deathly sick; my legs trembled beneath me, and I staggered against a fence. It was now noon, and with the hurry of the morning I had eaten scarcely a mouthful. As soon as my momentary weakness passed off, I went to a farm house near by to solicit a cup of coffee.

The farmer was just sitting down to a table upon which stood viands of a most tempting character. I was heartily invited to partake with the family, and, with a few draughts of the delicious coffee felt my strength rapidly returning.

The host seemed wonderfully interested in me when he learned where I had been and whither I was going. He was well acquainted with Bentley's people, he said. The atrocities at Belle Isle had been pretty thoroughly published throughout the country by this time, and he questioned me as to the general truth of the newspaper statements.

With many thanks for his kindness—he had indignantly refused pay—I bade the family farewell, and resumed my journey. I pushed along more rapidly than ever now, feeling invigorated by the dinner, and travelling straight toward the school house on Pollock's Hill, where I had attended fifteen years before. I could hardly realize that this was the hallowed spot when my eyes fell upon it. The change was great; the forest had

506

gone down beneath the axe of the woodsman, and long lines of fences inclosed most of the ground for cultivation. The old log cabin had disappeared, and in its stead, though not exactly upon its site, stood a neat frame building. The few huge walnut trees that once sheltered the spring were gone; the old beech at the upper end of the playground laid prone upon the earth in a state of decay.

I did not remain long here to moralize upon the mutations of life. A mile further stretched before me, and I hurried across Pollock's Hill, and down to Farmer Hindman's house. The old folks had gone visiting, and some little girls were in charge. The happy creatures were so pleasant with me, and so pressing in their invitation to come into the house and be seated by the fire, that I felt a little puzzled. Strange soldiers were sometimes dangerous customers, I had been taught when a child.

"Are you not afraid of me, little girl?" I said, taking the proffered chair, and drawing it close up to the hearth.

"Oh, no, sir," said the largest. "I know who you are very well. You used to live at Bentley's."

"I can't be changed so much after all," I thought.

After resting a few moments, I bade the little girls farewell, and passed down through the orchard and into the woods that surround the hills overlooking the river. In fifteen minutes I stood by the old coal mine just above and in full view of the homestead, and paused to take a view of the premises before descending. There stood, as in the olden times, the stone mansion, the barn, the stable, the dilapidated distillery, with its surroundings of stys and squealing hogs; and there, too, was poor old father, bent low, with long white locks drifting upon his shoulders, carrying upon his arm a basket of corn. It was feeding time, and across in what was known as the "slop yard", five or six dozen cattle thronged around the troughs. The fields along the river side seemed to be narrower than in the olden times, but the stream looked natural enough.

Bowing my head reverently, I thanked the Father of humanity for this happy opportunity, and descended the hill. In a few moments I stood beside father. He did not notice me at once, but presently looked up, and nodded his head.

"How do you do sir?" he said.

"Very well; how are you?"

"I see you are a soldier?"—then, looking at me closely, "Why, Sid, is that you?"

507

"It certainly is," I responded, taking the basket off his arm. "How have you been, father?"

"Right well. I am glad you have come."

Thereupon, we went over to the mansion together.

If time had wrought no great changes in the externals of the farm, it had effected many within the house. Of all its occupants when I had gone to the war, there now remained not one. Levi was dead; Mrs. Samuels was no longer the housekeeper; George, who in former days lived on the farm across the river, was now installed on the homestead.

For over sixty years some member of the Bentley family had lived here, most of them beginning and ending their earthly existence within these four heavy stone walls. A small graveyard occupied a portion of the orchard just east of the house, where were buried several of their members.

I met George at the door, and was cordially received. He had changed but little during the interval of my absence.

I remained on the farm a couple of weeks, visiting friends in the neighborhood, and enjoying myself very well. Quite a number of persons called to see me, and among them old Patrick Barry, the father of James, who had been killed near Warrenton in 1862.

"You have got your boy home, John," said he to father, as he shook my hand. Then, bursting into tears, he added, "mine will never come."

To avoid wasting my time in idleness, I went to Pittsburg and secured work upon the *Dispatch* newspaper. My "document," by way of precaution, was entrusted to the care of Mrs. Cook, and was subsequently of service to me. To dispense with even the appearance of evil, I retained my uniform, lest a civilian suit of clothing might give rise to comments of an unfavorable character. As my term of service was rapidly drawing to a close, I felt that I could not afford to be deemed a deserter. My earnings were carefully husbanded, and deposited in a savings bank on Fourth Street.

I had a rather curious experience a day or two after my arrival at 151 Third Street, after having been at home in Washington County. Mrs. Cook introduced me to a Mr. McLaren, a compositor, at that time, on the Commercial.

"I have met you before," said that gentleman, on the conclusion of the formalities of the occasion.

"I guess not," I responded. "I do not recollect you."

"Were you not out with me, one night about two weeks ago, and did we not have several glasses together?"

As I prided myself on being a "teetotaler," this information rather startled me.

"I was not, sir."

"And did you not give me your card?"

"No, sir."

McLaren deliberately put his right hand into his pocket, and brought out a piece of pasteboard. I took it, and read thereon, to my great astonishment, the following inscription:

"Sidney M. Davis, Company F, Sixth United States Cavalry."

My surprise was increased when McClaren also informed me that the party who gave him the card bore an exact resemblance to me "perhaps his hair was just a little longer, and he wore a fatigue cap somewhat different from yours, with a yellow band around it," he said.

This affair has ever since been to me a profound mystery. I felt positive that no one outside of Annapolis, save Dawson, knew of my presence in Pittsburg, and his appearance was entirely different from mine. Whoever personated me on the occasion referred to, seemed to be thoroughly acquainted with my business, and spoke of it as naturally as I should have done under ordinary circumstances.

I had been working in the *Dispatch* office perhaps a month, when one of the old employees on that paper, who had been drafted into the military service, but who was now, under the appointment of its editor, Mr. Foster (the provost marshal of that district) serving as a detective, arrested me as a deserter and took me before the deputy provost marshal. The whole affair was managed in such a polite way that I was not aware of being a prisoner until after my release, which occurred immediately upon the production of the "documents."

On the night of the 12th of March, 1864, while at work, my attention was attracted to a telegraphic dispatch to the associated press, which stated that all prisoners delivered at City Point up to a given date were declared exchanged by the commission of the United States. Being included in the list, I went to Washington County next morning to bid my friends farewell, returning to the city the following evening, and leaving on the first train for Baltimore, occupying, perhaps, twenty hours from the time of notification. I am thus particular in stating the time and the intermediate events to show how groundless were the subsequent proceedings at Annapolis, which assumed that I was a deserter, in view of the promptitude with which I responded to the declaration of

509

exchange.

On the train that left Pittsburg I was assigned to the "soldier's car." In one end was a squad of white soldiers, just returning from their re-enlistment furloughs, and in the other, a dozen or so colored recruits, on their way to join Burnside's army corps. For a time the veterans were jubilant under the influence of liquor and the excitement of travel, and bandied jokes with their colored brethren; but, as the reaction came, and the effects of the stimulating beverage "grew small by degrees, and beautifully less," the old prejudice of race began to manifest itself. A little corporal among the veterans made a jocular remark to a colored sergeant of huge proportions, the purport of which I do not now remember.

"Are you acquainted with Manassas Junction?" remarked the latter, with a grin.

"I am, casually; I met him once."

The comical conversation went on for a few moments, when some remark was made that insulted the little corporal, and he deliberately walked up and struck the huge colored sergeant in the mouth. Instantly there was a springing to arms and a drawing of bayonets at each end of the car, and a simultaneous advance along the whole line. Though an innocent spectator of the scene, I could not very well be an idle one, occupying, as I did, the vacant space between the belligerent armies, and having a fair opportunity of being shot or impaled by a bayonet from either side; and I became actively engaged in trying to dodge the issue. Fortunately, just at that critical moment several officers unlocked the car door and entered, and quelled the disturbance by removing the colored soldiers to other quarters. One or two punctures, not of a serious character, had been the result.

I experienced no difficulty, whatever, in reaching Annapolis; indeed, the facilities for going south in those days were ample. It was only when your face was turned to the rear that guards and detectives thronged your footsteps.

I reached the camp a little after dusk on the 16th of March, and attempted to cross the guard line as had been our wont in the olden time.

"Halt!"

The guard brought down his musket to a ready with a promptness that startled me. I halted without delay.

"Why do you attempt to pass my beat?" said he. "Why don't you go over to the guard house, and come in the regular way?"

"I don't know why, exactly," I said, "I don't happen to have a pass."

"Officer of the guard, post number six!" he shouted.

The call was taken up by the sentinels, and in a few moments, the functionary whose presence was required made his appearance, took charge of me, and we went together to the guard house. As we walked along the officer of the guard asked—

"Where is your pass?"

I explained to him that I had none, stated the circumstances of my absence from camp, and mentioned that I had been at home, but took occasion to return as soon as an exchange of prisoners was announced.

"That declaration of exchange has not yet been confirmed by the Secretary of War," said the officer of the guard; "it is not yet complete, is of no effect until so confirmed. The prospect of an exchange seems to be, in fact, as far off as ever."

On our arrival at the guardhouse, I was turned into a room about fourteen feet square, ventilated by two very small windows, in which I counted thirty-two prisoners, excluding myself. Most of these were huddled together upon the floor like a drove of hogs.

"Fresh fish! Fresh fish!"

The cry arose from thirty-two throats as I entered the place. It was a prison phrase—this "fresh fish"—indicating the advent of a new captive, and the yell was quite startling to the ears of the uninitiated.

I certainly felt bad enough just then. The prospect of sleeping upon the floor, now almost afloat with tobacco spit, without even a blanket to shelter me above or below, and to be jammed so tightly between two fellow unfortunates as to have scarcely breathing room, and to be smothered almost to death by the sum of a thousand foul odors, was enough to reduce the stoutest spirit to the verge of despair. A friendly soldier, whose name has now escaped me—and it ought to be written in letters of gold in my "recollections"—perceiving my predicament, offered me a share of his blanket, which was gratefully accepted.

There was little rest during that night—or, indeed, for that matter, any night in that enclosure. At intervals of an hour or two, a new face would be thrust in upon us (sometimes two or more together) and the yell, "fresh fish," would rise with fiendish intonation. The already prostrate crowd would be jammed still closer together to give the newcomers their quarter of room upon the floor. Most of these were sadly, blindly drunk, and, in their frantic endeavors to maintain an erect position in the dark would come plunging over us like wild horses, and then, amid the general jumping to feet and gathering of blankets, one would think of "chaos come again." Occasionally, by way of variety, a tremendous fight would ensue, in which billets of firewood that had been piled behind a stove in the corner, made mysterious though amazing flights through the thick darkness. Then all would quiet down in a few minutes, to be succeeded by a chorus of snores from all directions, that to be appreciated only need be heard. In addition to these various noises came, every two hours, the mustering of the guards in the adjoining room, with their heavy tramping and clattering of muskets.

The experience of this night, as I discovered afterwards, was a fair sample of that of other nights, though from sheer exhaustion, and a sort of adaptation to circumstances that comes to one under all difficulties, I became familiar with such scenes and rather enjoyed them. There was some fun, if little rest.

Daylight came at last, and with it to me a sense of relief. I expected to be released at guard mounting, and, as I did not care to have my friends in camp see me in such a horrible place, I sent no word to the barracks in regard to my breakfast. To my great disappointment, when the roll of prisoners was called, my name did not appear on the list of those who were to go to their quarters. With a heavy heart I returned to the loathsome room, and sat down in a corner. At dinner time I sent over for my acquaintances and something to eat. They came, with faces expressive of astonishment and concern. From them, I learned that after we had left the barracks an order from the War Department at Washington reached Camp Parole, in which all prisoners absenting themselves therefrom without leave should be deemed deserters. A letter had been written to notify me of that event, but unfortunately it never came to hand.

The reflection that, after a conscientious performance of my duty under all circumstances for nearly three years, my hard-earned reputation as a faithful soldier was about to be destroyed by the stigma of desertion, roused me to a determination to defend myself with all honorable means. A large number of the men in the guard house were held for trial under the same order, though they did not number a hundredth part of those absentees that were liable. Three or four had been tried, and, being virtually without counsel—the judge advocate, who is also supposed to see that the case of the prisoner is fairly presented, usually allows that part of his duty to go by default—and of timid dispositions, they were convicted and sentenced to various sorts of punishment. A few of us combined, selected one (that of Austin M. Foulk of the Twentieth Indiana) as a test case, and bent all our energies to secure for him an acquittal.

Colonel Root, of the Ninety-fourth New York Volunteers, had, in the meantime, relieved Colonel Chamberlain from the command of Camp Parole. Most of his regiment was here, on duty as guards, although they were really paroled prisoners themselves, and had not yet been declared exchanged, as was asserted. As they were returned to the federal lines at Gettysburg, instead of Vicksburg or City Point, the pledges they had given the confederates not to take up arms until duly exchanged were set aside.

To Colonel Root I made a written statement of the whole affair, so far as I was concerned, and asked to be released or granted a trial, as the army regulations provided that I was entitled to one within ten days after arrest, unless the exigencies of the service will not permit. Of this appeal no notice seemed to be taken.

When Foulk's trial came off, with three others, they were acquitted without much effort on their part. The president of the court martial, to whose attention it had been called, admitted the fact that, at the time they left the camp, under the peculiar condition of affairs, they were under no legal obligation to remain. The order from the War Department could not apply to their cases. They were released.

Days, and weeks, and months rolled on, and no further action was taken in regard to those remaining in prison under the charges, except a few were released. To bring the matter to a culmination, I wrote for relief to every source of official power of which I was cognizant—the President of the United States, the Secretary of War, the commanding general of the army, the commander of the military district, etc. Growing restive, I indited savage letters to Colonel Root, declaring that I should hold him responsible for the indignities I was suffering. Perhaps this mode of expression did not benefit me, but my patience had become utterly exhausted by the delay.

By his experience at Annapolis, the Common Soldier learned of just how little weight were the "regulations" which once he had deemed infallible as an authority in the army, when it is necessary that they should be set aside to allow a commanding, or other officer, to display his personal likes and dislikes toward his inferiors in rank.

The guard house at Camp Parole was quite an institution. It was a frame building, twenty-five or thirty feet square, and contained two large

513

and six small rooms. The latter were called cells, and were separated from the large rooms by a hall. They were about four feet wide and six long in dimensions, and were ventilated by an opening over the door perhaps six inches by ten. The entrance to each was from the hall. At each end of the hall was a common window, protected by iron rods running perpendicularly from top to bottom, with each end secured in the sills. The cells were for the detention of persons accused of misdeeds of an aggravated character. The room for the guards was duly fitted up with "bunks" and gun racks, and warmed by a huge stove. The prisoner's room has been sufficiently described heretofore.

In one of the cells there was a man confined for murder. As a precaution he was shackled hand and foot. One morning, however, he was not to be found. The bars at one of the windows were slightly bent, and beside a fence, a quarter of a mile from Camp, were found the broken shackles. How he could break his iron fetters was one mystery; how he could get out of a six-by-ten inch hole was another; how he could do all this, with a guard pacing up and down the hallway, within a few feet of whom, and whom he must pass of necessity, was another; but he was equal to the occasion. I do not know that the prisoner has been heard from since; he did not return to Camp Parole, at all events. I think his name was Burns, and that he belonged to a New York regiment.

Amid all their troubles, the prisoners made themselves happy, after a fashion. They organized a mock court martial, and tried each newcomer, or "fresh fish," with all due formality, the penalty applied being, as a general thing, so many "spanks" with a board which contained a hole. Poker playing occupied much of the time, the stakes, in most instances, consisting of beans rather than greenbacks. One was obliged to "hang one's clothes up on the floor" and sit upon them to protect the sanctity of the pockets.

By the judicious use of a pen-knife the prisoners cut open the double-planked floor, through which they were able to descend, and then crawl out through a hole in the foundation wall. The boards were easily refitted, and when replaced disclosed nothing of a suspicious nature. To prevent the guards from hearing the carpenters while at work, a "walk around"—a sort of dance—was organized, keeping time to vicious vocal music. One half would go to Annapolis one night, and return before daylight, without their absence being observed, and the next night the others would go. To obviate suspicion, the absentees were under a

514

mutual pledge to return, lest this source of pleasure should be extinguished.

Occasionally there would be a mock battle, in which half loaves of dry bread, and hats, and all sorts of things would darken the air, amid a chorus of wild yells. One was obliged to take good care of one's eyes during these sanguinary engagements.

One method of amusement was to call a friend from the outside, and have him place his ear to the keyhole to receive a confidential communication, and then bring the muzzle of a squirt-gun to bear directly upon the orifice. The laugh came in when you heard your victim consign the perpetrator to the lowest depths of theological perdition.

In some instances, when a "fresh fish," drunker than usual, was thrust into the thick darkness of the room, two or three guard house veterans would converse in an assumed dialect of the south, as though they were confederate soldiers. The newcomer would listen a short time in stupid amazement, and, on inquiring, would be grandly assured that he was in the encampment of southern troops. Occasionally the victim of the joke would curse the administration vehemently, and declare his pleasure at escaping from the damned Yankee army. The confusion of the party on the following morning, when daylight showed him his surroundings, and he vaguely recalled some of his wild declarations, was amusing to see. As a punishment for his disloyalty, the court would sentence him to a number of applications of the paddle.

At Camp Parole, there was established a branch of the Sanitary Commission,[1] under charge of a Miss Williams. A cavalry soldier, named McGrath, who, by the explosion of a shell near his head during one of the fights along the Rappahannock, had been rendered partially idiotic, was detailed to assist her in the menial duties of the Commission. Over poor McGrath, she exercised all the authority of a commanding general. On the most unheard of pretexts, he was thrust into the guard house like a common criminal; one time, for instance, because he went into her room without his coat; at another, because he went to church without her permission. As his malady partook of a religious character, he was very devout at all times.

I recollect the first night McGrath came into the guard house. Some one, who knew of his peculiarity of disposition, asked him to pray. He

[1]   The Sanitary Commission was organized in 1861 by civilians for the care of wounded soldiers. As the war continued, the range of their services expanded considerably. They maintained convalescent camps, wrote letters home for wounded soldiers, and assisted soldiers with pension applications.

immediately acceded to the request, and, kneeling down in one corner, began his supplications. At first, the matter was quite amusing, but, as time rolled on, we began to weary of it. Tattoo came, but McGrath still prayed. We wanted to go to sleep; but it was of no use. He went over the same phrases again and again, with a voice so peculiarly moderated, that the flesh of his listeners crept upon their bones. Toward morning it grew husky and cracked, but the supplications continued with unabated fervor. All efforts to stop him were in vain; he was elevated in the air, patted on the back, called pet names; swore at and threatened; offered money, whisky, circus tickets, bean soup, shooting-crackers—all to no purpose. At last, from sheer exhaustion, he fell asleep.

That was the last time McGrath was requested to hold religious services in the guard house.

The "fresh fish," among other embarrassments, were occasionally robbed of their money and jewelry, especially if they were of timid dispositions. A squad of roughs would deliberately throw them down and rifle their pockets with a nonchalance that fairly astounded their victims. It was of little use to complain of these outrages to the authorities; the only recourse was to make a vigorous fight for one's property.

On the 27th of April a "horse" was erected on the parade ground near the guard house. It consisted of a platform on posts, elevated a distance of perhaps twenty-five feet, and so constructed that the only mode of access was by a ladder. About twenty men could be crowded upon it with little difficulty. On this arrangement we were obliged to take our daily airing, in full view of the whole camp. It was much better, however, than the close confinement of the room in which we slept. Sometimes, by way of punishment, the men were kept up there night and day without blankets or overcoats, and, it was stated that, on one occasion, as a consequence, two died soon after their release. One night, when several men were thus kept exposed, the weather was such that, although in the guard house, with my usual quota of covering, I suffered much from the extreme cold. How the poor fellows managed that night to keep their blood in circulation is a mystery.

Sometime during the early part of 1864, Gavitt, of the First New York Artillery, the broker of Belle Island, made his appearance at Annapolis. He was arrested on charges preferred by some of his victims and confined in the jail at Annapolis. In a few weeks, however, he was released. As his presence, on account of the peculiar character of his offenses, was distasteful to his fellows, the authorities were obliged to protect him from personal injury. The men who had been confined for months charged with offenses which, in themselves, were insignificant, and for which they were unable to secure a trial, were fond of instituting comparisons between their "crimes" and those of Gavitt, and the course of justice toward each.

After Gavitt had been released from the jail in Annapolis, and sent to Camp Parole, he was obliged to take up his abode with the guards for self-protection. One evening, he was decoyed over to the barracks, and, when inside one of the buildings, about a hundred of his Belle Island victims made a vigorous assault upon him. Their very numbers saved him from an ignominious death; for in the rush and darkness he managed to escape from the clutches of his assailants. He reached the guardhouse in a rather dilapidated condition, breathless, hatless, ghastly, and bloody.

This experience was sufficient to deter Gavitt from venturing out of sight of the guards for a long time. One day, however, while wandering around rather carelessly, he was abducted and carried in triumph to a rather secluded spot, and thrown up in a blanket. As he weighed perhaps two hundred pounds or more, it required some effort to toss him to the ordinary altitude. When this was attained, however, the swinging committee forgot to catch him when he fell, and his thigh was broken. His persecutors escaped.

Since that time I have heard nothing of Gavitt.

Being thrown up in a blanket was rather amusing when properly conducted. The modus operandi was about as follows: Six men would arrange themselves around a strong blanket. The victim to be offered up was then seized, and laid prone upon his back in the middle thereof, and in the twinkling of an eye he would be swung bodily sixteen or seventeen feet into the air, coming down with astonishing facial expressions. The blanket was ready to receive him, and then up again he must go to an altitude that was absolutely frightful to contemplate. To appreciate the feelings of the victim, one only needed this experience. A solitary mishap—the bursting of a blanket, the slipping of a hold—might have been fatal to the "tossee."

Another of the amusements at Camp Parole, and one which, whenever I witnessed the performance, always threw me into convulsive laughter, was known as "Blind Davy." It is impossible to do this sport justice by a description. It was inexpressibly ludicrous.

One of the many curious characters that found their way into the guard house was known as "Lord Lyons." Pale, thin, long face, straight black hair that fell over his shoulders, a skeleton-like frame, upon which the clothes hung loosely, he presented a rather peculiar appearance. Although deemed demented, there was some method in his eccentricities that demonstrated his ability to take care of himself under most circumstances. He claimed to be a British subject, and seemed to carry on a voluminous correspondence with the British minister at Washington. He threatened the United States with all sorts of dire disaster if he was not released from the military service.

Clem, with his violin, supplied the music for our stag dances. These, though, perhaps, not always conducted strictly in accordance with the principles of terpsichorean amusements, served to enliven many a weary hour. I may never forget the well executed jigs of Bugler Lockwood, with their comical supplements by Hubbard, of the First Massachusetts Cavalry.

Checker playing was another method of amusement, in which I took such an intense interest that my dreams were haunted by the same, and when, in my waking hours, I looked upon the parade ground, it instantly resolved itself into a huge board, with "sure enough" men upon imaginary black spots. In time I became quite proficient as a player.

My communication with Miss Wahl was reopened shortly after my arrival at Annapolis. We temporarily exchanged pictures, and then closed up a correspondence which had been mutually pleasant, if not profitable, and which, begun in romance, closed in a matter-of-fact manner, with the best of feeling on each side.

On the 16th of May, the Ninety-fourth New York was relieved by a regiment of one-hundred-day men from Ohio.[2] These were, for the most part, middle aged, staid farmers. The newcomers furnished an abundance of amusements to the prisoners, who kept them in a chronic condition of exasperation by their vicious annoyances. There were the usual number of jokes about the want of butter, etc., cracked at their expense. The veterans ran away from their escorts at every opportunity, or invented unheard-of excuses for going to unheard-of places. The men of Ohio,however, were not long in becoming accustomed to their harness, and paid their tormentors back in their own coin.

On the 12th of May all prisoners paroled prior to that date were

[2]   Short-term enlistments such as these were rare and usually occasioned by political accomodation. In this instance, it is probably due to the state failing to meet its quota of men, and the one hundred day enlistment period provided enough volunteers to reach the required number.

declared exchanged, and those at our camp, except such as were held for trial, were sent to their respective regiments. By this means I was deprived of the presence of those upon whom I relied as witnesses in my case; and though I entered a strong protest against my continued incarceration under these circumstances, no notice whatever was taken of it. Although thus crippled, I did not despair of being able, sometime, to overthrow what I now had learned to look upon as a personal persecution.

At length, I managed to find access to the judge advocate of one of the courts martial that had been organized at Camp Parole, and to him stated the facts in my case in detail. There had been four of such courts in operation, I said, since my arrest, and before none of them had my name been laid, although it was entitled to precedence from priority of confinement. My time of service was fast drawing to a close; my witnesses were being discharged, and otherwise passing beyond my control, and, if the matter were much longer delayed, I should be entirely helpless.

The lieutenant examined his list, and informed me that my name did not appear upon it. However, he promised to see what could be done, and admitted the justice of my claims.

That afternoon, an orderly appeared at the guard house, and escorted me to the headquarters of the provost marshal. That officer stated to me, that, in consequence of my honorable conduct while a prisoner, it had been deemed advisable to give me the liberty of the camp, if I should pledge myself not to leave its limits without permission. Of course, I gave my assent, and then, after having been confined nearly five months, walked over to the barracks with a light heart in my bosom.

The Common Soldier had yet another lesson to learn in the school of experience. The long-looked-for day in July came, closing the term of my service, and I was still under a cloud. The next morning I called on the provost marshal, and suggested that my contract with the government was at an end. He assured me that my case should receive early attention, and I returned to my quarters.

Jubal Early was making his celebrated demonstrations around Washington about this time.[3] The excitement in camp reached such a height that the barracks were abandoned, and the men withdrawn into Annapolis, and preparations made to defend that ancient borough.

[3] On July 12, 1864, Confederate General Jubal A. Early attacked Fort Stevens, part of the defenses of Washington. It is currently located at 13th and Quackenbos Streets, N.W., Washington, D.C.

The officers had mustered to the number of perhaps two thousand, with seven pieces of artillery; but the material was not such as to inspire confidence in a vigorous defense. Our little party of paroled men offered their services to the commanding officer, but that functionary said we were prisoners, and could not be allowed to do duty under any circumstances; so we hunted up a nice shade tree in rear of the lines, just where we would be able to see the fury, if a demonstration was made, spread our blankets, and made ourselves comfortable. The expected attack, however, did not come off, though the rebels were certainly within twenty miles of us, and three of their scouts were reported to have penetrated much further towards Annapolis. It seems that Early's campaign met with a sudden and serious check near Washington, and he retired rapidly across the Potomac into Virginia. After the scare was all over, the troops returned to Camp Parole and reoccupied their old quarters, the paroled party following them.

Matters soon resumed their old status again, but I confess time hung heavily on my hands now. I wanted to go home. Finally, one morning the provost marshal sent for me, and smilingly informed me that Colonel Root had sent a communication to Baltimore, to General Lew Wallace,[4] commanding district, recommending that I be released and returned to my regiment upon certain conditions. I thanked the provost marshal for the announcement and returned to the barracks.

Upon the road I pondered thoughtfully the words "upon certain conditions." What could that mean? It was strange that these conditions had not been laid before me, as they were proposed to the commanding general. Altogether, the problem was too knotty a one for me, and I gave up all attempts to solve it. The more I thought of it, however, the firmer grew my conviction that all was not right. When I got to my barracks I resolved to cut the Gordian knot at once, and sat down and wrote a letter to General Wallace, informing him of the information I had received from our provost marshal, and the mention therein made of my being released "upon certain conditions." What these conditions were I could not say, but if they were such as would compromise my personal honor, if the acceptance of them by me was capable of being construed into a confession of guilt on my part of any offense whatsoever

---

[4] Lewis Wallace was born in Brookville, Indiana, on April 10, 1827. He raised the 11th Indiana Infantry at the outbreak of the Civil War and, on September 3, 1861, was appointed a Brigadier General. He resigned from the army after the war and later achieved fame as the author of *Ben-Hur*. He died in Crawfordsville, Indiana, on February 15, 1905.

against the government, I would suffer death before I should agree to such acceptance. This letter was immediately mailed, and was heard of by me no more.

The next morning the provost marshal sent for me again. A reply had been received from General Wallace, he said, and thereupon he proceeded to read off a paper, which went on to say that I should lose all back pay and allowances due me, and should make good the time of absence, and that I should be returned to my regiment without delay. I was then notified that I should leave for Washington within an hour. Without a word I turned on my heel and went to my quarters, and began packing up my clothes. My determination was already taken, nothing now remained for me to do but to push it through to the bitter end. I saw plainly the cruel advantage that had been taken of me; I had been denied all my rights under the regulations and laws relating to the army; I had been allowed no trial while my witnesses were available; I was to receive all this punishment upon the approval of an order by an officer who had no knowledge of the conditions of my arrest or the responsibility I had incurred; all this, too, in the face of the fact that of those tried who had made any defense, all had been acquitted. I resolved that, should an attempt be made to enforce this infamous order at the regiment, I should resist it to the last, and, if necessary, make it the business of my life to have it reversed.

At the appointed time, I was ready for the train. Two other prisoners, who had been released on the same conditions, were sent along, our little party being under charge of Lieutenant Leonard of the New York infantry. A slight smash up on the cars was the only incident of our journey worth of record; no one hurt, however. From the depot at the Capital we were marched over to the cavalry dismounted camp, beyond the Insane Asylum of St. Elizabeth's,[5] which we at length reached, tired and hungry. Here I rejoined a fragment of the Sixth Cavalry—dismounted men—and was released from arrest. I confess the night following was a long and anxious one for me, and I slept but little. The prospect before me was not reassuring, but I felt I had a duty to perform, which justice to myself and friends at home and in the regiment demanded I should fulfill. I felt, however, that there I should have at least fair play, for the regulations were a law among the regulars, and to

[5] At that time the institution was known as the Government for the Insane of the Army, Navy and District of Columbia. It acquired the name St. Elizabeth's during the Civil War. In 1916 the name was officially changed to St. Elizabeth's Hospital (the name derives from the original grant of land on which the hospital was established).

them I could appeal in perfect confidence.

To my great joy I learned, early next morning, that the regiment was expected to arrive at Giesboro Point, on the Potomac just below camp, that day. They were then on route to the Shennandoah Valley under the gallant Sheridan, as whose escort they were detailed. I made hurried preparations to meet them, so that, by the time the schooner had landed I was down at the wharf. It was a queer looking regiment by this time, not over twenty or thirty strong, apparently a few enlisted men being all that remained. I confess that the temptation to renew my term of service in the old Sixth grew strong in me as I stood looking at its remnant that day.

It seemed hard to part from such an old friend and true. I hunted up Company F, but all of Company F I could find was Corporal—now Sergeant—Miller, the man I had packed off dangerously wounded from the field at Brandy Station, on that red 9th of June, 1863. His wound still bothered him some, but he was in far better condition than I had expected to find him. The sergeant treated me to a splendid dinner of fried ham and eggs, and real butter and milk and coffee he had successfully foraged for at some place. After this we rode to the place where the regiment was ordered to encamp, on the side of the hill near Uniontown. The company books were not yet unloaded, but this was soon done, and the duplicate final statements, and those pieces of parchment so delicious looking to a soldier anxious for his liberty, were all duly made out and signed by Lieutenant A. Coates, commanding; and bidding good by to the brave boys with whom I had been associated off and on for three years, one month, and seven days, and saluting the regimental colors as I passed out of camp, I bade farewell to the service and turned my face towards the Paymaster General's office in Washington.

Going into the office where the accounts of the United States troops were adjusted, I presented my papers to a clerk to whom I was directed. After waiting half an hour these were all ready, and then he called me to him.

"Do you see that?" he said, pointing at the figures.

I read off "four hundred and sixteen dollars," quite slowly, to be sure that it was right.

"Well," I replied, "that does not surprise me. I have drawn no pay for fifteen or sixteen months, and have had no clothing to be charged for some two years, and I think something should be coming to me."

522

A check was made out and immediately cashed by the paymaster's clerk, and I went on my way rejoicing. Half an hour after I left camp, I afterwards understood, the order from Camp Parole came, causing some little excitement among the officials, but it was too late. What action, if any, would have been taken in the matter had I been there, I cannot say; but I know I should never have yielded my right to a trial by court martial, by which I am assured I should have been acquitted.

And now, to you who have worn the coarse blue, and who can of all others, appreciate the trials and manifold difficulties of the Common Soldier in the service, he has only to say, after wishing you a long and happy life, full of honor, "Hail and farewell!"

We can deduce from this letter, discovered amongst his papers, that Sidney found the publisher disinterested in his memoirs. With the terrible tragedies and consequences of the Civil War still fresh in the public mind, the rejection was understandable.

Though some books had been written about the war, mostly by officers on both sides of the conflict and by some few privates, perhaps none had been written by a common soldier of his remembrances of his experiences throughout his full term of service, specifically a cavalryman in the 6th U.S. Cavalry.

Now, a hundred and thirty years after the war, we are making this account of Sidney's Life in the Civil War available to interested readers for their pleasure.

The Editor

In writing to ask if you have examined my manuscript, I am not prompted by impatience, but by anxiety. With a family to support, with a home that is in daily peril through financial misfortune, with a sickly boy by whose little bed I linger, desperate because I cannot relieve his suffering; and without employment at present, I am constrained to appeal to you to consider the matter at your earliest convenience.

Understand me, I do not ask a concession because of these circumstances. If my narrative does not posses interest, or if it lacks that grace of expression which makes a story readable, or if there are literary defects of any character that in your judgment render it objectionable, I will thank you not to print it. I propose to enter the field of literature, and am conscious that in its case of publication I would be the chief sufferer.

No considerations induce me to put forward "A Very Common Soldier" as my vanguard in that field: First, because the subject and the ground are new and comparatively unknown in the books of our libraries; second, because in its preparation I had the advantage of an intimate acquaintance with the "Character", and the circumstances that surrounded him. My experience enables me to paint from the life the picture of an American Soldier as he existed in the late war; but whether the portrait be presentable in its details, or whether, if a faithful likeness, the features be pleasant to contemplate, it is first for the public to judge.

I know that my "Character" occupies a sphere that is circumscribed in spirit and that not one in 1,000 of the world's readers have a special interest in either him or his experiences as a individual; but I hope to bring out in relief those elements of human nature which has an abiding and a universal interest. While he is to be a soldier, and as such is allied to the events of our war, in a general sense he is to be found in any army in any war. To do this successfully, I have endeavored faithfully to describe, not only scenes but to depict, also, the emotions, sympathies, or other mental phenomena manifested in connection with these scenes. I may better illustrate my meaning by referring to the tale of Don Quixote. No one feels a particular interest in the common place adventures of that warrior, but only in the happy exaggerations of human passion and prejudice as exhibited in those adventures.

Probably you may think me presumptuous, and that I aim too high. Well, I do aim high. I aspire to extraordinary achievements with the pen and I shall seek them. I may be presumptuous too!

I will have about a hundred more pages ready by the close of the week, if everything goes right.

Respectfully,

Sidney M. Davis,
219 East, Northeast.

BIBLIOGRAPHIC ESSAY

Charles F. Cooney

A preeminent place to start for this Civil War memoir is the War of Rebellion: A Compilation of the Official Records of the Union and Confederate Armies (130 volumes, Washington, D.C.: Government Printing Office, 1880-1901). The reports, correspondence, and collateral documents relating to the actions of the unit in which the writer served may be found here.

For the 6th U.S. Cavalry, there is a regimental history, From Yorktown to Santiago With the Sixth U.S. Cavalry, by William G.H. Carter (Baltimore: Lord Baltimore Press, 1900). The first 130 pages of this volume deal with the actions of the regiment during the Civil War.

Two volumes provide information on Washington, D.C. and the defense of Washington during the Civil War. Margaret Leech's Reveille in Washington (New York: Harper Brothers, 1941; currently available in paperback reprint) deals with the social, economic and military milieu of the District of Columbia during the war. Symbol, Sword and Shield: Defending Washington During the Civil War by Benjamin F. Cooling (Hamden, Connecticut, Archon Books, 1975) provides a wealth of detail on the construction, utilization and purposes of the ring of forts erected to encircle the city.

The Peninsula Campaign 1862: McClellan and Lee Struggle for Richmond by Joseph P. Cullen (Harrisburg, Pennsylvania, Stackpole Books, 1973) provides an account of the 6th Cavalry's first campaign.

The Antietam campaign is described in James V. Murfin's The Gleam of Bayonets: The Battle of Antietam and the Maryland Campaign of 1862 (New York: Thomas Yoseloff, 1965; currently available in paperback reprint).

Edward J. Stackpole recounts the massacre at Fredericksburg in Drama on the Rappahannock: The Fredericksburg Campaign (Harrisburg, Pennsylvania: Stackpole Books, 1957).

The largest cavalry clash in the United States is reported in The Great Cavalry Battle of Brandy Station, 9 June 1863 by Heros Von Borke and Justus Scheibert (Winston-Salem, North Carolina, Palaemon Press, 1976).

Gettysburg may well be the most written about battle in American history. The Gettysburg Campaign: A Study in Command by Edward B. Coddington (new York: Charles Scribner's Sons, 1968; currently available in paperback reprint) is perhaps the best single volume available. Edward G. Longacre recently published The Cavalry at Gettysburg: A Tactical Study of Mounted Operations During the Civil War's Pivotal Campaign, 9 June—14 July 1863 (publisher not yet known to me) which may provide more specific detail on the 6th Cavalry's encounter at Fairfield.

Civil War Prisons by William B. Hesseltine (Kent, Ohio, Kent State University Press, 1962) provides a good overview of life in prison and should be used in conjunction with his Civil War Prisons: A Study in War Psychology (New York: F. Ungar, 1964) for information on this aspect of the war.

Useful books on the cavalry in the Civil War generally are Randy Steffen's The Horse Soldier (4 volumes, Norman, Oklahoma: University of Oklahoma Press, 1977-79) and Stephen Z. Starr's The Union Cavalry in the Civil War (3 volumes, Baton Rouge, Louisiana: Louisiana State University Press, 1979-85). The former provides useful information on equipage and the later is more a narrative of cavalry operations.